Foundations Of Behavioral Research

A Basic Question Approach

Kenneth M. Rosenberg
*State University of
New York at Oswego*

Helen B. Daly
*State University of
New York at Oswego*

Harcourt Brace Jovanovich College Publishers

Fort Worth   Philadelphia   San Diego   New York   Orlando   Austin   San Antonio
Toronto   Montreal   London   Sydney   Tokyo

For Hilde and Josef Bohmer, parents of Helen B. Daly, our spouses, Carol and John, and our teachers, Victor H. Denenberg, Bernard W. Harleston, James Ison, and Dorothy and Wallace McAllister.

Publisher: Ted Buchholz
Acquisitions Editor: Christina Oldham
Developmental Editor: Karee Galloway
Project Editor: Mike Hinshaw
Production Manager: Mandy Manzano
Book Designer: Jeanette Barber

ISBN: 0-03-055558-2

Library of Congress Number: 92-73715

Address editorial correspondence to:
301 Commerce Street, Suite 3700
Fort Worth, TX 76102

Address orders to:
6277 Sea Harbor Drive
Orlando, FL 32887
1-800-782-4479 outside Florida
1-800-433-0001 inside Florida

PRINTED IN THE UNITED STATES OF AMERICA

3 4 5 6 7 8 9 0 1 164 9 8 7 6 5 4 3 2 1

Copyright acknowledgments continued on page 493.

PREFACE

Behavioral researchers gather accurate information and render meaningful interpretations of their data in the same way all well-trained researchers do: they apply the precise, logical, and objective techniques of discovery that, collectively, constitute the scientific method. But because the research methods that apply to the study of behavior are somewhat specialized, students of psychology and other behavioral and social sciences require special preparation before they can effectively read and evaluate scientific literature and design and execute their own research projects. *Foundations of Behavioral Research: A Basic Question Approach* provides that preparation. Its class-tested approach provides detailed and comprehensive coverage of the methods of behavioral research, while remaining consistently engaging and accessible to students of wide-ranging academic ability. Here are some of its most effective features.

Features

The Basic Question Approach. Using easily understood examples and analogies, we show the reader that the great variety of issues that interest behavioral scientists can be expressed and explored in a surprisingly small set of questions. The seven basic questions are introduced in Chapter 5 (Recipes for Research) and provide a transition to Part II (Researching Answers to Basic Questions). As the title of Part II suggests, the Basic Questions anchor the discussion in the four chapters of Part IIA (Description: The First Level of Research Inquiry) as well as in the seven chapters of Part IIB (Experimentation: The Next Level of Research Inquiry).

Throughout Part II the text emphasizes two important aspects of research: (1) the need to focus on the question the research is supposed to answer and (2) the need to match the question(s) under study to an appropriate research methodology. Thus, the basic questions serve as a natural and meaningful organizer by keeping the *purpose* of methodology, which is to provide a framework for answering questions, constantly in the forefront. In Part III, in which we present published research to exemplify the methodological concerns of selected subdisciplines (see below), we continue the theme by relating the goals of each study to one or more of the Basic Questions.

Proposal Assignments. At the end of each chapter in Parts I and II we include a *Proposal Assignment*, a class-tested technique that helps students define and develop their own research problems and prepare a written report in APA style. Since these assignments build on one another in successive chapters, you will no doubt find that by the end of the course many students will have designed sophisticated and interesting studies.

We have used proposal assignments very successfully with our own students to supplement the hands-on research experience they get in our laboratory curriculum. Immersion in the intricacies of their very own research project motivates students to practice *applying* the research methods they are learning. Since the proposal assignments are usually not completed with the intention of actually carrying out the project, the students are free to be creative and ignore limitations of time, money, personnel, and apparatus.

Extensive Exposure to Published Research. The last section of the text (Part III: Review of Research Methodologies and Control Conditions Used by Selected Subdisciplines in Psychology) prepares students to read and evaluate real research by providing exposure to published scientific literature. The excerpts included have been carefully chosen for both content and reading level. Using the articles as a springboard, each chapter addresses the particular methodological concerns of some of the different subdisciplines of psychology through a thorough examination of the methods section of an original and current journal article representative of the subdiscipline. Thus, while students are learning to become knowledgeable consumers of published research, they are also becoming familiar with a few of the subdisciplines of psychology.

Part III contains excerpts from published articles and explores seven different subdisciplines: developmental and lifespan psychology, sensation and perception, transfer, neuropsychology, behavioral toxicology, industrial/organizational psychology and program evaluation, and social psychology.

Illustration of Key Concepts. Many research methods textbooks appear to have been written to satisfy two educational objectives at the same time: to teach students the *process* of behavioral research and to familiarize them with the *content* of behavioral research. Such books include numerous citations from behavioral science literature (the content) and use selected elements from published studies to exemplify the application of abstract methodological principles (the process). The dual focus can work well with some student populations, but we have found that students often dwell on learning the factual content of the examples at the expense of mastering the methodological principles the examples were intended illustrate. In the process-oriented approach we take in *Foundations of Behavioral Research*, we avoid extensive citations from the literature in Parts I and II, and, instead, maintain the students' focus on methodology by using carefully crafted hypothetical scenarios that draw on familiar life experiences. The use of hypothetical examples also provides a vehicle for continuity, as when we use the same hypothetical example in several different chapters to illustrate contrasting or expanded methodological approaches to the same research problem.

Repetition of Key Concepts and Gradual Escalation of Complexity. Although all the features of this textbook were designed to have broad appeal, the one that makes it most accessible is the *gradual* escalation of complexity. Thus, not only do we include repeated examination and review of key concepts, we also provide additional details to *expand* the coverage each time the concept is revisited. For example, the concept of association, which is introduced initially in Chapter 3, is repeated and expanded in Chapters 4 and 5, and, finally, is given its own chapter (Chapter 9: Describing the Association between Variables). The concept again becomes relevant and is discussed further in Chapter 15 (Quasi-Experimental Research) and throughout Part III.

Study Aids. The study of research methods requires students to master an extensive nomenclature. To help, each key term is printed in boldface the first time it is used, and it, together with its definition, appears in the page margin for ready reference. And, each time a term that was defined in Parts I or II comes up in the discussion in Part III, the student is encouraged to refer back to the specific page in Part I or Part II where the term was first introduced and defined.

All the key terms included in a chapter are listed at the end of the chapter along with a chapter summary and chapter exercises (review questions). A complete glossary of terms and definitions is provided at the back of the book for general reference.

Review of Statistics. Since research design and statistical reasoning are interdependent, we weave a review of many basic statistical concepts into our coverage of research methods. Some concepts are presented in Boxed Features (e.g., Box 4.1—Scatterplots: Picturing Association, Box 4.3—Describing Data with Statistics, and Box 4.4—The Meaning of Statistical Significance), and some are included in the main body of the chapter (e.g., The Logic of Hypothesis Testing and Regression to the Mean). The inclusion of a statistics review means that students don't have to search out a separate book for the information.

Creating Enthusiasm. The last feature to be highlighted may be the most important because it enhances the effectiveness of all the others: a strategy to create enthusiasm for research. The theme embodied in Chapter 1 ("Why Learn About Research Methods?") sets the tone for the rest of the book. With selected examples, we show that understanding the logical foundation of research methods and their practical application to research problems has value that extends far beyond academic life. Such knowledge also promotes career success and fosters intelligent behavior as responsible citizens and wise consumers.

Integrating the Laboratory Curriculum

It is very useful to read and discuss appropriate sections of Parts II and III before each laboratory experience. The material in Part III makes it possible to supplement the basic coverage of Parts I and II with detailed analyses of the methods, control groups, and experimental designs that are employed in the published research of mainstream psychology. For example, if a laboratory exercise involves measuring the sensory threshold of a subject under two different conditions of background noise, reading the material in Part III on sensation/perception and the relevant material in Part II (e.g., Chapter 12: Two-Treatment Designs With Correlated Observations) would be valuable preparation. And because the individual topic sections in Part III are freestanding units, there is no commitment to a particular sequence of topics.

Integrating a Statistics Curriculum

In some behavioral science curricula, students take a course in elementary statistics before they study research methods, whereas in other curricula the two topics are combined in a single one- or two-semester course. *Foundations of Behavioral Research* is compatible with either approach. The division of Part II into sections on descriptive research and on experimental research parallels nicely the topic sequence of descriptive statistics and inferential statistics universally used in behavioral science statistics textbooks. Furthermore, the content of individual chapters (e.g., "Describing the Association Between Variables") parallels the selection of topics in most statistics textbooks (e.g., correlation and linear regression).

Appendices

Appendix A ("Communication of Scientific Research Findings") contains all the information students will need to prepare their laboratory reports in APA style, including an annotated sample manuscript. In addition, Appendix A contains valuable advice to students on the preparation and delivery of oral presentations. Appendix B (Statistical Analyses of Selected Examples) presents data analyses of examples that appear in the text. Since substantial detail is provided in Appendix B, it can serve as a review of statistical

procedures when students are required to analyze their laboratory data.

Instructor's Manual with Test Items

For each chapter of the text, the Instructor's Manual provides an outline, teaching objectives, and suggestions for lectures and class activities. We pay particular attention to helping professors plan to use the chapters in Part III as part of their methods curriculum. To assist instructors in evaluating their students, we have assembled a broad sample of multiple-choice test items and essay questions related to the material in specific chapters, as well as a set of integrative questions that address material throughout the book.

Acknowledgments

The writing of *Foundations of Behavioral Research: A Basic Question Approach* was a complex undertaking, and it could not have reached its present form without the guidance we received from our Developmental Editor, Karee Galloway, and the many valuable and insightful suggestions of our professional colleagues who carefully read and critiqued each chapter. We thank the following for their contributions to this project: Michael M. Granaas, University of South Dakota; Ellen P. Susman, Metropolitan State College; George M. Diekhoff, Midwestern State University; Eric F. Ward, Western Illinois University; Barry H. Cohen, New York University; Bernardo J. Carducci, Indiana University Southeast; Dana S. Dunn, Moravian College; Paul J. Wellman, Texas A&M University; James H. Beaird, Eastern Oregon State College; Joseph Palladino, University of Southern Indiana; Sami Gulgoz, Auburn University at Montgomery; James J. Ryan, University of Wisconson-LaCrosse; Mary Ann Foley, Skidmore College; Brian Healy, Ithaca College; Richard M. Wielkiewicz, College of St. Benedict; B. Runi Mukherji, State University of New York, College at Old Westbury; and A. Richard Brayer, University of Hartford.

CONTENTS

Part II Researching Answers to Basic Questions

The Logic and Language
of Research Methods

C H A P T E R

1

Introduction to Behavioral Research

Why Learn about Research Methods?

Have you ever wondered why eating disorders and depression are so common among teenagers? Are you curious about how advertising sells us products we do not need? Why do some people "give up" when they fail, whereas others become more determined than ever to succeed? Psychological researchers study behavior and report findings concerning every aspect of our lives, including human sexuality, the development of thinking and motor skills in children, the hazards of environmental pollution, the effects of substance abuse, the effects of stress, and the control and eradication of psychological disorders. The knowledge of research methods you gain from *Foundations of Behavioral Research* will serve you far beyond your formal academic experience.

Decisions in our daily lives

Professional researchers are not alone in the need to understand the research process. As both consumer and citizen you will often need to evaluate and act upon research results. Have emissions from the smokestack of a local chemical plant resulted in a significant increase in respiratory problems in your neighborhood? Is day care beneficial for children? Does eating food with high sugar content contribute to hyperactivity? Are DWI convicts less likely to drive while intoxicated if they are required to attend a special workshop following their initial sentence?

To find the answers to such questions you must rely on **data** — the information that research produces — and interpretations of data provided by experts. (A **datum** is a single piece of data.) Leaving the resolution of controversial issues to professionals seems reasonable — except that many expert spokespersons, whether from industry, government, or the scientific community, have a vested interest in how particular issues are resolved (see Box 1–1). In many instances, laypeople who can think critically and reason logically, such as consumer activist Ralph Nader and his colleagues, have embarrassed experts by pointing out flaws in the data-collection process and in the logic the experts used to arrive at their opinions about the meaning of the data.

Data: The information research produces.

Datum: A single piece of data.

BOX 1–1

Color Additives: Botched Experiment Leads to Banning of Red Dye No. 2

The research described below occurred many years ago, but it had such a widespread impact (the initial approval and eventual banning of the most widely used food coloring in the United States) and was so widely reported in the media that it continues to be a primary example of a "botched" experiment. Fortunately, scrutiny of the work by the scientific community revealed the numerous procedural flaws and erroneous interpretations of the data.

Even though it may be reasonable to expect that such errors would not be repeated, even well-trained scientists occasionally have lapses. If you pay close attention to media reports, you will occasionally encounter similar revelations of mismanaged investigations.

Red 2 has been the most widely used food color in this country, and it has always been touted as the "most thoroughly tested" of all the food colors. Yet questions were raised in the early 1970's, largely on the basis of tests conducted in the Soviet Union, as to whether the dye might cause cancer or reproductive damage.

In an effort to answer these questions, two major tests were conducted by FDA. One, a collaborative effort involving two FDA laboratories and a commercial laboratory, concluded that Red 2 does not cause reproductive damage. The other, also originally launched as a reproduction study but then adapted to examine the question of carcinogenicity, soon became such a muddle that it is routinely referred to by FDA scientists as the "botched" or "bungled" study. Yet it is this study which formed the basis for the recent regulatory decision on Red 2.

The study involved feeding Red 2 to four different groups of rats, each at a different dosage level, and then comparing the health of these treated groups with the health of a control group. There were 500 rats in all — seemingly enough for a solid evaluation. But the study was left unsupervised for a long period of time after a scientist was transferred, and it developed two serious flaws. To begin with, the animal handlers managed to put some of the rats back in the wrong cages part way through the experiment, so that an undetermined number of rats were shifted among the control group and the four treated groups. Second, the animal handlers were lackadaisical about retrieving dead rats from their cages and rushing them off to the pathologists for examination. As a result, virtually all of the rats that died during the course of the experiment were so badly decomposed as to be of little use for evaluation. Only those rats that survived to the end of the experiment and were killed — some 96 in all — were available for detailed histopathological examination.

"It was the lousiest experiment I've seen in my life," commented one scientist who reviewed the data.

Yet the study was not considered a total loss by the FDA, which reasoned that it would be possible to treat the intact animals which had been fed the largest dose of Red 2 — 3 percent of their diet — as a "high dose" group and all the other intact animals as a "low dose" group. By comparing the two groups, the reasoning went, it might be possible to learn *something* about whether Red 2 is carcinogenic. . . .

The pathology division of the Bureau of Foods submitted a report on the "botched" experiment which concluded that Red 2 had "no apparent adverse effect" on the rats. And many members of the advisory committee seemed to agree, offering such comments as, "I have a feeling that this is an innocuous color" and, "There has been no evidence that I have seen which makes me think that this compound is a significant or major carcinogen."

Still, just to be certain, the committee ordered up three further analyses by experts within its membership. One of those studies — a statistical analysis of the results of the "botched" study performed by David W. Gaylor, principal biological statistician at the FDA's National Center for Toxicological Research in Arkansas- — revealed that the Bureau of Foods may have been a bit too hasty in drawing its rosy conclusions. Gaylor found that, while it was indeed true that there was no significant difference in the *total* number of tumors, both benign and malignant, in the high-dose and low-dose groups, there was in fact a significant increase in the number of *malignant* tumors found in the female rats fed the high dose. . . .

A working group of scientists from the Toxicology Advisory Committee, the FDA, and the National Cancer Institute met on 14 January to review Gaylor's analysis. . . .

The working group noted that the "botched" study was of such poor quality that it could never be used to demonstrate the safety of Red 2, but it suggested further evaluations of the data in an effort to determine whether Red 2 is carcinogenic. However, the FDA commissioner, who had recently been given a rough time on Red 2 by various senators and congressmen, the General Accounting Office, and reporters on a nationwide television interview show, was not about to wait for more evaluations. On 19 January, he announced that he would act immediately to terminate the approval for use of Red 2 in foods, drugs, and cosmetics. . . . The burden of proof, he added, lies with those who manufacture or use Red 2 to prove that it is safe and useful. Then, since he had not exactly ruled that Red 2 is unsafe, he explained that there would be no recall of existing products containing Red 2 since there is "no evidence of a public health hazard."

Source: Boffey, P.M. (1976). Color Additives: Botched Experiment Leads to Banning of Red Dye No. 2. *Science*, 191, 450–451. Copyright 1976 by the AAAS.

You do not have to be a consumer activist or plan a career in a science-related field to benefit from knowledge about research methods. As a citizen of planet Earth you must make many personal, professional, and political decisions. The information you use to guide your decision-making is only as valuable and useful as the data-gathering process is logically and procedurally sound. To the extent that your study of research methods makes you aware of the logical constraints that apply to the conduct of research and the interpretation of research data, you will be better able to tease the truth from available data on your own without depending upon an "expert" to do it for you. As a result, many important decisions throughout life can be based on research, reason, and critical thinking rather than on impulse or the unchallenged opinions of others.

Decisions in the workplace

Understanding the research process will enable you to make intelligent career choices. Professionals are drawn to the most recently developed methods and technologies in their fields but adopt them only if they represent a significant improvement over current methods. If, for example, you choose a career in human services and read or hear that a new way of servicing clients appears to be far more effective than a traditional method, you will not want to adopt the new method until satisfying yourself that it is truly superior. Training in research methods will enable you to critically evaluate experimental data used to test the effectiveness of a new technique so you can decide for yourself whether it would be advantageous to use it with your clients. Similarly, if you are planning a career in marketing or sales, are you going to guess which strategies work? How much better it would be to evaluate scientifically the effectiveness of your business practices. In general, the critical thinking skills you gain from your study of research methodology, and the understanding you develop concerning the limits the gathering of information places on its interpretation, will prepare you to deal with a wide range of personal and professional concerns with confidence.

If you do become a researcher

The third reason you should learn how to do good research is that you may become excited about what researchers do: They create new knowledge and verify what other researchers represent as new knowledge. It can be very gratifying to realize that, before your experiment, a particular set of facts was unknown. Whether the knowledge you create is the solution to a mundane problem (What conditions will minimize the mortality rate of my tropical fish?) or a more weighty problem related to your work, the discovery of knowledge is a joy.

A Joy?

Every college curriculum, from anthropology to zoology, contains a relatively difficult required course or two that some students look upon only as an academic hurdle, a curricular curiosity they see as largely irrelevant to their educational or career goals. For example, the anxiety or apathy some students feel toward mathematics is a significant problem for educators. If you have taken an introductory statistics course in preparation for your study of research methods, you may well understand the anxiety that the study of mathematics causes in some students.

The prospect of studying research methods has similarly worried its share of students. However, as students become aware of how essential an understanding of research methods is to understand the origins of our present body of knowledge and the creation of new knowledge, the anxiety engendered by "research" is replaced with curiosity.

The Research Mystique

Consider the word *research*, defined as the activity of "studious inquiry ... critical and exhaustive investigation." This description conjures up images of highly trained, sophisticated, white-coated, hard-working Ph.D.s who live in their laboratories, publish articles with strange titles in specialized scientific journals, communicate in a language that can be understood only by their colleagues, and delight in arguing with each other about their conflicting views of reality. If being that type of professional researcher is not on your list of career goals, you might well question the need to be exposed to the concepts and methods that govern the conduct of scientific research. But, as you progress through your study of research methods, you will develop an increasing awareness that the methodological and critical thinking skills you are acquiring will be useful in many ways throughout your life.

Finding a Research Problem

Most students of the behavioral sciences are very curious about the causes of certain behaviors. In fact, knowing that you are enrolled in a psychology course, a friend or family member may already have asked your opinion about the causes of a strange or antisocial behavior. If you have felt awkward trying to come up with a scholarly explanation, rest assured that this emotion is often shared even by trained and experienced psychologists.

Incomplete understanding of behavioral phenomena can be very frustrating, but it can also be very exciting. Think of all the mysteries waiting to be solved! And you can make a meaningful contribution even as an undergraduate student. You will learn how to design a research project, collect data, and prepare the results for publication. As you progress through the course of study offered in this text you will be given proposal assignments related to the development of your own research project. You may not get to collect data for your original proposal assignment at the same time you are being introduced to research methods, but you may be able to complete the project in a more advanced course or independent study. Even as an undergraduate you may be able to publish your research results in a scientific journal. Many of the authors' students have published research that began as a proposal assignment for the research methods course.

How Do Psychologists Develop Research Ideas?

There are many sources for research ideas, but all require some familiarity with existing knowledge. There may be a *gap in our knowledge*. For example, travelers who cross several time zones can suffer a phenomenon called jet lag, which makes them feel physically fatigued and mentally sluggish. Similarly, day workers reassigned to a night shift tend to suffer fatigue and loss of productivity. Both phenomena cause economic loss and personal discomfort. What specific factors are responsible for these behavioral phenomena? How can we minimize jet lag and the problems associated with day–night reversals? Research devoted to answering such questions seeks to narrow and, eventually, to close the gaps in our knowledge.

There may be *conflicting results* in the scientific literature. Can you really be motivated to buy a soft drink at a theater concession stand if a message ("Drink Coke!") is flashed on the screen too briefly even to be consciously noticed? Will losses from shoplifting decrease if background music at the shopping mall includes a very soft "stealing is wrong" message? A more general question is whether or not people can be influenced to behave in a certain way by stimuli presented at intensities too low to enter conscious awareness. The phenomenon, called subliminal perception, was once highly controversial. One study supported the position that subliminal perception is a real phenomenon; other studies failed to find such evidence.

When separate sets of research results are inconsistent in their support of a proposed explanation for a phenomenon, it is important to conduct a critical evaluation and comparison of the conflicting studies. In the case of subliminal perception, the study that seemed to support the phenomenon was run incorrectly. The intent was to compare the behavior of theater patrons who saw no subliminal messages to those who did — and, indeed, there was a difference in the behavior of these two groups: Those who saw a movie that included the subliminal messages purchased more soft drinks. The problem was that the subliminal messages were flashed on the screen only during the summer months, whereas the behavior of the theater patrons who saw no messages was assessed during the winter months. Even though the results of the study are consistent with what one would expect if subliminal advertising is effective, there is a competing explanation: People consume more beverages in the summer than during the winter. Thus the two groups in the study differed by more than exposure to the experimental variable: the presence or absence of subliminal messages. There was a second systematic difference between the two groups: the season of the year during which testing was conducted.

A factor that can exert a systematic influence on experimental results apart from any influence of the actual experimental variable, such as the season of testing in this example, is called a **confounding variable**. The flaw was relatively obvious here, but in later chapters you will learn to identify and avoid some much more subtle and deceptive causes for conflicting results.

A third approach to developing a research problem is *testing the predictions of a theory*. The quality of a theory rests on its capacity to predict the results of an experiment designed to test it ("If you do X, Y should happen"). Sometimes two or more theories offer competing explanations of the same phenomenon. When such a rivalry exists, a well-designed study often permits one theory to emerge as the most factual. For example, one theory of memory (Anderson, 1974) predicts that the more one knows, the longer it should take to retrieve information. Another theory (Smith, Adams, & Schorr, 1978) predicts the opposite. Which is correct? A study (or a coordinated series of studies) must be done to determine which theory correctly predicts the effect knowledge has on retrieval speed, or to determine if one theory is true under one set of circumstances and the other is true under another set of circumstances (Reder & Wible, 1984). It can take years to test and compare the predictions of alternative theories (notice the decade span between Anderson's original article and the Reder & Wible report), and the struggle to gain acceptance for different theoretical views can be intense among rival teams of researchers.

Confounding Variable: A factor that can influence experimental results apart from the influence of the actual experimental variable.

Basic and Applied Research

Research may be described as basic or applied, although not all research falls neatly into one category or the other. In general, the question is one of motivation.

Basic Research:
Acquiring information for its own sake rather than for practical application.

Applied Research:
Research to solve practical problems and improve the quality of life.

The scientist who does **basic research** wants to acquire information for its own sake and is not driven by the desire to find the solution to some practical problem. In contrast, the scientist who does **applied research** is oriented to solving problems, the solutions of which will improve the quality of life.

If you scan the titles of the articles in a selection of scientific journals from various disciplines you will see research-article titles that appear both strange and unrelated to anything "important." A typical reaction of people unfamiliar with the content of scientific journals is "Why would anyone want to spend time and money just to find out..." or "How is this knowledge going to help people?" Such studies, done in search of fundamental information, are typical of basic research. If the data do turn out to have some practical application, all to the good, but the original intent was not any readily identifiable practical goal.

Despite the basic thrust of some research, sometimes a wonderful practical application of basic information is discovered. Interestingly, such applications are often thought of by people not connected to the original research, which underlines the importance of disseminating research results in the scientific press. Nobody really set out specifically to invent a microcomputer. The idea grew from basic research into the physics of silicone and electricity. Discovery of the physical properties of silicone led to the invention of integrated circuits on silicone chips, the miniaturized brain of the modern computer. In the same way, eventual cures for cancer, AIDS, and other health problems are as likely to grow out of the findings of basic research as they are to come from more narrowly focused applied medical research.

Many researchers are drawn into an applied research project after being confronted with *a question that affects them* or someone they know directly. For example, many factors under the control of a college instructor affect the rate and ease with which students learn, and it is not always clear which teaching practices are best for any one type of class. Is it more effective to present certain materials using an overhead projector than with a chalkboard? Is it better for the class to meet for three one-hour sessions or for two hour-and-a-half sessions? Will giving numerous short quizzes result in more learning than giving a midterm and a final examination? Teachers interested in the answers to these questions would search the educational research literature and, if no relevant studies had yet been published, would possibly be motivated to research the problem themselves. Until there is a formal study comparing various approaches to teaching, the only recourse a teacher has is to guess (either as a hunch or from informal observations gleaned from past classroom experience) as to what ought to work most effectively. Scientific research is not the only source of our knowledge but, as chapter 2 suggests, for problems of interest to psychologists the scientific method is the best approach.

Summary

Research methods embrace far more than a formal academic discipline. An understanding of the research process will lead to your making more informed decisions both as a citizen and a professional. One experience that will greatly contribute to your understanding of research methods is the development of an original research proposal. (The proposal assignments at the end of each chapter will help you build an original research proposal.) The process of developing a proposal starts with an idea, and coming up with an idea that is good enough to justify the time and effort required to execute a research project can be a significant hurdle. To help you get started with Proposal Assignment 1, we discussed some sources of ideas and the difference between the basic and applied approaches to research.

Key Terms

Applied Research, p. 8

Basic Research, p. 8

Confounding Variable, p. 7

Data, p. 3

Datum, p. 3

Chapter Exercises

1. Explain the difference between basic research and applied research.

2. The text states that training in research methods is essential to an understanding of the origins of knowledge and to create new knowledge. What insights can you contribute in support of this statement? Why should nonscientists as well as scientists understand the research process?

3. What are some of the reasons that motivate people to do research? Can you think of some not mentioned in the text that reflect your personal curiosity about some phenomenon?

Proposal Assignment 1: Finding a Research Topic

Developing a research proposal is an effective way to practice applying the principles of research methods presented in this textbook. (A proposal is a description of a study you plan to do.) As we progress through the following chapters and as your knowledge of research methods becomes more extensive, you will be able to make your research proposal more complete, sophisticated, and detailed. Your assignment here is to come up with an idea for a study.

Deciding what to study is a very easy task for some, but difficult for others. One helpful suggestion is to select a behavior that relates to your own career goals so the practical significance of the problem will be readily apparent to you. For example, if you intend to become a clinical psychologist, you may build your proposal around a study of teen suicide, bulimia, anorexia, depression, or types of therapies for these disorders. If you plan to become a first-grade teacher you may be interested in techniques that help children learn to read. Combining interests (for example, business and psychology) is also possible in addressing interdisciplinary questions. For example, does on-site day care provided by an employer for the children of workers result in an increase in worker morale and productivity?

You can also use noncareer interests to guide your selection. If you are worried about the pollution released from a local factory, you may want to test the effects of exposure to pollution on behavior. Or select a behavior of your own, or one you have observed in others. Some students review the topics covered in Introductory Psychology to find proposal ideas.

Since you will not have to carry out the study you propose, you have license to be creative, remain on a conceptual level, and not worry about such practical aspects of research as how you might pay for all the expensive apparatus you would need to run your study.

The written part of this assignment is very short: a paragraph reviewing your topic. Remember, finding the idea for a research proposal may be the hardest proposal assignment for the entire semester. (Keep copies of your proposal assignments; you will need to refer back to them.)

C H A P T E R

The Origins of Knowledge

Have you ever tried to win someone over to your point of view only to have one of your premises challenged with "How do you know that's true?" Perhaps you responded with "It's simple common sense!" or "My Uncle Albert once told me, and he should know!" Would such responses advance the credibility of your argument in an earnest debate? Is a premise true just because it is logical? Could Uncle Albert's expert opinion possibly be wrong? In this chapter we explore the origins of knowledge and examine the degree to which each is useful and verifiable as a source of the truth.

Sources of Knowledge

Authority and faith

Much of the information we accept as truth is communicated to us by experts — **authority** figures in whom we place our faith and trust. We consult doctors, lawyers, stock analysts, clergy, advice columnists, and the like and heed their advice if we believe they have a greater understanding of our personal

Authority: Knowledge based on faith and trust in an individual or institution.

dilemmas than we do ourselves. But, aside from a cursory examination of an expert's credentials (do you read those degrees and certificates on the wall of your doctor's office?) we are usually not in a position to judge a professional's expert qualifications based on objective evidence. Instead, our acceptance of the professional's ability to dispense the truth is based on trust.

To trust an authority is to accept another person's view of the truth without verification. Similarly, faith is the unquestioning trust we place in the truth of ideas, from whatever source. Such faith can be remarkably steadfast despite the complete absence of any substantiating data. Some people believe we have been visited by beings from other planets and that psychics can communicate with the dead despite the absence of any objective evidence. Inconsistent or absent data are seldom a problem for the passionately faithful. Apparent inconsistencies between beliefs and objective data can be "explained" by our inability to understand the data. ("The prehistoric drawings carry an account of visitors from outer space. Don't you see the spaceship?") The lack of supporting data may be blamed on the inability of current technology to measure and record a phenomenon (the spaceship, which did not show on the radar screen, must have been equipped with a cloaking device) or, perhaps, to a conspiracy (the Air Force will not let its pilots talk to the media about UFO sightings).

Even when data are available for public scrutiny and there is agreement on what the facts are, experts commonly disagree on what the facts *mean*. Each expert may represent his or her differing interpretation of data as the truth, but only one can be correct. For example, in a criminal court proceeding in which experts have been called to testify concerning the sanity of the defendant, the psychiatrist called by the defense will testify that the defendant did not know right from wrong and was not in full control of his faculties when the crime was committed, whereas the psychiatrist called by the prosecutor will offer the opposite expert testimony. Similarly, one doctor's interpretation of medical test results may be that the patient must undergo surgery to have any chance of survival, whereas another equally qualified expert, after viewing the same test results, may recommend noninvasive medical management of the health problem. How can we resolve differences among experts when they have the same information available? Because there can be only one truth and experts do not always agree on what facts mean, expert opinion is potentially flawed as a standard of truth.

Rationalism

Rationalism: Knowledge based on logical deductions from true premises.

Discovery of the truth through reason is called **rationalism**. The rational approach rests on the assumption that the rules of logic, in their mathematical purity and elegance, will permit only correct conclusions to follow from true premises. For example:

> Animals that nurse their young are mammals.
> Bats nurse their young.
> Therefore, bats are mammals.

But how can we determine whether or not the premises themselves are true? Much of the time the premises we use to draw rational conclusions derive from our own personal experiences and our interpretations of those experiences. To the extent that the subjectivity involved in this process is a source of disagreement as to the truth of the premises, disagreements will arise concerning the truth of the conclusion. For example, conservation of volume is a cognitive skill that a four-year-old child does not yet have. When a four-year-old is presented with two equal volumes of fluid in identical tall and slender cylinders, the child will say they are "the same" (Figure 2–1). But when all the fluid in one tall cylinder is poured into a shorter

The perception of the four-year old child:

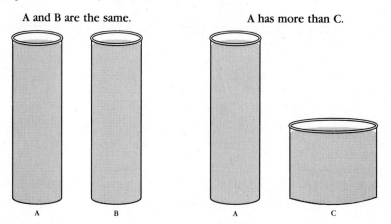

The four-year old child agrees that containers A and B have equal volumes, but when the contents of B are poured into C, the child reports that A has a greater volume of fluid than C because the fluid level in A is higher.

The perception of the seven-year old child:

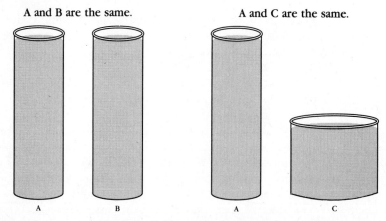

Beginning at about seven years of age, children agree that containers A and B have equal volumes, and when the contents of B are poured into C, they see the volumes of the dissimilar containers as equal. If asked to explain the different heights of the fluid in containers A and C, the child correctly communicates that the increased width of container C is responsible.

Figure 2–1. The perception of comparative volumes among children who can and cannot conserve volume.

wide-mouth beaker, the child will report incorrectly that the remaining tall cylinder has more fluid in it than the shorter beaker.

Of course, the wider diameter of the beaker is the reason for the reduced height of the equal fluid volume, but the immaturity of the four-year-old child's thinking skills does not permit a correct assessment of the situation. The four-year-old's thinking is guided by the premise "higher means more," so the higher fluid level in the cylinder compared to the wide-mouth beaker is, to the four-year-old, a clear and unambiguous indication that more fluid is present in the cylinder. When the fluid in the wide beaker is returned to its original slender container and the child again sees the fluid levels in the two cylinders as equally high, the child will once again report the two volumes as "the same." Note that the four-year-old reverts to the judgment of "the same" even though the fluid volumes were described as different moments earlier and no fluid was added to or subtracted from the original amounts.

Adults know that this is illogical. We may try to explain to the child as patiently and as gently as we can why the two volumes must remain the same regardless of the shape of the containers. But, even if the child who cannot yet conserve volume has a genius IQ, the child knows that higher *does* mean more and no amount of explanation can shake the belief in what, to the child, is perfectly rational:

Higher means more.
Container A has a higher level than Container B.
Therefore, Container A has more fluid in it than Container B.

To the extent that the truth of our logical deductions is compromised by the truth of our personal perceptions, a conclusion may be logical, as in this example, and yet be untrue. Rationalism is therefore not by itself an adequate standard for truth.

Intuition

When we act on the basis of a hunch or "gut feeling" without a rational justification or reference to supporting data, we are operating on the basis of **intuition**. Personal and subjective though it may be, intuition is more than a wild guess. We can think of it as a belief that was not formed from a systematic examination of all the relevant data: an educated guess the reasons behind which cannot be fully articulated. For example, an archeologist selected a rather ordinary-looking site for a major excavation but could not explain the decision to her graduate students other than to say "I have a feeling we should dig here." Naturally, since the graduate students had to do most of the digging and there was no line of reasoning implied or intended to support the decision, worker morale was a significant problem — until exciting discoveries were made. Reflecting on this success, the archeologist remembered finding a rock in a nearby layer of sediment that did not appear to be of local origin. Could it be a primitive artifact, some kind of tool or weapon? This discovery, not considered particularly significant at the time, may have been the origin of the archeologist's intuitive notion that an ancient civilization once inhabited the area. Occasionally, then, intuitions prove to be correct. Nevertheless, a strong feeling of truth, even when that feeling is our own, is not an adequate standard of truth.

Intuition: Knowledge based on a personal hunch.

Science and the scientific method

The fourth source of knowledge is **science**: the collection and interpretation of observations according to rules that preserve and protect objectivity and accuracy. One type of scientific investigation is the **experiment**: the implementation of a formal strategy to reveal cause–effect relationships between variables. By controlling and manipulating scientific aspects of the research environment and recording information (data), the experimenter can test a **hypothesis**: a speculation about the truth. The hypothesis may be a tentative view of the truth or a working assumption based simply on a hunch, or it may be a carefully reasoned conjecture based on a scholarly analysis and interpretation of previously published scientific research. Some examples of hypotheses: Eating foods that contain high levels of refined sugar causes hyperactivity in young children; training in stress-management techniques can increase the productivity of managerial staff; students who use a published study guide to review before examinations will perform better than students who review only by studying the text; the more time children spend watching television, the lower their level of academic achievement will be.

Many logical principles, procedures, rules, and conventions must be followed to design sound experiments for testing hypotheses and will be the subject of study in later chapters. For now it is sufficient to recognize that, unlike the other three sources of knowledge, the scientific method holds truth to an objective standard. That is, research data gathered to support a view of the truth must be untainted by personal impressions, systematic biases, or prejudices.

Scientists must also be able to repeat (replicate) a research effort to see "the truth" for themselves: Good science is public and repeatable. By publishing an article in a scientific journal or reading a paper at a professional conference, researchers are able to communicate to their colleagues around the world precisely how and under what conditions they carried out the experiment. The open invitation scientists extend to their colleagues to challenge their research results and their interpretations of results is at the heart of the self-corrective mechanism of science.

In addition to the stress the scientific method places on accuracy and objectivity, scientific discourse is often punctuated with expert opinions. These opinions differ, however, from the dogmatic pronouncements of an authority figure. They contribute greatly to the progress of science because they are recognized only as opinions by other scientists ("Here are some hypotheses we should test") rather than statements of fact ("Here are some truths you should accept").

Science: The systematic collection of information according to rules and procedures that preserve objectivity and accuracy.

Experiment: The implementation of a formal strategy to reveal cause–effect relationships between variables.

Hypothesis: A speculation about the truth.

Some Limitations of the Scientific Method

Assumptions

Despite the importance they place on the objectivity and verifiability of information, scientists cannot proceed without accepting on faith the underlying assumptions of science. Naturally, the value of science is limited by the degree to which its underlying assumptions are true. Perhaps the most fundamental assumption of science is that our universe is orderly rather than disorderly. Scientists assume that events have causes, and for any specific event the set of possible causes is assumed to be finite. This basic assumption, applied to behavioral science, means that every behavior is assumed to have a finite number of causes.

Think of the implications if the opposite assumption were true — that each behavior has an infinite number of potential causes. No matter how much we were able to discover about the causes of a behavior, there would always remain an infinite number of undiscovered causal factors. The futility of never being able to gather enough information to understand the causes of a phenomenon would destroy any incentive to do research. Since an important goal of science is to understand the underlying causes of phenomena, and since such understanding can only be attained if an event has a finite number of causes, this is the assumption under which scientists operate.

Science also assumes that cause–effect relationships are stable over time; without that assumption, advancement in science would be impossible. For example, in psychology, once a circumstance is known to be the cause of a behavior, we assume that it will continue to be a cause next week, next month, next year. If it were possible for lawful relationships to change, what was the truth in the past would not necessarily still be the truth in the present, and what is known to be true in the present could cease to be true in the future. Can you imagine the world's scientists periodically having to scrap all their research findings in order to rediscover the natural order of a new alternative reality?

A course called Philosophy of Science, offered by the philosophy department of most colleges, deals with the structure and assumptions of science. If you are interested in these issues, you should take the philosophy of science course at some point in your college career. But even if you do not, there is little reason to worry about whether the assumptions discussed above are really true. There has never been an indication in any field of science that the two assumptions, finite causes and stability, are untrue, and scientists proceed in confidence that they will never have to confront an alternative universe and rewrite the laws of science.

Disagreements among respected scientists

Most people recognize science as the least problematic avenue to the truth, but the ability of the scientific method to answer new questions is limited by the present body of knowledge. New information builds on old information, and if our understanding of a phenomenon is incomplete, subjective opinion can appear more accurate than a scientific analysis. For example, some stock analysts occasionally ignore objective data, preferring to trust their intuitions ("Rising economic indicators be damned! I say the stock market is headed for a crash"). Incomplete data can also mislead ("I'm sorry, Mrs. Smedley. His vital signs were so strong I thought for sure he was going to pull through"). Some physicians say we will live longer if we restrict our intake of cholesterol, whereas others claim that the data linking dietary cholesterol to heart disease do not warrant such a conclusion. Of course, the current limitations of science are unlikely to remain limitations forever. In time, most limitations that result from lack of knowledge will inevitably fall to the advances of science.

Sometimes scientists take conflicting positions on issues even though the same objective data are available to all. Disagreement among scientists may appear to be a limitation, but it is actually an asset. Disagreement is at the root of the public and self-correcting aspect of science: Findings are on display in published reports for all to read and at professional meetings for all to hear. The competitive spirit among scientists that can lead to differences of opinion is not a weakness. It leads to encounters reminiscent of a Darwinian struggle for survival. The idea that lives through the attacks of one's peers and all manner of public scrutiny, the idea that survives the gauntlet of competing explanations and apparently inconsistent data will be more polished, more precise, and more likely to be correct.

Even when exhaustive objective data are available for all to evaluate, those data may not necessarily be unambiguous as they relate to the experimental hypothesis. Thus it is sometimes unclear whether the experimental data truly support the researcher's hypothesis or whether some rival explanation is more likely to be correct. Because conclusions about what the data of an experiment mean are sometimes open to personal interpretation, scientists unavoidably inject a subjective element into their objective search for the truth. How can scientists resolve their different interpretations of a set of experimental results? By doing more research!

Testable, potentially testable, and untestable hypotheses

An experimental test of a hypothesis requires the availability of objective data that will either support or fail to support the hypothesis. When such a test is possible with available technology, we term the hypothesis **testable**. Thus, a researcher who wanted to test a hypothesis relating to the effects of weightlessness on the behavioral development of the laboratory rat could test the hypothesis by arranging for an experiment in a spacecraft. Of course, that same hypothesis would have been only **potentially testable** if it had been advanced before the dawn of the space age. Sometimes we must wait for technology to catch up with our research ideas.

Psychologists are aware that science cannot provide the answers to all questions that arise in their discipline (see Box 2–1). If it is apparent from the nature of a hypothesis that objective data are not available and never will be available, the truth as it relates to that hypothesis will never be known in a scientific sense. For example, no hard data are available either to verify or disprove the notion that some instances of deviant behavior are caused by demonic possession. Neither are the data *potentially* available, so the hypothesis is **untestable**. To collect data that could reflect on the existence of demonic possession, we would have to have a way of detecting the presence of demons (presumably with a "demonometer") that would satisfy the standards of objectivity. But even if the absurdity of developing such an instrument fails to confirm the untestable nature of the demonic possession hypothesis of behavior disorders, we would still have to assume that demons, being demons, would be uncooperative and, with their powers and perverse nature, manage to sabotage the demonometer and evade detection, create false readings, or both. No instrument can provide objective and accurate data that is subject to unpredictable influences.

Testable Hypotheses: Hypotheses that are verifiable by gathering and analyzing objective data.

Potentially Testable Hypotheses: Hypotheses that are not currently testable but may one day be testable as technology advances.

Untestable Hypotheses: Hypotheses that cannot be supported or rejected on the basis of objective data.

BOX 2–1

Is Psychology a Science?

This chapter explores some major aspects of the scientific pursuit of knowledge and such sources of knowledge as authority, rationalism, and intuition. It presents science as a *method* of knowledge acquisition: a system of rules and conventions that exist to preserve the objectivity and precision with which to pursue knowledge and maximize the accuracy of interpretations of data. Science, as a method, is suitable for addressing a vast range of questions over many different disciplines. It is not aligned with any particular research discipline more than with another. Yet, for many people, researchers in such so-called hard sciences as physics, chemistry, and biology are more readily identified as scientists than are researchers in the behavioral sciences.

The public image of psychology is of significant concern to psychologists. Like researchers in other disciplines, psychologists want to promote awareness of their discipline so the public will know what they are about. Stressing the commitment psychology has to the scientific method is, in effect, a declaration of membership in the scientific community.

Is psychology a science? Can we study behavior effectively using the scientific method? Some psychologists are interested in matters that may not at first appear suitable for precise scientific study. For example, will we ever be able to analyze the content of dreams scientifically, or, for that matter, design an experiment to determine if dream analysis really does provide insight into personality dynamics? Why do we fall in love? Why do some criminals feel no guilt or remorse for the crimes they have committed? It is difficult to imagine such questions as topics of scientific investigation, given all the precision and objectivity the term *scientific* implies. Even though there are concepts and variables in psychology that are difficult to define and measure, the difficulty merely calls our attention to the challenge of psychological research. It does not, by itself, disqualify the discipline as a science. It is the *method* that is applied to answer the questions of a discipline, not the subject matter of the study, that determines whether the research is scientific or not.

Parsimony

Advancing hypotheses to explain observations is by no means limited to the research problems of formal scientific disciplines. We also generate hypotheses as we contend with everyday problems: Why won't the car start? Why won't the stereo play? Why am I so tired all the time? In troubleshooting life's little pitfalls the most sensible approach is to investigate the simplest possible explanations first and pursue more complex explanations only when we must. Thus we test the hypothesis that an absence of gasoline in the fuel tank is responsible for the failure of a car to start before we have it towed to the garage for a comprehensive engine and ignition-system analysis. We make sure the stereo is properly connected to a working electrical outlet before we consider the hypothesis that a more complicated cause such as a blown transistor or a damaged printed circuit board underlies the malfunction. And we get more rest to test the hypothesis that inadequate sleep is responsible for our fatigue before we consent to undergo expensive and possibly painful medical tests for ailments that have fatigue as a symptom.

The approach we use to deal with common daily problems, to explain the greatest possible number of facts with the fewest possible principles and assumptions and to evaluate the simplest explanation first, is the same guiding principle scientists use when constructing theories: the principle of **parsimony**. William of Occam, a fourteenth-century philosopher, is generally credited with articulating the principle of parsimony, which is also known as **Occam's Razor**. What William of Occam actually said was that "Entities should not be multiplied without necessity." Translation: We should avoid framing explanations of phenomena founded on numerous assumptions. If two or more explanations are equally well reasoned and consistent with available data, the simplest explanation is the preferred one — at least until it is shown to be inconsistent with new, carefully collected evidence.

Morgan's (1906) application of the principle of parsimony to the study of animal behavior is known as **Morgan's canon**: "In no case is an animal activity to be interpreted in terms of higher psychological processes if it can be fairly interpreted in terms of processes which stand lower in the scale of psychological evolution and development." Morgan originally formulated his statement in 1894, using somewhat different wording, in reaction to the writings of Romanes, a contemporary of his who used anecdotal reports (informal observations) of animal behavior to support the view that some animals possess humanlike thinking and reasoning skills.

Imparting human motives, emotions, and intellectual abilities to animals in the absence of carefully controlled scientific observations is called **anthropomorphizing**. Thus we hear new parents talk of how "jealous" their pet dog is of the new baby, and how the once house-trained dog is "taking revenge" and being "spiteful" by soiling the new rugs. A more parsimonious explanation is that the harried new parents have not been adhering to the walking schedule the dog was used to and/or, in their understandable preoccupation with their new child, have become less sensitive to the behaviors that signal the animal's need to go out.

Parsimony: Principle that the simplest of two or more equally well-reasoned explanations is the preferred explanation.

Occam's Razor: We should avoid framing explanations based on numerous assumptions.

Morgan's Canon: "In no case is an animal activity to be interpreted in terms of higher psychological processes if it can be fairly interpreted in terms of processes which stand lower in the scale of psychological evolution and development."

Anthropomorphizing: Imparting human motives, emotions, and intellectual abilities to animals in the absence of carefully controlled scientific observations.

Starting the Scientific Process

Induction versus deduction

Two logical approaches for the discovery and description of lawful relationships are used in science: **induction** and **deduction**. Both logical processes play an important role in the advancement of science. Induction is the process of integrating information from known facts (available data) in order to explain why the facts are as they are. As suggested in Figure 2–2, induction starts with an examination of facts and progresses to a **theory** — a formal proposition or set of propositions that serve to explain, integrate, and in general make sense of a set of facts. Deduction works in the opposite direction: from theory to facts. A properly stated and scientifically valuable theory yields predictions (testable hypotheses) of what the

Induction: Integrating information from facts in order to explain why the facts are as they are.

Deduction: A statement of the facts a researcher should find if a theory is correct.

Theory: A proposition or set of propositions that serve to explain and integrate a set of facts.

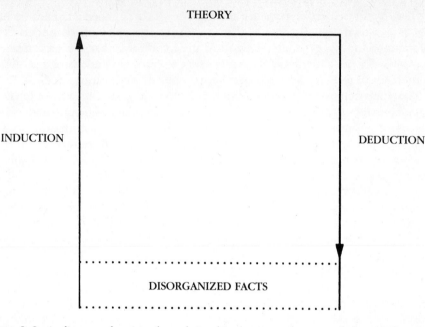

Figure 2–2. A diagram showing the relationship between theory and facts. Proposing a theoretical structure that will explain the arrangement of a set of facts is an inductive process, whereas a prediction from theory that certain facts will be found if we search for them is a deductive process.

researcher should find if he or she searches systematically for certain facts (collects certain data).

The terms *inductive* and *deductive* are used as descriptors for different types of research as well as for the logical processes they represent. Research described as inductive is not a logical extension of a formal theory, it is done primarily to discover facts. For example, some experiments are done simply to satisfy curiosity ("I wonder what would happen if...") or simply to answer a question arising from conflicting interpretations of existing data. Inductive research is driven by the notion that if enough facts become known and if enough questions are answered through research, a unifying theoretical framework will tend to emerge just as surely as the picture in a jigsaw puzzle becomes more recognizable with each successful fitting of the pieces.

When, on the other hand, the direction of reasoning progresses from theory to facts, from an abstract logical explanation to a search for empirical data that will support or call into question the accuracy of that explanation, the idea behind the research effort has been deductively inspired. For example, assume a genetic theory that can predict the genetic makeup of offspring from the controlled breeding of certain male-female genotypes is formulated. Once the experiment is carried out, the data would be compared to the theoretically predicted (deduced) results. The experimental data would either support the theory or, if the data are inconsistent with the theory, support the view that the theory is incorrect in its present form and must be modified or abandoned.

In a sense, the distinction between inductive and deductive research is somewhat artificial. In deductive research, if the data do not support the theory, the theory must either be modified to accommodate the data or, if unsalvageable, discarded entirely. This is an inductive process because the reasoning flows from data to theory construction. In inductive research the questions addressed by a research effort very often stem from some logical framework. That is, the set of known facts has a conspicuous void — a hole that cries out to be filled even if the reason for doing the experiment is not represented as a test of a formal theory. So, in the latter sense, inductive research is also deductive.

Summary

This chapter approaches science, a method for answering questions by means of the collection and interpretation of objective data, in terms of its relationship to other sources of knowledge: authority and faith (unquestioning trust in the truth of a person or idea), rationalism (using logic to reveal the truth), and intuition (the "gut feelings" or hunches we sometimes get from incomplete information). Scientific research, despite its objectivity and logical elegance, does, however, have limitations. Science cannot be used to evaluate the truth of all propositions because not all propositions are testable. Some are only potentially testable because their testing must await technological advances or the occurrence of a natural event. Other propositions are untestable because they do not pertain to the physical world ("It is possible to communicate with the dead"). Even science must accept some untestable assumptions ("events have causes" and "cause–effect relationships are stable over time"). This chapter also addressed the importance of parsimony (advancing the simplest explanation for a set of observations) to theory construction and the role of induction (facts → theory) and deduction (theory → facts) in the research process.

Key Terms

Anthropomorphizing, p. 19
Deduction, p. 19
Experiment, p. 15
Hypothesis, p. 15
Induction, p. 19
Morgan's Canon, p. 19
Occam's Razor, p. 19
Parsimony, p. 19
Potentially Testable Hypotheses, p. 17

Sources of Knowledge
   Authority, p. 11
   Rationalism, p. 12
   Intuition, p. 14
   Science, p. 15
Testable Hypotheses, p. 17
Theory, p. 19
Untestable Hypotheses, p. 17

Chapter Exercises

1. Select several beliefs you are confident are true. Then examine the source of your knowledge of the truth (authority, rationalism, intuition, and science). Do these sources of knowledge complement each other, are they incompatible, or both?

2. If science is objective, why do scientists sometimes disagree?

3. Discuss the limitations of science as a way of finding the truth.

4. Why are some questions regarded as unsuitable (untestable) for scientific investigation?

5. Compare and contrast inductive research to deductive research.

6. Janet came home late from work and flipped the switch for the light on her front porch. Nothing happened. Generate some testable hypotheses that could account for the failure of the porch light.

7. Assume that one day you find your usually outgoing friend strangely uncommunicative and grouchy. Formulate a theory concerning the cause that is consistent with your observation of uncommunicative and grouchy behavior and generate some testable hypotheses that you could use to support your theory.

Proposal Assignment 2: Are You Having Trouble with Proposal Assignment 1?

If you are having trouble finding a topic for a research proposal maybe the material covered in chapter 2 will help. Have you ever tried to convince someone to agree with you without having persuasive evidence? If you recall such an incident, perhaps you could design a study to collect information to prove your point.

Or perhaps you have an idea for your proposal, but it appears too simple. It is better to begin with a simple idea, because projects that initially appear simple often become complicated during development. If you have a few ideas and cannot decide which is most interesting, or if you are having trouble finding a topic, ask friends their opinions.

CHAPTER

The Characteristics of Data and Variables

Some of the material in this chapter may already be familiar, especially if you have taken other psychology courses. But, new or review, it is an important foundation of basic terminology that you must master to prepare for more advanced topics.

Data: Information for Answering Questions

The information research produces is called *data*. Assuming that a research plan conforms to the logical principles and procedural rigor of the scientific method, data can provide the answers to questions and the information to support or reject hypotheses. But there is one problem every researcher must face. Data are recorded in code, using numbers. So, before drawing conclusions from data, we must process them by means of **statistical analysis**, a tool for highlighting, extracting, and organizing the information in data. However, just as a skilled artisan is careful to use only tools appropriate for the job, researchers must also exercise care when selecting an approach to data analysis. The choice is partly dependent on understanding *scaling*, the level of measurement reflected in data values.

The Scaling of Data

Research data belong to one of four **measurement scales**: nominal, ordinal, interval, or ratio. Two points are particularly important here. First, scaling defines the level of information represented in the numerical code we use to record data, so data cannot be properly interpreted without knowing their scaling. Second, statistical tests for data analysis have underlying assumptions, one of which specifies the scaling that must be present in the data. If, for example, analyses that assume one level of scaling are performed on data with a more superficial scaling level, the results of the analysis may be uninterpretable. To illustrate the importance of scaling, consider one set of values (1, 2, 3, 4, 5, and 6) in four different contexts: as the player numbers (labels) on athletic jerseys, the order in which six competitors finished a race, temperature (either Fahrenheit or Celsius), and measures of distance.

Nominal scaling

When numerals are used only as labels, they serve a naming, categorizing, or classification function and are described as having **nominal scaling**. Nominal data communicate the relationship equal or unequal. For example, assume you went to a track and field competition and, over the course of the afternoon, saw a tall blonde competitor on three separate occasions. On one occasion the competitor wore the numeral 2 on her jersey, on another occasion a 4, and the third time a 6. Even though the athletes were very similar in appearance, you know that because each wore a different numerical label, the three competitors were not the same person. You attach no significance to the fact that 4 is more than 2, that 4 is twice the value of 2, or that the two units that separate 2 and 4 are the same number of units that separate 4 and 6. As athletic-jersey labels, the values can only represent the relationships equal (same value equals same person) or unequal (different value equals different person).

Some variables are simple labels or names (ethnic group, gender, eye color, nationality, social security number, political affiliation). No number is needed to record an individual datum (the singular of data): we simply classify subjects' attributes or behaviors into discrete categories and keep a tally of how many subjects belong in each category. For example, Republican, Democrat, and Independent are three categories of the variable *political party*.

It makes no sense to add, subtract, multiply, or divide values that reflect nominal measurement. For example, the mean value of all the players' jersey numbers is an uninterpretable value. It is possible to compute it by adding up all the jersey numbers and dividing by the number of players, but what possible interpretation could we give the mean of a set of numerical labels? The only numerical operation permissible with nominal data is the calculation of the frequency or percentage in each category. For example, in Table 3–1 the political party affiliations of a group of

Statistical Analysis: A tool for extracting, highlighting, and organizing the information in data.

Measurement Scales: The four levels of information data can convey (nominal, ordinal, interval, or ratio).

Nominal Scale: Numerals are used to name, categorize, or label.

	Republican	Democrat	Independent	Total
Frequency	54	98	48	200
Percentage	27	49	24	100

Table 3–1. Nominal measurement (political party affiliation) of 200 citizens shown as category frequencies and percentages.

200 citizens are displayed both as frequencies (the number of people in each party) and as percentages of individuals in the three qualitative categories. Notice from Table 3–1 that although we do not need numbers to record an individual datum (the variable values are Republican, Democrat, and Independent), we do use numbers to summarize the frequencies and percentages of individuals who belong to the various categories.

Ordinal scaling

Ordinal Scale: Numerals of different magnitude convey only "more" or "less."

Numerals that have **ordinal scaling** reflect relative magnitude in addition to the equal versus unequal information in nominal data. That is, ordinal data express the relationship "more versus less" in addition to "equal versus unequal." For example, if the same three competitors who wore numbers 2, 4, and 6 on their jerseys finished the race in first, second, and fourth positions, we would, of course, know that the race results posted for these runners (1, 2, and 4) refer to the performances of three different athletes. But we would also know that the competitor who finished in position 1 ran faster than the other two and that the competitor who finished in position 4 was the slowest of the three. When used to represent race results, the information on order reflected in the values 1, 2, and 4 means that the scaling of these numerals is at least ordinal.

Notice that no significance is attached to the size of the intervals between the values 1, 2, and 4. The fact that one unit separates 1 and 2 and two units separate 2 and 4 is irrelevant. For example, it is quite possible that the fourth-place runner was equally as close to the second-place runner as the second-place runner was to the first-place runner. Also, the fact that four is twice the value of two has no meaning in this context. It does not mean, for example, that the runner in fourth position finished twice as far back as the runner in second position. In general, data in the form of ranks (1st, 2nd, 3rd, etc.) or in the form of subjective ratings (as in scoring a beauty pageant, cooking contest, or works of art) are assumed to have ordinal scaling.

Sometimes ordinal data appear as an ordered series of categories that, like nominal data, do not require the use of numbers to record an individual datum. For example, instead of recording the order in which 90 marathon runners finish a race using numerals (1st, 2nd, 3rd, ... 90th), we could categorize the first 30 runners to finish the race as "fast," the second 30 to finish as "average," and the last 30 to finish as "slow." The scaling is ordinal because the categories not only represent different classifications of performance (nominal), the categories also differ by more or less of something (in this example, speed). Thus it is legitimate to argue that when category labels convey information on magnitude, measurement is ordinal rather than nominal.

Interval scaling

When data have **interval scaling**, we have more precise information on magnitude than ordinal data can provide. Specifically, numerically equal intervals reflect equal magnitudes of the variable being measured. Thus, when the values 1, 2, 3, 4, 5, and 6 represent temperature in Fahrenheit or Celsius, we know that different values represent different levels of heat (the equal versus unequal relationship of the nominal scale), higher values represent more heat (the more versus less relationship of the ordinal scale), and the difference in heat between equal intervals is the same: the two-degree difference in heat between 1° and 3° is the same quantity of heat that separates 4° and 6°.

The fact that equal intervals are known to reflect equal magnitudes represents a substantial increase in the information content of interval data compared to ordinal data. There is, however, an interesting limitation on the information we have when a variable has interval scaling. Even though 4° is (a) different from 2°, (b) more than 2°, and (c) different from 2° by the same amount that 4° is different from 6°, we cannot say that 4° is twice as hot as 2°. This is because the Fahrenheit and Celsius scales, which are interval, have an arbitrary rather than a true zero point. For example, 0° Celsius, the temperature at which water freezes, does not represent the temperature at which all heat is absent.

Interval Scale: Different variable values reflect different magnitudes, and equal intervals between magnitudes reflect equal quantity.

Ratio scaling

Data with **ratio scaling** contain all the information inherent in nominal scaling (equal versus unequal), ordinal scaling (more versus less), and interval scaling (same-size intervals represent equal magnitudes). But, unlike the latter three measurement scales, the ratio scale has a true zero point, which means that zero represents the true absence of what is being measured. For example, the value zero as applied to the measurement of volume, time, distance, and weight represents a true zero quantity for those variables.

The most noteworthy aspect in comparing ratio scaling to interval scaling is that statements concerning the relative magnitudes of data values (such as when we say value A is "twice as much as" value B or quantity C is "half as much as" quantity D) are meaningful only if the data have ratio scaling. Thus, whereas the comparison of two distances — "four miles is twice as far as two miles" — is meaningful, "4°C is twice as hot as 2°C" is not meaningful. Since distance is a ratio-scaled variable, the distance of four miles is not only a *different* distance than two miles, it is not only *more* of a distance than two miles, it is not only *equally different* from six miles (four plus two) as it is from two miles (four minus two), it is also *twice* the distance of two miles. By comparison, the amount of heat in 4°C is *not* twice the amount of heat in 2°C. There is one scale of temperature that, unlike the Fahrenheit and Celsius scales, permits ratio statements. In the Kelvin scale, in which the value zero does represent the true absence of heat, 4° is twice as hot as 2°.

Sometimes, to differentiate nominal and ordinal data from interval and ratio data, nominal and ordinal values are referred to as *numerals*, whereas interval and ratio values are referred to as *numbers* (also called *cardinal numbers*). Only cardinal numbers can be meaningfully subjected to mathematical operations (addition, subtraction, multiplication, division, square root, etc.). Table 3–2 gives a summary of the properties of the four measurement scales.

Ratio Scale: Equal intervals reflect equal quantity and the variable has a true zero point.

If the data are...,	the numerals 0, 1, 2, 3, 4 signify...
nominal	different labels for naming or categorizing
ordinal	different ranks to represent "more" or "less"
interval	values that are separated by an equal quantity (Zero is set arbitrarily, so 4 is *not* twice as much as 2.)
ratio	values that are separated by equal quantity (Zero represents the true absence of that being measured, so 4 *is* twice as much as 2.)

Table 3–2. A summary of the different levels of information that the same numerals (0, 1, 2, 3, and 4) can contain when belonging to each of the four different measurement scales.

The Reliability of Data

Reliability: Consistency of a measurement taken at different times.

    Reliability is discussed in various research contexts in later chapters, but it is not too soon to become familiar with this very important concept. A reliable measurement is one that shows consistency over time. If, for example, a psychologist tested your intelligence on two separate occasions, using the same test each time, and reported that you obtained similar or identical IQ scores, the consistency of the IQ assessments would indicate that the test was a reliable measure of intelligence. Similarly, if an experiment yields essentially the same data each time it is repeated, the data are reliable. If, instead, there is wide variation in the data across replications of the experiment despite all attempts to duplicate the original experimental conditions, the data are not reliable.

    The failure to reproduce experimental results is usually an indication that there are one or more confounding variables (chapter 1) present of which the experimenter is unaware. Let us examine this concept using an example of an actual student experience. George had a reliable method for removing various stains from his clothing. The spot-removing method had been passed down through the family for generations, and it worked consistently. Yet, when George moved more than a thousand miles away from his home town to attend college and tried to remove some stains from his clothes, the method did not work consistently. Could it be that the coin-operated machines in the dormitory just did not do as good a job as Mom's supercharged model? Was the water temperature inappropriate for maximum stain-removing action? Because George was so busy in school, did he wait too long after staining the garment before laundering it, allowing the stain to set? Any or all of these variables could cause the stain remover to yield unreliable results, but, in this case, it turned out that the hard, mineral-laden water of the region was the culprit. George discovered this by going to a laundromat that provided softened water for its machines. When he did his laundry in the dormitory and added a little water softener, the stain remover was restored to its usual level of reliability.

The Validity of Data

Validity refers to the capacity of a measurement to reflect accurately the variable under study. Experienced researchers never lose sight of the importance of validity because the more valid a measurement is, the easier it is to interpret the data. For example, to evaluate the health of their patients, physicians measure variables such as body temperature, white cell count in the blood, the presence of lesions, inflammation, and/or swelling, and other assorted instrument readings and sounds. Once analyzed, these data allow the physician to evaluate the patient with respect to the presence and severity of disease, trauma, or infection and, if intervention is warranted, the data are used to arrive at a recommended course of treatment. If the presence of certain symptoms and instrument readings do not accurately reflect the presence or absence of medical problems, we would say that the measures are not valid indications of whether or not a medical problem exists. Because physicians have confidence in the validity of their measurements, the answer to the question "What do the data mean?" is rather straightforward.

As an example of invalid measurement, consider the instructor who administers a poorly constructed test to her students (the questions are vague, ambiguous, or do not relate in a direct fashion to the knowledge of course material the students are expected to have). In such a case the test will not accurately reflect the extent to which the students know the assigned material because the question "What do the data mean?" cannot be answered with any confidence. Did the students fail to learn the assigned material or were the test questions so confusing that even a thoroughly prepared student would have performed poorly? Because the measuring instrument was flawed and did not yield an accurate measure of student achievement, the instructor cannot know how much of the assigned material the students really did or did not know. In this case we would say that the examination was not a valid instrument for measuring student achievement.

It is interesting to note that a measurement can be reliable without being valid, but a measurement cannot be both unreliable and valid. For example, consider a person who is not fluent in English and whose experiences have been largely restricted to growing up in a somewhat isolated ethnic community. If that person gets the same (reliable) low score on repeated administrations of an IQ test, would the tester be justified in describing the person as mentally impaired? Not necessarily. Some tests are culturally biased because they refer to information outside the normal realm of the test taker's experience. Cultural bias is a problem in IQ tests, and, to the extent that it is present, the test is not a valid measure of intelligence. Thus the culturally biased test may be reliable without being valid. On the other hand, a valid IQ test would also be reliable because an accurate (valid) measuring device will result in the same (reliable) measurement each time it is used.

Reactivity

One phenomenon that can have a negative effect on both reliability and validity is **reactivity**, an extraneous influence on measurement that occurs when the act of measuring a response itself produces a reaction in the subject. Reactivity is particularly common in the measurement of physiological responses such as blood

Validity: The capacity of a measurement to reflect accurately the variable under study.

Reactivity: An extraneous influence on measurement that occurs when the act of measurement produces a reaction in the subject.

pressure. The mild discomfort that occurs when the air-filled cuff closes tightly about the patient's arm can, in some individuals, cause a stress response and initially elevate the blood pressure reading. The first reading is often unreliable because it tends to be higher than subsequent readings taken when the patient is more relaxed. Similarly, if you were measuring a behavior that reflected problem-solving ability in an animal population and used apparatus that tended to frighten some of the animals, poor performance would not necessarily be a valid indication of poor problem-solving ability.

Variables

Variable: That which is subject to change, such as an experimental condition (independent variable) or a behavioral measure (dependent variable).

In the dictionary **variable** is primarily an adjective: It describes something that is subject to change. In a research or mathematical context, however, the term *variable* is usually a noun, referring to the identity of that which is subject to change. Independent and dependent variables (commonly designated variable X and variable Y, respectively) are discussed at length in Part II, but these terms are so important they are introduced in a brief preview in the next two sections.

Independent and Dependent Variables

Experimental Research: A method for documenting cause–effect relationships between variables.

Independent Variable: A manipulated variable that defines the treatment conditions of an experiment.

Treatments (Treatment Conditions): Conditions manipulated by and under the direct control of the experimenter.

Dependent Variable: A measurement that changes in response to different values of an independent variable.

When we define **experimental research** as a method for documenting cause–effect relationships between variables, we use *variable* as a noun. Values of the **independent variable** of an experiment define its **treatments** or **treatment conditions**, conditions that are manipulated by and under the direct control of the experimenter. The **dependent variable** is a measure used to register the effect(s) of one or more treatment conditions.

Assume, for example, that a psychologist is trying to find the answer to a relatively straightforward research question: Does a newly synthesized drug reduce the craving for cocaine that addicts experience? The fundamental strategy she intends to use to address this question is to document changes in one variable (craving for cocaine) that take place following the systematic manipulation of another variable (degree of exposure to the new drug).

Since degree of exposure to the new drug is the variable the experimenter intends to manipulate in a systematic fashion, it is the independent variable. The measure that is likely to change value in response to the manipulation of the independent variable is craving for cocaine, so craving is the dependent variable. The distinction between independent and dependent variables as used in an experimental context should be relatively easy to remember if you keep in mind that the value of the dependent variable *depends* upon the value of the independent variable.

To help remember the distinction between independent and dependent variables keep in mind some examples that relate to common experience. Let us say an automobile owner bought a different brand of gasoline each of the last four times he filled his fuel tank. The owner's goal was to evaluate the four different brands for fuel economy. In this case fuel economy, as measured in miles per gallon of gasoline, is the dependent variable and the brand of fuel is the independent variable. Similarly, if you plotted three different routes on your road map to get from City A to City B and, over time, tried all three routes to see which was the fastest, the specific routes (Routes 1, 2, and 3) would be the independent variable and travel time would be the dependent variable.

Operational Definitions of Variables

You may have noticed that the descriptions of the independent variable (degree of exposure) and dependent variable (craving) offered above in the drug study are far too vague to permit precise manipulation of drug exposure or measurement of craving in a research setting. The solution is to define the concepts "degree of exposure" and "craving," the independent and dependent variables of the study, in objective, unambiguous, methodological terms. That is, we must provide **operational definitions** for the independent and dependent variables. An operational definition of an independent variable is a detailed description of the specific operations used to *manipulate* the independent variable, and an operational definition of a dependent variable is a detailed description of the specific operations used to *measure* the dependent variable. In the case of the independent variable in the cocaine study, the researcher would have to decide on an operational definition for "degree of exposure." The most obvious systematic manipulation for varying the degree of exposure in the present context would be to vary the dose level (200 mg, 400 mg, etc.) of the new drug that is administered to the cocaine-addicted subjects of the experiment.

Similarly, "craving," the dependent variable, would have to be operationally defined so that it could be measured objectively. Because of ethical considerations that govern the conduct of research with humans, virtually all initial evaluations of experimental drugs use animal populations. (Complete coverage of ethical principles of psychological research, including APA guidelines for research involving human or animal subjects, appears in chapter 16.) So, let us assume that the laboratory rat was used as an animal model of a cocaine addict. Let us further assume that by pressing a lever to activate some sort of cocaine-delivery system, the rats could administer cocaine to themselves. With such an arrangement the researcher could operationally define the dependent variable "craving for cocaine" in an objective and quantifiable manner in terms of the number of lever presses that occurred in, say, a two-hour test period. If lever-pressing behavior is truly being driven by craving, the more lever pressing that occurs, the greater the craving the animal is presumably experiencing.

Other operational definitions

In addition to independent and dependent variables, researchers must also operationally define important terms and labels that are used in any research project. For example, the term *addict* may mean different things to different people. To arrive at a precise definition, addict, too, should be operationally defined. This could be done by listing the specific behavioral characteristics used to characterize individual rats as addicts. For example, the researcher could define an addicted rat as one that, even after a 24-hour period of food and water deprivation, spends more time self-administering cocaine than eating or drinking, or a rat that would cross a

Operational Definition: An objective definition of a variable stated in terms of the specific methods used to manipulate (independent) or measure (dependent) the variable.

30-cm wire grid charged with 0.5 mA of electricity to gain access to cocaine. To leave the definition of an addict to opinion or a vague standard would violate the objective standards of science.

Quantitative versus qualitative operational definitions

Qualitative: Representing different values of a variable without reference to a quantifiable characteristic (e.g., ethnic group, job title, and brand name.)

Quantitative: Representing different values of a variable as numerically coded expressions of magnitude (e.g., intelligence, drug usage, and time).

Since the distinction between **quantitative** and **qualitative** variables is referred to often in later chapters let us deal with the distinction itself before applying it to operational definitions. Chemistry provides an easily understood example. A chemist who analyzes a sample of unknown contents to determine what chemicals are present in the sample is doing a qualitative analysis. The analysis answers the question "*What* is in the sample?" When the chemist knows *what* is in the sample and wishes to determine *how much* of each chemical is present, the chemist does a quantitative analysis. In similar fashion, the operational definitions of the independent and dependent variables developed above were stated in quantitative terms: the drug dosage (quantity) of the experimental anticraving drug the animal received before being given the opportunity to lever-press for cocaine (the independent variable) and the number (quantity) of lever-press responses given in the test situation.

Operational definitions of independent and dependent variables may also be stated in qualitative terms. For example, if the experimental objective was to compare the relative therapeutic effectiveness of two different drugs, the independent variable (Drug 1 versus Drug 2) would be a qualitative rather than a quantitative difference. The distinction between the two treatment conditions is the identity of the drug used rather than the quantity of the drug used. Qualitative measures usually relate to a characteristic of a variable that cannot readily be represented using numbers. By contrast, quantitative description (amount, intensity, speed, and so forth) always involves numbers.

The distinction between quantitative and qualitative variables, however, is actually not as clear-cut as the preceding discussion may suggest. It is often possible to quantify qualitative differences. For example, in addition to counting lever presses to get a measure of cocaine self-administration, the researcher could record the style of the responses. That is, it is possible for two animals to lever-press an equal number of times within a given time interval but exhibit very different patterns of responding. One animal could press in bursts, resting in between, whereas another animal could spread out the same number of responses over roughly equally spaced intervals. Assuming each lever press delivered an equal amount of cocaine, both animals would receive the same overall dose, but the burst pattern would result in larger swings in dose level over time. The two patterns are analogous to differences in drinking patterns among alcoholics. Some sip throughout the day, maintaining a relatively low but constant level of intoxication; others go on periodic binges followed by periods of abstinence.

In the context of the lever-pressing example, assume that a burst is operationally defined as the occurrence of five or more lever presses within a five-minute period. At the completion of the experiment we could count the number of bursts performed by each subject and, by doing so, quantify a qualitative difference in substance-abuse behavior (steady responders versus burst responders).

Manipulated versus Nonmanipulated Variables

A **manipulated variable** is an independent variable, a condition that is under the direct control of the experimenter. Experimenter control of the independent variable is evident not only in the role the experimenter has in determining its values (low dose versus high dose of a drug treatment, for example), but also in the control the experimenter has over which subjects are exposed to which values. In true experimental research both elements of control must be present. (This characterization of experimental research is consistent with the preceding discussion of independent and dependent variables, which pointed out that the independent variable of an experiment is the variable that is systematically manipulated by the experimenter.)

Sometimes, however, psychologists wish to study the behavior of subjects who differ in systematic ways not as a consequence of some experimenter-controlled manipulation but because of the natural variety that exists in life experiences, physical characteristics, personality traits, age, IQ, aptitude, and so forth. When we define an independent variable that is *not* under the direct control of the experimenter, the variable is a **nonmanipulated variable** (also called a **subject variable** because the variable is a measurable subject characteristic).

There are two categories of nonmanipulated variables. When a nonmanipulated variable is a personal descriptor, such as career choice, years of formal education, degree of assertiveness, sexual preference, age, physical condition, or dietary habits, it is called a **selected variable**. Alternatively, when a nonmanipulated variable is defined by the subjects' exposure to or isolation from an unplanned event that has the potential to influence behavior, it is referred to as a **natural treatment**. Examples include being the victim of a crime, suffering an illness or family tragedy, winning a lottery, changing jobs, and so forth. Selected variables and natural treatments are described as ex post facto (after the fact) because the subjects are not recruited for the study until after the selected variables already exist and after the natural treatments have already occurred. When psychologists study the relationships between nonmanipulated variables (selected variables and natural treatments) and behavior, they are engaged in **correlational research**, *not* experimental research.

Gender is an example of a nonmanipulated variable because it is a result of biological and genetic determinants removed from any purposeful experimenter-controlled manipulation. Like so many other nonmanipulated variables that are connected to behavioral research (heredity, birth order, age, early versus late maturation of adolescents, deprivation and/or abuse during childhood, substance abuse, physical attractiveness, and so on), there is great interest in studying the role of gender as a predictor of behavior. Indeed, there are scientific journals devoted solely to gender-related topics (such as *sex roles*).

Confounding (Extraneous) Variables

A *confounding variable* is a factor in addition to the independent variable that can exert a systematic effect on experimental results. When a confounding variable is allowed to contaminate an experimental research environment, it is impossible to determine whether any observed differences among the different treatment

---

Manipulated Variable:
An independent variable; a condition under the direct control of the experimenter.

Nonmanipulated (Subject) Variable:
A subject characteristic or experience over which the researcher has no control.

Selected Variable:
A personal subject characteristic, such as age, years of formal education, or gender.

Natural Treatment:
Exposure to or isolation from an unplanned event.

Correlational Research:
Study of the relationships between nonmanipulated variables (selected variables and natural treatments) and behavior.

conditions of the experiment were caused by an action of the independent variable, by an action of the confounding variable, or both.

As an example of confounding we reported in chapter 1 a finding that theater patrons purchased more beverages when subliminal messages were flashed on the screen during movies than when no messages were flashed. The independent variable was therefore the presence or absence of messages, and the dependent variable was the number of beverage purchases. This result appears to support the notion that subliminal advertising is capable of boosting sales of soft drinks. But we also reported that the flashing of subliminal messages was done during the summer season, whereas collection of the supposed baseline data (beverage purchases in the absence of subliminal messages) was done during the winter. Since beverage purchases are typically higher during the warm summer months for obvious weather-related reasons unrelated to subliminal advertising, there are two rival explanations for the experimental finding. That is, the difference in beverage purchases is just as likely to have arisen from the confounding variable (summer versus winter) as from the independent variable of the experiment.

Extraneous Variables:
A variable that introduces confounding and, thereby, rival explanations of an experimental result. Another name for confounding variable.

The term **extraneous variable** is often used interchangeably with *confounding variable* and, as the label implies, such variables can introduce "extra" influences on the experimental results that allow for more than one interpretation. For example, you have decided to compare the quality of two different brands of frozen French-fried potatoes. If you prepare Brand A in a conventional oven and Brand B in a microwave oven, your negative evaluation of Brand B will most likely be a consequence of the method of preparation (microwaved French fries tend to be soggy) rather than a function of any difference in the quality of brands. Your attempt to compare the two brands is thus complicated by the presence of a confounding variable: the method of preparation. Obviously, the only fair way to compare the two brands is to prepare them in an identical manner. By cooking both brands in a conventional oven you would be neutralizing any possible effect of the method-of-preparation variable by holding it constant.

Unfortunately, the intrusion of extraneous variables into an experimental situation is rarely as obvious as in this example. Even without training in research methods, most individuals would see the folly of comparing the two brands of oven-ready potatoes using different methods of preparation. (In chapter 10 you will get a more realistic view of the struggle researchers engage in to eliminate, or at least limit, the influence of extraneous variables on their experimental data.) The effort to eliminate confounding variables from a study is a worthy investment because, if confounding is present, the inevitable question that follows a study — "What do the data mean?" — cannot be answered with confidence.

Causally Connected versus Associated Variables

Association: The systematic and orderly paralleling of the values of different variables.

When the values of two variables parallel each other in a systematic and orderly way, we say that an **association** exists. But it is important to recognize that association *alone* does not allow us to conclude that there is a causal link between the variables. For example, the finding that males tend to have higher wages than females is a description of the relationship between gender and wages: males = high, females = low. Sexism may indeed be the underlying cause of the wage differential, but because gender is a nonmanipulated variable, the possibility of a causal connection cannot be scientifically verified. Factors other than sexism may be responsible for the correlation between the gender and wage variables. In short, a correlation between variables is not evidence of a cause–effect relationship.

Perhaps the reason females tend to have lower wages than males is because the entry of women into the labor force in large numbers is a relatively recent phenomenon. Employees with fewer years on the job usually do have lower wages than their more experienced coworkers. So, in terms completely unrelated to gender, maybe on-the-job experience, a third variable, explains why differences in wages are *associated* with the gender variable.

Naturally, it is quite another matter if men and women are found to be equally experienced, equally competent, and are performing the same or equivalent jobs for unequal pay. Under such circumstances, after discounting all known possible competing explanations, when an explanation related to gender is all that remains, most people would agree that the wage differential between men and women is, at least in part, *caused* by sex bias. Nevertheless, as tempting as this causal interpretation may be and as much intuitive sense as it may make, *in doing research with nonmanipulated variables we can never be completely sure that we have ruled out all competing explanations.* For this reason we must describe the gender-related difference (men tend to have higher wages than women) as an *association*, as we did at the end of the last paragraph, rather than as a *causal* determinant of the wage differential.

Even though it can be very risky to offer causal interpretations when studying the behavioral significance of nonmanipulated variables, we must also recognize that it makes no sense to *exclude* causal explanations out of hand. For example, if a study should find that systematic behavioral differences exist between adolescent children whose parents decided to send them to day care during their preschool years and children whose parents kept them at home, there would be no reason to exclude day-care experience as a causal factor in the development of the observed behavioral differences just because it is a nonmanipulated variable. We could correctly hypothesize that day-care experience is a *potential* cause of the observed behavioral differences and test the hypothesis by manipulating the day-care variable in an experiment. (Of course the experiment is only hypothetical because obvious ethical considerations prevent a researcher from systematically manipulating which children do or do not attend a day-care center.)

Summary

This chapter reviewed the terms and concepts that comprise a fundamental research vocabulary. We began with *data* and explained how the information content of data is determined by its scaling. Then we discussed *reliability* (the consistency of measurement) and *validity* (the accuracy of measurement) and pointed out how the loss of one or both attributes can affect the interpretation of data. *Reactivity* and *confounding* (extraneous) *variables* were presented as threats to validity. We explained the distinction between *independent* and *dependent variables, manipulated* versus *nonmanipulated variables, causally related variables* (as revealed by experimental research) versus *associated variables* (as revealed by correlational research), and discussed the importance of operationally defining all the variables and important terms that relate to a research project. The terms explored in this chapter will recur in a variety of different contexts throughout the text, so it is imperative that you become thoroughly familiar with them and the issues to which they relate.

Key Terms

Association, p. 34
Confounding (Extraneous) Variables, p. 34
Correlational Research, p. 33
Dependent Variable, p. 30
Experimental Research, p. 30
Independent Variable, p. 30
Manipulated Variables, p. 33
Nonmanipulated (Subject) Variables, p. 33
Selected Variable, p. 33
Natural Treatments, p. 33

Measurement Scales: Nominal, Ordinal, Interval, or Ratio, p. 25, 26, 27
Operational Definitions of Variables, p. 31
Qualitative, p. 32
Quantitative, p. 32
Reactivity, p. 29
Reliability, p. 28
Statistical Analysis, p. 25
Treatments and Treatment Conditions, p. 30
Validity, p. 29
Variable, p. 30

Chapter Exercises

1. Identify the scaling of the following behavioral variables:
   a. Time to complete a task
   b. The number of persons who agree versus the number who disagree with a controversial statement
   c. Your rank in your high school graduating class
   d. Your cumulative grade-point average in college.
2. Which is the only scale with a true zero point?
3. Which scale performs only a naming or labeling function?
4. Is a person with an IQ of 150 "twice as smart as" a person with an IQ of 75?

5. Is the difference in intelligence between a person with an IQ of 100 and someone with an IQ of 120 the same difference in intelligence that exists between individuals with IQs of 140 and 160?

6. Glen, a college student, has a very reliable technique that he uses to prepare for examinations. What does it mean to describe Glen's technique as reliable?

7. Mr. Lisk developed a test for young children that has proved a valid indicator of musical talent. What does it mean to describe the test as valid?

8. The so-called lie detector test, which involves hooking up a subject with various electrodes and transducers, has been called reactive. Explain the use of the word *reactive* as it would apply to the ability of the test to detect deception.

9. Manfred tested the relative effectiveness of orange juice versus Fruit Loops as reinforcement in his teaching of dressing skills (such as putting on and tying shoes) to mentally handicapped children. Identify the independent variable in Manfred's experiment.

10. Operationally define a measure that would be suitable for measuring the acquisition of dressing skills in Manfred's children.

11. Assume that Manfred used your operationally defined measure of learning and found Fruit Loops the more effective reinforcer. Would the difference be quantitative or qualitative?

12. Why must variables be described using precise operational definitions?

13. A school psychologist took advantage of some unstructured time following an emergency evacuation of the school building (a bomb hoax) to administer a short test to some students. He found that students who had seen a very graphic horror film at the local theater displayed more anxiety on a psychological test than the students who had not yet seen the film. (The students had to respond "agree" or "disagree" to such statements as "I sometimes become afraid when I am home alone.") When the test was repeated, however, the difference was no longer evident.

    a. What variable(s) other than seeing versus not seeing the horror film could have accounted for the initial test results?

    b. Can you identify one or more confounding variables that could affect your interpretation of the test results?

    c. Do the inconsistent findings call the validity of the test into question?

    d. Do the inconsistent findings call the reliability of the test into question?

    e. If we assume the test for anxiety is both valid and reliable, what could account for the failure to find differences on the retest?

    f. Would you describe seeing versus not seeing the horror film as a manipulated or nonmanipulated variable? Why?

    g. Would you be comfortable with the interpretation that seeing the horror film caused an increase in student anxiety level? Defend your answer.

Proposal Assignment 3: Statement of Hypotheses

For this proposal assignment you are to name the independent and dependent variables of your proposed project (without operationally defining them at this point) and state the hypotheses (see chapter 2).

To help you with this proposal assignment, we shall provide a sample research proposal. As educators, the authors are interested in the variables that affect a student's ability to learn new material. Specifically, we have selected your acquisition of knowledge about research methods as the behavior to be studied (our *dependent variable*). Assume that we have untested, tentative beliefs (*hypotheses*) concerning the factors that affect student learning, and our research proposal is to test whether or not these factors, called *independent variables*, really do affect learning. Some independent variables we believe affect student learning are:

1. The amount of time students are told they are expected to study and do homework assignments for their Research Methods in Psychology class during a typical week.

2. The incentive students are given to learn the material.

3. Whether or not class attendance is strictly enforced.

4. The use of a tape recorder versus handwritten notes to record the lecture material.

5. The use or nonuse of a student study guide to accompany the text.

Some sample hypotheses:

1. Students who are told they are expected to study a lot for the Research Methods course will do better than those who are told that they are expected to study little.

2. Students who are given a big incentive to learn will do better than students who are not given this incentive.

3. The more classes students miss, the worse they will do in the class.

4. Students who normally tape lectures and use the recording to supplement their class notes will do better than students who are not allowed to use a tape recorder.

5. Students who are instructed to use the study guide provided with the textbook will do better than students who are told to ignore the study guide, but only if they are told they are expected to study a lot for the Research Methods course, and not if they are told that they are expected to study little.

Your assignment is to:

1. Write down the behavior you propose to study.

2. List five independent variables that you hypothesize may influence the dependent variable.

3. Give a sample hypothesis for each independent variable you list.

The Origins and Interpretations of Data

The Levels of Observation

This chapter examines four approaches to behavioral research, commonly referred to as *levels of observation* because their data convey different information. The first three approaches, naturalistic observation, survey research, and correlational research, are classified as **descriptive research** because, as the label implies, their data are limited to describing behavior. The data of the fourth level of observation, experimental research, go beyond description and are suitable for documenting cause–effect relationships between variables. Each method places unique demands on the researcher and each is capable of making important contributions to the body of scientific knowledge. Naturalistic observation (chapter

Descriptive Research: Investigations limited to describing behavior.

6), survey research (chapter 7), and correlational research (chapter 9) receive additional coverage in Part IIA, and experimental research is the topic of Part IIB.

Naturalistic Observation

Conducting some research projects requires such exotic and expensive equipment that, without support from government agencies or private foundations, the projects cannot be carried out. **Naturalistic observation**, the unobtrusive recording and description of animal or human behavior as it takes place in an unaltered natural setting, can be a pleasant exception. With a pencil, a pad of paper, a pair of binoculars, or perhaps even a video tape recorder, a trained observer can record the most minute details of animal and human behavior as they unfold. Some of the more common categories of behavior that have been studied in animal populations using naturalistic observation include courtship behavior, aggressive behavior, predatory behavior, parental behavior, and social organization.

Before recording observations, behaviors must be clearly defined to avoid confusion. For example, aggression involves hostility between members of the same species, whereas predatory behavior (the killing of prey for food) is directed at other species. Once the observer becomes familiar with the components of behaviors, such as the menacing postures, submissive postures, vocalizations, and the biting, clawing, and other components of aggressive behavior, observers can use checklists to facilitate the recording of *what, when,* and *how often* various behaviors occur.

In general, as little as possible is left to the subjective impressions of the observer. A notation that an adult male became *angry* with a juvenile male is inappropriately subjective. Instead, by using checklists of very specific behavioral actions, the event could be recorded as an instance of adult *growling* behavior that was followed by the *retreat* of the juvenile male. It is often not possible to remove all ambiguity from naturalistic data (Did that baboon yawn, or was it a dominance display?), but the use of checklists of specific behaviors tends to work well.

Naturalistic observation may not always refer to observing people or animals in their normal surroundings. As long as the act of observation itself does not affect the character of the environment and as long as the presence of the person or animal in a habitat is a matter of free choice, it is reasonable to describe observational data as naturalistic. For example, in Springfield, Massachusetts, a unique opportunity for naturalistic observation presented itself when a pair of peregrine falcons decided to nest on a high window ledge of a hotel. When the nest was vacant the hotel installed one-way glass in the window, kept the room vacant, and the local cable television company agreed to provide 24-hour coverage on an available cable channel. Urban America is clearly not the environment one usually associates with falcons, yet, because the living arrangement was undisturbed and the falcons themselves chose the nesting site, it is fair to call the situation natural.

One-way glass, which prevents the subjects from seeing the experimenter, and hidden film or video cameras are also used to observe humans in their natural setting. Facilities set up to study child development typically have rooms with one-way glass so that interactions among children can be studied without the children knowing that they are being observed. For example, in studying sharing behavior in children it is reasonable to assume that willingness or reluctance to share toys

Naturalistic Observation: The unobtrusive recording and description of animal or human behavior in an unaltered natural setting.

would be influenced by the presence of an adult observer. To view the *natural* inclinations of the children to share their toys it would be necessary to view the scene while behind a one-way glass, or perhaps by using a hidden video camera to record the behavior for later observation and analysis. The advantage of recording the behavior on tape or film is that you and other researchers can view the behavior sequence numerous times and see if there is general agreement that a certain behavior did or did not occur. The greater agreement there is among the observers about what behaviors did or did not occur, the more we have what is called **interobserver reliability**. The discussion of the reliability of a measuring instrument in chapter 3 stressed reliability as a measure of consistency. The only difference here is that, as observers, humans are the measuring instruments, and the consistency that exists between their recorded observations is expressed as the interobserver reliability.

Interobserver Reliability: The extent of agreement among observers about what did or did not occur.

The observer as a participant

Remaining out of sight is by no means the only way to be unobtrusive. Some researchers have taken a rather radical approach: to become so familiar and nonthreatening to the creatures being observed that the observer is virtually ignored. This tactic of participant observation was used by Diane Fosse in her studies of the mountain gorillas of Rwanda. (Her life was the subject of the motion picture *Gorillas in the Mist.*) Through great patience and perseverance, the turmoil within the gorilla troupe that resulted from her initial visits ceased to be a problem. She became accepted as a de facto member of the gorilla troupe and, as such, became part of the very natural environment she had set out to observe. Anthropologists frequently use this technique to study other societies: They live with and become accepted by the people they are studying.

Naturalistic observations provide valuable data as to what behaviors occur, when they occur, and how often they occur, but they can only generate conjecture as to *why* certain behaviors occur and what variables affect the development, quality, and quantity of the behavior. Studying observational data, and using them to form hypotheses as to the causes of behavior, is an example of the inductive type of research discussed in chapter 2. On the other hand, first having a theory about behavior (e.g., frustration increases aggressive behavior) and then observing behavior in a natural setting to test a prediction of the theory would be an example of deductive research.

Ethical considerations

Observing the behavior of children from behind one-way glass or with hidden cameras is unlikely to be challenged as an invasion of privacy because children are routinely supervised closely to ensure their safety and comfort. But doing the same with adults is quite another matter. The capacity of the neighborhood peeping Tom or keyhole eavesdropper to invade our privacy ("Honest, officer, I was just doing research!") has been greatly enhanced by the latest technology. There now exist spying devices of all sorts, many of them used for such security purposes as the detection of shoplifting or trespassing, that could also be used just as effectively to collect data on unwary people, even in the privacy of their own homes. Because, in many instances, the desire to record naturalistic observations on humans may be outweighed by the ethical considerations that relate to the right to privacy, we

■■■■■■■

cannot always watch human behavior directly. An alternative is to administer a carefully composed questionnaire and trust subjects' willingness to be honest and share information about personal perceptions (beliefs, attitudes, preferences, and the like), characteristics, and experiences.

Survey Research

Survey Research: A technique for exploring the nature of personal characteristics and perceptions by analyzing the answers to a set of carefully developed questions.

Survey research is a technique for exploring the nature of personal character- istics and perceptions by analyzing the answers to a set of carefully developed questions. Students commonly have the impression that survey research is relatively easy to do. No expensive apparatus or technical skill appears to be necessary. You just ask questions, get answers, organize the data, and interpret the results. You will discover in chapter 7 that this is a simplistic impression of survey research and is seldom accurate. Even though we do not discuss the procedural details of survey research here, some aspects of survey research parallel aspects of naturalistic observation.

One concern in using surveys and naturalistic observation to collect descriptive data on human behavior is how well the data recorded for an observed group represent the behavior of the population as a whole. Surveys of public opinion and the naturalistic observation of animals or humans usually involve intensive study of a relatively small sample, and, for the sample to be an accurate representation of the population, it must reflect the behavioral diversity that is present in the overall population. For example, pollsters often seek to describe the voting behavior of the American electorate. They cannot, of course, violate the privacy of the voting booth with a hidden camera to gain firsthand knowledge of citizens' voting behavior through observation, but they can survey citizens for an account of their voting behavior by conducting an exit poll.

Exit polling is not done in an intensive manner at only one voting precinct. Only by choosing a variety of nationwide precincts that reflect the cultural, ethnic, and political diversity of America can the media generalize their findings to the population at large with a minimal amount of error. This important characteristic of the survey sample—to be representative of the population at large—is what enables the media usually to predict a winner of a national election before all the polls close. Survey data are gathered to describe television-viewing habits, radio-listening habits, consumer preferences, and all manner of public opinions and beliefs.

Correlational Research

Correlation Analysis: A statistical technique for quantifying the strength of association between variables.

The systematic description of behavior usually entails taking many different measurements on each subject being studied. When we have two or more measurements on the same set of subjects, we can progress to another level of description. Specifically, we can determine whether or not a *relationship* or *association* exists between variables, and we can quantify the strength of the association using a statistical tool called **correlation analysis**.

Correlational research was defined in chapter 3 as the study of the relationships of selected variables and natural treatments with measures of behavior. Say, for example, that each member of a group of cigarette smokers was assessed with respect to two selected variables: the mean (average) number of cigarettes smoked per day (variable X) and the mean ounces of alcohol consumed per day (variable Y). Since we have two measures on each individual, it is possible to examine the data for a pattern of association. In general, if the individuals with high scores on variable X tend also to have high scores on variable Y and the individuals with low scores on variable X also tend to have low scores on variable Y, a **positive relationship** exists. In this example, if we assume that the direction of association between the drinking and smoking variables is positive, the heavy smokers would tend to be heavy drinkers, and the light smokers would tend to be light drinkers.

Conversely, if the pattern in the data shows that the individuals who score low on variable X tend to score high on variable Y and the individuals who score high on variable X tend to score low on variable Y, a **negative relationship** exists. We might, for example, expect to find such a relationship among students for the variables grade-point average and alcohol consumption: Poor grades would tend to be associated with high alcohol consumption. The strength and direction of association between variables with interval or ratio scaling is described using the **Pearson r** statistic; the **Spearman rho** is used when one or both variables has at least ordinal scaling. The strength of association is reflected in the magnitude of the correlation statistic. The range from 0 to $+1.00$ is the scale for reflecting the strength of a positive association, and the range from 0 to -1.00 is the scale for reflecting the strength of a negative association. See Box 4–1 for a graphic representation of the strength and direction of association: the scatterplot.

Curiously, one form of descriptive research, although commonly referred to as correlational, does *not* involve measuring the strength of association between different behavioral measures on the same set of individuals. Instead, the goal appears to be the opposite: to compare the *same* behavioral measures between *different* groups of subjects, as when comparing the language development of children who have an older sibling to the language development of children of the same age who have no older siblings. The latter type of correlational research resembles experimental research in that the focus is on studying the behavior of different groups of subjects who have had different experiences. But the identifying characteristic that reveals the research to be correlational rather than experimental is that neither of the variables (the level of language development and the presence or absence of siblings) is manipulated.

Two categories of nonmanipulated variables, selected variables and natural treatments, were discussed in chapter 3. There we saw that when we assign subjects to different groups on the basis of such a selected personal attribute as gender, age, race, political affiliation, sexual preference, income level, life-style, and the like we are forming groups on the basis of a selected variable. Similarly, when we assign subjects to different groups according to their level of exposure to a historical event (accidental exposure to toxic substances in the environment, a natural or manmade disaster, political or economic crisis, and the like) we are forming groups on the basis of a natural treatment.

The label *correlational research* serves to remind us that the data only provide evidence of an *association* between the selected variable or natural treatment and the behavioral measures we take on the different groups of subjects. We cannot conclude that the selected variable or natural treatment is the *cause* of any measured difference between the groups. For example, let us say we segregate infants into two groups, those whose mothers went scuba diving six or more times

Positive Relationship: The direction of association between variables when pairs of measurements on the same subjects both tend to be of the same relative magnitude (high,high; low,low).

Negative Relationship: The direction of association between variables when pairs of measurements on the same subjects tend to be of opposite magnitudes (high, low; low, high).

Pearson r: A measure of the strength and direction of association between interval- or ratio-scaled variables.

Spearman rho: A measure of the strength and direction of association that is appropriate when one or both variables have at least ordinal scaling.

during their first trimester of pregnancy and those whose mothers did not. If we compare the behavioral development of the two groups of infants and find differences, it would be proper to conclude that atmospheric compression during pregnancy is *associated* with a particular course of development. But, from these data alone, a causal explanation ("Compression from scuba diving during the first trimester of pregnancy affects the course of infant behavioral development") is inappropriate. Many explanations for the finding that have nothing to do with

BOX 4–1

Scatterplots: Picturing Association

When we have two measurements on the same set of subjects, we can plot the two scores for each subject as a dot on a graph. The dot is placed at the intersection of the two values. For example, the dot at the extreme lower left of the first scatterplot (Figure 4–1) represents a subject with an X-score (horizontal axis) of 20 and a Y-score (vertical axis) of 25. The greater the resemblance of the scatterplot to a straight-line (linear) trend, the greater the strength of association. In other words, a scatterplot with no discernible linear trend is indicative of no relationship between the two variables, and a scatterplot with all dots on the same straight line is indicative of perfect association. As seen in Figures 4–1 through 4–4, the direction of a linear trend can be either positive (from lower left to upper right) or negative (from upper left to lower right).

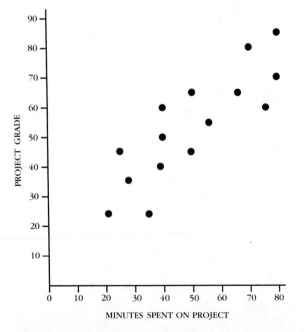

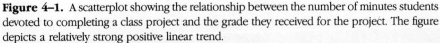

Figure 4–1. A scatterplot showing the relationship between the number of minutes students devoted to completing a class project and the grade they received for the project. The figure depicts a relatively strong positive linear trend.

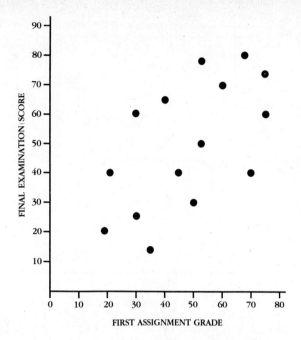

Figure 4–2. A scatterplot showing the relationship between the grades students earned on their first class assignment and their final examination scores. The figure depicts a relatively weak positive linear trend.

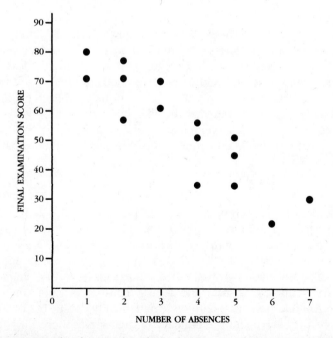

Figure 4–3. A scatterplot showing the relationship between the number of class absences recorded for students and their final examination scores. The figure depicts a relatively strong negative linear trend.

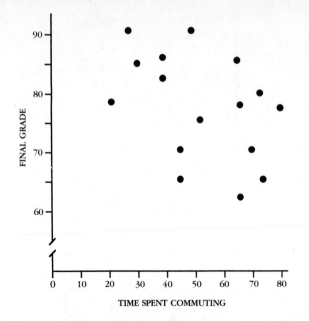

Figure 4–4. A scatterplot showing the relationship between time needed to travel to and from campus each day for a group of commuting students and their final course grades. The figure depicts a relatively weak negative linear trend.

compression are possible. For example, females who can afford to travel to tropical locations and scuba dive for recreation are likely to be wealthier and, thus, obtain more thorough prenatal care during pregnancy compared to the less affluent group of nonswimmers. Maybe the children of very athletic mothers, for reasons unrelated to compression, tend to develop skills at an abnormal rate. Each possible alternative explanation that emerges reduces the likelihood that any observed association between compression and developmental phenomena is rooted in an underlying causal relationship between prenatal compression and postnatal behavioral development.

Contingency

In addition to measuring the strength of association that exists between variables with interval/ratio scaling (using the Pearson r statistic) and between variables with ordinal scaling (using the Spearman rho statistic), it is also possible to evaluate nominal variables for association. In the special case of nominal data, the existence of an association is often called a **contingency**. For example, suppose we assessed the attitudes of male and female consumers by asking "Assume that Restaurant A and Restaurant B both serve high-quality cuisine but differ in the size of the portions they serve and the intimacy of their atmospheres. If you were dining out and had to choose between Restaurant A and Restaurant B, which would be the more important consideration, the atmosphere of the restaurant or the size of the portions?"

Contingency: Association between categorical (nominal) variables.

The variables of gender (male versus female) and selection criterion (portion size versus atmosphere) are categorical (nominal) because the data are simple frequencies assigned to categories. They are also both nonmanipulated (subject) variables. If the results of the survey were as presented in Table 4–1, even without a statistical analysis it is fairly easy to see that a contingency or dependent relationship exists between the gender variable and restaurant-selection criteria: Males tend to regard portion size as more important (27 "votes") than atmosphere (only 13 "votes"), whereas females tend to have the opposite attitude (24 "votes" for atmosphere versus 16 for portion size). In other words, if, on the basis of these data, we wished to make a statement concerning the relative importance people place on these two restaurant-selection criteria (portion size and atmosphere), we would have to say that the primary consideration determining an individual's restaurant selection is *contingent* on or *depends* on the gender of the selector.

Notice that when we collapse the table across the gender variable and focus on the responses of people in general, we get 37 and 43 for the atmosphere versus portion-size totals. The near-even split means that people *in general* do not regard portion size to be more important than atmosphere; the difference in preference emerges only within each gender.

If, by comparison, the data were as shown in Table 4–2, we do not see evidence of an association between the gender and selection-criteria variables because both

Which is more important?

	Atmosphere	Portions	Total
Male	13	27	40
Female	24	16	40
Total	37	43	80

Table 4–1. The responses of 40 men and 40 women to the question "Which is more important to you when selecting a restaurant, the atmosphere or the size of the portions?"

Which is more important?

	Atmosphere	Portions	Total
Male	27	13	40
Female	24	16	40
Total	51	29	80

Table 4–2. The responses of 40 men and 40 women to the question "Which is more important to you when selecting a restaurant, the atmosphere or the size of the portions?"

males (27 versus 13) and females (24 versus 16) responded similarly to the survey question. In describing this pattern of results we would say that the relative importance attached to the atmosphere and portion-size selection criteria is *independent* of or *not contingent* on the gender of the selector. In other words, there is a uniform pattern among consumers of both genders to prefer atmosphere over portion size.

Two-dimensional tables of **frequency data** (tally totals, such as those displayed in Tables 4–1 and 4–2) are called **contingency tables**, and the statistic researchers use to test for contingency between the row and column variables of such tables is the chi-square statistic. (See Appendix B for the chi-square analysis of the Table 4–1 and 4–2 data.) The contingency tables shown above were 2×2 tables because the row and column variables each had only two levels. Technically, however, any dimension is possible for a contingency table, such as 2×3, 4×4, 6×3, and so forth.

Prediction

Correlation analysis allows us to describe the strength and direction of association that exists between variables. But once association is known to exist, a further level of analysis is possible. Specifically, when variables are associated we can *predict* the value of one variable with the knowledge of the other, as when a medical researcher predicts lifespan based on the ratio of "good" to "bad" cholesterol in a person's blood. **Prediction**, estimation of one variable value from knowledge of another, is done using the statistical procedure called **regression analysis**. In simple linear regression, we predict variable Y with the knowledge of variable X. Variable X is called the **predictor variable** because it is used for making the prediction, and variable Y is called the **criterion variable**, the value that is estimated using a predictor variable. It is also possible to use more than one predictor variable when estimating criterion scores, as when medical researchers predict lifespan (Y) from the knowledge of serum cholesterol (X_1), subcutaneous ("Can you pinch more than an inch?") body fat (X_2), and life-style variables such as the level of stress (X_3), smoking (X_4), and exercise (X_5). Using several predictor variables to predict a criterion variable rather than only one requires an advanced statistical procedure called **multiple regression**.

Experimental Research

We saw in chapter 2 that an experiment is the implementation of a formal scientific strategy to reveal cause–effect relationships between variables. Carrying out an experiment presents several challenges to the researcher, among them defining the independent and dependent variables, composing a formal statement of the experimental hypothesis, including appropriate controls, and establishing procedures for data collection. Whereas all research data are the recorded values of some variable(s), there is a difference between the kinds of conclusions we may draw from the data of experiments and the data of naturalistic observations, surveys, and correlational research: Experiments permit the documentation of causal relationships among variables, whereas descriptive data do not. Even so, there is nothing wrong with using descriptive data as a source for testable hypotheses.

Temporarily setting ethical considerations aside, we can design a simple experiment to test the hypothesis that alcohol causes humans to smoke more cigarettes. Without going into all the procedural elements at this time, one requirement of the experiment would be to randomly divide into two groups a large number of subjects who both smoke and drink as part of their life-style (see Box 4–2). (To describe the assignment of subjects to the different treatment groups of an experiment as **random** means that the assignment was determined by chance alone.) The treatment condition for one group would be to drink a measured amount of a nonalcoholic beverage blended to taste like an alcoholic fruit punch. The treatment condition for the second group would be to drink an alcoholic version of the same fruit punch. The volume of alcohol administered to the second group of subjects would be calculated to raise their blood alcohol level to 0.1%, the operational definition for intoxication. In this simple experiment, alcohol consumption is the independent (manipulated) variable and a behavioral measure of cigarette consumption (say, the total number of cigarette puffs taken during the hour following the drink) is the dependent variable. Since the study is an experiment, if the subjects assigned to the alcohol condition smoke more than the subjects assigned to the no-alcohol condition we can conclude that alcohol *caused* the subjects to smoke more.

Random: A determination based on chance alone, as in the random assignment of subjects to different groups.

The experimental data of the latter study are on a different logical footing than the correlational data described earlier in this chapter. Even though the variables are the same in both examples (alcohol consumption and smoking cigarettes), the experiment generates new data on smoking behavior (the dependent variable) that are inextricably linked to the *manipulation* of alcohol consumption (the independent variable). By contrast, the correlational data are not the result of any controlled manipulation of an independent variable. In fact, as behavioral measures, cigarette and alcohol consumption may both be regarded as dependent variables. Within the correlational research framework, both variables are measures of voluntary and self-determined levels of alcohol and cigarette consumption that are after-the-fact (ex post facto) consequences of unspecified influences (that is, whatever causes people to drink and smoke).

Random assignment and initial equivalence

In the alcohol and smoking experiment we described the assignment of subjects to the two treatment conditions as random without pointing out the specific rationale behind this very important step: the achievement of **initial equivalence**. Initial equivalence exists when any pre-existing differences among subjects that could influence the results of an experiment are evenly distributed across all groups.

Initial Equivalence: An even distribution across treatment conditions of any pre-existing differences among subjects.

For the assignment of subjects to the treatment conditions of an experiment to be truly random, every *individual* subject should have an equal chance to be assigned to a treatment condition, and no one *group* of subjects should be any more likely than some other group to be assigned to a treatment condition. Box 4–2 describes some techniques to accomplish the randomization of subject assignment. Randomization procedures must be followed rigorously, because any deviation — no matter how apparently innocent or well-intended — can threaten the achievement of initial equivalence.

BOX 4–2

Some Techniques for Random Assignment

Once the subjects for an experiment have been selected from a subject pool, the next step is to assign them to their respective treatment conditions. When there are only two treatment conditions in an experiment, a coin flip is a very simple random procedure upon which we can base treatment assignment. A head outcome could be used to assign the subject to Treatment Condition 1, and a tails could be used to assign the subject to Treatment Condition 2.

Of course, there is no guarantee that the number of heads and tails outcomes will be even, so the group sizes could be uneven. If it is your intention to run the study with equal group sizes (the more common practice) and you have a list of the subjects who will be participating in your experiment, you can set up your random assignment in advance using the following method. Write the identity of each subject on a slip of paper and place the papers in a container. In another container put n_1 slips of paper that say *Treatment 1* and n_2 slips that say *Treatment 2* (n_1 and n_2 are the numbers of subjects you plan to assign to treatment conditions 1 and 2 respectively). The last step is to draw successive pairs of slips, one from each container, to assign each subject drawn from the first container to the treatment condition listed on the slip from the second container.

If the nature of the experiment does not require advance planning, the assignment of subjects to different groups can take place at the experimental session itself. The simple flip of a coin can be used to determine subject assignment so long as you are not concerned about having unequal sample sizes. To assure equal sample sizes, one easy method is to draw randomly from the container of Treatment 1 and Treatment 2 slips, as just described. Either of the above methods can easily be adapted for experiments with more than two treatment conditions by including the appropriate variety of differently labeled slips (*Treatment 1, Treatment 2, Treatment 3* for a three-treatment experiment).

Another choice is to use random sequences of numbers, found in many statistics texts and books of statistical tables. For example, assume that the goal is to split a group of subjects randomly into three groups. One method would be to prepare numbered cards that correspond to the page numbers of the random-numbers table. Mix the cards and pick one blindly to select a table page. In a similar manner, use random selections from a deck of numbered cards (50 is adequate for most random-number table formats) to select both a row number and a column number on the selected page. Then blindly select a direction (right, left, up, or down) using four additional cards. Random numbers are picked beginning at the intersection of the selected row and column, and in the direction selected. The procedure is to search up or down a column or across a row for the digits 1, 2, and 3. Each time we come across a 1, 2, or 3 we select the name of a subject at random and match the treatment number to the subject. If we want equal group sizes we assign subjects in sets of three. That is, if we first come across a 2 in the table and assign the first subject to Treatment 2, we next look only for a 1 or a 3. If we then find a 3, we assign the second subject to

Treatment 3, and the third subject is automatically assigned to Treatment 2. With one subject assigned to each of the three treatments, we again look for a 1, 2, or 3 to begin the next set of three subjects. We continue the process until we reach the desired group size or until the supply of subjects is exhausted.

Do the steps researchers take to ensure random assignment seem overly bothersome and complex? Researchers take every possible measure to assure random assignment because the stakes are so high: achieving initial equivalence between groups. To save work, the techniques for random assignment discussed above can easily be simulated on a computer in cases in which the numbers of subjects and/or the complexity of the experiment make coin flipping or preparing slips of paper and numbered cards unmanageable. In your initial research experiences, however, you are unlikely to need anything more exotic than the methods presented here.

If all subjects scheduled to participate in an experiment were equal in all respects, we would not need to use random assignment to achieve initial equivalence among different treatment groups. Any method of assigning subjects to treatment conditions, random or not, would be just as likely to achieve initial equivalence as another. In the real world, however, no two individuals are identical, so no two individuals have exactly the same behavioral potential. We refer to the natural diversity among people and their behavior as **individual differences**, and we count on random assignment to distribute individual differences across treatment conditions in a way that will produce initial equivalence.

Individual Differences: The natural physical and behavioral diversity among people.

We must achieve initial equivalence in order to link a set of experimental results unequivocally to the values of a manipulated variable. For example, some subjects to be included in a study may have great inner resources for coping with stress, whereas others may become easily distraught. If the experiment was designed to study the relative effectiveness of a drug to help addicts cope with withdrawal symptoms, it would clearly lead to a deceptive set of experimental results if all the subjects who received no drug had ineffective strategies for coping with the stress of withdrawal and all those who did receive the drug had very effective coping strategies. Random assignment of subjects to the treatment groups should, according to the laws of probability, make such an extreme distribution of an individual difference (all inwardly strong persons in one group and none in another) very unlikely. Thus the random assignment of subjects to different treatment conditions results in groups that we may assume are identical, or nearly so, even though we know that substantial individual differences between subjects are likely to exist.

Sample size and initial equivalence

In an experiment, the **sample size** is the number of subjects we assign to the different treatment conditions; the larger the sample size, the stronger the likelihood that all the groups will be initially equivalent. For example, if a group of four subjects contains two individuals with assertive personalities and two with passive personalities, random assignment is far more likely to result in an unequal split (all assertive people in one group and all passive people in the other) than if we had to split a similarly constituted group (half assertive and half passive) of, say, 20 people.

Sample Size: The number of subjects in an experiment assigned to the different treatment conditions.

It is easy to demonstrate the role of sample size in the achievement of initial equivalence. Prepare four slips of paper, two marked with an X and two marked with an O. Then randomly draw them one at a time from a container as you alternate group assignment (assign the first one drawn to Group 1, the second to Group 2, the third to Group 1, and the fourth to Group 2). You will either achieve perfect equivalence (an X and an O in each group), or you will fail utterly (one group has two Xs and the other has two Os). Try the experiment several times to give you an indication of how often you fail to achieve initial equivalence and how often you succeed. Now repeat the same sampling experiment with 10 Xs and 10 Os. You may not achieve *perfect* equivalence (five Xs and five Os in each group) very often with the larger sample size, but the likelihood of a markedly uneven ratio of Xs and Os in a group is now much more rare than was the case with the smaller sample size of four.

Assignment error: The failure to achieve initial equivalence

When the random assignment of subjects to the various treatment groups of an experiment fails to achieve initial equivalence, the experimental data are subject to a distortion we call **assignment error**. Theoretically, although we *expect* an assignment procedure based on chance alone to distribute individual differences evenly across treatment groups, there is no guarantee that random assignment will successfully accomplish this desired result.

Assignment Error: A possible but statistically improbable failure of random assignment to achieve initial equivalence.

For example, if we randomly split a group of subjects characterized by large individual differences along several dimensions (say, athletic ability, intelligence, and age), we would theoretically expect, since the assignment is random, that just as many athletic, intelligent, and young subjects would be assigned to one group as to the other. Random assignment cannot, however, guarantee this result. By chance alone all the older subjects could be assigned to one group and all the younger subjects to the other.

It is important to keep in mind that it is statistically rare for random assignment to fail to achieve initial equivalence, but it is possible. Despite our best efforts to achieve initial equivalence, subjects randomly assigned to different treatment conditions will, in rare instances, have markedly different behavioral profiles prior to any experimental manipulation. The possibility that differences between groups can exist independent of any experimental manipulation is one reason demonstration of even large behavioral differences across treatment groups cannot be offered as absolute proof of the capacity of an experimental treatment to affect behavior. Thus, even though the logical structure of an experiment permits us to conclude that documented behavioral differences between differently treated groups were caused by the manipulation of the independent variable, there is always the chance, however slight, that the result is really a product of assignment error.

What can we do to avoid assignment error? One solution is to use relatively large sample sizes. The larger the sample size, the less likely it is that assignment error will be a problem. How can we determine if our data have been affected by assignment error? Although we can never be absolutely sure that we have avoided assignment error, it is possible, before the experiment begins, to compare the randomly assigned groups on a number of selected measures to determine if they are equal on those measures. If pre-existing differences among treatment groups are suspected of contributing to the pattern of experimental results, we always have the option, perhaps even the duty, to repeat the experiment with different subjects.

The importance of control groups

The **control groups** of an experiment are standards against which we can compare the performance of experimental groups. Without standards for comparison we would be unable to determine what effect, if any, the treatment(s) had on the subjects' behavior. How would we know if the anticraving drug was working unless we could compare the behavior of the treated subjects to some that did not receive treatment? How would we know if drinking alcohol during pregnancy really is the cause of postnatal physical and behavioral abnormalities without comparing the behavior of treated subjects to an appropriate control group that consumed no alcohol? Without appropriate controls to serve as standards of comparison, it is logically impossible to document the existence of an experimental effect.

In general, *a control group is treated as identically as possible to the experimental group except for exposure to the specific treatment that the experiment was designed to evaluate.* For example, in the experiment to evaluate the effectiveness of the anticraving drug there were two groups, one (the experimental group) received treatment with the anticraving drug. The other group was treated in an identical fashion except that the "medication" the subjects were given contained no active ingredient. A bogus treatment condition is called a **placebo** and, in line with the general concept of a control group stated above, a placebo treatment ideally encompasses all elements of the treatment *administration* (as in swallowing a tablet) without actually receiving the treatment (placebo tablets contain no active ingredient). Without going through the motions of medicating subjects with bogus medicine, the experiences of the two groups in the experiment would not meet the standard of being "as identical as possible."

To illustrate the advantage of the methodological refinement of a placebo treatment, consider a similar two-group drug experiment in which the control group receives no treatment at all. If the experiment were run and the results revealed a difference between the drug-treated group and the untreated group, rival interpretations would be possible. Maybe the observed difference between the groups means the drug was indeed effective in reducing the addicts' craving. But another equally plausible interpretation is that the experience of receiving medication itself, through the power of suggestion ("This medicine is likely to help me with my problem"), tended to modify addict behavior quite apart from any action of the drug itself.

Comparing the experimental group to a placebo-treated group avoids this problem. Both the experimental group and the placebo control group experienced the secondary elements of the treatment, so the psychological interpretation, that an expectation of a therapeutic effect caused a change in behavior, can be eliminated as a possible explanation of differences between the two groups.

To see if a placebo effect exists in addition to the experimental effect, the experiment must include three groups: an experimental group, a placebo control group, and an untreated group. By comparing the performance of the placebo control group to the performance of the untreated control group we can see what effect on behavior, if any, results from subject expectancies and assumptions about what the treatment would do.

The placebo-treated group is only one type of control that researchers routinely use. Parts IIB and III discuss various types of experiments in detail, and many different kinds of control groups are introduced. They are all, however, faithful to

Control Groups: Standards against which we can compare the performance of experimental groups.

Placebo: A bogus treatment condition in which subjects experience the elements of the treatment administration without receiving the treatment itself.

the same standard: *to be as similar to the experimental group as possible except for exposure to the specific treatment the experiment was designed to evaluate.* Developing the skill to apply the latter standard in the great variety of research contexts and topic areas that exist in psychology is of paramount importance for anyone either doing research or reading the research reports of others.

Interpretations of Data: Why We Need Statistical Analysis

Behavioral scientists seek formal training in statistics to learn how to describe data (see Box 4–3), test hypotheses, and become familiar with the considerations that dictate the use of various statistical tests for processing certain kinds of data and answering certain kinds of questions. But what really is the function of statistics? In a nutshell, statistical analysis is a tool for making decisions in the face of uncertainty. Some experimental results are so consistent or inconsistent with a hypothesis that they can be interpreted easily and unambiguously: either there is no trace of the anticipated experimental effect (as when the subjects from all treatment conditions have essentially the same scores) or there is an obvious experimental effect (as when the scores from different treatment conditions are so different in magnitude that their ranges do not overlap [see Box 4–3]).

Most of the time, especially in the behavioral sciences, experimental results are not so clearly defined. Specifically, when the scores of the subjects in one treatment group overlap with the scores of subjects in a different treatment group, it is not obvious whether the data do or do not support the experimenter's hypothesis. How different do the scores in the two groups have to be before the data can be said to support the existence of an experimental effect? Is the magnitude of the observed difference large enough to discount the possibility that it occurred by chance alone?

BOX 4–3

Describing Data with Statistics

For students who have already taken a course in statistics the material in this box can serve as a brief review. Those studying statistics along with research methods may find this a useful supplement to their primary statistics text.

Central Tendency and Dispersion

One function of data analysis is to express, with specially computed values called statistics, the magnitudes of two important data characteristics: central tendency and dispersion. Measures of **central tendency** are ways to describe the average or typical value of a distribution, and measures of **dispersion** describe the extent to which the scores in a distribution deviate from the central value.

Central Tendency: The "average" or typical value of a distribution as reflected in the mean, median, and mode.

Dispersion: The extent to which the scores in a distribution deviate from the central value as reflected by the range and standard deviation.

Consider the following sets of score values:

Set A: 9, 9, 6, 3, 3   Set B: 9, 8, 6, 4, 3   Set C: 9, 6, 6, 6, 3

Let us examine what is the same and what is different about these three sets.

1. The *mode* of a data set is the score value that occurs most often. Only Set C has a single mode (mode = 6). Set B does not have a mode because all values occur with equal frequency, and Set A is **bimodal**, because its most frequently occurring values (3 and 6) occur equally often.

    Bimodal: Distribution in which the two most frequent values occur equally often.

2. The *median,* the score value above which and below which half the scores fall, is 6 for all three sets.

3. The *mean,* a measure of central tendency represented by the symbol $\bar{X}$ (read "X bar"), is simply the arithmetic average of all the values in a set: the sum of a set of scores divided by the number of scores in the set. The formula for the mean is: $\Sigma X/n$. (X is the general designation for a single score value, ΣX is statistical notation for the sum of a set of scores, and n is the number of scores in the set.) The means of the three sets all equal $30/5 = 6$ (i.e., $\Sigma X = 30$, $n = 5$, so $\bar{X} = 6$).

4. The *range,* a relatively crude measure of dispersion, is the spread between the lowest and highest values in a distribution. For the present data, the range is the same for all three sets: The value 3 is the lowest score in each set and 9 is the highest score, so the range is 9 minus 3, or 6.

    In one important aspect, the sets are different. Overall, the scores in Set A tend to deviate the most from the mean of 6:

$$
\begin{array}{ccccc}
(9-6) & (9-6) & (6-6) & (3-6) & (3-6) \\
3 & 3 & 0 & -3 & -3
\end{array}
$$

overall, the scores in Set B deviate to a lesser extent:

$$
\begin{array}{ccccc}
(9-6) & (8-6) & (6-6) & (4-6) & (3-6) \\
3 & 2 & 0 & -2 & -3
\end{array}
$$

and, overall, the scores in Set C deviate the least from 6:

$$
\begin{array}{ccccc}
(9-6) & (6-6) & (6-6) & (6-6) & (3-6) \\
3 & 0 & 0 & 0 & -3
\end{array}
$$

5. We can quantify the dispersion in a set of data with the *variance statistic* (s^2). Here is the formula:

$$
s^2 = \frac{\Sigma(X - \bar{X})^2}{(n-1)}
$$

Substituting the scores of Sets A, B, and C into the formula yields the three variances, 9.00, 6.50, and 4.52 respectively. Notice how the sizes of the variance statistic parallels the dispersal evident from simple inspection of the three sets: The greater the dispersion, the greater the variance.

The numerator and denominator of the variance formula have special names. The numerator is the *sum of squares* (often abbreviated SS), and the denominator, $n - 1$, is *degrees of freedom*. In general, the degrees of freedom by which we must divide the sum of squares to compute the variance of a set equals the number of score values in the set (the number of X values substituted in the numerator of the variance formula) less one.

Just as dividing ΣX by n gives us the mean value of a set with n elements, the variance is also a mean of sorts. Dividing the sum of squares by $n - 1$ gives us the mean squared deviation per degree of freedom, a statistical estimate (s^2) of the variance of the population (σ^2) from which the sample was drawn.

6. Some of the deviations are negative (e.g., $3 - 6 = -3$), and the squaring operation in the variance formula eliminated all negative deviations ($-3^2 = 9$). But rather than use the mean of the squared deviations to reflect dispersion, we can "unsquare" (take the square root of) the variance to compute the statistic known as the *standard deviation*. Here is the formula for the standard deviation (s or SD). Notice that it is the same for the variance formula except for the square root operation.

$$s = \sqrt{\frac{\Sigma(X - \bar{X})^2}{(n - 1)}}$$

For Sets A, B, and C, the standard deviations are 3.00, 2.55, and 2.13 respectively. As with the variance, the relative magnitudes of the three standard deviation values are in line with the obvious differences in the dispersion of Sets A, B, and C. The standard deviation is a very useful statistic with which to describe the dispersion in a distribution of raw scores. Perhaps you have noticed that many college instructors report examination results in standard deviation units (z scores).

7. If we collected many different random samples from a population, we would theoretically expect the value of each sample mean to equal the value of the population mean. For example, if you knew that the mean test score of a large psychology lecture class ($n = 400$) was 85, you would expect any random sample of students from that class to have a mean test score of 85. Of course, because of chance, some sample means would be less than the population mean, and some would be greater. The measure of the dispersion present in a distribution of sample means is called the *standard error*. The smaller the standard error of a mean (the closer it is to zero), the more confident we can be that the sample mean is a relatively close approximation to the population mean. In general, the larger the sample size, the smaller the standard error of the sample mean will be, and the more precision there will be in using the sample mean as an estimate of the population mean. Here is the formula for computing the standard error of the mean (SEM) from a set of sample data.

$$s_{\bar{x}} = \sqrt{\frac{\Sigma(X - \bar{X})^2}{n(n - 1)}}$$

For Sets A, B, and C, the standard errors of the mean are 1.34, 1.14, and 0.95 respectively.

Conclusions drawn from the inspection (eyeballing) of **raw data** (research results that have not yet been statistically described or analyzed) are, at best, only tentative and may even be misleading. To determine whether or not the groups differ, we must evaluate and interpret raw research results with the aid of statistical analysis.

The Logic of Hypothesis Testing

In a two-group experiment described in chapter 3, an anticraving drug was administered to cocaine-addicted rats to see if it could cause a reduction in lever-pressing for cocaine. If the data of this experiment showed that all the placebo-treated addicts continued to lever-press for cocaine and all the drug-treated addicts ceased lever-pressing, it would be logical to conclude that the drug was responsible for the difference in lever-pressing behavior. If, on the other hand, there was no difference in the mean number of lever presses between the placebo- and drug-treated groups, we would have no trouble concluding that the drug dosage had no effect on reducing the desire for cocaine.

But what if the drug-treated animals neither stopped lever-pressing altogether nor continued at the same rate as the placebo animals? What if they were observed to have "some" reduction in lever-pressing and some rats reduced their pressing more than others? How much of a reduction in lever-pressing must occur to justify the conclusion that chance alone is an unlikely explanation for the reduction? (See Box 4–4.)

In general, we examine data for statistical evidence of an experimental effect indirectly, by first stating a **null hypothesis**. In experimental research in the behavioral sciences, a null hypothesis is a tentative, working assumption that exposing subjects to different treatment conditions will fail to produce systematic behavioral differences attributable to those treatment conditions. For example, in preparing to analyze the data of the anticraving-drug experiment, we would tentatively assume that any observed differences in the lever-pressing behavior of the two differently treated groups (exposed versus not exposed to the anticraving drug) arose through chance alone rather than as a consequence of the experimental manipulation. With the null hypothesis in place, the next step is to evaluate whether the null hypothesis is consistent or inconsistent with the pattern observed in the experimental data. This is accomplished by applying an appropriate statistical analysis.

If a statistical analysis of a set of research data reveals only minimal differences in the behavior of differently treated groups of subjects, we retain (fail to reject) the null hypothesis and judge any apparent effect of the experimental variable to be **insignificant**: a consequence of chance alone (see Box 4–4). But if the pattern in the data is demonstrably inconsistent with the null hypothesis, as when differences in the behavior of differently treated subjects are too large to be attributed to chance alone, we reject the null hypothesis and, by default, we report the magnitude of the behavioral difference to be **significant**. The criteria for rejecting chance as an explanation for the existence of behavioral differences among differently treated groups are agreed on by convention: if the magnitude of an observed difference is so large that it could occur by chance alone only 5% of the time (5 out of 100 times), we reject chance alone as an explanation and, by default, adopt an interpretation that recognizes the contribution of the experimental variable in producing that difference.

Raw Data: Research results that have not yet been statistically described or analyzed.

Null Hypothesis: A tentative assumption that exposing subjects to different treatment conditions will fail to produce systematic behavioral differences attributable to those treatment conditions.

Insignificant: Description of an experimental result attributable to chance alone.

Significant: Conclusion that a research result is attributable to other than chance factors.

BOX 4–4

The Meaning of Statistical Significance

If you were serving as a juror in a court of law, how much incriminating evidence would have to be presented for you to judge a defendant guilty? In our legal tradition jurors are instructed to retain an initial assumption of innocence until the accumulation of evidence presented during the trial becomes so inconsistent with innocence (beyond a reasonable doubt) that they must reject the initial assumption of innocence and, by default, vote "guilty."

There is a direct logical parallel between the judgment of guilt/innocence in a courtroom proceeding and the evaluation of research data for evidence of a phenomenon. The only difference is that researchers replace the relatively vague "beyond a reasonable doubt" criterion with the concept of statistical significance: the determination that an observed pattern of results is unlikely to have occurred by chance alone. Evaluating research results requires a decision whether an observed pattern in the data is *insignificant* (merely a consequence of chance factors) or whether the observed pattern is *significant* (too prominent to attribute to chance alone). In other words, to describe a feature of data as statistically significant means that chance alone is rejected as an explanation for the feature.

How prominent does a feature of the data have to be before researchers reject chance as the explanation? In research "beyond a reasonable doubt" is supplanted by a probability value called "the level of significance" or "alpha level." Alpha is usually set by convention at .05, although .01 is also used. A statistical analysis that reveals a set of research results could have occurred by chance with a probability of more than alpha (say, $p > .05$), chance is retained as a possible explanation for the results. If, on the other hand, the analysis reveals that chance alone cannot realistically account for the results ($p < .05$), chance alone is rejected as an explanation. Every statistical test of significance, whether for comparing groups of differently treated subjects or to test for an association between variables, permits the determination of a probability value that must be compared to the .05 or .01 standard.

Why bother stating a null hypothesis?

The null hypothesis of a psychological experiment describes a single logical state: The experimental manipulation will have *no* effect on the subjects' behavior. An **experimental hypothesis** is a formal statement of the effect an experimental manipulation should produce. Like the null hypothesis, the experimental hypothesis also describes a single logical state, which is that the experimental manipulation will have *some* effect on the subjects' behavior. Evaluating which view is a more accurate reflection of reality — *no* experimental effect (retain the null hypothesis) versus *some* experimental effect (reject the null hypothesis) — is what the statistical analysis of experimental data is all about.

Experimental Hypothesis: Formal statement of the effect an experimental manipulation should produce.

In reality, however, an experimental hypothesis is consistent with many logical states. There are many levels of *some* effect (very small, very large, or anywhere in between), but only one conceivable pattern in a set of data is consistent with the description of *no* effect: uniformity in subject behavior across the various experimental and control conditions. Adopting the null hypothesis of "no experimental effect" as a working assumption enables the researcher to make decisions in an efficient way. Instead of attempting to specify which of many possible magnitudes of experimental effect should be regarded as *some* effect and comparing the experimental data to that criterion, the researcher instead compares the data to the one outcome that is consistent with no effect.

This indirect tactic is, by the way, the same approach used in legal proceedings. The defendant is presumed innocent (there is only one way to be innocent but many ways to be guilty) and the evidence is evaluated in terms of its consistency with the assumption of innocence (a legal version of the null hypothesis). If the evidence is incriminating beyond a reasonable doubt, the assumption of innocence is discarded (the null hypothesis is rejected) and a guilty verdict is rendered (the jury moves from the assumption of no illegal behavior to some illegal behavior).

Researchers must accept that the indirect method for evaluating experimental hypotheses will not always result in an accurate explanation of the experimental results. For example, in a legal proceeding it is possible for an innocent person to be convicted following the presentation of incriminating circumstantial evidence, as when the defendant had a motive, was placed near the scene of the crime, and was linked to physical evidence found at the crime scene. Similarly, it is possible for experimental results to appear consistent with the experimental hypothesis when, in fact, no effect linked to the independent variable is responsible. When the data lead us to such an incorrect conclusion, rejecting the null hypothesis when it should not have been rejected, we have committed a **Type I error**. A Type I error has a probability of occurring that equals the level of significance of the statistical test (usually .05). Thus, the stricter the standard we use to determine statistical significance (.05, .01, or even as strict as .001), the less vulnerable we are to making a Type I error. In general, the greater the costs of making a Type I error (the more dire the consequences are should we incorrectly determine that an experimental effect is significant), the stricter the standard we use for statistical significance.

It is also possible for a guilty person to go free because not enough incriminating evidence is found to warrant the jury's rejection of the initial assumption of innocence. Likewise, experimental results can appear to be consistent with the null hypothesis and in line with the assumption that only chance is responsible for any observed differences across treatment conditions, when, in fact, an experimental effect really does exist. This type of incorrect conclusion — retaining the null hypothesis when it should have been rejected — is called a **Type II error**.

There is thus no guarantee that subjecting data to formal statistical analysis will lead to an accurate interpretation of the data. Just like jurors sitting in judgment of the guilt or innocence of a defendant, on occasion researchers make incorrect decisions from an analysis of available evidence. Mistakes are made even when all mandated procedures are carefully and rigorously followed. The chance for making decision errors may be perceived as a weakness of the indirect null hypothesis approach to hypothesis testing, but, like our legal system, in comparison to any

Type I Error: Rejection of the null hypothesis when it should have been retained.

Type II Error: Retention of the null hypothesis when it should have been rejected.

other standard for drawing conclusions from evidence, it is the best we have. The remedy for dealing with a dubious experimental result is the same one we use to remedy a flawed legal decision: a retrial or replication of the experiment.

Comparing decision errors

Jurors are sometimes asked which error of judgment they are more concerned about: voting to reject the assumption of innocence and thereby convicting a person who was really innocent, or voting to retain the assumption of innocence and thereby letting a guilty person go free? Most respond that voting to convict an innocent person is the greater wrong. Similarly, if faced with the possibility of designating as significant research results that are really insignificant (a Type I error) or the possibility of designating as insignificant research results that really are significant (a Type II error), most researchers consider the Type I error more serious than the Type II error. The main reason is that most published results are reports of significant findings and, once a result is published and becomes part of the scientific body of knowledge, it is not so easy to correct the mistake. Failures to replicate the finding of significance can be blamed on even slight departures from the original methodology. It is far better, therefore, for a researcher to suffer the disappointment of insignificant research results than to taint the accuracy of the literature.

Power

Power: The capacity to detect an effect of the independent variable on the dependent variable when one truly exists.

Part of avoiding a Type II error is making every attempt to maximize **power**. In the context of an experiment, power is the capacity to detect an experimental effect of the independent variable on the dependent variable when one truly exists. In statistical terms, it is the capacity of the statistical test to reject the null hypothesis (and declare the existence of a significant experimental effect) when the null hypothesis is untrue and should be rejected.

Power and variability

The more dispersed the values in a set of experimental results for reasons unrelated to the manipulated (independent) variable, the more difficult it is to detect an experimental effect. For example, assume that you have decided to compare the effectiveness of two weight-reduction programs, using female subjects. You randomly divide your subject pool of overweight women into two groups and have each group follow a different diet program. You run this experiment with two different methods of data collection. In Method 1 subjects are weighed while wearing only a hospital gown, whereas in Method 2 they are weighed in their street clothes. When using Method 2, you notice that some subjects elect to take off their shoes before getting onto the scale, whereas other subjects do not. Also, because of variations in the weather, on some weigh-in days you observe that the subjects wear relatively bulky and heavy clothing, whereas on other days they tend to wear lighter warm-weather attire.

If you assume that there is only a slight difference in the relative effectiveness of the two weight-reduction programs, the first method, which eliminates the clothing variable from the weight data, would be the more powerful methodology. That is, following Method 1 you would be more likely to detect a difference in weight loss between the two groups. If you followed Method 2, all the fluctuations among the data values introduced by the uncontrolled clothing variable would tend to make the slight difference in the diets' effectiveness impossible to detect. In general, the more variability in a set of experimental data that arises from extraneous sources, the more difficult it is to detect an experimental effect when one exists.

Of course, researchers accept that they will not be able to eliminate all sources of extraneous variability from an experimental method. To maintain or increase power in the face of anticipated extraneous variability and/or in the face of an anticipated weak experimental effect, the most straightforward tactic is to increase the sample size.

Power and the choice of a dependent variable

Another enemy of power is using a dependent measure that is not sensitive to manipulations of the independent variable. For example, instead of weighing subjects on a scale accurate to the nearest half pound, assume you used changes in dress size to reflect weight loss among the female dieters. As a rule of thumb, a woman will go down one dress size for each 10 pounds lost, so a change in dress size is clearly a less sensitive measure of weight loss than measuring weight itself.

Summary

This chapter opened with a discussion of the different approaches researchers use to collect data, the so-called levels of observation. Distinction was made between psychological data from naturalistic observations, surveys, and correlational research, which are descriptive in character, and the data of true experiments, which provide information about the causes of behavior. As part of our coverage of correlational research, we explained the characteristics of data that indicate the presence of strong and weak positive and negative association between ordinal, interval, and ratio scaled variables and contingent relationships between categorical variables. The term *correlational research* is also used to refer to studies that use selected variables and natural treatments as independent variables. The discussion of correlational research concluded with a brief explanation of the concept of prediction and a reminder that descriptive data cannot be used to make a case for the existence of a causal relationship between variables.

The discussion of some of the principal characteristics of experimental research called attention to the importance of random assignment (to achieve initial equivalence) and control groups (to provide a standard for comparison) to the design of experiments and gave an overview of the role of statistics in the research process. Included in the latter discussion were the key concepts that pertain to the logic of hypothesis testing, including null hypothesis, experimental hypothesis, Type I error, Type II error, alpha level, statistical significance, and power.

Key Terms

Assignment Error, p. 52
Bimodal, p. 55
Central Tendency, p. 54
Contingency, p. 46
Contingency Table, p. 48
Control Groups, p. 53
Correlation Analysis, p. 42
Criterion Variable, p. 48
Descriptive Research, p. 39
Dispersion, p. 54
Experimental Hypothesis, p. 58
Frequency Data, p. 48
Individual Differences, p. 51
Initial Equivalence, p. 49
Insignificant, p. 57
Interobserver Reliability, p. 41
Multiple Regression, p. 48
Naturalistic Observation, p. 40
Negative Relationship, p. 43

Null Hypothesis, p. 57
Pearson *r*, p. 43
Placebo, p. 53
Positive Relationship, p. 43
Power, p. 60
Prediction, p. 48
Predictor Variable, p. 48
Random Assignment, p. 49
Random Sampling, p. 49
Raw Data, p. 57
Regression Analysis, p. 48
Sample Size, p. 51
Significant, p. 57
Spearman rho, p. 43
Survey Research, p. 42
Type I Error, p. 59
Type II Error, p. 59

Chapter Exercises

1. What are the four levels of observation as described in the text?

2. Why do we classify naturalistic observation as descriptive rather than as experimental research?

3. What does it mean to say that there is a positive association between infant birth weight and the scholastic achievement of school-aged children?

4. What does it mean to say that there is a negative association between a measure of cardiovascular fitness and average daily caloric intake?

5. What does it mean to say that political-party affiliation is contingent on the ethnic background of the citizen?

6. Speculate how the positive and negative correlations referred to in questions 3 and 4 could exist in the absence of a causal connection between the birth weight and achievement variables and between the fitness and intake variables.

7. If you were a teacher in an elementary school and found out that one of the children in your class had been a premature baby with low birth weight and you were aware of the relationship described in question 3, what general prediction could you make about the student's prospects for academic success?

8. What are the specific characteristic(s) of experiments that permit causal interpretations of independent–dependent variable relationships?

9. Review the description of the alcohol and cigarette consumption experiment in the Experimental Research section of this chapter.

    a. Which group was the control group?

    b. Was a placebo control used? Explain.

    c. What does it mean to describe the two groups of the experiment as initially equivalent?

    d. How was initial equivalence between the treatment groups achieved?

    e. State the null and experimental hypotheses for this experiment.

10. Explain the function statistical analysis of research data plays in the research process. Will statistical analysis always lead to correct conclusions about the meaning of the data? Why or why not?

11. Explain the concept of statistical power and its relationship to sample size.

Proposal Assignment 4a: Operational Definitions of Variables in Experimental Research

In Proposal Assignment 1 you selected a behavior, and in Proposal Assignment 3 you listed five independent variables you thought might influence the behavior and stated five experimental hypotheses. Now you will select the hypothesis that most interests you and operationally define your independent and dependent variables.

Proposal Assignment 3's first sample hypothesis was that students who are told they are expected to study a lot for the Research Methods course will do better than those who are told that they are expected to study little. The *independent variable* was how long students were told they were expected to study, and the *dependent variable* was how well the subjects did in the class.

In designing an *experiment* to provide evidence for a cause-and-effect relationship between the independent and dependent variables researchers must *manipulate* the independent variable. You must *randomly assign* some subjects to one level of the independent variable and the others to the other level, and not leave it to the individual student's discretion how much time he or she should spend studying. Before a study can be carried out, you must decide exactly what "told they are expected to study" and "will do better" mean. In other words, you must *operationally define* the independent and dependent variables. For example, the two different groups of students (Group H and Group L) could be told:

Group H: "In order to do well in this Research Methods in Psychology class you are expected to study and do homework assignments for 15 hours per week, and we will check to see that you follow our instructions."

Group L: "In order to do well in this Research Methods in Psychology class you are expected to study and do homework assignments for 5 hours per week, and we will check to see that you follow our instructions."

There are, of course, many ways to operationally define study time. Any values could have been picked, but a precise definition is required. It would have been meaningless to just say a "large" or "small" number of hours; operational definitions communicate the exact values to be used in a study.

The dependent variable must also be operationally defined. One possibility is the number of correct answers on a comprehensive 100-question multiple-choice test given at the end of the semester. (There are many ways you could have defined learning, but — as with the independent variable — you have to pick one operational definition and state it so precisely that other researchers could repeat the experiment.)

To complete this assignment, go back to Proposal Assignment 3 and pick the hypothesis of greatest interest to you. Then decide how you are going to manipulate the independent variable and provide an operational definition. You may discover that it is unethical to manipulate the variable. If this is the case, state how you would manipulate the variable if ethics were of no concern, then state that the experiment could not be done. Your next task is to operationally define the dependent variable.

Proposal Assignment 4b: Operational Definitions of Variables in Correlational Research

You may have discovered in working on Proposal Assignment 4a that some independent variables cannot be manipulated. To study such variables you would have to find support for your hypothesis using the correlational approach. Correlational research simply measures two or more subject characteristics or behaviors and determines if there is a positive, negative, or no relationship between them.

The objective of the sample proposal was to explore the relationship between the amount of time students spend on work related to the Research Methods in Psychology class and how well they do. We must decide how to measure both time spent studying and how well students do by operationally defining both behaviors. One way to measure the amount of time students spend studying for the Research Methods in Psychology course is to have students keep track of the number of minutes they work on the course each day. At the end of the semester the students would be asked to turn in their data sheet to the experimenter (who would, of course, not let the instructor know how much each student studied). The experimenter would then add up the total number of minutes for the entire semester for each subject to arrive at a study–time score. Measurement of how well they did in the class for the correlational design would be the same as for the experimental design: by recording the number of correct answers on a 100-question multiple-choice test.

A high positive correlation between time spent studying and grades could lead to the conclusion that there is an association between the two behaviors, but not that studying *caused* the higher grades. It is possible that some third factor caused both. Perhaps people of high intelligence (high IQ) both enjoy studying and have better test-taking strategies. Thus, high versus low levels of studying and high versus low test performance may both be manifestations of the third variable, the level of a subject's intelligence.

Your assignment is to show how the same hypothesis you selected in Proposal Assignment 4a can be studied using the correlational technique. In doing so, be sure to write down the operational definitions of both behaviors.

Recipes for Research:
The Seven Basic Questions

Behavioral Stew

The Seven Basic Questions

Nonmanipulated Variables: Basic Questions 1, 2, and 3
Basic Question 1. What are the dimensions along which behaviors naturally vary?
Basic Question 2. Does the classification of behavior into discrete categories conform to a specific theoretically expected or hypothesized pattern of results?
Basic Question 3. Does an association exist between two (or more) variables?
Association: categorical data
Association: ordinal, interval, and ratio data
Prediction and association

Manipulated Variables: Basic Questions 4, 5, 6, and 7
Basic Question 4. Will introducing subjects to a specific change in an otherwise standard context cause their behavior to change?
Basic Question 5. Will introducing subjects to qualitatively different conditions cause them to exhibit systematic differences in behavior?
Contingency with causality
Basic Question 6. Will introducing subjects to quantitatively different conditions cause them to exhibit systematic differences in behavior?
Basic Question 7. Will introducing subjects to two or more systematically different conditions cause an additive and/or interactive effect on behavior?

Behavioral Stew

Behavior is the output of a complex dynamic system that is shaped and nurtured by past experiences, current conditions, and heredity. Like an elegant goulash that is the end product of a complex recipe, behavior is determined by the blending and processing of many ingredients. Moreover, no two animals or people are products of the exact same genetic and experiential recipe.

Because of the variability of behavior (individual differences) and gaps in our knowledge concerning the determinants of behavior, attempts to influence behavior experimentally sometimes yield unexpected results. Imagine, for example, how surprised psychiatrists were to find that certain drugs used as stimulants for adults tend to calm rather than excite the behavior of hyperactive children. The systematic study of behavior in the context of formal laboratory research is a relatively recent phenomenon compared to the study of chemistry, physics — and cooking. Researchers understand some aspects of behavior, such as the learning paradigms of classical and operant conditioning, rather well and are able to study them with substantial precision. Studying other aspects of behavior, such as the development of personality traits, remains more of a challenge to behavioral scientists. In general, psychologists have not identified all the ingredients of behavior — the variables that determine the characteristics of specific behaviors — let alone the effects of modifying and blending the many ingredients. Psychologists accept that the determinants of most behaviors are complex, not unlike the determinants of weather phenomena, earthquakes, or the controlling variables of any other incompletely understood dynamic system.

Faced with such complexity and sparse knowledge of the forces that determine behavior, you may wonder how psychologists meet the challenge of gathering meaningful and fundamental information about behavior. They do it in much the way a chef creates a new dish: from a reasonable base of knowledge together with some experimentation. By systematically adding or deleting ingredients, changing the amounts, proportions, or brands of the ingredients in use, and/or changing the preparation (blending, cooking) of the dish, a picture eventually emerges of the relationship between the ingredients of the recipe, the processing of the ingredients, and the characteristics of the end product.

It is unrealistic to expect an experiment, or even a series of experiments, to result in a clear understanding of *all* the factors that determine the characteristics of a behavior. Nevertheless, following accepted principles of scientific methodology, researchers can, like the chef, systematically alter the recipe balance of prior experience, heredity, and current conditions to increase knowledge of the ways in which *some* variables act and interact to determine behavior.

An important premise of behavioral science research — and indeed, a premise that defines the approach in this text, is that it is possible to use the scientific method to unravel even the most complex mysteries of behavior, *if we are careful to apply research methodology appropriate to the question being asked.*

The Seven Basic Questions

Research, whether descriptive or experimental, is done to answer questions and, judging by the large number of journals (1,061 in psychology alone, according to *Ulrich's International Periodical Directory*) published to serve the almost equally large number of behavioral science disciplines, researchers ask a great many questions. Some of the questions addressed by research are so complex and demand such a detailed knowledge of the discipline to understand them that scientists within one subdiscipline (say, social psychology) may not understand the important research questions within a different subdiscipline (say, biopsychology), let alone understand the answers provided by the data.

Considered on a general level, however, the vast number of research problems that have been and continue to be articulated in the quest for information about behavior and its causes can be expressed in the form of a surprisingly small set of general questions. Specifically, almost all research problems can be expressed in the form of one or more of what we call *the seven basic questions*. In this chapter we use a unifying theme to explain and exemplify the character of each of the seven basic questions. It is built around an analogy to cooking, since tinkering with recipes is something you should be able to relate to even if you have very little science background. The cooking examples will be supplemented with more psychologically relevant examples that illustrate how researchers investigate animal and human behaviors.

Keep in mind that this brief preview is to *introduce* you to the fundamentally different questions about behavior that researchers in the behavioral sciences try to answer. In Part II the basic questions are articulated in somewhat more detail, and the emphasis will be on matching the structure of a descriptive or experimental research endeavor to the type of question that the research is intended to answer. Part II also discusses the advantages and disadvantages of some approaches to answering research questions compared to others, data-analysis options associated with various experimental designs, and, most important, the characteristics of the experimental designs that make them suitable for addressing research issues in the form of one or more of the seven basic questions.

Nonmanipulated (Subject) Variables: Basic Questions 1, 2, and 3

Research in the form of any of the first three basic questions is descriptive rather than experimental. That is, the data are measures of behavior that exist outside the influence of any purposeful and controlled manipulation of a variable. Chapter 3 refers to such data in a variety of ways: nonmanipulated variables, subject variables, and ex post facto (after-the-fact) variables.

Basic Question 1
What are the dimensions along which behaviors naturally vary?

The first step in the study of behavioral phenomena is to document, in as rich detail as possible, the natural behavioral repertoire of the subject under study. We must have descriptive information that tells us *what* a subject does, *how frequently* the subject does it, *where* the subject does it, *when* the subject does it (that is, under what circumstances), and *how long* the behavior continues when it appears before we can research *why* the subject does it.

Research in the form of Basic Question 1 is done by watching and recording observations, as in naturalistic observations of animal or human behavior or conducting a survey to reveal human behavioral practices. The data of such research provide descriptive details of overt behavior and, in humans, beliefs and attitudes recorded as they exist in nature, free of the influence of any manipulated variables.

With respect to the cooking analogy, we would expect a chef to be familiar with the dimensions along which food can vary before attempting to alter the characteristics of foods through experimentation. For example, in addition to the four basic tastes of salt, sour, sweet, and bitter, food can also be described as crunchy, chewy, spicy, bland, fluffy, heavy, soggy, rich, gooey, greasy, tender, and so forth. Before experimenting to alter the degree to which any of these characteristics are present in a dish, the characteristics themselves must be identified and a way devised to define them operationally so they can be measured.

Similarly, before exploring the variables that contribute to diversity in behavior between genders, a researcher must identify the specific behaviors that take different forms in males and females (the technical term is *sexually dimorphic behavior*) and have the ability to measure them. If, for example, a researcher wanted to study the effects of certain manipulated variables (such as hormonal status, odors, and visual cues) on the reproductive behavior of an animal species, the specific behaviors that comprise the courtship ritual, mating, and the rearing of the young would have to be identified and methods devised to measure them. The measurement of a behavior need not be complex. For example, in studying the mating behavior of the laboratory rat, one tactic is simply to count the number of times the male rat mounts the female rat within a given test interval.

Basic Question 2
Does the classification of behavior into discrete categories conform to a specific theoretically expected or hypothesized pattern of results?

Once we are aware of an organism's behavioral repertoire, it is possible to classify observed behaviors into distinct categories and use the resulting behavioral record to test hypotheses. For example, to evaluate consumer acceptance of a new cookie recipe, a baker made a large batch of cookies and had a panel of volunteers taste the results. After tasting a cookie, each volunteer had to answer the question "Would you buy this cookie for your family?" The possible responses were "yes," "no," and "maybe." The baker hypothesized that a significant majority of the tasters would respond yes. When inspecting Table 5–1, keep in mind that the behavioral measure of the study (each subject's opinion of the cookie) was not influenced by any manipulated variable. That is, whatever qualities in a cookie a subject happens to like or dislike were presumably in place as a personal preference before participation in the study.

We have categorized the behavior of each of 129 tasters as indicating acceptance of the product (a "yes" response), nonacceptance of the product (a "no"

	Yes	No	Maybe
Actual Taster Responses	85	21	23
Expected Responses Assuming No Clear Consumer Preference	43	43	43

Table 5–1. A summary of the preferences voiced by 129 consumers who responded to the question "Would you buy this cookie?"

response), or a noncommittal ("maybe") response, so the data in Table 5–1 are simple frequency tallies. Do the tallies indicate a significant preference for one type of response over the others? When researchers refer to a difference as *significant* they mean that, in their judgment, more than chance alone is responsible for an observed pattern of results (see Box 4–4). In the present example, if only chance were determining the consumers' evaluation, we would expect the frequencies to be equal in the three categories, as shown in Table 5–1. However, the actual subject responses to the survey question are far from equal across the categories and appear to offer strong support for the baker's assessment that the majority of consumers will like the new cookie.

Of course, researchers usually do not evaluate data and offer an interpretation from appearances alone. The more typical course of action — even, as in the present case, when the meaning of the data appears obvious — is first to subject the data to a formal statistical analysis. We examine the interdependence between research methods and statistical analysis more fully in chapter 8 and at various points throughout other chapters.

With respect to sexually dimorphic behavior, assume that a researcher wishes to study the aggressive behavior of a recently developed strain of laboratory mouse. The first step would be for the researcher to acquire the necessary knowledge of mouse behavior so he or she would know *when* mice tend to behave aggressively and *what* specific behaviors make up aggression and submission in social situations (issues in the form of Basic Question 1). Then the researcher would be prepared to classify each mouse as passive or aggressive on the basis of their behaviors and could test the hypothesis that the males of the new strain are more aggressive (or less passive) than the females.

Basic Question 3
Does an association exist between two (or more) variables?

Once we are sophisticated enough to describe what an organism does and how to classify and quantify what it does, the next level of study is often to demonstrate the existence of an association between measures of behavior. Two behavioral measures taken on the same set of subjects show evidence of association when the values of one variable parallel the values of the other in an orderly (positive or negative) way (see chapter 4). By comparison, two variables are unrelated to each other when the values of one variable fail to parallel the values of the other. Variables that are associated are often described as **functionally dependent** because, in a mathematical sense, the value of one variable *depends* on the value of the other. Similarly, variables are **functionally independent** when their values fail to parallel each other in an orderly fashion. *Functionally* means only that the relationship between the variables can be expressed in the form of a mathematical equation and will form a characteristic shape when plotted as a graph. Box 4–1 indicated that one possible relationship between two variables is a linear (straight line) relationship. (Because the dots in the scatterplots shown in Box 4–1 do not all fall on the same straight line, the relationships depicted are not perfectly linear and are best described as linear trends.)

Functionally Dependent: Referring to the existence of an association between variables.

Functionally Independent: Referring to the absence of an association between variables.

Association: categorical data

Consider the contingency table shown as Table 5–2. In this study restaurant patrons who ordered the daily special were offered one complimentary bottle of wine with their dinner. They had to choose which type they wanted, red or white, and after the meal were asked to cast a ballot to indicate their positive or negative evaluation of the meal. Did customer reaction to the chef's new creation (positive versus negative) depend upon the customer's choice of red versus white wine?

Two behavioral measures were recorded for each subject in this study and both are categorical: the type of wine (red versus white) the patrons chose to accompany their meal and their evaluation of the dish (positive versus negative). Neither behavioral measure has any link to an experimental manipulation, so they are both subject variables. The entries in Table 5–2 are frequency counts and were determined by assigning each of the 80 customers to a row/column combination (or **cell**) according to the type of wine they selected (the row variable) and their reaction to the dish (the column variable). By analyzing the four cell frequencies we can determine if a dependent relationship or *contingency* exists between the row and column variables.

Cell: A row/column combination in a table.

The pattern of the customer responses to the restaurant survey indicates that of those customers who chose red wine to be served with their meal, 32 out of 40 (80%) said they liked the new dish. By contrast, only 16 of 40 (40%) who chose white wine to be served with their meal said they liked the new dish. Even without statistical evaluation of these data (with the chi-square test of independence), inspection reveals that the customer reaction to the dish *depends* on the type of wine the customer selected to be served with the dish: The selection of red wine tends to be more heavily associated with positive ratings, whereas the selection of white wine is more heavily associated with negative ratings.

As an example of a study in the form of Basic Question 3 within the research area of gender differences, consider this hypothetical study to examine gender differences in the assessment of conflict outcomes. Male and female subjects (80 per group) view a videotape segment set in a singles bar in which professional actors depict the development of a potentially explosive social confrontation between two young, macho male customers. The tape ends at a tense moment without showing how or if the conflict was resolved. After viewing the tape, the subjects are asked to register one of three opinions: the conflict would be settled without a fist fight, the conflict would escalate to a fist fight, or undecided whether or not a fight would

Reaction to the Daily Special

	Positive	Negative
Red Wine	32	8
White Wine	16	24

Table 5–2. Ratings of the daily special, a new culinary creation submitted by 80 restaurant patrons. Either red or white wine was selected to accompany the meal.

	Will Fist Fight Occur?		
	Yes	No	Undecided
Male	44	17	19
Female	23	34	23

Subject Gender

Table 5–3. The likelihood of an aggressive solution to a staged social confrontation as predicted by male and female subjects.

ensue. The data for this study would be cast in a 2 × 3 contingency table, as shown in Table 5–3.

As in Table 5–2, the data in Table 5–3 are frequency data: tallies of the number of males and females who fall into each of the three response categories. Inspection of these fictional data reveals that roughly twice as many males as females predicted the confrontation would end in a fist fight and twice as many females as males predicted a nonviolent outcome. Responses in the undecided category were roughly equal.

Association: ordinal, interval, and ratio data

When data have ordinal, interval, or ratio scaling we can do more than document whether or not an association exists between two variables, we can also describe the strength and direction of the association. Consider the type of data shown in Table 5–4, two measures (body weight and the number of victories scored during aggression testing) on 26 laboratory mice. Is there an association between an animal's weight (in grams) and its social dominance?

We have included only four of the 26 pairs of data alluded to in the study's description to make it easier to illustrate a pattern of association between the weight and victory variables. Notice that the heavier animals are the ones credited with many victories, whereas the lighter animals tend to have fewer victories. Thus we would describe the relationship between the weight and aggression variables as

Subjects	Weight (X)	Victories (Y)
A	48	4
B	53	7
.	.	.
.	.	.
.	.	.
Y	62	9
Z	37	1

Table 5–4. A record of aggressive encounters for 26 laboratory mice (X = body weight in grams and Y = victories).

positive. To quantify the strength of the relationship we would have to analyze the 26 data pairs using a correlation statistic (here the Pearson r would be appropriate). In general, the closer the value of the correlation statistic to $+1.00$ for a positive association, or -1.00 for a negative association, the stronger the association between the two variables and the more pronounced the linear trend (see Box 4–1).

Prediction and association

The advantage of knowing that a significant linear trend exists between two variables extends beyond mere description. An association between two variables permits the prediction of a criterion variable (for example, lifespan) from a predictor variable (a measure of blood cholesterol). It is also possible to devise a prediction scheme based on the association among several variables. In fact, the reference in Basic Question 3 to an association between "two (or more) variables" was included specifically to encompass the more complex kinds of associative relationships that are often of interest to psychologists. For example, if we assume that high school grade-point average, SAT score, and IQ are all associated with academic success in college, a school psychologist who wants to predict the college performance of a student would use all these variables *together* to predict one criterion variable (college grade-point average). References in the psychological literature to multiple regression presuppose that more than one predictor variable is being used to predict a single criterion variable.

Manipulated Variables: Basic Questions 4, 5, 6, and 7

There is an important distinction between Basic Questions 4, 5, 6, and 7 and Basic Questions 1, 2, and 3. The research solutions to problems in the form of Basic Questions 1, 2, and 3 focus on gathering *descriptive* information. The *why* question, which is directed to finding the causes of behavior, is not addressed. As noted earlier, "We must have descriptive information that tells us *what* a subject does, *how frequently* the subject does it, *where* the subject does it, *when* the subject does it (that is, under what circumstances), and *how long* the behavior continues when it appears before we can research *why* the subject does it." By comparison, research projects designed to pursue the answer to issues in the form of Basic Questions 4, 5, 6, and 7 call for the researcher to manipulate one or more independent variables and then assess the impact of the manipulation(s) on behavior. The form of research in the form of Basic Questions 4, 5, 6, and 7 is therefore experimental rather than descriptive.

The latter point, first discussed in chapter 3, is a distinction so important that it will appear repeatedly in a variety of different contexts throughout the text. The goal of experimental research is to examine the capacity of variables *under the control of the experimenter* to affect behavior, and, by so doing, to document a causal linkage between the manipulated (independent) variable and the behavior being measured (the dependent variable).

Basic Question 4
Will introducing subjects to a specific change in an otherwise standard context cause their behavior to change?

Basic Question 4 is concerned with the behavioral consequences of superimposing a special condition on an otherwise typical set of behavioral determinants. Modification of the standard context of a behavior can be accomplished in one of two ways:

1. Introduce a condition that *is not* normally present and evaluate the effect of its presence on a behavior.

2. Remove a condition that *is* normally present and evaluate the effect of its absence on a behavior.

If a baker added or removed an ingredient of a cake recipe, would it affect the result? Researching this recipe problem would require the baker to compare the result (say, as reflected in cake sales figures) when the cake is prepared in the usual (standard) way to the result when the modified recipe is used. As long as the addition (or subtraction) of an ingredient is the only difference between the standard and experimental recipes, the baker could attribute any significant difference in cake sales to the experimental manipulation.

Suppose the baker noticed a decrease in the sale of cakes and, in trying to account for the drop, it occurred to him that he had been leaving out chopped raisins to cut back on costs. Would it be proper to attribute the drop in sales to the omission of the raisins? To be sure, that explanation is a possibility, but, because the change in recipe was not a purposeful manipulation *before* the evaluation of sales records, the data are ex post facto and cannot answer the *why* question unequivocally. Another event (say, the marketing of a similar cake by a competing bakery) could be the real cause of the drop in cake sales.

For a behavioral example in the form of Basic Question 4, imagine a systematic investigation into the aphrodisiac (love-potion) effects reputedly produced by preparations made from certain body parts of some endangered species (rhinoceros, gorilla, and certain species of bear). This is a serious issue among conservationists, because even though it is the animal poachers who directly threaten the survival of the endangered species, the illegal poaching is driven by consumers who believe in the medicinal properties of the animal-derived products. Unfortunately, folk-medicine preparations are rarely subjected to the kind of scientific scrutiny given to the drugs occupying the shelves of the local pharmacy, so it is possible that some species may be hunted to extinction for tissues that do not even possess medicinal properties. We can use the methods of behavioral research to fill such gaps in our knowledge.

A research problem in the form of Basic Question 4 is: Does powdered rhinoceros horn have medicinal properties that result in an increase in sexual motivation? The strategy, as articulated in the basic question, is to introduce subjects to a change in an otherwise standard context (expose subjects to the aphrodisiac) and take one or more behavioral measurements that are capable of registering any effect of the change.

Asssume that we initially decided to test the rhinoceros horn preparation for a possible effect on sexual motivation by doing an experiment with male laboratory rats. The first step would be to operationally define one or more specific male rat behaviors that reflect sexual motivation, such as the latency (time) to mount a receptive female or the number and duration of attempts to mount an unreceptive female. With such data in hand we could compare a baseline measure (the standard amount) of activity among subjects who do not receive the reputed aphrodisiac to the level recorded for subjects who do receive it. We would manipulate which subjects were and were not exposed to the powdered rhinoceros horn by assigning subjects randomly either to a control condition (a placebo control would be appropriate) or an aphrodisiac condition. This type of experiment is called a two-treatment **between-subject design** because the manipulated variable is hypothesized to cause a difference in behavior *between* subjects in different treatment groups. (Expanded coverage of between-subject designs is reserved for chapter 11.)

We could also choose to test the same subjects twice, once with the aphrodisiac and once without it. In the latter configuration the experiment is a two-treatment **within-subject design.** (Two-treatment within-subject designs are discussed in detail in chapter 12.) The within-subject label is used because the design calls for comparing two measurements of behavior, one after treatment with a placebo and another after treatment with the aphrodisiac, within the same subjects.

Before moving on, consider another situation: A study of the personal habits of a group of people reveals that some use powdered rhinoceros horn, believing that it has an aphrodisiac effect on behavior, whereas others in the group disdain such folk medicine and never use it. Thus, like the between-subject experiment, one group is exposed to the rhinoceros horn and the other group is not. Would the discovery that the two groups, users and nonusers, differed on some measure of sexual motivation demonstrate that powdered rhinoceros horn does indeed affect behavior? Since there is no manipulated variable in this study of personal habits, the answer is no. In the descriptive study of personal habits, the use or nonuse of powdered rhinoceros horn is under the control of the subjects, not an experimenter. The data are therefore ex post facto, and an explanation of a difference between the two groups causally linked to the use or nonuse of powdered rhinoceros horn would not be justified. Even if it is true that the two groups do differ, the finding is a description of *what* is true, not *why* it is true.

Between-Subject Design: Experimental design in which each treatment condition is administered to a separate group of subjects.

Within-Subject Design: Experimental design in which two or more treatment conditions are administered to the same group of subjects.

Basic Question 5
Will introducing subjects to qualitatively different conditions cause them to exhibit systematic differences in behavior?

A cooking problem in the form of Basic Question 5 would be: Will there be a difference in the taste of a dish if the chef prepares it using vintage burgundy instead of ordinary burgundy? Here we are not adding an ingredient to or subtracting an ingredient from an established recipe as we did to illustrate a study in the form of the fourth basic question. Instead, we are varying the quality of an ingredient: specifically, the quality of wine used in the recipe.

To clarify what a qualitative difference is, let us briefly review the difference between a qualitative difference and a quantitative difference. There are some quantifiable differences between different vintages of the same wine variety, such as sugar content, viscosity, and tannic acid content, but the differences in taste between wine vintages are not readily attributable to quantitative differences on one specific dimension. Rather, it is the unique blend of many characteristics that gives a wine its unique quality.

In general, we refer to a difference that cannot readily be quantified as a *qualitative* difference. A common idiom to express unique quality is "apples and oranges." An apple may be less juicy than an orange, its skin may be thinner, its seeds smaller, its sugar and water content may be different, and so forth, but changing any of these quantitative characteristics of an apple through selective plant breeding is not going to change an apple into an orange. The apple would still be an apple and the orange would still be an orange, so we say they are qualitatively different.

Contingency with causality

As an example of one type of behavioral experiment in the form of Basic Question 5, we modify the recipe problem in our discussion of Basic Question 3. There, restaurant patrons who ordered a new daily special were given the opportunity to select a complimentary bottle of either red or white wine. Before leaving the restaurant they rated the meal either positively or negatively by secret ballot. In a modification of this study, the gift of a red versus white wine was randomly determined by the restaurant manager rather than by customer prefer- ence. Would the evaluation data (shown as Table 5–5) still be limited to an interpretation of association?

With the methodological modification transforming red versus white wine to a manipulated variable, the original descriptive study in the form of Basic Question 3 is now an experiment in the form of Basic Question 5. The type of wine is the "qualitatively different condition," and the positive versus negative reaction to the new daily special is the measure of behavior. Any contingency that is documented to exist between wine type (the independent variable) and ratings (the dependent variable) is indicative of an underlying causal relationship as well as an association. The data show that providing complimentary red wine resulted in a more positive evaluation of the meal than providing white wine. Perhaps the red wine enhanced the flavor of the food, whereas white wine clashed with the flavor.

Reaction to the Daily Special

	Positive	Negative
Red Wine	32	8
White Wine	16	24

Table 5–5. Positive or negative reaction to the daily restaurant special as a function of which wine the restaurant patrons were selected to receive. In this form the study is an experiment.

Most experiments in the form of Basic Question 5 yield data with a higher level of scaling than the categorical data of the restaurant illustration. For example, a clinical psychologist could do an experiment to examine the relative effectiveness of group therapy sessions versus aversive conditioning in diminishing dependency on alcohol. Subjects assigned to the group-therapy condition would attend regular group psychotherapy sessions, whereas the subjects assigned to the aversive conditioning treatment would take Antabuse, a treatment option for recovering alcoholics. By itself, the drug has no effect. But if a person drinks when Antabuse is present to react with the alcohol, the result is nausea and vomiting. This treatment does not differ from group therapy on any obvious quantitative dimensions; one therapy does not have more or less than the other of some comparable attribute. Because the therapeutic approaches differ in *type* of treatment rather than *amount* of treatment, they are qualitatively different.

Again, to use the terminology introduced in the discussion of Basic Question 4, the therapy experiment is a two-treatment between-subject design, because subjects are randomly assigned either to the group therapy or Antabuse treatments. (In chapter 13 you will see that some research issues in the form of Basic Questions 4, 5, and 6 require the use of many treatment conditions. In this chapter, however, to maintain the focus of the discussion on fundamental issues, the examples are limited to experiments with only two treatment conditions.)

Basic Question 6
Will introducing subjects to quantitatively different conditions cause them to exhibit systematic differences in behavior?

To investigate research issues in the form of this basic question we must manipulate the amount (quantity) of the experimental variable present as an influence on the dependent measure. Unlike Basic Question 4, we are not manipulating the presence or absence of the variable, and unlike Basic Question 5, we are not manipulating the variable qualitatively. For example, assume an experiment with food preparation that requires not simply adding an ingredient to an established recipe or subtracting an ingredient but, rather, systematically varying the amount of a particular ingredient that may or may not already be included in the recipe. In effect, the cooking experiment calls for the quantitative manipulation of a variable (say, 1 teaspoon versus 2 teaspoons of a recipe ingredient) and an assessment of the effects of the manipulation on the end product: taste, texture, appearance, and so on.

One of the most straightforward examples of behavioral science research in the form of Basic Question 6 is the dose-response study for comparing the effects on behavior of two or more doses of a drug. For example, a researcher interested in developing a course of drug therapy to calm the behavior of hyperactive children would, at some point in the research effort, systematically vary drug dosages (50, 100, and 200 mg) and measure the effect of the quantitatively different treatments on the children's behavioral symptoms. The results of the experiment would assist in documenting the dose level of the therapeutic agent required to achieve the desired behavioral result.

Basic Question 7
Will introducing subjects to two or more systematically different conditions cause an additive and/or interactive effect on behavior?

Basic Question 7 asks if the influence of one independent variable on behavior is affected by the simultaneous manipulation of one or more other variables. In the cooking context we could, for example, investigate whether the addition of both yeast and milk to a sourdough bread recipe will result in loaves that increase in size more than can be accounted for by the individual contributions of yeast and milk. The yeast in a bread recipe needs a food supply to multiply and enable the bread to rise. The sugars in milk provide that food, so, together, the yeast and the milk *interact* to produce a well-risen dough capable of producing large loaves. Alone, neither ingredient is responsible for an attractive and good-tasting loaf of bread.

The **factorial design** is the method researchers use to explore how two or more independent variables act in concert, so it is uniquely suited to investigating issues in the form of Basic Question 7. A **factor** is simply another term for an independent variable, and the **levels of a factor** refer to the specific values of an independent variable that comprise the treatment conditions of an experiment. The factorial experiments summarized in Tables 5–6, 5–7, and 5–8 are all two-factor designs because, in each case, two factors (such as test-chamber temperature and

Factorial Design: A method for exploring how two or more independent variables act in concert.

Factor: Independent variable.

Levels of a Factor: The specific values of an independent variable that comprise the treatment conditions of an experiment.

	Access to Mathematics Materials (Factor B)	
	Yes	**No**
Access To Verbal Materials (Factor A) Yes	250	90
No	80	40

Table 5–6. The mean change in combined verbal and mathematics SAT scores for low–achieving students between first and second test administrations as a function of access to study materials. The experimental design is a 2 × 2 factorial.

	Drug Condition (Factor B)	
	Aphrodisiac	**Placebo**
Test Chamber Temperature (Factor A) 65 degrees	75	56
85 degrees	10	40

Table 5–7. Mean sexual activity scores for a hypothetical 2 × 2 factorial experiment. The pattern of means is indicative of an interaction effect.

		Drug Condition **(Factor B)**	
		Aphrodisiac	Placebo
Test Chamber	65 degrees	75	56
Temperature **(Factor A)**	85 degrees	61	40

Table 5–8. Mean sexual activity scores for a hypothetical 2 × 2 factorial experiment. The pattern of means is not indicative of an interaction effect.

drug condition in Table 5–7) are manipulated together in the same experiment. Also, because each factor in our examples has two settings (in Table 5–7 the settings are 65 versus 85 degrees for test-chamber temperature and aphrodisiac versus placebo for the drug condition), they are described as two-factor experiments with two levels for each factor or, for short, 2 × 2 factorial designs.

Sometimes when two or more independent variables are present to influence behavior, we cannot account for the combined impact the variables have on behavior by adding their individual contributions. For example, say that a class of high school juniors obtained disappointing scores on the verbal and mathematics portions of the SAT. After becoming aware of the disappointing grades, the guidance counselor decided to do an experiment. After randomly dividing the class into four groups, he issued each one some study materials. Group 1 got the mathematics section of an SAT preparation manual, Group 2 got the verbal section of an SAT preparation manual, Group 3 got both the verbal and mathematics sections, and Group 4 received no study materials at all. After the students retook the SAT test some months later, the difference between the combined verbal and mathematics SAT score on the first versus second test administrations (a change score) was computed for each student. The mean change scores for each of the four groups are presented in Table 5–6.

Inspection of Table 5–6 reveals that the students who had access only to the mathematics-preparation materials improved their overall SAT score by an average of 80 points, the students who had access only to the verbal preparation materials improved their overall score by an average of 90 points, and the students who had access to both sets of materials improved their overall score by an average of 250 points. The 40-point improvement in the control group is especially revealing, because it shows that some improvement occurred on the second test without the benefit of studying either set of review materials.

If the effects of extra preparation on verbal skills (Factor A) and mathematical skills (Factor B) are additive, it would be reasonable, based on the performance of the subjects who received only one or the other set of materials, to predict a 170-point overall increase for the subjects who received both sets of materials (90 + 80 = 170). When the effect of two or more independent variables acting in concert equals the sum of their respective influences when acting separately, the outcome is described as an **additive result.**

But in the hypothetical illustration, the mean score change of subjects who prepared using both sets of materials (250 points) exceeded the sum of the separate

Additive Results: A result of two or more variables acting in concert that equals the sum of their respective influences.

influences (90 + 80 = 170 points) by 80 points (250 − 170 = 80). Perhaps studying both sections of the SAT preparation manual helped the students develop better test-taking strategies and increased attentiveness to detail more than studying only one or the other section alone. For whatever reason, it appears from the data in Table 5–6 that the two types of review experiences had a greater effect on test performance when used together than would be predicted from their effects when used singly. (Of course, in a real research environment it is necessary to test the significance of what "appears" to be present in a set of data using statistical analysis. Evaluating the results of factorial experiments is addressed in chapter 14 and Appendix B.)

Interaction: A result of two or more independent variables acting in concert that cannot be explained as the sum of their individual contributions.

Nonadditive Result: An interaction.

A result of two or more independent variables acting in concert that *cannot* be explained as the sum of their individual contributions is an **interaction** effect or, alternatively, a **nonadditive result.** The concept of interaction is closely related to the concept of synergism, which is often invoked to explain the results of drug therapy in medicine. Either of two drugs used alone may have minimal or no therapeutic action. But when used in combination, the therapeutic effect can often be quite dramatic — larger than (that is, not an additive result of) the combined health benefits of the drugs when administered singly.

In the SAT example, both kinds of preparation materials were either present (Yes) or absent (No). To illustrate a different way to manipulate two levels of a factor other than the presence or absence of a condition, consider another aphrodisiac example. A psychologist was given a compound with reputed aphrodisiac properties while traveling in Eastern Asia. When she returned, she decided to do a study with some male laboratory rats to evaluate any effect the compound might have on stimulating sexual behavior. The four cells in the diagram of the experimental design (Table 5–7) represent the four treatment combinations of the experiment. Assume that 10 rats were assigned to each of the four groups in the experiment, so each table entry represents the mean sexual activity for 10 like-treated animals. (As in Table 5–6, the cell entries in Table 5–7 are *means,* not frequency data of the type shown in Tables 5–2, 5–3, and 5–4.) Rather than focus on a particular measure of sexual activity, simply assume for interpretive purposes that the higher the value of a cell mean, the more vigorous the sexual activity of the subjects in that group.

The two independent variables of the experiment are ambient temperature (the temperature of the test chamber was set either to 65 or 85 degrees Fahrenheit), and treatment either with the aphrodisiac or a placebo. Note that the aphrodisiac manipulation is of the same present/absent variety used in the previous SAT-preparation example, but the temperature variable is not.

The treatment of male rats with the aphrodisiac does seem to have resulted in an increase in sexual behavior (mean score = 75) when testing took place at 65 degrees, but, curiously, the same treatment seems to have suppressed sexual behavior when the test chamber was maintained at 85 degrees (mean score = 10). If the researcher were asked "Does the aphrodisiac have an effect on the sexual behavior of male laboratory rats?" she would have to respond "It *depends* on whether the animals are tested under cool or warm conditions." In other words, the temperature variable is interacting with the aphrodisiac variable: In the cooler 65-degree temperature the aphrodisiac increases sexual activity, but in the warmer 85-degree temperature the aphrodisiac decreases sexual activity.

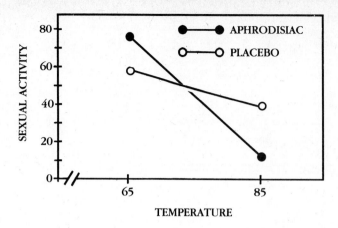

Figure 5–1. Sexual activity as a function of temperature and aphrodisiac ingestion.

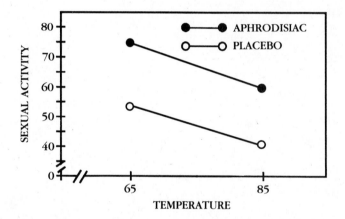

Figure 5–2. Sexual activity as a function of temperature and aphrodisiac ingestion.

A graphic plot of these cell means in present in Figure 5–1, which shows the characteristic absence of parallel lines (either crossing or converging lines) that is the signature of an interaction between variables. If, instead, the data were as shown in Table 5–8 and as plotted in Figure 5–2, we see no evidence of an interaction. The plots of the cell means form parallel lines, so we may say that neither independent variable depends on the value of the other with respect to the effects of the variables on the vigor of sexual behavior.

Summary

The chapter began by characterizing behavior as a complex dynamic system that, like the preparation of an exotic dish from a complex recipe, is the product of the action and interaction of many ingredients. The premise of the chapter is that most research that is geared to describing behavior and understanding the causes of behavior takes the form of one or more of seven basic research questions. Each of the seven questions was stated, its application to descriptive and experimental research contexts explained, and the features and interpretation of the research data required to answer the basic questions examined. The theme that ran through the initial explanation of each basic question was built on a cooking analogy, which was then followed by assorted examples of problems that relate to behavioral science. (The seven basic questions, only introduced in this chapter, are a running theme of the remainder of the text; the descriptive and experimental approaches to research covered in Parts IIA and IIB are presented as methodological solutions to the seven basic questions.)

Here are the questions themselves. The first three deal with the measurement of nonmanipulated (subject) variables and therefore constitute approaches to descriptive research. The remaining four questions deal with the manipulation of variables and are approaches to experimental research.

The Seven Basic Questions

1. What are the dimensions along which behaviors naturally vary?

2. Does the classification of behavior into discrete categories conform to a specific theoretically expected or hypothesized pattern of results?

3. Does an association exist between two (or more) variables?

4. Will introducing subjects to a specific change in an otherwise standard context cause their behavior to change?

5. Will introducing subjects to qualitatively different conditions cause them to exhibit systematic differences in behavior?

6. Will introducing subjects to quantitatively different conditions cause them to exhibit systematic differences in behavior?

7. Will introducing subjects to two or more systematically different conditions cause an additive and/or interactive effect on behavior?

Key Terms

Additive Result, p. 79

Between-Subject Design, p. 75

Cell, p. 71

Factor, p. 75

Factorial Design, p. 78

Functionally Dependent, p. 70

Functionally Independent, p. 70

Interaction, p. 80

Levels of a Factor, p. 78

Nonadditive Result, p. 80

Within-Subject Design, p. 75

Chapter Exercises

1. Assume that you have set out to do research on the behavior of the college sophomore. State a research problem in the form of each of the seven basic questions.

2. Which of the research problems generated in response to Question 1 can be addressed by descriptive data and which involve experimentation?

3. Give an example of how description can sometimes be the source of experimental hypotheses.

4. In your answer to Question 1 above, you stated a research problem the goal of which was to demonstrate a functional relationship (correlation) between two variables (the problem in the form of Basic Question 3). Design an experiment that would test for the existence of a causal relationship between the same two variables. Why would the existence of correlation alone not permit a causal interpretation of the relationship between the variables?

5. If ethical considerations were not a factor, design an experiment that would have the potential to support a causal connection between drinking and poor grades.

6. Explain the difference between a 2 × 2 contingency table (such as Table 5–2) and a 2 × 2 table of means (Table 5–6).

7. Explain why it is so important to be able to distinguish manipulated from ex post facto and naturally occurring variables when interpreting a research result.

8. Working parents sometimes defend the relatively scant contact they have with their children (the *quantity* of time) by pointing to the meaningful and fulfilling experiences they have when they do find time to spend with their children (the *quality* of time). Within the latter context, explain the difference between quantitative and qualitative manipulation of a variable.

Proposal Assignment 5: Basic Questions

Proposal Assignment 3 listed five sample hypotheses designed to answer some of the different basic questions introduced in this chapter. As the first part of this assignment, identify the basic question addressed by each of the hypotheses.

As the second part of the assignment, reword the hypothesis you selected for Proposal Assignments 4a and 4b and restate the hypothesis in the form of *three* different basic questions.

PART II INTRODUCTION

Part I built a vocabulary of fundamental concepts and terminology and introduced the basic questions that underlie most research in psychology and other behavioral sciences. Part II builds on this material by examining specific research methods and their capacity to address one or more of the basic questions.

Part IIA: Descriptive Research

Chapters 6 through 9 are devoted to descriptive and correlational methods. In general, methods that focus on the description of behavior (such as naturalistic observations, surveys, and the administration of standardized psychological tests) call for the researcher to compile a behavioral record without contributing in any way to the circumstances responsible for the form or frequency of the behavior being studied. Once we have two or more measures of behavior on the same set of individuals we can describe the strength of the association or *correlation* that exists between different behavioral measures.

Part IIB: Experimental Research

In descriptive studies the researcher measures behavior without systematically manipulating any conditions that affect behavior; in experiments (chapters 10 through 14) the researcher purposefully and systematically manipulates at least one variable that, hypothetically, is capable of causing a change in behavior. The question the researcher sets out to answer with an experiment can be a logical extension of information published in scientific literature; it can come from the desire to pursue the causes of facts documented by descriptive research; or it may be the result of simple curiosity. In these chapters you will see that experiments can take

many different forms (designs), depending on the form of the question the researcher is intent on answering.

Quasi-Experimental Methods

Sometimes researchers refer to studies with selected variables or natural treatments as quasi-experiments (in preference to *correlational studies*). Like true experiments, quasi-experiments require collecting behavioral data on groups of subjects who have had different experiences, and the objective of the quasi-experiment, like that of true experiments, is to link the discovery of behavioral differences among groups to the different experiences of the groups. The resemblance, however, stops there.

In one type of quasi-experiment, subject characteristics are determined by a selected variable or natural treatment rather than being produced by an experimental manipulation. Thus, instead of being initially equivalent prior to experiencing different treatments, the groups of the quasi-experiment are known *not* to be initially equivalent. The lack of initial equivalence identified with the selected variable or natural treatment takes the place of what, in an experiment, would be the manipulated treatment condition.

The reference to a study with a selected variable or natural treatment as an experiment, even though qualified as a quasi- (false or not-quite) experiment, is more revealing of the focus of the research. Specifically, the aim of quasi-experimental research is to go beyond the descriptive analysis and interpretations limited to association that characterize correlational studies and, instead, make a case for a causal linkage between a selected variable or natural treatment and between-group behavioral differences. Special research strategies called quasi-experimental designs are structured to minimize, to whatever extent is possible, the alternative explanations of research results that are inescapable when we compare

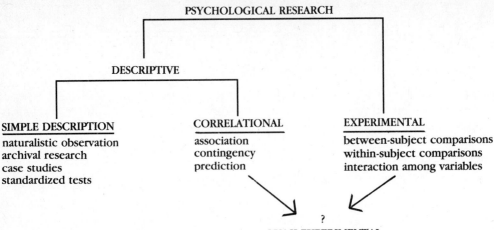

The goals of research include the simple description of behavior, the description of the association that exists among variables (correlational), documentation of a causal linkage between variables (experimental), and attempts to approach causal explanations of behavioral phenomena without the orthodoxy of true experiments (quasi-experimental research).

groups that differ ex post facto (after the fact) rather than from purposeful manipulation.

Another type of quasi-experiment involves exposing different groups of subjects to different values of a manipulated independent variable just as one would do in an experiment. The departure from proper experimental methodology that makes the experiment "quasi" is the questionable initial equivalence of the differently treated groups. As chapter 15 indicates, applying the techniques of random assignment to maximize initial equivalence and avoid confounding variables is not always practical and may even be impossible.

The research approaches covered in Part II are depicted above as a hybrid, that is, containing elements of both descriptive and experimental research. The question mark represents uncertainty about which of the two basic types of research, descriptive or experimental, is more characteristic of quasi-experimental research. Each study must be evaluated independently. Whether a given set of results from a quasi-experiment is limited to a descriptive interpretation or can support a causal interpretation ultimately depends on the degree to which the study has achieved control over confounding variables and the rival explanations they introduce.

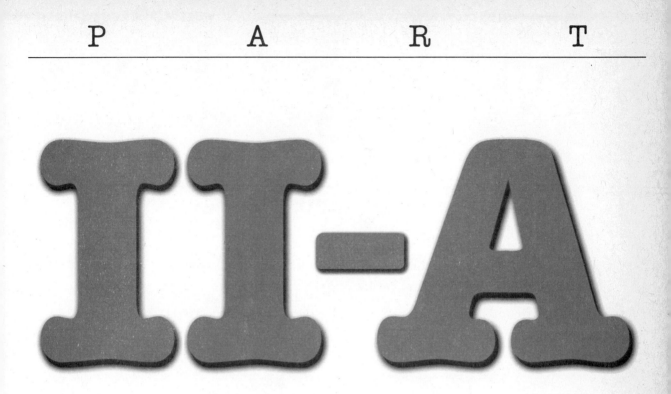

II-A

Description: The First Level of Research Inquiry

Methods for Describing Behavior

Overt Behavior: A directly observable behavior.

Covert Behavior: A psychological reaction or mental process that cannot be physically described or directly observed.

Gathering data for the description of behavior can be compared to harvesting wild edibles. Just as some food enthusiasts gather wild berries, mushrooms, and truffles without prior involvement in their planting or cultivation, researchers who use descriptive methods systematically gather information on behaviors that are governed by naturally occurring rather than by experimentally manipulated forces. Psychologists use descriptive methods to study both overt behaviors and covert behaviors. An **overt behavior** is directly observable, like the body language and facial expressions subjects engage in during a social encounter. A **covert behavior** is a psychological reaction or mental process that cannot be physically described or directly observed, like the impact of a social encounter on a subject's attitudes, beliefs, or emotional state. Of course, evidence of a covert behavioral reaction is often present in overt behavior, as when we hang or shake our heads after suffering a disappointment. The mission of descriptive research, regardless of the method employed, is to record the measurable characteristics of behavior in a manner as detailed, systematic, objective, and accurate as possible. Only with these attributes in place can research, either descriptive or experimental, be considered scientific.

The Issue Is Description

Basic Question 1 asks: *What are the dimensions along which behaviors naturally vary*? Description, the first level of research inquiry, is the method we must use to answer the question. We must record which member of a group is exhibiting the behavior (the "who" question), the specific elements that comprise the behavior, such as body movements and vocalizations (the "what" question), the frequency of the behavior (the "how often" question), and the duration of the behavior (the "how long" question). A description of the context in which the behavior tends to appear is also important information, but the association of a behavior with a particular environmental context (the "when" and "where" questions) is more germane to Basic Question 3: *Does an association exist between two (or more) variables*? Did you notice the omission of the "why" question? The "why" question deals with the issue of causality and is beyond our present focus on description.

The methods psychologists use to describe behavior include naturalistic observation, the case study, archival research, standardized psychological tests, and survey research. (This chapter is devoted to the first four methods; the last, survey research, is covered in chapter 7.) The naturalistic, archival, and case study methods are descriptive because, unlike experimental research, they do not involve assigning subjects to systematically varied treatment conditions together with appropriate control conditions. Standardized psychological tests are useful both for describing behavior and in experimental research. For example, a psychologist who uses a standardized test to assess a student's verbal ability is using the test as a descriptive tool, but a psychologist who uses the same test to compare the verbal skill of students assigned to a traditional rather than an experimental classroom is using the test as a dependent variable in an experiment.

Naturalistic Observation

The discussion of the levels of observation in chapter 4 introduced the notion that research data differ with respect to the depth of information they provide about behavior. The first level of observation is naturalistic observation: the unobtrusive recording and description of animal or human behavior as it takes place in an unaltered natural setting. (We encourage you to reread the section in chapter 4 on naturalistic observation to review some important aspects of the naturalistic method, such as the need for the observer to avoid being noticed by the subjects and the importance of objectivity and interobserver reliability.) **Natural setting** denotes the absence of any purposeful or controlled modification of an organism's living conditions. (By contrast, in experimental research, the fourth level of observation, control of the research setting, is intentionally and systematically

Natural Setting: An environment characterized by the absence of any purposeful or controlled modification of an organism's living conditions.

maintained by introducing, withdrawing, and manipulating some variables and by holding others constant.)

The rationale for describing naturalistic observation as the first level of observation is that we must first be able to describe a behavior as it exists in nature before we can present evidence of its association with other behaviors and/or variables (correlational research) or discover the underlying causes of the behavior (experimental research). Consider, for example, the study of reproductive behavior in animal populations. Our knowledge of the association that exists in many species between aggressive behavior among the males and the onset of receptive behaviors (courtship) among females had to have been preceded by accurate descriptions of what males and females do at different stages of the reproductive cycle. Once researchers were aware of the components of individual behaviors (stereotypic postures, threat displays, submissive displays, vocalizations, biting, chasing) and applied a label to categorize the behaviors as an interrelated set (these behaviors are all elements of aggressive behavior), they could evaluate the degree to which the set of behaviors in the male is associated with the reproductive cycle in the female.

Experimental research also relies on the descriptive record as a valuable source of information. Inspection of descriptive data often suggests a hypothesis concerning the underlying causality of a behavior. Thus detailed descriptions of the sniffing behavior of male monkeys and female posturing (presenting) while being sniffed suggested the importance of odor as a sexual attractant and initiator of courtship. Experimental research in which the role of odor was carefully examined verified that odor is indeed a key stimulus that initiates courtship and sexual interaction in monkeys (Michael, 1980).

A trip into the jungle or even to a zoo or animal laboratory for naturalistic observations of animal populations is not necessary. Observing the behavioral interactions of an intact dog or cat (one that has not been sexually neutered) with other animals when it or others in the vicinity are in estrus ("heat") quickly reveals aggressive and courtship behaviors. Pet owners unfamiliar with the behavioral manifestations of sexual receptivity by the females and rivalry and aggression by the males soon become familiar with the specific behaviors associated with canine and feline reproduction. The owner of a male dog who lives in the vicinity of a female dog in heat is likely to observe him howl, fail to respond to learned commands, become agitated, stay out all night, fight, and lose appetite. The uninformed owner may initially react to the display of these atypical behaviors with confusion and worry. Eventually, however, the observant pet owner recognizes the individual behavioral anomalies as a behavioral syndrome tied to the animal's natural reproductive urges.

Our common experiences with domestic animals mirror the progressive levels of understanding through which researchers progress in their formal study of behavioral phenomena. Researching a behavioral phenomenon typically begins with observational data: a listing of *what* occurs. From that point we progress to the study of associations that exist among behaviors and between behaviors and contextual variables. Eventually we reach the *why* question, which focuses on understanding the function and causes of behavior. How we accomplish this progressive understanding has more to do with our cognitive capacity as human beings than with the information content of research data. Observational data can easily appear as a list of disconnected facts, a detailed catalog of a subject's movements, mannerisms, and reactions to events and circumstances. No amount of objective, descriptive detail of individual behaviors will, by themselves, convey the function the behavior serves in the natural scheme or its underlying causes. So how do we gain insight into the meaning of observational data? Ultimately, the interpretation of descriptive data is partly subjective, relying on the personal creativity, inspiration, and insight of the scientist. This use of naturalistic data is an example of inductive research because it serves to impose order on an initially disordered array of facts (see chapter 4 and Figure 2–2).

Uses of Naturalistic Observation

Besides providing a data base of descriptive details that can lead to the deeper levels of observation called correlational and experimental research, naturalistic observation also serves a number of other useful purposes.

Establishing external validity

Naturalistic observation allows researchers to determine whether or not findings from laboratory studies can explain the behavior of organisms in their natural habitat. Gathering support for the interpretation of laboratory findings by comparing them with data from naturalistic observations is a way of establishing **external validity**, the extent to which one can generalize the results of carefully controlled laboratory studies to understand behavior in real-life situations. For example, assume that you observe in your environmentally controlled animal laboratory (with its uniform cage environment, temperature, humidity, and controlled day–night light cycle) that setting a 14 : 10 ratio of day to night hours (14 hours light, 10 hours dark) increases courtship behavior and improves the fertility of breeding pairs of a bird species. You could verify the importance of the 14 : 10 day-to-night ratio as a trigger for reproductive readiness by making some naturalistic observations of the birds at different seasons of the year. If you observe in a natural setting that maximum reproductive readiness coincides with 14-hour days, the consistency of this observation with your laboratory finding would support the external validity of your research results. If a behavior observed in the laboratory is *not* consistent with observations from a natural setting, it is likely to be viewed as an artifact of the unnatural, environmentally controlled laboratory setting.

External Validity: The extent to which researchers can generalize the results of carefully controlled laboratory studies to understand behavior in real-life situations.

When experiments are impossible

Another use of the naturalistic method is to study behavior that would be too difficult, costly, or unethical to study experimentally. For example, homeless people are a common sight in America's urban centers. To address this growing problem with effective social programs, planners must know as much as possible about the life-style and coping behaviors of the homeless. The successes and failures of the social welfare system in dealing with the problem of homelessness, the successes and failures of the legal and mental health systems, and the responses of police and politicians to the dilemma all have to be documented. (Politicians, social workers, police, predatory street criminals, and so on must all be included in the "natural" urban environment.) It would, of course, be unethical to contrive a disaster (manipulate a variable) that would place a random sample of financially stable citizens at risk of becoming homeless and not interfere with the lives of an equivalent sample of citizens just to study the determinants of homelessness experimentally. One can, however, be opportunistic and describe the predicaments of existing homeless populations using the method of naturalistic observation.

When behavior is rare or difficult to observe

Sometimes passive observation is inefficient, especially if the behaviors or the conditions that precipitate them are relatively rare or difficult to observe. In such cases researchers typically modify the natural setting in a way calculated to increase the flow of scientifically valuable data. For example, animals are fitted with transmitters to signal their location, birds are banded to study migration patterns, and animal and human habitats are surreptitiously modified to permit filming and videotaping. Modifying a natural setting is a manipulation and technically disqualifies the research as a pure example of naturalistic observation. Nevertheless, as long as the manipulations are minimally disruptive, the data are still likely to be valuable as a description of natural behavior.

Archival Research

Archival Research:
Retrieval of selected information from existing data bases.

Archival research is retrieval of selected information from existing data bases. Seldom do we get through a day without contributing information to one or more data bases. We fill out forms that relate to job, school, insurance, or medical care. We buy prescription medication, apply for credit, pay bills, get parking tickets, charge purchases using credit cards, make long-distance telephone calls, participate in surveys, vote in elections, subscribe to magazines and newspapers, and much more. Often a record of our behavior is available for public scrutiny even though it is not linked to us personally. For example, 1990 U.S. Census data revealed that the number of homes with young children headed by a single parent increased compared to 1980 data, but the names of the single parents are kept confidential to protect the privacy of census respondents. Similarly, a drug company reports to its stockholders that more than two million people bought its newly marketed diet pill in the past year. The purchasers' behavior was included in those data even though their names were not.

Records are the research environment of the archival researcher. Unlike other researchers, the archival researcher *selects* data from available records instead of collecting them. The archival researcher is a scavenger of sorts, retrieving information from printed, magnetic, or film records with a focus probably not imagined by the original collector of the information. For example, hospital records list both the date of admission and a diagnosis for each patient. This information makes it possible to examine the association of stress-related medical disorders (gastric ulcers, migraine headaches, skin eruptions) with the flow of good and bad economic news during the dates prior to the onset of the patients' medical difficulties.

Focusing information retrieval

In preparing to do archival research, investigators must take two important steps: specify with an operational definition the exact characteristics of the public record they wish to highlight, and formally state the hypothesis they are investigating. For example, assume that school officials noticed a wide discrepancy in the district regarding the number of school-age children identified in their medical records as developmentally delayed and the number of children identified as developmentally delayed by the district's school psychologists. An outside consultant is asked by the court to examine subpoenaed medical records for indices of developmental delay and to report on the credibility of the assertion that local pediatricians tend to under-report developmental delays in their patients.

Before beginning an examination of the records, however, the consultant would have to define developmental delay operationally. He or she might operationally define developmental delay as the failure to master skills appropriate for 75% of chronological age. Using this definition, a skill that children normally master by 9 months of age would be considered significantly delayed only if it had not occurred by 12 months of age. By comparing the recorded ages at which the children mastered various skills of coordination, balance, and language to published developmental norms, the researcher could label each behavior objectively as normal or delayed. Without an operational definition of developmental delay, the objectivity of the archival study would be lost.

Archival data versus experimental data

Archival research can yield extensive, detailed, and intensely interesting data on entire populations, and the temptation to go beyond description and conclude causality can be considerable. For example, if a researcher finds that Stanford Achievement Test scores declined steadily over the past 10 years for Milton Elementary School students at the same time class sizes increased dramatically, the researcher has demonstrated that a negative association exists between the achievement and class-size variables (Basic Question 3). But does the association also document the negative influence of large class size on effective teaching (Basic Question 6)? Clearly, it is incorrect to conclude from these data alone that large class size leads to low student achievement or that small class size enhances student achievement. To investigate the issue in the form of Basic Question 6 (Will students in small classes achieve at a different rate than students in large classes?) a researcher would have to do an experiment: manipulate class size by operationally defining *small* and *large*, randomly assign students to the different-size classes, and hold other relevant variables (such as the instructional materials and lesson plans) constant for both classes. In contrast to experimental data, archival data are inevitably ex post facto, and this fundamental characteristic limits the data to the description of behavior (what?) as opposed to explanation (why?).

Using Archival Data

Public records can be analyzed for a variety of enlightening purposes. One objective is to present data in a new light: to reveal descriptive characteristics of a population that had never been previously appreciated. For example, colleges have both high school and college records that describe the prior and present academic performance of all their students. It would be possible to analyze those records to assess the association of students' academic success in college with the particular high school from which the student graduated. Of course, if the college grades of mathematics majors who are alumni of Central High were found to be superior to the grades of mathematics majors who attended Valley High, we could not, on the basis of the ex post facto findings, *causally* attribute the students' achievement level to the high school they attended. Perhaps the parents of the brighter and more motivated students tend to gravitate to the Central High school district because of the rigor of its curriculum and its excellent reputation.

Another useful application of archival research is to justify the time, effort, and expense of future research. For example, the researcher who examined school and medical records for evidence of developmental delay in children found that school officials and physicians differed in their assessments of developmental delay—a research result that could be used to justify a program to open up more lines of communication between the two groups of professionals. Similarly, archival data showing that the college grades of Central High alumni were superior to the grades of Valley High alumni are consistent with the view that Valley High does not give students the same caliber of college preparation that is available at Central High and would likely prompt further comparisons of the educational practices of the two schools. Of course, a research result that describes the difference between two groups (the college performance of Central High alumni is superior to that of Valley High alumni) can be consistent with a causal explanation (Central High does a better job of preparing students for college than Valley High) but cannot, by itself, be used to verify a causal explanation. Only experimental research is capable of assessing the causal basis of group differences.

Like the data from naturalistic observations, archival data can also be used to demonstrate the external validity of experimental findings. For example, assume we find in the laboratory that when subjects hold and pet kittens, puppies, and other similarly cuddly creatures, their response to stress is less than subjects who are not holding pets. To demonstrate the external validity of this laboratory phenomenon we could compare the medical records of pet owners to non-pet owners with respect to the incidence and severity of stress-related disorders. If we found that pet owners are less likely than non-pet owners to suffer from a stress-related disorder, the association would be consistent with the hypothesis that owning a pet tends to weaken the impact of stress in the real world, not just in the controlled environment of the laboratory.

One final use of archival data is to examine the public record for evidence that a significant event (natural disaster, outbreak of war, technological breakthrough, the rise of a powerful public figure, and so on) had an impact on behavior. To be useful in this regard, data must have been recorded both before and after the significant event. For example, it would be interesting to compare crime statistics in a large American city both before and after the seizure of a major drug shipment. Some people who support the legalization of drugs contend that efforts to cut the supply of illegal drugs actually increases crime. They point out that if the supply of illegal drugs is significantly diminished, or if there is even the perception in the drug-using subculture that there might be a disruption in the supply of street drugs, demand increases and forces up the price of the drugs on the street. Consequently, drug users must commit more crimes to get the money to buy drugs. A comparison of selected crime statistics before the big drug seizure versus afterward would reflect on the relationship between the supply of illegal drugs and crime rate.

In interpreting the results of a before-versus-after comparison from archival data, we must be careful not to conclude that the significant event *caused* the change. If, for example, arrest statistics did document an increase in drug-related crime following the seizure, it would be improper to claim that the seizure was itself a direct cause of the increase. Another factor, such as the flare-up of a territorial dispute between rival drug lords, may have been the real cause of the increase in arrests. It is, however, correct to present the result as an association, as in the statement "The price of drugs on the street is positively associated with reported crimes: the higher the price, the more crimes are committed."

The Case Study

A **case study**, as it pertains to psychological research, is a very detailed and comprehensive study of the behavior of a single individual together with descriptions of past and present life events relevant to the behavioral record.

Sources of Data

There are many diverse sources of information from which to construct a case study. Elements of a case study could include information from job evaluations and school records (archival research), unobtrusive observations of the subject in a variety of situations (naturalistic observation), personal interviews (survey research), and the impact on the individual of either programed (therapeutic intervention) or unforeseen life events.

Idiographic versus Nomethetic Research

The case study is an **idiographic** form of research, which means simply that the primary objective is to describe, analyze, compare, and contrast the behavior of *individual* subjects. Most other descriptive and experimental behavioral research is **nomethetic**, which means that the primary focus is on the behavior of *groups*. Drawing a distinction between studies that focus on individuals instead of groups is by no means limited to behavioral research. In medicine, for example, the effectiveness of an experimental drug is typically evaluated by comparing the reactions of one or more control groups who do not get the drug treatment to one or more experimental groups who do. If only the treated subjects, taken as a whole, experience a significant therapeutic effect with minimal or no negative side effects, the drug would be considered effective and would be approved for its intended medical application. Since the character of the study is nomethetic, the fact that an occasional treated subject fails to benefit from the drug or suffers from a moderate and uncommon side effect is of relatively minor significance. But once the drug is no longer experimental and is approved for use by the public, the criteria for drug evaluation change. From the physician's viewpoint as a health-care provider, the primary benchmark of the drug's effectiveness becomes idiographic: the reactions of individual patients to the medicine.

An important advantage of nomethetic research over idiographic research is that it is more likely to provide accurate generalizations about population characteristics. The reason is straightforward: With data available for only one individual, it is impossible to determine whether an observed behavioral characteristic is unique

Case Study: A very detailed and comprehensive study of the behavior of a single individual together with descriptions of past and present life events relevant to the behavioral record.

Idiographic Research: Research with a primary objective to describe, analyze, compare, and contrast the behavior of individual subjects.

Nomethetic Research: Research that has the behavior of groups as its primary focus.

(idiosyncratic) to the individual or true of people in general. On the other hand, case-study data sometimes reveal small but important influences on an individual's behavior—variables that are so subtle and irregular in how they affect the behavior of different individuals that they might appear not to influence behavior if evaluated experimentally. For example, case-study data could show that modifying an established therapeutic practice produces a slight but noticeable improvement for a minority of clients, whereas an experimental comparison between traditional and modified treatment groups could easily fail to reveal the effectiveness of the modification (a Type II error).

Another disadvantage of nomethetic research is that the generalizations it produces about a population may not accurately describe the behavior of any of the individual group members. This curious result occurs when no single member of a group behaves the same as the group mean. For example, if you have an instructor who posts examination grades along with the class mean, compare the class mean to the list of individual student grades. You might find that no one student actually performed right on the mean. To take an extreme case, if a set of test grades consisted of an equal number of 40s, 50s, 80s, and 90s, none would even be close to the mean score of 65. By comparison, when the behavioral record of a single individual is compiled, perhaps over a period of many years, the psychologist can gain important insights about subtle variables that affect the individual's behavior that are less likely to be detected in studies comparing groups.

Uses of the Case-Study Approach

As in medicine, the case-study approach in psychology is most closely associated with clinical practice: carefully describing and documenting a patient's problem, the prescribed course of treatment, and the patient's progress during treatment. Of course, the clinician keeps careful records primarily to get the information needed to help the patient, but case-study data can also provide insights that may cautiously be generalized to other individuals. Thus, as in all research, the goal of the case study is to collect and disseminate useful information.

Taking advantage of an opportunity

Several specific applications of case-study research are widely recognized. One of the most common is taking advantage of the opportunity to study a rare phenomenon. For example, individuals who have had brain tissue excised because of a tumor or aneurysm are often studied to gain insight into the loss of function that occurs with unavoidable damage to specific neuroanatomical locations. Whereas researchers would never purposely inflict such injury on a healthy subject, they often take advantage of such medically necessary procedures to study the relationship between the site of brain damage and subsequent changes in memory capabilities, temperament, motivation, coordination, and the like.

Testing a treatment innovation

Innovative medical treatments such as heart transplants and genetically engineered drugs are initially developed and tested using nonhuman organisms. At some time, however, the treatment must be tried on a human before it will be accepted as clinically safe and effective. In the practice of clinical psychology, treatment innovations are unlikely to be as risky or invasive as in medicine, but new treatment strategies must still be carefully evaluated. The case-study approach can yield very valuable preliminary information about the potential effectiveness of a treatment innovation. The knowledge gained from the case study can be helpful in refining a treatment and perhaps lead to a recommendation to adopt the treatment strategy on a wider scale. At the same time, however, we must also keep in mind the limitations of case-study data. As pointed out earlier, we take a risk when we generalize case-study findings to a larger population because it is impossible to determine the extent to which the results of a case study are unique to the individual or true of people in general. Thus, interpretations of and generalizations from case-study data should be considered tentative until verified experimentally.

The Limitations of Case Studies

Keep in mind that the data of a case study are descriptive in character and, as such, are subject to the limitations that govern the interpretation of descriptive data. To the extent that the data of a case study consist of subjective clinical evaluations (expert opinion), they will lack the objectivity that comes from the measurement of operationally defined variables. Also, in a case study there are no true control subjects against which to compare the progress of the case-study subject. Nevertheless, there appears to be a certain tolerance in the human-services community for "impressions" and personal "insights" that result from case-study data, perhaps because tentative interpretations of case-study data can be such a rich source of testable hypotheses. In analyzing and interpreting case-study data one must balance the desire to give weight to intriguing aspects of the data with the capacity of the idiographic data to mislead and distort. As long as we are careful to allow for the subjective and possibly idiosyncratic character of case-study data, it will continue to occupy a useful niche in psychological research.

Standardized Psychological Tests

Standardized psychological tests are instruments that assess the behavioral characteristics, abilities, and aptitudes of individuals. The reference to a test as **standardized** means two things: First, that specific (standard) conditions must apply during the test administration and scoring to ensure interpretable results. Second, that an individual's performance on the test is interpreted by comparing it to a **norm**, a description of the average (mean, median, or mode) or standard form of a behavior derived from prior study of a relatively large group. Thus, a psychologist who administers an intelligence test to a 10-year-old follows the standard procedures for administering the test and assesses the child's intelligence by comparing his or her performance to the average score of 10-year-old children. With intelligence, the comparison to the norm is expressed as an intelligence quotient, commonly abbreviated IQ. As shown below, if a 10-year-old child is found to be

Standardized Psychological Tests: Instruments that assess the behavioral characteristics, abilities, and aptitudes of individuals with reference to group norms.

Standardized: Denotes adherence to uniform test administration and scoring procedures and the comparison of test results to norms.

Norm: The central (mean, median, or mode) or average form of a behavior derived from prior study of a relatively large group.

functioning at an intellectual level typical of the normal 12-year-old, the child has a 120 IQ.

$$IQ = \frac{\text{Mental Age}}{\text{Chronological Age}} \times 100$$

$$IQ = \frac{12}{10} \times 100 = 120$$

Standardization Sample:
The sample studied to determine the normative level of a behavioral capacity.

The sample we draw from a population and study to determine the normative level of a behavioral capacity is called the **standardization sample**. It is very important that the subject being tested not differ in any systematic way from the standardization sample. The concept of the standardization sample is at the root of much current controversy regarding the performance of ethnic minorities on standardized intelligence tests. If the items on an intelligence test are based on personal and educational experiences alien to the individual taking the test, we describe the test as having a **cultural bias**. In general, the usefulness of a test as a measure of behavioral capacity will suffer if the subject being tested differs in systematic ways from the subjects that made up the standardization sample.

Cultural Bias: A threat to the accurate measurement of a behavioral capacity arising from the subject's limited access to the personal and educational experiences on which the test items are based.

Standardized tests are used for a variety of purposes, including the assessment of intelligence, aptitudes, personality traits, clinical diagnosis of psychological disorders, and as a dependent measure in an experiment. Of the more than 1000 different psychological tests available commercially in English-speaking countries, each, in its own way, provides specialized information about the psychology of the individual. Some, like the Minnesota Multiphasic Personality Inventory (MMPI), are easily standardized because the statements that make up the test are unambiguous (such as "I give up too easily when discussing things with others") and responses are limited to "True," "False," and "Cannot say." By comparison, such projective psychological tests as the Rorschach present ambiguous stimuli (inkblots) to which the subjects can give an infinite variety of imaginative responses. Moreover, describing a subject's personality characteristics on the basis of his or her descriptions of the inkblot images is largely a subjective enterprise because it is more dependent on the examiner's skill and sensitivity than on the application of objective scoring criteria.

Historically, the demand for test development originated with governments. After public instruction was adopted as national policy in turn-of-the-century France, the wide variation in the intellectual capacity of French children became apparent: most were capable, but others were not responding well to formal education. In 1904, responding to the concern of the French minister of instruction, Alfred Binet (1857–1911) and his colleague Theodore Simon began the development of an objective test to identify children who would be unlikely to benefit from tradition educational curricula and methods of instruction. As intended, Binet and Simon's test of intelligence provided French officials the information they needed to make important decisions affecting the education and lives of individuals. Likewise, the government of the United States was an active supporter of the development of test instruments. The Army Alpha and Beta tests, as well as the present Armed Services Vocational Aptitude Battery, were developed in response to the need to match soldiers with a job and responsibility for which they were suited.

What Makes a Good Test?

Validity

To be useful as an assessment tool a test must be both reliable and valid. Validity, as we have seen, is the capacity of data in an experiment to reflect accurately the variable under study. Similarly, in the context of tests and measurement, validity is a measure of how capable a test is of measuring what it is supposed to measure. Thus, if a test instrument is supposed to measure the managerial potential of a job applicant, it is a valid test only if the items on the test permit an accurate determination of managerial potential.

On another level, validity is a statistical concept. **Criterion-related validity** is reflected in the size of the correlation (r value) between the test scores of a group and one or more relevant performance measures (criteria). The closer the association is between test score (variable X) and a performance measure (variable Y), the more confident we can be using the test as a measure of performance potential. When test scores are useful for predicting performance levels of behaviors that depend on the characteristic the test measures, we say the test has **predictive validity**. For example, to the extent that the Medical Aptitude Test predicts the level of academic success in medical school and peer evaluation of a physician's proficiency in the practice of medicine, it has predictive validity. Naturally, cultural bias is as damaging to predictive validity as it is to validity in general.

Measures of academic performance and professional qualifications constitute **performance criteria**, behavioral measures against which to compare predictions of a test. In Binet's case the performance criteria for his test of intelligence were school grades and teacher evaluations. His determination that the students' test scores were positively correlated with the measures of school performance (the better they did on the intelligence test, the better they tended to do in school) demonstrated that the test had predictive validity and could be used to identify students with special needs.

Sometimes we only assume that certain measures reflect underlying behavioral capacities. Thus, without a formal statistical evaluation of validity, it would be reasonable to assume that a test of strength and muscular coordination would be predictive of athletic success or that a child's fine motor coordination and ability to reproduce pure tones and keep a steady tempo would be predictive of success in mastering a musical instrument. When the validity of a measure as a predictor of behavior is assumed because of the obvious association between the measure and the behavior, we describe the measure as having **face validity**.

Whereas we describe tests in terms of their predictive validity, we describe constructs (psychological concepts such as anxiety, anger, guilt, hostility, and so on) in terms of their **construct validity**. It would be legitimate to ask, for example, if managerial potential is really a valid construct. If an industrial psychologist showed that several variables known or assumed to be associated with and/or predictive of success as a manager relate in a consistent fashion to several measures of managerial success (see Table 6–1), the construct of managerial potential would be validated. In the best-case scenario, high or good scores on all the predictors would be linked in a positive fashion to high or good scores on the measures of managerial success, and

Criterion-related Validity: The extent of association between a set of test scores and one or more relevant performance measures.

Predictive Validity: The degree to which a test can predict the type of performance it is supposed to predict.

Performance Criteria: Behavioral measures against which to compare the predictions of a test.

Face Validity: Assumption that a measure is a valid predictor of behavior owing to the obvious association between the measure and the behavior.

Construct Validity: The usefulness of a psychological concept as a measure of behavior.

Assumed Predictors of Managerial Success	Measure of Managerial Success
Rank in school graduating class	Growth in sales
IQ	Performance of supervisees
Academic honors	Profits
Leadership positions in clubs, etc.	New accounts
References from former teachers and employers	Employee morale
Psychological tests results	Customer satisfaction
Evaluation from personal interview	Adherence to company policies

Table 6–1. Some predictors and measures of managerial success.

mediocre or poor scores on the predictors would be consistently linked with poor scores on the measures of managerial success.

Reliability

The reliability of measurement, another equally important characteristic of a useful test, is the property of consistency over time (see chapter 3). That is, if a test instrument is reliable, its assessment of a stable psychological variable (such as intelligence) will be essentially the same over repeated test administrations (retests). The actual statistical procedures for computing reliability estimates— which, like the assessment of validity, involve correlation analysis—are beyond the present level of discussion. Nevertheless, the underlying logic of reliability estimation is itself not difficult to understand.

Reliability estimates are measures of the strength of association (see chapter 4). In **test-retest reliability**, we evaluate the association between the original test results and the retest results. The greater the association between the responses on the original test administration and the responses on the retest, the greater the reliability of the test. In the computation of **split-half reliability**, the test is first split into two equivalent halves. Then, as with test-retest reliability, we assess the association (consistency) that exists between the two sets of test data. The computation of **internal consistency reliability**, although mathematically related to the split-half method, is somewhat more complex. Instead of a single comparison between equivalent test halves, the internal consistency method compares the response made to each test item to the responses on every other test item. The internal consistency reliability estimate of the test will be the largest when every item on the test measures essentially the same dimension of behavior and the number of items on the test is relatively large. One advantage the split-half and internal consistency methods have over the test-retest method is that they provide a way to assess the reliability of a test without having to administer a retest.

No test will always yield consistent results on repeated measurements of the same sample, be it a physiological test (such as tests to detect the presence of illegal drugs in blood or urine) or a behavioral test (such as an attitude assessment instrument), but the experts who construct psychological tests strive for as much

Test-Retest Reliability: The strength of association between original test results and a set of retest results.

Split-half Reliability: The association between responses to two equivalent halves of a test.

Internal Consistency Reliability: The mean reliability measure one would obtain from all possible split-half analyses.

reliability as possible. After all, how useful would an instrument to assess intelligence be if a subject scored in the genius range on one test administration and in the mentally retarded range on a second test? The latter example also illustrates that some minimal level of reliability is required for any degree of validity to exist. That is, a test cannot be a valid measure of a stable psychological characteristic and at the same time yield opposite results on separate administrations of the same test to the same individual.

Differences Among Tests

Standardized tests not only vary with regard to their measurement objectives, they also vary considerably in how they are administered and how they are scored. Some tests require only paper and pencil to complete and can be administered to many people at once (called **group-administered tests**), whereas others, called **individually administered tests**, involve one-on-one interaction between the test administrator and the subject. Administering a test one-on-one usually requires extensive and intensive training both to present the test items properly and to interpret the test results. By contrast, only minimal training in testing procedures is necessary when administering paper-and-pencil tests.

Group-administered Tests: Tests that can be administered to many subjects at once.

Individually Administered Tests: Tests that must be administered one-on-one.

Most psychological tests are scored objectively, as in a multiple-choice format, whereas others are subjectively scored. When scoring is objective, anyone scoring the test will get the same results. When scoring is subjective, the personal interpretations and perceptions that contribute to the scoring make it most unlikely that multiple scorers will get exactly the same results. To maximize the interobserver reliability (discussed in chapter 4) of scoring procedures, it is important that testers be thoroughly trained. One diagnostic method to check for interobserver reliability is to correlate an expert trainer's scores with those of a trainee. A low correlation would indicate that the trainee is not using the same scoring criteria as the trainer, and further training would be in order. Of course, a subjectively scored test with scoring criteria too vague to ensure a reasonable degree of consistency among test administrators is, by definition as well as by evidence, not reliable.

The Uses of Standardized Tests

We have already noted the application of standardized tests to measure that elusive quality of mental agility and capacity we call intelligence. But psychologists are interested in measuring many other important personal characteristics besides intelligence. Here are a few of the more common ones. Achievement refers to a person's present knowledge of a subject or performance level of a skill, and aptitude is the potential a person has for future achievement. The measurement of both achievement and aptitude is central to meeting educational and economic objectives. Through your own high school experience you are familiar with the SAT, the American College Testing program (ACT), and the achievement tests that evaluate ability in individual academic subjects. When you complete your formal education you are likely to encounter another type of test: the personnel test. (No, you are not done taking tests when you are done with college!) Personnel tests also measure aptitude and achievement, but the focus is on aptitude and skills relating to the performance demands of various jobs rather than the academic demands of school.

Field	Typical Assessment Activities
Clinical Psychology	Assessment of intelligence
	Assessment of psychopathology
	Neuropsychological assessment
Counseling Psychology	Assessment of career interests
	Assessment of skills
	Assessment of social adjustment
Industrial/Organizational Psychology	
	Assessment of managerial potential
	Assessment of training needs
	Assessment of cognitive and psychomotor ability
School Psychology	Assessment of ability and academic progress
	Assessment of maturity and readiness for school
	Assessment of handicapped children

Table 6–2. Typical assessment activities for several fields of applied psychology. From Kevin R. Murphy and Charles O. Davidshofer, *Psychological Testing: Principles and Applications*, 2nd ed. (Englewood Cliffs, N.J.: Prentice-Hall, 1991), p. 12. Reprinted by permission of Prentice-Hall.

Typical assessment activities for several fields of applied psychology appear in Table 6–2.

Summarizing the Results of Descriptive Research

Descriptive Statistics: Computed values that reflect specific characteristics of data, such as central tendency and dispersion.

Inferential Statistics: Procedures that permit making generalizations about population characteristics from the analysis of sample data.

There are two principal ways to identify, organize, summarize, and communicate the information that resides in a set of results from survey, archival, and case-study research. The first is by computing **descriptive statistics**, computed values that reflect specific characteristics of the data. For example, the mean, median, and mode reflect central tendency, and the standard deviation reflects the dispersion of the data values. There are also statistical tests (many of which are described briefly in Appendix B), that comprise **inferential statistics**, procedures that permit making generalizations about population characteristics from the analysis of sample data. For example, one objective of market research is often to evaluate the effectiveness of an advertising campaign to increase public awareness of a product. Comparing survey data collected before the campaign with data collected after the campaign would indicate its impact on public awareness of the product. Of course, an alternative to the numerical representation of data characteristics with statistics is to use charts, figures, and tables. Statistical and nonstatistical summaries tend to complement each other, and every researcher uses these reporting techniques to full advantage to communicate the "heart and soul" of a set of data.

Summary

Basic Question 1 is concerned with the description of behavior, and this chapter discussed four methods useful for describing behavior: naturalistic observation, archival research, the case-study approach, and the application of standardized psychological tests. We presented descriptive research as an endeavor to record the measurable characteristics of behavior in as detailed, systematic, objective, and accurate a manner as possible. Only with the latter attributes in place can research be considered scientific.

Each descriptive method, in its own way, can make valuable contributions to our understanding of behavior. We pointed out the strengths, weaknesses, and potential pitfalls of each method, and the limitations we must observe in interpreting the data they offer. In particular, we pointed out the usefulness of naturalistic observation in establishing the external validity of a laboratory finding and as an alternative to experimental research when practical and ethical constraints make some studies impossible to carry out. The discussion of archival research stressed the great wealth of potentially valuable information that awaits discovery in public records and data bases and the importance of not concluding causality from archival data despite the illusion that the data can support it. Our coverage of the case-study approach highlighted the distinction between idiographic and nomethetic research and the advantages and disadvantages of each. The discussion of standardized psychological tests provided an opportunity to revisit and expand upon the concepts of reliability and validity. The chapter concluded with some comments on how psychologists summarize descriptive data.

Key Terms

Archival Research, p. 92

Case Study, p. 95

Construct Validity, p. 99

Covert Behavior, p. 88

Criterion-related Validity, p. 99

Cultural Bias, p. 98

External Validity, p. 91

Descriptive Statistics, p. 102

Face Validity, p. 99

Group-administered Tests, p. 101

Idiographic Research, p. 95

Individually Administered Tests, p. 101

Inferential Statistics, p. 102

Internal Consistency Reliability, p. 100

Natural Setting, p. 89

Naturalistic Observation, p. 89

Nomethetic Research, p. 95

Norm, p. 97

Overt Behavior, p. 88

Performance Criteria, p. 99

Predictive Validity, p. 99

Reliability, p. 100

Split-half Reliability, p. 100

Standardization Sample, p. 98

Standardized, p. 97

Standardized Psychological Tests, p. 97

Test-Retest Reliability, p. 100

Chapter Exercises

1. Why is naturalistic observation considered the first level of observation?

2. Give an example of how one might use the data of naturalistic observation, archival research, and case studies to support the external validity of a laboratory result.

3. Even though descriptive data may be consistent with a research hypothesis concerning the causes of a phenomenon, descriptive data do not by themselves reveal the causes of phenomena. Explain.

4. Describe the strengths and weaknesses of the idiographic and nomethetic approaches to research.

5. A group of high school teachers from Metropolitan City believes that there has been a steady and significant deterioration in the scholastic capabilities of their students from 1985 to the present. Describe how you would collect data to describe this suspected educational problem using the naturalistic observation, archival, and case-study methods.

6. Assume that you are still a high school senior and have unlimited access to all the records maintained at a particular college. What social, academic, and financial descriptive characteristics of the student and faculty populations could you retrieve from this data base that could help you decide whether or not to attend the college? For example, you would probably want to know the high school grade-point average of the freshman class to get an idea of the academic qualifications of the most recently admitted students. You would probably want to know the average class size to estimate the amount of individual attention you could expect if you attended the college. In your answer, strive for some creative uses of the school's archives.

7. What does *standardized* mean in reference to a psychological test?

8. Define *reliability* and *validity* in the context of psychological testing and explain why the usefulness of a psychological test is so closely tied to its reliability and validity.

9. What is the difference between a test that measures aptitude and a test that measures achievement?

Proposal Assignment 6: Searching the Literature

Now that you have an idea for a proposal, it is time to explore what research related to your idea has already been reported in the psychological literature. (Appendix A reviews the techniques researchers use to find published research in review articles, source books, psychological abstracts, and computer-search data bases such as PsycLIT.) Your initial search goal should be to find published research that has examined the independent variable you intend to manipulate and the behavior you intend to measure.

It is possible that you may not be able to find a study with the same independent *and* dependent variables included in your proposed study. Perhaps no one has ever asked a question similar to yours. As an alternative, your literature search should center on finding articles that report either manipulating the same independent variable *or* measuring the same dependent variable as your proposed study. You may cite journal articles in which only the independent variable is the same as in your experiment to provide evidence that your independent variable influences behaviors in addition to the particular behavior you have chosen to study. Journal articles in which only the dependent variable is the same as your proposed study may be used to provide evidence that your behavior is influenced by independent variables other than the one you have chosen to manipulate. (Begin by finding and reviewing just two articles. Your instructor will let you know how many articles you should eventually review.)

After you have found two articles related to your proposal, write the *first draft* of the introduction section. (Appendix A reviews how to write the different sections of a research article. The same format is used by many journals because locating the same type of material in the same section makes it easier to find specific information.) Be sure to start the Introduction with a brief statement of the topic of your proposal. Then review the research results you have found in the literature, and conclude with a statement of the purpose, the hypotheses themselves, and the bases for your hypotheses.

CHAPTER

Survey Methods and Questionnaire Construction

Of the five approaches to descriptive research covered in this text, the survey method is probably most familiar to you. At one time or another most of us have been asked to fill out a questionnaire or participate in an interview. This chapter builds on that familiarity by describing the preparation required to do a survey project, stressing the tricky task of questionnaire composition and the methodological alternatives available in survey research. The result should be greater understanding of the strengths and weaknesses of survey research.

Survey Research

Survey research, as noted in chapter 4, is a technique for exploring the nature of people's personal characteristics and perceptions (attitudes, beliefs, opinions, and the like) by analyzing the answers to a set of carefully developed questions. The survey is a valuable tool for describing and tracking changes in populations (Basic Question 1) and, if intelligently conceived and properly administered, can make an important contribution to our understanding of the fabric of contemporary social life. But surveys do have limitations. For example, most of the research methods presented in this text are appropriate for investigating phenomena in many different disciplines and with many different species. Surveys, which for obvious reasons can be administered only to human populations, tend to be more useful in some subdisciplines of psychology (such as social and developmental psychology) than in others. Surveys are also limited by their vulnerability to certain methodological pitfalls: sources of error that can render survey results useless for accurate description of population characteristics. For example, a common problem is the failure of all the subjects included in the sample to cooperate and complete the survey.

Students are often not sensitive to the many problems survey researchers encounter, and many tend to choose a survey project in preference to an experiment for a required research project. What could be easier? You make up a list of questions, find some people who are willing to answer those questions, and summarize and discuss the recorded responses. Students who embark on survey projects, however, inevitably become aware that there are many challenges to overcome in the quest for meaningful and accurate survey results — including the tasks of composing and pretesting the questionnaire, selecting a representative sample, selecting a method for conducting the survey, and selecting a survey design. The first challenge is composing the questionnaire.

Composing the Survey Instrument (Questionnaire)

If your research needs can be met by using an existing and respected survey instrument, you will, of course, have no need to develop your own. Researchers who find themselves in this situation are fortunate indeed, because developing a quality survey instrument is no simple matter. Also, by using an existing survey instrument of demonstrated quality researchers are better able to compare their findings to published reports from the literature of their discipline. The survey instrument is the heart of the survey effort. It must be written and organized in a way that will yield the information the researcher has set out to find. Failure to meet effectively the challenges of survey administration may threaten the quality of the survey data, but failing to develop a quality instrument in the first place is a guarantee of wasted effort and ultimate failure.

Step 1: Start with a Knowledge Base

In a sense, the composition of a survey instrument involves a catch-22 paradox: In order to compose pointed and understandable questions that will produce interpretable answers, the researcher must already be very familiar with the subject matter he or she wishes to explore. In short, to get knowledge you have to have knowledge. Surveys are, therefore, not useful for exploratory studies, which generally progress from a minimum base of prior knowledge.

Researchers who are not well informed about an issue must prepare for a survey by researching materials in books, professional journals, newspapers, and magazines. For example, you should know what radioactive waste is, what the dangers of radioactive waste are, and the real or perceived problems of people who live near waste storage facilities before trying to survey public NIMBY (not in my backyard) or NOPE (not on planet Earth) attitudes concerning a proposed site for dumping low-level radioactive waste. Observation is another method for exploring new issues and should precede a formal survey. After studying relevant materials in the library, attending a few town meetings devoted to the landfill issue, and talking to and observing protest groups, support groups, and public officials, you would be better prepared to develop an instrument that would focus on the major issues of contention.

Step 2: Draft a Set of Questions

In composing your initial draft of survey questions it is important to have a well-defined research objective in mind. You must place a limit on the breadth of information you intend to acquire so as not to sacrifice depth. Surveys are more often faulted for trying to address too many issues than for being too focused. When you are in the early stage of developing your survey instrument, the primary objective should be to get your thoughts down on paper so you can define a proper focus. Keep in mind that a survey instrument with too broad a focus will not only be lengthy and difficult to compose, it will also be a negative factor influencing subject cooperation with the survey administration.

Choose a question format

There are two question formats from which to choose: open-ended and closed. **Open-ended questions** do not place limits on the content of the response (What is your opinion of your employer's affirmative action policies?). **Closed questions** usually provide between two and seven discrete response categories (multiple choice), and the respondent is required to select the one that best represents his or her attitude. Survey researchers generally try to keep the question format as simple as possible and the instrument itself as short as possible in order to maximize the cooperation of survey subjects.

Several examples of closed-question survey items appear below. The items conform to what survey researchers refer to as **Likert-type scaling**. Likert's (1932) contribution was to improve on the two-choice agree-or-disagree, like-or-dislike format by expanding the scale of response alternatives to include less extreme and neutral choices. For example, instead of the item

One of the major reasons for getting married is to have children.

Agree ____   Disagree ____

the Likert-type item would read

One of the major reasons for getting married is to have children.

Strongly Agree	Agree	Uncertain	Disagree	Strongly Disagree
( )	( )	( )	( )	( )

Notice the variety of formats in the survey questions below. One obvious feature is that a survey "question" can be in the form of a statement rather than a question. Sometimes the response alternatives are numbered, at other times there are no numbers. Sometimes, as in the first example, each response alternative has a verbal label, and at other times some verbal labels are omitted from some response categories. Sometimes the verbal labels appear on top of the numbered response categories, at others they are placed beneath the numbers. In some surveys the response of maximum agreement with a statement (strongly agree) is placed on the left, in other surveys on the right, and frequently the right-versus-left placement of the response of maximum agreement changes in an irregular sequence from question to question. Also, there is no standardization either in the number sequencing (1, 2, 3, ... or 5, 4, 3,...) or in the number of response categories, although two, five, and seven categories are the most common formats. Sometimes the middle category is labeled *uncertain, neutral, neither agree nor disagree,* may be left blank, or there may not be a middle category. Alternative wordings of the middle category are not necessarily equivalent. In some surveys it may be desirable to differentiate between a neutral position on an issue (neither agree nor disagree) or no clear response due to lack of information (uncertain), whereas in other instances the distinction is not important to the aims of the survey.

The U.S. Congress should increase spending on social programs.

1	2	3	4	5	6	7
strongly disagree			neither agree nor disagree			strongly agree

My teeth often itch.

strongly agree	agree	uncertain	disagree	strongly disagree
(5)	(4)	(3)	(2)	(1)

I feel that the meeting time was used effectively.

1	2	3	4	5	6
strongly disagree					strongly agree

Overall, how satisfied are you with the election results?

(5)	(4)	(3)	(2)	(1)
very satisfied	somewhat satisfied	neither satisfied nor dissatisfied	somewhat dissatisfied	very dissatisfied

Closed questions may be more difficult to write and each one may yield a very limited amount of information, but, since each response has a numerical value, the answers to closed questions can be easily tabulated and analyzed. By comparison, the answers to open-ended questions often contain a wealth of information, but the researcher must score the answers according to a predetermined and often labor-intensive system. Also, because closed questions are generally easier for respondents to complete, cooperation with survey administration is likely to be greater if the survey instrument uses the closed-question format.

Inter-rater Reliability: The degree of consistency among multiple evaluators.

Content Analysis: The plan for evaluating an answer to an open-ended question with respect to objectively defined features of its content.

The technical aspects of scoring the answers to open-ended questions are beyond the scope of this chapter, but two aspects must be understood by anyone using that question format. The answers to open-ended questions are typically scored by several readers, and the project director must take steps to maximize **inter-rater reliability**, the degree of consistency among multiple evaluators. Equally important is establishing a clear approach to **content analysis**, the plan for evaluating an answer to an open-ended question with respect to objectively defined features of its content. Inter-rater reliability and content analysis are interdependent because separate evaluations of a subject's response to an open-ended question cannot be consistent in the absence of uniform scoring methods.

In scoring the open-ended question cited earlier (What is your opinion of your employer's affirmative action policies?), the plan for content analysis could include searching for and counting adjectives or phrases that denote favor with the policy (OK, morally correct, long overdue, reasonable, and so forth) or disfavor with the policy (favoritism, prejudice in reverse, unfair, unconstitutional, and the like). Then the answers could be rated on the whole as positive, negative, or mixed, based on the ratio of positive to negative adjectives and phrases. (For more detailed coverage of inter-rater reliability and content analysis consult the references listed at the end of this chapter.)

Step 3: Evaluate Questions for Focus and Interpretability

It is very important to pay careful attention to the phrasing of individual questions and how questions are ordered within the set of questions. Even trained professionals often seek expert advice in constructing and editing their survey questions, especially when the intention is to assess beliefs or opinions that are very controversial and divisive in the community. For example, if you intend to survey public attitudes about the problems that face the legal community (clogged court system, plea bargaining, prison life, the parole system, crime-punishment contingencies, and the like), you would be wise to have both a prosecuting attorney and a criminal lawyer read and comment on your questions. As active and opposing participants in the legal process, they would be more sensitive to the use of poorly defined or undefined terms; erroneous assumptions; imprecise, slanted, emotionally charged, racist, or sexist language; and other flaws that could redirect the intended focus of the questions and jeopardize the interpretability of the answers.

It is also advisable to consult laypeople who have opposing views on an issue, such as political conservatives and liberals with respect to the current operation of our legal system. Of course, when you seek outside opinions of your survey items, keep in mind that each type of reviewer may have a hidden agenda: to recruit more supporters of their respective points of view. For example, a police officer would likely have a different perspective on the right of an apprehended drug dealer to be free on bail than would a lawyer for the American Civil Liberties Union, whose major concern is the protection of constitutionally guaranteed rights. It is therefore very important to consider the perspective of the reviewer when evaluating comments on your draft of survey questions.

Specific pitfalls to avoid in composing questions

Questions should avoid challenging the intellectual capabilities of the respondents in ways unrelated to the survey goals. Thus, questions should be short (20 words maximum is a popular standard for question length), clearly written, and not contain vocabulary the respondents may not understand.

In composing questions the frame of reference that applies to key words must be clear. For example, if a question has a reference to family, it should be clear whether *family* refers to the respondent's parents and siblings, the respondent's extended family, or perhaps to the respondent's own spouse and children. Another feature of a well-constructed questionnaire is the progression of questions from general to specific. Early in the questionnaire you might ask if the respondent had been the victim of a crime during the previous 12 months and follow up a positive response with the pursuit of additional details. In the case of a negative reply, instructions would inform the subject to skip the follow-up questions for exploring details of the crime and its aftermath.

In composing questions you must avoid **double-barreled questions, loaded questions**, and **leading questions**. A *double-barreled question* contains two queries, so it is not clear which query the respondent is answering. For example, if a survey item read "Do you believe there are equal opportunities for minorities and women at your place of employment?" and the respondent answered in the negative, you would not know whether he or she was reporting a perception of sex discrimination, racial discrimination, or both.

A *loaded question* is one that contains emotionally charged language. For example,

To what extent do you think the values of the Ku Klux Klan are alive and well in the South?

1	2	3	4	5
not alive at all		uncertain		very much alive

conjures up images of white-hooded men burning crosses and terrorizing racial minorities. It would be better to have the question read:

To what extent do you think support for racial segregation still exists in the South?

1	2	3	4	5
very weak support		uncertain		very strong support

A *leading question* tends to channel a response in a certain direction and is therefore a source of bias. For example, in the survey item

I agree with the popular view that our current foreign policy is flawed.

Strongly Agree		Uncertain		Strongly Disagree
( )	( )	( )	( )	( )

Double-barreled Question: A survey item that contains two queries, which makes it impossible to tell which one the respondent is answering.

Loaded Question: A question that contains emotionally charged language.

Leading Question: A question that tends to channel a response in a certain direction.

the respondent would presumably be more likely to conform to the popular view than to deviate from it. It would be better to write the survey item

Our current foreign policy is flawed.

Strongly Agree		Uncertain		Strongly Disagree
( )	( )	( )	( )	( )

When questions lead the respondent by including a reference to a specific person or institution, the question has **prestige bias**. For example, instead of the reference to a popular view, the leading question could have read:

Do you agree with former Secretary of State Henry Kissinger that our current foreign policy is flawed?

or

Do you agree with the most recent analysis of the prestigious Brookings Institution that our current foreign policy is flawed?

A leading question can do more than bias the response to the leading question itself. It can also bias responses to the properly composed (neutral) questions that follow. For example, the bias inherent in the leading question: *Do you agree with the popular perception that our current foreign policy is flawed?* is likely to affect the answer to a subsequent question on the same general topic: *Do you believe the President should be able to initiate hostile action against another country without the consent of Congress?*

Other potential problems with questions include **double negatives** and **embarrassing questions**. In a question or statement with a double negative, two negatives are used to express a positive, which introduces an unnecessary source of confusion to the reader. For example, the explicit double negative in the statement:

I do not support the view that Bible study should not be a part of the public school curriculum.

could be fixed by rewording it to read

I support Bible study as a part of the public school curriculum.

Double negatives can be implicit as well as explicit. For example, consider the use of *eliminating* in this statement: *I am not in favor of eliminating government subsidies for tobacco growers* really means *I am not in favor of not continuing government subsidies for tobacco growers.* It would be better if the item read:

I am in favor of continuing government subsidies for tobacco growers.

Survey items that request information of a personal or intimate nature or deal with socially disapproved or illegal behavior can be embarrassing, and the stress they introduce may be considered an abuse of the subject's rights. Of course, in some instances such questions are inextricably tied to the goals of the research, as in the study of sexually transmitted diseases and patterns of illegal drug use. Often an explanatory cover letter or personal briefing before the survey is administered will minimize subject discomfort when the nature of the research requires the inclusion of potentially embarrassing survey items.

Prestige Bias: An influence on a survey response arising from references to popular people or institutions in the body of the question.

Double Negative: A potential source of confusion from using two negatives to convey a positive thought in a survey item.

Embarrassing Questions: Survey items that request information of a personal or intimate nature.

Finally, in composing survey items it is important to state all information that is intended to qualify the item at the beginning of the statement or question. Failure to observe this convention can affect the impact of the question. For example, it would be better to ask

> *If an interruption of oil imports threatened our way of life, would you support a new tax to fund solar energy research?*

than

> *Would you support a new tax to fund solar energy research if an interruption of oil imports threatened our way of life?*

In the latter form, the first bit of key information to strike the reader is "… support a new tax." Since everybody hates the thought of having to pay higher taxes, beginning the question without first describing the hypothetical reason for the proposed tax is likely to set a negative tone and encourage a negative response. Placing the qualifying information at the beginning of the question makes it more likely that the respondent will consider the whole question rather than just a fragment and avoid a knee-jerk "No!" response to the prospect of higher taxes.

To evaluate your success in focusing your survey items on clearly defined issues, it is often helpful to create a variety of responses to each item. Then reflect on the made-up results and ask yourself what the different responses mean. Does the answer to every question contribute to your understanding of the survey topic? Do the different responses to the same question lend themselves to unambiguous interpretation? Will the answers to your entire set of questions provide you the descriptive documentation you have defined as your research goal? If you can answer yes to such questions, your instrument is on its way to yielding properly focused and interpretable results.

Step 4: Pretest the Instrument

The pretest is a trial run and should be done to help you refine the instrument. You should administer your most recent draft of the questionnaire to a relatively small group that either belongs to or is similar to the population you will be studying. Then, following the survey administration, discuss the survey items with the subjects during a debriefing session to make sure the questions were understood as they were intended to be understood. During the debriefing session it is more important to find out *why* respondents answered as they did as opposed to examining *what* they answered. For example, a question could a be:

> *I would be uncomfortable sharing a taxicab for a 20-minute ride to the airport with a person suffering from AIDS.*

> _____ Agree   _____ Disagree

You could find during your debriefing of the subject that three respondents agree with the statement, but for different reasons. One respondent may agree because of the fear, however unfounded, of catching the deadly disease, whereas another, aware of the absence of risk from such casual contact, may agree with the statement because of a loathing of gays (homophobia) and the belief that AIDS is primarily an affliction of the homosexual community. Still another respondent may agree with the statement because she never shares taxicabs with strangers. Assuming that you intended to examine only the respondent's willingness to come in casual contact with an AIDS sufferer, you could rewrite the question:

Alice, a neighborhood acquaintance, contracted AIDS by receiving a transfusion of tainted blood. I would be uncomfortable sharing a taxicab with Alice for a 20-minute ride to the airport.

——— Agree   ——— Disagree

Step 5: Write Final Draft and Instructions

The final step in the preparation of your survey instrument is to incorporate all the valuable insights you have gained from your consultants and the debriefing of pretest participants into a final draft. You must also standardize (set a fixed procedure for) the administration of the survey by providing a set of explicit instructions for its use. Standardization is especially important if the survey is to be administered by telephone or face-to-face interview. The more uniformly the interviewers follow a set procedure of administering the survey, the less effect individual interviewers will have on the survey responses. (**Interviewer bias**, a systematic effect on the respondent's behavior that stems from the behavior of the interviewer toward the respondent, is discussed in more detail later in the chapter.)

Interviewer Bias: A systematic effect on the respondent's behavior that stems from the behavior of the interviewer toward the respondent.

Sampling

The overall goal of sampling is to select a subset of a population with a distribution of characteristics that matches the population. The result is a **representative sample**. By comparison, a sample with a distribution of characteristics that is systematically different from the population from which it was drawn is said to be a **biased sample**. Two types of bias are relevant to the current topic of survey research: selection bias and response bias.

Selection bias occurs when some segments of the population are over- or under-represented in the sample. Usually the cause of the selection bias lies in the failure to provide each element of the population an equal chance of being included in the sample. One of the most commonly cited examples of selection bias is the 1936 *Literary Digest* poll, which incorrectly predicted that Republican presidential candidate Alfred M. Landon would defeat Democrat Franklin D. Roosevelt. The sample of voters, drawn from telephone directories, magazine subscription lists, and automobile registration lists, did not adequately represent the segment of the electorate that was poor — and supportive of the Roosevelt candidacy. Because the sample had a built-in bias that favored the representation of Landon supporters to a greater degree than was true in the overall population, the results incorrectly pointed to a Republican victory.

Response bias is a term encountered in psychological contexts that have nothing to do with surveys (as in signal detection theory, addressed in chapter 18). In the context of survey research, response bias refers to a distorting influence introduced when some members of the population selected for the sample either

Representative Sample: A subset of a population that matches the characteristics of the population.

Biased Sample: A subset of a population with characteristics that are systematically different from the population as a whole.

Selection Bias: A flaw in the sampling process that results in an over- or under-representation of some segments of the population in a sample.

Response Bias: A distorting influence on the representativeness of a sample caused by the failure of some sampled people to respond to the survey.

refuse or are unable to participate in the survey. The problem caused by response bias is the same as for selection bias: an over- or under-representation in the sample of some segment of the population. But the reason for the imbalance is different. The degree of response bias that is present depends on the extent to which the absence of nonparticipants damages the representativeness of the sample. For example, there is some risk that returns of a mail survey sent to two-income households could under-represent families with preschool children compared to households with no children or older children. Balancing career and domestic responsibilities is so demanding of the time and energy of working parents who have young children that, in such households, filling out and returning surveys is likely to have a very low priority. The worse the return rate for two-income households with preschool children, the less representative the sample of survey respondents will be of the population of two-income families, and the greater risk there is of a response bias in favor of the views of childless and/or older survey subjects.

Unfortunately, with less than complete cooperation from the subjects of the selected sample (a virtual certainty in survey research), survey researchers must assume that response bias exists to some degree in their data. The procedure for estimating the magnitude of response bias involves comparing those who respond to the survey with the population at large on as many relevant dimensions as possible. For example, let us say that a survey instrument was designed to assess the attitudes of adult Americans toward the legalization of certain illegal street drugs. We could check for response bias by comparing the sample of survey respondents to population census data with respect to political affiliation, religious affiliation, socioeconomic level, age, ethnicity, and life-style variables such as urban/rural, marital status, and the like. A response bias, say, if the sample underrepresented rural dwellers, could damage the survey's goal to accurately determine the position of all Americans on this controversial issue. If the survey data show evidence of response bias, all is not lost. Sophisticated statistical techniques (multiple regression and correlation) can be used to assess and neutralize the influence of response bias on survey results. As you will see in the coming discussion, different methods of conducting surveys vary in their vulnerability to response bias.

Alternative Approaches for Collecting Samples

Keep in mind three important thoughts when designing a sampling plan:

1. A random sample is very likely to be representative of a population.

2. A sample from a population is random only if every element of the population had an equal chance of being included in the sample.

3. A sample must be representative. It is a group that, despite its small size relative to the population, exhibits the same qualitative and quantitative descriptive characteristics as the population from which it was selected. The more representative a sample is of a particular population, the more accurately we can generalize from what we *know* to be true of the sample to what we *believe* to be true of the population. If the sample fails to be representative, it will give a distorted (biased) view of the

population. Random sampling and the alternatives to random sampling we discuss below will, under ideal circumstances, result in the selection of a representative sample.

Simple Random Sampling

Often a list exists on which every member of a population appears. For example, if you define the student body of your college as a population, you could use a random sampling procedure to select a subset of that population from a list of all students. Interestingly, the way you go about selecting the sample may be nonrandom and yet retain all the desirable characteristics of a random sample. To use one popular method, called **systematic (or 1-in-k) sampling**, we first enter the list of potential subjects at a randomly determined point (say, a randomly selected page number and randomly selected line/column on the page). Then we select each kth subject on the list, with k being any constant value. The value selected for k depends on what proportion of the list the researcher wishes to include in the survey. With k set equal to 2, 50% of the list would be selected; with k set equal to 5, 20% of the list would be selected; and so on. The sample retains its random character because every person on the list has an equal chance of being included in the sample, and any one sample group is just as likely to be chosen as another. Since the 1-in-k method retains the random character of the sample, we can assume that the sample is representative of the population defined by the entire list. (See Box 4–2 for a discussion of random sampling.)

Systematic Sampling: Inclusion of every kth member of a list in the sample.

Although often overlooked, when 1-in-k sampling is applied to *alphabetized* lists, such as a student directory or a list of registered voters, the procedure is not truly random. Individuals with the same last name are more likely to be related than individuals with different last names, and they are also more likely to have adjacent positions on an alphabetized list. Since only one in every k^{th} subject is selected, the procedure tends to generate samples that, compared to random samples, are less likely to include relatives. The obvious solution, which is to randomize the alphabetized list before initiating 1-in-k sampling, is usually bypassed if the anticipated bias is considered tolerable.

Alternatives to Random Sampling

Sometimes the population about which we intend to generalize from a set of survey results is so enormous (say, U.S. citizens over 65, teenagers, and specific ethnic or religious groups) or inaccessible (as with homeless people) that sampling a random subset from a list of the entire population is not a realistic alternative. Complete lists of very large or relatively inaccessible populations usually do not exist or, if they do, researchers may not have ready access to them. For example, personal data collected from citizens of the United States by the U.S. Bureau of the Census and the Internal Revenue Service are kept confidential. When circumstances preclude every member of a population from having an equal chance of being included in a sample, we must rely on alternatives.

The sampling frame

Sampling Frame: A relatively large, clearly defined group assumed to be an accurate microcosm of the even larger target population.

One alternative to sampling from an entire population is to specify a **sampling frame**, a relatively large, clearly defined group assumed to be an accurate microcosm of the even larger target population. The key word in the last sentence is *assumed*, because it takes a leap of faith to regard the sampling frame as representative of a larger population. For example, before a market researcher would evaluate consumer acceptance of a new food product by test-marketing it in one city, she or he would look for evidence (socioeconomic variables, ethnic mix, data from previous surveys in the city) that the tastes, habits, preferences, and attitudes toward food among the residents of the test-market city are representative of the entire population of consumers.

The problem with the 1936 *Literary Digest* poll cited earlier was that the various lists that comprised the sampling frame were not representative of the target population: all registered voters. No matter how rigorous the pollsters were to select subjects randomly from the lists to ensure that everybody on the list had an equal chance of being included in the sample, the distorting flaw, a sampling frame (telephone owners, magazine subscribers, and automobile owners) with a socioeconomic profile that was systematically different from the larger population of eligible voters, was already built in to the research effort.

Of course, the generalizations that the *Literary Digest* made about the popularity of Alfred Landon with the electorate were quite accurate when limited to describing voters who were members of the sampling frame: predominantly Republican telephone owners and magazine subscribers. The characterization of voting behavior from the survey data became inaccurate only when the pollsters generalized beyond the sampling frame to the entire electorate. Sometimes, as in this classic example of the *Literary Digest* survey of 1936 voting preferences, researchers determine after the fact that their assumption of similarity between their sampling frame and the larger target population was invalid.

The accidental sample

When an individual is recruited to be part of a survey sample just because he or she happens to be at a particular location at a particular time, we refer to the sample as an **accidental sample**. (Another term for the accidental sample is **haphazard sample**.) If you were ever approached at your local shopping mall by someone holding a clipboard who asked "Would you help us out by answering a few questions?" and you consented to the interview, you have been part of an accidental survey sample. Had you passed by when the interviewer was occupied with another person, had your path taken you too far from the interviewer for a personal approach, or had you avoided eye contact because you were not inclined to participate, you would not have been included in the sample. Some television news programs allow viewers to call a special number at their own expense to register a yes vote on a question and a different telephone number to register a no vote. The sample of callers, people who happen to be watching the show and are interested enough in the issue to make and pay for a telephone call, is accidental.

Accidental samples are convenient, but because they are *not* random, they may not be representative of the researcher's target population. Bias is likely to be present because there is no control over which subjects in the pool of potential subjects will ever be asked to participate, and there is no guarantee that, if asked, the subject will agree to participate. Also, in the shopping-mall survey and others of its kind that use accidental samples, curious and/or sociable shoppers may actually volunteer for the survey by approaching the interviewer, whereas other shoppers, who may be in a hurry or simply do not want to be bothered answering questions,

Accidental Sample:
A sample that includes subjects simply because they are available at a particular time and/or location.

do not make eye contact with the interviewer and brush on by. In general, the burden of proof is on the researcher to show that other sampling methods can produce findings that are consistent with those obtained with an accidental sample. Without corroborating evidence from an independent source, we must assume the presence of some bias in the accidental sample and retain a healthy degree of skepticism for the results of the survey.

Purposive sampling

Purposive Sampling: Accidental sampling combined with some selectivity to ensure that a certain type of subject is included in the sample.

Accidental sampling that is combined with some selectivity to ensure that a certain type of subject is included in the sample is called **purposive sampling**. The goal of the purposive sampling procedure is to maximize the value of the information the subjects have to offer. So, if the objective of a survey conducted in a public place is to assess brand recognition and opinion of certain high-tech luxury items, the pollster would likely approach only those subjects who, in his or her expert judgment, appeared to have the economic means to purchase the item if they wished to do so.

Purposive sampling retains elements of an accidental survey because the pollster is limited to soliciting only those subjects who happened to pass by when he or she is not busy interviewing somebody else and those subjects who agree to participate. Because of the lack of control in selecting the pool of potential subjects and the application of subjective judgment in selecting subjects, purposive samples are not random. Therefore, as in the case of the accidental sample, we must retain a healthy degree of skepticism when interpreting survey results gathered from a purposeful sample.

Enhancements of Simple Random Sampling

A simple random sample from a population will *probably* be representative of that population, especially if the sample size is relatively large. There is, however, the chance, especially if the sample size is relatively small, that a randomly selected sample will not accurately reflect the behavioral diversity of the population members. For example, the Interfaith Council of a large city maintains a master list of all members of the city's many religious institutions. In a random sample from the master list, one would rightly expect the various religious denominations to be represented in the sample in the same proportion that they exist on the master list. Thus, if 50% of the residents of the city are Roman Catholic, 46% are Protestant, 2% are Mormon, and 2% are Jewish, the religious affiliations of sampled individuals would be expected to reflect these known percentages. Instead of trusting such an outcome to chance, however, we can maximize representativeness by imposing some structure on simple random sampling. One approach is called **stratified random sampling**.

Stratified Random Sampling: Random sampling conducted within defined subgroups of a population.

To stratify a random sample we must select randomly within each defined subgroup (stratum) of the population. The number of elements from each stratum included in the sample can either be equal or, as an alternative, the sample size from each stratum can be in proportion to the size of the stratum. Thus, in our selected city we could randomly select the same number of people from within each of the religious denominations (say, four equal-sized strata of 50 Roman Catholics, 50 Protestants, 50 Mormons, and 50 Jews) or, alternatively, assemble a sample made up of 50% Roman Catholic, 46% Protestant, 2% Mormon, and 2% Jewish (proportional strata).

In choosing equal versus proportional strata we must consider the goals of the survey. If the main focus of the survey is to characterize the population as a whole, only proportional strata will result in a true microcosm of the city's population. But if a goal of the survey is also to provide detailed descriptive information about each stratum of the population, we could, even with a relatively large overall sample, be faced with the problem of trying to characterize one or more strata with very limited data. For example, in a proportionately stratified sample of 200 subjects from the population of our survey city, how likely is it that only four Jews and four Mormons (2% each) will adequately represent the diversity of opinion that exists in their respective communities? In summary, if some population strata are proportionately small and if there is the intention of using the survey results to describe individual population strata, using the equal rather than the proportional method will avoid the pitfall of using a very small sample to represent a proportionately small, but numerically large, segment of the population. See Table 7–1 for a comparison of equal and proportional strata.

Quota sampling includes elements of both proportional stratified sampling and accidental sampling. With quota sampling, as with proportional stratified sampling, we match the representation of subjects included in the survey sample to the strata in the population. But unlike proportional stratified sampling, the sampling of subjects is haphazard rather than random. For example, let us say we wished to assess public attitudes about introducing a sex education curriculum into the public schools as a function of religious affiliation. If we used quota sampling, we would first determine the proportions of different religious groups in the population (the quotas), and then we would seek out subjects as best we could in a haphazard manner (as in door-to-door solicitation) to fill the quotas. One possible strategy would be to approach subjects as they leave their places of worship for the parking lot following religious services. But the fact that quota sampling is not random does not excuse the survey researcher from making a good-faith attempt to gather a representative sample. We know, for example, that not all persons who identify with a religious group regularly attend religious worship. Thus it would not be an acceptable sampling strategy simply to take the path of least resistance and sample people who are on their way into or out of church.

Quota Sampling: Sampling that fills strata quotas using an accidental sampling method.

	Equal Strata	Proportional Strata
Roman Catholic	50	100
Protestant	50	92
Jewish	50	4
Mormon	50	4

Table 7–1. A comparison of sample sizes within strata using equal versus proportional representation of a target population. The total sample size is 200, and the assumed proportions are 50% Roman Catholic, 46% Protestant, 2% Jewish, and 2% Mormon.

Cluster Sampling:
Sampling groups
as opposed to
sampling individuals.

Another alternative to simple random sampling is **cluster sampling**, a technique for randomly selecting groups rather than individuals for inclusion in the survey. For example, to survey the attitudes of hospital interns regarding various aspects of their training, we could assemble a list of all the hospitals in the United States and randomly pick some hospitals from the list. (We could stratify the sampling to ensure that small-town hospitals, city hospitals, and metropolitan hospitals were all represented in the sample.) Then, at the selected hospitals, we could survey all the interns or a random sample of the interns. The cluster sample approach is far more practical than attempting to compile a sampling frame consisting of all hospital interns in the entire country and then taking a random sample from that master list. This is especially so when the survey method is to conduct a personal interview. It is much easier to travel to a cluster of cities to collect data than to several hundred.

Methods of Conducting Surveys

There are three principal ways to conduct a survey: using face-to-face *personal interviews*, through the *mail*, and by *telephone*. Each method has its own strengths and weaknesses (see Table 7–2). An advantage of the personal interview is that

Survey Interview Format

	Telephone	Face-to-Face	Mail
Lowest expense[1]			X
Least labor to administer			X
Best respondent cooperation		X	
Capability to explain questions	X	X	
Least problem with interviewer bias			X
Best method to reach large numbers of potential respondents			X
Easiest to organize[2]			X

[1]Assumes paid interviewers
[2]No need to train interviewers or arrange for telelphone facilities

Table 7–2. A general comparison of the advantages and disadvantages of telephone, face-to-face, and mail survey administration methods.

subjects have a greater tendency to be cooperative when in the physical presence of the person conducting the survey than they might if contacted by telephone. Also, in a personal interview it is possible for the subject to ask the interviewer to clarify a question and for the interviewer to ask the subject to clarify an answer. The word *possible* should be stressed because interviewers are trained not to clarify survey items in some cases in order to keep the presentation of questions uniform. In response to the survey question "Do you support gun control?," one of the authors asked the telephone interviewer "Are we talking about keeping convicted felons and mentally ill persons from owning handguns or denying law-abiding citizens the right to own handguns?" only to be denied clarification by the interviewer, who responded "I can only read the question as written."

There are also some disadvantages to gathering survey data using personal interviews. One disadvantage is the time and money required to train an interviewer to administer the survey. Also, during training the interviewer must be taught to avoid saying or doing anything that might reflect approval or disapproval of a subject's response to a question. To react to a subject's answer with, say, a facial expression of surprise, a frown of disapproval, or an affirmative nod of support would introduce interviewer bias, defined earlier as a systematic effect on the respondent's behavior that stems from the behavior of the interviewer toward the respondent. Besides the potential for interviewer bias, another disadvantage of personal interviews is the reluctance of people to provide very personal information or information on very controversial subjects to a stranger.

Response bias is a potential problem for all three survey methods but is usually more closely associated with mail and telephone surveys than with personal interviews. Perhaps people find it easier to ignore a survey or deny a voice on the telephone the opportunity to conduct an interview than refuse the request of a person who is physically present. The greater the disparity between the number of mailed surveys or telephone contacts and the number of returned surveys or successfully completed telephone interviews, the less likely the sample is to be representative of the sampling frame. The worry about response bias in a mailed survey is, however, partially offset by the absence of interviewer bias: The survey is self-administered, so there is no interviewer to bias the results. Also, while mail surveys do incur the expense of postage, they do not require the hiring or training of interviewers, and this saves both time and money.

Many reasons can account for the failure of solicited subjects to respond to a mail survey, including an unwillingness or inability to take the time to complete the survey and an inability to read and/or understand the questionnaire or write intelligible responses because of language deficiencies or health problems. Unlike the U.S. census, it is unlikely that you will be pressed to make an appointment for an interview if you fail to mail in a survey questionnaire. So, whatever reasons subjects have for failing to return a mail survey, the researcher only gets to see the data of a nonrandom subset of the initial sample. As noted in the discussion of response bias, we can assess the degree to which response bias is present by comparing the sample to the population on as many relevant dimensions as possible.

Maximizing returns

Researchers are, however, not totally dependent on the good will of subjects to complete and return mail surveys. The clever use of incentives can produce some remarkable results. On the authors' college campus, members of the senior class were surveyed in connection with the development of a general education curriculum. Similar surveys in the past had suffered from poor rates of return. This time the seniors were told that their completed and returned survey forms would serve as a raffle ticket for a $50 bill. The return rate was over 80%, and the $300 prize money (six $50 bills were raffled off) was judged to be a small price to pay for the excellent return rate and the value of the information received for curriculum planning.

During a time when there was no money in the budget to fund any prizes, a survey was sent to members of the student body promising selected respondents a free dinner, cooked and served by the college president at her home. The return rate was a startling 97%. Another strategy was to tell subjects that a shortage of funds made it impossible to pay them adequately for completing the survey; however, if they returned the survey they would be eligible to win more than one million dollars. When they returned the survey they were sent a current New York State Lottery ticket for a chance of winning several million dollars.

Another tactic to maximize the rate of survey returns is somewhat more devious than the prize approach because it employs a mild form of intimidation. A code is printed on each survey and the cover letter that accompanies the survey instrument explains that "There is a code on each form, but the code will *not* compromise the anonymity of your responses to the survey questions. The code will only be used to help us avoid making unnecessary and frequent telephone contacts to ensure the survey's return." When a professor used this tactic with college students it was a bluff. There was no intention to blitz nonrespondents with telephone calls. In the college environment the tactic was successful and there were no complaints about it. Nevertheless, because of the deception and mild intimidation, the morality of the tactic is questionable.

Which method is best?

There is, of course, no one method that is always better than the others for conducting a survey. From reading this section and inspecting Table 7–2, you know that each method of survey administration has its advantages and disadvantages. Moreover, weighing the various pros and cons of the different methods can be very difficult. How, for example, would one go about weighing the relatively low cost, low labor, and typically low respondent cooperation of the mail survey against the greater cost and greater respondent cooperation of the face-to-face interview? In the absence of a clear-cut best choice for a given survey enterprise, practical considerations (such as time, money, the availability of personnel capable of administering the survey, and anticipated problems reaching the subjects selected for the survey sample) usually dictate the method of survey administration.

Survey Design:
A strategy that guides the administration of the survey instrument.

Cross-sectional Study: A study conducted within a single time frame.

Survey Designs

With sampling and survey methods in place, the researcher must still decide on a **survey design**, a strategy that guides the administration of the survey instrument. In a **cross-sectional study** the survey instrument is administered once to the sample within a single time frame. The single-time-frame feature is noteworthy because the attitudes and opinions reflected in survey responses can be unstable and are subject to change over time. Thus, even under the best of circumstances (no response bias, a representative sample, and so on), cross-sectional data are limited to describing population characteristics that existed *at the time the survey was taken*.

When the focus of the research is to track the *changes* that take place in descriptive characteristics of a population over time, one choice is to repeat the cross-sectional study with different samples over a specified time span. In the latter configuration the study is sometimes referred to as the **successive independent samples design**.

The final choice of survey design mentioned here is a close cousin to the successive samples design. It is called the **panel (or longitudinal) study**. The panel study resembles the successive independent samples design in that the survey is administered on successive occasions, but instead of administering the survey to different samples, the same sample is used for each successive administration. Here, as with the successive independent samples design, the focus is on tracking changes that occur in the pattern of survey responses across time.

Note that in a longitudinal study it is necessary to keep track of the sample as closely as possible so that, when the time for retesting the subjects arrives, as many of the original subjects as possible can be retained. Of course, there is no guarantee that subjects will agree to continue their participation when contacted for retesting. So, like other survey designs, response bias can also be a factor in longitudinal research.

Strengths and Weaknesses of Survey Designs

The cross-sectional design is the least controversial of the three designs described. If the sample is representative and an adequate percentage of the selected sample is successfully surveyed (at least 50%), the characteristics of the survey responses can be assumed to apply to the population as a whole. With the successive independent samples design and the longitudinal design, which tend to focus on the changes in a population that take place over time, there are rival explanations for differences that exist between successive survey administrations.

One rival explanation for the appearance of a change in population characteristics applies to the successive samples design: Observed differences in the data of successive survey administrations may be reflecting systematic differences in sample characteristics without necessarily being indicative of systematic changes in the population. The label for this phenomenon is **noncomparable successive samples**. When systematic differences can be shown to exist among several samples, we may not be able to tell which sample is the most accurate representation of the population — if, indeed, any one of them is. Let us assume that we administer a survey at the start of the fall semester and find that a sample of college freshmen have generally positive perceptions about campus life. Toward the end of the semester, however, the same survey with a different sample of freshmen indicates a negative shift in attitude. It could be that the attitudes of the class as a whole have shifted, but a rival explanation is that the make-up of the two samples may have been systematically different. For example, more students in the second sample may have been from very distant locations and may be experiencing substantial homesickness.

Successive Independent Sample Design: A series of cross-sectional studies with different samples.

Panel Study: A study that uses the same sample on successive occasions.

Noncomparable Successive Samples: A source of bias in the successive samples design that arises when the successive samples have different characteristics.

Another disadvantage of the successive independent samples design is its vulnerability to what researchers call the historical pitfall. Briefly, the survey researcher is likely to try to explain shifts in attitudes, beliefs, and the like that have occurred over time as consequence of a natural or manipulated event. Survey data collected before the event are compared to survey data collected after the event, and the event is credited with producing the change in survey responses. The problem with attributing the change in survey responses to the event is that there may be plausible explanations for the shift that are unrelated to the event. For example, assume that we had survey data reflecting satisfaction with the quality of life in San Francisco both before the severe earthquake of 1989 and one year later, in 1990. It would be possible to interpret a negative shift in attitude about the quality of life in San Francisco to a fear of future earthquakes and the consequences of the 1989 earthquake (loss of loved ones, economic disruptions, traffic problems), but the real reason may lie elsewhere. The San Francisco economy is very sensitive to the level of government expenditures on defense spending, which were cut in 1990. Thus, the impact of the earthquake is confounded with the changes wrought by reduced defense spending and the resulting negative impact on the local economy.

The longitudinal design is not as prone to the problem of noncomparable successive samples because the intention is to use the same sample on each successive survey administration. The problem, however, is not truly eliminated because it is very difficult to maintain a complete sample throughout the duration of a longitudinal study. Subjects may balk at repeated administrations, they may move without leaving a forwarding address or telephone number, they may become too ill to participate, and so on. This problem is called **subject loss** (as well as **subject attrition** and **respondent mortality**). Sometimes it is possible to estimate the extent of the bias introduced by subject attrition if the researcher happens to notice that the lost subjects differ in systematic ways from the remaining subjects. Nevertheless, to the extent that the loss of subjects impairs the representativeness of the sample, the appearance of change in the pattern of survey responses over repeated administrations may be an illusion rather than real.

Subject Loss: The failure of sampled subjects to participate fully in a study.

Another problem is akin to the problem of reactivity discussed in chapter 3 and the problem of carryover effects discussed in chapter 11. The essence of the problem centers on the effects that prior survey administrations can have on the behavior of the subjects during subsequent survey administrations. Responding to questions on an initial survey can raise a subject's awareness of the possibilities for opinion and belief that pertain to various issues. A "Do you enjoy" question on the initial survey could prompt the respondent to try something that she or he had never done or even considered doing. The subject may also be more attentive to media reports and more likely to engage in discussions that pertain to the survey issues. Subjects have even been known to try to "help" the researcher by offering the answers they think the researcher wants to hear or, in an effort to be consistent, trying to respond in a manner consistent with the responses given during previous survey administrations.

Reading Survey Results

The preceding material on survey methods not only gives you the basic information necessary to conduct a survey but also helps you be a sophisticated consumer of survey results. When you read an article or attend an oral presentation in which survey results are reported, take into account your knowledge of survey methods in gauging your support for the researcher's conclusions. Identify the design of the survey, examine the survey items, and consider the sampling techniques used. If the article does not include a reproduction of the original survey items, or if you become aware of the survey through television or radio, write or call for a copy of the actual survey instrument. The more information you have to evaluate the methodological rigor of the survey, the more confidence you can have in the results.

Summary

This coverage of survey methods presented the principal considerations that govern the composition and administration of the survey instrument (questionnaire). The preparation for a survey was broken down into steps that include establishing a knowledge base sufficient to write good questions, choosing a question format, evaluating the questions for focus and clarity, specific pitfalls to avoid when writing survey questions, and pretesting the survey instrument and instructions. Alternative approaches to sampling, the strengths and weaknesses of the different approaches, and the kinds of sampling bias that can lead to a nonrepresentative sample were examined. Methods of survey administration (personal interviews, mail, and telephone) and survey designs (cross-sectional and panel studies) were explained and compared, followed by a discussion of the limitations one must observe in interpreting survey data.

Additional Sources

Now that you are familiar with the basics of survey methods, you can appreciate the hard work that goes into the composition, design, and administration of a survey. For greater depth and detail refer to the following books:

Babbie, E. R. (1973). *Survey research methods.* Belmont, CA: Wadsworth.

Babbie, E. R. (1986). *The practice of social research (4th ed.).* Belmont, CA: Wadsworth.

Bailey, K. D. (1987). *Methods of social research (3rd ed.).* New York: Free Press.

Fink, A., & Kosekoff, J. (1985). *How to conduct surveys.* Newbury Park, CA: Sage.

Fowler, F. J. (1988). *Survey research methods.* Newbury Park, CA: Sage.

Marsh, C. (1982). *The survey method.* London: Allen & Unwin.

Mendenhall, W., Ott, L., & Scheaffer, R. L. (1971). *Elementary survey sampling.* Belmont, CA: Wadsworth.

Oppenheim, A. N. (1966). *Questionnaire design and attitude measurement.* New York: Basic Books.

Key Terms

Accidental Sample, p. 117
Biased Sample, p. 114
Closed Questions, p. 108
Cluster Sampling, p. 120
Content Analysis, p. 110
Cross-sectional Study, p. 122
Double-barreled Question, p. 111
Double Negative, p. 112
Embarrassing Questions, p. 112
Haphazard Sample, p. 117
Inter-rater Reliability, p. 110

Interviewer Bias, p. 114
Leading Question, p. 111
Likert-type Scaling, p. 108
Loaded Question, p. 111
Longitudinal Study, p. 123
Noncomparable Successive Samples, p. 123
Open-ended Questions, p. 108
Panel Study, p. 123
Prestige Bias, p. 112
Purposive Sampling, p. 118

Chapter Exercises

1. Before administering a survey, one must have a carefully composed survey instrument. Explain the steps of questionnaire construction and the pitfalls to avoid.

2. What are the different approaches to sampling for a survey project and what are the advantages and disadvantages of each?

3. A survey on a sample will reflect reality in the population only if the sample is representative. What are the threats to representativeness and what steps can you take to maximize the representativeness of your sample?

4. Can a survey sample be representative without being random? Explain.

5. Surveys can be conducted by means of personal (face-to-face) interviews, telephone interviews, or by mail. What are the advantages and disadvantages of each method of collecting survey data?

6. The selection of a survey design depends on the research question the study is supposed to answer. Describe the different kinds of research problems that are suitable for investigation with the survey designs discussed in the text. Include in your answer a comparison of the cross-sectional and panel designs.

7. Using the ideas described in the text as a guide, create some original strategies to maximize respondent cooperation with mailed, face-to-face, and telephone surveys.

Proposal Assignment 7: Writing Survey Questions

In this assignment you will practice writing a few survey questions. Pretend that you are interested in surveying opinions about the causes of the behavior you selected for your proposed project. (1) Explain how you would go about getting your sample; (2) Describe the survey method you would use, and why; and (3) Compose three survey questions, using a different format for each one.

To help you get started, we will use our sample proposal as a model. If you recall, the topic of our sample proposal was to investigate the variables that affect a student's ability to learn new material. We are especially interested in how to increase learning of the material covered in a Research Methods in Psychology course. Therefore, one group of people we should survey is those students who have recently taken such a course. Our plan is to obtain a list of all the students who were enrolled in this class during the previous two semesters and randomly select a sample to survey. Because the time and resources we have for this project are limited, we will mail our questionnaire to the students rather than do personal interviews or a telephone survey.

Here are our three items. They deal with student perceptions of the relationship between elements of their behavior and the degree of academic success that is likely to follow. Notice that each of the three questions appears in a different format.

1. The more time students spend studying and doing their homework assignments in the Research Methods in Psychology course the more they will learn.

1	2	3	4	5
strongly disagree		neither agree nor disagree		strongly agree

2. Students will learn more in the Research Methods in Psychology class if class attendance is strictly enforced.

    _____ Agree   _____ Disagree

3. In your opinion, what are the important factors that determine how well a student will do in the Research Methods in Psychology class?

8

Reporting the Results of Descriptive Research

All the descriptive research methods covered in the preceding chapters (naturalistic observation, archival research, the case study, and surveys) rely on the numerical coding of observations and measurements to produce the qualitative and quantitative records of behavior we know as data. Sometimes data convey a clear meaning from the superficial inspection of data (sneak preview or eyeballing) that often precedes a formal descriptive analysis. Most often, however, getting an accurate impression of the information that is in the data and determining the meaning of the information in the context of the research problem requires substantial effort. The reason is that research data in their raw form are most often inscrutable, like a complex labyrinth in which numerous discoverable treasures of information are present but hidden from view.

Statistical analysis and graphic techniques handle the task of description. Together they allow us to detect the meaningful information contained in the data and summarize it so it can be assimilated and understood. Although in this chapter we occasionally discuss some concepts that relate to statistics and measurement and refer by name to some specific statistical tests, statistical analysis is not the focus. Rather, the purpose is to highlight the different kinds of data researchers collect, the differences in the levels of information data can convey, and the importance of using a statistical approach compatible with the data and the questions that the data are supposed to answer.

Selecting a Descriptive Method for the Data

In selecting an approach for describing research results, it makes no sense to proceed with a powerful and sophisticated statistical analysis to search for information that is not in the data. Neither does it make sense to look for information that *is* in the data with a weak or inappropriate descriptive tool that will not reveal it. The explanation of the four measurement scales (nominal, ordinal, interval, and ratio) in chapter 3 pointed out that the scaling of data defines its information content. Therefore, in order to apply a method of descriptive analysis that is an appropriate match for our data, we must first ascertain its scaling.

The remainder of this chapter explores the application of descriptive methods to data belonging to each of the four measurement scales. The presentation centers on a single research problem (teacher evaluation) in order to illustrate that many different kinds of data can contribute to the investigation of a single research problem.

A Hypothetical Research Scenario: Teacher Evaluation

The president of the Psychology Club commissioned one of its officers, Gail, to research student perceptions of the department of psychology faculty, the courses they teach, and their grading practices. Part of the psychology major curriculum at Gail's school consists of a sequence of three courses. Psychology 100 is taught by Professor Stein, Psychology 200 by Professor Macko, and Psychology 300 by Professor Ramirez. Thus, by the time the students reach their junior year, they have been in the classes of all three professors. In her initial study of the faculty, Gail decided to survey student attitudes of all junior and senior psychology majors toward the three teachers with whom they all studied during their freshman and sophomore years.

Data in the Form of Categorical Assignments

One of the questions on the survey was "Of the three instructors who teach Psychology 100, 200, and 300 (Stein, Macko, and Ramirez), which was your favorite teacher?" Gail's data for this question appear in Table 8–1.

Recognizing nominal data

Briefly turning our attention from Table 8–1, the summary of all 276 responses, let us examine the information content of a single response to the survey question. This step is necessary, because the scaling of data is truly revealed only when we examine the nature of a single datum. As stressed in chapter 3, when the record of a behavior is only a label, name, or classification rather than a measurement-reflecting quantity, the data have nominal (naming) scaling. This is the case in the present example because the response of each of the 276 surveyed students was recorded as a single tally in a precisely labeled category, much as we would keep a tally of votes in an election. Each response indicated an individual student's preference for Stein, Macko, or Ramirez and did not require a numerical representation to record the response. Only when the tallied responses of all the surveyed subjects are added within each response category, as shown in Table 8–1, do we benefit from a numerical representation of the survey results.

Describing nominal data

We may summarize nominal data by reporting category totals, as in Table 8–1, or, as shown in Table 8–2, with percentages. (We convert to percentages by dividing the individual cell frequencies of 84, 114, and 78 by 276, the total of all the

	Stein	Macko	Ramirez
Tallies	84	114	78

Table 8–1. The votes for "favorite freshman/sopohomore teacher" of 276 junior and senior psychology majors.

	Stein	Macko	Ramirez
Tallies	30.4	41.3	28.3

Table 8–2. The percentages of junior/senior psychology majors who voted for one of three people as their favorite freshman/sophomore instructor. The percentages are based on 276 responses.

frequencies, and multiplying by 100.) When using raw frequencies, the highest value may be regarded as a mode, the most frequent response and the only statistic that is appropriate for describing the central tendency of nominal data. (See Box 4–3 for a review of the measures of central tendency and dispersion.)

When using percentages it is best also to report the numbers on which the percentages are based (as we do in the caption for Table 8–2). You will realize why if you consider that the same percentage shown in Table 8–2 would apply if only 46 subjects were surveyed and the distribution of responses across the three response categories were Stein = 14, Macko = 19, and Ramirez = 13. It is inappropriate and misleading to hide relatively small and, therefore, less impressive sample sizes by displaying results as percentages instead of raw frequencies.

The potential for abuse when reporting results as percentages is especially acute when describing the magnitude of a change. For example, the report of a 200% one-year increase in the student dropout rate would be accurate if a school lost 30 students in the past year and 90 students in the present year. But a change from one student dropout in the past year to three student dropouts in the present year would also be a 200% increase. The increase in the former case is more disturbing than in the latter, even though the percentage of the increase for both is 200%. Similarly, a report that a neighborhood watch program has cut the local crime rate by 50% is much more impressive if reported burglaries changed from 50 per year to 25 than would be the case if the change was only from 6 to 3.

True discrete categories versus forced categories

Sometimes the task of describing data is simplified by representing raw data that have ordinal, interval, or ratio scaling as tallies in discrete categories. As such, they are forced into a format that we *usually* associate with nominal data. For example, when instructors assign letter grades (A, B, C, D, or E) to their students on the basis of their performances on a 100-item objective test, the instructor is forcing a quantitative measure of student performance into discrete categories. The quantitatively defined limits of categories are commonly called cutoffs, as in: A = 91 − 100 points; B = 81 − 90; C = 71 − 80; and so forth. Unfortunately, the rigid adherence to cutoffs by instructors is a source of much student-teacher controversy. Missing an A by only one point is frustrating, but no matter where the cutoffs are positioned, somebody is going to be the highest in the B category and be the person who "just missed" getting an A.

One factor that contributes to student frustration about letter grades is that forcing data with ordinal, interval, or ratio scaling into discrete categories results in a loss of information. For example, going by letter grades alone, we would consider the performances of two students equivalent if they both received a grade of B on an objective test. But it is possible for one B student to have scored only one point below the cutoff for an A and the other to have scored just above the cutoff for a C. The measurable difference in their performances (low B versus high B) is lost when both are assigned the same letter grade. The loss of information resulting from categorization is evident in the labeling of many behavioral characteristics (developmentally delayed, normal, and gifted) as well as biological characteristics (underweight, normal, and overweight).

Hypothesis Testing with Nominal Data: Comparing Frequencies

It is possible to compare frequency data (categorical data, such as the tally totals in Table 8–1) to a hypothetical set of frequencies using the chi-square statistic (see Appendix B for an illustration of the **chi-square goodness of fit test** or consult your statistics text). The values of the hypothetical (expected) frequencies depend upon the nature of the research issue under study.

Chi-Square Goodness of Fit Test: A statistical test to evaluate whether the deviation of obtained frequencies from expected frequencies is significant or due to chance.

When equal frequencies are expected

Assume that one of Gail's research goals was to examine the data for evidence of a significant difference in popularity among the three instructors. The null hypothesis assumption would be that there is *no* difference in popularity among the three instructors, so the frequencies Gail would use for the chi-square goodness of fit test would be equal portions (92) of the total frequency (276), as shown in Table 8–3. The results of the chi-square test $\chi^2(2, N = 276) = 8.08, p < .05$) support rejection of the null hypothesis that the three teachers are equally preferred. Since Macko's score of 114 is the most deviant from the expected frequency of 92 and is the only cell entry greater than 92, the data support the view that Macko is the most highly regarded teacher of the three.

When unequal frequencies are expected

The chi-square goodness of fit test is also appropriate for comparing obtained frequencies to expected frequencies when the expected frequencies are different across categories. For example, Gail could use her data to see if they are consistent with a specific claim: Macko is preferred over Stein and Ramirez two to one. Before evaluating the claim statistically, expected frequencies that conform to the hypothesized two-to-one breakdown would have to be entered in the table. As shown in Table 8–4, the expected frequencies are 69, 138, and 69. They were computed by assigning half of the 276 tallies to Macko ($276 \div 2 = 138$) and splitting the remaining 138 tallies among Stein and Ramirez. The chi-square goodness of fit test ($\chi^2(2, N = 276) = 5.99, p < .05$) shows that the difference between the obtained frequencies and the two-to-one configuration of expected frequencies is significant.

Votes for Favorate Instructor

	Stein	Macko	Ramirez	Totals
Obtained Frequencies (raw data)	84	114	78	276
Expected Frequences (from null hypothesis)	92	92	92	276

Table 8–3. The obtained data for favorite instructor and the theoretically expected frequenices if the 276 students had no preference for any of the three instructors.

	Votes for Favorate Teacher			
	Stein	**Macko**	**Ramirez**	**Totals**
Obtained Frequencies (raw data)	84	114	78	276
Expected Frequences (from null hypothesis)	69	138	69	276

Table 8–4. The obtained data for favorite instructor and the theoretically expected frequenices if the 276 students had a two-to-one preference for Professor Macko.

Therefore, even though the students clearly prefer Macko over the other two instructors, the preference is not as extreme as two to one.

Description versus Experimentation

When we compare frequencies in discrete categories to hypothetically expected frequencies as we did for the data in Table 8–3 and 8–4, an outome of statistical significance means that the difference between the obtained frequencies and the expected frequencies was too large to be attributed to chance alone. But by itself, there is nothing about the results of a statistical test that indicates whether the data come from a descriptive study (as do all the data in this chapter) or an experimental study in which a variable was manipulated. Therefore, when we interpret the finding of a statistically significant difference we must discriminate between descriptive results, which answer the *what* question, and experimental results, which have the power to explain *why* the data appear as they do. For example, following the analysis of the Table 8–3 data with the chi-square goodness of fit test, Gail can describe the student preference for Professor Macko as significantly higher than the preferences for Stein or Ramirez ($\chi^2(2, N = 276)$ $= 8.08$, $p < .05$), but this significant result does not tell Gail *why* the preference exists. Whenever we seek to answer the *why* question, we must run a carefully controlled experiment in which the independent variable is manipulated, not assessed as a subject variable (see chapter 3) as it is here.

Data in the Form of Subjective Ratings

Another approach Gail used to describe the students' perceptions of the three freshman/sophomore instructors was to ask all students currently taking a course from one of the professors to rate their instructor on a scale of 0 to 10. (Zero was the worst possible rating, and 10 was the best.) When Gail was done collecting the data, she had 30 **subjective ratings** (personal student perceptions of instructional performance) for each instructor, which is a formidable number of observations to try to describe and interpret from inspection alone. In order to use the data for a comparison of student perceptions of the teachers' job performance, Gail wanted to

Subjective Rating: Assignment of a value to an observation based on the subject's personal perception.

express the central tendency of each set of ratings with a single value. But which measure of central tendency, the mean, median, or mode, should she use to describe the central tendency of ratings? Before addressing that issue, let us first discuss some of the characteristics of data in the form of subjective ranks or ratings.

Recognizing ordinal data

As we saw in chapter 3, whenever scores reflect subjective ratings or ranks, the scaling of the data is ordinal. Ordinal measurements reflects only *more, less,* or *equal.* Equal numerical intervals between different values do not necessarily represent the same quantitative difference, and the relative size (ratio) of one value to another is without meaning. Thus, with teacher ratings or any other variable with ordinal scaling, a one-unit difference between two values (say, ratings of 6 and 7) does not necessarily represent the same difference in teacher performance that separates other values (say, ratings of 7 and 8). Similarly, we cannot defend a ratio interpretation of proportionately different rating values. Thus, a performance rating of 10 is not "twice as good as" a performance rating of 5, despite the fact that 10, viewed in absolute terms as a quantity, is twice 5. As in the case of categorical data, the limited information held by numerals with ordinal scaling places limits on how they can be processed for description. To ignore the limits is to risk invalid and misleading interpretations, as explained in the following section.

Describing ordinal data

To be technically correct, we should use only the median or the mode to describe the "average" or "typical" score when data have ordinal scaling. Consider the data summary in Table 8–5. It is not difficult to compute and report the arithmetic mean of a set of ratings, but without an objective unit of measurement, the meaning of the number is questionable. In other words, if the mean of 30 ratings equaled 6.0 units, we would have to ask 6.0 units of what. We cannot specify the unit value because subjective ratings, which are only personal impressions, are not precise enough to be divisible into units of equal quantitative magnitude. The mode, the rank that was assigned most often, and the median, the rating value above which and below which half the ratings fall, may not have quite the quantitative elegance of the arithmetic mean, but their meaning is clear. For Professor Macko, the most frequent rating (the mode) was an 8, and half of his students rated him higher than 8.5 (the median) and the other half rated him below 8.5.

	Stein	Macko	Ramirez
Median Rating	7.5	8.5	5.5
Mean Rating	7.0	8.5	7.0
Mode	8.0	8.0	5.0
Class Size	30	30	30

Table 8–5. The median, mean, and modal teacher ratings (on a scale of 0 to 10) obtained from three classes of students.

The above notwithstanding, using the arithmetic mean to describe the central tendency of ranked data or data with questionable interval scaling is fairly common practice in the behavioral sciences. Researchers who tend to be conservative in their data-analysis methods shun the practice. But as long as we are careful not to interpret the differences between mean ranks as if they were on an interval scale, we can avoid letting our interpretations go beyond the information in the data. Thus, if we did report a mean rating, as in Table 8–5, we could not assume that the 1.5 unit difference between Stein's mean rating of 7.0 and Macko's 8.5 rating represents the same difference in teacher performance that separates mean ratings of say, 6.5 and 8.0.

Describing dispersion in ordinal data

Technical considerations also limit the options we have in describing the dispersion of ordinal data. In fact, computing the range of a set of ratings (the highest rating minus the lowest), crude measure that it is, is the only noncontroversial way to describe the dispersion of ranked data. Let us examine why. To compute the standard deviation of numerical values we must first compute the sum of squares (see Box 4–3). Here is the formula in deviation notation:

$$SS_X = \Sigma(X - \bar{X})^2$$

The formula directs us to compute the sum of the squared deviations of each score to the mean. But what sense does it make to compute the $(X - \bar{X})$ deviation score for each raw score when equal deviation scores do not necessarily reflect the same quantity of the measured entity? We have no way of knowing if the deviation $9 - 6$, which is three units, means the same thing as the deviation $10 - 7$, which is also three units. Thus, in squaring numerically equal deviation scores to compute a measure of dispersion, we would be squaring and adding noncomparable quantities (apples and oranges). The results would most certainly be without clear meaning.

Nevertheless, using the standard deviation and similar measures to describe the dispersion of ranked data or data with questionable interval scaling is fairly common practice despite its being technically incorrect. The practice is unlikely to lead to misleading descriptions of results as long as the researcher takes the scaling of the raw data into account. For example, assume we compute the standard deviations of three sets of subjective ratings: $SD_1 = 4.00$, $SD_2 = 6.00$, and $SD_3 = 8.00$. We could legitimately describe the dispersion in Set 3 as being more than the other two sets, but, because the raw data are ordinal rather than interval or ratio, it would be misleading to describe the dispersion in the Set 3 ranks as being "twice as much as" the dispersion in Set 1.

Hypothesis testing with ordinal data: comparing ranks

Like the categorical data of Table 8–1, a comparison of median ranks in Table 8–5 suggests that there is a difference in the student perception of the three instructors: Macko is preferred over Stein and Ramirez. The median score of 8.5 means that half of Macko's class of 30 students rated him at or above 8.5 on a scale of 0 to 10. A statistical test called the **Kruskal–Wallis H** test is used to compare differences among three or more sets of ranked data for statistical significance. The computational method for the Kruskal–Wallis H test is most likely to be found in statistics texts devoted to the coverage of nonparametric statistical tests. In general,

Kruskal–Wallis H Test: A test used to compare differences among three or more sets of ranked data for statistical significance.

nonparametric statistics tend to have minimal assumptions about the scaling and distribution of data and are especially useful for the analysis of nominal and ordinal data. Applying the Kruskal–Wallis H to the raw rankings (not shown) would tell us whether the differences in student ratings of the three teachers is statistically insignificant (so small as to be attributable to chance alone) or statistically significant (too large to have arisen from chance alone).

Data in the Form of Objective Quantitative Measurements

All three professors administer final examinations consisting of 100 objective questions (true/false and multiple-choice). Gail thought she could gain some insight into the relative difficulty of the three courses by comparing final examination scores. Specifically, Gail decided to examine the three distributions of final examination scores of the 276 junior/senior students who, as freshmen and sophomores, took courses from the three professors. All three teachers agreed to dig into their archives and submit the examination scores, but the names of the students were withheld.

Recognizing interval and ratio data

Since the methods for describing research results must be appropriate for her data, Gail's first task would be to reflect on the scaling of her data. If we assume that the examination scores have interval scaling, the difference between a score of 60 and a score of 70 (70 represents 10 more correct responses than 60) is assumed to represent the same difference in performance that separates any other scores separated by 10 units (e.g., 85 and 95). Thus the interval scaling of these data means that a higher score not only represents a level of performance that is *unequal* to a lower score (nominal), a higher score not only represents a *better* performance than a lower score (ordinal), but, in addition, equal intervals between scores on different points of the scale represent the same difference in test performance (interval).

Are the data also ratio? As we saw in chapter 3, data on a ratio scale must have a true 0 point. It is possible for a student to get a 0 on a test by failing to respond correctly to any questions, but does a score of 0 really mean a complete lack of knowledge of course material? Does a student who got a 75 really know three times as much as a student who got only 25? With respect to the questions on the test we can say a score of 0 does represent a complete lack of knowledge, so we could defend treating the data as ratio data. With respect to the course itself, however, the point is arguable. Surely even a student with a 0 score would know *something* of the course content even if that level of mastery was too slight to permit making any correct responses to the test. Since the methods for processing interval and ratio data do not differ, researchers seldom pursue drawing the latter distinction and seldom agonize over whether their data are interval or ratio.

Describing interval and ratio data

Unlike nominal and ordinal data, when data have interval or ratio scaling, equal numerical intervals between different variable values (say, $10 - 7 = 3$ units versus

9 − 6 = 3 units) represent the same quantity. Because mathematical operations using data values with either interval or ratio scaling will yield meaningful results, Gail can describe the three grade distributions (one from each professor) using the mean as a measure of central tendency and the standard deviation as a measure of dispersion and be assured of obtaining descriptive statistics that are relatively easy to interpret. The values of the mean and standard deviation for the three grade distributions are shown in Table 8–6.

Hypothesis testing with interval/ratio data: comparing means

From the summary statistics of Table 8–6 Gail observed that the mean student performance tended to be the best on Macko's final examination, but the dispersion of the scores around the mean also tended to be the greatest on Macko's examination. Are the differences among the three final examination means attributable to chance alone or are they significant? The statistical procedures we use to compare means include the *t* **test,** for comparing only two means, and the **one-way analysis of variances (ANOVA),** for comparing more than two means. (Here, in the context of descriptive research, we refer to the use of the *t* test and ANOVA to compare the mean performance measures of nonmanipulated conditions. Further comments concerning the application of these statistical techniques to compare manipulated treatment conditions appear in the coverage of experimental research in chapters 11, 12, and 13.)

Before leaving our discussion of Gail's teacher-evaluation project, pat yourself on the back if you noticed a problem in her descriptive study that is rather common in evaluation research: the presence of confounded variables. Specifically, in Gail's study there are two nonmanipulated variables that are confounded: the subject matter of the course (Psychology 100, 200, or 300) and the instructor teaching the course (Stein, Macko, or Ramirez). Also, the order in which students took the three courses (first Stein's course, then Macko's, and finally Ramirez's) was also fixed by circumstances rather than by Gail, the researcher. Remember from chapter 3 that in experimental research we can often manipulate and hold variables constant to eliminate confounding. In the present evaluation scenario, however, no variables are manipulated. In fact, since program evaluation is often descriptive research in the form of Basic Questions 1, 2, or 3, the manipulation and control of variables that would be necessary to eliminate all confounding is not only impossible to apply, it is inappropriate as well.

t **test**: A statistical test for evaluating the difference between two treatment means for significance.

Analysis of Variance (ANOVA): A statistical procedure for comparing multiple treatments or treatment combinations.

	Stein	Macko	Ramirez
Mean Examination Score	74.0	78.5	71.0
Standard Deviation	4.5	7.0	4.0
Sample Size	276	276	276

Table 8–6. The summary statistics of three hypothetical distributions of final examination scores. All final examination data are from the same group of 276 students.

So, assuming that statistically significant differences exist among the means shown in Table 8–6, the obvious question is "What, if anything, do the differences mean?" Are the differences among the three final examination means more closely associated with the course instructor, with differences in course content, or the order in which the courses were taken? Because of the confounding of these three nonmanipulated conditions, we cannot answer the question definitively. Also, because the study is descriptive, we can only speculate about the reasons *why* the differences in examination performance occurred. Is the course material easiest in Macko's course and the most difficult in Ramirez's? Does Macko make up easier examination questions than Ramirez? Do the teachers differ in the effectiveness with which they prepare their students for the examinations?

In program evaluation research, confounding variables can complicate the task of interpreting the data, but confounding is not as disruptive to the goals of descriptive research as it is to the goals of experimental research. In an experiment, the focus of the research is to establish a cause–effect relationship between the manipulated values of an independent variable and the recorded values of a dependent variable. By comparison, the aim of program evaluation research is frequently to reveal the presence of strengths and weaknesses in a program and *suggest* steps to remedy deficiencies and build upon strengths. For example, one worthwhile result that typically follows teacher evaluations is for colleagues to work with low-rated professors on improving their course materials and teaching techniques. Both the faculty members and the students benefit from the exchange of ideas even though the apparent need for a teacher to improve certain policies and behaviors may have been inferred from a descriptive evaluation study with confounded variables.

When the Scaling of Data Is Arguable

As mentioned briefly above, the scaling of data and the choices for descriptive analysis are not always clear-cut. Many variables that psychologists measure (such as IQ scores, grade-point averages on high school and college transcripts, numerical records of survey results) are difficult to defend as pure representations of interval scaling but are commonly treated as such. For example, is the difference in academic achievement between a student who has a grade-point average of 2.50 and a student with a 3.00 the same difference in achievement that separates 3.50 and 4.00? Is the difference in intelligence between people with IQs of 90 and 100 the same difference in intelligence that separates persons with IQs of 130 and 140?

Recall this survey item from chapter 7:

The U.S. Congress should increase spending on social programs.

1	2	3	4	5	6	7
strongly disagree			neither agree nor disagree			strongly agree

The opinions of subjects are coded numerically using values 1 through 7. Is the difference in positive regard between "moderately disagree" (a 2 response) and "slightly disagree" (a 3 response) the same difference that exists between "slightly agree" (a 5 response) and "moderately agree" (a 6 response) because the differences are one unit in each case?

It is controversial whether or not numerical representations of academic achievement, intelligence, attitudes and beliefs (from survey responses), and other behavioral measures with a subjective component can be treated as if they have interval scaling. Yet the research community tends to tolerate processing data with questionable interval scaling as if they were interval. For example, to justify processing the responses to survey items (say, the values 1 through 7) as interval data, a common assumption is that the respondent to the questionnaire *perceives* the intervals in the response scale to be equal.

Is it a violation of statistical orthodoxy to compute means and standard deviations for variables such as IQ scores, grade-point averages, and survey responses that may not truly meet the criteria of interval scaling? On the one hand, we need guidelines in order to avoid producing uninterpretable values through the indiscriminate entry of raw data into statistical formulae. On the other hand, it does not serve the best interests of behavioral science to put undue emphasis on the correctness or incorrectness of an approach to descriptive analysis solely on the basis of the scaling of the data. Perhaps it is more fruitful to focus on the capacity of the descriptive analysis to support a particular interpretation of the data rather than on the analysis itself. As long as you are aware that the match between the scaling of your data and the assumptions that underlie the statistical procedure you are applying may not be perfect, you can approach your interpretation of summary statistics with a healthy amount of caution.

Answering Questions

Are you able to match the research objectives in the examples in this chapter to the basic questions that were outlined in chapter 5? Viewed as an effort to describe the overall student perceptions of the three professors (the *what* question), the studies summarized in Tables 8–1 and 8–5 address Basic Question 1 (What are the dimensions along which behaviors naturally vary?). The research summarized in Tables 8–3 and 8–4, however, goes a step beyond simple description because it involves comparing an obtained pattern of results to a hypothetical outcome (either no difference or a two-to-one preference for Macko). The latter feature changes the objective from a simple descriptive issue to one in the form of Basic Question 2 (Does the classification of behavior into discrete categories conform to a specific theoretically expected or hypothesized pattern of results?). Notice that a survey showing one teacher to be more highly regarded than another carries no deeper message that would hint at *why* this is so. It is simply a description of reality, which only tells us *what* is so.

The next step

We can do more with description than represent the information reflected in the measurements of a single variable. We can also describe the *association* that exists between different variables. For example, is Gail able to predict how well a student will do in Macko's class with the knowledge of how well the student did in Stein's class? The research issue fits Basic Question 3 (Does an association exist between two [or more] variables?). The next chapter reviews the concept of association (introduced in chapter 3 and covered briefly in chapters 4 and 5) and discusses the techniques used to assess it. As with the descriptive techniques available to describe measurements of a single variable, the techniques used to assess association also vary as a function of the scaling and other characteristics of the data.

Summary

This chapter emphasized two main points: (a) Many different kinds of data can contribute to the investigation of a single research problem; and (b) The techniques used to summarize the results of descriptive research should, under ideal circumstances, be matched to specific scaling characteristics of the data values and to the questions we propose to answer with the data. In the context of a hypothetical teacher-evaluation research scenario, we reviewed how to recognize the scaling of data, the problems that arise when we use descriptive measures that are not appropriate for the scaling of the data, and we saw examples of hypothesis testing with different kinds of descriptive data. We also pointed out the difference between true categorical data and data that really have higher scaling but are forced into the categorical format, and explained why, when the data are ordinal, some researchers frown on using the mean as a measure of central tendency and the standard deviation as a measure of dispersion. As a reminder that the scaling of data and the choices for descriptive analysis are not always clear-cut, we pointed out that the scaling of some behavioral data is arguable. We also called attention to the fit between the research examples and the basic questions presented in chapter 5 and stressed that the various results were descriptive rather than experimental.

Key Terms

Analysis of Variance, p. 138   Subjective Rating, p. 134
Chi-Square Goodness of Fit Test, p. 133   *t* test, p. 138
Kruskal–Wallis H Test, p. 136

Chapter Exercises

1. Information provided by the 1991 graduates of Ivory Tower University and North Central State University reveal that the graduates of Ivory Tower were employed at a significantly higher mean starting salary ($27,000) than the graduates of North Central State ($24,000).

    a. Without even seeing the raw salary data, can you determine the level of measurement reflected in the salary data?

    b. Which basic question is addressed by comparing the mean starting salaries of the two groups of graduates?

    c. Should we interpret the existence of a significant salary differential between the two groups of graduates as a descriptive result only, or is it appropriate to suggest that an Ivory Tower education is a direct cause of the increased market values of its graduates?

    d. What explanations unrelated to attendance at one or the other university could account for the existence of a significant salary differential between the two groups of graduates?

    e. If ethical considerations were not an issue and you could be assured of the cooperation of school officials and prospective employers, what experiment could you devise that *would* permit you to causally attribute the finding of a salary differential to the different educational experiences offered by the schools?

2. A recent survey of an inner-city high school revealed that 80% of the students agreed with the statement "I feel hassled most of the time." In an earlier study, only 55% of the students agreed.

   a. What is the scaling of the agree/disagree response data?

   b. If the data were used only to describe the past and current attitudes of the students, what basic question is addressed?

   c. In testing whether the current data are indicative of a significant increase in perceived stress among the students compared to the earlier survey, what basic question is addressed?

3. A psychologist "graded" the preschoolers in two systematically different day-care situations (segregation of different-aged children versus a mingling of younger and older children) on a variety of behavioral dimensions, including willingness to share, sensitivity to the concerns of others, activity level, and attention span. The grading was done using a 10-point scale.

   a. If the data were used simply to describe the respective populations, what basic question is addressed?

   b. What is the scaling of the behavioral ratings?

   c. If the ratings reveal that systematic differences exist between the two classes of preschoolers, is this an experimental or descriptive result? What features would have to be present in the research approach to permit an experimental comparison of the two day-car situations?

   d. What basic question is addressed in an experimental comparison of the two day-care environments?

4. Why is it inappropriate to manipulate (add, subtract, multiply, or divide) data that have only nominal scaling?

5. Why is the median used to describe the central tendency of ranked data rather than the mean?

Proposal Assignment 8: Writing the Method Section

It is now time to specify the procedural details of your proposed research project. Remember, though, for this class you are just designing your study and not collecting data. We stress the hypothetical nature of the exercise so you will not feel constrained by limitations of resources, such as money, research space, the availability of apparatus, etc. (Naturally, if your proposal is especially good, it is possible that your professor could get excited and support your efforts to run the study as a student project in a future semester.) In the process of writing a Method section, you will discover all the difficult decisions you have to make before data collection can begin. The material that must be included in a Method section is reviewed in Appendix A. Your assignment is to write a Method section in APA style. It must include three main subsections: Subjects, Apparatus (or Materials), and Procedure.

Proposals for research projects are normally written in the future tense, but the Method section is always written in the past tense. Since you are just learning how to write in APA style, it might be easier for you to write your proposal in the past tense. Ask your instructor for his or her preferred approach to this exercise.

Your assignment is to write the *first draft* of the Method section. Because there may be a number of decisions that you cannot make without help, do the best you can and place three question marks (???) after each decision you make that you suspect could be incorrect or inappropriate. For example, how many subjects should you test? Is there a commercially available apparatus that measures the response you are interested in, and if so, who is the manufacturer?

CHAPTER

9

Describing the Association Between Variables

We briefly examined the concept of association in chapter 3 and continued with a limited discussion of association, correlation, contingency, and prediction in chapters 4 and 5. Here we review and expand our coverage of these very important concepts by discussing the evidence that is indicative of an association between variables, how researchers describe the trend and strength of association both graphically and statistically, and what the existence of an association between variables does and does not mean.

The Meaning of Association

Basic Question 3 asks: *Does an association exist between two (or more) variables?* We say that an association exists between two variables when the changing values of one variable correspond in a consistent and orderly way to the changing values of the other. For example, when a psychologist characterizes the association between age and verbal skill as positive, it means that as people get older their verbal skill also tends to increase. In a negative relationship, such as the one between time spent in social/recreational activity and academic grades, as one measure increases in value, the other measure tends to decrease in value. Thus, we would expect the "party animals" of a student population, who spend substantial time in the pursuit of fun, to perform academically at a poor to satisfactory level, whereas the students who spend less time in recreational pursuits and, presumably, more time studying would be more likely to get relatively high grades. (See Box 4–1 for graphic displays of positive and negative relationships.)

Association and Prediction

On a personal level, we become aware of the existence of associations between variables through life experiences, and that knowledge enables us to make predictions. For example, some senior citizens report that they do not need to listen to weather reports to know the weather forecast. Their joints tend to stiffen and old injuries start to ache the day before the onset of wet weather. Sailors know that "Red sky at night, sailor's delight. Red sky at morning, sailor take warning." At some point in time seafarers became aware of the tendency for a red evening sky to be followed the next day by fair weather and a red morning sky to be followed by a day of inclement weather. Without necessarily understanding the atmospheric phenomena that underlie the relationship, sailors came to use the association to predict the next day's weather. Anecdotal reports from zoo employees and patrons, as well as those who are in contact with farm and domestic animals, frequently report that animals begin to behave in a very erratic and excited manner about an hour prior to an earthquake. Presumably, the animals are able to sense prequake tremors arising from geological phenomena that are beyond human sensory capacity. Once we are aware of the association between erratic animal behavior and impending seismic activity, we can use animal behavior as a predictor of earthquakes.

The concept of association also underlies the measurement of aptitude, a measure of a person's suitability for a particular endeavor. Once we find that people who have met or exceeded their career goals are consistent in their knowledge of a particular body of information and/or are consistent in their mastery of a particular skill, we can use the association between knowledge and success to predict success for those who aspire to the career (such as medicine, law, music, or athletics). Interestingly, the accuracy of the prediction can be impressive even if the aptitude test items bear no direct relationship to the skill to be achieved. For example, one old test item on the Medical Aptitude Test, which is taken by college students with medical career aspirations, asked "How many symphonies did Beethoven write?" The developers of the test had determined that successful medical students tended to know that Beethoven wrote nine symphonies and, for whatever reason, unsuccessful students tended not to have that information. Thus the test item contributed to a prediction of academic success or failure in medical school even though having certain musical knowledge bears no direct relationship to the practice of medicine. Perhaps the students' familiarity with classical music and their successful performance in medical school are both consequences of the intellectual stimulation they got in the family environment of their youth.

In general, in the behavioral sciences we are unlikely to observe perfect consistency in the association between variables. So, even though we know that high scorers on the Scholastic Aptitude Test also tend to have high academic achievement in college, we know that, for a variety of reasons (such as illness, emotional problems, and financial pressures) not all high scorers will live up to their academic potential. Also, some students with modest SAT scores will have the self-discipline and motivation to summon every resource and perform at a level that exceeds statistical predictions. Because there are usually some exceptions to any trend we may observe in a set of behavioral data, we describe association in terms of the type of functional relationship that *best fits* the pattern in the data. So, when the plot of the X-Y values (a scatterplot, as shown in Box 4–1) resembles a straight line, we describe the trend as **linear.**

Linear: Pertaining to a straight line.

Association versus Causality

We must be careful to draw a distinction between concurrent changes in variable values that rest solely on an association, and concurrent changes that rest on both an association *and* a causal linkage between variables. Specifically, we cannot tell if the association between variables is or is not rooted in an underlying causal relationship if the variable values are assessed after the fact (ex post facto). We may conclude that an association between two variables is indicative of an underlying causal relationship only when one variable has been systematically manipulated. For example, assume we take two measurements on a group of workers: a measure of job satisfaction and a measure of a person's typical level of alcohol consumption. We may find that a negative association exists: low job satisfaction is associated with high alcohol consumption and high job satisfaction is associated with low alcohol consumption. Even though the interpretation may be intuitively pleasing, we cannot presume that low job satisfaction *causes* workers to numb their despair with alcohol. In fact, the reverse could be true. Alcohol abuse could be present for reasons unrelated to the work environment, and the stress of working while trying to recover from an ever-present hangover might be the source of morale problems.

It is easy to be seduced into rendering a causal interpretation of correlational data, especially when the causal interpretation is consistent with our presumptions, prejudices, and other research data. For example, we are all aware that some individuals respond to stress by increasing alcohol consumption, and we are also probably aware that poor working conditions can be stressful. Can an interpretation that makes so much intuitive sense — "Low job satisfaction causes workers to drink more" — really be incorrect just because the job satisfaction and alcohol intake variables were measured ex post facto? The answer is: Not necessarily. Inferring the existence of a causal relationship between variables when the data show only an association is indefensible in a logical sense, but the inference may nevertheless be correct. The reason is that a causal linkage between variables cannot exist without the simultaneous existence of an association. In other words, an association between variables will always accompany a causal relationship, but a causal relationship will not always accompany as association.

At this point you may be wondering if there is a way to tell when a condition of underlying causality is responsible for an observed association between variables. In general, unless the data represent responses to the manipulation of an independent variable (that is, unless the data are *experimental*), we can only speculate about the possibility that an underlying causality between variables is responsible for an observed association.

Association and Risk

Risk: An association between variables that carries an element of danger.

Risk Factor: A variable that is predictive of an undesirable consequence.

When the association between variables carries an element of danger, predictions from variable X to variable Y are often expressed in terms of **risk.** For example, above we described the hypothetical discovery of a negative association between job satisfaction and alcohol consumption in a group of workers. From this knowledge we could predict that workers with very low job satisfaction are likely to have a relatively high level of alcohol consumption. In other words, low job satisfaction could be described as a **risk factor** for alcohol abuse because it is predictive of that undesirable consequence.

Interestingly, once we know that an association exists between variables, it is proper to make predictions from the knowledge of one variable to the value of another even though the data do not provide any information as to *why* the association exists. Medical statistics reveal that women over the age of 40 are more likely than younger women to bear a child with Down syndrome, a mentally and physically handicapping condition, so it is proper to describe advancing age as a risk factor for bearing a Down syndrome child. A third variable, the presence of an imperfectly formed chromosome 21, which is more likely to occur in the babies of females who become pregnant after the age of 40, underlies the association between the age of the female and the incidence of Down syndrome.

Sometimes the documentation of statistical risk is acted upon as if the data were experimental rather than ex post facto. The attitude is "We cannot be sure that we are aware of all possible competing explanations, and our data do not have all the necessary attributes to support a causal interpretation, but a causal interpretation is consistent with the data, and we cannot afford to ignore this." For example, a finding that males convicted of child and/or spouse abuse were themselves victims of abuse during childhood is evidence that a history of suffering abuse in childhood places the victim at risk of growing up to become a violent adult and/or an abusive parent. But, technically, this finding would not warrant the conclusion that suffering abuse in childhood *causes* one to become an abusive adult. It is conceivable that factors unrelated to the suffering of abuse are present and remain a pathological factor in family dynamics across many generations and that these factors are the true underlying cause of the relationship between suffering abuse in childhood and violent behavior in adulthood. Nevertheless, the mental health of our children is so important that there is a tendency to bend the orthodox distinction between experimental and ex post facto data and do everything we can through education and intervention to break the hypothetical cycle of abused children becoming abusive and criminal adults.

The blurring of the distinction between statistical risk and causality is especially evident if the data base is very large and all known plausible explanations for the existence of the functional relationship have been ruled out. Most scientists thus accept the assertion that it is the extra genetic material on chromosome 21 that is the underlying *cause* of Down syndrome even though no study has been (or ever will be) done to manipulate the genetic makeup of chromosome 21 in otherwise healthy human fetuses in an attempt to produce Down syndrome experimentally. The data base (the number of documented cases) in which the chromosome 21 anomaly and Down syndrome occur together is very large; no third variable has ever explained (or been proposed as an explanation) for both the appearance of the genetic anomaly *and* Down syndrome; and the observable manifestations of Down syndrome do not appear in the absence of the genetic anomaly. Thus, despite the absence of an experimental test of the hypothesis, the *idea* of a causal connection between the genetic anomaly and the syndrome is defensible because it is consistent with all observations to date.

Predictor and Criterion Variables

When we make use of an association to predict one variable from the knowledge of another (chapter 4), the variable we use to make the prediction is the predictor variable (X), and the variable we predict is the criterion variable (Y). So, if we use the job-satisfaction variable to identify workers who may be at risk of developing an alcohol dependency, job satisfaction is the predictor variable and alcohol consumption is the criterion variable. Similarly, if we use our knowledge of the amount of time a student prepared for an examination to predict the student's examination score, study time would be the predictor variable and examination score would be the criterion variable. Of course, there is no reason the variable designations could not be reversed, as when the predictor variable becomes the criterion and the criterion becomes the predictor. For example, once we are aware of the association between job satisfaction and alcohol dependency, we can use our knowledge of a person's alcohol dependency as a predictor of low job satisfaction just as readily as we can use low job satisfaction as a predictor of alcohol dependency. Similarly, we can predict that a student with a high examination score is likely to have studied for many hours just as readily as we can predict that a student who studied for many hours is likely to do well on an examination.

Measuring Association: Variables with Interval/Ratio Scaling

We can often detect orderly patterns in the data that indicate the trend of an association both by organizing and inspecting the raw data values and by inspecting graphic displays of the data. In a mathematical sense (as in an equation), a pattern refers to the function that best characterizes the trend of the relationship between variables. We discussed *linear* trends in chapter 4, but sometimes the relationship between some variables is best described as a *curvilinear* trend (see Figure 9–1). In

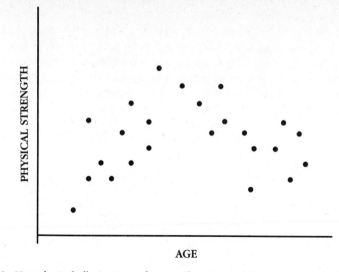

Figure 9–1. Hypothetical illustration of a curvilinear trend between age and a measure of physical strength for 24 subjects.

a curvilinear relationship, as the predictor variable increases so does the criterion variable Y — up to a point; then further increases in the predictor variable are paired with decreases in the criterion variable. For example, age and physical strength are related in a curvilinear fashion: as we progress through childhood and adolescence to our peak of physical fitness, our strength grows. But further increases in age, through adulthood, middle age, and, eventually, old age, are associated with some decrease in strength.

Although some variables of interest to behavioral scientists are related to each other in a curvilinear fashion, the reports in the literature of linear (straight-line) associations between behavioral variables are much more numerous than reports of curvilinear associations. In fact, undergraduates are unlikely either to encounter reports of curvilinear association between behavioral measures in the literature they are assigned to read or to design studies that require familiarity with the measurement of curvilinear association. For this reason, even though we recognize that some variables of interest to behavioral scientists are related in a curvilinear fashion, the present discussion is limited to the measurement of linear association.

Assessing the Strength of Linear Association: Correlation Analysis

Whenever we record two variable values on the same individuals we can measure the strength of the association between the variables. Consider the video-game data shown in Table 9–1. Ten right-handed male subjects were assigned to play a video game that requires a considerable amount of eye–hand coordination and speed to avoid being devoured by the dragon and "losing a life." During one test session each subject manipulated the game's action with a joystick controller. In a different session each subject was required to use a computer keyboard to control the action.

Subject	Type of Controller (X) Keyboard	(Y) Joystick
1	2	0
2	4	2
3	5	2
4	11	7
5	15	10
6	7	9
7	3	4
8	14	9
9	8	5
10	14	12

Table 9–1. The number of video game lives lost when 10 subjects played one session of a video game with a keyboard controller and one session with a joystick controller.

We assume that the behavioral measure of performance skill, the number of "lives" lost while playing the video game, reflects at least interval measurement. That is, we shall assume that the skill that separates a score of 2 and a score of 4 is the same degree of skill that separates a score of 10 from a score of 12. Inspection of the data reveals that each subject exhibited roughly equivalent game proficiency regardless of the type of controller used. Those players who lost few lives when using the keyboard controller also tended to lose few lives when using the joystick controller. Conversely, those who lost many lives using the keyboard controller also tended to lose many lives using the joystick controller. The pattern we have just described for the Table 9–1 data is, of course, the pattern of a positive association.

We do not cover the computational procedures of correlation and regression analysis in this chapter. (Consult either Appendix B or your statistics text.) But we explain, in general terms, how we can visually represent the pattern of association that exists between the keyboard and joystick performances, how we can solve for the mathematical function that best fits the data, how we can measure the strength of the association that exists between variables, and how we can use our knowledge of association to make specific predictions from one variable to another.

The Scatterplot

To draw a scatterplot (see Box 4–1), we must label one variable Y, the other X, and place a dot at the location defined by each pair of X–Y coordinates. The scale for variable Y, the criterion variable, is on the vertical axis (the ordinate), and the scale for variable X, the predictor variable, is in the horizontal axis (the abscissa). The scatterplot of the video game data in Table 9–1 (Figure 9–2) reveals the same trend we noticed from our inspection of the raw data: as variable X (lives lost when playing the game with a keyboard controller) increases in value, variable Y (lives lost when using the joystick controller) also tends to increase in value, and vice versa.

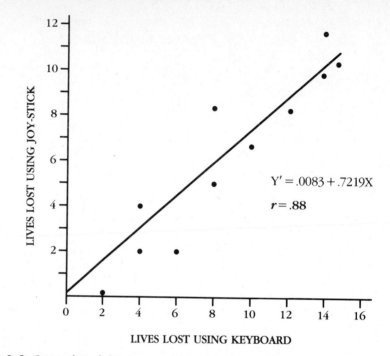

Figure 9–2. Scatterplot of the data in Table 9–1 with the Pearson *r* value, the regression equation, and the best-fit regression line.

Regression: Plotting a Best-Fit Linear Function on a Scatterplot

Line of Best Fit: The straight line that best represents the trend in a scatterplot.

Linear Regression Analysis: A statistical procedure for determining the regression constants.

Regression Constants: The slope and Y-intercept of the best-fit linear function.

We can summarize the information in the scatterplot by drawing a straight line, or **line of best fit,** through the main axis of the scatterplot. The line of best fit, also called the *regression line* or *best-fit linear function,* summarizes the trend of a scatterplot in the same sense that the arithmetic mean summarizes the values of a distribution. We find the line of best fit by applying **linear regression analysis** to the data. The first step is to determine the two **regression constants**. The symbol a_Y represents the Y-intercept, which is the value of variable Y when X = 0 or, in other words, where the regression line intersects the Y-axis. The symbol b_Y is the slope of the regression line, which is the rate of change in the value of variable Y relative to a change in the value of variable X. (If relatively small changes in variable X are accompanied by relatively large changes in variable Y, the slope of the regression line will be steep. Conversely, if relatively large changes in variable X are accompanied by relatively small changes in variable Y, the slope will be shallow.) Once we know the values of the regression constants, a_Y and b_Y, we can write the equation for the regression line in the form

Predicted value for Y equals the value at the Y-intercept plus the product of the slope times the value of variable X

or

$$Y' = a_Y + b_Y X$$

For the data in Table 9–1 the Y-intercept equals .0083 and the slope equals 0.7219, so, with substitutions, the regression equation takes the form

$$Y' = .0083 + 0.7219X$$

By substituting arbitrary X values in the equation and solving for Y, we can plot some of the points on the regression line. Then, by connecting the points, we can plot the regression line through the scatterplot. Thus, for the data in Figure 9–1, when we let X = 2 and solve the regression equation, Y = 1.47, and when we let X = 12, Y = 8.67. To plot the regression line we simply connect the dots plotted at the two pairs of coordinates: X = 2.00, Y = 1.47 and X = 12.00, Y = 8.67.

Even though solving for the slope and Y-intercept of the regression line allows us to represent the linear trend that exists between two variables in the form of a mathematical equation, the regression equation of the best-fit linear function does not describe the *strength* of the linear trend. In fact, it is possible for one scatterplot that represents a relatively weak linear trend and another with a relatively strong linear trend to have regression lines with the same constants. The **envelopes** (lines sketched around the periphery of the scatterplot to indicate its general shape) of Figures 9–3 and 9–4 show, respectively, weak and strong linear trends, but notice that the slope and Y-intercept of the regression lines (and, therefore, the equations of the lines) are the same.

From a visual standpoint, the more tightly clustered the dots of the scatterplot about the regression line, the stronger the linear trend between variables X and Y. So the strength of the linear association between the X and Y variables is more pronounced in a scatterplot with minimal dispersal of the points about the regression line (Figure 9–4) than it would be for a scatterplot with more extensive dispersal (Figure 9–3).

We need not, however, rely on vague visual impressions of the strength of association ("fat" versus "skinny" scatterplots). It is possible to quantify the strength of association between two variables by computing a correlation coeffi-

Envelope: Sketch around the periphery of a scatterplot that indicates its general shape and trend.

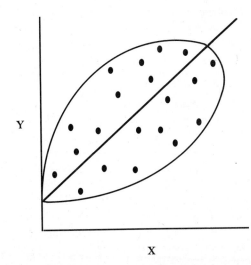

Figure 9–3. An envelope representative of a relatively weak linear trend.

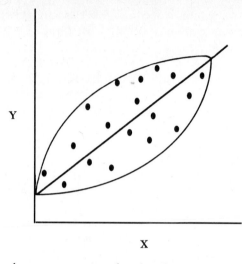

Figure 9–4. An envelope representative of a relatively strong linear trend.

cient (see chapter 4). For the data in Table 9–1, which we assume to reflect measurement of normally distributed variables with at least interval scaling, the Pearson *r* is the appropriate correlation statistic. The Pearson *r* statistic for the data in Table 9–1 equals .88. The more closely the dots of a scatterplot are clustered about the regression line, the closer the *r* values will be to the maximum of + 1.00 (for a positive relationship) or − 1.00 (for a negative relationship). The maximum value of + 1.00 or − 1.00 can be reached only if the dots of a scatterplot form one straight line.

The formulae for computing the Pearson *r* statistic and regression constants involve substantial number-crunching, so data analysts tend to rely more and more on computers. (It is well worthwhile to pursue learning how to do data analyses on a computer. In fact, many instructors of research methods and statistics already require their students to use main-frame or microcomputer statistical programs [software]. Computers will save a great deal of time and spare much effort in the long run, although some frustration during the learning process is not unusual.)

Statistical Significance

As discussed in Box 4–4, statistical significance means that more than chance factors account for a set of research results. With respect to correlation analysis, statistical significance means that the association between the X and Y variables is sufficiently strong to be considered real. Conversely, the finding of no significant association means that we attribute the results to chance alone. For example, with respect to the data in Table 9–1, a significant correlation would mean that the degree of positive association between keyboard and joystick performance (*r* = + .88) is too large to attribute to chance factors alone. Had the correlation analysis failed to reveal a significant association, we would conclude that a person's skill with one type of game controller is unrelated to the skill he or she displays with the other controller.

The computed value of the Pearson r ($r = .88$) is significant because it is greater than the appropriate critical value (for 10 pairs of scores and at the .05 level of significance) published in a table of critical values for the Pearson r statistic ($r_{critical} = .63$). In fact, even if we decided to use a stricter standard of significance by using the critical values for the .01 level ($r_{critical} = .76$), the r value of .88 would still be significant. Take note that the critical values for the Pearson r change with the sample size. For example, the critical value (at the .05 level of significance) we used to evaluate the significance of the association between the 10 joystick and keyboard measures in Table 9–1 equals .63. But if we had data on 50 subjects instead of only 10, the critical value would have been a much smaller .28.

The level of significance we use to conduct a statistical test (usually .05 or .01) is the same as the probability of making a Type I error — concluding that significance exists when it really does not. (If necessary, review Box 4–4.) Thus, the determination that a significant positive association exists between the keyboard and joystick performance measures at the .01 level of significance means that there is only a 1 in 100 chance that the observed level of association occurred by chance.

The Coefficients of Determination and Nondetermination

The square of the Pearson r, written r^2, is called the **coefficient of determination**. It is the proportion of variability in variable Y that is predictable from knowledge of the value of variable X. The proportion of variability that is unpredictable equals $1 - r^2$ and is called the **coefficient of nondetermination**. For the data in Table 9–1, the Pearson r equals .88, so $r^2 = .78$ and $1 - r_2 = .22$. To convert the proportion to a percentage we need only multiply by 100. As a percentage, we can state that 78% of the variability among the joystick scores (Y) is predictable with the knowledge of the keyboard scores (X), and 22% is unpredictable (see Figure 9–5).

In simple terms, the coefficient of determination is a translation of the Pearson r, which quantifies the strength of the association between variables, into a value that quantifies the strength of our ability to predict one variable with the knowledge of the other. Since the size of the r^2 statistic is determined by the size of the r statistic, the greater the strength of association, the more accurate the predictions from X to Y will be. The latter relationship also becomes evident from inspecting the appearance of a best-fit line through a scatterplot: The more closely the dots of the scatterplot cluster about the regression line, the higher the r value will be, and the greater the accuracy of predictions will be.

If we calculate r^2 for a range of r values we notice that predictive power diminishes rapidly as r decreases. An r value of .50, even if statistically significant, only makes it possible to predict of 25% of the variability ($.5^2 = .25$) in Y with the knowledge of X. Three times as much variability (75%) remains unpredictable. Similarly, r must be greater than .71 just to be able to predict more than half ($.71^2 = .50$) the variability in Y with the knowledge of X. If the author of a research report provides an r value without also reporting the r^2 value, a reader would be wise to calculate it personally. It can be sobering to realize how little predictive power exists even when r is statistically significant. For example, an r value of .3 computed on 50 pairs of scores is significant, but, since $r^2 = .09$, only 9% of the

Coefficient of Determination: r^2, the proportion of variability in the criterion variable that is predictable.

Coefficient of Nondetermination: $1 - r^2$, the proportion of variability in the criterion variable that is *not* predictable.

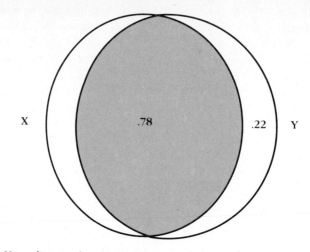

Figure 9–5. A Venn diagram showing the proportion of total variability in the criterion variable (Y) that is predictable (.78) and the proportion that is unpredictable (.22) with the knowledge of X when $r_{XY} = .88$.

variability in the criterion (Y) variable is predictable with the knowledge of the predictor (X) variable.

Measuring Association: Variables with Ordinal Scaling

When one or both variables are in the form of ranks, we can assess the degree of association using the Spearman rho statistic. Rho is really just a Pearson r computed on ranked (ordinal) data. Like the Pearson r, the Spearman rho quantifies the strength of association on a scale that ranges between -1.00 and $+1.00$.

The data in Table 9–2 represent two measurements on the same set of subjects, and both variables have ordinal scaling. Variable Y is a report of perceived pain following a diagnostic medical procedure on a scale from 0 (the subject reports no pain) to 10 (the subject reports excruciating pain). Variable X is a rating of patient resistance to the procedure from 0 (very willing to undergo the procedure) to 10 (strongly resisted the physician's and family's advice to undergo the procedure). The patients provide the pain ratings, and the physician had the task of scoring the patients on the resistance-to-treatment scale.

The Spearman rho value for the Table 9–2 data equals $+.75$, which represents a significant positive association at the .05 level of significance. As with the Pearson r, we know the computed r value is significant if it exceeds the critical value published in a table of the rho statistic. (For 12 pairs of values, rho$_{critical} = .59$ at the .05 level of significance.) The determination that the resistance data and the pain data are positively associated to a significant extent means that the more a patient resists advice to undergo the procedure, the more likely the patient is to experience postprocedural pain.

Subject	(X) Resistance	(Y) Pain
1	2	1
2	4	2
3	4	5
4	9	7
5	5	3
6	7	9
7	3	4
8	8	6
9	2	3
10	4	5
11	7	8
12	1	3

Table 9–2. Resistance-to-treatment ratings (X) and patient pain rating (Y) for a group of 12 patients subjected to a diagnostic medical procedure. The data are hypothetical.

Measuring Association: Variables with Nominal Scaling

As indicated in chapters 4 and 5, even research data with only nominal scaling can reflect a dependent relationship between variables. Consider the row and column variables listed in Table 9–3.

Forty subjects were surveyed within each of three different age groups. They were shown three images that were being considered for use in an advertising campaign for a new low-calorie beverage. The only task the three groups of different-aged subjects had to complete was to register their opinion as to which advertising image was the most appealing. As each subject registered a response, a

AGE	IMAGE 1	IMAGE 2	IMAGE 3
10–30	///	### ### ### ### ...	### ///
31–50	### ///	### ### ### ### ...	### /
51–70	### ### /	### ### ### ### ...	//

Table 9–3. A partially filled-in 3 × 3 contingency table (each slash represents one data point) with nine row/column combinations (cells) that are defined by the three levels of the row variable (Age) and the three levels of the column variable (Image). The complete data summary appears in Table 9–4.

tally (check mark, tick) was recorded in the appropriate cell. For example, if a 35-year-old subject preferred Image 2 over Images 1 and 3, the scorer would record a tally in the second column and second row of the table. The summary of all 120 individual tallies appear as the nine cell totals in Table 9–4.

The display of frequency data as tallies in a two-dimensional table with r rows and c columns is called a contingency table, and any association we may find to exist between the row and column variables is called contingency. The rows and columns of the contingency table define **mutually exclusive response categories**, which means that the definitions of the categories exclude the possibility that a subject's response could fit in more than one cell of the contingency table. In the present example, a subject can be only one age and register a preference for only one image.

The goal of the study summarized in Table 9–4 was to determine whether or not the appeal of the advertising image is contingent on the age of the potential consumer. Since there are three age categories (the row variable) and three image categories (the column variable) the table is a 3×3 contingency table and has nine cells. The pattern indicating the absence of contingency could be for some image (or images) to be uniformly preferred over others, regardless of the age of the consumer. For example, in Table 9–4 notice that Image 2 tends to be preferred over Images 1 and 3 across all age categories. Therefore, the results shown in Table 9–4 suggest that image preference is *independent* of the age variable.

By contrast, if the pattern of preference for the three images *depends* on (or, in other words, is *contingent* on) the age of the consumer, the pattern would lack uniformity. One such pattern is evident in the data of Table 9–5: the two groups of older subjects tend to prefer Image 2 (cell tallies of 26 and 27), whereas Image 2 was the least favorite among the youngest category of subjects (a cell tally of only 3). Thus, the pattern in the data of Table 9–5 suggests that the relative appeal of the

Mutually Exclusive Response Categories: Nonoverlapping response categories.

AGE	IMAGE 1	IMAGE 2	IMAGE 3
10–30	3	29	8
31–50	8	26	6
51–70	11	27	2

Table 9–4. A pattern of frequencies that is indicative of the independence of the row and column variables. Image 2 was uniformly preferred by all age groups.

AGE	IMAGE 1	IMAGE 2	IMAGE 3
10–30	29	3	8
31–50	8	26	6
51–70	11	27	2

Table 9–5. The data summary of the responses of three groups of 40 like-aged subjects to the question of image preference.

three advertising images *depends* on (varies in a consistent fashion with) the age of the consumer.

Statistical Significance

As with the Pearson *r* and the Spearman rho statistics, there is a procedure for determining whether the extent of the contingency evident in the table is strong enough to discount chance as the sole reason for the pattern. The widely used chi-square test of independence (see Appendix B or a statistics text) is the test of choice (assuming its assumptions have been met) for determining the dependence/independence of two categorical variables). For the data in Table 9–5, that, from inspection, seem to indicate the presence of a contingency between the row and column variables, the computed value of the chi-square statistic equals 39.38. By comparison, the chi-square computed from the data of Table 9–4, which was offered as an example of a pattern of independence, equals 8.12. The critical value of the chi-square statistic for a 3 × 3 contingency table and with the level of significance set at .05 is 9.49. So, in line with our impression from inspection, only the data in Table 9–5 reveal a statistically significant contingency between the row and column variables.

Other Measures of the Strength of Association

There are other statistical measures of the strength of association between variables besides the Pearson *r* and Spearman rho correlation coefficients, and like the *r* and rho statistics, their application depends on the characteristics of the data. Below we list and describe four additional measures of association with respect to the unique kinds of data they describe. Also, in Figure 9–6, we present a flow chart to illustrate the process for choosing a measure of association based on the characteristics of the data. The brief descriptions should give you enough familiarity with the various measures of association that, when you encounter them in your reading of the psychological literature, you will understand why they were used in the particular research context and the information they provide about variable relationships.

The point biserial correlation coefficient (r_{pbi}) is used to measure the strength of association between a variable with at least interval scaling and a dichotomous variable with nominal scaling. (A dichotomous variable can take on only two values, such as male/female.) Thus, if we wished to compute the correlation between the gender variable (male/female) and a variable with interval scaling, such as grip strength measured in pounds, the point biserial *r* would be the statistic of choice.

Sometimes we wish to correlate two variables that both have at least interval scaling, but one is artificially divided into two categories (dichotomized) such as "high and low" or "pass and fail" when applied to test scores with interval scaling. If the data fit the latter description, the biserial correlation coefficient (r_{bi}) is the appropriate statistic to represent the strength of association. Thus, if we wished to compute the correlation between grip strength measured in pounds and height measured in inches, we would use the Pearson *r*. But if we artificially dichotomized the height scores into tall and short categories, we would have to use the biserial r for the analysis.

The tetrachoric correlation coefficient (r_{tet}) is also used for the analysis of dichotomized data that are fundamentally of at least interval scaling, except that both variables, not just one variable as in the case of biserial r, have been artificially dichotomized. Thus, r_{tet} would be used to correlate grip strength and height if we first dichotomized the grip strength scores into "strong" and "weak" and the height scores into "tall" and "short."

The phi correlation coefficient (r_{ϕ}) is a close relative of the chi-square statistic. It is used to measure the strength of association between two categorical variables (nominal scaling), both of which are dichotomous. Thus, to measure the strength of

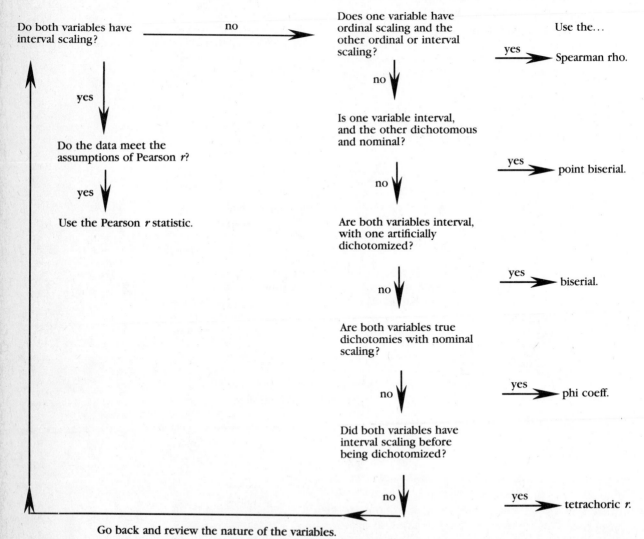

Figure 9–6. A guide to the application of the various correlation statistics.

association between the gender of a shopper (male/female) and the response of the shopper to a sales pitch (a choice either to buy or not to buy the merchandise), r_ϕ would be appropriate.

Correlational Research That Resembles Experimental Research

Studies designed to address research issues in the form of Basic Questions 4, 5, 6, and 7 were identified in chapter 5 as forms of experimental research because they all share one important characteristic: exposing initially equivalent groups of subjects (or the same group of subjects on different occasions) to one or more manipulated conditions. Keeping the latter common characteristic in mind, let us briefly review the statements of the last four in the set of seven basic questions:

- *Basic Question 4.* Will introducing subjects to a specific change in an otherwise standard context *cause* their behavior to change?

- *Basic Question 5.* Will introducing subjects to qualitatively different conditions *cause* them to exhibit systematic differences in behavior?

- *Basic Question 6.* Will introducing subjects to quantitatively different conditions *cause* them to exhibit systematic differences in behavior?

- *Basic Question 7.* Will introducing subjects to two or more systematically different conditions *cause* an additive and/or interactive effect on behavior?

Notice that the word *cause* appears in all four questions. As we have stressed repeatedly, arguing that a systematic change in behavior is a direct consequence of a subject's experience is justified only when the experimenter (a) manipulates the variable characteristics of the experience, (b) can randomly assign which subjects get which experiences, and (c) has one or more reference (control) conditions against which to compare the effects of the experimental condition. The wording of Basic Questions 4 through 7 was carefully crafted to convey the notion of manipulation through the use of the phrase *introducing subjects to.*

Now let us modify the above basic questions and replace the emphasis on experimental manipulation with an emphasis on researching the effects of nonmanipulated variables: selected variables and natural treatments. The language of manipulation ("introducing to") is gone, and in its place appears language that expresses the ex post facto character of the variables ("identified as having experienced"). In their changed form we refer to the questions as the **descriptive corollaries**: questions that, although similar to Basic Questions 4, 5, 6, and 7, represent types of correlational rather than experimental research.

Descriptive Corollaries: Questions that, although similar to Basic Questions 4, 5, 6, and 7, represent types of correlational rather than experimental research.

- *Basic Question 4 Corollary.* Is there a measurable change in behavior among subjects identified as having experienced a change in an otherwise standard context?

- *Basic Question 5 Corollary.* Are there systematic differences in behavior among subjects identified as having experienced qualitatively different conditions?

- *Basic Question 6 Corollary.* Are there systematic differences in behavior among subjects identified as having experienced quantitatively different conditions?

- *Basic Question 7 Corollary.* Are additive and/or interactive effects evident among subjects identified as having experienced two or more systematically different conditions?

Original Basic Questions Compared to the Descriptive Corollaries

Since nonmanipulated (ex post facto) variables are *associated* with behavioral differences rather than viewed as the *cause* of behavioral differences, research in the form of the descriptive corollaries cannot be considered experimental. The forms of research defined by the descriptive corollaries may *resemble* true experiments and may *appear* to justify causal interpretations because, just as in experiments, they call for comparing the behavior of subjects who have had different experiences. Nevertheless, because research in the form of the descriptive corollaries presumes the collection of ex post facto data, we call it *correlational,* a label that reminds us the results are limited to interpretations of association.

Interestingly, correlational research in the form of the descriptive corollaries, although called correlational, does not involve the application of a correlation analysis such as the Pearson *r* or the Spearman rho to the data. This is because a requirement of correlation analysis — that the data consist of two or more measures on the same set of subjects — is lacking. Instead of correlating different measures on the same set of subjects as we would when researching an issue in the form of Basic Question 3 (say, measuring the association between birth weight and IQ at five years of age), the goal of correlational studies in the form of the descriptive corollaries appears to be the opposite: to compare the *same* behavioral measures between *different* groups of subjects (as in comparing the five-year-old IQ of firstborn versus lastborn children from two-parent homes with three children).

In some experimental research (between-subject designs) we also compare the same behavioral measure between two or more groups. (Between-subject experimental designs were mentioned briefly in chapter 5 and will be covered in chapters 11 and 13.) But, unlike the design of a between-subject experiment, which presumes exposing initially equivalent groups to different manipulated levels of a variable, the wording in the descriptive corollaries presumes that selected variables or natural treatments have left their mark on behavior *prior to* the inception of the research project. Thus the researcher's role in carrying out a correlational study is fundamentally different from the role of an experimenter. Instead of manipulating a variable that is hypothesized to affect behavior, in a correlational study the researcher measures the behavior of subjects who are *identified,* after the fact, as having had certain experiences (natural treatments) or possessing certain physical or behavioral attributes (selected variables) that are associated with behavioral differences.

Comparing the original wording of the basic questions to the descriptive corollaries sensitizes you to the difference between correlational research and experimental research, the topic of Part IIB. Focusing on the question addressed by the research and the circumstances that surround data collection enables you to distinguish correlational studies in the form of the descriptive corollaries from true experiments. This, in turn, will enable you to determine whether the results of a study reflect causality or only association.

Multiple Correlation and Regression

As noted in chapter 5 in the discussion of Basic Question 3, multiple correlation is a relatively advanced statistical technique that permits us to assess the association between several predictor variables and a criterion variable. The Pearson r and Spearman rho statistics can, by comparison, measure the association between only two variables.

Since this chapter is devoted to correlational methods, we review here why it is both possible and desirable to assess the association that exists between a composite of several predictor variables and a single criterion variable rather than just between two variables. Academicians use several predictors in deciding the suitability of a student for an academic program. For example, students applying to graduate school are evaluated using several criteria such as grade-point average, rank in class, Graduate Record Examination scores, faculty ratings of academic potential, and Miller Analogy Test scores. Taken alone, each of these measures of academic achievement and aptitude has a degree of association with success in graduate school, and each could be used singly to predict a level of success in graduate school. But, by combining all the individual predictor variables into one composite index of academic aptitude, it becomes possible to harness their combined predictive power and thereby make more accurate predictions.

The computational procedures for multiple correlation and multiple regression are usually beyond the scope of an introductory level statistics text and are not covered here. Be aware, however, that the study of the relationships between variables and the derivation of mathematical expressions for making predictions is by no means limited to the one-to-one portrayal (use X to predict Y) in this chapter's tables and graphs.

Summary

We began chapter 9 by restating Basic Question 3 ("Does an association exist between two [or more] variables?") and reviewed the concept of association. We then explained the characteristics of data that are indicative of association and why the existence of an association between variables permits the making of predictions from the knowledge of one variable (the predictor variable) to another variable (the criterion variable). After pointing out how important it is not to confuse an association between variables with a causal linkage, we discussed the relevance of association to the concept of risk factors, the statistical measurement of the strength of association for different types of data, the use of regression analysis to formalize the prediction of one variable from another, and the concept of statistical significance as it applies to the strength of association between variables. We pointed out that a significant association between two variables does not necessarily mean that one variable will be useful for predicting the value of another. The proportion of variability in the criterion variable that is predictable with the knowledge of the predictor variable (r^2) can be very low even in the presence of a significant association. We then contrasted experimental and correlational research that share a common goal: exploring effects of different experiences on subjects' behavior. First we reviewed Basic Questions 4, 5, 6, and 7, which define approaches to experimental research. Then, after a slight change of wording to change the variables from manipulated to ex post facto, we explained why the research becomes correlational rather than experimental. In their changed form, we refer to the questions as descriptive corollaries. We concluded by describing, in general terms, the usefulness of multiple regression and correlation as analytical tools.

Key Terms

Best-Fit Linear Function, p. 152

Coefficient of Determination, p. 155

Coefficient of Nondetermination, p. 155

Descriptive Corollaries, p. 161

Envelope, p. 153

Line of Best Fit, p. 152

Linear, p. 147

Linear Regression Analysis, p. 152

Mutually Exclusive Response Categories, p. 158

Regression Constants, p. 152

Regression Line, p. 152

Risk, p. 148

Risk Factor, p. 148

Chapter Exercises

1. Describe the telltale patterns in data that reveal positive and negative associations between variables.

2. What is the relationship between the strength of the association that exists between variables and the accuracy with which we can predict the value of one variable from the knowledge of another?

3. What is the rationale for regarding some performance measures as indicators of aptitude for other performance measures?

4. How can you tell if the trend evident in a scatterplot is linear versus curvilinear?

5. Explain: Causally linked variables are also functionally associated, but not all variables that are associated are causally linked.

6. What is the difference between identifying divorce/separation as a *risk factor* for neurotic depression and labeling this stressful life event as a *cause* of neurotic depression? What kind of data is required to document divorce/separation as a cause versus a risk factor for neurotic depression?

7. What is the pattern of frequency data in a contingency table that is indicative of an association between the row and column variables?

8. What feature of a scatterplot provides a visual impression of the strength of association between the X and Y variables?

9. What does it mean to say that the association between variables is statistically significant?

10. Both the original basic questions (4–7) and their corollaries refer to comparing the behavior of subjects who have had different experiences. Why are we restricted to interpretations of association when the research is in the form of the descriptive corollaries?

Proposal Assignment 9: Rewriting the Introduction

For Proposal Assignment 6 you searched the literature for two articles related to your study and wrote the first draft of the introduction section to your proposal. Now go back to the library and find additional references (your instructor will tell you how many more to find) to expand the literature review in the introduction section. Finding additional articles is not difficult, because the two articles you have already located probably cite between 15 and 20 articles in their reference section, which appears at the end of a report. In addition, you can use Social Science Citation Index to find articles that have referenced the ones you have already found (see Appendix A).

In addition to finding more articles, rewrite your introduction. Assuming that you have obtained critical comments from your instructor on your first draft, rewrite the section based on those suggestions. Remember, rewriting is the key to clear and accurate communication. Be your own worst critic. When you compare your later drafts with early ones, you may be amazed at the improvement.

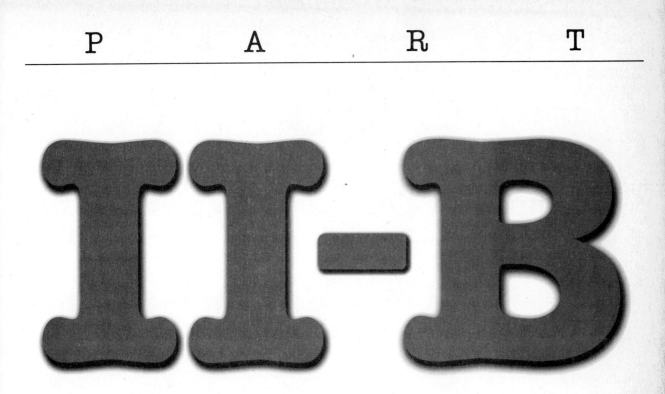

II-B

**Experimentation:
The Next Level
of Research Inquiry**

10

A Sampler of Research Strategies and Procedures

Treatment Effect: An influence on behavior that is attributable to the manipulation of the independent variable.

Having discussed descriptive methods for addressing research issues in the form of Basic Questions 1, 2, and 3, we now turn our attention to the next level of research inquiry: the experiment. An experiment is the implementation of a formal strategy to reveal cause–effect relationships between variables. When psychologists do experimental research, they harvest information by recording measurable aspects of behavior, just as they do when they conduct descriptive research. But, to continue with the agricultural analogy, the information is cultivated rather than wild. In an experiment the researcher purposely interferes with the natural order by manipulating one or more conditions that he or she expects will affect behavior, just as farmers apply fertilizers, control pests, irrigate, modify soil acidity, and rotate plantings to counteract and improve upon the influences of natural forces. If the experimental hypothesis is accurate, the result is a **treatment effect**, an influence on behavior that is attributable to the manipulation of the independent variable. Experiments are often successful in identifying the causes of behavioral phenomena, but we must also keep in mind that the behavior studied by the psychologist and the produce grown by the farmer are both subject to natural forces about which psychologists and farmers have little or no knowledge and/or over which they have little or no control.

The Design of Experiments

Despite the great variety of questions that can be answered through experimentation, there are a limited number of ways to organize an experiment for the pursuit of accurate and interpretable information. Collectively, the various methodological approaches we use to answer formally stated research questions are called **designs**. This chapter introduces an assortment of relatively uncomplicated research designs in the context of some hypothetical research problems. It is important to appreciate early, prior to the more detailed coverage of experimental research in the following chapters, how several of the core concepts already covered (such as control groups, experimental groups, and confounding variables) as well as some new concepts pertain to a typical research effort.

Designs: The various methodological approaches we use to answer formally stated research questions.

The single-sample study

In a **single-sample study** one group of subjects is exposed to an experimental condition. Then the behavior of this experimental group is compared to an established norm, defined in chapter 6 as the central (mean, median, or mode) or average form of a behavior derived from prior study of a relatively large group. For example, assume that a new medication has been developed that shows promise for alleviating the severe depression that so often leads to suicidal behavior. All indications are that the medicine is safe, but it has not been tried on a large scale with humans who suffer from depression. The plan is to medicate a group of 200 patients, all of whom have a history of depression and one suicide attempt, and to keep careful records of the incidence of suicidal behavior for five years. At the end of the study it would be possible to compare the incidence of suicidal behavior recorded for the medicated subjects to established norms concerning the incidence of a second suicide attempt within five years of an initial attempt.

Single-sample Study: The behavior of a single treatment condition is compared to norms of behavior from some data base.

If the suicide rate is lower than the population norm for the patients who received the new medication, can we conclude that the new medication is responsible for the reduction? Before considering this question, let us first turn our attention to a single-sample design as it might be used in an experiment with animal subjects.

Assume that a researcher plans to use a single-sample design to assess the effects of infant stimulation on the course of behavioral development in laboratory rats. Every day for the first 20 days of life, several litters of baby rats are removed from their nursing mothers and isolated in one-gallon containers lined with wood shavings. Infant animals disturbed daily in this way receive substantial stimulation that is not part of the normal rearing experience in the laboratory. The researcher's hypothesis is that the stimulation will accelerate the maturation of various behaviors and developmental milestones (say, the age at which the animal begins reflexively to roll over on its stomach when placed on its back and the age at which the animal's eyes first open). Once the developmental data of the experimental animals are collected they may be compared to the developmental norms that are known from prior study of the species. The normative data serve as a standard of comparison as if they were measures from an untreated control group. If the behavior of stimulated animals deviates from the established developmental norms, can we conclude that the differences have been caused by the extra stimulation we gave the animal? Maybe yes, maybe no!

In both the human and animal research examples offered above, drawing a conclusion that the treatment is the cause of change requires making a rather bold assumption: that the norms being used as the standard of comparison accurately reflect what the behavior of the subjects would have been had they not been exposed to the experimental condition. Because it is possible, even likely, that the procedures and conditions under which the research data were collected and the procedures and conditions under which the normative data were collected are not exactly the same, it is possible for factors other than the experimental treatment to be responsible for any deviations from the normative data.

In the animal study, perhaps after the normative data were collected the experimenter changed the brand of chow fed to the animals, modified the test apparatus, or hired new technicians to test the animals. In the human study, maybe improved prospects for world peace and economic prosperity led the subjects to refrain from second suicide attempts. For these and similar reasons, most researchers regard interpretations of data from single-sample experiments as equivocal and quite risky. In fact, because of the shaky foundation for a causal interpretation of results, one may reasonably argue that a single-sample study is not a true experiment at all.

There is, however, a place for single-sample studies in science. Consider, for example, the developmental phenomenon called fetal alcohol syndrome, or FAS. Physicians began to notice (among them Abel, 1980; Streissguth, 1976) that the babies of women who were heavy consumers of alcoholic beverages during pregnancy tended to deviate from the norms of infant development in a number of ways, including growth deficiencies, mental deficiency and performance problems, and behavioral problems. The apparent association between maternal ingestion of alcohol and developmental problems in babies advanced the hypothesis that alcohol can cause mental and physical abnormalities in babies.

Hypothetically (that is, if we did not attend to ethical considerations), we could test this hypothesis experimentally in humans using the single-sample approach. We would randomly select a group from a population of recently impregnated women and put them on a heavy drinking regimen. From the time of birth onward the behavior of the babies would be monitored and compared carefully to the norms of human development that are known from prior research on infant development. But, even if such a study were done, could we draw a meaningful conclusion from the data? Could we say that any abnormalities we document were *caused* by alcohol? We could not unequivocally attribute observed departures from established behavioral norms to the exposure to alcohol unless, with a leap of faith, we assume that the norms are an accurate representation of what the behavioral development of the babies would have been like without exposure to alcohol.

The two-sample experiment

Instead of making the latter assumption, a more precise approach to the problem would be to randomly divide a group of newly impregnated women into two treatment conditions: those assigned to the drinking (experimental) condition and those assigned to a nondrinking (control) condition. The study, which now has both a control group *and* an experimental group, is a **two-sample experiment** (also called a **two-treatment experiment**). Expectant mothers assigned to the drinking condition would have to consume a fixed daily portion of alcohol, whereas the nondrinking mothers would have to abstain from any drinking. By maintaining the care of all the expectant mothers in as consistent a manner as possible (with the exception of alcohol consumption, the experimental variable), we would be on firmer logical footing in drawing a causal connection between alcohol consumption and any developmental differences we observe between the children of drinking and nondrinking mothers.

Of course, we would probably also be in jail if we attempted to carry out either of these alcohol experiments. As discussed more fully in chapter 16, both technical and ethical constraints place strict limits on the kinds of experimentation we can do with animal and human subjects. The limits that are in place to protect human welfare are more strict than the limits to protect animal welfare, so, when faced with a public health problem of the magnitude of FAS, researchers often turn to animal models. An **animal model** is a nonhuman biological preparation used as a substitute to study a phenomenon that is fundamentally human, such as drug dependency.

Two-sample Experiment: An experiment for comparing the effects of two different experimental conditions or comparing an experimental treatment condition to a control condition.

A Walk Through a Typical Experiment

In the remainder of the chapter we give you a flavor of the methodological alternatives and procedural details that a researcher is likely to struggle with when planning and carrying out a relatively simple experiment. We also introduce some new methodological principles in the context of the FAS research scenario.

Developing an Animal Model for Fetal Alcohol Syndrome (FAS)

Suppose, recognizing the limitations for studying FAS in humans, you decide to develop an animal model. (Indeed, you may decide that an animal experiment is most appropriate for your choice of a research problem in developing your proposal assignment.) The first step, should you decide to investigate FAS using a simple two-group experimental design, would be to randomly divide a group of newly impregnated females into two groups. You would randomly designate one group as the experimental group and the other as the control group. The experimental treatment is to expose developing fetuses to alcohol by administering controlled doses to their mothers during pregnancy. Assuming the pregnancies of the treated animals are, with the exception of prenatal exposure to alcohol, as normal as possible, the obvious reference (control) group against which to compare the offspring of alcohol-treated mothers is a group of animals born of parents not given alcohol. If there are no other systematic differences between the treated and untreated groups except the alcohol treatment, it is reasonable to attribute any observed differences between the two groups to the alcohol treatment.

So far, the general plan for the experiment is uncomplicated: expose some pregnant mothers to alcohol, leave others untreated, and compare their offspring on some behavioral dimension. If we carried out this research plan would we be able to conclude that any systematic differences we observed between the offspring of alcohol-treated mothers and the offspring of untreated mothers was caused by the alcohol? If only it were that simple! *The real challenge of designing an experiment that can support a causal interpretation of the results begins when the specific procedural details of the experiment are planned.* In general, when we plan the procedures we intend to use to administer the treatment and collect the data, we must be careful not to violate a basic principle of experimental design: *isolate exposure to the experimental variables(s) as the only systematic difference between treated subjects and the control group(s) against which they will be compared.*

Controlling Unwanted Sources of Variation

Researchers are trained to be suspicious and vigilant, always concerned about the undetected presence of confounding variables that could compromise the unambiguous interpretation of their data. These variables, if not controlled, are loose cannons rolling around on the experimental deck. They can ruin the test of an interesting hypothesis by creating the illusion of an experimental effect when none exists. Within the FAS research problem, let us explore some possible sources of confounding variables.

Selecting subjects

We use laboratory rats for this experiment. They are relatively inexpensive, easy to house and feed, and have a short gestation period (21 to 22 days). We do not, however, want to use just any laboratory rats that happen to be handy. We would want to make sure that the animals that would be the mothers of our subjects had not participated in any previous experiment that could affect the health of their offspring. Researchers describe such previously unused subjects as **experimentally naive**. It is always best to use experimentally naive subjects, either human or animal, to avoid any residual effects on behavior from prior treatments.

Since there are systematic genetic and behavioral differences between various strains of laboratory rats, we should settle on one specific strain. Holding the heredity variable constant for both treated and untreated animals further increases the likelihood that no systematic difference other than from the manipulation of the experimental variable will affect the magnitude of the difference *between* the control and experimental groups. Equally important, it will also reduce the random, nonspecific variability present among the scores *within* these two groups. It is such within-group variability in data values that can make even what appears to be a relatively large difference between group means fail to achieve statistical significance (see chapter 4).

Ideally, we would also hold constant certain environmental variables, such as the rearing history of the mothers. If we buy adult animals from a supplier we must accept on faith that the animals had uniform rearing conditions. It would be better

Experimentally Naive: Description of subjects who have never before participated in an experiment.

to raise the animals in our own laboratory from breeding stock. This would spare the experimental animals the stress of shipping as well as afford us the opportunity to maintain strict control over their rearing conditions (such as the availability of food and water and the regulation of temperature, humidity, sanitation, and noise level). The tighter control we maintain over such rearing conditions, the more similar in constitution the mothers of our research animals are likely to be, and the less we have to worry that variables other than alcohol will act to influence the data.

Administering the treatment

We are faced with many decisions concerning the administration of the treatment in our hypothetical alcohol study. Will we put alcohol in the animals' drinking water for them to drink whenever they wish or will we administer a fixed dose directly to each of the alcohol-treated animals — say, through a gastric tube (a thin flexible tube passed through the mouth, down the esophagus, and into the stomach)? The former plan has the advantage of causing minimum trauma to the animal because no handling is required to administer the alcohol. The disadvantage is that the animals may not drink equivalent amounts of alcohol solution, and this could lead to wide variations in the dose levels.

Coaxing the animals to swallow a gastric tube creates a new problem. The stress on the pregnant female resulting from daily gastric-tube insertions may have consequences for the development of her babies quite apart from any influence of alcohol. Thus, if we used a gastric tube to administer the alcohol to the treated mothers and left the untreated mothers alone, the stress associated with the experimental treatment would be a confounding variable, a difference between the treated and untreated mothers in addition to exposure to alcohol.

There is also a possible confounding variable in the water-delivery method. Perhaps the animals who have alcohol in their water would drink less because they may not like the taste, or perhaps they would drink more because they like the "high" they get from the alcohol. In any event, to the extent that water-consumption patterns differ for treated and untreated animals, a confounding variable exists. In addition, alcohol is a depressant and has long been known to affect appetite. It is therefore also likely that the food-consumption patterns of the alcohol-treated animals would differ from the untreated controls, introducing another possible confounding variable. Of course, if we choose to administer both food *and* liquid by means of a tube, appetite would be eliminated as a confounding variable.

Remaining on guard for confounding influences

Mother rats are very busy around the time of birth. They have no help. They must deliver their pups and, rapidly, before the pups suffocate, remove the thin birth membrane in which the pups are wrapped. If she does not do this the pups will be deprived of oxygen and will die or, perhaps, be brain damaged. She must also assemble the pups and huddle over them to keep them warm because baby rats cannot regulate their own body temperature. Is an intoxicated female going to be able to function adequately in this situation? If she does not, how much of the damage to the pups will be caused by this postnatal neglect rather than by an effect of alcohol on prenatal development? Even if we stop the alcohol treatment a couple of days before birth, the possibility remains that the consequences of alcohol withdrawal could affect the competency of the mother's behavior. Researchers must observe their subjects closely and be sensitive to confounding influences that become apparent only after the experiment has begun. To the extent that confounding exists in the FAS experiment, we have a diminished capacity to make a causal connection between prenatal exposure to alcohol and the dependent variables(s) of the experiment.

Neutralizing Confounding Variables with Partially Treated Control Groups

From the preceding discussion it may appear that we are stuck in a morass of methodological problems. There are, however, solutions for neutralizing the confounding variables we have identified. Specifically, we can include **partially treated control groups**, subjects who have some or all of the experiences of the experimentally treated subjects except for the treatment itself. Including partially treated control groups in the design of an experiment allows us to distinguish effects arising from the procedures used to administer the treatment from effects that are the result of the treatment itself.

Partially Treated Control Groups: Subjects who have some or all of the experiences of the experimentally treated subjects except for the treatment itself.

The placebo control

Let us assume that we decide to administer a constant daily dose of alcohol to the experimental animals using a gastric tube. As noted above, the experience of receiving a gastric tube could, by itself, affect behavior apart from any alcohol delivered through it. To provide an appropriate reference group for the alcohol-treated animals we must therefore include in our experiment a group that receives a gastric-tube insertion and a volume of water equivalent to the volume of alcohol solution administered to the treated rats. Since both the alcohol-treated group and the control group would undergo the same stress of daily gastric tube insertion, any differences in the behavior of the offspring of these animals could be attributed to the exposure to alcohol itself rather than to the stress of the procedure that was used to administer the alcohol.

This type of partially treated control group is commonly referred to as a placebo (discussed in chapter 4) because subjects receive only elements of the treatment administration without receiving the treatment itself. The placebo control is especially important in research with humans because people tend to develop expectancies and assumptions about the effects a procedure will have on them. Inclusion of a placebo control group as well as an untreated group in an experimental design allows us to evaluate the experimental effect separately from a possible placebo effect.

Controlling for differences in subjects' experience

The potential that exists for the pups to experience different maternal care has already been discussed. The alcohol-treated mothers could be experiencing the symptoms of alcohol withdrawal whereas the untreated animals would not. To control for this confounding variable we must find a way to provide the same quality of maternal care for the pups born of alcohol-treated mothers that the pups born of untreated mothers are getting. The answer is what animal researchers call the *crossfoster control.* The strategy is to provide foster mothers to the pups of both groups by replacing biological mothers with lactating females who have themselves recently given birth. Notice how important it is to crossfoster *all* the pups, in both the alcohol- and partially treated control groups, to keep this experience constant for all subjects. As long as we give foster mothers to all the pups and thereby maintain crossfostering as a constant, we control for possible differences in the postnatal environment of the pups without introducing a new treatment variable.

Implementing this control group would require some planning to ensure an adequate supply of foster mothers. We could exchange mothers between untreated litters so that none of the pups of untreated females would be raised by their biological mothers, but we would have to have another source of lactating females to provide foster mothers to the pups of alcohol-treated females.

Controlling for differences in diet

To the extent that the pattern of food and water consumption differs systematically between treated and untreated mothers, the potential for confounding exists. In theory, there is a solution to this possible confounding variable but, in the context of this particular experiment, it would be somewhat difficult to implement.

We could create pairs of untreated and alcohol-treated mothers at the beginning of the experiment and link the amount of food and water we provide to the untreated animals to the consumption we observe in the experimental animals. In general, when the experience of a control subject is linked to a voluntary behavior of an experimental subject we have defined a **yoked control**. To set up a yoked control in the present context we would have to measure food and water consumption each day for each alcohol-treated female animal. On the next day, we would provide those exact amounts to the yoked controls matched to these animals. Thus, consumption patterns could be matched but would be one day out of phase.

Yoked Control: A subject whose treatment is linked to a voluntary behavior of an experimental subject.

A more technological solution for yoking the food and water consumption of animals was used by Joffe, Rawson, and Mulwick (1973). The experimental animals lived in a special chamber in which they had to press levers for the delivery of food, water, and light. Subjects in the control condition also lived in special chambers, but they did not have the same control over their supply of food, water, and light that the experimental animals had. Instead, every time an experimental animal pressed a lever, the precise consequence occurred in the chamber of the experimental animal's yoked control.

Of course, in the two methods of yoking food and water consumption we have described, there is no way to guarantee that the yoked control will eat and drink all the food and water allotted to them. If, for example, the alcohol treatment causes the experimental animals to eat more than the normal amount of food, there is no guarantee that, when given a larger-than-normal daily allotment of food, the yoked control will eat it all. This type of control group, while very useful in some research contexts, is unlikely to contribute much to the precision we are seeking in designing an animal model of FAS.

Controlling for subject expectancy effects and experimenter bias

The saying goes that "Too much knowledge can be a dangerous thing." In research, the danger is that intimate knowledge of an experiment, either on the part of subjects or experimenters, can give rise to speculations and beliefs about the methods and purpose of an experiment. The speculations and beliefs, in turn, have the potential to bias the results of the experiment. To explore the strategies researchers use to eliminate bias and protect the integrity of experiments, imagine that extraterrestrial invaders have control of earth's population and their scientists have decided to study the effects of maternal alcohol abuse on the behavioral development of human children in much the same way we have proposed studying the phenomenon in laboratory rats.

Single-blind methodology

Single-blind Methodology: Withholding methodological details of an experiment from subjects to avoid biasing their behavior.

Expectancy Effect: A bias in subjects that arises from some degree of knowledge about the methods and/or purpose of an experiment, or assumptions (correct or incorrect) about the experiment.

Single-blind methodology is a precaution to ensure that subjects remain unaware of any methodological details of an experiment that could generate an expectancy and thereby distort the results of an experiment. Its implementation is usually quite simple: Do not reveal to subjects the treatment condition to which they have been assigned. The alternative is to risk an **expectancy effect**, a bias that arises from some degree of knowledge about the methods and/or purpose of an experiment, or assumptions (correct or incorrect) about the experiment. For example, assume that the alien scientists take a random sample of expectant mothers and administer alcohol to some but not to others. The children of both groups are fostered to other caretakers at birth, and their behavioral development is monitored. If the children of the foster parents somehow found out their true parentage, alcoholic or nonalcoholic, that knowledge could affect subjects' expectations about their own future, their self-perception, ability to cope, and so on. Therefore it would be necessary to keep such information from the children to prevent the knowledge from influencing the experimental results as an additional (extraneous) variable.

Maintaining confidentiality

Informed Consent: A description of an experiment with enough detail for subjects to decide whether or not it is in their best interests to participate.

Researchers generally assume that expectancy effects will be a problem in human research and try to keep as much nonessential information from subjects as possible. Ethically, however, researchers must have the **informed consent** of human subjects before using them in an experiment. That is, the researchers are obligated to provide subjects enough information about the study for them to understand the potential the study has for objectionable, inconvenient, or unpleasant consequences. If, after being so informed, subjects freely declare their willingness to participate, the consent is informed. Outside of participating in a psychology experiment, your most likely experience with informed consent will be in connection with a medical procedure. After explaining the procedure to you, your physician will ask you to sign a document attesting to the fact that you were informed of the nature and risks of the procedure, and that you give permission for the physician to do the procedure.

Debriefing: Explaining an experiment to a subject upon its completion, including the nature and purpose of any deception that may have been used.

Even waiting until *after* a subject is tested before revealing any information about an experiment can influence experimental results. After an experiment, subjects undergo **debriefing**. The researcher explains the goals of the experiment to the subject, as well as the nature and purpose of any deception that may have been used. If the subject then talks about the experiment with potential future subjects, their expectancies are likely to influence their behavior when they serve as subjects. Yet, as with informed consent, ethical guidelines require researchers to debrief subjects.

Double-blind methodology

The subjects of experiments are not the only potential source of bias in a research environment. Experimenters themselves can, either consciously or unconsciously, allow their fears, hopes, expectations, and/or prejudices to affect how they conduct an experiment. We refer to the phenomenon as **experimenter bias**. **Double-blind methodology** controls experimenter bias in much the same way that single-blind methodology controls subject expectancy effects: by giving out information about the experiment on a need-to-know basis. Specifically, in a double-blind study both the subjects who generate the data and the person who collects the data have only enough knowledge of the experiment to enable them to fulfill their respective functions. All information other than the need-to-know details, such as subjects' treatment assignments or whether a treatment is real or a placebo, are withheld until the experiment is over. The application of double-blind methodology both neutralizes subject expectancy effects and, at the same time, assures the even-handedness of the experimenter's conduct. Let us assume the alien scientist expects the alcohol treatment of the parents to result in behavioral deficits in the children. Moreover, even though the knowledge is not necessary to carry out the data-collection phase of the experiment, the scientist happens to be aware of the parentage of each child in the experiment. Perhaps, as a consequence of having this knowledge, the alien has a bias, conscious or unconscious, that causes him (it?) to assess the development of the children of alcohol-treated parents more negatively than the evidence warrants.

The potential for experimenter bias is especially probable if the alien, like many human scientists, *wants* to find a specific pattern of results to enhance his prestige in the alien science community. Thus, subject expectations, as explained in the discussion of single-blind methodology, as well as the expectations of experimenters themselves, have the potential to bias research results. Only the careful application of single- and double-blind methodology can eliminate the threat of these biases. In general, the more dependent the data are on subjective assessments of behavior, the greater is the risk of experimenter bias. Conversely, the risk of experimenter bias is minimized when the data of an experiment are recorded as instrument readings or other objective measurements that are unlikely to be influenced by variability in human judgment. To avoid any chance of compromising an experimenter's objectivity, another person, who takes no part in the data-collection process, must safeguard all the subject assignment codes and treatment information.

A familiar example of a double-blind approach to a research problem can be seen in the clinical tests of fluoride toothpaste. Neither the subjects nor the dentists who examined them were aware of which toothpaste, fluoride or not, the subjects were using. If the subjects knew whether or not their toothpaste contained fluoride, the knowledge could have affected the thoroughness with which they brushed ("I don't have to brush well because the fluoride will prevent my having cavities!"). If the dentists knew which of the subjects they examined did or did not brush with a fluoride toothpaste, that knowledge could compromise the objectivity of their evaluations of the patient's teeth. For example, an irregularity on a tooth may be less likely to be classified as tooth decay if a subject is known to belong to the fluoride-treated group. With double-blind methodology in place, the researchers could confidently point to the effectiveness of the fluoride treatment without worrying

Experimenter Bias: The influence of an experimenter's fears, hopes, expectations, and/or prejudices on the conduct of the research.

Double-blind Methodology: Neither the subjects nor the experimenter know any details of the experiment that could bias their behavior.

that different brushing behavior on the part of the placebo and experimental subjects or different standards of tooth evaluation contributed to the reported experimental effect.

Internal Validity

Internal Validity: The determination that an obtained pattern of experimental results is a direct and unambiguous consequence of the experimental manipulation.

We describe the fluoride toothpaste experiment as having **internal validity**, the determination that an obtained pattern of experimental results is a direct and unambiguous consequence of the experimental manipulation (here, the presence or absence of fluoride). In general, to achieve internal validity experimenters must eliminate any influence on the dependent measure that can obscure, distort, or masquerade as an experimental effect. Researchers maximize the logical precision of their experiments by including all necessary control conditions and by executing all aspects of the experimental plan with careful attention to minute detail. To the extent that extraneous (confounding) variables threaten the internal validity of an experiment, the researcher's capability to render a meaningful and focused interpretation of the experimental results is diminished. (See Box 10–1 for a discussion of some threats to the internal validity of experimental research.)

In our earlier walk through a typical experiment we defined various control conditions that serve to enhance internal validity. The control conditions provided the standards of reference necessary to isolate the independent variable, maternal alcohol consumption, as the cause of abnormalities in offspring. (Of course, to explain the control of extraneous variables that would be necessary to achieve internal validity, we had to imagine a relaxation of the usual ethical restraints that are imposed on research with human subjects.) Only with the necessary controls in place would a researcher be assured of the validity of a causal inference linking maternal alcohol consumption to abnormalities in the offspring.

BOX Box 10–1

Some Threats to the Internal Validity of Laboratory Experiments

All of the threats to internal validity reviewed in this box have been mentioned in this or in earlier chapters as sources of extraneous variability in experiments. They are gathered together here to complement the chapter's discussion of internal validity.

Reactivity

Reactivity refers to the influence an observer has on the behavior of the subject being observed. If you think of how much harder you would try to excel in a sports competition if you knew your family and friends were in the gallery cheering, you will appreciate why the mere act of observing behavior can introduce an extraneous influence on the measurement of behavior. (The reactive behavior in the latter example is called *social facilitation*.)

One type of reactive behavior occurs when subjects behave according to their impressions of what the experimenter expects or wants. The cues subjects use to form their reactive posture are sometimes referred to as **demand characteristics**. For example, if a subject is interviewed to determine whether or not she is a heavy smoker and is then asked to give informed consent prior to being hypnotized, the subject could draw a conclusion that the intent of the hypnosis is to help her cut down or quit her smoking habit. The demand characteristics, an awareness of the experimenter's interest in smoking behavior and hypnosis, could create a subject expectancy and thereby bias the results of the experiment.

Even when researchers mask the true purpose of their experiments with clever deception, it may be impossible to eliminate demand characteristics entirely. Subjects can use cues to guide their behavior even when the cues bear no relation to the experiment. For example, a subject could interpret an experimenter's grimace as an expression of disfavor with his performance when the true cause is a physical ailment. Discussions with subjects after the experiment will usually reveal the presence of demand characteristics.

Demand Characteristics: Cues that lead subjects to have an impression of what an experimenter expects or wants to happen in a study.

The reliability of the stimulus delivery and the measuring instrument

The stimuli subjects respond to in a research environment and the sensitivity and accuracy of the instruments used to measure their responses can change over time and bias experimental results. It is therefore important to check apparatus periodically for proper operation. For example, consider an experiment in which a tape recorder plays a series of pure tones at a predetermined rate. Upon hearing a certain interval between the preceding note and the present one, the subject must press a key, which records the subject's reaction time. A careful experimenter would periodically check both the tape player (a worn motor, dirty head, or damaged tape could affect both the rate and the pitch of the tone delivery) and the key device for recording reaction time. A key that sticks or becomes sluggish toward the end of the experiment or a stimulus display that fails to cycle properly could sabotage the experiment.

Extraneous variability from inconsistent treatment administration

Failure to control precisely the manipulated values of the independent variable will introduce extraneous variability. In a worst-case scenario, the values of the independent variable could overlap among different treatment conditions to such an extent that a Type II error is practically guaranteed. For example, if dosages in a dose-response drug study were measured in a sloppy manner, some subjects in the low-dose group could conceivably get as much of the drug as some subjects in the high-dose group. Also, exposing subjects *within* a treatment condition to variable levels of an independent variable rather than a constant level will increase the variability of the subjects' performance within that treatment condition. Since excessive variability within treatment conditions makes an experimental effect more difficult to detect, you will no doubt recognize the loss of power (discussed in chapter 4) that could result from imprecise regulation of independent variable values.

Selective subject loss

Human subjects may decline to participate in an experiment by not showing up when scheduled to meet with the experimenter, by exercising their right to deny informed consent prior to the beginning of the experiment, or even by terminating their participation after the experiment is underway. If the subject loss is selective, as when only those who are desperate for the compensation they will receive for being subjects agree to participate fully, the selective loss can seriously distort the randomness of the sample.

It is possible for some treatments to place subjects at greater risk for health problems and result in a nonrandom pattern of subject loss. For example, in using animal subjects to screen a new tranquilizer for sedative action, animals assigned to a high-dose group would likely be more at risk for experiencing toxic side effects than animals receiving lower dosages. The result would be the loss of initial equivalence.

Experimenter bias

When an experimenter's expectation of finding a certain pattern of results is not effectively isolated from the data-collection process, experimenter bias can exist. Most of the time, the word *bias* has the connotation of voluntary favoritism or prejudice; in research, however, bias is probably more likely to be unintentional than intentional. Thus, we must introduce controls to guard against the *possibility* of bias even if we believe the researcher to be scrupulously objective.

Nonrandom assignment

As with experimenter bias, violations of random assignment procedures are usually unintentional. Of course, the violations are no less serious even if they are unintentional — as one embarrassed research assistant found out. The assistant was given the task of randomly dividing a cage of six very aggressive adult male laboratory rats. He reasoned, quite correctly, that his risk of being bitten would be minimized if he removed and rehoused only three animals from the cage. The three captured animals would be designated Group 1 and the remaining animals, who were able to avoid capture, would be Group 2. Had the procedural error not been discovered before the start of the experiment, the two groups would have lacked initial equivalence. Presumably, the three rats that remained in the original cage avoided capture by virtue of their greater speed and intimidating aggressive displays.

Contamination

Contamination of the subject pool usually refers to the spreading of information about an experiment by former participants to future participants. Subjects are usually told not to discuss the experiment with anybody else in the subject pool, but this behavior is impossible to control. Contamination can also be a problem in animal research. If an experimenter has a problem removing an animal from a cage for testing and thereby disturbs and upsets other animals that

Contamination (of the subject pool): The spreading of information about an experiment by former participants to future participants.

are also scheduled for testing, their behavior in the experiment can be affected by the incident.

Carryover effects

In some experimental designs (covered in chapter 12) subjects are tested two or more times rather than just once. If a subject's knowledge of an experiment from prior experience or a residual effect from the experience of receiving some treatment carries over to influence the subject's behavior on subsequent behavioral testing, a carryover effect exists. Sometimes the carryover effect is the very phenomenon of interest to the researcher, but at other times it is a confounding variable that must be controlled to preserve the internal validity of the experiment.

Omission of a key group from the experimental design

An experiment is internally valid only if its logical structure permits one to relate systematic variability in the dependent variable to a causal action of the independent variable. If a control group is missing from the design of an experiment, its internal validity cannot be documented because the possibility remains that some other variable (an extraneous variable) is the real force behind the observed pattern of experimental results. For example, drug studies usually include a placebo control to help distinguish a possible treatment effect from any effects that are consequences of the method of treatment administration. Unfortunately, defining appropriate control conditions in some research areas is far more subtle and challenging than the relatively straightforward placebo condition of drug research. In fact, even accomplished researchers are sometimes chagrined to discover that they have omitted an important control group from a study.

External Validity

Inevitably, the structure and control necessary to achieve internal validity comes with a price tag. Put simply, findings from the carefully controlled environment of the laboratory do not always generalize to more realistic environments. When we take a research problem into the laboratory, the specific characteristics of the subject population, the precise methods we use to administer the experimental treatment, and the measurement capability we have to assess the effects of the treatment may not resemble reality. As a result, internally valid experimental results can sometimes be very weak with respect to the insight they provide into the relationships that exist between variables in the real world. Consider, for example, the hypothetical study of maternal alcohol consumption. Women who abuse alcohol during pregnancy do not come from a single ethnic background (our animal subjects are all from the same strain), women are likely to drink a variety of alcoholic beverages (our rats would get diluted ethanol), and the amount of alcohol in the beverages (the dose levels) would probably vary widely over time and between different subjects (our rats would get controlled doses). What, you may rightly ask, does this highly contrived experimental situation, which used animals as subjects, have to do with patterns of real-life alcohol abuse in pregnant women and the effects on their children?

The price of strict methodological control, which is so necessary for internal validity, is often the erosion of external validity (defined in chapter 6 as the extent to which we can generalize the results of carefully controlled laboratory studies to understand behavior in real-life situations). Consider, for example, the hypothetical alien invader who did the alcohol experiment on pregnant humans. The alien's controlled manipulation of alcohol consumption and the crossfostering control procedure that was used to eliminate the contribution of confounding variables distorts the true patterns of alcohol abuse in pregnant women. To the extent that such experimental methods represent a caricature of the real-life problem, to the extent that the conditions of the experiment do not accurately reflect the events that place children at risk for developing FAS, the alien's ability to make meaningful generalizations from the experimental data to the real sociological problem of excessive alcohol consumption among pregnant women would be reduced.

To achieve *both* internal and external validity, in the initial phase of a research program one strategy is to sacrifice external validity for internal validity by maintaining very high levels of control. Once the behavioral phenomenon has been established in the laboratory, we then test for the phenomenon in a more realistic, less controlled setting to see if the results remain consistent with the original laboratory finding. If the results are consistent, we have internal validity by virtue of the earlier highly controlled laboratory experiments, and we have external validity from our experiments in more realistic, but less controlled, settings.

Pilot Work

In the remaining chapters of Part IIB we discuss how researchers apply various experimental designs to address research issues in the form of Basic Questions 4, 5, 6, and 7. But executing an experiment involves much more than selecting a design that is appropriate for answering a question. Before making the commitment of time, work, and money to a project, researchers usually attempt to rehearse the methods they will use in the research, the administration of the treatment conditions, and the collection of data. The preliminary work done before full-scale execution of the experiment is called **pilot work**. For example, a researcher may have a tentative operational definition of the dependent variable of a planned experiment (thickness of subcutaneous body fat) and must determine whether or not the measure is sensitive enough to respond to manipulated values of an independent variable (a program of high- versus low-impact aerobic exercise).

Similarly, it is often wise to pretest the treatment conditions of an experiment for their capacity to produce observable differences between differently treated subjects. For example, assume you intended to demonstrate that the acquisition of a learned response is more rapid under conditions of continuous reinforcement (reward every correct response) than under a fixed-ratio reinforcement schedule (reward only a specific proportion of correct responses). If the fixed-ratio schedule

Pilot Work: The preliminary work done before full-scale execution of the experiment.

specified reward delivery on 9 out of 10 correct responses, there could be a problem demonstrating a difference in response acquisition between the continuous and fixed-ratio groups. The reason is that rewarding 9 out of 10 correct responses is very close to the condition of continuous reinforcement.

In general, before committing to do a large-scale study with minimally different independent variable values, it is often useful to do some pilot work with the same values. A promising pilot result (say, a trend toward different behavioral responses to similar experimental conditions) would support the decision to proceed with a more intensive experimental investigation. But even if the pilot work does not reveal a trend, the decision to proceed may still be justified. Pilot work, which is usually on a small scale, is less likely to detect a subtle effect (that is, is more vulnerable to Type II error) than a larger-scale experiment. Ultimately, the researcher must weigh the potential fruitfulness of an experimental approach against the time, labor, and expense of running a large-scale experiment.

We also do pilot work to make sure the research equipment will work as planned, to train the researchers who will be administering the treatments (if the research is experimental), and/or to train the researchers who will be collecting the research data. Sometimes pilot work is a complete but small-scale version of the planned experiment. At other times pilot work may not include all the control groups that are planned for the complete experiment. The philosophy behind the latter approach is to do an initial study without sophisticated control conditions to see if the behavior of the subjects in the various experimental conditions differs. This avoids the commitment of time, money, and resources to a sophisticated study of a hypothetical experimental phenomenon until there is some evidence, imprecise and ambiguous though it may be, that there really is a phenomenon to study.

In the context of the fetal-alcohol research scenario, we may want to evaluate a particular amount and method of alcohol administration for its ability to produce behavioral or physiological indices of intoxication among the pregnant females and consequences for their offspring. That is, we may ask how effective our operationally defined independent variable is in producing a treatment effect.

Similarly, we may wish to evaluate the sensitivity of our dependent measures (the behavioral indices of an FAS syndrome in the animals) to manipulated levels of the independent variable (prenatal exposure to alcohol). Also, the pilot study offers an opportunity for the researcher to master technical skills, such as learning how to administer alcohol through a gastric tube. Assured that there is a phenomenon to investigate and that we have the expertise to carry out the experiment, we would then be concerned with designing a more sophisticated experiment to rule out confounding variables. If an effect observed in the pilot data failed to hold up after incorporating the appropriate controls, the failure would be evidence that a confounding variable rather than the alcohol caused the apparent treatment effect in the pilot study.

Knowing What Controls to Use

Perhaps the most difficult task a researcher faces is to design an experiment that can support an independent variable–dependent variable causal connection. There is no universal solution to ensure internal validity except to heed the following dictum:

> To gauge accurately the effect of an experimental variable on behavior it is necessary to have data from control subjects who do not experience the experimental condition but who, *in every other way*, are as identical as possible to those who do experience the experimental condition.

All the controls brought into the discussion of the alcohol example were governed by this basic principle. The principle, some creativity, and a basic familiarity with the accumulated knowledge of a research area is really all one needs to design internally valid experiments.

A search of the relevant literature, to learn how other researchers have worked with the variables of interest, is an indispensable part of preparing to design an experiment with all the appropriate control groups. Also, personal communications (by letter, telephone, or a visit) between students and scholars who have the same research interests can be tremendously beneficial to the course of a research project. Established researchers are usually more than happy to share their expertise with less experienced researchers.

When bad things happen to good scientists

Even if the design of an experiment is logically sound and even if the procedural details of the experimental method are carefully and expertly carried out, it is still possible for the data of an experiment to give an inaccurate view of reality. One cause of such a distortion was covered in chapter 4 as assignment error, an unlikely but possible failure of the random assignment of subjects to equalize the behavior potential of the various treatment and control groups.

Other problems that are typically uncontrollable and have been known to interfere with the running of an experiment include subjects not showing up for an experiment, terminating participation before the experiment is completed, illness among the subjects or experimenters, apparatus breakdown, unannounced fire drills during data collection, power/air-conditioning/heat disruptions, and so on. One strategy for coping with such unanticipated problems is for the experimenter to record detailed notes of all the problems encountered as the planning and execution of the experiment progress. Periodically, the list should be evaluated. If only a few unforeseen problems disturb the integrity of the experiment, it is reasonable for the experimenter to complete the study and simply report the disturbances in the final report. But if the disturbances severely compromise the integrity of the experiment, it is time to stop the experiment, take steps to avoid a repeat of the problems, and begin anew. Should you ever have to take such a step, you will find your detailed notes an excellent resource for identifying procedural difficulties.

Summary

In this chapter we introduced the concept of experimental design as a logical structure for examining the causal relationships between variables. After explaining the underlying logic of single-sample and two-sample experiments, we walked through a typical research scenario, the study of FAS, to give a feel for the types of design decisions, interpretive issues, and challenges that researchers must confront on a regular basis. These included subject selection, the need to hold some variables constant, solving technical problems in the administration of a treatment, neutralizing confounding variables with partially treated control groups, and controlling for subject expectancy effects and experimenter bias.

Some of the challenges researchers confront require skills (such as knowledge of subject matter, creativity, and insight) that are common to all problem-solving situations. In other instances, meeting the challenges of research requires specialized knowledge of methodological techniques to employ and insidious pitfalls to avoid. One measure of the quality of an experiment is its internal validity, the attribution of apparent treatment effects to a causal action of the independent variable. There are many threats to the internal validity of laboratory experiments, such as reactivity and demand characteristics, unreliable apparatus, inconsistent treatment administration, selective subject loss, contamination of the subject pool, and others (the complete discussion is in Box 10–1). Sometimes, however, in striving for internal validity we sacrifice external validity, the degree to which laboratory findings generalize to the real world. In doing research we must strive for a balance between internal and external validity.

As we prepare for the detailed coverage of experimental design in the coming chapters, it is important to keep in mind that matching a research question to a design that is appropriate for answering that question is only the beginning of a research effort. Pilot work, the preparation that precedes full-scale execution of a project, is an important ingredient for success in research in much the same way that rehearsal allows actors and stage personnel to refine their performances prior to the opening night of a play. Designing even a "simple" experiment requires a great deal of thought and attention to detail.

Key Terms

Contamination, p. 180

Debriefing, p. 176

Demand Characteristics, p. 179

Designs, p. 169

Double-Blind Methodology, p. 177

Expectancy Effect, p. 176

Experimentally Naive, p. 172

Experimenter Bias, p. 177

Informed Consent, p. 176

Internal Validity, p. 178

Partially Treated Control Groups, p. 174

Pilot Work, p. 182

Single-Blind Methodology, p. 176

Single-Sample Study, p. 169

Treatment Effect, p. 168

Two-Sample Experiment, p. 171

Two-Treatment Experiment, p. 171

Yoked Control, p. 175

Chapter Exercises

1. What are the important differences between descriptive research and experimental research?

2. Why is the single-sample design not considered a true experiment?

3. Why do researchers sometimes turn to the study of animal models?

4. What characteristic(s) of a true experiment support the interpretation that different values of the independent (experimental) variable *caused* differences between treatment groups?

5. Explain how extraneous sources of variation, such as those that are unavoidably introduced as a part of the treatment administration, can distort the results of an experiment and the accuracy of our interpretation of experimental data.

6. How does including a group of partially treated controls in the design of an experiment help to rule out extraneous sources of variation as the cause of an observed difference between treatment conditions? Give some examples of the kinds of partially treated controls researchers use.

7. What is accomplished by introducing single- and double-blind controls into the design of an experiment?

8. Differentiate between internal validity and external validity. Why is one kind of validity sometimes achieved at the expense of the other?

9. If an experiment has only two groups, one that receives exposure to the experimental treatment and one that does not, what steps can we take to maximize internal validity?

10. Explain the role pilot work plays in the conduct of experimental research.

11. Even if a researcher follows all the rules for designing internally valid experiments and carefully executes a procedurally sound experimental approach to a problem, success in obtaining an accurate assessment of the effect of the experimental treatment is not 100% guaranteed. Why?

Proposal Assignment 10: What Controls Do You Need?

In chapter 10 you saw how difficult and detailed a task it is to design an internally valid experiment. To eliminate rival explanations of the results (those that are not tied to the experimental manipulation) we must include all appropriate controls. List the control conditions you have decided should be included and explain what rival explanation each control condition takes into account.

A good way to go about completing this assignment is to imagine how a nitpicking critic would respond to your proposal. Assume that your results support your hypothesis. Have you left yourself vulnerable to an attack on your conclusions? Another source of information for completing this assignment is in Part III. If you read the chapter that has subject matter similar to your proposed project, you may gain valuable insights into the types of controls you must consider for your project.

If you have chosen a correlational study, the issue of controls is somewhat different. Discuss possible alternatives that may be the reason for the correlation other than a cause-and-effect relationship. For example, at the end of chapter 3 we discussed the correlation between gender and wages and pointed out that a third variable, number of years on the job, could explain why differences in wages are correlated with the gender variable.

C H A P T E R

11

Two-Treatment Designs with Independent Observations

As we saw in the last chapter, for experimental data to answer the question(s) of interest to the researcher, the arrangement of the experimental and control conditions must conform to a predetermined and carefully constructed research plan or *design*. Our coverage of experimental designs begins with a relatively simple one: the two-treatment experiment with independent observations. However, we first review our use of the terms *treatment condition, between-subject design, within-subject design* and introduce two new terms: *independent observations* and *correlated observations*.

A treatment condition is *any* experimenter-controlled state to which a particular group of subjects is exposed. Thus, if the design of a two-treatment experiment includes an untreated control group and a group that receives an experimental treatment, both groups experience a treatment condition even though the treatment for one group is really no treatment at all. Likewise, a partially treated control condition, such as a placebo-treated group, is a treatment condition even though exposure to the full experimental manipulation is withheld.

Within-subject designs call for administering two or more different treatment conditions to the same subjects on different occasions. Because the same subjects provide the data for all treatment conditions, it is possible to evaluate the association (correlation) between the scores they obtain under one treatment condition and the scores they obtain under another. The data of within-subject experiments are **correlated observations** because of their potential for association. Conversely, in a between-subject experiment each treatment is administered to a different group of subjects, so any difference across treatment conditions is in the form of a difference in behavior *between* the subjects in one group and the subjects in the other. Since there is no reason for the data of subjects in one treatment condition to be associated with the data of different subjects assigned to other treatment conditions, we refer to the data of between-subject experiments as **independent observations**.

Correlated Observations: The data of within-subject experiments, in which repeated measures are taken of the same subjects.

Independent Observations: The data of between-subject experiments, in which subjects experience only one treatment condition.

The Two-Treatment Between-Subject Design

The general strategy of a two-treatment between-subject design is to expose each of two initially equivalent groups of subjects to a different treatment condition, collect data, and then examine the data for evidence of behavioral differences between the two differently treated groups. Table 11–1 shows 20 subjects randomly split into 10 subjects per treatment. (As discussed in Box 4–2, the assignment of

Treatment Condition 1	Treatment Condition 2
S_1	S_{11}
S_2	S_{12}
S_3	S_{13}
S_4	S_{14}
S_5	S_{15}
S_6	S_{16}
S_7	S_{17}
S_8	S_{18}
S_9	S_{19}
S_{10}	S_{20}

Table 11–1. Subject assignment for the two-treatment between-subject experimental design. The illustration depicts 20 subjects who have been randomly split into two groups of 10.

equal numbers of subjects to the two treatment groups is the more common approach, but equal group sizes are not required for between-subject designs.) The subscripted Ss in Table 11–1 represent individual subjects 1 to 20.

The custom of displaying the data of a two-treatment between-subject experiment as two columns of values sometimes leads to an erroneous tendency to view each row of the data table as a pair of scores that "go together." It is important to remember, however, that in the case of a between-subject experiment, the row of the table on which a data value happens to be recorded is arbitrary. Only column placement (Treatment 1 versus Treatment 2) is relevant, so any positive or negative association that appears to exist between pairs of values on the same row of the table must be regarded as a meaningless coincidence.

The assumption of initial equivalence between differently treated groups is fundamental to the between-subject design. Specifically, we assume that any systematic differences among the subjects (such as differences in intelligence, aptitudes, physical characteristics, personality, or prior experience) that could affect the recorded values of a dependent variable are equally represented in all treatment groups. We assume that the random assignment of subjects to different treatment conditions achieves initial equivalence, and this permits us to attribute any significant between-treatment behavioral differences to the experimental manipulation.

Answering Questions with the Two-Treatment Between-Subject Design

The two-treatment between-subject design is suitable for answering a variety of different research questions. For example, we can:

1. Compare an untreated or partially treated control group to an experimental group (Basic Question 4).

2. Compare qualitative Condition 1 to qualitative Condition 2 (Basic Question 5).

3. Compare quantitative Condition 1 to quantitative Condition 2 (Basic Question 6).

An Untreated Control Group versus an Experimental Group

One use of the two-treatment between-subject design is to address research problems in the form of Basic Question 4: Will introducing subjects to a specific change in an otherwise standard context cause their behavior to change?

In its simplest form, Basic Question 4 asks for a comparison between subjects who do not receive any exposure to an experimental variable (the control group) and subjects who do receive exposure to an experimental variable (the experimental group). You will recall from chapter 5 that the experimental manipulation may take two forms:

1. Introduce a variable that *is not* normally present and evaluate the effect of its presence on a behavior.

2. Remove a variable that *is* normally present and evaluate the effect of its absence on a behavior.

For example, assume that you decide to conduct a study to evaluate the effectiveness of a tutoring program being run by the Office of Student Services at your college. We will further assume that because the demand for tutors exceeds their availability, assigning tutors to students is done through a lottery system. The study will compare the final examination grades of 10 students who were randomly chosen to be assigned tutors for four hours per week to 10 students who applied to the program but were not assigned tutors.

Referring to the terminology used in the statement of Basic Question 4, if we define doing without the services of a tutor to be the standard context of a particular college scene, then the tutoring represents the experimental variable being introduced into the standard context. If, on the other hand, we are dealing with a school at which the availability of tutors is the norm, we would define the availability of tutors as the standard context and the lack of tutors to be the removal of a variable that is normally present. One question asks whether the introduction of tutoring services is working to produce an improvement in academic performance and the other asks if the withholding of services has had a negative impact on academic performance. However you view the issue, the comparison is still *between* students who receive tutoring and students who receive no tutoring.

A Partially Treated Control Group versus an Experimental Group

Another use of the two-treatment between-subject design calls for comparing a partially treated control group to an experimental group. Because this variation also addresses Basic Question 4, it is really just a refinement of the untreated control group versus experimental group design described above and should not be thought of as a fundamentally different design. To understand why the use of a partially treated control group represents a refinement, recall a research dictum first introduced in chapter 10:

> To gauge accurately the effect of an experimental variable on behavior, it is necessary to have data from control subjects who do not experience the experimental condition but who, *in every other way*, are as identical as possible to those who do experience the experimental condition.

To adhere strictly to this fundamental methodological principle, we often need more than just an untreated control group as a standard of comparison for a treated group. When, in a two-group experiment, some aspect of the treatment administration is likely to influence behavior *by itself* (that is, even in the absence of the actual experimental variable) it is desirable to expose the single group of control subjects to as many components of the treatment administration as possible short of exposing them to the treatment itself. Such a group, as we saw in chapter 10, is referred to as a partially treated control group to distinguish it from an untreated control group — which, by definition, is not subjected to any manipulation at all. Placebo and yoked controls are categorized as partially treated controls because they receive many of the experiences associated with the treatment administration without being exposed to the experimental variable itself.

Controlling extraneous variables

It is especially important to include partially treated controls in studies in which the administration of the experimental treatment may be considered invasive, such as experiments that require hypodermic injections or surgical procedures. If, for example, an experiment called for injecting laboratory animals with a behavior-altering substance, it would be desirable for *both* the control and experimental groups to have an injection experience. The typical procedure is to inject the experimental subjects with the drug dissolved or suspended in its vehicle (a water or oil medium, depending on whether the drug is water- or lipid-soluble), whereas the control group is "treated" with the vehicle alone (see chapter 20).

If only the subjects in the experimental group of a two-treatment drug study receive injections and the subjects assigned to the control group remain totally undisturbed, any effect resulting from the treatment administration itself, such as the stress associated with capturing, holding, and injecting the animal, would be confounded with the effect of the drug. The confounding variables, in turn, open the door to explanations for behavioral differences that have nothing to do with the manipulation of the independent variable.

Although we used the example of a placebo control in a drug study to illustrate how partially treated control groups can neutralize confounding, the use of partially treated controls extends to all types of research. Earlier, for example, we described an experiment to evaluate a tutoring program by comparing the performance of tutored subjects to a group of untutored controls. Note that the experience of the two groups, tutoring versus no tutoring, differs by more than contact or no contact with a tutor. The tutored students have two separate dimensions of experience: four hours of structured study time *plus* the personal supervision of a tutor. Perhaps the study time *by itself* would produce a beneficial effect on grades, without personal contact with a tutor. To neutralize the confounding between the study-time and tutor variables we could require the nontutored subjects to report weekly to the Tutoring and Advisement Center along with the tutored students. They would be required to work independently on their assignments in a private room for the same amount of time that the other students spend working with a tutor. By equating as many experiences as possible for the two treatment groups, except for the opportunity to interact with a tutor, we can have greater confidence that any differences in student performance that may occur on the final examination are a result of the tutors' ability to clarify and communicate the course content rather than just the additional structured study time in a specific environment.

In general, whether animals or humans are the subjects of a research project, the only way we can rule out rival explanations for an observed phenomenon that are tied to elements of the treatment administration is to include a control group that is treated just like the experimental group except for the experimental treatment itself. Although it is not always possible to neutralize confounding totally, the more nearly we approach that ideal the more confident we can be in an interpretation that links our research results solely to an action of the experimental treatment.

Limitations of the two-treatment design with a partially treated control group

The use of a partially treated control group in a two-treatment experiment provides a standard against which to compare the behavior of the experimental group and, at the same time, allows us to neutralize the possible contributions of confounding variables. But, in an experiment that is limited to two groups, we obviously cannot have more than one control group (say, both an untreated control and a placebo control) if we also wish to include an experimental group. As subsequent chapters show, this is not a limitation of multiple-treatment experiments. In a three-treatment drug study, for example, we could have an untreated control group, a placebo control group, and a drug-treated group. With data for all three groups, we would be able to *test* for the existence of a placebo effect by comparing the untreated group to the placebo group. We would not have to *assume* that a placebo effect exists, as we must do in a placebo-group versus experimental-group two-treatment study.

Qualitative Condition 1 versus Qualitative Condition 2

Making a comparison between two qualitatively different treatment conditions is the third use of the two-treatment between-subject design. The essence of the research issue is embodied in Basic Question 5: *Will introducing subjects to qualitatively different conditions cause them to exhibit systematic differences in behavior?*

The distinguishing feature of experiments that address Basic Question 5 is that they focus on the relative effects of two qualitatively different experimental treatments on behavior rather than on the effects of a single experimental treatment relative to an untreated (or partially treated) control. For example, pretend that we wish to compare the academic performance of students who are assigned tutors to the academic performance of students who are issued student study guides to supplement their primary texts. As in all versions of the between-subject design, we assume that students are randomly assigned to one or the other condition.

In this type of experiment notice that neither group really fits the description of a control group: Each group is exposed to a variable (personal tutoring versus self-instruction with a study guide) qualitatively different from the variable to which the other group is exposed. It is possible *arbitrarily* to designate one treatment group as a control group when one of the conditions is the procedural norm, as when self-instruction with a study guide is the traditional practice and personal tutoring is an innovation that is being tried on an experimental basis. Even if one of the treatment groups in this variation of the between-subject design is referred to as a control group, the study still addresses Basic Question 5 rather than Basic Question 4 because neither group is untreated.

Quantitative Condition 1 Versus Quantitative Condition 2

The fourth use of the two-treatment between-subject design is treatment with different quantitative levels of the same experimental variable. The issue is captured in Basic Question 6: *Will introducing subjects to quantitatively different conditions cause them to exhibit systematic differences in behavior?*

The two-treatment experiment used to address research problems in the form of Basic Question 6 can also fit Basic Question 4. Specifically, in a two-treatment experiment, if the quantitatively manipulated levels (Basic Question 6) of an independent variable are set at zero and some nonzero value, it is reasonable to label the group receiving zero exposure as an untreated control. Thus, as a comparison between untreated and treated groups, the study also fits the form of Basic Question 4. On the other hand, if two treatment conditions are defined by two quantitatively different settings of an independent variable that are *both* nonzero, there is no untreated control group in the experiment. Instead, as expressed in Basic Question 6, the focus is on the relative effects on behavior of two quantitatively different exposures to the same independent variable.

Continuing with the tutoring scenario, we could ask whether students who are assigned to attend two tutoring sessions per week will show a level of academic performance different from that of students assigned to attend only one session per week. The different experiences of the two groups of students would be quantitative because, presumably, more instruction of the course material occurs in two tutoring sessions than in one. The independent variable is therefore quantitative and the question we seek to answer from a comparison between the two groups fits the form of Basic Question 6. Table 11–2 presents some hypothetical data to illustrate the type of quantitative comparison just described.

GROUP 1 Tutored Once Per Week		GROUP 2 Tutored Twice Per Week	
S_1	78	S_{11}	80
S_2	73	S_{12}	82
S_3	66	S_{13}	76
S_4	83	S_{14}	94
S_5	73	S_{15}	88
S_6	88	S_{16}	72
S_7	70	S_{17}	91
S_8	74	S_{18}	85
S_9	82	S_{19}	86
S_{10}	63	S_{20}	76
$\bar{X} = 75$		$\bar{X} = 83$	
SD = 7.82		SD = 7.09	

Table 11–2. The final examination grades, means, and standard deviations for two groups of students ($n = 10$ per group) who received either one or two tutoring sessions per week.

The Two-Treatment Experiment and Type II Error

A Type II error in an experiment (as we saw in chapter 4) is failing to find an effect on behavior from manipulating an independent variable when, in fact, the variable really does influence behavior. One feature of any experiment that can lead to making a Type II error is selecting an inappropriate level of the independent variable for a treatment. For example, assume that a psychiatrist planned a two-treatment experiment (placebo versus experimental) to evaluate a new antianxiety drug. Further assume that the drug really is effective, but the psychiatrist selected a dose level that was not strong enough to produce a therapeutic effect. In the latter case a Type II error is guaranteed: A truly effective treatment would appear to be ineffective.

Whereas the results of any experiment can give a misleading view of reality if the values of an independent variable are inappropriately set, two-treatment experiments are especially vulnerable. The reason is quite simple. In a two-treatment experiment we are restricted to setting only one level of the independent variable (to address an issue in the form of Basic Question 4) or two levels of the independent variable (to address issues in the form of Basic Questions 5 and 6). By comparison, when an experimenter sets several different levels of an independent variable (experiments with multiple treatment conditions are the subject of chapter 13), it is less likely that he or she would set all the levels of the independent variable inappropriately. One or more dose levels could be too low to register an effect, but probably not all. Some dose levels could be too similar quantitatively for them to cause different effects, but probably not all. Thus, in terms of avoiding Type II error, the choices we make in setting the levels of the independent variable are more crucial in a two-treatment experiment than when selecting several levels for a multiple-treatment experiment. In this regard, pilot work, a key preparatory step for all types of research, is particularly valuable in determining the optimum independent variable settings in a two-treatment experiment.

How Many Subjects Are Needed?

Once you have designed an experiment to address your research problem, operationally defined the independent and dependent variables, and worked out procedural details, one more important element must be in place before you can run your experiment: the matter of sample size. "How do I know how many subjects to run in my experiment?" is one of the most common questions asked by students who are developing a research proposal. Unfortunately, there is no simple answer to this question.

There are, however, some considerations that should be weighed carefully before setting the sample size of an experiment. One has to do with the *precision of the dependent variable*. Precision is reflected in how exclusive the changes in the dependent variable are with respect to changes in the independent variable. The ideal circumstance (and one seldom achieved) is to use a dependent variable that is affected only by the particular independent variable you happen to be manipulating.

The second consideration is the *sensitivity of the dependent variable*. The issue of sensitivity concerns the extent to which changes in the independent variable will be reflected in changing values of the dependent variable. To clarify, assume that a test uses a special chemical compound to detect the presence of a specific enzyme in the blood. The test is **sensitive** if the compound will react to very small amounts of the enzyme in a blood sample, and the test is **precise** if the compound reacts only to the one specific blood enzyme.

The third consideration is the *difference between manipulated settings of the independent variable*. In general, the more extreme the set values of the independent variable are from each other, the more likely there is to be a noticeable effect on the dependent measure. For example, if you intend to compare the performance of two groups on a task as a function of different incentive levels, the promise of $10 versus $100 on successful completion of the task is more likely to result in a detectable difference in level of motivation and vigor of performance than potential payoffs of $10 versus $11.

A fourth consideration is the *behavioral characteristics of the subjects*. If subjects are known to differ substantially with respect to a behavioral measure, there will likely be extensive variability among the data values for reasons unrelated to any action of the experimental treatment. This normal behavioral diversity would tend to mask an experimental effect, especially if the effect is weak. In such a case it is necessary to use a relatively large number of subjects to avoid a Type II error. Conversely, if subjects tend to be similar with respect to a behavioral measure, the effect of an experimental treatment will be more easily noticed when we compare experimental and control conditions, so fewer subjects will be required to maintain power.

In chapter 4 power was defined as the capacity to detect an effect of the independent variable on the dependent variable (that is, a treatment effect) when one truly exists. Experimental treatments vary in the power they have to produce a significant change in behavior: Some produce effects that are quite dramatic and others produce only subtle effects. The greater the potential a treatment has to affect behavior and the more precisely and sensitively we can measure its impact on behavior, the fewer subjects we need to be able to document the effect scientifically. Conversely, the more subtle a treatment effect is and the less precision and sensitivity we have to measure it, the more subjects we need to document the effect.

One way to conceptualize power is to draw an analogy from the study of sound detection. Let us assume that we are interested in studying how loud a sound has to be before a person with normal hearing would be able to detect it. The ability to detect a sound obviously depends, among other things, on the volume of the sound and the level of background noise present when the sound is turned on. The softer a sound is and/or the louder background noise level is, the more difficult it is to detect the sound. Conversely, the louder a sound is and/or the softer background noise level is, the easier it is to detect the sound.

We can equate the level of background noise in a sound-detection study to the random, unsystematic, extraneous factors that operate in an experiment outside our control and/or awareness. Undue "noise" from random factors will increase the variability in our dependent-variable measurements and will tend to mask relatively subtle treatment effects, just as a relatively high level of background noise will tend to mask an otherwise detectable sound. Naturally, a loud sound or a powerful treatment effect is less likely to be obscured by noise.

How can we possibly evaluate the power of our treatment condition to affect our dependent behavioral measure, and thereby prepare to use a relatively small or large sample size, before we have ever run the experiment? One possible solution lies in searching the literature for relevant publications to see what other investigators have used with success when they have done experiments similar to the one you are planning. As you read reports of studies that used independent and/or dependent variables that are similar or, perhaps, even identical to the ones you intend to use, take note of the sample sizes that were used and the magnitude of the experimental effects.

In the absence of information from the literature, it is often helpful to do pilot work (discussed in chapter 10) and get an indication of the level of "noise" (variability of behavior among subjects who get the same treatment) you are likely to encounter in your experiment as well as an indication of the capacity of the experimental treatment to affect behavior. Of course, sometimes practical considerations (money, time, space, the availability of subject volunteers, and the like) force decisions of sample size on us, and in such instances we must simply do the best we can with the available resources.

What Do the Data Mean?

At the completion of an experiment there is a sense of anticipation, an eagerness to immerse oneself in the data to determine what they mean and to find the answers to the research objectives of the experiment. Every set of experimental data has the potential to document new information — evidence of a causal relationship never previously known or understood by the scientific community. A researcher might sift through data to look for some individual score values that stand out from the others, or even try to compare the raw data of different subjects from different treatment conditions. But, to repeat an important point made in chapter 4, raw research results usually fail to project a clear meaning because there is usually too much information to assimilate and interpret in an objective manner. The exceptions are clear-cut cases in which the magnitude of the experimental effect is very large and easily noticed.

To overcome our information-processing limitations when confronted with a large and/or complex collection of data, and to gather evidence that reflects on the accuracy of the experimental hypothesis, we must first subject the raw research results to statistical analysis. Only then is the important information that resides in a complex set of experimental data likely to be revealed in a form we can grasp and interpret, and only then will we be able to render a meaningful and defensible answer to the question, "What do the data mean?"

Statistics as an ally

Even though you are aware of the important role the statistical analysis of data plays in the research process, you would probably admit to some lack of enthusiasm for stepping through the mathematical procedures of an actual statistical analysis. Students initially express attitudes about doing statistical analyses that range from bland acceptance to outright distress, and we are delighted when students learn to appreciate the value of statistical analysis. If you are convinced that doing a statistical analysis must be a painful experience, your attitude probably stems from your earlier academic training in the methods of data analysis, at which time you were probably limited to analyzing data from assigned problems and exercises. Once you are in the position of having to analyze the data of your very own research, you will be more likely to view statistical analysis as a valuable and helpful ally rather than an unpleasant chore. This is especially true in the present age of computers, which make the statistical analysis of data relatively quick and easy.

Computers, however, have their limitations: Despite the savings in work and time, no computer is capable of weighing the considerations that dictate the proper statistical test to use for the analysis of a given set of data. Any numbers you feed into a computer for processing by a data-analysis program will, in general, be accepted, but the output is likely to be meaningless unless the program in residence is appropriate for the analyzing the input. (The popular acronym GIGO — "Garbage in, garbage out" — reflects this limitation of computers.) The responsibility is still yours to use the computer program that is appropriate for analyzing your data. Toward this end, if the curriculum at your school requires you to take statistics before rather than together with research methods, we urge you to review relevant portions of your old statistics text whenever you feel it is necessary.

Plan ahead

The decision concerning which statistical analysis is appropriate for your data should be made *before* the data are collected, not after. Thinking about data processing as a part of the total research plan guarantees that once you have completed collecting your data, an analytical approach is indeed available that will enable you to find the answers you are looking for. Researchers who fail to include data analysis as part of their overall planning and strategy may find their data unsuitable for testing their hypotheses. As careful as researchers try to be, they sometimes fail to neutralize confounding variables with appropriate control conditions. As a result, data are sometimes useless for retrieving specific kinds of information, no matter what statistical test is employed. Logical flaws, either in research design or methodological procedures, are more likely to become apparent early enough to correct them if the planning of the research project includes the consideration of an appropriate analysis for the research data. Not all scientists are expert statisticians, and they frequently consult with other scientists who are. Students should likewise feel free to consult with more advanced students and faculty to evaluate their intended uses of statistical analysis.

Analyzing and Displaying the Data of Two-Treatment Experiments

The analysis and subsequent interpretation of data are greatly simplified if recordkeeping has been orderly and the data can be clearly displayed. Thus we shall emphasize the conventions that are observed for displaying research data in tables and figures as well as the considerations that dictate the kind of analysis that should be applied to different types of research data.

Data Analysis Options for Two-Treatment Between-Subject Experiments

The primary consideration in choosing the correct statistical approach to your data should be: What question do you wish to answer with the information the statistical procedure will extract from the raw data? For example, in the present context of two-treatment experimental designs, the mission is simply to contrast the effect(s) of two different treatment conditions on behavior and evaluate the differences for statistical significance.

Two statistical tests are widely used to compare two treatment conditions. One is a *parametric* test (the *t* test), and the other is a *nonparametric* test (the Mann–Whitney U test). The *t* test evaluates the magnitude of the difference between the treatment means for significance, whereas the Mann–Whitney statistic assesses the degree of overlap between the ranked data of Treatment 1 versus Treatment 2. The less overlap, the more pronounced the treatment effect. Statistical tests that are classified as parametric tend to have several underlying assumptions about the variable under study, such as the requirement that the distribution be normal (bell-shaped) and the scaling be interval or ratio. As a class, nonparametric tests do not require most of the assumptions of the parametric tests, but they tend to be less powerful. Fortunately, the Mann–Whitney U test is an exception to this general characterization of nonparametric statistics: Its results are almost always consistent with the results of its parametric cousin, the *t* test.

Summarizing Research Results

Statistical analyses (such as the *t* test) and graphic displays (such as histograms and line graphs) are ways to present and make comprehensible the information contained in a set of experimental results. Figure 11–1 plots the mean final examination scores shown in Table 11–2 (75 and 83) against the values of the independent variable values of the experiment (one versus two tutoring sessions per week) in the form of a histogram. According to convention, the dependent variable (Y) is assigned to the vertical axis (the ordinate), and the independent variable (X) is assigned to the horizontal axis (the abscissa). Thus the dependent variable, EXAMINATION SCORES, is the label of the Y axis of the graph (Figure 11–1), and the independent variable, TUTORING SESSIONS PER WEEK, is the label of the X axis.

The top of each histogram bar in Figure 11–1 is located at the value of the mean (75 and 83) on the vertical axis. In addition, we have included an interval of one standard error unit (reviewed in Box 4–3) above and below the top of each histogram bar (± 2.47 and ± 2.24, respectively). In general, the less standard-error intervals around treatment means overlap, the more likely it is that the difference between the treatment means is statistically significant. In Figure 11–1 the intervals do not overlap at all: The top of the interval for Condition 1 (77.47) is lower than the bottom of the interval for Condition 2 (80.76). This is consistent with the significant results of the *t* test for the Table 11–2 data: the computed value of the *t* statistic equals -2.40, which is more extreme than the -2.101 critical value of *t* (from the *t* table) with df = 18 and, α, the level of significance, set at .05.

Did you notice that the *t* statistic has a negative value? It is the *magnitude* of the difference between the treatment means and how extreme (far from zero) the

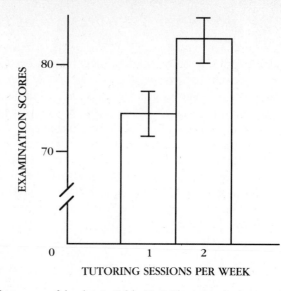

Figure 11–1. A histogram of the data in Table 11–2. The intervals above and below the treatment means (at the top of each bar) represent plus and minus one standard error unit.

computed value of t is that is the determinant of statistical significance, not the *sign* of the difference. The data of Table 11–2 show mean values of 75 and 83, and $(\bar{X}_1 - \bar{X}_2) = (75 - 83) = -8$. If the columns of data representing the results of the two treatment conditions were reversed from their appearance in Table 11–2, the difference between the means would have been $+8$: $(\bar{X}_1 - \bar{X}_2) = (83 - 75) = 8.00$. In this case the t value from the analysis would have been positive $(+2.40)$.

Summary

The chapter began with a review of some terminology (experiment, experimental design, treatment condition, independent groups, and between-subject design) and continued with a discussion of the role of random assignment in achieving initial equivalence between groups of subjects. We then explored the capacity of two-treatment between-subject experimental designs to address research issues in the form of Basic Questions 4, 5, and 6. The types of two-treatment experiments discussed include comparing an untreated control group to an experimental group, comparing a partially treated control group to an experimental group, comparing two qualitatively different conditions, and comparing two quantitatively different conditions. In addition to highlighting the capacity of the designs to answer questions, we also stressed the necessity to control for extraneous variables and the importance of an adequate sample size for statistical power. We then focused on the task of determining what experimental data mean. Both statistical and visual displays of data were discussed and encouraged as a means for revealing and communicating the information residing in data.

Key Terms

Correlated Observations, p. 189
Independent Observations, p. 189

Chapter Exercises

1. In a two-treatment experiment, what does it mean to describe the observations (data) collected under Treatment Condition 1 as being *independent* of the observations collected under Treatment Condition 2?

2. Explain how the achievement of both independent observations and initial equivalence is tied to the procedure for assigning subjects to the different treatment conditions?

3. Why are two-treatment experimental designs with independent observations also called between-subject designs?

4. Explain the advantage of including partially treated as opposed to untreated controls in the design of an experiment.

5. What is accomplished by subjecting raw research data to formal statistical analysis? Explain the importance of statistical analysis to the research process. (In addition to this chapter, you may wish to reread sections of chapter 4 in preparing your answer.)

6. What are two important considerations that must be carefully evaluated before applying a statistical procedure to raw research data?

7. What are the consequences of choosing an inappropriate statistical test for your data?

8. Why is it so important to plan the statistical approach to your data before the experiment is even run?

9. Which of the seven basic questions can be answered by research of a descriptive nature and which require experiments?

10. Why is it so important to assign subjects randomly to the different treatment conditions when setting up a between-subject experiment? (This issue was also discussed in chapter 4.)

11. What characteristics of the data of a two-treatment experiment would cause us to analyze the data using a nonparametric statistical alternative to the *t* test?

12. In the experiment represented in Table 11–2, the experimental hypothesis is that Group 2 will score higher on the final examination than Group 1. Using your statistics text as a resource, do a *t* test and a Mann–Whitney U test on the data of Table 11–2. What do the data mean? Do the results support the experimental hypothesis? Does it make any difference which treatment condition (tutored once per week versus tutored twice per week) is designated Treatment Condition 1 and which is designated Treatment Condition 2?

Proposal Assignment 11: Drawing Figures

In Proposal Assignment 4a you operationally defined the independent and dependent variables in your proposed experiment. Now use these variable names as labels for the X and Y axes of a figure. The first step is to make up the means for your conditions (*not* raw data) that are consistent with the hypothesis you stated in Proposal Assignment 3. Then draw two figures: a bar graph (or histogram) *and* a line graph.

In Proposal Assignment 4b you selected and operationally defined two behaviors in preparation for evaluating their association (correlation). After creating a data set indicative of either a positive or negative association, draw a scatterplot of your hypothetical results. (For this exercise you will have to make up *two* scores for each subject.)

C H A P T E R

12

Two-Treatment Designs with Correlated Observations

In chapters 5 and 11 we discussed two different approaches for the design of two-treatment experiments. One requires the random assignment of subjects to one or the other of two treatment conditions (the between-subject approach); the other requires using the same subjects under both treatment conditions (the within-subject approach). The fundamental difference between the independent observations of the between-subject approach and the correlated observations of the within-subject approach becomes readily apparent when we inspect the tables that are commonly used to display the two types of data. For example, consider the arrangement of Table 12-1: The two columns are for recording the data of Treatment Conditions 1 and 2, and the 10 rows are for the data of subjects 1 to 10. Two data values must be recorded for each subject: one for Treatment Condition 1 and another for Treatment Condition 2. Since the two columns in the table represent pairs of data values from the same subjects, we refer to them as correlated observations.

For comparison, refer back to Table 11–1, which is a general representation of the between-subject design, and notice that there are no row labels. It is, of course, important to record the dependent variable value for each subject in the appropriate column, but there are no restrictions with regard to row placement. The two values that do happen to appear together on each row of the completed table are therefore *arbitrary* pairings of the data of different subjects, and this eliminates any meaningful assessment of correlation between the Treatment 1 and Treatment 2 data sets.

We also refer to the design feature of recording more than one observation on the same subject as the taking of repeated measures, so the term **repeated measures design** is used interchangeably with within-subject design. Both names reflect the unique feature of the design, which is to compare the behavior of the same subjects under different treatment conditions.

Repeated Measures Design: Within-subject design.

Three Variations of the Two-Treatment Within-Subject Experiment

Sometimes we can use either form of two-treatment design, a between-subject or within-subject experiment, to compare the effects of two different treatment conditions on behavior. In the case of some research problems, however, we are

Treatment Condition 1	**Treatment Condition 2**
S_1	
S_2	
S_3	
S_4	
S_5	
S_6	
S_7	
S_8	
S_9	
S_{10}	

Table 12–1. A blank raw data summary table (using a sample size of 10 subjects) for the two-treatment within-subject experimental design. Each row of the table will accommodate two measurements: one under Treatment Condition 1 and a repeated measurement on the same subject under Treatment Condition 2.

Test-Retest Design:
Subjects are evaluated twice under the exact same set of experimental conditions and data-gathering procedures.

The Test-Retest Design

One type of two-treatment within-subject design is the **test-retest design**. As diagramed below, it calls for evaluating a single group of subjects twice under the exact same set of experimental conditions and data-gathering procedures.

The Test-Retest Design
Initial Test → (time interval) → Retest

Trial: A single unit of test experience.

For example, let us assume that we give a subject a **trial** (a single unit of test experience) consisting of a one-minute study session during which the task is to memorize a list of words. After testing the subjects' memory (by having them write down all the words they can remember from the list) and allowing them a short rest period, we administer a second identical trial — the retest. After another one-minute study session of the same list of words, the subjects must again write down as many words as they remember from the list. Any increase in the number of words remembered on the retest compared to the number of words remembered on the initial test is presumably attributable, at least in part, to the experience of taking the initial recall test. That is, we assume that the subjects' memory capability on the retest will build on the learning that took place on the initial test.

The test-retest design does not call for manipulating a variable in the usual sense, such as having subjects memorize semantically similar words (big, huge, large) in Treatment Condition 1 and semantically dissimilar words (key, dam, bus) in Treatment Condition 2. Assuming we are careful to maintain a uniform testing environment during the test and retest sessions and thereby prevent the intrusion of extraneous variables, the experience of the initial test session will itself be the only variable that affects performance on the subsequent retest. In reference to Basic Question 4, we may regard the initial test condition as a standard context because the subjects have had no prior experience completing the test and are, therefore, experimentally naive. At the same time, the experience gained from completing the initial test represents the "change in an otherwise standard context" that we presume will affect performance on the retest. Since the goal of evaluating the effect of a subject's initial test experience on subsequent retest performance cannot be accomplished without collecting two measures on the same subjects, the research issue requires the application of a within-subject design.

The Pretest-Posttest Design

Pretest-Posttest Design:
An initial evaluation occurs before a significant event and is followed by another evaluation after the significant event.

The **pretest-posttest design**, like the test-retest design, requires us to collect the same type of data twice: once from an initial test and again from a later test.

The Pretest-Posttest Design
Pretest → (significant event) → Posttest

Also, as in the test-retest design, we must strive to carry out both the pretest and the posttest under uniform conditions to prevent the intrusion of extraneous variables (confounds). Unlike the test-retest design, however, in the pretest-posttest design a "significant event" occurs *between* the pretest and the posttest. Sometimes the event is the introduction of an experimenter-controlled condition, and sometimes the event is an unforeseen and unplanned occurrence outside any experimental control. We refer to the former as a **planned pretest-posttest study** and to the latter as an **unplanned pretest-posttest study**. In both forms, the pretest-posttest design addresses Basic Question 4. The pretest is carried out in a standard context (the subjects are naive prior to the occurrence of the significant event), and the significant event is the "change in an otherwise standard context."

An example of a planned pretest-posttest study would be examining a group's attitude toward a racial minority before and after seeing an educational film on the irrationality of prejudicial attitudes and their harmful consequences both to individuals and society as a whole. The film presentation would be the significant event intervening between the pretest and the posttest, both of which would be an administration of an attitude-assessment instrument. Since an attitude shift is a change in behavior within a subject, the research question (Will viewing a film cause a group of subjects to experience a shift in attitude?) is the type of experimental issue that requires repeated measurements on the same subjects (a within-subject design).

An example of an unplanned pretest-posttest study would be to compare the number of prescriptions for tranquilizers dispensed from a city's retail pharmacies for the month before versus the month after the announcement of major personnel cuts by the city's principal employer. Notice how the collection of the pharmaceutical sales data provides a clue to their descriptive (as opposed to experimental) character. The records of tranquilizer purchases were in the stores' archives and were clearly not measurements of behavior following the controlled introduction of an experimental variable between a pretest and a posttest. We therefore cannot explain a change in tranquilizer consumption as having been *caused* by a rise in unemployment. Rather, we would describe increased purchases of tranquilizers as *associated* with the rise in unemployment.

Even if the pretest-posttest study is planned, we could still be in error concluding that a difference between pretest and posttest performance was caused by the designated significant event. It is possible for additional significant events to occur between the pretest and posttest and, without control groups that would allow us to evaluate the impact of such other events, how we are to know which event (or combination of events) caused the pretest-posttest difference? For example, in addition to the educational film on prejudice that the subjects see between the pretest and posttest attitude assessments, one or more subjects may have seen, and been deeply affected by, a televised address by a human rights advocate such as antiapartheid activist Nelson Mandela or a diatribe by an opposite-minded segregationist. Exposure to either of these additional significant events would confuse any attempt to attribute attitude change from pretest to posttest, or the lack thereof, to the film alone.

As the latter example portrays, even when exactly the same testing conditions are maintained for both the pretest and the posttest, the underlying cause of a pretest-posttest difference may not necessarily be caused by the significant event. In

Planned Pretest-Posttest Study: The significant event that occurs between the pretest and the posttest is planned.

Unplanned Pretest-Posttest Study: The significant event that occurs between the pretest and the posttest is unplanned.

fact, the capacity of the design to link a pretest-posttest difference causally to a particular significant event is so questionable (that is, its internal validity is so weak) that it is usually represented as a quasi- (pseudo or false) experimental design rather than a true experimental design. In chapter 10 we saw that internally valid experiments support a causal linkage between independent and dependent variables. Conversely, a study lacks internal validity when factors other than the independent variable are identified as possible causes of differences between treatment conditions. In chapter 15, which is devoted to a detailed discussion of various types of quasi-experimental designs and their associated pitfalls, we return to the pretest-posttest design and discuss ways to strengthen its internal validity.

The Condition 1 versus Condition 2 Design

Let us design a two-treatment within-subject experiment that would be capable of answering the question: Does performance on a video game differ as a function of the type of controller (keyboard versus joystick) that is available? Table 9–1 presented an example of a research scenario geared to evaluating the degree of association between keyboard-controlled and joystick-controlled video-game performance. The study was in the form of Basic Question 3: *Does an association exist between two (or more) variables?* Now we modify that research scenario so it is in the form of Basic Question 5: *Will introducing subjects to qualitatively different conditions cause them to exhibit systematic differences in behavior?*

The modification changes the study from a correlational study, in which no variables were manipulated, to an experiment, in which the type of game controller is a manipulated variable:

The Condition 1 versus Condition 2 Design
Condition 1 → (time interval) → Condition 2

Ten subjects were assigned to play a video game that required a considerable amount of eye-hand coordination and speed to avoid being devoured by the dragon and "losing a life." During one test session each subject manipulated the game's action with a joystick controller. In a different session each subject was required to use a computer keyboard to control the action. We use the same data for the two-treatment experiment (Table 12–2) that we presented for the correlational study (Table 9–1) to make the point that the appearance of a data set (in this case, two columns of numbers with labeled rows and columns) does not necessarily reveal the question the data can answer. The data of Table 9–1 address the association issue of Basic Question 3, whereas the data of Table 12–2 address the cause-effect issue of Basic Question 5 (qualitatively different treatment conditions).

The data in Table 12–2 show the number of lives lost during each one of the five-minute test sessions for the 10 subjects who participated in the experiment. Notice that any comparisons we make between joystick performance and keyboard performance (the keyboard and joystick treatment means are 8.3 and 6.0, respectively) involve within-subject comparisons, since every subject yields data for both experimental conditions.

The research question (Does performance differ as a function of the type of controller that is used?) could just as easily have been examined using a between-

| | Type of Controller | |
Subject	Keyboard	Joystick
1	2	0
2	4	2
3	5	2
4	11	7
5	15	10
6	7	9
7	3	4
8	14	9
9	8	5
10	14	12
	$\bar{X} = 8.30$	$\bar{X} = 6.00$

Table 12–2. The number of video game lives lost when 10 subjects played one session of a video game with a keyboard controller and one session with a joystick controller.

subject design. This is because we are not necessarily concerned, as we were in the test-retest and pretest-posttest designs, with a within-subject change in behavior from one test session to another.

Maintaining Internal Validity in the Condition 1 versus Condition 2 Design

Taking repeated measures on the same set of subjects, once under each of two different treatment conditions, would, at least on the surface, appear to maximize initial equivalence and therefore contribute greatly to the internal validity of the within-subject experiment. In the test-retest design, for example, data from the initial test provide a performance baseline (performance with *no* prior test experience) against which we compare performance on the retest (performance *with* prior test experience). Similarly, in the pretest-posttest design the pretest data provide a performance baseline against which we compare performance on the posttest. In both designs the same subjects generate both baseline and experimental data. Therefore each subject, in effect, serves as his or her own control, because nobody is more equivalent to a given individual than the individual himself or herself.

Carryover Effects

In the within-subject version of the condition 1 versus condition 2 design, however, there is a built-in threat to internal validity: It is possible for the initial test experience to affect the subjects' performance on the second test aside from any reason connected to the independent variable. Examples of such residual influences,

Carryover Effects:
Residual effects on a subject's behavior from having experienced one or more prior treatment conditions.

called **carryover effects** (or **sequence and order effects**), include a warm-up or practice effect, fatigue, boredom, and more specific residual effects (such as a hangover from a drug treatment) that are consequences of experiencing the initial treatment condition. In the test-retest version of the within-subject experiment, the experience of initial testing is itself the treatment, so we *expect* it to affect the subjects' performance on the second test. But in the condition 1 versus condition 2 design, the influences of the first test session on a subject's performance during the second test session are extraneous to the independent variable and will introduce rival explanations for between-treatment differences. In order to ensure that between-treatment differences in condition 1 versus condition 2 experiments can unambiguously be attributed to the experimental manipulation, we must neutralize carryover effects.

As an example of a carryover effect, consider the industrial psychologist who was hired to evaluate the impact on worker morale and productivity of two different product-assembly methods. Two work facilities were set up in separate areas of the plant. One was set up for manufacturing using Method 1 and the other for Method 2. The plan was to evaluate a single group of workers first under Method 1 and then switch facilities and collect data on the same workers under Method 2. If the data showed that Method 2 resulted in better productivity and/or worker morale, would you have confidence in the apparent superiority of Method 2 over Method 1?

Whereas we cannot *exclude* the possibility that Method 2 may be superior, there are rival explanations for such a result if the research plan were as described above. It is possible, for example, that the experience the workers gained under Method 1 provided a practice or warm-up that had a positive effect on their Method 2 performance. A warm-up effect would be very likely if one component of the two experimental manufacturing processes required the workers to learn how to use exotic new equipment and tools. When beginning Method 2 they would already have learned how to use the new tools and would therefore have a tendency to get off to a better start under Method 2 than they did for Method 1. The influence of such carryover effects on the data of within-subject experiments can be minimized using the methodological refinement called **counterbalancing**.

Counterbalancing: A method to neutralize the impact of carryover effects.

AB/BA Counterbalancing

To counterbalance carryover effects in the condition 1 versus condition 2 within-subject design and thereby enhance the internal validity of the experiment, we randomly assign half the subjects to be tested first under Treatment Condition 1, then Treatment Condition 2, and the other half are tested first under Treatment Condition 2, then Treatment Condition 1. Because half the subjects experience the treatments using a one-two (or A–B) sequence and the remaining half experience the treatments using a two-one (or B–A) sequence, this technique is referred to as **AB/BA counterbalancing** (see Table 12–3). Note that counterbalancing requires us to use an even number of subjects and randomly assign exactly half of the subjects to each order of treatment presentation. If we used an odd number of subjects, the symmetry needed to balance the carryover effects would be missing.

AB/BA Counterbalancing: The treatments are administered to half the subjects in an A–B sequence, with a B–A sequence for the other half.

We must take care when doing a two-treatment counterbalanced experiment to make sure we record all Treatment A scores and Treatment B scores in their respective columns, as shown in Table 12–4, and not confuse the different order of

Subject	Treatment Sequence
1	A–B
2	A–B
3	A–B
4	B–A
5	B–A
6	A–B
7	B–A
8	A–B
9	B–A
10	B–A

Table 12–3. One possible pattern of random assignment of five A–B treatment sequences and five B–A treatment sequences administered to 10 subjects.

	Treatment	
Subject	A	B
1	A	B
2	A	B
3	A	B
4	A	B
5	A	B
6	A	B
7	A	B
8	A	B
9	A	B
10	A	B

Table 12–4. Recording of experimental results using the testing sequences portrayed in Table 12–3.

treatment presentations, first versus second, with Treatment Conditions 1 and 2. Table 12–4 also shows that, despite the fact that two different groups of subjects experience different testing sequences, which might remind you of a between-subject design, the counterbalancing does not disturb the within-subject character of the design.

By counterbalancing we do not prevent a subject's experience with Treatment Condition 1 from carrying over to affect the subject's subsequent behavior under Treatment Condition 2, and we do not prevent nonspecific order effects (boredom, fatigue, loss of attention span, habituation to apparatus) from having a different impact on second- versus first-treatment experimental data. We do, however, attempt to balance these effects and thereby neutralize them as an extraneous source of systematic variability between treatment conditions.

Symmetrical Transfer:
The assumption that any carryover effect from Treatment A to Treatment B can be offset by the carryover effect from B to A.

The success we experience in counterbalancing carryover effects depends on the degree to which the carryover effects meet the assumption of **symmetrical transfer**. Specifically, we assume that any carryover effect that results from having experienced Treatment A before Treatment B will be offset by an equal and opposite effect of experiencing Treatment B before Treatment A. For example, if the initial experience of Treatment A results in a three-unit decline in the subjects' subsequent performance under Treatment B, the assumption of symmetrical transfer is that under the reverse testing order, the initial experience of Treatment B will also result in a three-unit decline in the subjects' performance under Treatment A.

If the assumption of symmetrical transfer is valid, carryover effects will be counterbalanced (that is, will cancel each other out). If the assumption is not valid, then AB/BA counterbalancing will fail to neutralize carryover effects. How can we tell when the assumption is valid? Unfortunately, the presence of symmetrical transfer is not verifiable and, indeed, may not be present even though we assume that it is. Nevertheless, despite the uncertainty, it is better to counterbalance in order to have a chance of neutralizing carryover effects than not to counterbalance and be *guaranteed* to have an imbalance of any carryover effects that may exist. When we counterbalance the presentation of treatment conditions, differences in the behavior of subjects under Treatment Condition 1 versus 2 can be more confidently attributed to a causal action of the independent variable as opposed to a rival explanation involving the sequence or order of treatments.

In the two-treatment experiment to compare different video-game controllers, if the "lives lost" data (shown in Table 12–2) were collected using the AB/BA counterbalancing scheme illustrated in Table 12–3, and if the assumption of symmetrical transfer is valid, any positive carryover effects (such as developing a game strategy) or negative carryover effects (such as the confusion that could result from the dissimilar movements required to operate the keyboard and joystick controllers) would be balanced. The balancing, in turn, excludes carryover effects as an explanation for the superiority of the joystick controller.

ABBA Counterbalancing

ABBA Counterbalancing: All subjects experience both orders of both treatments in ABBA sequence.

In the AB/BA counterbalancing scheme we just discussed and illustrated in Table 12–3, half the subjects are tested using an A–B order, and the other half are tested using a B–A order. By contrast, in **ABBA counterbalancing** (note the absence of the slash: ABBA and AB/BA counterbalancing are different) all the subjects experience both orders of the treatment. ABBA counterbalancing is illustrated in Table 12–5.

Linear Progressive Error: The assumption relevant to ABBA counterbalancing that the carryover effect grows progressively and in equal amounts with each repeated testing.

The success of ABBA counterbalancing in neutralizing carryover effects is also tied to an assumption: the assumption of **linear progressive error**. Specifically, in ABBA counterbalancing we assume that the carryover effect grows progressively and in equal amounts with each repeated testing.

As shown in Table 12–6, there is no carryover influence on the first administration of Treatment A because no treatment preceded it. All successive administrations are assumed to be affected by a constant carryover effect (three units) that accumulates with repeated treatments ($0 + 3 = 3$, $3 + 3 = 6$, and $6 + 3 = 9$). The total carryover effect for the two administrations of Treatment A ($0 + 9 = 9$) exactly equals the total carryover effect for the two administrations of Treatment B

| | | Treatment | | |
Subject	A	B	B	A
1				
2				
3				
4				
5				
6				
7				
8				
9				
10				

Table 12–5. An illustration of ABBA counterbalancing showing that all subjects are tested under the same ABBA testing order. Each row of the table contains the data of a single subject, so, unlike AB/BA counterbalancing, each subject is measured four times (A–B–B–A) rather than only two times (A–B or B–A).

	A	B	B	A
Treatment:	A	B	B	A
Magnitude of Carryover Effect:	0	3	3	3
Progressive (Cumulative) Carryover Effect:	0	3	6	9

Table 12–6. A hypothetical illustration of linear progressive error. Each treatment is represented as contributing a 3-unit carryover effect.

$(3 + 6 = 9)$, so we say the carryover effects have been counterbalanced. The illustration in Table 12–6 is described as hypothetical because we cannot really assess the magnitude of the carryover effects (the illustration assumes a shift of 3 units in the dependent variable values), whether or not they are linear, or even if they are truly progressive. Nevertheless, to repeat, it is better to counterbalance in order to have a chance of neutralizing carryover effects than not to counterbalance and be *guaranteed* to have an imbalance from any carryover effects that may exist.

Mixed-Stimulus Counterbalancing

In some within-subject experimental situations it is practical to mix two treatment conditions together within one testing period. For example, assume an experimenter wanted to measure the time it takes subjects to press a button (reaction time) in response to two different stimulus displays (say, bright light A versus dim light B) during the same testing session. One approach is to create a mixed random order consisting of an even number of A and B trials (such as A–B–A–B–B–A–B–A–A–B) and then compare the reaction times following the type A

Mixed-Stimulus Counterbalancing:
Neutralizing carryover effects from type A and type B trials by arranging the trials in random sequence.

versus type B stimulus presentations. The method is called **mixed-stimulus counterbalancing**, and, like AB/BA and ABBA counterbalancing, there is no guarantee that it will succeed in neutralizing carryover effects. But it is better to incorporate counterbalancing and attempt to neutralize carryover effects than to ignore the likelihood of carryover effects and be guaranteed of having ambiguous experimental results.

When to Avoid the Within-Subject Design

The within-subject design is a poor choice for condition 1 versus condition 2 experiments in which the goal is to compare the capacity of two treatment conditions to effect a relatively permanent change in behavior. For example, some research is done to compare the effectiveness of different medical or psychological therapies in promoting recovery from an illness. If the first therapy is effective, it would be unwise, unethical, and maybe even impossible to return the subject to an ill condition in order to evaluate the relative effectiveness of a different therapeutic approach. In such cases, a between-subject design is the only feasible approach to the research problem.

The Presence of Correlation in the Data of Within-Subject Experiments

In examining the data in Table 12–2, note that the scores within each of the treatment conditions reflect a considerable amount of variability in the skill level among the 10 subjects. Within Treatment Condition 1 (the keyboard condition), Subjects 1 and 2 are the most skilled, having been devoured by the dragon 2 and 4 times, respectively. By comparison, Subject 9 was moderately skilled, having been devoured 8 times, and Subject 10 was devoured 14 times over the five-minute test session and, hence, was a relatively unskilled performer. If you inspect the data for Treatment Condition 2 (the joystick condition) in a similar manner, you will also find that there is noticeable variability in the skill shown by different subjects, just as in the keyboard condition. *In addition*, the performance of the subjects tends to be consistent across the two conditions: The best performers with the keyboard controller also tended to excel when using the joystick, and the relatively poor keyboard performers also tended to experience difficulty when using the joystick.

It is this tendency for individual subjects to behave in a consistent manner across different treatment conditions (relatively high scores on both or relatively low scores on both), together with substantial variability in behavior between subjects, that is the signature of a positive correlation. In general, we assume that a correlation will exist between the data of Treatment Condition 1 and the data of Treatment Condition 2 in any within-subject experiment. The reason is quite straightforward: It is more likely than not for a subject to behave in a consistent manner across different treatment conditions. The subject who makes the most correct responses and is the most alert, attentive, coordinated, focused, and so forth under Treatment Condition 1 is also more likely than not to exhibit similar degrees of those behavioral traits when tested under Treatment Condition 2.

Experiments with correlated observations versus correlational research

It is very important that you maintain the proper focus when examining the condition 1 versus condition 2 experiment summarized in Table 12–2 or, for that matter, the data of any two-treatment experiment with correlated observations. The fact that two sets of data are measurements on the same subjects and, therefore, must be regarded as correlated observations should not mislead you into viewing the research as correlational research. The goal of correlational research is to assess the *association* between variables, whereas the goal of experimental research is to evaluate the effect of manipulating an independent variable on the value of a dependent measure. For example, the goal of a correlational study (Basic Question 3) would be to assess the *relationship* between joystick and keyboard performance, as we did in chapter 9. ("If players vary substantially in their ability to play the game, will players who perform well with the joystick also tend to perform well with the keyboard? Will players who perform poorly with the joystick also tend to perform poorly with the keyboard? Can we predict lives lost under keyboard control from the knowledge of lives lost under joystick control?") By contrast, the *experiment* (Basic Question 5) examines the effect of manipulating the controller variable. ("Do players lose a different number of lives when they control the game with a joystick versus a keyboard?")

Achieving Initial Equivalence by Matching Groups

The primary advantage of the within-subject design is that we *know* the subjects tested under all treatments are initially equivalent because they are the same individuals. By contrast, when using the between-subject design we must *assume* that the random assignment of subjects to different treatments will achieve initial equivalence between groups. As an alternative to the within-subject and between-subject approaches, we can also enhance initial equivalence by using a mix of the within-subject and between-subject approaches. In the **matched-groups design** separate groups of subjects are assigned to different treatment conditions, which is a between-subject feature, but, like the within-subject design, the observations are correlated. For example, consider the random assignment of two subjects from the same family to different treatment conditions (as shown in Table 12–8) or, in animal populations, two subjects who come from the same brood or litter. The design calls for splitting pairs of different individuals between two treatment conditions, but the common bonds of heredity and experience that link the members of each pair mandate that the data be regarded as correlated observations and be analyzed as such (see Box 12–1). Also, when subjects cannot be assumed to be similar because of like experiences, similar histories, or genetic constitutions, we can *arrange* for them to be similar by using some selection criterion (such as intelligence, aptitude, physical traits, and the like) to form matched pairs. Thus, if you feel you would rather not count on random assignment to produce initially equivalent groups of subjects and you do not think you can eliminate carryover

Matched-Groups Design: Subjects are paired on the basis of some attribute or behavioral measure, then assigned to different treatment conditions.

effects by using one of the three counterbalancing techniques, you can impose some structure on random assignment by using matched pairs of subjects.

The variable that is used for forming matched pairs should be one that is correlated with the dependent variable. If you wished, for example, to compare student achievement as a function of two different methods of instruction, you would most likely want to use pairs of subjects that were matched in scholastic aptitude. This would relieve you of the doubt that, just by chance, a disproportionate number of very able students happened to be assigned to one particular group and a disproportionate number of underachievers happened to be assigned to the other group. Similarly, if you wanted to compare the progress of athletes who were being trained in the methods of sports psychology to maintain concentration and control anxiety against athletes who did not receive such training, it would be wise to match the subjects in the two groups on their initial athletic ability.

Forming matched pairs

To form matched pairs, the first step is to pretest all the subjects either on the dependent variable itself or on a variable that is known or assumed to be correlated with the dependent variable. If, for example, a coach wanted to compare two programs of physical fitness training to prepare athletes to race a metric mile (1500 m), he or she could pretest subjects using the same dependent measure planned for use in the experiment itself (such as time needed to complete a metric mile course) or a variable that is assumed or known to be correlated with racing ability (such as endurance on a fast-moving treadmill). The data from the pretest would then be used as the matching criterion.

After rank-ordering all the subjects with respect to their performance on the pretest, we form the first matched pair from the two top-ranked subjects, the second matched pair from the third- and fourth-ranked subjects, and so on down the list. After the pairs are formed, one subject from each pair must be randomly assigned to one treatment condition. The remaining subject in the matched pair is, by default, assigned to the other treatment condition.

An alternative procedure is to take the top two scores from the ordered list (assume eight subjects in all):

Ordered Criterion Scores: <u>110, 108</u>, 104, 96, 83, 72, 62, 61

then randomly assign these two subjects to the two treatment conditions,

Treatment 1	Treatment 2
110	108

and then "flip-flop" the treatment assignments of successive pairs on the list with respect to their magnitude following a high-low, low-high, high-low, etc. pattern as illustrated below.

Treatment 1	**Treatment 2**
110	108
96	104
83	72
61	62

By assigning matched pairs of subjects to two treatment conditions, as opposed to forming two independent groups, we can be more confident that any systematic differences in behavior we observe between the treatment conditions is truly a function of the experimental variable rather than due to any pre-existing difference between two groups of subjects.

Is matching better?

Matching groups on the basis of a selection criterion has great intuitive appeal as a method for achieving initial equivalence, but it is not a perfect solution. In fact, famed statistician R. A. Fisher (1953) rejected matching as a favored strategy for achieving group equivalence. He trusted the random assignment of subjects to different treatment conditions in preference to matching because it is possible for a matching procedure to create an illusion of group equality even when true initial equivalence is absent.

Let us assume, for example, that you intended to recruit subjects to participate in the comparison of two rival weight-loss programs. You further decide to set up the two groups as a series of matched pairs, pairing subjects according to their weight. From your population of volunteers you randomly select the subjects and then, for your first pair, you match Bubba, the 250-pound guard on the school's football team, with Findlay, a 250-pound couch potato. Bubba is determined to lose body fat in the off season so he can compete in body-building competitions, whereas Findlay is somewhat more apathetic to the idea of weight reduction. There are differences between the subjects in motivation, the level of physical activity (since only one is an athlete), the ratio of muscle mass to fat, and perhaps other relevant characteristics that escape being equated by the matching procedure. To the degree that other "matched" pairs are also different in ways that are not remedied by the matching procedure, the equivalence of the two groups is an illusion. Thus, despite the intuitive appeal of matching, it is arguable that equality between the groups of an experiment may be more readily achieved with random assignment.

In practice, the random assignment of subjects to different treatment conditions (the between-subject approach) tends to be the favored strategy when the researcher has the resources to use a relatively large sample size for each treatment condition. But when the total number of available subjects is relatively small (say, only 12) and individual differences that correlate with the dependent variable are present, matching is a popular approach. Consider, for example, a researcher who plans to run a small-sample experiment to compare the speed with which two differently treated groups master a learning task. Since the ability to perform on a learning task correlates with intelligence, it would be reasonable to match the two groups on intelligence, especially if it were known that intelligence is highly variable among members of the subject pool.

The Two-Treatment Matched Groups and Between-Subject Designs: A Comparison

If, despite the reservations discussed above, you conclude that the investigation of your two-treatment research problem would be best served by matching the subjects across the two treatment conditions, your experiment would be a two-treatment matched-groups design. The two-treatment matched-groups design is similar to the two-treatment between-subject design in that two separate groups of subjects are assigned to one or the other of two treatment conditions. In setting up a matched-groups design, however, an extra step is taken to optimize the initial equivalence of the two groups. As illustrated above with Bubba and Findlay, each subject in the matched-groups design has a mate to whom he or she is matched on any nonmanipulated physical or behavioral dimension the experimenter feels could, if not properly managed through matching, constitute an extraneous influence on the recorded values of the dependent variable.

Perhaps the ultimate matched-groups design is the two-treatment experiment with identical twins as subjects. (Naturally, identical twins are not absolutely identical in their behavior. Nevertheless, it is reasonable to assume that, because of identical genes and the likelihood of shared experiences, twins tend to be more alike than other matched individuals who do not share this unique biological status.) When identical twins are used in the matched-groups design, one twin of each pair is randomly assigned to one treatment condition and the other is assigned to the second treatment condition. To illustrate the advantage that can be derived from matching subjects (or the advantage of having several sets of identical twins for subjects), imagine an experiment to compare the achievement of students taught using two different methods of instruction. Further, we shall imagine running the experiment using two different designs: the two-treatment between-subject design and the two-treatment matched-groups design.

The data in Table 12–7 represent the test results of 12 unrelated students who were randomly assigned to be taught using one or the other of the teaching methods. Notice that Instruction Method 1 resulted in an average two-point increase in performance over Instruction Method 2, but the independent groups t test shows that this difference is not significant. ($t = 1.46$ and the critical value of the t statistic at the .05 level of significance with df $= 10$ is 2.228.) (See Box 12–1 for the analysis of the Table 12–7 data.)

Subject	(Group 1) Instruction Method 1	Subject	(Group 2) Instruction Method 2
1	4	7	1
2	3	8	2
3	5	9	3
4	7	10	5
5	9	11	6
6	8	12	7
	$\bar{X} = 6.00$		$\bar{X} = 4.00$
	SD $= 2.37$		SD $= 2.37$

Table 12–7. The number of correct responses on a 10-item test following two different methods of instruction administered to two independent groups (a between-subject design).

Now let us look at the results of the experiment run as matched-groups design with identical twins for subjects. Each set of twins was split by randomly assigning one twin to be taught using Instruction Method 1 and the other to be taught using Instruction Method 2. For the matched groups experiment we assume, unlikely though it may be, that we obtained exactly the same results in the matched-groups experiment that were obtained in the independent groups (between-subject) experiment. That is, although the experimental designs differ, the data in Tables 12–7 and 12–8 are the same.

Unlike the data in Table 12–7, each row of data in Table 12–8 is assumed to contain the scores for one matched pair (Twin Set). The row totals provide a measure of high or low overall performance across both methods of instruction for each matched pair, and the differences between the scores of twins (the D scores) reflect the magnitude of the treatment effect. By scanning down the row totals it is easy to see the variability in task performance across twin sets. Neither twin from Set 1 did very well on the test, both twins from Sets 5 and 6 did relatively well, but in all cases the twin taught using Method 2 scored higher. Thus, because each twin serves as a reference (that is, a standard of comparison) for the other, the experimental effect is apparent despite the variability of performance within each treatment condition.

Same scores, different results

The data are the same in Tables 12–7 and 12–8, the group means are the same, and the variability among the scores within each of the two groups is identical, but the values of the t statistic are different. Instead of an insignificant 1.46, which resulted from the independent groups t test on the Table 12–7 data, the t value computed from the matched-groups version of the experiment shown in Table 12–8 equals 5.48. Since the computed value of the t statistic is more extreme (larger) than the critical value of t published in the t table ($t_{crit} = 2.571$ when df = 5 and $\alpha = .05$), the difference in the performances resulting from the two methods of instruction is statistically significant for the matched-groups experiment.

Twin Set	Instruction Method 1	Instruction Method 2	Row Total	Difference (D) Scores
1	4	1	5	3
2	3	2	5	1
3	5	3	8	2
4	7	5	12	2
5	9	6	15	3
6	8	7	15	1
	$\bar{X} = 6.00$	$\bar{X} = 4.00$		$\Sigma D = 12$

Table 12–8. The number of correct responses on a 10-item test following two different methods of instruction administered to matched groups of subjects. Differences among the row totals reflect the degree of individual differences that exist among the subjects, and the difference scores (D scores) reflect the magnitude of the experimental effect.

Why, if both *t*-test analyses were done on the same data (Tables 12–7 and 12–8), are the results of the analyses so different? The cause lies in the alternative ways in which the two analyses estimate error (see Box 12–1). In the *t* test for independent observations it is not possible to discriminate systematic individual differences in behavior among subjects from random unsystematic sources, so the estimate of random error tends to be inflated:

$$(s_{\bar{X}_1 - \bar{X}_2} = 1.366).$$

In the *t* test for correlated observations, it is possible to remove systematic individual differences from the estimate of error. This tends to result in a smaller value:

$$(s_{\bar{X}_1 - \bar{X}_2} = 0.365),$$

and the smaller the estimate of random error is (the denominator of the *t* statistic), the larger the value of *t* will be.

Answering Questions Using Two-Treatment Within-Subject Designs

Like between-subject designs, within-subject and matched-groups designs can be used to address Basic Questions 4, 5, and 6. Using either a single group that is measured twice or matched pairs, we can compare the effects of introducing an experimental condition to an untreated or partially treated condition, we can compare the effects of administering different qualitative levels of an experimental variable, and we can compare the effects of administering different quantitative levels of an experimental variable.

BOX 12–1

The *t*-test Analyses for Independent and Correlated Observations

Below are independent and correlated *t* test analyses of the same scores taken from different research contexts (Tables 12–7 and 12–8). The numerators of the two formulae equal the same 2.00 units obtained by taking the difference between the two treatment means $(\bar{X}_1 - \bar{X}_2)$ and the $\mu_1 - \mu_2$ value stated in the null hypothesis. (For most applications the null hypothesis is that no difference exists between the two treatment means, so the null hypothesis is that $[\mu_1 - \mu_2]$ equals zero.)

The difference between the two computational methods can be seen by inspecting the denominators of the formulae. In the analysis that is appropriate for correlated data, the estimate of random error is computed using the difference scores (see Table 12–4). Systematic individual differences are thereby removed from the estimate of random error, which typically results in a relatively small estimate of error. By comparison, the method for estimating error in the analysis that is appropriate for independent observations does not differentiate individual differences from truly random error, and so its estimate of error is likely to be relatively large. Review your statistics text for additional details of the independent and correlated t test analyses. If you find formulae that use different notation, don't be confused. There are many different ways to write the formulae of both the independent and correlated versions of the t test.

General Formula

$$t = \frac{(\bar{X}_1 - \bar{X}_2) - (\mu_1 - \mu_2)}{S_{\bar{X}_1 - \bar{X}_2}}$$

Computational Formulae:

Independent Observations	Correlated Observations

$$t = \frac{(\bar{X}_1 - \bar{X}_2) - (\mu_1 - \mu_2)}{\sqrt{\left[\dfrac{SS_1 + SS_2}{n_1 + n_2 - 2}\right]\left[\dfrac{1}{n_1} + \dfrac{1}{n_2}\right]}}$$

$$t = \frac{(\bar{X}_1 - \bar{X}_2) - (\mu_1 - \mu_2)}{\sqrt{\dfrac{\Sigma\, d^2}{(n(n-1))}}}$$

$$t = \frac{2.00}{\sqrt{\left[\dfrac{28 + 28}{6 + 6 - 2}\right]\left[\dfrac{1}{6} + \dfrac{1}{6}\right]}}$$

$$t = \frac{2.00}{\sqrt{\dfrac{28 - \dfrac{(12)^2}{6}}{6(6-1)}}}$$

$$t = \frac{2.00}{1.366}$$

$$t = \frac{2.00}{0.365}$$

$$t = 1.46$$

$$t = 5.48$$

Next, we must find the critical values of the t statistic ($\alpha = .05$) from the t table with degrees of freedom (df) equal to 10 and 5. (Find a t table in the appendix of your statistics text.)

Independent Observations: with $\alpha = .05$ and df $= 10$, $t_{critical} = 2.228$. Thus, the computed t value of 1.46 is not significant.

Correlated Observations: with $\alpha = .05$ and df $= 5$, $t_{critical} = 2.571$. Thus, the computed t value of 5.48 is significant.

We categorize the test-retest version of the within-subject experiment as one that addresses Basic Question 6, since it is usually the quantity of experience in the initial task that is thought to affect subsequent performance in this type of experiment. The pretest-posttest experiment is more closely associated with Basic Question 4 because the significant event that occurs between the pretest and the posttest is the "change" that is introduced into the standard context. The condition 1 versus condition 2 within-subject or matched groups experiment is as versatile as its two-treatment between-subject counterpart in addressing Basic Questions 4, 5, and 6.

Comparing Two-Treatment Designs

Since between-subject, within-subject, and matched groups designs can all be used to answer Basic Questions 4, 5 and 6, it is natural to wonder if one approach is better than the other and, if so, when. In general, when the measurements of a given dependent variable tend to be highly variable, the extra precision it is possible to achieve when using a matched-groups or within-subject design can provide the extra degree of statistical power (see chapters 4 and 11) needed to detect a relatively subtle experimental effect. We must be careful, however, not to have unrealistic expectations about the capacity of matching to maximize initial equivalence. That is, although matching subjects on a relevant dimension *should* act to improve initial equivalence, there is no guarantee that it will. For example, in designing a two-treatment experiment to research the relative effectiveness of two contrasting teaching methods, it would make sense to set up pairs of subjects that were matched on scholastic aptitude. But matching on scholastic aptitude is no guarantee that other variables known to effect performance on a learning task (motivation, attentiveness) would also be equated for the subjects in the two treatment conditions.

When we plan to collect data that are appropriately analyzed using the t statistic and we know ahead of time that the dependent measure is not likely to be characterized by broad individual differences, there is little advantage, and maybe even a disadvantage, to running the study as a matched-groups or within-subject design. There is little advantage because the principal statistical feature of a design with correlated observations, removing systematic individual differences from the estimate of random error (the denominator of the t statistic), is not needed when individual differences among the data values within a treatment condition are minimal. The possible disadvantage of a design with correlated observations stems from the loss of degrees of freedom in the statistical analysis. Specifically, for any given number of raw data values (say, $n = 15$ for each treatment condition), the between-subject design will have twice the degrees of freedom ($n_1 + n_2 - 2 = 30 - 2 = 28$) than the analysis for correlated observations ($n - 1 = 14$). As illustrated in Box 12–1, the fewer degrees of freedom, the larger the critical value of the t statistic will be, and the less power the t test will have to detect a significant difference between the treatment conditions.

The above notwithstanding, sometimes the within-subject design is the more desirable choice for an experiment. If, for example, the availability of subjects is a problem, you may be better off running the experiment using a within-subject design with a reasonable number of subjects (say, 10 to 12) rather than splitting the subjects into two very small groups of only five or six.

Summary

The chapter began by contrasting two-treatment designs that produce independent observations (between-subject designs) versus correlated observations (the within-subject and matched-groups designs). We then discussed three variations of the within-subject experiment: the test-retest design, the planned and unplanned pretest-posttest design, and the condition 1 versus condition 2 design. The distinguishing characteristic of the test-retest design is that the initial test experience is itself the independent variable. The distinguishing characteristic of the pretest-posttest design is that the independent variable is a significant event that occurs between the initial measurement and a later measurement. In the condition 1 versus condition 2 design, the two different treatment conditions are qualitatively or quantitatively defined manipulated variables.

Next we discussed the problem of maintaining internal validity in the execution of within-subject designs, the counterbalancing of carryover effects using the AB/BA, ABBA, and mixed stimulus approaches, and when to avoid the application of a within-subject design to a research problem. Because the proper analysis and interpretation of data is such an important aspect of research, we pointed out how to identify a pattern of correlation between sets of experimental data and stressed that the existence of correlation in the data of within-subject or matched-groups experiments does not make the study correlational research (the topic of chapter 9).

After discussing the matched-groups design as an alternative to the within- and between-subject approaches, we presented some methods for matching subjects, compared designs with correlated observations in terms of their ability to address some of the Basic Questions introduced in chapter 5, and, with examples and a computational comparison, discussed the strengths and weaknesses of designs with independent versus correlated observations.

Key Terms

ABBA Counterbalancing, p. 212
AB/BA Counterbalancing, p. 210
Carryover Effects, p. 210
Counterbalancing, p. 210
Linear Progressive Error, p. 212
Matched-Groups Design, p. 215
Mixed Stimulus Counterbalancing,
    p. 214
Pretest-Posttest Design, p. 206
   Planned Pretest-Posttest Design,
    p. 207
   Unplanned Pretest-Posttest Design,
    p. 207

Repeated Measures Design, p. 205
Sequence and Order Effects, p. 210
Symmetrical Transfer, p. 212
Test-Retest Design, p. 206
Trial, p. 206

Chapter Exercises

1. Why do we describe a within-subject or matched-groups design has having correlated observations?

2. The display of the data of two-treatment experiments, whether the data be independent or correlated observations, consists of two columns of numbers: one set of observations for Treatment Condition 1 and one set of observations for Treatment Condition 2. But, despite appearances, the rows of the table of correlated observations form meaningful pairs, whereas the rows of the table of independent observations form arbitrary pairs. Explain.

3. Why is an experiment in which identical twins are assigned to different treatment conditions analyzed in the same way as a within-subject experiment?

4. Explain the difference between an experiment with correlated observations and correlational research. Discuss the different basic questions addressed by correlational versus experimental research.

5. Explain how it is possible for groups not to be initially equivalent despite their being matched on some dimension.

6. Explain the difference between the research objectives of the test-retest design, the pretest-posttest design, and the condition 1 versus condition 2 design.

7. Explain why "all one-group pretest-posttest designs are repeated measures designs, but not all repeated measures designs are pretest-posttest designs."

8. What are some steps we can take to minimize the threats to internal validity that can affect the results of repeated measures designs?

9. A within-subject design was presented to test the relative effectiveness of keyboard versus joystick controllers (see Table 12–2). How would you compare the effectiveness of the two types of controllers using a between-subject design?

10. What are the considerations that dictate the choice of a design with independent versus correlated observations and what are the strengths and weaknesses of each type of design?

Proposal Assignment 12: Within-Subject Designs

In Proposal Assignments 4a and 4b you designed your study both as a two-treatment experiment (probably as a between-subject design) and as a correlational study. Now you are to design it as a two-treatment within-subject design. Do this three times, using the following designs: the AB/BA design, the ABBA design, and the mixed-stimulus design.

In the two-treatment within-subject design all subjects in your experiment are going to be tested under both levels of the independent variable. For example, in the study we described to compare the effects of different study times on grades, we would have to test all students twice: once when they are instructed to study for 20 hours per week, and then again when they are instructed to study only 5 hours per week. The problem is that the experience from participating in the first condition may influence how well, or how poorly, they do in the second condition. To solve the problem of a potential carryover effect, we must *counterbalance* the conditions.

In the *AB/BA design* we counterbalance the carryover effect by having half the subjects experience the 20-hour study condition first and the other half the 5-hour study condition first. We shall arbitrarily label studying for 20 hours per week the A condition and studying for 5 hours the B condition. All the subjects must be randomly divided into two equal-size groups. One group is then assigned to the AB order of testing and the other group to the BA order. If there is a carryover effect, we hope that the size of the effect going from A to B is equal to the size of the effect of going from B to A (the assumption of *symmetrical transfer*).

In the *ABBA design* all subjects receive both the AB and the BA order. This means that they are tested four times: the 20-hour condition, then the 5-hour condition, the 5-hour condition again, and then the 20-hour condition again. The assumption in this design is that the error due to the carryover effect grows progressively with repeated testing but that the size of the effect grows in equal amounts (linearly) with each additional test.

In the *mixed stimulus* design we mix the two conditions together within one testing period. This design is difficult to apply to our example and would probably not be used. We could, however, assign some material to the 20-hour study condition (A), and other material to the 5-hour study condition (B), and tell the subjects to study the A and B material a number of times in random order.

You may have discovered that there is an additional problem using the AB/BA or ABBA design when testing the effects of study time: we cannot give the subjects the same material to learn both times they are tested. One strategy is to counterbalance which material they learn first versus second in addition to counterbalancing the study-hours condition.

Again, your assignment is to design your experiment using each of the three within-subject designs:

1. AB/BA design
2. ABBA design
3. mixed stimulus design.

If you have problems designing your study using these three within-subject designs, do the best you can. It is a useful exercise even if you only *identify the problems* with each design and explain why you think they may not work for your experiment.

13

Single-Factor Experimental Designs with More Than Two Treatments

By this point in your study of research methods you know a great deal about the descriptive (chapters 6, 7, 8, and 9) and experimental (chapters 10, 11, and 12) methods researchers use to study behavioral phenomena. Also, in completing your proposal assignments and other class and laboratory exercises you have had some hands-on experience applying many research skills, such as creating partially treated control conditions and operational definitions of variables. You should be starting to feel like a scientist!

Perhaps you are nevertheless frustrated with the limitations of the investigative tools examined in the preceding chapters. Specifically, coverage of the experimental methods for studying behavior has, up to now, been limited to the application of two-treatment experimental designs. The basic two-treatment design is adequate for answering questions if all we are interested in is comparing measurable aspects of a behavior that exist under "normal" or "typical" circumstances to measurable aspects of the same behavior that are evident after introducing subjects to an experimental condition (Basic Question 4). The two-treatment design is also adequate if our interest is limited to comparing two qualitatively different conditions (Basic Question 5) or two quantitatively different conditions (Basic Question 6). Realistically, however, exploring the causes of behavior often requires making comparisons among many more than two treatment conditions.

Limitations of the Two-Treatment Design

Let us, then, examine the limited capacity of the two-treatment experiment for gathering scientific information within the context of a relatively uncomplicated research problem: Does injection with an experimental mood-altering drug (Compound X) alleviate the symptoms of clinical depression? What aspects of this question can we answer with the two-treatment design, and what aspects require running an experiment with more than two treatment conditions?

Untreated versus treated

Assume that we randomly split a group of depressed subjects and assign one group to receive no treatment at all (the untreated condition) and the other to be treated with Compound X. We would likely be pleased if, following the course of drug therapy, we were able to document a significant improvement in the clinical status of the treated patients relative to the untreated patients. Unfortunately, with only that experimental result available, it would be unclear whether the improvement was a sole result of the drug treatment, a product of some aspect of the treatment administration (for example, a placebo effect), or both. To pinpoint Compound X, the independent variable of the experiment, as the sole cause of the improvement, we must be able to rule out alternative explanations by incorporating appropriate control groups into the experimental design.

Partially treated versus treated

The use of one or more partially treated control groups (discussed in chapter 10) allows the researcher to isolate the contribution of experiences tied to the treatment administration from the effect of the experimental variable itself. Thus, instead of comparing subjects treated with Compound X to a control group of subjects who receive no treatment whatever, we could compare the drug-treated group to a placebo-treated group — one that has all the experiences of the experimental group minus actual treatment with Compound X. If we designed the two-treatment study as a simple placebo versus Compound X comparison, the elements necessary for the delivery of the experimental treatment would be constant for both groups. As a result, it would be unclear how much, if at all, aspects of the treatment administration *by themselves* contributed to post-treatment changes in the patients' level of depression. In other words, even if treatment with Compound X led to a more profound recovery than treatment with a placebo, we still would not know if subjects treated with *only* a placebo would recover faster than untreated subjects.

Untreated versus partially treated

We could resolve the issue as to whether or not the recovery from depression is, in part, linked to a placebo effect by comparing an untreated group to a partially treated group. But in this two-treatment experiment no subjects would be exposed to Compound X. Thus the comparison, which is between two control conditions, would tell us nothing about the potential influence of the experimental treatment on behavior.

In summary, each of the two-treatment comparisons discussed above, which are all in the form of Basic Question 4, can answer an important question, but each also leaves another question unanswered. Our example was in the form of a drug study, but the same principles apply to any kind of experimental research that is limited to two treatment conditions. In general:

- The *untreated versus treated* experiment answers the question: *Will subjects who are given the experimental treatment behave differently from untreated controls?* But it does not answer the question: *If the subjects who receive the experimental treatment do behave differently from untreated controls, is it the experimental treatment alone, an aspect of the treatment administration alone, or a combination of the two that led to the behavioral difference?*

- The *partially treated versus treated* experiment answers the question: *Will subjects who receive the experimental treatment behave differently from partially treated controls, who get everything but the actual experimental treatment?* But it does not answer the question: *Can aspects of the treatment administration affect behavior by themselves, without the presence of the experimental variable?*

- The *untreated versus partially treated* experiment answers the question: *Can aspects of the treatment administration affect behavior by themselves, without the presence of the experimental variable?* But it does not answer the question *Does the experimental variable affect behavior?*

Other kinds of two-treatment experiments for researching problems in the form of Basic Question 5 (qualitative level 1 versus qualitative level 2) and Basic Question 6 (quantitative level 1 versus quantitative level 2) can also be difficult to interpret and generalize, because the effects of only two manipulated levels of the independent variable are available for comparison. If the independent variable is quantitative in character (say, in an evaluation of a relatively low- versus high-dose level of a therapeutic agent) and we failed to find any differences between two differently treated groups, it would be natural to wonder if we would have been successful had we used values for the independent variable other than the two selected for the experiment. Similarly, if the independent variable were qualitative and we defined only two treatment conditions (say, drug therapy versus electroconvulsive therapy for relieving depression), it would be natural to wonder about the relative effectiveness of other potentially effective therapies for depression, such as group therapy, various talk therapies, or antidepressive medicines that are different from the ones used in the two-treatment experiment. Making numerous comparisons between several different forms of therapy is obviously impossible within the framework of a single two-treatment experiment.

Expanding the Two-Treatment Experiment

How do we investigate research issues that are too complex for the limited design structure of the two-treatment experiment? In many cases, the incorporation of more than two treatment conditions into a single experimental design is the answer. If our research goal were to determine if Compound X has a significant antidepressant effect (Basic Question 4), a design with three treatment conditions (that is, one that includes untreated, partially treated [placebo], and experimentally treated subjects) would allow us to detect the existence of both placebo and experimental effects *and* assess the relative magnitude of each — all within the framework of a single experiment. Similarly, if the treatment conditions of our experimental design consisted of many fundamentally different kinds of therapy for depression (Basic Question 5) or systematically varied the amount of drug therapy or psychotherapy given to the subjects (Basic Question 6), we would be able to compare the relative effectiveness of a wide range of qualitatively or quantitatively different treatments within the framework of a single experiment.

To expand or not to expand?

We must maintain some restraint when deciding how many treatment conditions to include in an experiment and not try to answer too many questions with a single experimental design. One reason is that the more complex an experimental design becomes, the more work it will take to execute the experiment and the more likely it is that some form of extraneous influence will affect the experimental results. "More work" in a large-scale experiment takes many forms, such as recruiting more subjects (or buying and maintaining more subjects, if the subjects are animals), building or buying more apparatus and supplies, making more decisions about the exact experimental procedures to follow, and recording and analyzing more data. If the demands of the project are beyond the capacity of a single experimenter, he or she must recruit helpers to administer treatments, collect data, maintain the apparatus, recruit subjects, organize testing schedules, and so on. You might assume that an experimenter would actively seek to be relieved of such tasks, which can be both time-consuming and difficult, but every responsibility that the experimenter relinquishes to a helper represents some loss of control over the precision and consistency of the experimental procedures.

If the researcher's response to the additional workload is to spread out the running of the experiment over a relatively long period of time, this also increases the risk that extraneous variables may intrude to affect the experimental data. For example, people who suffer from depression and live in northern locations sometimes experience their symptoms in a cyclic manner that varies with the season of the year. The pattern is called Seasonal Affective Disorder (SAD). During the summer months, when light is abundant, the symptoms subside or disappear. In the winter, however, the relative absence of light is likely to trigger an episode of depression among people who have a history of the disorder. Therefore, if the evaluation of a therapy for depression were extended across more than one season, it is likely that the "season" variable would affect the recovery rate of the treated subjects and increase the variability among the recovery scores. Subjects who began therapy in early spring might tend to recover more rapidly, not because of the effectiveness of the experimental therapy, but because of the eventual onset of summer and the increasing light of summer's days. Conversely, subjects who began therapy in the fall could fail to recover significantly, not because the therapeutic approach was completely without merit but because of the onset of the short days of winter.

Terminology

In preparation for the discussion of experimental design that follows we should briefly review a few terms originally introduced in chapter 5. A factor is simply another name for an independent variable, and the levels of a factor are the specific values of an independent variable that comprise the treatment conditions of an experiment. Thus, a treatment condition is defined both by reference to a particular factor (the independent variable) and by specifying the manipulated level of the factor. A research plan in which only one independent variable is manipulated is a **single-factor design**, and the number of treatment conditions in the single-factor experiment is the same as the number of levels of the factor.

Single-Factor Design: A research plan in which only one independent variable is manipulated.

All the between-subject and within-subject experimental designs we presented as examples in chapters 11 and 12 called for the manipulation of only one independent variable, so all were single-factor designs. Also, because all the designs had two treatment conditions, the factor of each experiment had only two levels. The examples of factors used in our discussions of two-treatment experiments include the number of tutoring sessions per week (see Table 11–2) and the type of game controller (see Table 12–2). Notice that the two levels of the factor we called the number of tutoring sessions per week are quantitative (one session per week versus two sessions per week), whereas the two levels of the factor we called the type of game controller are qualitative (keyboard versus joystick). Because all two-treatment designs are single-factor designs, the titles of chapters 11 and 12 could just as easily have been "Single-Factor Two-Treatment Designs with Independent Observations" and "Single-Factor Two-Treatment Designs with Correlated Observations."

Multiple-treatment single-factor designs are simply single-factor designs in which the factor has more than two levels. For example, if a researcher compared the effects of one versus two versus three tutoring sessions per week on student achievement, the quantitative factor of the experiment (number of tutoring sessions per week) would have three levels (one, two, and three tutoring sessions per week). Similarly, if a researcher compared performance with three types of game controllers (keyboard, joystick, and trackball), the qualitative factor of the experiment (type of game controller) would have three levels. Thus, multiple-treatment single-factor designs are simply extensions of the two-treatment single-factor designs discussed in chapters 11 and 12. As extensions, they are used to address the same basic questions for which we use two-treatment designs. But, by including more than two levels of the experimental factor in the design of the experiment, multiple-treatment experiments are capable of providing a more complete answer to the basic question being addressed. To begin we extend the between-subject two-treatment design to a multiple-treatment design and examine its enhanced ability to answer basic questions.

Multiple-Treatment Single-Factor Designs: Single-factor designs in which the factor has more than two levels.

Between-Subject Multiple-Treatment Designs

The assignment of subjects to the treatment conditions of a multiple-treatment between-subject design is done using basically the same random assignment procedures we used for two-treatment designs. The only difference is that we randomly assign subjects to three or more treatment conditions instead of only two. An illustration appears in Table 13–1 with k, the number of treatments, set at four, and n, the number of subjects assigned to each treatment, set at 10. Notice that each subject (S) is labeled with a different subscript and experiences only one treatment

Treatment Condition 1	Treatment Condition 2	Treatment Condition 3	Treatment Condition 4
S_1	S_{11}	S_{21}	S_{31}
S_2	S_{12}	S_{22}	S_{32}
S_3	S_{13}	S_{23}	S_{33}
S_4	S_{14}	S_{24}	S_{34}
S_5	S_{15}	S_{25}	S_{35}
S_6	S_{16}	S_{26}	S_{36}
S_7	S_{17}	S_{27}	S_{37}
S_8	S_{18}	S_{28}	S_{38}
S_9	S_{19}	S_{29}	S_{39}
S_{10}	S_{20}	S_{30}	S_{40}

Table 13–1. Subject assignment for a multiple-treatment between-subject experimental design. In this illustration 40 subjects have been randomly assigned, 10 each to four treatment conditions.

condition, thus confirming that the observations collected for each treatment condition are independent of each other.

Multiple-Treatment Designs for Answering Basic Question 4

Multiple-treatment experiments that address Basic Question 4 have a single experimental treatment condition and two or more control conditions. The groups against which we compare the experimental condition are referred to as control groups because they serve as a standard of comparison by which we judge the magnitude of the experimental effect. This type of design is applied in many areas (including neuropsychological research; see chapter 20) when the experimental manipulation calls for a surgical procedure, such as the production of a brain lesion in animal subjects. The animals assigned to receive the experimental treatment are anesthetized and surgically altered. One group of control subjects typically receives no treatment whatever, a second control group is anesthetized only, and a third group is both anesthetized and operated on without any alteration or removal of tissue that is likely to affect the dependent measure. The latter group is often described as having undergone a **sham procedure**, a treatment condition that contains all the invasive elements of the experimental treatment (the neurosurgery) short of the treatment itself (the production of a lesion). (Whether one describes the group as a sham group or a placebo group, as we did earlier in the description of a study to examine Compound X for its antidepressant effect, is not important. The two terms refer to the same kind of partially treated control condition, although the sham designation is more common when aspects of the treatment administration, such as surgery, are invasive and therefore potentially stressful.)

In summary, we answer Basic Question 4 by comparing the behavior of subjects who receive exposure to an experimental variable (the experimental group) to control subjects who either remain totally undisturbed (the untreated control group) or who experience certain aspects of the treatment administration without actually experiencing the treatment itself (one or more partially treated control groups). As introduced in chapter 5, experimental manipulation can take either of two forms:

1. Introduce a condition that *is not* normally present and evaluate the effect of its presence on a behavior.

2. Remove a condition that *is* normally present and evaluate the effect of its absence on a behavior.

In general, whenever an experimental manipulation involves introducing a condition into or removing a condition from a normal or typical environmental context, we must control for the procedures we use to accomplish the introduction or removal. That is, we do not want effects linked to the treatment administration masquerading as experimental effects.

An Extension of a Two-Treatment Between-Subject Experiment

To build on your understanding of control procedures and how several control groups are sometimes necessary to assess accurately the effect of a single experi-

Sham Procedure: A treatment condition that contains all the invasive elements of the experimental treatment short of the treatment itself.

mental treatment, we re-examine a problem in the form of Basic Question 4 that was presented in chapter 11: Will subjects who receive tutoring at the Student Advisement Center benefit from the experience?

Students were randomly assigned either to be tutored or not to be tutored, and their performances on an examination were used to reflect the effectiveness of the tutoring experience. Let us assume that we were able to demonstrate that, as hypothesized, the tutoring experience resulted in superior performance on an examination relative to the performance of untutored subjects. We may be pleased to have confirmed the value of private tutoring for academically at-risk students, but, expected result or not, the confirmation of our experimental hypothesis is not necessarily the end of our interest in our evaluation of tutoring effectiveness.

Sometimes answers raise questions

The results of an experiment, whether expected or not, often raise more questions than they answer. In fact, some would argue that the questions raised by an experiment are as much a measure of its quality as the questions the experiment answers. For example, with respect to the tutoring research scenario, it is natural to wonder what specific aspects of the tutoring experience caused the improvement in the students' test scores. To what extent was an improvement in test performance among tutored students linked to the quality of the review materials used by the tutor? To what extent was the improvement linked to the nature of the personal relationship and rapport between student and tutor? Was a student perception of emotional support a key factor ("My tutor really cares how well I do. I can't let her down!") or was the improvement in test performance in part due to the confidence and motivation the tutor instilled ("You can do it!")? Do students learn more from same-gender tutors or from different-gender tutors? Perhaps the principal condition enabling the tutored students to perform in a superior fashion was not at all linked to the tutors' presentation of specific course-related information. It may have been nothing more complicated than the opportunity the students had to study in the distraction-free atmosphere of the Student Advisement Center or the development of a better test-taking strategy.

In the original two-treatment experiment, which called for comparing the performances of untutored to those of tutored students, we could not tease apart the contributions various aspects of the tutoring experience made to an improvement in the students' test performance. In a multiple-treatment design, however, we are not as limited.

By adding two treatment conditions to the original design, we could assess the contribution of quiet study time and access to special review materials to the tutoring effect. The groups would be:

Treatment Condition 1: Untutored controls, as in the original two-treatment study.

Treatment Condition 2: Untutored controls, as in the original two-treatment study, but the students have to come to the Student Advisement Center for one hour per week of quiet unsupervised study of the course material.

Treatment Condition 3: Untutored, but students come for one hour per week of quiet study time at the Student Advisement Center and use the same special review materials as the tutored subjects.

Treatment Condition 4: Tutored in a quiet environment with special review materials, as in the original two-treatment study.

Interpretations of Four Patterns of Experimental Results

Four sets of hypothetical results from this experiment are shown in Table 13–2.

Result 1. If only the tutored subjects had high test scores (Treatment Condition 4), we would be more confident of the value of the tutor's role in promoting an improvement of the students' academic performance. There is nothing in this pattern of results indicating that access to special review materials or the opportunity for quiet study time can, by themselves, cause an improvement in test scores.

Result 2. If subjects in Treatment Conditions 2, 3, and 4 were similar in their test performance and all three groups performed better than the untutored subjects of Treatment Condition 1, we would have evidence that the opportunity to have a quiet place to study undisturbed is, by itself, sufficient to produce a positive influence on the test scores.

Result 3. If Treatment Conditions 3 and 4 performed similarly and both obtained better test scores than Treatment Conditions 1 and 2, we would have evidence that providing students access to the special review materials used by the tutors was sufficient to improve test scores, and we would have to question whether the personal involvement of a tutor was necessary for the instructional benefit to occur.

Result 4. In this pattern we assume that all four treatment conditions were different from each other. The interpretation would be that each additional educational benefit (a quiet study environment, access to special review materials, and personal instruction and coaching by a tutor) is sufficient to promote some improvement in test performance, and that the more elements present, the better test performance is likely to be.

A Multiple-Treatment Experiment to Follow a Result 1 Outcome

Let us assume that Result 1 was the experimental outcome, which indicates that personal instruction and coaching is a necessary component of the Student

	Treatment Condition 1	Treatment Condition 2	Treatment Condition 3	Treatment Condition 4
Result 1	71	73	75	91
Result 2	68	88	87	90
Result 3	72	69	92	90
Result 4	67	77	86	95

Table 13–2. Four hypothetical patterns of mean test results from the experimental evaluation of four study methods (Treatment Conditions 1, 2, 3, and 4).

Advisement Center's efforts to raise the test scores of academically at-risk students. We can attempt to find further support for the latter conclusion by moving from a Basic Question 4 conception of the problem (Does the experience of being tutored increase students' test scores?) to a Basic Question 5 conception (To what extent is an improvement in test performance among tutored students linked to the *style* of personal instruction that takes place between student and tutor?) An experimental design to explore the relative effectiveness of three study environments on test grades is shown below.

Treatment Condition 1. A one-hour study session per week, with special review materials available, held in the same location used by the tutored subjects, but without the assistance of any tutor. (The tutor proctors the study session but does not interact with the student.)

Treatment Condition 2. A one-hour study session per week, with special review materials available, with the tutor present, but "tutoring" is limited to answering student questions. The tutor is responsive when the student pauses during the self-paced review to ask a question, but does not initiate any discussion of the material.

Treatment Condition 3. A one-hour study session per week with the same special review materials used by the other students, but presented by the tutor in the form of a structured lesson plan. (This is the same condition that was used in the original two-treatment experiment to compare the performance of untutored to tutored subjects.)

Holding variables constant

In the three-treatment experiment described above we have held study time, study location, and study materials constant for all three groups (a benefit first described in chapter 10). In the original two-treatment (untutored versus tutored) experiment, any of these three variables could have contributed to the superiority of the tutored students. They may have studied more than the untutored students because of their required attendance at the weekly tutoring session; when they did study it was in an ideal atmosphere; and they had the advantage of using specially developed review materials. By contrast, the only variable we are systematically manipulating in the three-treatment experiment described above is the level of personal involvement between the tutor and the student. If the students who experience Treatment Condition 3 get better grades than the other two groups, in this particular study we could eliminate the three variables we held constant as an explanation for the superior test performance and argue for an interpretation that links the benefit to the student/tutor relationship.

Basic Question 5 versus Basic Question 6

Because the levels of the independent variable in the latter experiment differ qualitatively (the style of tutoring), the experiment addresses Basic Question 5. Had we, instead, systematically varied the *time* allotted for tutoring (say, 0 minutes, 30 minutes, and 45 minutes) while keeping the style of instruction constant (say, the structured lesson plan of Treatment Condition 3), the experiment would be in the form of Basic Question 6 (quantitatively defined levels of the independent variable) rather than Basic Question 5 (qualitatively defined levels of the independent variable).

Research as a Chain of Experiments

We began our re-examination of the tutoring scenario with a review of the original two-treatment result: Tutoring promoted superior academic performance. Then we explored one of many questions raised by that finding (Is personal tutoring both necessary and sufficient to improve test scores?). We followed one possible outcome (Result 1) of that experiment (only the tutored subjects obtained high test scores) by posing yet another question (Will varying the amount of tutoring students get lead to different levels of academic improvement?). This is the nature of research: Experiments progress in chainlike fashion leading to ever more detailed questions and experimental approaches that probe every facet of a behavioral phenomenon. When you conduct a search of the literature to gather background material for an intended research project, you will find that a single journal article is often used to report the results of several experiments. Each individual experiment may leave some important questions unanswered, but together they are likely to answer at least one important research question.

Manipulated versus Nonmanipulated Independent Variables: A Reminder

Instead of assigning subjects to each of the three tutoring conditions described above, wouldn't it have been easier to let subjects decide for themselves how they wished to handle their preparation for examinations? Those subjects who chose to work independently would be regarded as having experienced Treatment Condition 1, those who wanted a tutor *available* to answer questions but did not want a formal tutoring session would be regarded as having experienced Treatment Condition 2, and those subjects who preferred the structured lesson from the tutor would be regarded as having experienced Treatment Condition 3.

Without careful consideration, the latter arrangement may appear a legitimate alternative to *assigning* subjects to the various treatment conditions. But, recalling the distinction between manipulated and nonmanipulated (ex post facto) variables originally drawn in chapter 3 and repeated in several places since, you know that when an independent variable is not under the control of the experimenter the study is an example of *correlational* research rather than *experimental* research. The data of a correlational study allow us to assess the *association* between the type of test preparation the student elects (a subject variable) and test performance (a behavioral measure), but we cannot conclude that one or the other methods of preparation *causes* relatively good or poor test performance. This interpretive limitation of correlational data becomes clear if you consider that the less able students, who probably perceive that they could fail the course, may be more likely than the better students to elect structured tutoring (Condition 3). The uneven distribution of high- versus low-achieving students across the Condition 1 and 3 treatment groups would therefore be confounded with the method-of-preparation variable, and the internal validity we need to draw a causal connection between the method of preparation and the level of test performance would be absent.

Error: Noise in the System

When an analysis of experimental results fails to support a hypothesized pattern of behavioral differences among the treatment conditions, there are two possible interpretations. Either the manipulated levels of the experimental factor are incapable of causing the hypothesized pattern or they are indeed capable but did not produce the pattern in strong enough fashion to be detectable against an error-filled ("noisy") background.

We examine throughout this book how error can mask the effects of manipulating an independent variable in many different contexts and in many different ways, including discussions of power (chapters 4 and 11), confounding and extraneous variables (chapters 3 and 10), initial equivalence and random assignment (chapters 4 and 11), and individual differences (chapter 4). Here we will again discuss elements that can contribute "noise" to an experiment and ways of dealing with the problems that are appropriate for multiple-treatment experiments.

Individual differences

In analyzing the data of a single-factor between-subject experiment it is possible to identify two sources for the variability that exists among the dependent variable measurements: the treatment effect and error. But part of the variability identified as error from random sources is really due to systematic individual differences: the physical and behavioral characteristics of individual subjects that represent their uniqueness as individuals. In a psychological experiment, individual differences among subjects influence the behavioral data in addition to any effects of the experimental treatment(s). Sometimes, as in the case of a within-subject experiment (chapter 12), it is possible to estimate the variability introduced by individual differences and, in effect, remove it from the estimate of error. But, in a between-subject experiment, the contributions of individual differences and random factors are inseparable, so individual differences add to the estimate of error and make it more difficult to detect the effect of a manipulated variable.

One obvious tactic to avoid large individual differences is to use only those subjects who meet predetermined criteria. For example, if you were to do a reaction-time study to see how rapidly subjects could respond to a signal from different instrument displays, you would want to screen all your subjects to make sure they all had good vision and were free of any health problems that could affect their usual ability to respond to a stimulus.

Another tactic for minimizing nonexperimental sources of variability is to make the methods involved in data collection as uniform as possible for all the subjects. The apparatus must function reliably as intended; the subjects in any given treatment condition must be given precisely the same instructions; the experimenter must, if personally involved in testing, behave in a consistent manner for all subjects; and so forth. The more features of the research environment you can hold constant or within narrow limits, the more successful you will be in controlling sources of error, and the more successful you are likely to be in demonstrating a significant experimental effect if one truly exists.

Block Randomization in Between-Subject Designs

Sometimes variability that appears to be random can be caused by the intrusion of systematic extraneous influences that are tied to the execution of the experiment, and this is especially likely when the execution of an experiment extends over a long period of time. Consider, for example, the possibility of systematic changes in a subject population that can take place over time. Students in introductory psychology are often asked to volunteer to serve as subjects for student and faculty research projects for extra course credit. A legitimate worry is that the students who volunteer early in the semester could tend to be mostly the high achievers, who are eager to have new experiences and want to contribute to science. Conversely, the students who volunteer later in the semester could tend to be less motivated, reluctantly deciding to sign the subject roster only when they become aware that they need the extra credit to avoid getting a poor grade. Any difference in the motivation level of early versus later volunteers would, of course, be a source of extraneous variability.

Even animal populations maintained in laboratory environments are vulnerable to influences that fluctuate over time. For example, the control that is maintained over temperature, humidity, and other living conditions (food, water, and sanitation) can occasionally falter due to equipment breakdown, power failure, or human error. Also, changes in the animal maintenance staff that take place over time can affect the laboratory environment with respect to noise, cleanliness, and the general quality of animal care.

Some systematic changes that take place over the administration of a lengthy experiment are related to changes in the experimenter and in the experimental apparatus. Wear and tear on experimental apparatus can affect both treatment administration and data collection. Personnel in charge of testing can, over time, become more expert at conducting the experiment or, on the negative side, become less proficient because of fatigue, the loss of initial enthusiasm, the crush of other responsibilities, and the like. Also, if there are staffing changes over the course of a long experiment, the techniques of the new experimenters are unlikely to match exactly the techniques of the previous ones.

There is a way to balance the impact of extraneous variables across all treatment conditions of a multiple-treatment between-subjects design to improve the capacity of the experiment to document treatment-induced behavioral differences. The method, called **block randomization**, requires assignment of subjects randomly to treatment conditions in **blocks** — subgroups containing one subject per treatment condition. For example, the criterion for membership in a block could be the date on which the subject volunteered for the experiment. If the experiment has four treatment conditions, each of the first four subjects to volunteer would be randomly assigned to one of the four treatment conditions in the first block (see the first row of Table 13–3). The next four would be assigned to the second block in a similar manner, and so on.

Block Randomization: The random assignment of subjects to treatment conditions in blocks.

Block: A subgroup containing one subject per treatment condition.

	Treatment 1	Treatment 2	Treatment 3	Treatment 4
Block 1	S_3	S_1	S_2	S_4
Block 2	S_7	S_5	S_6	S_8
Block 3	S_9	S_{10}	S_{12}	S_{11}
Block 4	S_{14}	S_{16}	S_{13}	S_{15}
Block 5	S_{19}	S_{17}	S_{20}	S_{18}
Block 6	S_{21}	S_{22}	S_{23}	S_{24}
.	.	.	.	.
.	.	.	.	.
.	.	.	.	.

Table 13–3. The assignment of subjects to four treatments by blocks. The illustration stops with the assignment of the first 24 subjects.

The subjects within a block are all tested under their assigned treatment condition before testing the next set of subjects in the next block. As we proceed through the experiment, forming blocks from successive waves of volunteers, each block represents a particular time frame in the execution of the experiment. Presumably, any extraneous variables unique to that particular time frame (changes in the functioning of apparatus; a new experimenter takes over data collection; changes in the subject pool) will have a uniform impact on all the subjects within a particular block and, therefore, an equal impact on all treatment conditions.

Within-Subject Multiple-Treatment Designs

Chapter 12 presented three variations of the two-treatment within-subject experiments: the test-retest design, the pretest-posttest design, and the condition 1 versus condition 2 design. All of these designs may be expanded to include more than two treatment conditions.

The Extension of the Test-Retest Design

As in the two-treatment version, the extension of the test-retest design (test-retest — retest — ... — retest) is most useful when prior test sessions are themselves the variable we presume will affect subsequent measures of performance. In the memory task, Treatment Condition 1 consisted of having the subjects study a list of words for one minute and then write down as many words as they could remember from the list. Treatment Condition 2 was an exact repeat of the first, and we presumed that the experience gained from the first study session would contribute to the subjects' subsequent capability for recalling words after the second one-minute study session. The latter test-retest arrangement can be expanded to include any number of retest sessions.

Criterion: A level of performance used to designate successful achievement of a task.

When the independent variable is prior test experience, it is more common to designate the original test and each subsequent retest as a *trial* (a unit of test experience) rather than a treatment condition. In some experiments subjects are given a set number of trials. In other experiments subjects continue to be tested until they reach a predetermined **criterion**, a level of performance used to designate successful achievement of a task. We could, for example, decide to terminate the experiment on the trial when a subject successfully recalled 90% of the list of words, thereby designating "number of trials to criterion" as the dependent variable.

The raw data of a multiple-treatment test-retest experiment is commonly presented as in Table 13–4. Notice the repeated measurement aspect of the design: Each trial represents a test (Trial 1) or a retest (Trials 2 to *k*) of the same subjects.

Sometimes the analysis of data in the form of Table 13–4 centers on simple description of the subjects' progress from trial to trial, whereas in other research contexts it is important to examine the different levels of performance between specific trials for statistical significance. It might be important, for example, to determine if the subjects recalled significantly more words on Trial 4 than on Trial 2.

The Extension of the Pretest-Posttest Design

The pretest-posttest design was presented in chapter 12 as a close cousin of the test-retest design because both involve an initial and a later test that, ideally, are carried out under uniform test conditions. The difference is that in the pretest-posttest scenario a "significant event" occurs *between* the pretest and the posttest, which is presumably reflected in a difference in the posttest scores compared to the pretest scores. An extension of the pretest-posttest design is shown in Table 13–5.

As in the case of the two-treatment pretest-posttest design, the extended version is vulnerable to extraneous influences that, along with the significant events, can affect the subjects' behavior. Thus, we cannot really be sure that the significant events are the cause of demonstrable differences between pretest and posttest performances, and internal validity suffers.

To establish a basis for the conclusion that the intervening events are the cause of behavioral change and thereby introduce internal validity, we must include a control group against which to compare the experimental group. The appropriate

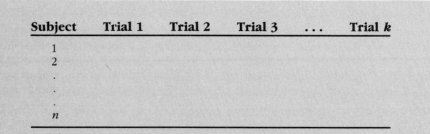

Subject	Trial 1	Trial 2	Trial 3	. . .	Trial *k*
1					
2					
.					
.					
.					
n					

Table 13–4. The form of the table for recording the data from *k* trials for a group of *n* subjects. Each row of the table contains the data for one subject, so each trial is a repeated measurement on the same subject.

Subject	Pretest	[Event 1]	Posttest 1	[Event 2]	Posttest 2
1					
2					
.					
.					
.					
n					

Table 13–5. A one-test extension of the pretest-posttest design. Each row of the table contains the data for one subject, so each posttest is a repeated measurement on the same subject.

control group consists of subjects who are comparable to the experimental subjects, who are tested on the same schedule as the experimental subjects but who do not experience the intervening events (see Table 13–6). In other words, initial equivalence must exist between the experimental and control groups. In the latter form, the design is called the **pretest-posttest design with an equivalent control group**, and the initial equivalence is achieved through the random assignment of subjects to the control and experimental groups.

Pretest-Posttest Design with an Equivalent Control Group: Two groups of randomly assigned subjects receive the pretest and the posttest but only one experiences the significant event.

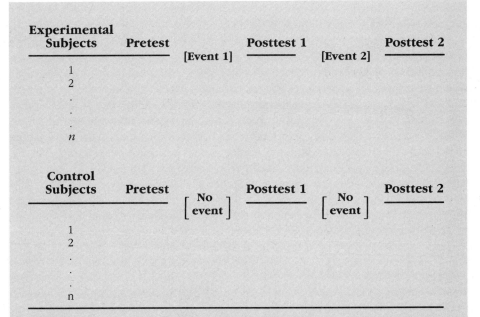

Experimental Subjects	Pretest	[Event 1]	Posttest 1	[Event 2]	Posttest 2
1					
2					
.					
.					
.					
n					

Control Subjects	Pretest	[No event]	Posttest 1	[No event]	Posttest 2
1					
2					
.					
.					
.					
n					

Table 13–6. A one-test extension of the pretest-posttest design with a control group that does not experience the intervening events. Each row of the table contains the data for one subject, so each posttest is a repeated measurement on the same subject.

The design shown in Table 13–6 is particularly useful when evaluating the effects of specific programed experiences on behavior. Imagine, for example, an attempt to evaluate the effectiveness of two different messages on smoking behavior. After assigning smokers randomly either to the control or experimental condition, we would pretest each one to evaluate the strength of the cigarette habit (say, by recording the number of cigarettes each subject smokes in a day). Next, the smokers assigned to the experimental condition see a film with a mild fear message (Event 1) that explains how smoking can be damaging to one's health. The film is followed at some point by a re-evaluation (Posttest 1) of the strength of each subject's smoking habit. Then the experimental subjects see another film (Event 2), but this time the health message is delivered with a strong fear message. As before, we re-evaluate the smoking habit (Posttest 2) some time after the subjects see the film. Since we do not know how much the subjects' smoking would have decreased without their seeing the films, we must use an equivalent control group as a standard of comparison. The controls are the smokers who do not see the film but are evaluated on the same schedule as those who do see the film. To compare the posttest behavior of the experimental and control groups, one tactic is to compute a set of change scores for both groups by subtracting each subject's posttest measure from his or her pretest measure. Then the two sets of change scores are compared using a t test. A significant finding would mean that the change in behavior between pretest and posttest was greater for one group than the other.

The pretest-posttest label is also applied to investigations in which the significant intervening event is accidental rather than manipulated. For example, instead of randomly assigning smokers to the experimental group (which experiences the intervening events) and the control group (which does not), imagine this scenario. Two television specials dealing with the dangers of smoking are shown six months apart. Some smokers tune in to both specials, whereas others do not. Like the experiment described earlier, we have two groups of subjects to evaluate, one that experienced both antismoking messages and one that did not. But the absence of a random assignment procedure for determining which smokers do and which smokers to not experience the intervening events disqualifies the study as a true experiment. Instead, it is a **quasi-experiment**, a study that takes the general form of an experiment but does not have the elements of control or the random assignment of subjects to treatment conditions that characterize true experiments. In general quasi-experiments are useful when truly experimental approaches are impossible or impractical to implement. Since they are not true experiments, they tend to suffer from threats to internal validity, which compromises our ability to infer a causal relationship between the subjects' experiences and the subjects' subsequent behavior. (In chapter 15, which deals with quasi-experimental designs, we describe strategies to increase the internal validity of quasi-experimental pretest-posttest studies.)

Quasi-experiment: A study that takes the general form of an experiment but does not have the elements of control or the random assignment of subjects to treatment conditions that characterize true experiments.

The Extension of the Within-Subject Condition 1 versus Condition 2 Design

The multiple-treatment within-subject design with k conditions is the same as the between-subject design with k treatment conditions (see Table 13–1) except that, as shown in Table 13–7, the same subjects are exposed to all the treatment conditions.

Subject	Treatment Condition 1	Treatment Condition 2	Treatment Condition 3	Treatment Condition 4
1				
2				
3				
4				
5				
6				
7				
8				
9				
10				

Table 13–7. Subject assignment for a multiple-treatment within-subject experimental design. Since each row of the table contains the data for one subject, filling in the data for each row requires four repeated measurements of the same subject.

We now expand a hypothetical research problem we addressed earlier so it will fit the multiple-treatment design shown in Table 13–6. Specifically, chapter 12 described an experiment to compare subject performance on a video game as a function of the type of game controller (keyboard versus joystick) the subject used to play the game. All subjects were tested with both controllers. To extend that simple design we could add two other controllers to the experiment: a trackball (a sphere for controlling movements with the fingertips) for Treatment Condition 3, and a glove controller (basically a glove equipped with sensors to respond to hand movements) for Treatment Condition 4. Unfortunately, as explained below, it is now no longer a "simple" design.

Carryover Effects

The threat to internal validity posed by carryover effects was discussed in chapter 12 in the context of two-treatment within-subject experimental designs. It may already have crossed your mind that the problem is likely to be even more severe when subjects experience multiple treatment conditions, and, of course, you would be correct.

Sequence and order effects

There are really two kinds of carryover effects: sequence effects and order effects. In the last chapter we mentioned but did not emphasize the distinction between sequence and order effects. In the context of two-treatment experiments, sequence and order effects cannot be teased apart. The second treatment can follow only one other treatment (the first), so both its order (second) and its sequence (following the first treatment) are bound together. Now, however, in the context of repeated measures experiments with more than two treatment conditions, it is possible to tease apart sequence effects and order effects.

A sequence effect is more tied to a specific effect from a preceding treatment, whereas an order effect is associated more with the position a treatment condition occupies in a set of several treatment conditions (first, second, third, and so on). Let us examine a design with three treatments to illustrate the difference between a sequence effect and an order effect. Consider the six possible orders (see Table 13–8) of three treatment conditions (1, 2, and 3) in a within-subject design:

Notice that the treatments differ both with respect to order of administration (each treatment is administered either first, second, or third) *and* with respect to the treatment (or treatments) that precede them. For example, when we compare Testing Order 1 to Testing Order 6, we see that the *order* of Treatment 2 is the same (second in both testing orders), but its *sequence* is different: In Testing Order 1, Treatment 2 follows Treatment 1, but in Testing Order 6, Treatment 2 follows Treatment 3. If the results from Treatment 2 in Testing Order 1 differed from the results of Treatment 2 in Testing Order 6, we could describe the phenomenon as a sequence effect.

Fortunately, even though it is possible to differentiate sequence effects from order effects, in most cases we need not be concerned about the distinction between these two kinds of carryover effects. The influence of both sequence and order effects on the data of within-subject experiments may be minimized using counterbalancing measures similar to the procedures used for the two-treatment within-subject condition 1 versus condition 2 design.

Counterbalancing with All Possible Orders

Inspect the six orders of treatment presentation shown in Table 13–8. The illustration depicts a within-subject design with three treatments. Did you notice that every possible treatment order was represented? In general, there are *k!* possible testing orders where *k* is the number of treatment conditions and the exclamation point (!) is mathematical notation for the factorial operation. To compute *k!* we must multiply [the * symbol is a multiplication dot] $k * (k - 1) * (k - 2) * (k - 3)$, etc. until the value 1 is reached. For example, if $k = 3$, as it does in Table 13–8, $k! = 3! = 3 * 2 * 1 = 6$. The answer ($k! = 6$) is the number of treatment orders that are possible when $k = 3$. Similarly, $6! = 6 * 5 * 4 * 3 * 2 * 1 = 720$.

To counterbalance carryover effects, all we have to do is randomly assign the same number of subjects to each of the possible treatment orders. Therefore, we could run a counterbalanced three-treatment within-subject experiment with 6

Order Number	Treatment Numbers
1	1–2–3
2	1–3–2
3	2–1–3
4	2–3–1
5	3–1–2
6	3–2–1

Table 13–8. All possible orders of three treatment conditions.

subjects (one subject in each order), 12 subjects (two subjects in each order), 18 subjects (three subjects in each order), and so on.

Counterbalancing with Selected Orders: The Latin Square

Counterbalancing by running the experiment with all possible treatment orders becomes progressively unwieldy as the number of treatment conditions increases. The value of 4! is 24; 5! = 120; 6! = 720; etc. Thus, even with as few as four treatment conditions, we would have 24 possible orders and would have to run at least 24 subjects to have a counterbalanced design that would include all possible orders of four treatments. The alternative is to use *selected* orders by constructing a Latin square.

We do not present the steps for constructing a Latin square, since that relatively complex solution for neutralizing counterbalancing is not likely to be attempted in an undergraduate research proposal. Nevertheless, you may encounter Latin square designs in your reading of the psychological literature, so you should have a basic understanding of what one is. A **Latin square** is a matrix of k rows and columns (remember, k stands for the number of treatment conditions) that contains a subset of all the possible treatment orders in a multiple treatment experiment. A Latin square is shown in Table 13–8 for a within-subject experiment with $k = 6$. To preserve balance, an equal number of subjects would be assigned to each of the 6 treatment orders.

As in the case of all possible orders, the Latin square design designates each treatment to be administered once in each ordinal position (first, second, third, and so forth), *and* for each treatment both to precede and follow every other treatment equally often. For example, the arrangement of treatments in Table 13–8 is a Latin square because each treatment appears once at each ordinal position, each treatment follows each of the other five treatments only once, and each treatment precedes each of the other five treatments only once. However, unlike the set of all possible treatment orders, each treatment does not precede and follow every other treatment equally often *at each ordinal position*. For example, in Table 13–8 notice that Treatment 3 follows Treatment 6 only when Treatment 3 is fourth in the treatment order. Thus, even though the counterbalancing offered by the Latin

Latin Square: A square matrix (k rows and columns) that contains a subset of all the possible treatment orders in a multiple-treatment experiment.

Order Number	Treatment Numbers					
1	1	2	6	3	5	4
2	2	3	1	4	6	5
3	3	4	2	5	1	6
4	4	5	3	6	2	1
5	5	6	4	1	3	2
6	6	1	5	2	4	3

Table 13–9. A Latin square with $k = 6$. The numbers are labels for treatment conditions, and each row is an order of treatment administration to one or more subjects.

square is not quite as complete as running all possible treatment orders, the sacrifice in precision is generally not worrisome relative to the unmanageable alternative: running $6! = 720$ different treatment orders.

Block Randomization in Within-Subject Designs

Some research problems, most notably those related to the study of perceptual phenomena, require measuring subject responses to repeated displays of a limited set of individual stimuli. A researcher might, for example, wish to display six different stimuli, one at a time, and repeat each stimulus five times, resulting in a total of 30 separate trials for each subject. Simple randomization of the 30 trials could result in uneven sequencing, as when early in the 30-trial sequence one or more stimuli appear repeatedly and, late in the sequence, do not appear at all. To avoid the imbalance in carryover effects that uneven sequencing is likely to introduce, we can present the stimuli in blocks using essentially the same block randomization procedure we applied to subject assignment in the between-subject design (see Table 13.3). Table 13.10 demonstrates the application of block randomization to the within subject design. Each block contains a randomized order of the complete set of stimuli, and the number of blocks designated for each subject corresponds to the number of repetitions planned for the stimuli (here, five). As with the more systematic counterbalancing techniques we have discussed, block randomization does not guarantee that existing carryover effects will be balanced, but it does not make it more likely they will be balanced.

	Block 1	Block 2	Block 3	Block 4	Block 5
S_1	6-4-3-1-2-5	3-4-1-2-5-6	2-5-1-6-4-3	1-6-4-5-3-2	4-3-2-5-6-1
S_2	3-6-4-1-2-5	5-2-4-3-1-6	1-6-5-2-4-3	2-6-5-3-1-4	2-1-6-4-3-5
.	.	.	.	.	.
.	.	.	.	.	.
S_n	2-1-6-4-3-5	5-3-6-2-4-1	4-2-6-5-1-3	6-3-5-1-2-4	1-2-6-4-3-5

Table 13–10. Block randomization for a within-subject design that calls for each of n subjects to be presented with five repetitions of six different stimuli.

Analyzing the Data of Single-Factor Experiments

ANOVA: The analysis of variance; a statistical analysis for comparing the means of two or more treatments or treatment combinations.

If the experimental data meet the underlying assumptions of the analysis of variance (**ANOVA**), it is the method of choice to determine if any differences exist among the set of k treatment means. The assumed data characteristic that is most easily verifiable is the interval or ratio scaling of the data. There is a version of the single-factor ANOVA that is appropriate to compare the treatment conditions of between-subject experiments, and a somewhat different version to compare the treatment conditions of within-subject experiments. Both computational methods are illustrated in Appendix B.

What Does the ANOVA Tell Us?

It is important to understand what the ANOVA tells us about the outcome of a single-factor experiment and what it does not tell us. A significant result means only that the variability among the set of treatment means is too large to be attributable to chance alone. That is, we know only that among the set of k treatment means, some mean or combination of means is/are significantly different from some other mean or combination of means. No more explicit information is implied by the finding of statistical significance. For example, a significant result could take the form of any of the patterns of results listed in Table 13–2. If an ANOVA on the data of such a four-treatment experiment revealed a significant treatment effect, we could not tell from the ANOVA alone which pattern of between-treatment differences (if, indeed, it was even represented by one of the four described in Table 13–2) is present. Therefore, following the determination of statistical significance in the "overall" ANOVA, the researcher should pursue running a **post-ANOVA test**, an analysis to follow the overall ANOVA that can reveal additional details about the specific pattern of the differences among the treatment conditions.

Post-ANOVA Test: An analysis to follow the overall ANOVA that can reveal additional details about the specific pattern of differences among the treatment conditions.

Post-ANOVA tests

Several methods are available for making comparisons between specific treatment conditions after the overall ANOVA has been completed. A requirement of one class of tests, called **a priori tests** or **planned comparisons**, is that the differences between the treatment conditions we wish to test for significance must have been hypothesized before the experiment was run. (It is legitimate to do *planned* comparisons even if there is no statistical significance evident in the overall ANOVA as long as the "planning" occurred prior to seeing the research results.)

A Priori Test: A technique for executing a comparison between treatment conditions that was planned prior to running an experiment.

If, instead, following a significant result in an ANOVA, we notice what appears to be a relatively large difference between two treatment means and we decide to evaluate the difference after the fact (**a posteriori**), we cannot use an a priori test. If we did, we would almost certainly make a Type I error (concluding a difference is significant when it really is not) in one or more of the comparisons. Three often-used a posteriori (also called **post hoc**) tests are the Tukey HSD test, the Neuman–Keuls test, and the Scheffe test. Post hoc tests allow us to make all possible comparisons among the treatment means (that is, to compare each treatment mean to every other treatment mean) after the fact while maintaining strict control over the probability of Type I error.

A Posteriori Test: A technique for executing a comparison between treatment conditions that was not planned prior to running an experiment.

The computational methods for ANOVA and post-ANOVA tests are readily available in most statistics texts, but, to renew the suggestion made in chapter 9 when discussing correlation, for anything other than a very limited data set, do your statistical analyses using a computer. Learning to use data-analysis software is well worth the effort.

Data analysis options for ordinal data

If the data to not meet the assumptions that underlie the ANOVA, there are alternatives. If the experimental design is between-subject and the data have at least ordinal scaling, the Kruskal–Wallis H test is the test of choice. If the experimental design is within-subject and the data have at least ordinal scaling, the Friedman test is appropriate. The computational methods for both tests can be found in any text that includes extensive coverage of nonparametric statistics.

Summary

The two-treatment designs covered in the previous two chapters can be used effectively to address some research questions, but, because of their limited scope, they also leave some questions unanswered. Often, the solution is to expand the two-treatment design to a multiple-treatment design. After pointing out the additional work that inevitably goes along with running more treatment conditions and the vulnerability of multiple-treatment designs to the intrusion of extraneous variables, we illustrated the advantages of multiple-treatment designs: the greater capacity the design has to answer questions. To provide continuity with previously discussed material, the examples we used to illustrate multiple-treatment designs were expanded versions of the between-subject and within-subject two-treatment experimental designs included in chapters 11 and 12. We defined the terminology that applies to multiple-treatment designs, and, using the basic questions as an organizing theme, we discussed the interpretation of various possible patterns of experimental results from a multiple-treatment study. Next, the strategy of holding variables constant was discussed in the context of multiple-treatment designs along with a reminder of the distinction between manipulated and nonmanipulated (subject) variables in a multiple-treatment context. Carryover effects are even more of a problem in within-subject multiple-treatment designs than they are in within-subject two-treatment designs, so we expanded the two-treatment counterbalancing procedures presented in chapter 12 to show how using all possible treatment orders and the Latin square design compare as tactics to neutralize carryover effects. The chapter concluded with a brief discussion of the choices for the statistical analysis of the data of multiple-treatment between-subject and within-subject experiments.

Key Terms

A Posteriori Test, p. 247
A Priori Test, p. 247
ANOVA, p. 246
Block Randomization, p. 238
Block, p. 238
Criterion, p. 240
Latin Square, p. 245
Multiple-Treatment Design, p. 231

Planned Comparisons, p. 247
Post-ANOVA Test, p. 247
Post Hoc Test, p. 247
Pretest-Posttest Design with an
    Equivalent Control Group, p. 241
Quasi-Experiment, p. 242
Sham Procedure, p. 232
Single-Factor Design, p. 230

Chapter Exercises

1. Discuss the limitations of the two-treatment experiment with respect to research in the form of Basic Questions 4, 5 and 6.

2. How does expanding a two-treatment design to a multiple-treatment design add to the capacity of an experiment to answer Basic Questions 4, 5, and 6? Use examples that draw on the two-treatment between-subject and within-subject experiments you designed for Proposal Assignments 4a and 12.

3. Review the hypothetical cooking and aphrodisiac research scenarios used to explain Basic Questions 4, 5, and 6 in chapter 5 and expand these two-treatment experiments to multiple-treatment experiments. Offer operational definitions for all independent and dependent variables. What are the factors and the levels of the factors in your experimental designs? With the expanded designs, what questions do you have the potential to answer that you could not answer with the two-treatment designs?

4. Explain your use of sham procedures and placebo conditions in the multiple-treatment designs you presented in your answers to question 3.

5. Design a two-treatment experiment to test the effectiveness of regular exposure to bright lights as a therapeutic measure to combat Seasonal Affective Disorder. Offer operational definitions for all independent and dependent variables. Assuming that the light therapy worked to ease the symptoms of depression, design some experiments to explore the importance of duration of exposure and the light intensity used in the treatments. Explain your use of sham/placebo groups in your experiments.

6. Assume you have been assigned to explore the effects on body weight of lowering daily caloric intake to 90%, 80%, 70%, 60%, or 50% of normal. What variables would you strive to keep constant for all the treatment conditions? What control group(s) would you include in your experimental design? Generate some hypothetical patterns of results for the means of the k treatment conditions in your experiment and offer an interpretation for each pattern.

7. Some researchers hypothesize that when some young children eat food with high levels of refined sugars they tend to become hyperactive. Present both an experimental and a correlational research approach to the hyperactivity hypothesis. In your experimental approach to the problem, try both a between-subject and a within-subject design. What control groups should you include in your experimental approach to this research problem? Generate some different patterns of results and offer an interpretation for each pattern.

8. A large group of colleges and universities in the Boston area pooled the Scholastic Aptitude Test data of their freshman classes. From the master list, a researcher randomly selected 50 students who had SAT verbal scores between 500 and 550, 50 students who had scores between 600 and 650, and 50 students who had scores between 700 and 750. All 150 students were contacted and all agreed to participate in a memory experiment, which found significant differences in the performance levels of the three groups. Was this an experiment? Why or why not?

Proposal Assignment 13: More Than Two Treatments

For Proposal Assignment 12 you modified your proposal from a two-treatment between-subject design to a two-treatment within-subject design. Now add a third treatment: Describe the third treatment. Then explain how you would assign subjects to groups in a between-subject design and how you would assign subjects to treatment orders in a within-subject Latin square design.

14

Experiments with Two or More Factors

Perhaps you have noticed that our own coverage of experimental design has progressively increased in complexity. First we discussed different types of between-subject (chapter 11) and within-subject (chapter 12) single-factor experiments with only two treatment conditions. Then, in chapter 13, we discussed between-subject and within-subject single-factor experiments with more than two treatment conditions. These single-factor experimental designs were presented as approaches to research problems in the form of Basic Questions 4, 5, and 6. Since research problems in the form of Basic Questions 1, 2, and 3 were addressed in Part IIA, that leaves only one basic question from the list originally presented in chapter 5 that we have not yet discussed. Appropriately, the last question is the most complex of the seven basic questions:

Basic Question 7: *Will introducing subjects to two or more systematically different conditions cause an additive and/or interactive effect on behavior?*

Two key terms in Basic Question 7 must be understood to capture the essence of the question as a whole: additive effect and interactive effect. They first appeared in chapter 5 in the discussion of Basic Question 7 and the application of factorial designs to research problems. To describe the combined effects of two treatment conditions on behavior as additive means that the effect one treatment condition has on behavior is independent of (is separate from or does not influence) the effect the second treatment condition has on behavior. When additivity is present in the results of a factorial experiment, the behavioral response to the manipulation of two factors is, as the label *additive* implies, simply the sum of two influences on behavior: the effect of manipulating independent variable 1 plus the effect of manipulating independent variable 2. By comparison, when the combined influence of two manipulated variables is characterized as interactive, the impact on behavior *cannot* be accounted for as a sum of two individual contributions. That is, an interactive effect (also called an interaction) is present when the effect of two variables acting in combination is either greater than (a **synergistic effect**) or less than (an **antagonistic effect**) what we would expect the combined effects of the two variables to be if each was acting independently of the other.

Specially contrived (model) sets of experimental data can be helpful in explaining and describing additive and interactive effects. But before we examine the model examples that illustrate the principal topic of this chapter—how two independent variables (factors) can combine their influences on behavior in additive and/or interactive fashion—let us consider a model of a single factor acting alone. The design is a between-subject two-treatment single-factor experiment (for review see chapter 11).

Synergistic Effect: A combined action of two or more variables that is greater than the sum of their individual contributions.

Antagonistic Effect: A combined action of two or more variables that is less than the potential of their individual contributions.

A Model of a Single Factor Acting Alone

Imagine that members of a hypothetical population of student subject volunteers possess only one or two levels of performance capability with respect to Task Y, a behavioral measure. Specifically, we assume that if tested on Task Y, half the population would get the score of 10 (low) and the remaining half would score 30 (high). If we randomly sampled 20 subjects from the population of high and low scorers and randomly assigned the selected subjects to two equal-sized groups, the result should be two groups of 10 subjects with equal representation of low and high scorers—the same ratio of low to high scorers that is present in the population. Thus, with respect to the subject's ability to perform on Task Y (see Table 14–1), we would describe the two groups as initially equivalent (see chapter 4 to review the concept of initial equivalence). Overall, the mean performance potential of the two groups on Task Y is the same medium (mean = 20) performance ability. Of course, in a true experiment we would not know a subject's performance ability in advance of any behavioral testing. Also, it is most unlikely that performance ability on a task would ever exist among members of a population in only two specific magnitudes, such as 10 and 30, and random factors always exist to some degree in a true research environment to influence experimental results. Nevertheless, for simplicity's sake, imagine the situation as described for the model: *Prior* to being exposed to any experimental condition, the subjects would, if sampled and tested above, perform on Task Y as shown in Table 14–1.

	Group 1	Group 2
	10	10
	30	10
	30	30
	30	10
	10	30
	10	10
	30	30
	10	10
	10	30
	30	30
Mean:	20	20

Table 14–1. Two groups that are initially equivalent with respect to performance potential on Task Y ($n = 10$ subjects per group) because random assignment resulted in equal numbers of high and low scorers in the two groups.

An Experiment with Factor A Alone

Now we introduce an experimental factor into the model. Imagine a research program for exploring the effects of rewarding subjects for their Task Y performance. For the first experiment assume that Factor A is the promise of a cash payment for completing Task Y. Subjects assigned to Level 1 of Factor A are promised only $1 for completing Task Y, whereas subjects assigned to Level 2 are promised $20. The performance on Task Y under Level 1 of Factor A ($1) does not change the subjects' initial performance potential, but the promise of $20 does result in a change: a 10-unit increase over the subjects' original Task Y performance potential. A hypothetical representation of the results of this two-treatment between-subject experiment appears in Table 14–2. Notice how the promise of the $20 payment raises the Task Y score by a constant 10 units for every individual, whereas the promise of only $1 has no effect (that is, a zero contribution).

After adding the hypothetical experimental effects to the initial performance potentials, the result would be Table 14–3. With the behavioral effects of the promised $1 and $20 payments added in, the means for Task Y performance (20 versus 30) now differ by 10 units, which is statistically significant. We would conclude that subjects who were promised $20 performed better on Task Y than subjects who were promised only $1 for their efforts.

An Experiment with Factor B Alone

Now let us imagine another experiment that is almost identical to the two-treatment, between-subject model just described for Factor A. The only difference is that in this experiment the compensation variable (Factor B) is in the form of extra course credit rather than money. Subjects assigned to Level 1 of Factor B are promised only 1 extra point toward their grade for completing Task Y, whereas the subjects assigned to Level 2 are promised 20 extra points. Assume that the prospect of receiving only 1 extra point enhances Task Y performance by 3 units over the

Factor A (Cash Payment)

Level 1 ($1.00)	Level 2 ($20.00)
10 + 0	10 + 10
30 + 0	10 + 10
30 + 0	30 + 10
30 + 0	10 + 10
10 + 0	30 + 10
10 + 0	10 + 10
30 + 0	30 + 10
10 + 0	10 + 10
10 + 0	30 + 10
30 + 0	30 + 10
Mean: 20 + 0	20 + 10

Table 14–2. The addition of a treatment effect causes the performance of two initially equivalent groups to differ. Two manipulated levels of Factor A, the promise of a $1 versus a $20 payment, contribute 0 versus 10 units to Task Y performance.

Factor A (Cash Payment)

Level 1 ($1.00)	Level 2 ($20.00)
10	20
30	20
30	40
30	20
10	40
10	20
30	40
10	20
10	40
30	40
Mean: 20	30

Table 14–3. These data, a collapsed representation of Table 14–2, represent the addition of experimental effects (0 and 10) to two initially equivalent groups. The 10-unit difference between the means of 20 and 30 is statistically significant, $t(18) = 2.12$, $p < .05$.

subjects' initial performance potential, and the prospect of receiving 20 points of extra course credit enhances performance by 11 units. A hypothetical set of results for the Factor B experiment appears in Tables 14–4 and 14–5. Table 14–4 shows the assumed initial performance potentials and the hypothetical experimental effects from Factor B as separate contributions to the data values, and Table 14–5 is a collapsed representation of Table 14–4. The two hypothetical treatment effects from manipulating Factor B, 3 units and 11 units, are represented as constant additions to each subject's initial performance potential. Unlike the experiment with Factor A, in this case the difference between the two treatment means, 23 and 31, is not significant.

Factor B (Extra Credit)	
Level 1 **(1 Point)**	**Level 2** **(20 Points)**
10 + 3	10 + 11
30 + 3	10 + 11
30 + 3	30 + 11
30 + 3	10 + 11
10 + 3	30 + 11
10 + 3	10 + 11
30 + 3	30 + 11
10 + 3	10 + 11
10 + 3	30 + 11
30 + 3	30 + 11
Mean: 20 + 3	20 + 11

Table 14–4. The addition of a treatment effect causes the performance of two initially equivalent groups to differ. The two levels of Factor B, 1 extra point versus 20 extra points, contribute 3 versus 11 units to Task Y performance.

Factor B (Extra Credit)	
Group 1 **(1 Point)**	**Group 2** **(20 Points)**
13	21
33	21
33	41
33	21
13	41
13	21
33	41
13	21
13	41
33	41
Mean: 23	31

Table 14–5. These data are a collapsed representation of Table 14–4 and represent the addition of experimental effects to two initially equivalent groups. The 8-unit difference between the means 23 and 31 is not significant, $t(18) = 1.69$, $p > .05$.

Combining Two Factors: Additive Effects

Instead of evaluating the effects on Task Y performance of a low versus high cash payment and a low versus high award of extra course credit in separate experiments, it is possible to manipulate *both* factors within the body of a single experiment. Using the terminology introduced in chapter 5, the combined form of the experiment is described as a 2×2 factorial design (see Table 14–6). The two levels of Factor A and two levels of Factor B define four treatment combinations or cells. In a between-subject design, subjects are randomly assigned to each cell, so there are four independent groups participating in the experiment. The letters AB within each cell of Table 14–6 refer to Factors A and B, and the *i* and *j* subscripts for the AB cell entries denote the levels of Factors A (subscript *i*) and B (subscript *j*) that are operative within that cell. In other words, each cell defines a different AB_{ij} treatment combination. Subjects assigned to cell AB_{11} ($i = 1$ and $j = 1$) receive the promise of $1 and 1 point of extra credit (Level 1 of both factors). Similarly, subjects assigned to cell AB_{12} ($i = 1$ and $j = 2$) are promised $1 and 20 points, those in AB_{21} are promised $20 and 1 point, and those in AB_{22} are promised $20 and 20 points.

A hypothetical set of *additive* experimental results from exposing four initially equivalent groups of subjects to the effects of *both* Factor A and Factor B on Task Y performance is shown in Table 14–7. Just as we did for the two single-factor experiments (see Tables 14–2 and 14–4), we shall assume that Levels 1 and 2 of Factor A add, respectively, 0 and 10 units to the subjects' original performance potential, and that the effects of the Levels 1 and 2 of Factor B add, respectively, 3 and 11 units.

Recalling that the initially equivalent groups assigned to each of the four AB_{ij} cells (treatment combinations) of the experiment all had a mean performance potential of 20 (see Table 14–1), each of the four cell means can be seen as the sum of two experimental effects added to a baseline value. That is, each AB_{ij} cell mean is represented as the original mean performance potential for that cell (20 in each

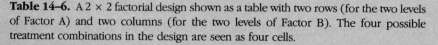

		Extra Credit (Factor B)	
		1 point (Level 1)	20 points (Level 2)
Cash Payment (Factor A)	$1 (Level 1)	AB_{11}	AB_{12}
	$20 (Level 2)	AB_{21}	AB_{22}

Table 14–6. A 2×2 factorial design shown as a table with two rows (for the two levels of Factor A) and two columns (for the two levels of Factor B). The four possible treatment combinations in the design are seen as four cells.

		Extra Credit (Factor B)	
		1 Point (Level 1)	**20 Points (Level 2)**
		10 + 0 + 3	10 + 0 + 11
		30 + 0 + 3	10 + 0 + 11
		30 + 0 + 3	30 + 0 + 11
		30 + 0 + 3	10 + 0 + 11
	$1 (Level 1)	10 + 0 + 3	30 + 0 + 11
		10 + 0 + 3	10 + 0 + 11
		30 + 0 + 3	30 + 0 + 11
		10 + 0 + 3	10 + 0 + 11
		10 + 0 + 3	30 + 0 + 11
		30 + 0 + 3	30 + 0 + 11
	Cell Means:	20 + 0 + 3	20 + 0 + 11
Cash Payment (Factor A)			
		30 + 10 + 3	30 + 10 + 11
		10 + 10 + 3	10 + 10 + 11
		10 + 10 + 3	30 + 10 + 11
		30 + 10 + 3	10 + 10 + 11
		10 + 10 + 3	10 + 10 + 11
	$20 (Level 2)	10 + 10 + 3	30 + 10 + 11
		30 + 10 + 3	30 + 10 + 11
		10 + 10 + 3	10 + 10 + 11
		30 + 10 + 3	30 + 10 + 11
		30 + 10 + 3	10 + 10 + 11
	Cell Means:	20 + 10 + 3	20 + 10 + 11

Table 14–7. The contributions of Factor A and Factor B to performance on Task Y. Each level of each factor is assumed to add a constant increment to each subject's initial Task Y performance potential.

case), plus the contribution from a level of Factor A, plus the contribution from a level of Factor B. In Table 14–7, for example, the cell mean of 41 (AB_{22}) is represented as 20 + 10 + 11: initial performance potential plus the influence of Level 2 of Factor A (10 units), plus the influence of Level 2 of Factor B (11 units). In general, when we describe the effects on behavior of two independent variables as additive, it means that the effect on behavior of the combination of variables can be understood as the sum of two separate effects.

Table 14–8 is the Table 14–7 data collapsed into composite scores that are representative of what real experimental data would look like. We say "real" because, outside a hypothetical model, we can never partition data values to identify the contributions of individual differences and treatment conditions in the manner shown in Table 14–6.

The individual contributions of Factors A and B to the results of a factorial experiment are called **main effects**. For the hypothetical data in Table 14–8, both

Main Effects: Differences among the treatment conditions of a factorial design that are attributable to a single factor.

**Extra Credit
(Factor B)**

		1 Point (Level 1)	20 Points (Level 2)	Factor A Means
		13	21	
		33	21	
		33	41	
		33	21	
		13	41	
	$1 (Level 1)	13	21	
		33	41	
		13	21	
		13	41	
		33	41	
	Cell Means: $\overline{AB}_{11} = 23$		$\overline{AB}_{12} = 31$	$\overline{A}_1 = 27$
Cash Payment (Factor A)				
		43	51	
		23	31	
		23	51	
		43	31	
		23	31	
	$20 (Level 2)	23	51	
		43	51	
		23	31	
		43	51	
		43	31	
	Cell Means: $\overline{AB}_{21} = 33$		$\overline{AB}_{22} = 41$	$\overline{A}_2 = 37$
	Factor B Means: $\overline{B}_1 = 28$		$\overline{B}_2 = 36$	

Table 14–8. The results of a model experiment with two treatment conditions. The effects of the treatment conditions are assumed to be additive. The subscripted $\overline{A}$ and $\overline{B}$ table entries are the means of the levels of Factors A and B.

the A and B main effects are statistically significant, but there is no evidence of an interaction between Factor A and Factor B (see Appendix B for details of the analysis). Specifically, the main effect from Factor A is apparent when we compare two overall Factor A means located in the far-right column of Table 14–8. One is the mean performance of all subjects who experienced Level 1 of Factor A (27), and the other is the mean performance of all subjects who experienced Level 2 of Factor A (37). The significant difference between these two means indicates that the promise of a $20 cash payment resulted in a higher level of Task Y performance than a $1 cash payment. Similarly, the main effect from Factor B is apparent when we compare the two overall column means at the very bottom of Table 14–8. One is the mean performance of all subjects who experienced Level 1 of Factor B (28), and the other is the mean performance of all subjects who experienced Level 2 of Factor B (36). The significant difference between these two means indicates that the promise of 20 points of extra credit resulted in a higher level of Task Y performance than 1 point of extra credit. Incidentally, in the single-factor experiment to evaluate Factor B (Table 14–5) discussed earlier, the same magnitude of experimental effect (3 units for Level 1 versus 11 units for Level 2) did not produce a statistically significant difference. The experimental effect was significant in the factorial experiment because of the extra power (see chapters 4 and 11) we get from using 20 versus only 10 subjects under each level of Factor B.

When two factors fail to interact, which is the pattern we purposely incorporated into the hypothetical data in Table 14–8, the plot of the cell means has a characteristic appearance: parallel lines. This graphic "signature" is apparent in the plot of the four cell means (see Figure 14–1) from Table 14–8. Of course, Figure 14–1 shows only one pattern of parallel lines: one that is consistent with the statistical significance of both A and B main effects. With other data, in which one or the other or both main effects are absent, the parallel lines would appear with different slopes and/or with varying degree of separation between them (see Figure 14–2).

Combining Two Factors: Interactive Effects

Just as cell means will plot as parallel lines when factors fail to interact, when factors do interact the cell means will plot as *non*parallel lines. In Figure 14–3, we

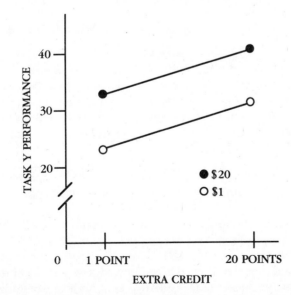

Figure 14–1. Task Y performance as a function of cash payment and extra credit. The plotted values are the four cell means from Table 14–8. The parallel lines indicate the absence of an interaction effect.

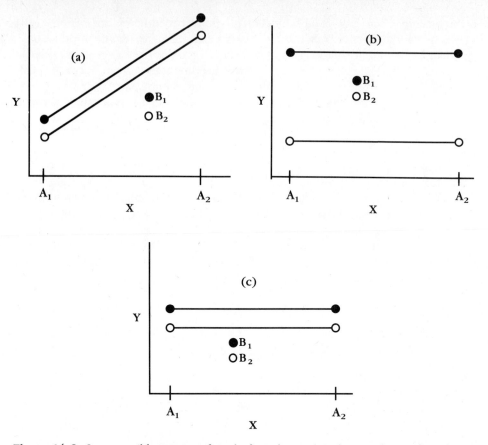

Figure 14–2. Some possible patterns of results from the combined manipulation of two factors that do not interact. (a) A main effect for Factor A is present, but not for Factor B. (b) A main effect for Factor B is present, but not for Factor A. (c) Neither an A nor a B main effect is present.

represent some possible patterns of interaction that are possible in a 2 × 2 factorial experiment. In general, when the lines cross (illustrations a and d in Figure 14–3), the results are dominated by the interaction effect, and main effects are unlikely to register as significant. When the lines diverge or converge (illustrations b and c in Figure 14–3), both main effects and interactions may be statistically significant.

Interaction as an Antagonism to Main Effects

Consider first a data set (Table 14–9) with cell means that, as shown in part a of Figure 14–3, plot as crossing lines. (The statistical analysis of the Table 14–9 data, which shows a significant interaction with no main effects, is summarized in Appendix B.) The data in Table 14–9 are the same as in Table 14–8 with one notable exception: each performance score in cell AB_{22} has been reduced by 22 units. The components of each score are viewed hypothetically (we can never *actually* dissect data values in the way represented in cell AB_{22}) as a composite of initial performance potential, plus the constant experimental effect assumed for Level 2 of Factor A ($+10$ units), plus the constant experimental effect assumed for Level 2 of Factor B

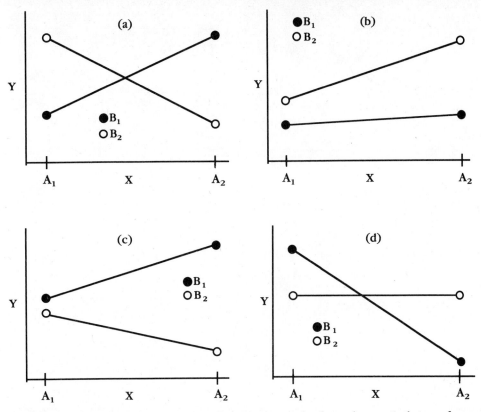

Figure 14–3. Some possible patterns of interactive results from the manipulation of two independent variables. The plots of cell means are all nonparallel.

(+11 units), plus an effect (−22 units) that is unique to the combination of Level 2 of Factor A with Level 2 of Factor B. Thus, in this case, the A × B interaction takes the form of a negative influence on performance that tends to counter (is antagonistic to) the positive influences of Factors A and B (+10 and +11 units, respectively) when they are acting independently of each other.

The mean of cell AB_{22} is now a relatively low 19 compared to the 41 for the same cell in Table 14–8, in which no interaction effect was incorporated. Thus, the most heavily compensated group ($20 and 20 points of extra credit) performed relatively poorly even though the effect on behavior of each type of compensation taken alone was to improve performance. (Perhaps the relatively poor performance of the most heavily compensated group was caused by the anxiety our hypothetical subjects felt from having to perform for such high stakes.) In contrast to the parallel lines of Figure 14–1, which reflect the absence of interaction, in Figure 14–4 we see that with an interaction present, the cell means plot as crossing lines.

In answer to the question "How did the 1-point versus 20-point incentives affect Task Y performance?" the answer would have to be "It depends." When the two levels of extra-credit incentive were offered in combination with a $1 payment, the mean of the 20-point group was higher than the 1-point group (31 versus 23). But when the two levels of extra-credit incentive were offered in combination with a

		Extra Credit (Factor B)		
		1 Point (Level 1)	20 Points (Level 2)	Factor A Means
Cash Payment (Factor A)	**$1 (Level 1)**	13 33 33 33 13 13 33 13 13 33	21 21 41 21 41 21 41 21 41 41	
	Cell Means:	23	31	$\overline{A}_1 = 27$
	$20 (Level 2)	43 23 23 43 23 23 43 23 43 43	$30 + 10 + 11 - 22 = 29$ $10 + 10 + 11 - 22 = 9$ $30 + 10 + 11 - 22 = 29$ $10 + 10 + 11 - 22 = 9$ $10 + 10 + 11 - 22 = 9$ $30 + 10 + 11 - 22 = 29$ $30 + 10 + 11 - 22 = 29$ $10 + 10 + 11 - 22 = 9$ $30 + 10 + 11 - 22 = 29$ $10 + 10 + 11 - 22 = 9$	
	Cell Means:	33	$20 + 10 + 11 - 22 = 19$	$\overline{A}_2 = 26$
	Factor B Means:	$\overline{B}_1 = 28$	$\overline{B}_2 = 25$	

Table 14–9. A set of hypothetical results to illustrate an antagonistic interaction between cash and extra credit compensation. Only cell AB_{22} is presented in the partitioned form of the two-factor model to show the contributions of Factor A (10 units), Factor B (11 units), and the antagonistic interaction effect (-22 units) to Task Y performance.

$20 payment, the relationship was the reverse: the mean of the 20-point group was lower than the 1-point group (19 versus 33).

Simple Effects

Do the relatively small differences between the Factor A means (27 versus 26) and the Factor B means (28 versus 25) indicate that neither Factor A nor Factor B affected performance on Task Y? An inspection of the cell, row, and column means, summarized in Table 14–10, reveals that when an interaction is present, we cannot

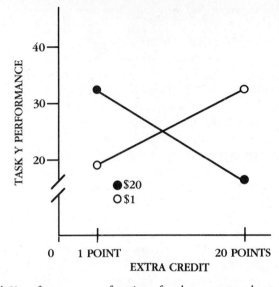

Figure 14–4. Task Y performance as a function of cash payment and extra credit. The plotted values are the four cell means from Table 14–9. The nonparallel lines reflect the interaction effect.

draw the latter conclusion. In the presence of an A × B interaction, the absence of significant main effects must be interpreted with caution. Instead, we must look at the effects of Factor A on performance *separately* within each level of Factor B (23 versus 33 and 31 versus 19), or the effects of Factor B *separately* within each level of Factor A (23 versus 31 and 33 versus 19).

The process of examining the experimental effect of one factor within each level of another factor is called an analysis of **simple effects** (also called **simple main effects**). Following the documentation of an interaction effect, it is generally necessary to focus on an analysis of simple effects rather than the overall main effects. We may very well find that Factor A alone is capable of affecting behavior, *but only within one or more specific levels of Factor B*, or that Factor B alone is

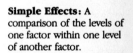

Simple Effects: A comparison of the levels of one factor within one level of another factor.

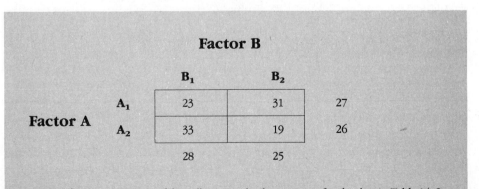

Table 14–10. A summary of the cell, row, and column means for the data in Table 14–9.

capable of affecting behavior, *but only within one or more specific levels of Factor A.*

The analysis of simple effects for the data in Table 14–9 (see Appendix B for details) shows that for those subjects who received 1 point of extra credit (that is, for those subjects assigned to Level 1 of Factor B), the mean performance of the $20 group (33) was significantly *higher* than the mean of the $1 group (23). For those subjects who received 20 points of extra credit (that is, within Level 2 of Factor B), the pattern was reversed: the mean performance of the $20 condition (19) was significantly *lower* than the mean of the $1 condition (31). We can just as easily analyze the simple effects of 1 versus 20 points of extra credit separately within the $1 condition and within the $20 condition. The results are that the 1 point versus 20 point comparison is significant within the $20 condition (33 versus 19) but is not significant within the $1 condition (23 versus 31). Note that the comparisons described above for the cell means of Table 14–10 were between values located in either the first or second row of the table or the first or second column. The two remaining comparisons, between the diagonals of the table (23 versus 19 and 33 versus 31), will not yield any useful information. The reason is that diagonal cells differ from each other on two dimensions (the levels of both Factors A and B) rather than only one, making it impossible to attribute the cause of a difference to any one factor.

Interaction as a Synergism of Main Effects

Another possible pattern of interaction can easily be illustrated by changing the interactive effect of -22 units in cell AB_{22} to $+22$ units, as shown in Table 14–11. These hypothetical results indicate that the incentive value of the two high levels of compensation, $20 and 20 extra points, resulted in a better performance (the cell mean equals 63) than can be accounted for by adding the independent contributions of Factors A and B to the mean initial performance potential: $20 + 10 + 11$ equals 41, not 63. The extra 22 units, the degree to which the experimental effect of the two variables acting in combination exceeds the combined effects of the two variables considered singly, is a synergism. In Figure 14–5, the interaction effect shows up as two diverging lines (see Table 14–12 for a summary of the means). In addition to an interaction effect, both A and B main effects are significant. The main effect for Factor A is that the promise of $20 resulted in better overall performance than the promise of only $1 (48 versus 27). The main effect for Factor B is that the promise of 20 extra points of course credit resulted in better overall performance than the promise of only 1 point (47 versus 28).

Even though both the A and B main effects are significant for the Table 14–11 data, the simultaneous presence of an A × B interaction means that Factor A did not have the same influence on behavior across all levels of Factor B, and Factor B did not have the same influence on behavior across all levels of Factor A. An analysis of simple effects, which should be done whenever an interaction effect is present, reveals important additional details of the contributions of Factors A and B to the experimental results. For example, the 20-point incentive (Factor B) resulted in significantly better Task Y performance than the 1-point incentive only under the $20 condition (a cell mean of 33 compared to 63) and not under the $1 condition (a cell mean of 23 compared to 31).

	Extra Credit (Factor B)		
	1 Point (Level 1)	**20 Points (Level 2)**	**Factor A Means**
$1 (Level 1)	13	21	
	33	21	
	33	41	
	33	21	
	13	41	
	13	21	
	33	41	
	13	21	
	13	41	
	33	41	
Cell Means:	23	31	$\overline{A}_1 = 27$
$20 (Level 2)	43	$30 + 10 + 11 + 22 = 73$	
	23	$10 + 10 + 11 + 22 = 53$	
	23	$30 + 10. + 11 + 22 = 73$	
	43	$10 + 10 + 11 + 22 = 53$	
	23	$10 + 10 + 11 + 22 = 53$	
	23	$30 + 10 + 11 + 22 = 73$	
	43	$30 + 10 + 11 + 22 = 73$	
	23	$10 + 10 + 11 + 22 = 53$	
	43	$30 + 10 + 11 + 22 = 73$	
	43	$10 + 10 + 11 + 22 = 53$	
Cell Means:	33	$20 + 10 + 11 + 22 = 63$	$\overline{A}_2 = 48$
Factor B Means:	$\overline{B}_1 = 28$	$\overline{B}_2 = 47$	

Cash Payment (Factor A) (row label for Factor A)

Table 14–11. A set of hypothetical results to illustrate an interaction between cash and extra credit compensation. Only cell AB_{22} is presented in the partitioned form of the two-factor model to show the contributions of Factor A (10 units), Factor B (11 units), and the interaction effect ($+22$ units) to Task Y performance.

Different Types of 2 × 2 Factorial Designs

Our coverage of single-factor designs compared between-subject and within-subject designs and pointed out the advantages and disadvantages of each experimental approach. We now expand that discussion to include two-factor between-subject and within-subject factorial designs as well as the so-called mixed design, which is a hybrid of the between-subject and within-subject approaches.

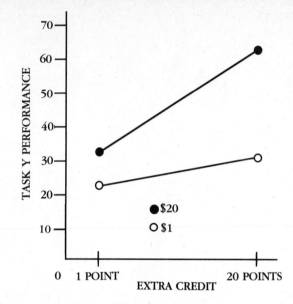

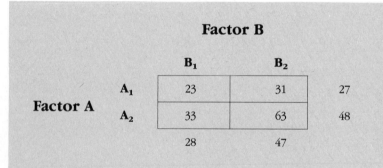

Figure 14–5. Task Y performance as a function of cash payment and extra credit. The plotted values are the four cell means from Table 14–11 as summarized in Table 14–12.

Factor B

		B₁	B₂	
	A₁	23	31	27
Factor A	A₂	33	63	48
		28	47	

Table 14–12. A summary of the cell, row, and column means for the data in Table 14–11.

The Between-Subject 2 × 2 Factorial Design

In the 2 × 2 factorial experiment we used to illustrate additivity and interaction, different subjects were assigned to each of the four treatment combinations or cells (see Table 14–13). Therefore the evaluation of experimental effects stemming from the manipulation of Factors A and B will always involve comparisons between different groups of subjects, which is why we refer to the design as a between-subject factorial design.

		Factor B	
		Level 1	**Level 2**
Factor A	**Level 1**	S_1 S_2 . . . S_{10}	S_{11} S_{12} . . . S_{20}
	Level 2	S_{21} S_{22} . . . S_{30}	S_{31} S_{32} . . . S_{40}

Table 14–13. A diagram of a 2×2 between-subject factorial design. Each of the four treatment combinations is administered to a different group of subjects. In this illustration the sample size is 10 subjects per group.

The Within-Subject 2 × 2 Factorial Design

If we had run the hypothetical cash payment/extra credit experiment as a within-subject design, a single group of subjects would have received all four treatment combinations, as shown in Table 14–14.

One advantage of the within-subject design is that the taking of multiple measurements on the same subjects under each one of the possible treatment combinations permits the experiment to be run with only one-fourth the number of subjects (only 10 subjects in the Table 14–14 illustration) that would be required for an equal-sized between-subject design (40 subjects in the Table 14–13 illustration). However, as you may already have surmised, carryover effects are likely to contribute to the subjects' performance and be confounded with any experimental effects that are present. Counterbalancing treatment administrations must be incorporated into the administration of a within-subject factorial experiment to neutralize carryover effects, just as in the cases of single-factor experiments. To counterbalance the presentation of the four treatment combinations shown in Table 14–14 using all possible treatment orders (see chapter 13) would require a minimum of $4! = 4 * 3 * 2 * 1 = 24$ subjects. Sometimes, however, either a treatment or a data-collection procedure causes a subject to be unsuitable for further testing (as when, following an experimental treatment, tissue is surgically removed from an animal donor for analysis). Thus the elimination of counterbalancing as a possible or practical solution for dealing with carryover effects precludes running an experiment as a within-subject design.

		Factor B	
		Level 1	**Level 2**
Factor A	**Level 1**	S_1 S_2 . . . S_{10}	S_1 S_2 . . . S_{10}
	Level 2	S_1 S_2 . . . S_{10}	S_1 S_2 . . . S_{10}

Table 14–14. A diagram of a 2 × 2 within-subject factorial design. Each of the four treatment combinations is administered to the same group of subjects. In this illustration the sample size is 10 subjects per treatment condition.

The Mixed Between-Subject/Within-Subject 2 × 2 Factorial Design

Mixed Design: A hybrid design with between-subject and within-subject elements.

A third version of the 2 × 2 factorial design is a hybrid of the between-subject and within-subject cases. Instead of the four independent groups of the between-subject design and the single group of the within-subject design, the **mixed design** uses two groups. One group is assigned to Level 1 of Factor A and is tested under both levels of Factor B. A second group is assigned to Level 2 of Factor A and is also tested under both levels of Factor B (see Table 14–15).

As with any within-subject experiment, we must be concerned with counterbalancing carryover effects. In the 2 × 2 case we could simply test half of each group first under Level 1 of Factor B and, second, under Level 2 of Factor B. The other half of each group would be tested in the reverse order.

Extensions of the 2 × 2 Factorial Design

At the beginning of chapter 13 we discussed the limitations of the two-treatment experiment and explained how the limitations can be overcome by designing single-factor experiments with more than two treatments. For the same reasons, it is often desirable to increase the dimensions of the 2 × 2 factorial design. For example, to extend the hypothetical experiment shown as Table 14–6, in which there were only two manipulated levels of cash payment (Factor A) and extra credit (Factor B), we could include a "no compensation" level of each factor (zero dollars

		Factor B	
		Level 1	**Level 2**
		S_1	S_1
		S_2	S_2
Level 1		.	.
		.	.
(Group 1)		.	.
		S_{10}	S_{10}
Factor A		S_{11}	S_{11}
		S_{12}	S_{12}
Level 2		.	.
		.	.
(Group 2)		S_{20}	S_{20}

Table 14–15. A diagram of a 2 × 2 mixed factorial design. One group of subjects is assigned to each level of Factor A, and all subjects in each group experience both levels of Factor B. In this illustration the sample size is 10 subjects per group.

and zero points of extra credit) to form a 3 × 3 factorial design. Similarly, if we added another level to the 3 × 3 design by including subjects who were promised a payment between the $1 and $20 levels (say, $10), the result would be a 4 × 3 factorial, as shown in Table 14–16.

As with the basic 2 × 2 design, factorial designs with more than two levels per factor can be run as between-subject, within-subject, or mixed designs. In practical terms, however, in any given research environment one type of factorial design

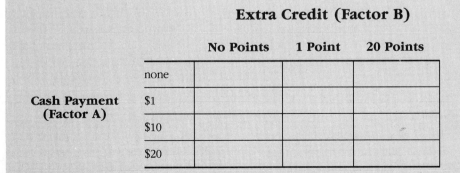

		Extra Credit (Factor B)		
		No Points	**1 Point**	**20 Points**
	none			
Cash Payment	$1			
(Factor A)	$10			
	$20			

Table 14–16. An extension of the 2 × 2 factorial design illustrated in Table 14–6 to a 4 × 3 factorial design.

(between-subject, within-subject, or mixed) of one particular size (say, 4 × 3) is likely to emerge as the most suitable for pursuing a particular research goal. The availability of human and financial resources, such as subjects, experimenters to run the subjects, and the expense of apparatus and supplies, also limits the scope of the factorial experiments that researchers design and execute.

Factorial Designs with More Than Two Factors

Higher Order Designs: Experimental designs that include the manipulation of more than two factors.

Experimental designs that include the manipulation of more than two factors are often referred to as **higher order designs**. For example, in addition to studying the effects of different monetary rewards (Factor A) and extra credit (Factor B) on performance, we could expand the experiment depicted in Table 14–5 to include a third factor, which we would designate as Factor C. For example, two levels of Factor C could be how we prepared the subjects to perform the task: Instruction Set A versus Instruction Set B. The addition of a third factor with two levels forms a 2 × 2 × 2 factorial design (read "2 by 2 by 2"), and, as shown in Table 14–17, the experiment would have 2 × 2 × 2 = 8 different treatment combinations.

The advantage of applying a higher order design to a research problem is that it permits us to examine the effects of many variables in all possible combinations, which can be crucial to understanding the interplay of the many variables that influence behavior. The disadvantage of a higher order design is that interpreting the information it produces can be extremely challenging. It is one matter to point

Factor A	Factor B	Factor C	Group
$1 Cash Payment	1 Point Extra Credit	Instruction Set A	1
		Instruction Set B	2
	20 Points Extra Credit	Instruction Set A	3
		Instruction Set B	4
$20 Cash Payment	1 Point Extra Credit	Instruction Set A	5
		Instruction Set B	6
	20 Points Extra Credit	Instruction Set A	7
		Instruction Set B	8

Table 14–17. A diagram of a 2 × 2 × 2 factorial experiment showing the eight possible treatment combinations. Since a separate group is assigned to each of the eight treatment combinations, the illustration represents a between-subject design.

to the significance of an interaction among, say, three factors (A × B × C), and another matter to figure out what, if any, meaningful information about behavior is conveyed by the discovery of the statistically significant three-way interaction.

Theoretically, there is no limit to the number of factors we can include in a factorial design, and there is no limit imposed on the number of levels each factor may have. In practical terms, however, experiments with many different factors and/or several levels of each factor require either large numbers of subjects (between-subject designs) or testing the same subjects many times (within-subject designs). Thus, large-scale experiments can be very time-consuming and expensive to carry out. Also, as already mentioned, higher order experimental designs can yield results that are difficult, maybe even impossible, to interpret. For example, a four-factor design with only the minimum two levels for each factor still has $2 \times 2 \times 2 \times 2 = 16$ different treatment combinations, four main effects (Factors A, B, C, and D), six possible two-way interactions (A × B, A × C, A × D, B × C, B × D, C × D), four possible three-way interactions (A × B × C, A × B × D, A × C × D, B × C × D), and one possible four-way interaction (A × B × C × D)! To add to the possibilities for complexity, higher order designs, as with any factorial design, can be set up as between-subject experimental designs, within-subject experimental designs, or mixed between-subject and within-subject experimental designs.

Despite the complexity of higher order designs, some research issues are too complex to approach any other way. In fact, the experiment we use to represent the subdiscipline of social psychology (chapter 23) employs a higher order design ($2 \times 2 \times 2 \times 2 \times 2$). When faced with making sense out of a complex set of results from a factorial experiment, simply keep three ideas in mind: (a) The effects on behavior from two or more experimental conditions administered in combination can be additive or interactive; (b) If the combined influence of the treatment conditions is additive only, any experimental effects that exist will show up as main effects; and (c) If the combined influence of the treatment conditions is interactive (either antagonistically or synergistically), the contribution of individual factors can only be understood as a set of simple effects (the effects of one or more factors within the levels of one or more other factors).

Using Factorial Designs for Correlational Studies

All the illustrations we have used thus far in our discussion of factorial designs have been in the context of experimental research. That is, all factors were manipulated levels of independent variables, which is a requirement for a study to be a true experiment. But factorial designs are also useful in correlational research. As pointed out in chapter 9, a study is correlational when the levels of the independent variable are "selected" or result from "natural treatments" rather than from experimental manipulation.

In the context of an *experiment*, a factorial design can address a research problem in the form of Basic Question 7: *Will introducing subjects to two or more systematically different conditions cause an additive and/or interactive effect on behavior?*

But, in the context of a *correlational study*, the question addressed by a factorial design is in the form of a corollary to Basic Question 7: *Are additive and/or interactive effects evident among subjects who are identified as having experienced two or more systematically different conditions?*

Introducing (*manipulating*) conditions is, as you surely know by now, very different from identifying (*assessing*) conditions after the fact (ex post facto). The data of experiments and correlational studies are handled the same way as far as statistical analyses are concerned, but interpreting the significant main effects and/or interactions that emerge from the analysis of the results of a correlational study must be limited to description. Regarding the results to have been *caused* by the selected variables or natural treatments is not justified. For example, suppose you collected data on cigarette smoking as a function of income level (Factor A) and gender (Factor B) and got the results shown in Table 14–18. We shall assume that you were able to locate 20 people for each of the four cells: 20 men with annual incomes greater than $30,000, 20 women with annual incomes greater than $30,000, 20 men with annual incomes less than $20,000, and 20 women with annual incomes less than $20,000. The numbers in Table 14–18 represent the mean number of cigarettes smoked per day by each group.

The pattern of the data in Table 14–18 suggests that smoking is uniformly higher among persons earning less than $20,000 per year compared to those who earn over $30,000 per year, but the difference is larger between males than between females. This interactive pattern among the four cell means is evident when we view Figure 14–6. Assuming that the statistical analysis of the research results summarized in Table 14–18 revealed a significant interaction and that you performed the required analysis of simple effects, what would it mean to find that males of different income levels have different smoking habits and that females do not differ? Can we go beyond the simple description? Do the data tell us what is it about the combination of being male and having an income of less than $20,000 that contributes to the relatively high smoking rate of this group? The Table 14–18 data cannot provide an answer to such a question; they are just descriptive of groups of individuals whose

		Gender (Factor B)		
		Male	Female	Factor A Means
Income (Factor A)	> $30,000	10	12	11
	< $20,000	28	18	23
	Factor B Means:	19	15	

Table 14–18. Mean cigarettes smoked by four groups of smokers. The groups are defined by income level and gender characteristics. The pattern of means for these hypothetical data are indicative of an interaction effect.

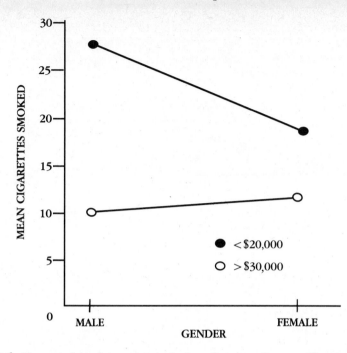

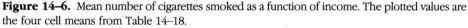

Figure 14–6. Mean number of cigarettes smoked as a function of income. The plotted values are the four cell means from Table 14–18.

different characteristics (their gender and whether or not they smoke) exist apart from the influence of any experimental manipulation.

Mixed Experimental/Correlational Factorial Designs

Earlier we mentioned a type of mixed factorial design that was a hybrid of between-and within-subject conditions. There is another type of mixed factorial design that is a hybrid of manipulated treatment conditions and nonmanipulated (subject) variables. We call it a **mixed experimental/correlational design**. For example, the design in Table 14–19 depicts a study that was designed to examine the effectiveness with which two types of weight-training regimens (Program 1 and Program 2) add muscle mass to male and female athletes. Because the type of training program *is* a manipulated variable and gender *is not* a manipulated variable, the design of the study is a hybrid of experimental and correlational methods.

Assuming we find that only the A and B main effects of the 2 × 2 factorial are significant, the pattern of cell means in Table 14–19 suggests that, overall, men derived more benefit from the training programs than women, and the athletes achieved better results from Program 1 than they did from Program 2. The gender

Mixed Experimental/ Correlational Design: A research design that includes both manipulated and nonmanipulated factors.

| | | Gender (Factor A) | | |
		Male	Female	Factor A Means
Weight Training (Factor B)	Program 1	19	11	15
	Program 2	15	5	10
	Factor B Means:	17	8	

Table 14–19. Mean increase in muscle mass that was achieved when male and female athletes followed two weight-training regimens.

difference is descriptive (women do not gain muscle mass from weight training as readily as men), and the different training programs *caused* the athletes to respond with different degrees of muscle gain.

Summary

Research issues in the form of Basic Question 7 require the simultaneous manipulation of two or more independent variables, or factors. Using hypothetical sets of results, we devoted a large part of chapter 14 to explaining two key concepts: (a) Two factors act in an additive fashion when their combined influence on the experimental results is the sum of their individual contributions; and (b) two factors act in an interactive fashion when their combined influence *cannot* be explained as the sum of their individual contributions. Experimental effects that are tied to the manipulation of individual factors are main effects, and effects that are unique to specific combinations of factor levels are interaction effects. We stressed the importance of analyzing simple effects when an interaction is present. Also, by plotting the mean performances for each treatment combination (the cell means) as a figure, we showed that the presence of an interaction shows up as nonparallel lines and that main effects in the absence of interaction show up as parallel lines. Next, we described three types of 2 × 2 factorial designs: between-subject, within-subject, and mixed designs. We then described two-factor designs that have more than two levels of each factor and higher order designs, which have more than two factors. The chapter ended with a discussion of the use of factorial designs in correlational research and mixed experimental/correlational research.

When we began this chapter we presented Basic Question 7 as the most complex of the seven. After reading the chapter you probably agree. There is, however, no need to be intimidated by factorial designs as long as you keep the important distinctions in mind: additive effects versus interactive effects, antagonistic versus synergistic interactions, the stress put on simple effects versus main effects when an interaction is present, and factors that are the selected variables or natural treatments of correlational research versus the manipulated variables of experimental research.

Key Terms

Antagonistic Effect, p. 252
Higher Order Design, p. 270
Main Effects, p. 257
Mixed Between-Subject/Within-Subject
  Factorial Design, p. 268

Mixed Experimental/Correlational
  Factorial Design, p. 273
Simple Effects, p. 263
Synergistic Effect, p. 252

Chapter Exercises

1. What does it mean to describe the effects of two variables acting in combination as additive?

2. What does it mean to describe the effects of two variables acting in combination as interactive?

3. What is a factorial experiment, and what information does it provide that is not available when we study the effects of variables singly in separate experiments?

4. When figures are prepared from the cell means of a 2 × 2 factorial experiment:

   a. What pattern indicates the absence of an interaction?

   b. What pattern indicates the presence of an interaction that is antagonistic to main effects?

   c. What pattern indicates an interaction that is synergistic with main effects?

   d. What pattern is consistent with a set of experimental results that show both main effects and interactions?

5. What is the difference between interaction as an antagonism to main effects and interaction as a synergism of main effects?

6. What is a simple effect (or simple main effect) and why is it necessary to follow the detection of an interaction effect with an analysis of simple effects?

7. Discuss one advantage and one disadvantage of running a factorial experiment using a within-subject design.

8. Discuss one advantage and one disadvantage of doing research using higher order factorial designs.

9. What considerations would warrant extending the basic 2 × 2 factorial design to a larger dimension (such as 3 × 3 or 2 × 6)?

10. Explain the difference between an experiment in the form of Basic Question 7 and a correlational study in the form of the corollary to Basic Question 7.

Proposal Assignment 14: Adding a Second Independent Variable

In Proposal assignment 4a you designed an experiment with one independent variable. Now we would like you to add a second independent variable. First, draw a figure of the results that shows both of your independent variables influencing the dependent variable (parallel lines) and write a summary of the results. Second, draw a figure that shows an interaction effect (nonparallel lines) and write a summary of the results.

We will help you with this proposal assignment by giving you an example. Earlier proposal assignments described the manipulation of expected study time (15 or 5 hours a week) for a Research Methods class. Pretend that we are also interested in the effects of having the instructor assign the use of a study guide or not. We would have a 2 × 2 factorial design, diagramed:

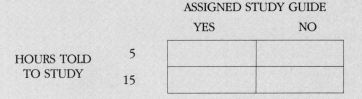

We would test four different groups: Groups 15-SG, 5-SG, 15-NSG, 5-NSG (SG = Study Guide, NSG = No Study Guide). The following figure shows the results if both main effects are significant:

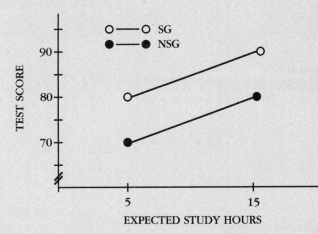

Test scores as a function of expected study hours and use of study guide (SG = Study Guide; NSG = No Study Guide).

Students who were told to study 15 hours per week did better than students who were told to study only 5 hours per week. Also, students who were required to use a study guide did better than those students whose instruction did not include the use of a study guide.

The following figure shows the results if the interaction effect was significant.

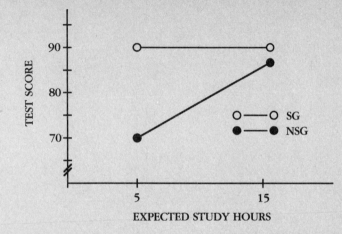

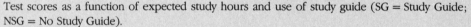

Test scores as a function of expected study hours and use of study guide (SG = Study Guide; NSG = No Study Guide).

If tests of simple effects showed that Groups 15-SG and 5-SG did not differ, but Groups 15-NSG and 5-NSG did differ, and that Groups 15-SG and 15-NSG did not differ, but Groups 5-SG and 5-NSG did differ, then we could make these conclusions: Among those students who were told to study only 5 hours, those who used the study guide scored higher than those who did not use the study guide. But among those students who were told to study 15 hours, those who did use the study guide failed to score higher than those who did not use the study guide. Also, among students who did not use the study guide, those who were told to study for 15 hours scored higher than those told to study for 5 hours. But among those students who did use the study guide, those students who were told to study for 15 hours failed to score higher than those who were told to study for 5 hours.

C H A P T E R

15

Quasi-Experimental Research

The preceding chapters have discussed the elements of experimental methodology and research design that enable researchers to document cause-effect relationships between manipulated variables and behavioral measures. We have stressed that to the extent we stray from the fundamentals of experimental methodology and allow avoidable flaws to tarnish the scientific process (see Box 10–1), we invite the intrusion of extraneous variables. In turn, a loss of precision and control can introduce explanations of experimental results that are not linked to the manipulation of the independent variable, and the research suffers a loss of internal validity. (As explained in chapter 10, the internal validity of an experiment refers to the degree to which behavioral differences among treatment conditions can be considered to have been caused by the experimental manipulation.)

Nevertheless, doing research to discover useful and important knowledge entails more than documenting cause-effect relationships between variables in artificially controlled laboratory environments. Researchers also take advantage of opportunities to gather important information in natural settings ("in the field"), in which many of the methodological refinements of laboratory research (such as the random assignment of subjects to different treatment conditions) are either impractical or impossible to implement. When we cannot structure and organize a research environment to fit the mold of true experimental methodology, we must make do with approaches to research that *resemble* experiments but fall short of meeting one or more of the criteria of true experiments. The term *quasi-experiment*, introduced in chapter 13, refers to studies that lack the rigor of experimental methodology, not because of negligence or a lack of sophistication on the part of the researcher, but because of aspects of a field environment that limit or block the researcher's ability to design, plan, and execute true experiments.

Despite its failure to measure up to all the characteristics of true experimental research, there are three reasons why quasi-experimental research is a valuable companion to laboratory research. First, a quasi-experimental approach may be the *only* possible way to take advantage of a unique research opportunity, such as the impact of an unforeseen natural event on behavior. Second, we can use quasi-experimental research to determine how consistent data from laboratory research are with data we gather in natural settings. Comparing data gathered in natural settings to the data of laboratory research is a key step to establishing external validity: the relevance that laboratory findings have to our understanding of real-world phenomena. Third, we can use the data of field research as a rich source of testable hypotheses, as when researchers use a carefully controlled laboratory experiment to establish the internal validity of a cause-effect interpretation of a quasi-experimental result.

Quasi-Experiments Compared to True Experiments

As the prefix *quasi* indicates, quasi-experimental research approximates but is *not* real experimental research. Therefore, it will help you to recognize quasi-experimental research and compare and contrast it to true experimental research if we review the characteristics of a true experiment. Once you understand the difference between true experimental research and quasi-experimental research, you will understand the threats to internal validity that must be taken into account when interpreting the results of quasi-experimental research. In general, the more aware researchers are of the problems they face when working in a field environment, the more cautious they will be when offering an interpretation of results.

A Review of the Characteristics of a True Experiment

In preparing to run a typical between-subject experiment, we use random assignment to create initially equivalent groups. Then we systematically manipulate the experiences of the different groups and assess the impact on behavior. We accomplish the isolation of the independent variable (the experimental treatment) as the only systematic difference between the treated and control groups of an experiment either by holding other variables constant for all groups (see chapter 10) or by eliminating confounding variables from the experimental environment. Thus, for an investigation to qualify as an experiment three principal elements must be in place: (a) The groups assigned to experience the different treatment conditions must be initially equivalent; (b) The experimental treatment must be a *manipulated variable*; and (c) There must be one or more appropriate reference groups (control groups) against which to compare the behavior of the experimentally treated subjects. If any one of these three characteristics is missing, a study is not a true experiment. Because it is so important to be able to recognize the elements of a true experiment, we review each of them in some detail.

The importance of initial equivalence

Initial equivalence strengthens a causal interpretation of an independent variable–dependent variable linkage by eliminating one rival explanation for between-treatment differences: that the subjects assigned to the various control and treatment conditions differed in systematic ways *prior* to the beginning of the experiment. In experimental research we assume that the random assignment of subjects to the various treatment conditions of a between-subject experiment will achieve initial equivalence. Conversely, it is the *absence* of random assignment of subjects to different conditions that is characteristic of quasi-experimental research. Because, in the absence of random assignment, we cannot assume that subjects who have experienced the different conditions of a quasi-experiment were initially equivalent, we must be cautious when offering a causal explanation of a quasi-experimental result.

The importance of a manipulated variable

The second important element of the internally valid experiment is that the treatment condition be a *manipulated* variable rather than a selected variable or natural treatment (chapter 3). Testing the impact of a variable on behavior ex post facto rather than through purposeful manipulation opens the door to rival explanations linked to the actions of one or more other variables (called extraneous or confounding variables). Let us say, for example, that we identify two groups of people: those who consume only artificially sweetened soft drinks and those who consume only drinks sweetened with natural sugars. Our behavioral measures indicate that those who drink only naturally sweetened beverages tend to have a more positive self-image. Is the difference in dietary habits (consumption of natural versus artificial sweeteners) responsible for the behavioral differences between the two groups? Should those who drink only artificially sweetened beverages be advised to switch to naturally sweetened products so they too could enjoy a more positive self-image? As you might expect, another possible explanation for the between-group behavioral differences has nothing to do with the difference in sweetener consumption: Perhaps people who drink only artificially sweetened beverages are more likely to have a problem maintaining a desirable weight compared to people who drink only naturally sweetened beverages. The confounding variable of obesity might be the real cause for the lower self-esteem of consumers of artificially sweetened products. The only way to link the consumption of artificial sweeteners causally to a behavioral phenomenon that would eliminate confounding variables and rival explanations would be to manipulate the sweetener variable using initially equivalent groups. (The procedure would be to randomly assign subjects to two groups, randomly determine which group would drink the artificially sweetened beverage and which would drink the naturally sweetened beverage, and measure the self-image of all subjects after a fixed level of exposure to each type of beverage.)

The importance of control groups

The importance of the third requirement of an experiment — that appropriate reference groups be available against which to compare the behavior of the experimental subjects — was expressed in chapters 10 and 11:

> To gauge accurately the effect of an experimental variable on behavior, it is necessary to have data from control subjects who do not experience the experimental condition but who, *in every other way*, are as identical as possible to those who do experience the experimental condition.

An experimental design that includes all appropriate control groups has the logical structure that is necessary for a causal interpretation of an independent variable–dependent variable linkage. As we saw in chapter 10, the ideal control condition differs from the experimental condition only by the absence of the manipulated experimental variable. In the absence of such a reference group, it is logically impossible to separate the contributions that aspects of the treatment *administration* make to the results from the contributions of the experimental treatments themselves.

Control groups are formed differently in between- versus within-subject designs. In between-subject designs different individuals are randomly assigned to the control and experimental conditions. In within-subject designs, each subject is tested under both experimental and control conditions, and so serves as his or her own control. Regardless of which design strategy (between-subject or within-subject) the experimenter decides to use, the control conditions serve the same purpose: to provide a reference against which to compare the behavior of the experimental subjects.

Studies That Are Not Experiments: Correlational, Quasi-Experimental, and Sloppy Research

In general, psychological research usually involves comparing the behavior of subjects who have experienced one or more specific events to the behavior of subjects who either have not experienced the event(s) or who have experienced different specific events. Any study conforming to the latter generic structure that does not meet the three criteria of experimental research set forth above is, depending on the nature of the departure from experimental methodology and the aims of the research, either a correlational study, a quasi-experiment, or simply a flawed experiment. As mentioned in the introduction to Part II, both correlational and quasi-experimental studies depart in similar ways from the requirements of a true experiment. Both can include a selected variable or natural treatment and/or nonrandomly formed groups rather than the manipulated variables and initially equivalent groups required of a true experiment.

We prefer to differentiate between correlational and quasi-experimental studies by drawing attention to the focus of the research. If the focus of research involving selected variables and natural treatments is to describe the association between the experiences of subjects and behavioral measurements on those subjects, we favor the designation *correlational research*. If the focus is to imply a causal connection between the selected variable or natural treatment and subsequent behavior, we favor the designation *quasi-experiment*. Notice the use of the word *imply* in the last sentence. It is meant to convey a soft or equivocal causal linkage in contrast to the confident inferences we can make from a logically unassailable experimental design.

Nevertheless, some studies that meet the experimental requirement of manipulating a variable are not true experiments. Sometimes the flaw is that some or all of the control conditions necessary for an unambiguous interpretation of the experimental results are absent. Sometimes, if the experimental design is between-subject, the groups of subjects who were exposed to the control and treatment conditions are known to have been formed in a nonrandom fashion. In a within-subject experiment, the flaw could be the omission of appropriate counterbalancing measures. In such cases it is necessary to make a distinction between a quasi-experiment and a study that falls short of being a true experiment because of avoidable human error. In the laboratory environment, in which an experimenter can exert the maximum amount of control over the conduct of the research effort, the failure to assign subjects to treatment conditions in a manner likely to achieve initial equivalence is almost always an avoidable error. Likewise, the omission of one or more important control groups is almost always attributable to a mental lapse in designing the experiment (see Box 10–1). In contrast, in a field research environment removed from the control of the laboratory, nonrandom assignment of subjects to different treatment conditions and/or the absence of important control conditions is often dictated by practical considerations and is, more often than not, unavoidable.

For example, say that we wished to study the psychological impact of parental separation on the children of military personnel who participated in Operation Desert Storm in Saudi Arabia and Kuwait in 1991. In some two-parent military families, both parents were called to active duty overseas, and in other families only the father or the mother was sent overseas. Single-parent families were also split by the activation of the mother or father for overseas duty. In still other military families there was no assignment to the Persian Gulf, so the conflict with Iraq did not result in separation of children from parents. Can we assume that assignment to overseas versus domestic duty was randomly determined and thereby regard the children of intact military families as an initially equivalent control group against which to compare the children of separated families?

We doubt that military decisions are random, so we cannot assume initial equivalence among the groups of children (separated from one or both parents or not separated) prior to the military event with the same confidence that would be justifiable following a random assignment procedure. The researcher would have no control over which military families would experience a separation, which families with two parents in the armed forces would experience a dual separation, which families would temporarily lose only a mother and which only a father, which parents would be in the war zone and which would not, the ages of the children and the number of children in the affected families, and so forth. Clearly, the requirements of a true experiment are impossible to meet because of the ex post facto character of the variables. Yet, to the extent that the focus of the study is to imply a causal connection between parental separation and behavioral consequences for children rather than a simple association, it is more revealing of the aims of the study to refer to it as a quasi-experiment rather than as a correlational study. Both designations are, however, correct.

In the case of a known but unavoidable departure from orthodox experimental methodology, the internal validity of the study is at risk. But the researcher who is aware of the quasi-experimental character of a study and the equivocal interpretations of its data can take rival explanations into consideration and possibly make a case for ruling out one or more of them. According to Campbell and Stanley (1963), "because experimental control is lacking [in quasi-experiments] it becomes imperative that the researcher be thoroughly aware of which specific variables his particular design fails to control." The difficulty lies in the subtlety of some of the rival explanations that cannot be ruled out in a quasi-experiment. It is therefore very important for the researcher to understand exactly what variables have not been controlled in a study and take the lack of control into consideration when interpreting results.

Potential Threats to the Internal Validity of Quasi-Experiments

Cook and Campbell (1979) describe many rival explanations that are potential threats to the internal validity of quasi-experiments (sometimes referred to as the pitfalls of quasi-experimental research). We will discuss five of the threats to internal validity in the context of the pretest-posttest design, a traditional favorite for illustrating the rival explanations that can surface when trying to interpret the data of a quasi-experiment. In fact, the internal validity of the pretest-posttest design is so open to attack that it is sometimes referred to as a *pre*-experimental design rather than as a quasi-experimental design. We briefly review the elements of the pretest-posttest design (first introduced in chapter 12) before discussing its vulnerability to five specific rival explanations.

The Pretest-Posttest Design

In a pretest-posttest study, illustrated in Table 15–1 (and previously in chapter 12), we collect behavioral data twice on the same set of subjects: once before and once after the occurrence of a significant event. Sometimes the event is the introduction of an experimenter-controlled condition and sometimes the event is an unforeseen and unplanned occurrence outside any experimental control. In chapter 12 we referred to the former as a planned pretest-posttest study and to the latter as an unplanned pretest-posttest study. The unplanned pretest-posttest study, which, by definition, is removed from the types of environmental control that characterize laboratory research, is the more likely to suffer low internal validity.

An example of an unplanned pretest-posttest study would be to compare children's selection of war-related toys before versus after the Allies' victory over Iraq in 1991 (see Table 15–2). Since we are usually unable to predict the occurrence

The Pretest-Posttest Design

Measurement 1		Measurement 2
before the significant event (baseline)	→ significant event →	after the significant event

Table 15–1. A diagram of the pretest-posttest design.

Selections of War-Related Toys

Subject	Prewar	Postwar
Ernest	6	11
Laura	1	8
Susan	2	8
David	7	13
Tamara	2	7
Arthur	11	15
Richard	7	14
Sheila	0	6

Table 15–2. A hypothetical study showing a difference in toy-selection behavior before (the pretest) versus after (the posttest) the Persian Gulf War. The data are intended to represent the number of war-related toys each child selected as top-ten favorites from a comprehensive illustrated toy catalog, $t(7) = 15.71$, $p < .01$.

of an unplanned significant event, the availability of pretest data is often a matter of luck. That is, the availability of data collected before a significant event can present a unique and unanticipated opportunity for research. In the present example we assume that the invasion of Kuwait was not imagined at the time the pretest data on the children's toy preferences were collected and that the availability of the prewar data was simply good fortune. Thus, in our example, the Persian Gulf War is the significant event around which we opportunistically build the pretest-posttest study. The war was costly in terms of lives, money, and the destruction of property and natural resources. It was obviously not a manipulated event that some researcher introduced in order to study the effect of media coverage of international conflict on children's play behavior. Nevertheless, we can be opportunistic and research the impact of significant events even when they have tragic overtones.

The most obvious and tempting interpretation of a difference between a pretest measurement of behavior and a posttest comparison is to attribute the difference to the intervening significant event. ("Sheila is now demanding that her parents buy her military toys. She was never interested in anything of a military nature before the Persian Gulf War and all the media coverage of the contributions of women military personnel, so the war must be responsible for the shift.") But there are rival explanations for any pretest-posttest differences that are independent of any influence from an intervening significant event. (Perhaps Sheila's new interest in war-related toys is connected with her desire to build a friendship with a peer who happens to be very attracted to such toys.) The more difficult it is to rule out rival explanations, the less confident we can be that the intervening significant event is the cause of the pretest-posttest difference. Here are five sources of pretest-posttest differences that are independent of any effect from the intervening significant event.

History

History as a threat to internal validity: The attribution of pretest-posttest differences to a behavior-altering experience that occurs between pretest and posttest in addition to the significant event.

History threatens internal validity when subjects have a behavior-altering experience between the original measurement (the pretest) and the repeated measurement (the posttest) in addition to the intervening significant event that is the focus of the study's pretest-posttest comparison. For example, consider the case of the commissioner of public health for a large city who wished to evaluate the success of a family-planning curriculum in the city's schools. Her strategy was to compare the incidence of unwanted teen pregnancies before the introduction of the new curriculum to the incidence after the curriculum was in place for two years. In this pretest-posttest research scenario the significant event is the planned introduction of the curriculum. Some hypothetical data for the city's high schools are shown in Table 15–3. (Notice that the row labels, which usually identify the subjects participating in the pretest-posttest study [as in Table 15–2], identify schools in the present example. Thus, the experimental unit in the pretest-posttest study represented in Table 15–3 is a school rather than a person.)

Attributing the significant reduction of unwanted pregnancies to the implementation of the new curriculum is tempting. Nevertheless, other historical events that

The Number of Unwanted Teen Pregnancies

	School	Pretest	Posttest
	Valley	16	11
Macedon	Lyndon	4	0
Consolidated	Shaw	11	7
School	Campbell	7	3
District	Tech	2	5
High Schools	Academy	5	3
	Riley	8	4

Table 15–3. Hypothetical results of an evaluation of a family-planning curriculum. The scores are the numbers of cases involving an unwanted teen pregnancy reported by each high school in the Macedon School District before versus two years after the introduction of the family-planning curriculum, $t(6) = 2.76$, $p < .05$.

are capable of affecting the sexual conduct of teenagers may also have occurred during the two-year interval between the collection of pretest and posttest data. Perhaps, for example, the two-year interval coincided with a dramatic increase in media coverage and public awareness of AIDS and the risk of HIV infection between heterosexual partners. A significant decrease in unwanted teenage pregnancies could thus be attributed to the fear of AIDS rather than to an increased awareness of contraceptive measures.

Maturation

Sometimes **maturation**, the normal age-related development of behavioral characteristics, is responsible for changes in behavior between pretest and posttest measurements rather than the intervention of a significant event. An extreme example would be a pretest-posttest study with children in which the pretest data were collected before the onset of puberty and the posttest data were collected after the onset of puberty. The influence of puberty, a developmental milestone during which profound physical and behavioral changes take place, would rival any explanation for changes in behavior that we try to link to a significant event intervening between pretest and posttest evaluations. Thus, if we had behavioral data on children from troubled home environments both before (the pretest) and after (the posttest) court-ordered placement in a foster home (the significant event), we would have to consider the degree to which the children's behavior would normally change during the pretest-posttest interval before we could assess the harmful or beneficial impact of foster care on the behavior of the children.

Maturation as a threat to internal validity: The attribution of pretest-posttest differences to normal age-related developmental phenomena rather than to the significant event.

Testing

Sometimes simply participating in the pretest can affect subjects' performance on the posttest. Usually, the potential threat to internal validity from the **testing** factor rests in the familiarity with the apparatus, testing procedure, and so forth that the subject gains during the pretest that influences performance on the posttest. The influence of testing is, therefore, confounded with any effect on behavior that results from the significant event between the pretest and the posttest. For example, many high school juniors who are preparing to apply to colleges become quite concerned if they do not score well the first time they take the Scholastic Aptitude Test (SAT). Some students pay to take a special course to prepare for the SAT test, and they can expect a minimum 50- to 75-point increase in their score on their second try. But it is not unusual for SAT scores to go up on the second try even without any special intervening preparation. Presumably, the testing factor (familiarity with the testing procedure, the types of questions that appear on the test, the testing environment, and so forth) is responsible for the improvement.

Testing as a threat to internal validity: The attribution of pretest–posttest differences to the subjects' growing familiarity with experimental apparatus and procedures rather than to the intervening significant event.

Instrumentation

The threat to internal validity posed by **instrumentation** refers to the inconsistency (or drift) that is possible in the functioning of apparatus (either in the delivery of an experimental treatment or in the recording of data), the care and attention to detail that the experimenter exercises when running the experiment, and the criteria that the experimenter uses when his or her recording of behavior involves an element of subjective judgment. Naturally, any systematic change in the

Instrumentation as a threat to internal validity: The attribution of pretest-posttest differences to inconsistent experimental execution rather than to the significant event.

operational details of an experiment from pretest to posttest introduces an extraneous variable that will be confounded with the influence of the significant event. Apparatus can be regularly recalibrated against a set standard to avoid inconsistent function, but, when the experimenter is the instrument and the data are from subjective assessments, the risk of a drift in instrumental precision can be substantial. For example, unless precautions are taken to assure the application of consistent measurement criteria over the course of a study, a researcher studying play behavior in children could, at one point in the study, score a poking behavior as aggressive and, at a later point, come to regard the same behavior as playful. One solution to the latter problem is to make a permanent visual record of the pretest and posttest sessions (say, by videotaping) and rescore them as necessary to check for drift.

Regression to the mean

Nobody's behavior is perfectly consistent across time. We are all capable of a range of behavior with respect to most measurements, and our typical or average behavior can be found between two less frequently observed high and low extremes. For example, a basketball team with a relatively stable mean foul-shooting percentage of 80% per game could, during one particular game, successfully complete only 60% of their foul shots ("We were ice-cold!") and as much as 100% in another game ("We were red-hot!"). But we recognize the latter high and low scoring extremes to be atypical of a team with a fairly consistent (reliable) 80%-per-game foul-shooting performance.

Regression to the Mean as a threat to internal validity: Attributing a shift from an atypical level of performance on a pretest to a more normal level on a posttest to the statistical improbability of consecutive atypical performances rather than to the significant event.

Let us regard a basketball team's foul-shooting performance in a research context by viewing each game as a repeated measure of the team's foul-shooting ability. If the shooting percentage went from 100% in one game down to the team average of 80% in the following game, would you infer that the athletic ability of the team had diminished from some experience interposed between the original measurement and the repeated measurement? Similarly, if the foul-shooting percentage went from a low of 60% in one game up to the team average of 80% in the following game, would you necessarily infer that the team's athletic ability had substantially increased between the two measurements? Most likely you would correctly recognize that such changes toward the mean level of performance do not necessarily indicate a fundamental change in the team's performance capability. Instead, **regression to the mean** may be responsible. In general, if a subject's performance during the original measurement of a behavior is, for whatever reason, atypically high or low, on a repeated measurement we are likely to observe a change (regression) toward a more typical level of performance even without an intervening significant event.

Regression to the mean is particularly likely to contribute to the results of a pretest-posttest study when the pretest data are extreme. For example, imagine a company president hiring a dynamic personality to conduct a one-day workshop to motivate and rejuvenate those members of the sales staff who recently have been failing to meet their sales quotas. After the workshop, as hoped, sales for the underachieving salespeople increase. The improvement may very well have been caused by the workshop experience in the form of a more positive and energetic attitude among the weaker members of the sales staff. But it is also possible that the poor sales performance that preceded the workshop was a temporary downturn due simply to chance, and the improvement to a more acceptable rate of sales success would have occurred anyway—without the benefit of any workshop.

Quasi-Experimental Designs

Those who wish to make before-and-after comparisons of behavior in a field environment need not accept the loss of internal validity as inevitable. They can take steps to counter the threats to internal validity that we discussed above through the use of **quasi-experimental designs**, research strategies that tend to minimize one or more of the threats to internal validity that arise when we are unable to apply all the controls required of a true experiment. If successfully applied, quasi-experimental designs may not *eliminate* rival explanations, but they can often *strengthen* the case for attributing behavioral change from pretest to posttest to the intervening significant event.

The quasi-experimental designs we cover in this chapter are simple extensions of the basic pretest-posttest design. Like the original pretest-posttest design introduced in chapter 12, the modified designs deal with issues in the form of Basic Question 4: *Will introducing subjects to a specific change in an otherwise standard context cause their behavior to change?*

Quasi-Experimental Designs: Research strategies that tend to minimize one or more of the threats to internal validity that arise when we are unable to apply all the controls required of a true experiment.

The Pretest-Posttest Design with a Control Group

The improvements we will make to the one-group pretest-posttest design serve to rule out specific kinds of rival explanations and thereby add to internal validity. For the first modification of the pretest-posttest design, consider the hypothetical experiment summarized in Table 15–3. The goal of the study was to evaluate the impact of introducing a family-planning curriculum on the incidence of unwanted pregnancies among high-school students. The specific threat to internal validity cited in the example was the information the study may have acquired from media coverage concerning the danger of HIV (AIDS) infection among sexually active heterosexual partners.

To eliminate extraneous historical events as rival explanations for pretest-posttest differences, we must include a control group that shares the experiences of the experimental group *except for the significant event itself*. Such a design is shown in Table 15–4. Only the experimental group experiences the significant event. The control group, which is measured before and after the significant event along with the experimental group, serves as a reference against which to compare the experimental group.

The Pretest-Posttest Design with a Nonequivalent Control Group

When the researcher is able to assign subjects randomly, the two-group pretest-posttest design is a perfectly legitimate experimental design (the pretest-posttest design with an equivalent control group—chapter 13). We can assume initial equivalence between the two groups and, since the control group is subject to the same history as the experimental group, it provides a perfect reference for a posttest

The Pretest-Posttest Design with a Control Group

	Measurement 1 (Pretest)			Measurement 2 (Posttest)
Group 1 (experimental)	before the significant event occurs (baseline)	→	the significant event occurs	after the significant event occurs
Group 2 (control)	measured along with Group 1	→	no significant event	measurred along with Group 1

Table 15–4. A diagram of a pretest-posttest design with a control group. If subjects are randomly assigned to the two groups, the study is a true experiment.

comparison. Sometimes, however, the restrictions imposed by the field research environment make it impossible or impractical to assign subjects randomly to different groups. In the present family-planning example, randomly assigning some students within the same school to receive or not to receive family-planning education would probably not be an effective approach. The students who are not selected to participate could resent being left out. Also, since students in the same school are likely to share a great deal of information, the content of the family-planning curriculum would probably become known to the control group. Instead of randomly assigning subjects to control and experimental conditions, we could use as a control a comparable school district that has not implemented a family-planning curriculum (see Table 15–5). We must be careful to qualify such a nonrandomly formed control group as a **nonequivalent control group**: a group that resembles the experimental group but, because of the absence of random assignment, cannot be assumed to be initially equivalent to the experimental group. When the control group of the two-group pretest-posttest study is nonequivalent, the design shown in Table 15–4 is quasi-experimental: a **pretest-posttest design with a nonequivalent control group**. Table 15–5 shows what the study from Table 15–3 would look like if it were enhanced by adding a nonequivalent control group.

Interpreting the results of a two-group pretest-posttest design

With the control group added to the basic pretest-posttest design, it is possible to separate the influence of the significant event from the influence of historical factors. Any historical influence that might have been present will show up as a pretest-posttest difference in the control group. If both the experimental and control groups change from pretest to posttest in similar fashion (as shown in Figure 15–1), then the shift is from history rather than from the significant event. If the behavior of both groups shifts from pretest to posttest but the degree of change

Nonequivalent Control Group: A group that resembles the experimental group but, because of the absence of random assignment, cannot be assumed to be initially equivalent to the experimental group.

Pretest-Posttest Design with a Nonequivalent Control Group: A two-group pretest-posttest study that lacks the random assignment of subjects to the control and experimental conditions.

Unwanted Teen Pregnancies

	Measurement 1		Measurement 2
School District A (experimental)	before the introduction of the family-planning curriculum	→ the family-planning curriculum is introduced →	after the family-planning curriculum is in force for two years
School District B (nonequivalent control)	measured together with the experimental group	→ no family-planning curriculum →	measured together with the experimental group

Table 15–5. A pretest-posttest design can be extended by adding a control group that is comparable to the experimental group but does not experience the significant event. When the control group is nonequivalent, as it is in this illustration, the study is a quasi-experiment.

among the experimental subjects is greater than the degree of change among the control subjects (as shown in Figure 15–2), we may conclude that the significant event affected behavior, but historical factors may also have influenced the results. When measures of the experimental group change from pretest to posttest and measures of the control group do not (as shown in Figure 15–3), we may conclude that the significant event is the only influence promoting a change in behavior. (Figures 15–1, 15–2, and 15–3 were drawn assuming that the significant event would

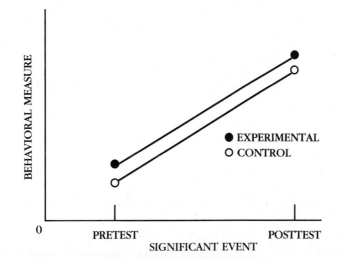

Figure 15–1. The behavior of both the experimental and control groups changes in similar fashion from pretest to posttest, which indicates that history is responsible for the change.

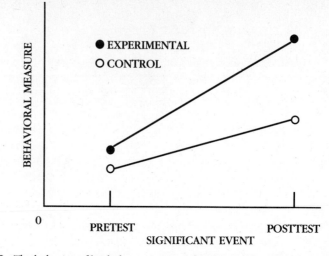

Figure 15–2. The behavior of both the experimental and control groups changes from pretest to posttest, but the change in the experimental group is greater. The pattern indicates that both history and the significant event are responsible for the change.

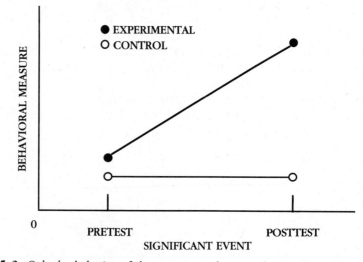

Figure 15–3. Only the behavior of the experimental group changes from the pretest to the posttest, so the change is attributed to the significant event.

increase the values of the behavioral measure. It is, of course, also possible for the values of a behavioral measure to decrease following a significant event.)

Of course, the confidence we have in drawing conclusions about the contribution of the significant event to changes in behavior depends on how comparable the control group is to the experimental group. The more the subjects in a nonequivalent control group resemble the subjects in an experimental group, the greater the internal validity of the study. However, whereas the addition of a nonequivalent control group to the pretest-posttest design may strengthen the internal validity of a study somewhat, only a randomly assigned control group is likely to achieve the level of internal validity we expect from a true experimental design.

The Interrupted Time-Series Design

Sometimes it is not possible to find a group to serve as a nonequivalent control in a pretest-posttest field study. There are, however, other modifications of the one-group pretest-posttest design we can employ to minimize rival explanations and improve internal validity. One such design is the **interrupted time-series design**, a pretest-posttest design with several pretests and several posttests before and after the significant event. The basic plan is shown in Table 15–6 with four pretests and four posttests.

The first phase of the interrupted time-series study requires taking a series of pretest behavioral measurements over time that, ideally, will prove to be stable and represent an established pattern of behavior. The second phase is the occurrence of the significant event. The last phase is a series of posttest measurements. If the behavior remains essentially the same on multiple measures before the significant event, changes immediately after the event, and stays changed during multiple measures after the significant event, we may conclude that the significant event is the instrument of behavior modification. This pattern is illustrated in Figure 15–4.

For history to introduce a rival explanation, the extraneous event would, just by chance, have to coincide with the significant event. For maturation to introduce a rival explanation, the maturational phenomenon would, just by chance, have to coincide with the significant event, and the same can be said for the remaining threats of testing, instrumentation, and regression to the mean. If we assume that such coincidences are very unlikely, we can discount the challenges to internal validity and accept an explanation of the shift that is linked to the significant event.

Many different patterns of results can emerge from interrupted time-series studies. For example, another pattern of results that tends to implicate the significant event but is opposite to that shown in Figure 15–4 is a stable positive shift (see Figure 15–5). In the context of the present example, a positive shift would be evident if the critics of family planning are correct in their assertion that covering explicit sexual information in a school setting encourages premarital sex and will ultimately exacerbate the problem of unwanted pregnancies among unmarried teens. Other possible patterns of interrupted time-series results (Figure 15–6) are either weak in their implication of the significant event as an instrument of

Interrupted Time-Series Design: A pretest-posttest design with several pretests and several posttests before and after the significant event.

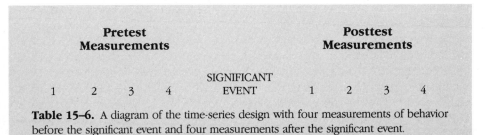

Pretest Measurements					Posttest Measurements			
				SIGNIFICANT EVENT				
1	2	3	4		1	2	3	4

Table 15–6. A diagram of the time-series design with four measurements of behavior before the significant event and four measurements after the significant event.

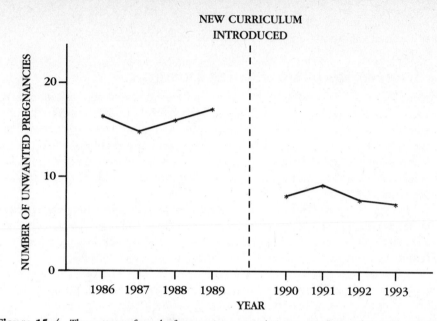

Figure 15–4. The pattern of results from an interrupted time-series design that is most indicative of the success of the family-planning curriculum in reducing unwanted pregnancies. The ideal result appears as an abrupt and stable shift from the pretest baseline.

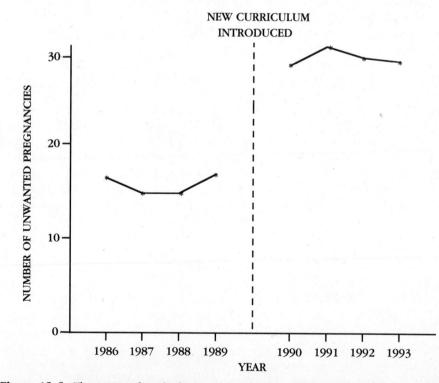

Figure 15–5. The pattern of results from an interrupted time-series design that is most indicative of an increase in unwanted pregnancies following the introduction of the family-planning curriculum.

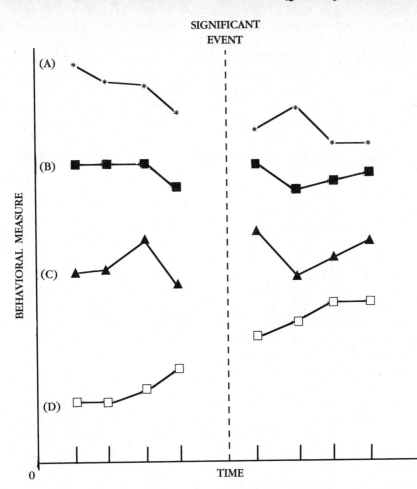

Figure 15–6. Four patterns that could emerge from an interrupted time-series experiment that provide weak (A and B) or no support (B and C) for the hypothesis that the significant event caused a behavioral change.

behavioral change (Result A) or indicate the absence of any effect on behavior from the significant event (Results B, C, and D). Result C would be consistent with a regression effect (a return to a stable level after an atypical flurry of high and low extremes), and Result D would be consistent with a maturation or testing effect.

The Multiple Time-Series Design

Even if we do obtain results that strongly imply an effect from the significant event (as in Figures 15–1 and 15–2), we still have to worry about the possibility that, coincidentally, another event occurred at the same time as the significant event and constitutes a rival historical explanation. We can attempt to neutralize this rival explanation by using the **multiple time-series design**, which is really just a

Multiple Time-Series Design: A pretest-posttest design with a nonequivalent control group that has been expanded into a time-series design.

pretest-posttest design with a nonequivalent control group that has been expanded into a time-series design. As was true for the nonequivalent control group extension of the pretest-posttest design, the more comparable the control group is to the original group, the better chance we have to eliminate historical events as confounding variables. The design is diagramed in Table 15–7.

If the pretest and posttest measurements of Group 2 (the nonequivalent control group) tend to parallel the measurements of Group 1 (the group that experienced the significant event), we cannot conclude that any change we observe in Group 1 is a consequence of the significant event (Figure 15–7). If, however, the two sets of

	Pretest Measurements						Posttest Measurements			
Group 1 (experimental group)	1	2	3	4	SIGNIFICANT EVENT		1	2	3	4
Group 2 (nonequivalent control)	1	2	3	4	NO SIGNIFICANT EVENT		1	2	3	4

Table 15–7. A diagram of the multiple time-series design with a nonequivalent control group. There are four measurements of behavior before the significant event and four measurements after the significant event.

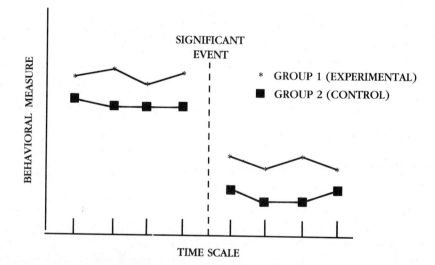

Figure 15–7. A possible pattern of results from a multiple time-series study. Even though the behavior of Group 1 changes after the significant event, the corresponding change in the nonequivalent control group indicates that the significant event is not responsible for the change.

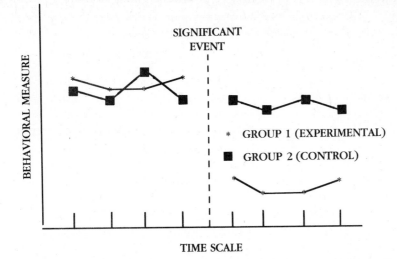

Figure 15–8. A possible pattern of results from a multiple time-series study. Only the behavior of Group 1 changes after the significant event, so the significant event is likely to be the cause of the change.

measurements diverge following the significant event (Figure 15–8), the significant event can be presumed to have influenced the change.

Single-Subject Designs

Some research strategies resemble the quasi-experimental time-series study but are, nevertheless, classified as experimental rather than as quasi-experimental designs. B. F. Skinner (1953) developed one such approach for his studies of learning phenomena: the **single-subject design**. It requires introducing and withdrawing an experimental condition and examining the effects on a reversible behavior of a single subject. Since learned behaviors are reversible (we can "unlearn" as well as learn a mode of responding), the single-subject approach is a suitable choice (maybe, according to Skinner [1963], even the *preferred* choice) for studying the influence of experimental conditions on the learning process.

The A-B-A Design

The most basic single-subject design (see Table 15–8), the **A-B-A design**, begins with a recording of a **baseline** (A) level of a behavior: the subject's level of performance prior to introducing an experimental condition or prior to making a change in an existing experimental condition. Next, the change (B) is introduced and maintained while performance is measured. The last phase of data collection begins with a return to the A condition that was originally in force during the baseline phase. Thus, the baseline data serve as a control or reference level against which to compare the data collected during the middle (B) experimental phase. For example, to examine the effectiveness of praise to get a chronically tardy student to

Single-Subject Design: Studying the effects of the introduction and withdrawal of an experimental condition on a reversible behavior using only one subject.

A-B-A Design: Tracking a reversible behavior first without (A), then with (B), and again without (A) the experimental condition present.

Baseline: The subject's level of performance prior to introducing an experimental condition or prior to making a change in an existing experimental condition.

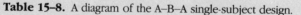

A	B	A
Measure baseline behavioral output (experimental condition not yet operative).	Measure behavioral output while under the influence of the experimental condition.	Measure behavioral output after experimental condition is withdrawn.

Table 15–8. A diagram of the A–B–A single-subject design.

arrive at class on time, an instructor could establish a baseline level of tardiness in Phase A, then, in Phase B, praise the student for every on-time arrival (tardy arrivals would be ignored), then, in Phase C, discontinue the praise. If the student's tardiness decreases with the introduction of praise and reverses back to baseline after praise is withdrawn, praise is implicated as an important determinant of the student's behavior.

Two possible patterns of A-B-A results indicate an effect on performance attributable to the experimental condition. In one pattern (Figure 15–9), the experimental condition increases the values of the dependent measure relative to the baseline phase, and the subsequent removal of the experimental condition causes the behavioral output to settle back down to the baseline level. In the other

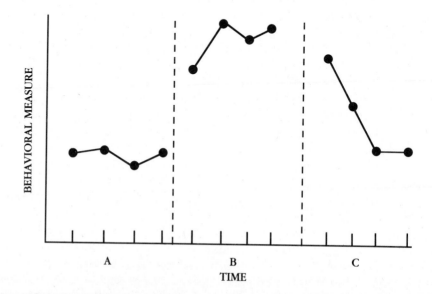

Figure 15–9. A pattern representing the responses of a single subject to the introduction and removal of an experimental condition following the measurement of a baseline level of responding. The experimental condition increased the value of the behavioral measure.

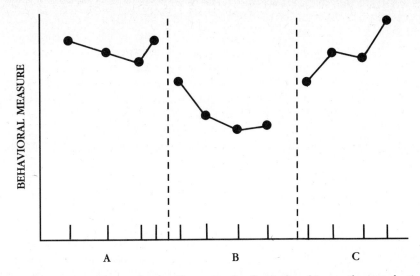

Figure 15–10. A pattern representing the responses of a single subject to the introduction and withdrawal of an experimental condition following the measurement of a baseline level of responding. The experimental condition decreased behavioral output.

pattern (Figure 15–10), the experimental condition suppresses the values of the dependent measure relative to the level that was present during the baseline phase. Then, after the removal of the experimental condition, the behavioral measure increases back to the baseline level.

Internal validity and the A-B-A design

For a design that requires only one subject, the A-B-A design has substantial internal validity for several reasons. First, the issue of the initial equivalence of subjects assigned to experimental and control conditions is addressed by using each subject as his or her own control. Second, extraneous variables are unlikely to be a problem in single-subject research because of the strict control it is possible to maintain in a laboratory environment. Third, the requirement that the behavior be reversible following the withdrawal of the experimental condition rules out the possibility that some event or circumstance unrelated to the experimental condition is the true reason for the movement away from the baseline level. For example, the rationale for ruling out the effect of history is that even if, by chance, some event occurred coincidentally with the onset of the experimental condition and had an effect on the subject's behavior, it is most unlikely that another random event with an opposite effect on behavioral output would also occur coincidentally just as the experimental condition is withdrawn.

Even if coincidences are discarded as a possible explanation for the orderly fluctuations of the behavioral measure from the A to the B and from the B to the A conditions, with the experimental observation of only one subject as evidence, a researcher might be reluctant to conclude that the experimental manipulation caused the fluctuations. To strengthen confidence in the internal validity of single-

Small-*n* Experiment: An experiment that requires only a few subjects, such as a multiple-baseline design or replications of a single-subject design.

subject results and to improve the ability to generalize from such data, one option is to run identical experiments with additional single subjects. If the reversible behavior measured in the additional single-subject experiments responds to the introduction and withdrawal of the experimental condition in a manner consistent with the behavior of the original subject, we can discount the possibility that the reaction of the original subject was idiosyncratic (that is, unique to the individual) and have more confidence in the internal validity of the study. (A report of several identical single-subject experiments is often described as a **small-*n* experiment**. In statistical notation, *n* represents the number of individuals who serve as subjects in an experiment.)

The A-B-A-B Design

Another tactic to enhance the internal validity of the single-subject experiment is to extend the A-B-A design to an A-B-A-B design. If the experimental condition is indeed the instrument of behavioral change, the behavioral output of the subject should rise and fall along with the introduction or withdrawal of the experimental (B) condition. Another advantage of the A-B-A-B design lies in its ability to defuse the ethical dilemma of withdrawing a beneficial treatment. In an applied clinical setting, in which experimental behavior-modification programs tend to be oriented toward the welfare of the client/patient, a successful A-B-A experiment would leave the patient with the same problem that was present during baseline. With the A-B-A-B approach, following the return to baseline under the second baseline (A) condition, the client/patient is restored to the desirable behavior pattern with another exposure to the experimental (B) condition.

A-B-A and A-B-A-B single-subject designs are not to be confused with the case study approach (chapter 6), which focuses on descriptive characteristics of an individual rather than on the effects of manipulating a variable. Neither should single-subject designs be confused with the quasi-experimental time-series study, which also requires taking several measurements before and after a change in conditions. The time-series study includes only the A and B phases of the A-B-A design. There is no attempt to reverse the behavior (if, indeed, it is even possible) by changing the conditions back to those that were in effect during the baseline measurement phase.

Laboratory Origins, Human Applications

Even though single-subject designs arose from the animal learning research of B. F. Skinner, who studied lever-pressing in rats and key-pecking behavior in pigeons, the research strategy can also be applied outside the laboratory environment to study any reversible behavior. For example, many overweight people who desire to trim down seek the counseling and expertise of support groups. Members are expected to follow a diet plan and attend weekly meetings to weigh in and get information about healthy weight-losing tactics. As many of us know all too well, the behaviors that lead to weight loss are reversible, and, following a successful diet program, people often gain back the weight they lost (and more!). Since the behaviors leading to weight loss are reversible, experimental conditions that are hypothesized to affect weight loss and the consequences of withdrawing those conditions can be evaluated using the single-subject design.

Assume, for example, that a support group for dieters has set up a schedule of weekly meetings on your campus for the spring semester. To use the single-subject approach to evaluate the contribution of group support to successful weight loss, it would first be necessary to establish a baseline for a program candidate by recording several weekly weight measurements before the beginning of the diet. Then we would continue to take weekly weight measures during the person's participation with the support group. The final phase would be to monitor weight at weekly intervals during the summer break, after the program is over. A result in the form of Figure 15–10 would indicate that the program worked to encourage weight loss, but that after the support group disbanded, the single subject regained the lost weight.

Multiple-Baseline Designs

Like the single-subject design, **multiple-baseline designs** require tracking a behavioral measure over time before and during the introduction of an experimental condition. But unlike the A-B-A and A-B-A-B single-subject designs, multiple-baseline designs do not require that the behavior under study be reversible. Thus, multiple-baseline designs are suitable even if the experimental condition results in changes of a relatively permanent nature. Here are two different types of multiple-baseline designs, both illustrated with behaviors that leave the subject better off if never reversed.

Multiple Baseline Designs: Small-*n* designs that require tracking a behavior across the introduction and withdrawal of an experimental condition and, unlike the single-subject design, do not require that the behavior be reversible.

The Multiple-Baseline Design Across Subjects

The first phase of the multiple-baseline design across subjects is essentially the same as for the single-subject design: to record baseline behavior. The difference lies in the fact that more than one subject contributes baseline data (hence the name *multiple-baseline*), and the experimental condition is introduced at a different time for each subject. For example, one way to study the effectiveness of an experimental method to eliminate bedwetting behavior in children would be to record bedwetting incidents for three children over different baseline periods and follow with the experimental condition (see Figure 15–11). Since the frequency of bedwetting dropped off for all the subjects regardless of the month during which the experimental condition was introduced, we can eliminate rival explanations tied to coincidental historical events, maturation, and so on.

The Multiple-Baseline Across Behaviors

This form of the multiple-baseline design requires only one subject, but instead of gathering baseline data with reference to a single behavior, we gather different periods of baseline data for several different behaviors. For example, let us assume that Sally intends to begin a formal diet program. Prior to beginning the diet we could have Sally write down everything she eats in a daily diary. Using the information in the diary we could then establish baselines for two different

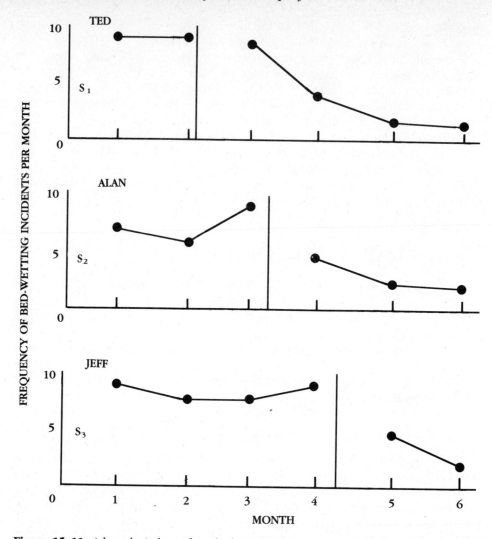

Figure 15–11. A hypothetical set of results from a multiple-baseline across subjects study. The vertical lines indicate the beginning of the behavior modification program to eliminate bedwetting for each of the three subjects.

behaviors: the frequency with which Sally eats foods that are forbidden on the diet program and the frequency with which she eats greater than allowable portions of permissible foods. After Sally begins the diet we could introduce a program of behavior modification to reward eating the correct foods. Then, at another time, using the same behavior modification strategy, we could reward eating appropriate portions. If the program can successfully modify behavior, the eating of forbidden foods and the eating of too much food should both drop off, as shown in Figure 15–12.

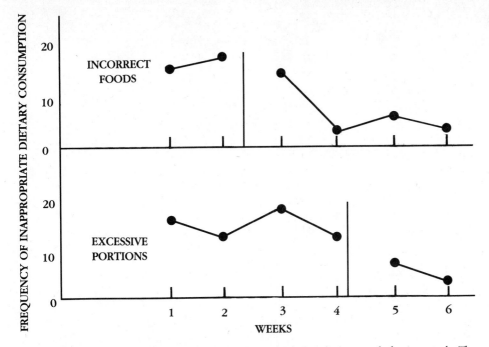

Figure 15–12. A hypothetical set of results from a multiple-baseline across-behaviors study. The vertical lines indicate the beginning of the behavior modification program to eliminate cheating on a diet program.

Summary

We began our coverage of quasi-experimental research by explaining what a quasi-experiment is and how quasi-experimental research differs from experimental research, correlational research, and just plain sloppy research. We then presented five potential threats to the internal validity of quasi-experiments (history, maturation, testing, instrumentation, and regression to the mean) in the context of a very shaky research design: the pretest-posttest design. Next, we discussed specific enhancements of the pretest-posttest design (the pretest-posttest design with a nonequivalent control group, the interrupted time-series design, and the multiple time-series design) that help to neutralize rival explanations (threats to internal validity). The chapter ended with a discussion of some experimental approaches that resemble the time-series design. Single-subject designs are useful when the behavior is reversible, and multiple-baseline designs are useful when the behavior either is not reversible or when it would be undesirable to reverse the behavior.

Key Terms

A-B-A Design, p. 297

A-B-A-B Design, p. 300

Baseline, p. 297

History (as a threat to internal validity), p. 286

Instrumentation (as a threat to internal validity), p. 287

Interrupted Time-Series Design, p. 293

Maturation (as a threat to internal validity), p. 287

Multiple Time-Series Design, p. 295

Multiple-Baseline Designs, p. 301

Nonequivalent Control Group, p. 290

Pretest-Posttest Design with a Nonequivalent Control Group, p. 290

Quasi-Experimental Design, p. 289

Regression to the Mean (as a threat to internal validity), p. 288

Single-Subject Designs, p. 297

Small-n Experiment, p. 300

Testing (as a threat to internal validity), p. 287

Chapter Exercises

1. If quasi-experiments are "almost" or "not quite" real experiments, why don't researchers simply make the procedural and design improvements that are necessary to qualify the study as a true experiment?

2. Why are quasi-experiments such a valuable supplement to the experimental investigation of behavior?

3. Explain the history, maturation, testing, instrumentation, and regression-to-the-mean threats to the internal validity of the pretest-posttest quasi-experiment. Then explain how true experimental designs avoid the challenges to internal validity that affect quasi-experiments.

4. What are the three characteristics of a true experiment?

5. Compare the focus of quasi-experimental research to that of correlational research.

6. The quasi-experimental designs we presented in this chapter are really just enhancements of the basic pretest-posttest design. List each quasi-experimental design covered in the text by name and describe how each enhances the internal validity of the basic pretest-posttest design.

7. Explain why the underlying rationale of the single-subject design demands that the behavior under study be reversible.

8. What patterns of results support the interpretation that the introduction and withdrawal of the experimental condition is responsible for behavioral changes across the phases of A-B-A and A-B-A-B single-subject experiments?

9. What features of multiple-baseline designs contribute to for their internal validity?

10. Pick out a significant natural event being reported by the print and/or broadcast media and describe how you would examine its impact on behavior using a quasi-experimental approach.

Proposal Assignment 15: Completing Your Proposal

It is now time to work on the remaining sections of your proposal. The sections of an APA style paper are reviewed in Appendix A. Your assignment is to write or revise the following sections:

Title page (new section)
Abstract (new section)
Introduction (one more revision is probably necessary)
Method (method sections often require several revisions)
Results

You have drawn a number of figures of your expected results. Include the figure that fits the design you decided to use. Be sure to include a verbal description of the results that match the figure. Also, state which statistical analysis would be appropriate, but do not calculate the results.

Discussion

Write two discussion sections. The first should be written assuming that the results supported your hypothesis. The second should be written assuming that the results did not support your hypothesis. Be sure in each discussion section to begin with a review of the results and state whether they support the hypothesis given in the introduction. Tie in the results with the literature you reviewed earlier. Then discuss problems with the way the study was run. Conclude by mentioning the implications of the results.

References
Figure caption(s)
Figure(s)

16

The Ethics of Research

All behavioral researchers have fundamentally the same agenda: to gather and assess information about behavior for its own sake and for the benefit of humanity. It is a noble goal, and thousands devote their careers to it. Yet researchers would not retain their high standing in the public eye if, in their gathering of information, they failed to carefully consider and protect the rights of the individuals who provide the information: their subjects. Behavioral scientists recognize that research is a probing process with the potential to infringe on subjects' rights. Despite their own sensitivity for the rights of others and their faith in the professionalism of their colleagues, behavioral scientists have come to recognize that a formal code of checks and balances is needed to preserve the ethical integrity of behavioral research.

Perhaps the most fundamental premise of any set ethical guidelines that place restrictions on interactions among people is that every individual wants and deserves respect. When we fail to get respect and the due consideration of our rights that respect brings, we feel diminished as human beings. Among the individual rights we cherish as prerequisites of respect are the right to be fully informed of matters that are of legitimate concern to us, the right to be protected from pain and discomfort, and the right of privacy. Behaviors that violate these rights are wrongful. Yet, with some careful thought and soul-searching, you can probably think of circumstances, perhaps from your own personal experiences, that can justify behaviors that, on their face, are wrongful. Here are some examples for consideration.

An elderly family member, hospitalized and in frail condition, is not told about a reversal of family fortunes. The information was withheld to spare the aged patient a devastating, perhaps unsurvivable, emotional shock. In this special situation, there is no denying that information the patient had a right to know was withheld, but the motive for withholding it was noble rather than base.

Medical procedures routinely involve significant pain and discomfort, but we do not generally characterize physicians as amoral sadists. We understand that even though the pain and suffering they inflict while diagnosing and/or treating an affliction sometimes seem to rival the discomfort of the affliction itself, it is in our own best interest to endure temporary discomfort for the long-range medical benefits.

Sometimes officials in law enforcement use deceit (so-called sting operations), invasion of privacy (wire taps and other surveillance measures), misrepresentation (undercover work), and various forms of harassment in their dealings with criminal suspects. Are these behaviors unethical regardless of their use for the pursuit of truth and justice, or do the ends justify the means?

Three Views on Exposing Research Participants to Risk

Researchers face similar conflicts when the strategies they intend to use to gather scientifically valuable data involve risks to research participants. Much of what follows in this chapter is concerned with how behavioral scientists carry out their formal obligation to consider and minimize the risks to research participants. First, however, we shall consider how risk assessment is affected by one's view of morality.

Sometimes a strategy for collecting valuable scientific information calls for the researcher to behave toward subjects in a manner generally considered wrongful (deceiving subjects about the nature of the research, inflicting discomfort, or purposely exposing individuals to mental and physical stress). In such cases the researcher is faced with a moral dilemma. Should ideas for research be abandoned if the proposed methodology requires wrongful behavior toward subjects, or must we consider the degree to which the negative aspects of a subject's experience can be balanced and, perhaps, outweighed by beneficial consequences? In other words, can a researcher's wrongful behavior toward subjects be redeemed as morally correct if, on balance, the potential for positive consequences appears to outweigh the risk of negative consequences? Here are three different views on what constitutes a proper answer to this question.

The first moral stance

One view is that ethical standards do not shift as a function of the consequences of their violation. That is, ethical standards are viewed as absolute and discoverable rather than as unstable and enigmatic. According to this relatively inflexible moral stance, lying to people, placing them at risk of discomfort, stress, or injury is *always* unethical regardless of the good intentions of the perpetrator or the benefits the wrongful act will ultimately bring.

Consider an extreme case of wrongful behavior: the taking of a human life. A person whose pacifist beliefs forbid the taking of a life under any circumstances would, if faithful to those beliefs, reject an opportunity for self-defense in a life-threatening situation if the act of defense would result in the death of the aggressor. The pacifist view that the taking of a human life is always wrong fits the philosophy that some behaviors are always wrong.

The second moral stance

Another view holds that standards for discriminating right from wrong are orderly and discoverable, but according to this view it is not possible to defend one particular set of ethical standards as the one true set to guide all people of all cultures. In other words, for the members of a defined social group to commit themselves to a carefully considered ethical code of behavior is marvelously civilized, but we cannot necessarily expect all other groups to accept the same code. Standards of morality have not evolved in the same form across all cultures, and moral standards continue to evolve within the same culture. Therefore, the second position supports conformity to a set of carefully thought-out ethical principles as a valuable and reasonable element of civilized behavior. But, because alternative sets of ethical principles will always exist, it is impossible to defend one particular set of ethical standards as the one true absolute guide.

Clearly, the second moral stance is more flexible and respectful of diverse opinion than the first moral stance. If the members of a society other than our own embrace certain standards of behavior and appear to thrive under their direction, according to the second moral stance it would be an act of arrogance and self-righteousness for us to proclaim their behavior as unethical just because their values differ from ours. Nevertheless, tolerance of diverse ethical standards is not without its controversial aspects. For example, should we always regard the denial of equal rights for women as unethical, or do we accept its existence in foreign cultures as morally correct? Do the countries who have abolished the death penalty hold the high moral ground over the United States, or do we retain the right to establish a legal system that we feel best suits our own sense of morality? These issues are the subject of vigorous debate. People who tend to think of moral dilemmas in terms of the first moral stance believe that they can have only one correct resolution. All others are incorrect and less than satisfactory. By contrast, the essence of the second moral stance is that the nature of pluralism will forever remain a barrier to the discovery of an absolute set of ethical standards.

The third moral stance

The third view is that judging the moral acceptability or unacceptability of a specific behavior should be tied to the consequences of the behavior rather than to any unconditional doctrine. This view can be thought of as the cost-benefit approach to moral judgment. According to this view, in one context a behavior could be considered appropriate, perhaps even admirable, yet be condemned as an outrage in another context. Thus, to refer once again to the extreme example of taking a human life, turning off the life-support system and causing the death of a recovering patient is an act of murder, but turning off life support to end the pain and suffering of a terminally ill patient is more likely to be considered an act of mercy.

Reconciling Research Goals with Human Values

Even though most behavioral research is benign, some research does have an element of risk to participants (subjects) that cannot be ignored. When risk is believed to be present, the standards investigators apply to protect subjects' rights most closely resemble the cost-benefit philosophy. Some costs (risks to the welfare of research participants) are tolerated if, after careful review, the potential costs are outweighed by the potential benefits (contributions to human welfare and/or the body of scientific knowledge), and if the subjects agree in advance to participate with full knowledge of the risks.

The American Psychological Association (APA) updated its Ethical Principles of Psychologists in 1990, and Principle 9 constitutes the primary reference for protecting the rights of human participants in psychological experiments. The 10 parts of Principle 9 (labeled 9a through 9j) are *not* a list of specific prohibitions with respect to research strategy and methodology with human subjects. Instead, they focus on the broad issues that must be considered when researchers are faced with weighing the potential a research strategy has for producing harmful consequences for the subjects against its potential for producing positive consequences for mankind and the body of scientific knowledge. Technically, the APA principles represent a code of professional conduct for psychologists rather than a code of law. They are, however, in synchrony with federal regulations issued by the Department of Health and Human Services (HHS) regarding the use of human subjects in research. We quote each APA principle as originally published and follow with a brief explanation and commentary on the issues each one raises.

APA Principle 9: Research with Human Participants

Principle 9 of Ethical Principles of Psychologists is introduced with this paragraph:

> The decision to undertake research rests upon a considered judgment by the individual psychologist about how best to contribute to psychological science and human welfare. Having made the decision to conduct research, the psychologist considers alternative directions in which research energies and resources might be invested. On the basis of this consideration, the psychologist carries out the investigation with respect and concern for the dignity and welfare of the people who participate and with cognizance of federal and state regulations and professional standards governing the conduct of research with human participants.

This introduction to Principle 9 calls attention to the freedom of investigators to pursue the research problems of their choice in a manner they consider to have the most scientific merit. The only mandate the current guidelines introduce to limit that freedom is the requirement that the investigator take steps to protect the welfare of research participants. Specifically, the investigator has the responsibility of being aware of and conforming to the federal and state regulations and professional standards that govern the conduct of research with human participants.

> a. In planning a study, the investigator has the responsibility to make a careful evaluation of its ethical acceptability. To the extent that the weighing of scientific and human values suggests a compromise of any principle, the investigator incurs a correspondingly serious obligation to seek ethical advice and to observe stringent safeguards to protect the rights of human participants.

Principle 9a is a general declaration of the investigator's responsibility to scrutinize all research procedures for their potential to compromise ethical principles. It implicitly recognizes that research endeavors can involve risk to the welfare of research participants, and it obligates investigators to evaluate the ethical acceptability of their treatment of subjects. If the investigator or those with whom the investigator consults identify a source of risk to a subject, the investigator must weigh the risk against the potential contribution of the study and work to minimize any violation of a subject's rights. The stipulation that the investigator seek the advice of other parties is in recognition of the difficulty a researcher is likely to have arriving at an unbiased evaluation of the ethical acceptability of the research goals and planned methods for achieving those goals.

> b. Considering whether a participant in a planned study will be a "subject at risk" or a "subject at minimal risk," according to recognized standards, is of primary ethical concern to the investigator.

Principle 9b calls for the investigator to characterize the degree of risk research participants will be exposed to in the planned study relative to the risks they normally experience. Making such a risk comparison can be quite challenging because the degree of risk that subjects normally endure can be quite variable. For example, children being raised by competent parents in wholesome environments are in a relatively low risk situation with respect to negative events that could affect psychological development compared to children who are being raised in under-staffed and underfunded state institutions.

Once the researcher has made a good-faith effort to understand the degree of risk normally endured by a subject population, two recognized standards must be met in order to classify a proposed project as minimally risky. The first standard of **minimal risk** is that a subject's participation in a study must not increase the likelihood of a negative event that is known to occur occasionally in the subject's normal environment. For example, children sometimes quarrel with each other over toys, so children are normally at some risk of becoming upset with each other when they are in the same play environment with a limited number of attractive toys. It would be a fair assumption that an experiment for studying toy-sharing behavior in children would also involve some risk of emotional upset for children. For the toy-sharing study to involve *minimal* risk, the probability that the child would become upset in the research environment should not be greater than the risk that is present

Minimal Risk: Risk is minimal if a subject's participation does not increase the likelihood of a negative event occurring or the magnitude of a negative event, should one occur unexpectedly.

in a normal play situation. The second standard of minimal risk is that participation in the study must not increase the *magnitude* of a negative event that is known to occur. For example, an experimental procedure in the toy-sharing study might not increase the likelihood of a quarrel, and thus satisfy the first condition of minimal risk, but if whatever quarrel did occur in the research environment was likely to be more severe than usual, the second standard of minimal risk would be violated.

Sometimes experiences that are not a part of a subject's typical daily routine are nevertheless still considered minimally risky. For example, administering routine physical or psychological examinations or tests to subjects does not by itself constitute a departure from minimal risk even though people tend to take such tests only on rare occasions.

Planned studies that involve minimal risk are, of course, much less controversial on ethical grounds than studies that involve more than minimal risk. If more than minimal risk is present, the investigator must carefully evaluate the extent of the risks, take measures to limit the risks, defend the risks as necessary for the pursuit of the research goal, make a case that the potential benefits of the study outweigh the risks, and follow special safeguards set forth in Principles 9d and 9g. In short, research can still be conducted with human subjects even when more than minimal risk is present, but the more risk, the more difficult it is to make a case that the potential value of the research outweighs the risk to subjects. The potential costs of each study to human welfare must be evaluated on a case-by-case basis against the study's potential benefits.

> c. The investigator always retains the responsibility for ensuring ethical practice in research. The investigator is also responsible for the ethical treatment of research participants by collaborators, assistants, students, and employees, all of whom, however, incur similar obligations.

Principle 9c affirms the responsibility of the principal investigator to oversee all elements of the research project for compliance to ethical standards but does not in any way diminish the obligation of other personnel to adhere to ethical principles. In projects supervised by several co-investigators who share equal authority, each co-investigator is as responsible for the ethical integrity of the project as if he or she were the only investigator. The number of personnel does not dilute the responsibility each has to oversee the project for conformity to ethical guidelines.

> d. Except in minimal risk research, the investigator establishes a clear and fair agreement with research participants, prior to their participation, that clarifies the obligations and responsibilities of each. The investigator has the obligation to honor all promises and commitments included in that agreement. The investigator informs the participants of all aspects of the research that might reasonably be expected to influence willingness to participate and explains all other aspects of the research about which the participants inquire. Failure to make full disclosure prior to obtaining informed consent requires additional safeguards to protect the welfare and dignity of the research participants. Research with children or with participants who have impairments that would limit understanding and/or communication requires special safeguarding procedures.

If a planned study will involve more than minimal risk, the researcher must describe the experiment to the subject before asking the subject to enter into a formal agreement to participate. The operative ethical principle in 9d is that subjects have a right to know what the researcher intends to expose them to before they agree to permit it. As part of the research description, the investigator should mention who is doing the study, the type of data that will be collected, and the broad research issue that the study addresses. The researcher must also answer truthfully any of the subjects' questions about the study, and *it must be clear that any agreement to participate can be withdrawn at any time before or during the study.* It is especially important that the researcher make known any feature of the study that could possibly expose subjects to unpleasantness and thereby influence their willingness to participate. When a subject agrees to participate in a study after being given a thorough orientation to his or her pending research experience, we say the subject has given informed consent. (Informed consent was defined in chapter 10 as a subject's declaration of willingness to participate in a study with full knowledge of the potential for objectionable, inconvenient, or unpleasant consequences.)

Once a subject gives informed consent, the obligations of both researcher and subject should be clarified. Items of clarification may include a request of the subject not to tell other prospective subjects about the study (see the discussion of contamination in Box 10–1), information about compensation (if any) for the subject (money, extra course credit, and so forth), and an offer to present the results of the experiment to the participants when completed and analyzed.

Several problems that can arise in a psychological research project are related to the issue of informed consent. One difficulty is that subjects are not always competent to understand the details of a research project well enough to give informed consent. In such cases (as when the subject is mentally retarded, mentally ill, mentally impaired because of medical problems, or very young) the investigator must obtain informed consent from the person who is responsible for the subject's welfare (such as a parent or guardian) and institute special procedures to monitor the welfare of the subject during and after the study. If, for whatever reason, a subject who is not competent to give informed consent expresses reluctance to participate as a subject, that reluctance must be honored despite obtaining the informed consent of a parent or guardian.

A second difficulty arises when informed consent will reveal to the subject information that is inconsistent with the aims of the study. Full disclosure is inconsistent with the aims of a study when the information will distort or negate the anticipated experimental effect. For example, if a research plan called for giving a subject a false report of an IQ evaluation to manipulate the subject's emotional state, the false feedback would be rendered useless as a research tool if the subject knew that the test information was false.

A third difficulty with informed consent is that it can disturb the degree to which the subjects can be considered representative of a population. Let us say, for example, that on the basis of the disclosures in informed consent, a high proportion of potential subjects from a population of college sophomores declined to participate in one or more conditions of an experiment. The subjects who agree to participate despite the risks they are made aware of during the researcher's request for informed consent can hardly be considered a representative sample of the population of college sophomores. The bias exists because all subjects who are intolerant of risk eliminate themselves from participation.

A fourth difficulty is that it is possible for subjects to use the information from informed consent to try to deduce the purpose of the experiment and then behave in a manner they believe is expected of them. When expectancies influence subjects' behavior in a manner unanticipated by the researcher, the subject is said to be responding to the demand characteristics (chapter 10) of the experimental situation. Demand characteristics, which can ruin an otherwise natural and spontaneous behavioral record, can be avoided with **deception**, the practice of describing a study with incomplete and/or false information in order to avoid contaminating the results. The additional obligations an investigator incurs when he or she uses deception are covered next, in Principle 9e.

Deception: The practice of describing a study to a subject with incomplete and/or false information in order to avoid contaminating the results.

> e. Methodological requirements of a study may make the use of concealment or deception necessary. Before conducting such a study, the investigator has a special responsibility to (i) determine whether the use of such techniques is justified by the study's prospective scientific, educational, or applied value; (ii) determine whether alternative procedures are available that do not use concealment or deception; and (iii) ensure that the participants are provided with sufficient explanation as soon as possible.

Principle 9e recognizes that, in selected instances, a full and accurate description of a research effort during informed consent can thwart the effectiveness of an experimental strategy. In such cases the researcher may purposely withhold information and/or provide false information when soliciting informed consent, but the researcher is obligated to justify the practice in terms of the potential the study has to contribute to human welfare or add substantively to the body of scientific knowledge. Naturally, the more the deception is seen as a risk to the subjects' welfare, the more difficult it is to justify it.

The second obligation the researcher has is to explore the development of an alternative research strategy (one that would not involve deception but would permit testing the same experimental hypothesis) prior to making the decision to use a deceptive strategy. Sometimes using deception is the path of least resistance when researchers are planning strategy to test a hypothesis. Principle 9e urges researchers to take the trouble to devise alternative strategies if at all possible. If further consideration of the research problem and some creative effort results in an effective approach that does not require deception, that is the approach the researcher should adopt for the experiment.

The third obligation researchers have when they use deception is to correct any misinformation or reveal information that was purposely withheld in order to execute the research strategy. The goal of debriefing (see chapter 10) is to give the subject a clear idea of what the study was all about, to explain how the deception worked to further the goals of the research, and to remove any misconceptions the deception may have created. For example, Schlenker, Weigold, and Hallam (1990) (reviewed in detail in chapter 23) gave subjects a test of social decision-making prior to the experiment and told them, regardless of how they actually performed, that they scored in either the 93rd (success) or 27th (failure) percentile. The deception was employed to manipulate the subjects' perception of success or failure on a previous task. Therefore, as part of debriefing, the authors had an obligation to explain to subjects why they did not report their true test results and that the feedback they were given during the experiment was not a true reflection of their ability.

If the use of deception poses a risk to the welfare of a research participant (such as emotional distress) too profound to be neutralized by debriefing, the experiment is in violation of the ethical guideline. Thus the investigator's willingness to include subject debriefing is not sufficient by itself. The investigator must also make a convincing case that the debriefing will be effective in neutralizing the impact of the deception on the subjects. Also, since debriefing is an educational experience for the subject as well as a mechanism to counteract any negative effects of deception, even studies that do not exceed the minimal risk criteria commonly include a debriefing session.

> f. The investigator respects the individual's freedom to decline to participate in or withdraw from the research at any time. The obligation to protect this freedom requires careful thought and consideration when the investigator is in a position of authority or influence over the participant. Such positions of authority include, but are not limited to, situations in which research participation is required as part of employment or in which the participant is a student, client, or employee of the investigator.

Principle 9f centers on the issue of **coercion**: inducing subjects to participate or to continue to participate against their own best interests. One important piece of information the researcher must include in the formal request for informed consent is the subject's option to withdraw consent at any time. The fact that the subject agreed to begin participation does not obligate that subject to carry participation through to completion. Also, a strict interpretation of Principle 9f means that if participation is compensated with money, extra course credit, or other similar incentive, the incentive should be awarded even if the subject declines or withdraws informed consent. The reason for such a generous policy is simple. If full compensation were permitted to be contingent on full participation, subjects in dire need of the incentive could be induced to place themselves at risk against their better judgment. For example, consider the case of a student who volunteers for an experiment that holds more than minimal risk. The student hopes that the extra course credit promised to volunteers will be enough to change a failing course average to passing. If the student were to deny consent after being informed of the details of the experiment or withdraw consent after the experiment begins, the student should, nevertheless, receive the full amount of extra credit—even though he or she did nothing more than show up at the appointed time. Again, without this provision subjects could be coerced to participate in a research project in which they felt uncomfortable or threatened.

Another form of coercion that relates to the issue of compensation is attempting to recruit subjects for risky research by promising them inordinately high compensation. The prospect of making a large sum of money for participating in a research project can cloud a prospective subject's judgment concerning his or her acceptable tolerance for engaging in risky activity. To the extent that high compensation causes subjects to consent to endure risks that would ordinarily be unacceptable, the offering of high compensation is unethical. It is especially important in this regard to protect the rights of those who are not competent to give informed consent, such as the mentally handicapped and the very young. It is not ethical, for example, to induce needy parents to consent to have their children participate in risky research activity by offering high compensation.

Potential for coercive abuse is especially high when the investigator is in some position of authority relative to the potential subject population. If, for example, your psychology instructor asked you to volunteer to participate in an experiment, you might feel pressured to give informed consent. You might worry that a refusal could harm your relationship with the instructor and, perhaps, affect the evaluation

Coercion: Inducing subjects to participate or to continue to participate in an experiment against their own best interests.

of your academic performance. Investigators must be especially sensitive to this type of concern and assure subjects that refusal to participate is perfectly acceptable.

> g. The investigator protects the participant from physical and mental discomfort, harm, and danger that may arise from research procedures. If risks of such consequences exist, the investigator informs the participant of that fact. Research procedures likely to cause serious or lasting harm to a participant are not used unless the failure to use these procedures might expose the participant to risk of greater harm, or unless the research has great potential benefit and fully informed and voluntary consent is obtained from each participant. The participant should be informed of procedures for contacting the investigator within a reasonable time period following participation should stress, potential harm, or related questions or concerns arise.

Fortunately, most psychological research carries minimal or no risk to participants, but the Ethical Principles for Research with Human Participants would be incomplete without specifically addressing the responsibilities of researchers who do engage in research that carries significant risk. Principle 9g states the same obligation alluded to in Principle 9d: to protect the subject from harm before, during, and after the study and give the subject an informed choice of participating. The only difference is that in Principle 9g the obligation is stated in more explicit terms, and the cost-benefit philosophy is emphasized as the means to judge the ethical correctness of proceeding with a study that puts subjects at risk.

> h. After the data are collected, the investigator provides the participant with information about the nature of the study and attempts to remove any misconceptions that may have arisen. Where scientific or humane values justify delaying or withholding this information, the investigator incurs a special responsibility to monitor the research and to ensure that there are no damaging consequences for the participant.

Principle 9h is a more detailed and explicit statement of the researcher's obligation to debrief subjects, first introduced in Part 3 of Principle 9e. Principle 9h also recognizes that debriefing subjects after their participation can sometimes be counterproductive to the aims of the study ("scientific . . . values") or the subjects' welfare ("humane values"). If the investigator is able to defend withholding debriefing on scientific or humane grounds, he or she incurs a special responsibility to monitor the subjects during and after the research even more closely than usual for damaging consequences. Delaying debriefing on the basis of scientific values is often related to the desire to keep prospective subjects from learning details of the experiment from debriefed subjects with whom they socialize (contamination of the subject pool, discussed in chapter 10). Also, when subjects such as young children or subjects with mental impairments, who are likely to misinterpret or fail to understand a proper debriefing, Principle 9h permits withholding the debriefing.

> i. Where research procedures result in undesirable consequences for the individual participant, the investigator has the responsibility to detect and remove or correct these consequences, including long-term effects.

Principle 9i recognizes that good-faith efforts to protect the welfare of subjects may not always be successful. Should a research participant suffer damaging consequences from participation in a study, the investigator has the responsibility to detect and remove the source of the problem and take remedial action to correct the damaging consequences to the extent possible.

An experiment can have damaging consequences either from the omission of a procedure that would minimize risk or from the commission of a procedure that introduces risk. For example, consider an experiment to evaluate how effective a new therapy is for curing seriously ill patients. If the therapy had some potentially damaging side effects, the research to evaluate it would introduce risk to the patients who get the treatment. But what if the therapy proved to be effective without side effects? Wouldn't withholding the experimental therapy from the untreated control subjects of the experiment deny them an equal chance to recover and thereby increase their risk? The message of Principle 9i is that once the beneficial effects of an experimental treatment are supported by hard data, every effort must be expended to extend the same benefits to subjects who, by chance alone, were denied the treatment.

> j. Information obtained about a research participant during the course of an investigation is confidential unless otherwise agreed upon in advance. When the possibility exists that others may gain access to such information, this possibility, together with the plans for protecting confidentiality, is explained to the participant as part of the procedure for obtaining informed consent.

Principle 9j is self-explanatory in its safeguarding of a participant's right to privacy. When the right to privacy cannot be guaranteed, the risk that research data could one day be released to other parties must be explained to the participant and agreed to as part of informed consent.

The Process of Ethical Review

All proposed research that places human subjects at risk must be reviewed by an **Institutional Review Board (IRB)** if the institution at which the research is to be carried out receives any government funding. (In practice, all proposed research at public and private academic, medical, and other similar institutions that places human subjects at risk must receive IRB review for conformity to Health and Human Services (HHS) regulations because, in one way or another, virtually all of them receive some measure of federal funding.) The HHS regulations are designed to cover *all* research with human subjects, not just behavioral research, so they are more encompassing and, in minor ways, somewhat different from the professional code represented by the APA Principles. Nevertheless, if a psychologist has met his or her professional responsibility to conform to the APA Ethical Principles of Psychologists, the proposed project is certain to conform to the legal guidelines set forth in the HHS regulations. The members of the IRB should include nonscientists as well as scientists, members of the local community as well as the research community, and members who have legal expertise.

According to federal regulations (Department of Health and Human Services, 1981), some research with human subjects is exempt from IRB review, and the regulations provide many examples to clarify the nature of such research. For example, surveys and interviews of a noncontroversial and noninvasive nature are exempt from review as long as the subjects remain anonymous (that is, are not identified by name in the research records). Similarly, observing people in public places (say, in restaurants or at sporting events) does not involve enough risk to warrant review, unless the intention is to observe subjects when they can reasonably assume they have privacy.

Institutional Review Board (IRB): A broad-based group of citizens entrusted with screening research proposals to make sure they comply with regulations governing the ethical treatment of human subjects.

Proposed studies that expose subjects to minimal risk (as when electrodes are attached to a subject's scalp to take an electroencephalograph) must be reviewed, but they are routinely approved. Proposed research that exposes subjects to more than minimal risk is the most challenging. It must be reviewed thoroughly by the IRB to assure conformity to accepted ethical standards. Any research proposal that is found to lack proper safeguards to guarantee the safety of subjects or a proper plan to obtain informed consent will not be approved in the form submitted and cannot be carried out unless it is modified to the satisfaction of the IRB. Perhaps the most accessible source of detailed information regarding the determination of risk and the safeguards that HHS deems necessary to protect the rights of human subjects is the IRB of your college. The IRB should have abundant materials to guide researchers in the preparation of their proposals.

Err on the side of conservatism

In practice, the wisest course of action a researcher can take with respect to the assessment of risk and conformity to legal guidelines is to submit *all* proposed research to the IRB—even if a project does not appear to involve risk. The reason for following such a conservative policy has more to do with possible financial consequences than virtue. Say, for example, a subject feels wronged by his or her research experience and sues the researcher. *If the researcher sought and received IRB approval* and followed the approved procedures, the institution will stand behind the researcher and pay legal costs. If, on the other hand, the project was not approved, the institution is not obligated to share the burden of mounting a legal defense.

The Use of Animals in Psychological Research

Sometimes students are puzzled why psychologists do so much research using animal populations. After all, aren't psychologists primarily interested in understanding human behavior? Three important issues underlie the relevance of animal research to human concerns: the issue of physical and behavioral continuity, the issue of special behavioral characteristics, and the issue of ethical treatment of humans. Any or all of the three reasons are likely to be raised on the benefit side of the cost-benefit ethical analysis that, as in studies with human subjects, precedes the approval of a research plan.

The issue of physical and behavioral continuity

This issue relates to Charles Darwin's view of the origin of species. According to Darwinian theory, there is continuity between relatively primitive and advanced species. Thus, of the many related species that are currently alive (say, all the mammalian species) all have a hereditary link to a more primitive common ancestor. If common ancestry is a fact, then at least some physical and behavioral continuity should exist between humankind and other mammals. Psychologists who work with animals and subscribe to the Darwinian view assume that some classes of variables influence animal behavior in the same lawful way in which they influence human behavior. Here are some examples to illustrate the similarities between human and animal physical and behavioral characteristics.

a. All mammals have a similarly configured nervous system, and the localization of function in the brain is basically the same. For example, the parts of the mammalian brain that receive sensory information, control motor responses, emotion, appetite, and so on are the same for all mammalian species.

b. The sensory apparatus is quite similar among mammals (eyes, ears, etc.), and the encoding of sensory information as electrochemical impulses that travel along neurons is also similar.

c. Both human and animal learning (such as classical and instrumental conditioning) tend to follow the same basic laws.

d. Developmental phenomena are influenced by the same classes of variables (although not necessarily in the same way) in both humans and animals. For example, the effects of environmental deprivation and environmental enrichment affect the development of intellectual and perceptual-motor skills in both humans and animals.

The issue of special behavioral characteristics

The second reason for studying animals rests on the fact that some animals possess special behavioral characteristics that relate to human concerns and make them uniquely appropriate for studying a particular research problem. For example, the males of some strains of laboratory mice are known for their high level of aggressive behavior; any intruder into their territory is almost certain to be attacked. It is natural for the experimenter who wishes to study the genetic, environmental, and physiological factors that are important to the development and exhibition of aggressive behavior to work with an animal that, by its nature, is aggressive.

The issue of ethics

Some well-organized and dedicated groups (among them the Society Against Vivisection and the Animal Rights Coalition) argue that it is unethical to use animals for research purposes. Animal rights activists have been known to picket research facilities, engage in civil disobedience and, in some instances, even engage in criminal behavior (such as a breaking into research facilities and destroying research equipment) to get their message to the public and the research community.

Animals cannot, of course, give informed consent, so it is a fair argument that intervention by concerned citizens on behalf of helpless animals is a humane and generous act. Yet most people recognize and accept that animals play a key role in the preservation and advancement of human welfare. Most people consume their muscle tissues for food and wear clothing made of their skin; their abilities are used to perform labors; and researchers use them as living preparations to investigate behavioral and biological phenomena too risky to investigate with human subjects. Is it morally defensible to be less concerned with an animal's health and welfare than we are for the health and welfare of our fellow humans? Just as there is debate on how to judge the propriety of placing human subjects at risk (the three moral stances discussed above), there are also alternative views on how to judge the propriety of placing animal subjects at risk.

Responsible researchers who use animals for research purposes do not do so frivolously. They are guided by the same cost-benefit philosophy used to screen and evaluate research proposals with human participants. Making a case for using animals in the pursuit of information (i.e., research) may not be as easy as making a case for using animals to ensure human survival (i.e., by those who depend on them as a food source), but using animals for research purposes is, in the view of animal researchers, morally justifiable on a case-by-case basis.

In general, the formal policies psychologists use to guide their use of animal subjects are not quite as protective as those that are in place to protect the welfare of human subjects. For example, investigators tend to regulate the nonresearch-related experiences of their laboratory animals very closely and maintain the strict environmental controls that are necessary to eliminate confounding variables from the research environment. Also, it may at times be impossible to avoid discomfort, stress, and even the death of the animal in the course of a research project and, at the same time, meet the goals of the research.

Below we reprint the tenth among the Ethical Principles of Psychologists (American Psychological Association [1990]: Care and Use of Animals). As with Principles 9a through 9j that protect the rights of human subjects, the principles set forth to protect animal subjects raise the issues the researcher must consider in the cost-benefit analysis of the proposed research project, and the professional code of conduct they represent is backed up by state and federal government regulations. (An institution's committee on animal research and experimentation, described below, fulfills the same role for nonhuman subjects as the IRB fulfills for human subjects.) As before, we first quote the text of each principle, then follow with a brief commentary.

APA Principle 10: Care and Use of Animals

> An investigator of animal behavior strives to advance understanding of basic behavioral principles and/or to contribute to the improvement of human health and welfare. In seeking these ends, the investigator ensures the welfare of animals and treats them humanely. Laws and regulations notwithstanding, the animal's immediate protection depends upon the scientist's own conscience.

Note two statements in this opening paragraph. The first calls attention to the justification for doing research with animals: "to advance understanding of basic behavioral principles and/or to contribute to the improvement of human health and welfare." Thus, these principles are guided by the same cost-benefit philosophy that guides our consideration of research with human subjects. Although not explicitly stated, the message is that subjecting an animal to unpleasant conditions is unethical unless justified by the potential for obtaining scientifically valuable information. The second statement makes mention of "the scientist's own conscience." Because, with the possible exception of vocalizations, animals cannot complain, the researcher has a special responsibility to monitor their welfare. The reference to the scientist's conscience makes this moral obligation explicit.

> a. The acquisition, care, use, and disposal of all animals shall be in compliance with current federal, state or provincial, and local laws and regulations.

Principle 10a simply puts the animal researcher on notice that there are strict rules that govern the use of animal subjects and that it is the researcher's responsibility to be familiar with them.

> b. A psychologist trained in research methods and experienced in the care of laboratory animals closely supervises all procedures involving animals and is responsible for ensuring appropriate consideration of their comfort, health, and humane treatment.

Principle 10b calls attention to the specialized knowledge it takes to maintain and handle a colony of laboratory animals in a manner protective of their comfort, health, and welfare. A person who has such knowledge must be available to supervise the animal-care personnel as well as student researchers and technicians who have less than expert knowledge of animal care and handling. To ensure compliance with Principle 10b, there are federal and some state regulations providing for unannounced inspections of animal facilities. Violations, such as overcrowding and unsanitary conditions, can result in the closing of the research facility and the withdrawal of funding for the project.

> c. Psychologists ensure that all individuals using animals under their supervision have received explicit instruction in experimental methods and in the care, maintenance, and handling of the species being used. Responsibilities and activities of individuals participating in a research project are consistent with their respective competencies.

Principle 10c says that all personnel who will have a direct role in running the research project must be competent to handle the animals and administer any necessary treatment or tests.

> d. Psychologists make every effort to minimize discomfort, illness, and pain of animals. A procedure subjecting animals to pain, stress, or privation is used only when an alternative procedure is unavailable and the goal is justified by its prospective scientific, educational, or applied value. Surgical procedures are performed under appropriate anesthesia; techniques to avoid infection and minimize pain are followed during and after surgery.

Principle 10d is a straightforward appeal to avoid, or at least minimize, discomfort to animal subjects both during and after the experiment.

> e. When it is appropriate that the animal's life be terminated, it is done rapidly and painlessly.

According to Principle 10e, psychologists who use animal subjects are obligated to conduct euthanasia in a prompt and humane manner when the need arises.

Cheating

All professions have scoundrels who ignore accepted ethical standards to pursue personal gain. In discussions of unsavory political intrigue it is sometimes referred to as the sleaze factor. In the financial community we hear of insider trading in the stock market and fraud and mismanagement in the savings and loan and commercial banking industries. In the manufacturing community we hear of companies that illegally export chemicals and weapons to despots, ignoring human welfare for the big profits. In the law-enforcement community we occasionally hear of police and elected officials who forsake their responsibilities to the public for a piece of the drug-money pie.

Do Scientists Cheat?

Scientists, being human and therefore fallible, have also been known to violate the ethics of their profession to pursue personal gain. Fortunately, ethical transgressions among scientists have not wreaked as much havoc on humanity as have the examples cited above. One reason is the self-correcting feature of science. Research results that do not replicate and are regarded as suspicious will eventually be ignored by the scientific community, whether or not they are ever demonstrated to have been dishonestly generated or reported. But, as is true for so many checks and balances that constrain wrongdoing, one compelling factor underlying scientific honesty is probably fear. A scientist can be eccentric, ill-tempered, egotistical, and exemplify all manner of human flaws and still be respected as a knowledgeable professional. But the scientist who cheats in his research, gets caught, and loses credibility is finished in the profession.

Let us for the moment reflect on science as a job rather than as a noble profession so we can appreciate the pressures that could drive a scientist to engage in unprofessional behavior. Scientists would not spend the time, effort, and money to plan and carry out research projects if they were not reasonably confident of getting provocative and valuable results. Unfortunately, creative effort, hard work, and attention to detail are not guaranteed to provide good data and, as in any job, failure can create stress. Specifically, there can be immediate negative repercussions on one's chances for promotion, job security, financial security, status in the scientific community, funding for research assistants and physical facilities, and success in obtaining funding from the government agencies and foundations that sponsor research. With these pressures it is no wonder that, on rare occasions, scientists feel they must create an illusion of success where none exists—even if it involves a betrayal of professional ethics. Here are some examples of unprofessional and dishonest conduct among scientists.

Fabricating data

Scientists are sometimes so convinced their theories are correct that they refuse to be held back by the inconvenience of data that do not support their views. One of the most often-cited examples of data fabrication is that of Sir Cyril Burt (1883–1971), the British psychologist who devoted his career to the study of the genetic and environmental bases of intelligence. There is a very strong case (Kamin, 1974; Dorfman, 1978) that Burt, in his studies of identical twins reared apart, made up data to support his view that heredity had an important influence on intelligence. Interestingly, the fraud was not discovered because subsequent research failed to support Burt's conclusions. The data were first suspected of being fraudulent when data from different Burt studies were revealed to be remarkably identical. Even if all aspects of Burt's theories were correct, the extreme degree of uniformity among results (correlations that were the same to the third decimal place) would be most unusual. After more digging, it turned out that individuals Burt named as co-investigators either were never involved with the project or were discovered not even to exist.

Selectively excluding data

Sometimes scientists fail to incorporate all the data they collect into the final report of their research. Simply put, they throw out selected pieces of data. Obviously, the practice is cheating when the intent is to bias results to conform better to the investigator's predictions. But excluding data is not *necessarily* dishonest. The researcher may discover that a subject was ill during testing, the apparatus may have malfunctioned during testing, the experimenter may have committed a procedural blunder during testing, and so on. In any event, to be beyond ethical reproach when reporting the results of a study, the researcher should disclose what data were omitted and the circumstances that, in the researcher's view, justified the omission.

Incomplete or Inaccurate reporting of procedures

All well-trained researchers know that in preparation for a between-subject experiment they must assign subjects to different treatment conditions on a random basis. Only then can we assume initial equivalence for differently treated groups of subjects, and only then is it logically correct to attribute behavioral differences between differently treated groups to an action of the experimental variable. Unfortunately, researchers do not always do the extra work necessary to carry out random assignment. For example, public television (PBS) reported (*Nova*: *Why Scientists Cheat*, 1988) a very ugly scandal that erupted in the medical research community. An assistant in the laboratory of an established researcher refused an instruction to embellish the report of a sloppy study. He was asked to state that the assignment of subjects to treatment conditions was random when it actually was not. He refused, but the senior researcher made the change himself and included the dishonestly described methodology when he presented the paper. The assistant publicly disavowed any association with the paper even though his name was listed among the authors. As you can imagine, this unusual step caused quite an uproar at the scientific meeting. Unfortunately, most of the acrimony was initially directed at the whistleblower rather than at the dishonest scientist. The scientists apparently found it easier to question the credibility of a research assistant than the reputation of the established and respected senior researcher he was attacking.

Failure to mention confounding variables

Unforeseen events and procedural errors sometimes justify discarding data, as noted above. A different but somewhat related problem is the intrusion of unforeseen events that *should* trigger concern over the usefulness of the data but are, incorrectly, ignored. For example, while you are running a study with laboratory animals a cage full of animals escapes as you are attempting to remove one for testing. All the animals in that cage have an experience (cavorting around the laboratory floor) that could affect their subsequent behavior apart from any action of the independent variable(s) in the experiment. Thus, the experience of the escape is an extraneous influence on the subjects' behavior (see chapter 10). Researchers have an obligation to mention such an irregularity in any report of the experiment to the scientific community, especially if the subjects are retained in the study.

To accuse or not to accuse

In general, scientists who accuse other scientists of cheating must be prepared for a bitter and prolonged struggle, which is not an attractive choice despite the ethical issues at stake. Public accusations of wrongdoing directed toward professional peers (police against police, doctor against doctor, judge against judge) are uncommon because, even when accusations are supported by good evidence, the ordeal of resolving the issue can be as much a nightmare for the whistleblower as for the accused. An accuser can expect the accused to fight for his or her professional life by whatever means (honest or dishonest) necessary. Smear tactics and counter-accusations are the norm and, unfortunately, the bitter struggle is likely to end with two losers and no winner.

It is, then, unwise and unfair to make an accusation of fraud unless the evidence points unmistakably in that direction. What may initially appear to be a fraudulent report might turn out to be a result of carelessness, incompetence, or an undetected instrument malfunction. Perhaps a better choice than accusation and confrontation is to rely on the self-correcting aspect of science: replicate and/or encourage others to replicate the questionable research. Additional data that do not replicate earlier work will call the *results* of the earlier work into question without attacking the integrity of the researcher. If, for whatever reason, the original results do not replicate, they will eventually be discredited.

Summary

Our coverage of research ethics began with a discussion of three ways in which people judge the moral correctness of exposing research participants to risk: by reference to an absolute standard, by reference to a standard that is stable but somewhat more acceptant of diverse opinion than an absolute standard, and by reference to the results of cost-benefit analysis. We then listed and discussed the APA Principles in the Conduct of Research with Human Participants one by one, pointing out the challenges and obligations they present to the researcher who uses human subjects. The concepts of informed consent and risk received particular attention. We next described the Institutional Review Board (IRB) and the role it plays in reviewing proposed research projects. The topic then shifted to a discussion of why behavioral scientists sometimes use animal subjects in their research and the ethical guidelines that the APA has put in place to protect the welfare of animal subjects. The last ethical issue raised in the chapter centered on the researcher rather than on the subjects participating in the research: the issue of cheating. We described the pressures under which professional researchers work that have been known to lead to cheating, and we described several forms of cheating. The chapter ended with a mention of how difficult it is for professionals to police their peers and the struggle that inevitably ensues when, as a matter of conscience, a researcher feels compelled to level a charge of wrongdoing against a professional peer.

Key Terms

Coercion, p. 315
Deception, p. 314
Institutional Review Board (IRB), p. 317
Minimal Risk, p. 311

Chapter Exercises

1. When the strategies that researchers create to study behavior present risks to the participants (subjects), what obligations must the researcher fulfill before proceeding with an investigation?

2. What is the distinction between minimal-risk and more-than-minimal-risk research? Name some kinds of research with human subjects that have so little risk they need not be approved by IRB review.

3. Why must the level of risk to subjects that is acceptable in a research project be judged on a case-by-case basis?

4. We stated that the underlying ethical philosophy of the APA Principles was the cost-benefit approach. Explain.

5. Explain how you would implement each of the APA principles (animal or human) for your proposal assignment research project.

6. What are the pressures that have been known to lead to fraudulent behavior on the part of professional researchers? What are some of the specific misdeeds perpetrated by dishonest scientists?

7. In the long term, why does science tend to be so resilient to the damage perpetrated by fraud?

8. Under what circumstances would a researcher describe an experiment to prospective subjects without providing full information or with incorrect and/or misleading information?

9. When obtaining informed consent, it is sometimes difficult, even impossible, to inform subjects fully because the subjects are not able to comprehend fully what they are consenting to. What are the responsibilities of the researcher in such instances?

10. Assuming the principal focus of behavioral science research is to understand human behavior, what reasons can you give to support the notion that the findings of animal studies can help us understand human behavior?

Additional Sources

In this chapter we have touched upon many ethical issues of concern to behavioral scientists. For more detailed and exhaustive coverage of the topic we recommend the following books:

Steininger, M. Newell, D. J., & Garcia, L. T. (1984). *Ethical issues in psychology.* Homewood, Ill: Dorsey Press.

Keith-Spiegel, P., & Koocher, G. P. (1985). *Ethics in psychology.* New York: Random House.

Proposal Assignment 16: Ethical Concerns

For your final proposal assignment, identify possible ethical concerns that arose as you developed your project. How would you convince the Institutional Review Board or the Animal Research and Experimentation Committee that the benefits of your project outweigh the costs?

P A R T

Review of Research Methodologies and Control Conditions Used by Selected Subdisciplines in Psychology

Because behavior is so varied and complex, studying behavior presents complex methodological challenges to research psychologists. They describe, categorize, and measure behavior using naturalistic observation, survey, and correlational techniques and determine cause-effect relationships using the experimental method. But instead of researching a diverse set of problems, individual psychologists tend to focus their research pursuits. They identify themselves as specialists in such subdisciplines of psychology as perception, developmental psychology, social psychology, and neuropsychology. Figure III–1 reviews many of these subdisciplines.

All subdisciplines of psychology and related fields are similar in that they share many of the research methodologies covered in Parts I and II. There are, however, some major procedural differences across the subdisciplines, most noticeably in the types of control groups that are necessary to neutralize confounding variables. Part III presents the *original abstract* and *method section* of published research reports from psychological literature and reviews the types of procedures and control groups that are fundamental to the respective subdisciplines.

It is important to learn about all the controls needed in the various subdisciplines of psychology so that when you read published articles you can determine if the study was executed correctly and adjust your confidence in its findings. Perhaps you think it unlikely that a student would catch a serious procedural error in the research methodology of a published report. But even established researchers are human, and they occasionally make mistakes. It is not unusual at meetings of professional societies for students in attendance, both undergraduate and graduate, to raise valid concerns about the procedural adequacy of a reported experiment. Naturally, if major controls are missing, we cannot accept the validity of the article's conclusions or the results on which they are based. A new experiment, designed to be free of damaging flaws, is required. If only minor controls are missing, you may still conditionally accept the conclusions, but take note of what control(s) is/are missing. As you read original research articles, it is your task to evaluate each one using all the expertise you have developed.

The discussion follows the order of presentation of the material in the original article, and periodically you should refer back to the original abstract and method sections as you read our discussion of their content. There is also frequent reference to key terms defined in earlier chapters. These key terms are *italicized*, and to help you review them we reference the chapter and page number where the term was first introduced. Each chapter ends with a discussion of additional techniques and controls used in the subdiscipline.

Neuropsychology
What is the role of the brain
in controlling behavior?
–How do chemicals, brain
injuries, brain tumors
influence behavior?

Sensation
How do we sense
simple stimuli
(vision, audition, taste
smell, touch)?

Comparative
How do species behave
similarly/differently
(humans vs. monkeys,
rats vs. turtles)?

Perception
How do we interpret
complex stimuli?
. . . Why are these
. . eight dots
. . . perceived as
a square?

Performance
How skilled are we
at doing what we do?

Learning
How do we modify our
behavior due to
outcomes and
experiences?

Development
How does behavior change from
infancy to old age?

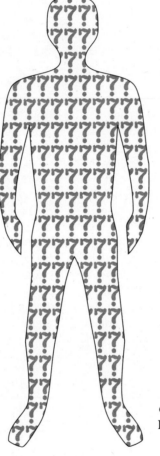

Social
What is the influence of others
on the behavior of the individual?

Memory
How do we remember
the information we
learned in the past?

Personality
Why do people behave in
characteristic ways?

Motivation
Why do we learn more and perform
better when we want something?

Abnormal
Why do some people
behave "strangely"?

Cognition
How do we think, process information,
and solve problems?

Language
How do we learn to speak and communicate?

Applied Areas

. Clinical	. Educational	. Industrial	. Program Evaluation
. Vocational	. Surveys	. Health	. Behavioral Medicine
. Personnel	. Advertising/	. Sports	. Behavioral Toxicology
. Testing	Consumer	. Law	. Human Factors

Figure III–1. Examples of research in the subdisciplines of psychology.

C H A P T E R

17

Research in Developmental and Lifespan Psychology

Using a broad selection of the research designs described in Parts I and II (naturalistic observation and correlational and experimental designs, for example), some developmental psychologists focus on the behaviors that are present at specific developmental ages such as infancy, early childhood, adolescence, or adulthood and the variables that influence those behaviors. For example, a correlational study to assess the relationship between preference for violent TV shows and the display of aggression in five-year-old children or an experiment (say, using a 2×2 factorial design) to evaluate two different strategies for teaching four- and six-year-old children to share their belongings would be representative of age-focused developmental research.

An alternative to the latter approach is called the lifespan approach: the study of changes in behavior that occur over the entire life cycle, from infancy to old age.

Cross-sectional Design: The behavior of different-aged subjects is measured at the same point in time.

Longitudinal Design: The same people are repeatedly tested as they grow older.

Figure 17–1 shows two possible patterns of a behavioral measure when evaluated across the entire lifespan. There can be an increase followed by a decrease not only in physical abilities, but also in mental abilities such as memory and reasoning. Lifespan psychologists determine how rapidly the increase occurs, the age of maximum behavioral capacity, and how steep the decline is if there is one.

Cross-sectional and longitudinal designs are frequently used by lifespan psychologists. In the **cross-sectional design** the behavior of different-aged subjects is measured at the same point in time (as in a *between-subject design*, chapter 11). In the **longitudinal design**, the same people are repeatedly tested as they grow older (as in a *within-subject design*, chapter 12). Each design has advantages and disadvantages, and we will review them later.

In this chapter we present the abstract and method section of an article by Schaie (1989). Subjects aged 22 to 91 years were tested on a perceptual speed matching task. Specifically, they were timed while trying to match a figure with one of four possible choices (Identical Pictures test) and while crossing out words that contain the letter A (Finding A's test). The research was in the form of Basic Question 3: Does an association exist between two (or more) variables (the age of the subjects and behaviors that are indicative of perceptual speed)? This article includes both cross-sectional and longitudinal designs and allows for a comparison of the two research approaches. Specifically, the author wanted to determine whether results using the cross-sectional design (the more commonly used and less time-consuming research approach) overestimate or underestimate behavioral changes that are apparent in longitudinal data. When you read the article, note how the subjects were selected, whether possible *confounding variables* (chapter 3, p. 33) were measured, and if the tasks seem appropriate for each age tested. Such scrutiny is necessary because these are the major control issues in developmental/lifespan psychology.

Please pause at this point to read the article on pages 334–35, and then return to the following discussion.

Discussion of Techniques and Controls in Schaie (1989)

Method

Subjects

The author used a relatively straightforward method for recruiting a large number of subjects between the ages of 10 and 84 (17 and 91 by the end of the study). He randomly selected members of a health maintenance organization and requested that they volunteer to participate in his research project. Those who volunteered became part of the study. Some were tested both in 1977 and again in 1984 (longitudinal subjects), and others were tested only once (cross-sectional subjects). As researchers commonly do, the author used a table to summarize how many subjects were tested and at what ages they were tested.

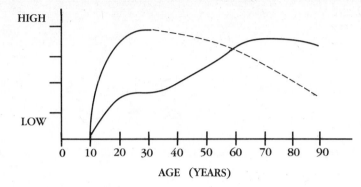

Figure 17–1. Possible patterns of results from studies of changes in behavior that occur during the entire life cycle.

Measures and Procedure

Two *standardized tests* (chapter 6) were used to measure speed of performance. It was expected that the older people would be slower on these tasks, which are assumed to measure a skill called perceptual speed. The five ability tests (verbal meaning, spatial orientation, inductive reasoning, number, and word fluency) had previously been adapted by the author from classic research in the area. The purpose of including the ability tests was to determine whether one could *predict* (chapter 5, p. 73) a decline on these tests based on declines in perceptual speed and to determine whether there are differences on these abilities when one **partials out** (statistically removes) the effects of slower perceptual speed through the use of the partial correlational technique. (The statistical procedure that is used to partial out effects of a confounding variable is beyond the scope of the present discussion, but it is a routine procedure for those with advanced statistical knowledge.) If you are interested in finding out which abilities are at their maximum level of proficiency at certain ages and their degree of decline when perceptual speed is partialed out, read the results and discussion sections of the Schaie paper. Fortunately, the results are encouraging for senior citizens: The "correlations between age and ability are reduced virtually to zero when perceptual speed is partialled out" (p. 448).

All tests were paper-and-pencil tests. Therefore, no fancy equipment was needed to run the study. Subjects were tested in small groups rather than individually, which is a clear advantage when testing 1,838 subjects.

Partial Out: Statistically remove the effects of a confounding variable in a correlational design through the use of the partial correlational technique.

Additional Techniques and Control Issues in Developmental and Lifespan Psychology

Although understanding age-related behavioral phenomena has broad-based appeal to laypeople and scientists alike (We are all aging!), age is impossible to study

Psychology and Aging
1989, Vol. 4, No. 4, 443–453

Perceptual Speed in Adulthood: Cross-Sectional and Longitudinal Studies

K. Warner Schaie
Pennsylvania State University

Cross-sectional data on age differences in perceptual speed are presented from the Seattle Longitudinal Study for the age range 22–91 years ($n = 1,620$, first assessed in 1977, $N = 628$, first assessed in 1984). In addition, 838 subjects were followed over the 7-year interval. Markers of perceptual speed were the Identical Pictures and Finding A's tests from the ETS Kit of Factor-Referenced Tests. Significant age differences, age changes, and cohort differences were found at both observed variable and latent construct levels. Cross-lagged correlations examine the role of perceptual speed in predicting later performance on other abilities (Verbal Meaning, Inductive Reasoning, Spatial Orientation, Number, and Word Fluency). When perceptual speed is partialled out of scores for these abilities, aging effects are reduced markedly for all abilities, but least for Spatial Orientation and Inductive Reasoning.

Method

Subjects

Study participants were volunteer subjects who had responded to a solicitation addressed to a random draw of persons 22 to 84 years of age who were members of a Pacific Northwest health maintenance organization (HMO). Included in the present analysis are data from 1,838 individuals. Of these, 1,420 subjects first received the perceptual speed measures in 1977 (809 subjects had previously been tested on other primary abilities, while 611 subjects were at first test). An additional 628 subjects were first tested in 1984. Longitudinal data are available for 838 subjects who were tested on both occasions. These subjects ranged in age from 29 to 91 years at retest. Table 1 provides the age by sex breakdown of these data sets. All subjects were community-dwelling individuals in good health. The sample is predominantly White and similar to the demographic composition of the sampling frame from which it is drawn. The sampling frame (the HMO), in turn, is a good cross-section of the upper 75% of the socioeconomic spectrum.

Measures

Several variables are represented in the present analysis. The two measures of perceptual speed are the Identical Pictures test, which requires subjects to match a stimulus stick figure from a set of four multiple choice figures, and the Finding A's test, which requires cancellation of words that contain the letter "a." Both tests are identified as markers of perceptual speed in the ETS Kit of Factor-Referenced Tests (Ekstrom et al., 1976). The five primary mental abilities measures are Verbal Meaning, a recognition vocabulary test; Spatial Orientation, a measure involving visual rotation in two-dimensional space; Inductive Reasoning, a letter series task involving the identification of rules; Number, a measure of simple arithmetic skill using addition checks; and Word Fluency, a measure requiring recall of words according to a lexical rule. The ability tests are adaptations of the work of the Thurstones (1949; Schaie, 1985).

Procedure

The tests are all pencil-and-paper tests that were administered as part of broader psychometric batteries that extended over $2\frac{1}{2}$ hr in 1977 and were expanded to a 5-hr battery in 1984. All subjects were tested in small groups using one examiner and one proctor. Subjects were paid for their time at a rate of $5.00 per hour.

Table 1
Age and Sex Distribution of Cross-Sectional and Longitudinal Study Participants

Age range	All 1977 subjects		New 1977 subjects		Longitudinal subjects		New 1984 subjects	
	M	F	M	F	M	F	M	F
22–28	28	28	28	28	16	10	28	56
29–35	39	57	29	33	23	31	27	28
36–42	60	73	36	36	36	53	30	40
43–49	79	109	33	36	59	68	26	39
50–56	109	110	40	38	81	82	33	33
57–63	99	119	35	38	73	83	36	43
64–70	75	99	35	38	63	75	40	42
71–77	70	76	36	33	27	32	39	36
78–84	54	71	28	31	9	13	24	28
85–91	8	9	—	—	2	2	—	—
Total	650	770	300	311	389	439	283	345

Note. M = male; F = female

experimentally. The reason is straightforward: Age is an independent variable that researchers cannot manipulate. One cannot designate a randomly assigned group of subjects to be 10 years old and another group to be 65 years old. Rather, subjects come to the experiment with their ages already fixed. Therefore, all research that tests the effects of age is restricted to the *correlational* approach, which means that rival explanations unrelated to age can account for observed changes in behavior across different-aged subjects. We will review the major problems researchers in lifespan/developmental psychology must address and aspects of the research on which you should focus when you read articles in this subdiscipline of psychology.

Subject Recruitment

Researchers who work in academic settings and test young adults have an easy time obtaining large numbers of subjects. The large numbers of students who study introductory psychology can provide researchers with hundreds of volunteers who are primarily between the ages of 18 and 21. Those who study developmental phenomena in animals simply buy subjects from suppliers or have an on-site breeding program. It is fairly easy to obtain both young and old animals, although older animals are more expensive. It is far more difficult for researchers to gain access to a subject pool of human infants, children, and the elderly. Researchers who work with these populations spend a lot of time finding and recruiting subjects. We will review different techniques appropriate for recruiting subjects in these less-accessible age groups.

Newborns and infants

Researchers can contact obstetricians (physicians who care for pregnant women) or can go to prenatal clinics to contact women during pregnancy for permission to test their newborn babies. Another tactic is to go to maternity wards in hospitals and request permission from the hospital and parents to allow testing of their newborn babies. At slightly older ages the parents can be reached through well-baby clinics or pediatricians. Sometimes researchers keep track of announcements of baby births in the local paper and contact the parents when the baby has reached the desired age.

Parents may be reluctant to have their baby tested, so researchers must take the time to build a good rapport with the parents. One step in this direction is to explain both the benefits of the study for knowledge in general and how the study may help their baby. If the infant is tested at home, it is important that the parent(s) select the time and date to avoid invasion of privacy. If the parent is asked to bring the infant to a testing laboratory, the researcher should offer to provide transportation or reimburse the cost of the trip.

Some babies are born prematurely, and there are ways of measuring how premature an infant is. It is common practice to use the gestational age (age adjusted for the degree of the infant's prematurity) rather than chronological age when assigning the age of the infant.

Preschoolers

The preschool population is fairly accessible since many children of preschool age attend a nursery school or a day-care center. It is the responsibility of the researcher to get permission to test these children from both the directors of the school or center and the parents (or legal guardians).

School-age children

After establishing a good relationship with the local school system, it is relatively easy to recruit children between the ages of 6 and 17 years. It is, of course, necessary to obtain permission from both the school officials and the parents (or legal guardian) before testing any student under the age of 18.

The Elderly

The elderly can be recruited through advertisements in the local paper, contacting organizations that serve the elderly, or visiting senior citizens' centers or nursing homes. They can also be recruited at public places such as libraries and museums or at health-care centers, as was done by the researcher of the article reviewed in this chapter.

Subject Selection

The way subject selection in longitudinal research is handled determines how readily the results can be *generalized* (*external validity*, chapter 6, p. 91). If subjects are restricted to one segment of a population, generalizing results to the entire population can be risky. Selection of a nonrepresentative sample does not, however, influence the analysis of the effects of age in longitudinal studies because the same individuals are tested repeatedly.

The way in which subject selection is handled in cross-sectional research is important for a different reason. If the sample in one age group is different from subjects in the other age groups on any dimension other than age, *confounding* (chapter 3, p. 33) exists. As a result, behavioral differences between age groups may have nothing to do with the different ages of the subjects. For example, pretend we select a sample of 18- to 21-year-old young adults from the student body of an expensive private college where most students are from wealthy families. We then compare their behavior to that of 80- to 85-year-old indigent residents of a substandard nursing home. It is highly probable that factors associated with rich versus poor life-styles (nutrition and education, for example) rather than age account for the differences in behavior between the two groups.

Confounding variables can also creep into the selection process when pre-schoolers are recruited from day-care centers or the elderly are recruited from nursing homes. Some day-care centers are part of a university and are attended primarily by children of faculty and other professionals who have a higher-than-average education level. Children from other centers, such as those located in the inner city of large metropolitan centers, would be likely to have parents who are less affluent and less educated. Similarly, the elderly who live in nursing homes and the elderly who live at home may both qualify to participate in a study because of their comparable ages, but those who live in nursing homes may tend to be less physically fit than those living at home.

If researchers identify potential confounds in a study of age-related developmental phenomena, two remedies are possible. They can try to *match* (chapter 12, p. 215) subjects at the different ages on one or more of the potentially confounding variables (e.g., income level and/or education level). It is also possible to *partial out* the effects of confounding variables using statistical techniques, which is the procedure followed by the author of the study reviewed earlier to remove the effects of perceptual speed on the ability tests. Both matching subjects and statistically partialing out the effects of confounding variables have the same goal: to try to isolate age as the only determinant of behavioral differences.

Subject Attrition

Both very young and very old subjects frequently refuse to carry through behavioral testing to completion. Babies become fussy, tired, hungry, wet, or simply fall asleep in the middle of testing. If *subject attrition* (chapter 7, p. 124) is random, there is no threat to the *internal validity* (chapter 10, p. 178) of the study. But if a certain type of subject tends to drop out, the remaining subjects form a *biased sample* (chapter 7, p. 114), and the study loses internal validity. For example, let us assume that both young adults and elderly subjects are tested on a complicated task. Let us further assume that those subjects who experience great initial difficulty with the task tend to resist continuing their participation and many ultimately decide to drop out of the experiment. If most of the subjects who experience great difficulty are in the elderly group, this would leave the elderly group with only higher-functioning members. By comparison, the initial group of young adults would survive relatively intact and would contain a broader range of lower- and higher-functioning subjects.

In order to neutralize the impact of nonrandom attrition, researchers have two alternatives. The first method requires the researcher to identify the characteristics of the subjects who dropped out and then find subjects in the second group who match these characteristics. The matched subjects are then dropped from the second group. This alternative is very risky because the researcher is unlikely to know all the reasons why subjects dropped out of the experiment. The second alternative is often more desirable: to begin the study over again with procedures that minimize the loss of subjects.

Although subject attribution can occur in any study, it is more likely to occur in longitudinal research. The reason is that large time spans, often several years, can pass between test and retest, and this creates the considerable problem of keeping track of and locating former subjects over the long term. Selecting people all of whom tend to visit a specific place on a regular basis (such as a health maintenance organization) minimizes the problem of locating subjects. Even if subjects should move away or die, the tendency of many clubs and medical-care organizations to keep detailed records would save the researcher a lot of work trying to trace the whereabouts of subjects. Researchers can also tell subjects of their intention to ask for a retest in the future and to please inform them if they move away. Self-addressed envelopes or postcards can be provided to increase the probability that subjects will comply. Another tactic is to give subjects a useful gift that displays a telephone number to call if they move. For example, a nightlight with the researcher's phone number on it can be given to the parents of babies who are going to be retested at an older age.

Researchers typically report how many subjects were lost during the course of testing, and, if they know why the subject dropped out, they report the reasons.

Because of the importance of minimizing subject attrition, researchers take steps to minimize its occurrence. Subjects should be told how important it is that they continue to be part of the study.

Measurement Equivalence

It is impossible to give the same test using the same procedures to subjects of very different ages. Obviously, babies cannot understand complex verbal instructions, three-year-old children cannot effectively complete a paper-and-pencil test, and the elderly may not be able to solve a relatively complicated problem in a very limited amount of time. **Measurement equivalence**, the application of behavioral testing procedures that are appropriate across a broad spectrum of age groups, is very difficult to achieve. Researchers approach the problem of measurement equivalence differently for each type of behavioral test. Although the topic is beyond the scope of this book, we urge you to determine how the authors solved the problem in every article you read in the developmental/lifespan subdiscipline.

> **Measurement Equivalence:** The application of behavioral testing procedures that are appropriate for a broad spectrum of age groups.

Cross-sectional and Longitudinal Designs: Advantages and Disadvantages

The advantages of the longitudinal design tend to be the disadvantages of the cross-sectional design, and vice versa. Longitudinal designs are excellent for determining changes in a group of individuals as they age. All subject characteristics are equated since the same subjects are tested repeatedly. Longitudinal designs are, nevertheless, very time-consuming: several years may elapse between the first and second tests. We must also consider the demands on the researcher who chooses to study changes in human behavior across, say, the first 30 years of life. The researcher has to be relatively young at the beginning of the study, or, to ensure continuity, make sure that a younger researcher joins the project before he or she retires. As mentioned above, problems with subject attrition and the effectiveness of the test instrument for measuring behavior in different-aged subjects are often encountered in longitudinal research. Also, if subjects are given the same test a number of times, there may be *carryover effects* (chapter 12, p. 210) from the previous test experience. Sometimes tests become old and dated, and an equivalent new test must be made up. Subjects cannot be tested **anonymously** (without knowing the subject's name) since the researcher must know the name of the person to contact for the next test session. Therefore longitudinal studies stress **confidentiality**; the names of the subjects are never reported and subjects are assigned secret code numbers when their data are analyzed.

> **Anonymous Testing:** Testing subjects without knowing their identities.
>
> **Confidentiality:** The names of subjects are known, but in order to maintain secrecy they are assigned secret code numbers when their data are analyzed.

The biggest disadvantage of the longitudinal design is that there is no control over what other events besides age may coincidentally exist to influence behavior. For some subjects, changes in family fortunes, the world economy, and international stability (war versus peace) may be more powerful instruments of behavioral change than age.

Cross-sectional designs provide complete results far more quickly than longitudinal designs because the subjects are only tested once. The one-time-only cross-sectional testing procedure is also compatible with maintaining anonymity for the subjects, which, as pointed out above, is not possible in longitudinal designs. A disadvantage, however, is the near-impossible task of equating all potential confounding variables between subjects of different ages (such as socioeconomic level, IQ, education level, birth order, and family size). The biggest disadvantage of the cross-sectional design, however, is that it is impossible to isolate the influence of the age variable from the influence of events that coincidentally surrounded them at some point in their lives. For example, if elderly subjects were born and raised during the Great Depression of the early 1930s and younger subjects were born and raised during a period of rapid economic expansion, these circumstances could exert more of an influence on behavior than the different ages of the subjects.

Additional Research Designs

There are modifications to the standard cross-sectional and longitudinal approaches that serve to minimize their potential disadvantages. In a cross-sectional study, subjects of many different ages are tested at the same point in time. By comparison, in a **cross-sectional–sequential design** (see Table 17–1) the cross-sectional study is repeated some time later (say, in 5 years) with a new set of subjects. The sequential modification decreases the problem of confounding the age of subjects with events surrounding the time of testing, because testing is done on two separate occasions. One can, of course, further reduce the possibility of rival explanations from confounding variables by testing a third set of subjects at a time even further removed from the time of original testing (say, after 10 years). Because different subjects are used during each test period, it is possible to avoid the problems of longitudinal designs that arise from repeated testing of the same subjects.

The longitudinal design calls for repeated testing of one group of like-aged subjects. But if subjects born in two different years are tested in the same year and then repeatedly tested, the design becomes a **longitudinal sequential design** (see Table 17–2). The sequential modification minimizes the confounding that can arise when all subjects in the experiment are **cohorts** — that is, born at the same time and therefore exposed to the same unique environmental circumstances

Cross-sectional–Sequential Design: The cross-sectional study is repeated some time later (say, in 5 years) with a new set of subjects.

Longitudinal–Sequential Design: Subjects born in two different years are tested in the same year and then repeatedly tested.

Cohorts: Subjects born at the same time and therefore exposed to the same unique environmental circumstances present at that time.

	Testing Year	
Year of Birth	**1990**	**1995**
1950	40	45
1955	35	40
1960	30	35
1965	25	30
1970	20	25
1975	15	20
1980	10	15
1985	5	10

Table 17–1. Age of subject in years at the time of testing in a cross-sectional design (1990 column only) and a cross-sectional–sequential design (1990 and 1995 columns).

Year of Birth	Year of Testing					
	1990	1995	2000	2005	2010	2015
1980	10	15	20	25	30	35
1985	5	10	15	20	25	30

Table 17–2. Age of subject in years in the year of testing in a longitudinal design (1980 row only) and a longitudinal-sequential design (1980 and 1985 rows).

present at that time. Further control over cohort confounding can be incorporated by including three or more cohort age groups as subjects. The procedure is to begin testing with three or more different age groups in the same year, and then follow up with repeated testing at specific intervals. Time of testing and age of subject are now no longer totally confounded.

There is another useful research design in developmental psychology that reveals if significant events or circumstances present during the years subjects were born or tested are confounded with age, although the data will not reveal which confound is present. The approach, named the **time-lag design**, calls for testing subjects of the same age in different years. For example, let us say a longitudinal study involves testing 10-year-old subjects in 1990 (Table 17–2, first row). To implement the time-lag feature we could follow with a new group of 10-year-old children in, say, 1995, another group of 10-year-old children in 2000, another group in 2005, and so on. Differences among the 10-year-old subjects tested in the different years would be evidence that either the year of birth or the year of testing was influencing the results in the longitudinal design. This realization would, in turn, caution the researcher to interpret the results of the longitudinal study with great care.

Time-lag Design: Subjects of the same age are tested in different years.

Use of the Longitudinal Design to Determine Direction of Possible Cause

Let us assume a researcher reports data showing that a positive correlation exists between preference for violent TV shows and aggressive behavior in children. Even though the data may only be capable of documenting an association, it is also possible for the result to be a manifestation of an underlying cause-effect relationship: maybe watching violence on TV *causes* aggressive behavior. But even if we were willing to assume that the association between the TV and aggression variables truly is rooted in a cause-effect relationship, we still would not know whether watching violent shows causes children to be aggressive or, conversely, if the aggressive nature of the child causes him/her to select violent TV shows. Researchers argue that the **cross-lagged panel design**, diagrammed in Table 17–3, can answer the question of the direction of possible cause.

The approach calls for measuring both behaviors (TV-show selection and the child's level of aggressive behavior) in the same children at two different times (a longitudinal design). The next step is to calculate the correlation (r value) between

Cross-lagged Panel Design: A research approach that points to the direction of a possible cause-and-effect relationship in correlational data.

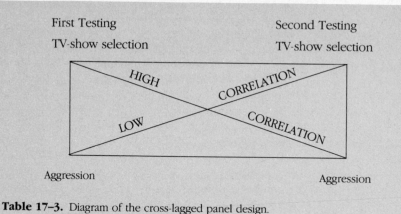

Table 17–3. Diagram of the cross-lagged panel design.

aggressive behavior at first testing and TV-show selection at the second testing, and TV-show selection at the first testing and aggressive behavior at the second testing (the diagonals in the table). If one of these r values is higher than the other, it points to the direction of the possible cause-effect relationship. Table 17–3 shows that the correlation is higher between TV-show selection at the first testing and aggressive behavior at the second testing. Therefore in our example it is more likely that watching violent TV programs causes children to be aggressive and less likely that aggressive children select violent TV shows to watch. Note that Schaie, the author of the first paper, used the cross-lagged correlation procedure to predict future abilities based on perceptual speed (see Abstract).

Summary

Developmental and lifespan psychologists test the same subjects at different ages (longitudinal designs) and different-aged subjects at the same point in time (cross-sectional designs). Because age cannot be a manipulated variable, the developmental researcher must work to minimize the influence of confounding variables on research results. Potential confounds include the bias from subject selection, subject loss, and the lack of measurement equivalence when behaviors are measured at different ages.

In the article we reviewed, subjects aged 22 to 91 years old were tested on matching tasks and various ability tests to determine the association between age and task performance, which is research in the form of Basic Question 3.

Key Terms

Anonymous Testing, p. 339
Cohort, p. 340
Confidentiality, p. 339
Cross-lagged Panel Design, p. 341
Cross-sectional Design, p. 332
Cross-sectional–Sequential Design,
    p. 340

Longitudinal Design, p. 332
Longitudinal–Sequential Design, p. 340
Measurement Equivalence, p. 339
Partial Out Statistically, p. 333
Time-lag Design, p. 341

Chapter Exercises

1. Schaie found a positive correlation between perceptual speed and inductive reasoning. Explain how it is now possible to use perceptual speed in people to predict level of inductive reasoning ability.

2. Why can't we conclude that slower perceptual speed caused the decreased ability to reason inductively?

3. Schaie was interested in determining if elderly people would still show decreased inductive reasoning ability after the contribution of their slower perceptual speed was removed. When he partialed out the effects of perceptual speed, he found that the differences between elderly and young subjects on inductive reasoning ability were much smaller. What implications does this finding have for elderly people?

C H A P T E R

18

Research in Sensation and Perception

Our bodies contain many specialized cells that react to specific forms of physical energy. The cells in the retina of the eye react to light, the cells in the skin react to pressure and temperature, and so forth. Collectively, these specialized cells make up the sense organs that enable us to receive information from the environment. Psychologists who do research in the area of sensation have developed a number of techniques to measure the sensitivity of our eyes, ears, nose, tongue, and skin to physical stimuli (light, sound, smell). Frequently, the goal of research in sensation is to determine the lowest value of stimulation we can detect and measure the limits of our ability to detect differences between physically similar stimuli.

We have selected two articles to represent the subdiscipline of sensation/perception. Gilmore and Murphy (1989) were interested in changes in sensitivity for detecting sweet taste (sucrose) and bitter taste (caffeine) as a function of the age of the subject. If we view the goal as an effort to document sensitivity for detecting sucrose and caffeine, the study addresses a descriptive issue in the form of Basic Question 1 (What are the dimensions along which behaviors [sensitivity to sweet and bitter tastes] naturally vary?). From a different perspective, the study also conforms to Basic Question 6 (Will introducing subjects to qualitatively different conditions [sucrose versus caffeine] cause them to exhibit systematic differences in behavior [taste sensitivity]?). The comparison between young adults and elderly subjects is an issue in the form of a corollary to Basic Question 6 (Are there systematic differences in behavior [taste sensitivity] among subjects who are identified as having experienced quantitatively different conditions [age]?). The interaction between the type of solution (sucrose versus caffeine) and the concentration of the solution can be viewed as an issue in the form of Basic Question 7 (Will introducing subjects to two or more systematically different conditions cause an additive and/or interactive effect on behavior?). Lastly, we must not lose sight of the fact that age can interact with the manipulated conditions (type of solution and concentration of solution). But since one of the "different conditions" referred to in Basic Question 7 is not manipulated (the age variable), the study is a *mixed experimental/correlational design* (chapter 14, p. 273). Thus, the interaction of age with the manipulated variables of the study is a hybrid of Basic Question 7 and its corollary (Are additive and/or interactive effects evident among subjects who are identified as having experienced two or more systematically different conditions?).

In the second article, Gardner, Morrell, Watson, and Sandoval (1989) used two procedures to test body-size judgments by obese and normal people. Because a subject's assignment to the obese or normal condition was on the basis of a *selected variable* (chapter 3, p. 33), the study is correlational and is in the form of the Basic Question 6 corollary: Are there systematic differences in behavior among subjects who are identified as having experienced quantitatively different conditions (body weight)?

Before you read the method sections of the articles, it will help you to become familiar with some key terms. The absolute threshold (abbreviated AL because *limen* means threshold in Latin) is the minimal amount of energy that can produce a sensation. Operationally, the AL is the level of stimulation that must be present for the subject to detect the presence of the stimulus 50 percent of the time. For example, if we present a series of tones that vary in intensity (some of them are possible to hear and others are too soft to hear) and ask the subject on each trial "Did you hear it?," we can determine how loud the tone must be to enable the subject to correctly detect it on half of the trials. Psychologists know that AL values can change under different conditions (for example, from drug treatment, lack of sleep, or illness). The change in AL caused by changing conditions is called the relative threshold.

To determine the AL of a stimulus (say, a tone), psychologists have traditionally used three different methods of stimulus presentation. If a fixed number of constant tone stimuli (typically between 5 and 11) that vary in loudness are presented in random order, the procedure for determining the AL is called the **method of constant stimuli**. If the tone is presented in fixed order many times, progressing from soft to loud and from loud to soft, the procedure is called the **method of limits**. If the subjects' task is to adjust the tone intensity gradually (say, by moving a dial) until they can no longer hear it, and then raise the tone intensity until they can once again hear it, the procedure is called the **method of adjustment** (also called **method of average error**).

Method of Constant Stimuli: A fixed number of constant stimuli (typically between five and eleven) that vary in a dimension (such as loudness or frequency of tones) are presented in random order to determine a threshold.

Method of Limits: To determine a threshold, stimuli, such as tones, are presented in a fixed order many times, progressing from soft to loud and from loud to soft.

Method of Adjustment (also called **Method of Average Error**): To determine a threshold the subject adjusts a stimulus until it can no longer be detected, then increases the intensity until it can once again be detected.

Standard Stimulus:
A reference against
which the subject must
contrast the
comparison stimulus
to determine the
difference threshold.

**Comparison
Stimulus**: The
stimulus against which
the standard stimulus
is contrasted.

Another measure of sensory capacity is the difference threshold (abbreviated DL because it is also called the difference limen): the minimal difference that must exist between two stimuli so they will be recognized as different. For example, to determine a DL for loudness we would start with two stimuli that are both above the AL but are so similar in loudness that it is difficult to tell them apart. The first tone we present serves as a reference and is called the **standard stimulus**. The similar tone presented after the standard stimulus is called the **comparison stimulus**. The subject's task is to report whether the comparison stimulus appears to be louder or softer than the standard stimulus. On the next trial we again present the standard stimulus followed by a different comparison tone. The procedure continues in this way for many trials. Typically, on half the trials the comparison stimulus is louder, and on the other half it is softer than the standard stimulus. Naturally, when there is a substantial difference between the standard stimulus and the comparison stimulus it is easy to tell which is the louder tone, but on trials with very similar tones, the discrimination tends to be very difficult. All presented stimuli are above the absolute threshold.

As with the determination of AL, presenting the tone pairs in random order is called the method of constant stimuli, presenting the comparison stimuli in fixed order is the method of limits, and having the subject adjust the comparison tone until it appears to be the same as the standard tone is the method of adjustment. Operationally, the DL is the difference between the standard stimulus and the comparison stimulus that permits the subject to hear them as different 50 percent of the time (the DL), although some researchers use a 75 percent criterion. The DL is also called the just noticeable difference (abbreviated JND).

To make sure you are prepared to read the sensation/perception articles presented in this chapter, three more terms need explaining. After a subject is tested using one of the procedures for determining the DL, the experimenter can determine the point of subjective equality (PSE), a value of the comparison stimulus so close to the standard stimulus that the subject cannot discriminate it from the standard stimulus. The magnitude of the difference between the PSE and the standard stimulus is called the constant error. After determining the PSE and the DL, we can calculate the Weber ratio (also called Weber fraction) by dividing the DL by the value of the standard stimulus. Knowledge of the Weber ratio lets us calculate the expected DL if we were to test subjects using a more or less intense standard stimulus. (We discuss the importance of the Weber ratio later.)

Please pause at this point to read the article on pages 348–49, then return to the following discussion.

Discussion of Techniques and Controls in Gilmore and Murphy (1989)

Method

Subjects

The authors were careful to describe not only the age of the subjects but also their physical status, cognitive abilities, and mental health. The researchers also measured many characteristics of the subjects so they would have the necessary information to interpret the data. What, for example, would it mean if the DLs for the elderly were larger? Was the difference caused by cognitive impairment (such as the possibility that the elderly subjects did not understand the instructions), or was some other aspect of aging responsible? If the researchers know from prior evaluation that none of the elderly subjects were cognitively impaired, they can rule out cognitive impairment as an explanation for the age-related DL difference.

The authors tested only female subjects. The advantage of the gender restriction is that, should the performance of males and females differ on this task, restricting subjects to one gender will reduce the *variability* (chapter 4, p. 55) between subjects. The disadvantage is that the data may or may not *generalize* (chapter 6, p. 91) to males. The authors of the next article solved the generalization dilemma by running both male and female subjects and using sex (gender) as a variable in the statistical analysis. Defining gender as a variable permits identifying the variability due to gender difference, reduces the statistical estimate of error variability, and adds to the *power* (chapter 4, p. 60) the experiment has to detect an effect on behavior attributable to the other independent variables. Of course, the decision to test both males and females meant running more subjects, which involved time and money.

Once you read the procedure section of the Gilmore and Murphy study it must have become clear why the subjects were paid: They were asked to spend between 4 and 8 hours as subjects.

Stimuli

Research to determine DLs typically involves testing subjects with several different standard stimuli. For both caffeine and sucrose, the authors used three different standard stimuli, and each one was compared with six comparison stimuli.

Procedure

The authors tested all subjects with both caffeine and sugar (*within-subject design*; chapter 12), and were careful to *counterbalance* (chapter 12, p. 210) the order of the tastes. The subjects were asked to make many comparisons over four days of testing. Since lengthy testing can become very tedious for subjects (especially older people), the experimenters let subjects work as slowly as they wanted to. Does the fact that the younger subjects worked more quickly represent a possible *confounding variable* (chapter 1, p. 7)? This is a difficult question to answer; even if allowing subjects to work at their own pace does introduce an extraneous variable, there may be no method that will succeed in avoiding some type of confounding. Allowing all subjects the same time to complete the task could force the older subjects to work more quickly than they would like to and introduce another confounding variable. An alternative is to test subjects under both types of instructions and see if the results differ.

Perception & Psychophysics
1989, 46 (6), 555–559

Aging is associated with increased Weber ratios for caffeine, but not for sucrose

MAGDALENA M. GILMORE and CLAIRE MURPHY
San Diego State University, San Diego, California

To investigate whether age-associated changes in the human taste system are quality-specific, we compared young and elderly subjects' suprathreshold discrimination abilities for caffeine and sucrose. The method of constant stimuli was used to obtain just noticeable differences and Weber ratios. The elderly generated larger Weber ratios than did the young for both the medium and high concentrations of caffeine, but not for the low concentration. For example, a 74% increase in .005 M caffeine was required to obtain a perceptible difference for the elderly, whereas a 34% increase produced a perceptible difference for the young. The Weber ratios for sucrose did not differ for the two age groups. The results of this study indicate that age-associated changes in the taste system are quality-specific.

METHOD

Subjects

The participants were 12 females, 67–77 years of age ($M = 72.42$, $SD = 3.20$), and 12 females, 18–25 years of age ($M = 22.92$, $SD = 1.51$). All of the elderly subjects were active, community-dwelling individuals who were able to drive themselves to the laboratory and had not been hospitalized within the previous year. All were members of a university-based education and enrichment program. All reported good to excellent health, and only 3 smoked. All but 1 of the young subjects were upper division or graduate students majoring in psychology, and 1 young subject smoked.

The cognitive status of the subjects was assessed with the Raven progressive matrices (Raven, 1956) and the digit-span portion of the Wechsler Adult Intelligence Scale (Wechsler, 1955). The cognitive testing indicated that all subjects were intellectually capable of performing the task. The mean Raven and digit-span scores, respectively, were 43.42 (95th percentile for age group) and 16.0 for the elderly, and 55.17 (95th percentile for age group) and 18.08 for the young. All subjects were paid $5.00 per hour for participating.

Stimuli

The stimuli were reagent grade sucrose and Baker grade caffeine, dissolved in deionized water. For the discrimination task, the standards for sucrose were .15 M, .30 M, and .60 M sucrose. The standards for caffeine were .0025 M, .005 M, and .01 M. Six comparison stimuli were prepared for each standard, three being more concentrated than the standard and three less concentrated. The six comparison stimuli for each standard were .70%, .82%, .94%, 1.06%, 1.18%, and 1.30% of the standard concentration (see McBride, 1983). The levels selected for the discrimination task were determined by pretesting with a recognition task, to be sure that the stimuli to be presented in the JND experiment were actually perceptible.

Procedure

The discrimination task was run according to the method of constant stimuli. For most subjects, a total of four sessions were run, usually on separate days. During each single session, the subject was presented with stimuli of only one taste quality, sweet or bitter. (One elderly and 1 young subject participated in a session in which sweet and bitter stimuli were both presented.) Half the subjects received bitter stimuli first, and half received sweet first. The subjects set their own pace, and a session lasted approximately 1 h for the young subjects and 1–2 h for the elderly subjects.

A session consisted of the tasting of 60 pairs of stimuli: the stimuli associated with two standards. (Two elderly and 1 young subject opted for three sets of 30 pairs in one session with intermittent breaks.) One stipulation was that of the 60 pairs presented, the subject first taste the 30 pairs in which the standard was lower in concentration. Each subject tasted 30 pairs of stimuli associated with each of the standards.

Within one set of 30 pairs were the six comparison stimuli, each paired with the standard. These six pairs were administered five times and randomly distributed. Within a pair, the stimuli were randomly placed so that each subject had an equal probability of tasting the standard first or second.

The experimenter instructed the subject where to begin, to always taste the left cup first, to taste both cups in the pair, and subsequently to choose the stronger of the two by placing a small piece of paper in the cup. The subjects were allowed to rest at any time, and they were encouraged to rinse thoroughly between pairs. The experimenter recorded the number of times the comparisons were judged to be stronger than the standards.

Data Analysis

The proportion representing the number of times a comparison stimulus was judged stronger than a standard was calculated for each of the six levels of comparison, for each of the standards. These proportions were then converted to z-scores, according to Reference Table 1 in Engen (1971). The least squares regression method described by Engen (1971) was used to determine JNDs by fitting normal deviates against concentrations. The JND was defined as the increment judged correctly 75% of the time. The point of subjective quality (PSE, the point at which the comparison stimulus is perceived as being equal to the standard) was also determined, and the ratio of the JND to the PSE yielded the Weber ratio.

A few values fell outside the distribution. These were replaced with data points three standard deviations from the mean of the distribution (Tabachnick & Fidell, 1983).

One-way analyses of variance were used to compare results for the two age groups.

Perceptual and Motor Skills, 1989, 69, 595–604. © Perceptual and Motor Skills 1989

SUBJECTIVE EQUALITY AND JUST NOTICEABLE DIFFERENCES IN BODY-SIZE JUDGMENTS BY OBESE PERSONS

RICK M. GARDNER, JAMES A. MORRELL, Jr., DEBORAH N. WATSON, and SUSAN L. SANDOVAL

University of Southern Colorado

Summary.—Body-size estimates by obese and normal-weight subjects were compared using two different procedures with a TV-video methodology. In the continuous method subjects adjusted an image larger or smaller until they judged a correct TV-image had been achieved. In the second procedure the method of constant stimuli was used wherein values corresponding to the point of subjective equality (*PSE*) and difference threshold (*DL*) were determined. No differences between obese and normal-weight subjects were obtained with these procedures. On the continuous task subjects slightly underestimated body size and were more accurate on descending trials where they adjusted the size of the image downwards. With the second procedure, an average *PSE* of − .62% was obtained, with an average *DL* = 7.27%. Different *PSE* values were obtained when subjects were judging whether their image was distorted too wide or too thin. Data from the two procedures are compared and ramifications for the study of body size are discussed.

Method

Subjects

Subjects were 40 volunteers from the university and local community, including 20 men and 20 women. One half of the subjects from each group were classified as obese. Obesity was defined by subject's weight being 20% or more over their recommended weight using the Metropolitan Life Insurance (1983b) standards according to body-frame size. Body-frame size was determined by measuring elbow breadth with calipers and referencing the tables in the Metropolitan Life Foundation Statistical Bulletin (1983a). Subjects were classified as normal weight if they weighed within ± 10% of their recommended body weight. The average control subject weighed 139.5 lb. which was +2% over the norms while the average obese subject weighed 197.5 lb. which was 39% over the norms. Subjects were paid $5.00 per hour for their participation.

Procedure

Subjects wore normal street clothes. They were positioned 60 in. in front of a TV camera. Background cues, which may aid the subject in gauging body size, were eliminated. Subjects stood against a plain white background. A high resolution 16-in. black-and-white TV monitor was positioned 68 in. in front of the subjects. The TV camera was modified so that the horizontal dimensions of the TV-image could be altered, causing the resulting body image to appear wider or thinner without affecting the height of the image. An Apple II computer controlled the random distortion of the presented body image.

Two tasks were performed by each subject. In the first task, subjects were presented an image that was initially distorted either too wide or too thin. The amount of distortion possible with this apparatus ranged between 162% too wide and 104% too narrow. A value of 100% reflects distortion of two times the actual body-size, while the value of −100% reflects a distortion of one-half the actual body-size. The subject held a control device mounted in a small hand-held box. By pressing one of the two buttons, the subjects could vary the width of the body image, making it either wider or thinner. Pressing the buttons caused the image to become wider or thinner at a constant rate, determined electronically. For one-half of the trials the subject was presented an initial body-image which was too thin and was asked to adjust the image wider until the image reflected an accurate representation of the subject's body (ascending trials). On the other one-half of the trials the initial image presentation was too large and the subject was asked to adjust the image thinner until an image was perceived as accurate (descending trials). The initial amount of distortion presented varied randomly between ± 100% from trial to trial so that subjects were required to use differing amounts of adjustments to arrive at the perceived correct image-size. Each subject was given ten practice trials, after which 20 data trials were completed. The order of ascending and descending trials was randomized. Subjects were allowed as much time and as many adjustments (wider or thinner) as needed to alter the image accurately. Subjects pressed another button on the hand-held control device when the perceived actual image had been produced. An Apple II computer recorded the amount of distortion present, in terms of percentage of overestimation or underestimation, the number of seconds required to make the judgement, and the number of adjustments (wider or thinner) the subject made in arriving at the final image.

The second task employed the psychophysical technique of method of constant stimuli to determine the point of subjective equality (*PSE*) and the difference limen (*DL*) score for each subject. Subjects viewed their body at 11 discrete levels of distortion ranging between ± 20%, with a 4% distortion separating each interval (i.e., −20%, −16%, −12%, −8%, −4%, 0%, 4%, 8%, 12%, 16%, and 20%). After one practice trial at each level of distortion, subjects made 50 judgments at each of the 11 intervals of size distortion. Using the hand-held device described earlier, subjects pressed one of two buttons to signify whether distortion was present or absent on a given trial. The order of distortion levels was randomized within each block of 11 trials. In one phase, subjects responded whether the image was "too wide" or normal, while in another phase they responded whether the image was "too thin" or normal. Subjects were presented 555 trials (50 at each distortion level) for each phase. Order of the two phases was randomized across subjects. The levels of distortion present for the two phases were identical, with the only difference being that subjects were looking for the presence/absence of distortion which was either "too wide" or "too thin," to determine whether such instructional set would affect the *PSE* and *DL*.

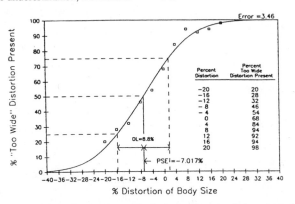

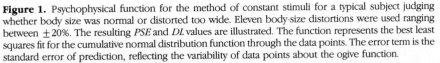

Figure 1. Psychophysical function for the method of constant stimuli for a typical subject judging whether body size was normal or distorted too wide. Eleven body-size distortions were used ranging between ±20%. The resulting *PSE* and *DL* values are illustrated. The function represents the best least squares fit for the cumulative normal distribution function through the data points. The error term is the standard error of prediction, reflecting the variability of data points about the ogive function.

Discussion of Techniques and Controls in the Gardner et al. Study

Method

Subjects

Both males and females were tested, even though gender was not one of the variables of interest to the authors. Unlike the authors of the first article, these authors can conclude that their findings apply to both males and females.

Although the authors did not state how they recruited subject volunteers, presumably they advertised in university and community newspapers. If subjects of a certain type are needed for an experiment (say, obese people), one option is to include the desired specifications in the request for subjects. Otherwise luck will determine whether or not the quota of subjects with the desired specification will volunteer to participate. The disadvantage of including subject specifications in an advertisement is that the information can lead subjects to speculate about the purpose of the research ("This study must be about weight reduction"), which could introduce *demand characteristics* (chapter 10, p. 179) and may influence the results in unpredictable and undesirable ways.

Procedure

Subjects were shown a distorted picture of themselves and were asked to adjust the image until it was perceived as accurate. To carry out this research the experimenters needed a device that could take the image of the subject and distort it by making the person appear wider or thinner. In addition, the subjects had to be able to vary their body image. The authors used a computer to present the distorted images, vary the image, and record a number of different responses (for example, amount of distortion present after the subjects determined the perceived correct image-size and the number of seconds it took to make the judgment).

All subjects were tested in two ways. The method of adjustment was used first, and the method of constant stimuli was used second. As in the first article, each subject was given many trials and was paid $5 per hour.

Analysis

To illustrate how the PSE and DL are calculated, we have included a figure from the article that shows the results of testing one male subject using the method of constant stimuli. First the authors plotted the percentage of times the subject stated that the presented image was "too wide" for each of the 11 distortion levels tested. Then they drew the best-fitting curve for the data (an ogive or S-shaped curve), and from this curve calculated the PSE and the DL as explained below. (It will help you follow the discussion if you refer often to the figure in the article.)

The PSE is the distortion of body size the subject reported as "too wide" on half of the trials (50% point), which is also the point he said was "too thin" on half the trials. This is clearly the setting of the device that produced an image the subject felt was equal to his true appearance. The figure shows that this subject perceived himself as 7.017% thinner than he actually was. The subject's constant error of −7.017 is the PSE minus the standard, which in this study is zero distortion of body size.

The DL is the value the subject reported as wider or thinner than the PSE on half the trials and is calculated by taking the difference between the 50% point and the 75% and 25% points (refer again to the figure). To help you understand why the 75% and 25% points on the curve are selected as limits for DL calculation, consider the following. If the subject judges the image at the 50% point to be equal to his size, the 100% point is obviously the point the subject thinks is always wider than his size. Presumably, the subject will judge the image that is halfway between the 50% and 100% points (the 75% point) to be distorted on half the trials. The difference between the 75% and 50% points (−7.017 and +1.7) equals 8.717 and is called the upper DL. The same reasoning is used to justify using the 25% point (halfway between the 50% and the 0% points) in the calculation of the lower DL. The lower DL equals the difference between the 25% and 50% points (−15.9 and −7.017) or 8.883. The mean of the upper and lower DLs equals a DL value of 8.8, which means that the image had to be distorted by 8.8% for the subject to notice any distortion of his self-image.

Additional Techniques and Control Issues in Sensation and Perception

Signal Detection Theory

The three methods for determining the sensitivity of organisms to stimuli and calculating the AL and DL (method of constant stimuli, method of limits, and method of adjustment) are called the **psychophysical methods**. Although they have been, and continue to be, used extensively by psychologists, there is one major drawback to these methods: They do not permit us to determine the response bias (also called response criterion) of the subject, which is the overall willingness of the subject to report that a stimulus event occurred. Response bias exists because, under some circumstances, people are very reluctant to say they detect a stimulus, and under other circumstances they are not. For example, assume your job is to watch a radar screen for enemy intercontinental ballistic missiles (ICBMs). If you see evidence of an incoming missile on your radar screen, you must notify the president of the United States, who would presumably order a missile launch and begin World War III. Under such circumstances you would probably be very reluctant to report seeing an enemy ICBM if the radar image was ambiguous and you were not sure. That is, you would adopt a conservative response criterion, a bias against reporting the detection of a stimulus. Conversely, if your job were to read slides of human tissue to detect cancer cells, you would be more likely to report the presence of such cells even if you were not absolutely sure they were present. That is, you would adopt a liberal response criterion, a bias in favor of reporting the detection of a stimulus. It would be less risky to the patient's long-term welfare to state that cancer cells were

Psychophysical Methods: Methods for determining the sensitivity of organisms to stimuli and calculating the absolute (AL) and difference (DL) thresholds (method of constant stimuli, method of limits, and method of adjustment).

Signal Detection Theory (SDT): An approach to threshold measurement that accounts for both the physical characteristics of the stimulus and the characteristics of the background (noise) against which the stimulus is presented.

present and have another test done to verify the first test than to tell the patient's physician there were no cancer cells when in fact there were.

Fortunately, another technique for measuring stimulus sensitivity has been developed that is independent of the response criterion. The technique is based on **Signal Detection Theory (SDT)**, an approach to threshold measurement that accounts for both the physical characteristics of the stimulus and the characteristics of the background (noise) against which the stimulus is presented. The SDT approach requires giving subjects a large number of trials. On some trials a stimulus is added to a particular background. On other trials no stimulus is added to the background. If the stimulus is presented, it is always the same one. The stimulus is intended to be difficult to detect, and all the subject has to do is report whether or not a stimulus was present during the trial. Table 18–1 shows the four types of results that are possible. When the stimulus is presented during a trial and the subject correctly reports that it was present, the subject has scored a hit. If the subject reports that the stimulus was absent during the trial when it really was present, the subject has scored a miss. When the stimulus is omitted from the trial but the subject incorrectly reports that it was present, the response is a false alarm, and when the subject correctly reports that the stimulus is absent, the response is a correct rejection. The results are usually graphed as the percentage of hits against the percentage of false alarms, and the figure is called a receiver operating characteristic (ROC) curve. If the subject was operating with a liberal response criterion, the ROC would show a high percentage of hits and false alarms. If the subject was operating with a conservative response criterion, the ROC would show a low percentage of hits and false alarms. Based on the percentage of hits and false alarms, both the *sensitivity* of the subject, called d' (d prime), and the *response bias* of the subject, called β (beta), can be calculated. You will learn the formulae used to calculate d' and β in specialized courses in sensation, perception, learning, cognition, memory, or social psychology.

When you read the last sentence were you surprised that signal detection theory relates to so many subdisciplines of psychology? A computer search using PsycLIT (a reference data base in psychology; see Appendix A) revealed that 470 articles published between 1983 and 1990 used the signal detection technique. Topics included "Detection of invalid response patterns on the California Psycho-

		Subject's Response	
		Present	Absent
Stimulus	Present	HIT	MISS
	Absent	FALSE ALARM	CORRECT REJECTION

Table 18–1. The four types of trials that can occur in a signal-detection experiment.

logical Inventory," "Recall, recognition and serial learning: A signal-detection measurement," "The impact of ratee performance characteristics on rater cognition processes and alternative measures of rater accuracy," "The use of signal detection theory to assess DSM-III–R criteria for autistic disorder," "Personality dimensions and memory as measured by signal detection," "Simulation studies of latency measures of components of the event-related brain potential," "Fluprazine hydrochloride: No influence on the odor detection performance of male rats," and "The effect of passive smoking on vigilance performance."

Scales Used by Psychologists and Physicists

Physicists measure the intensity of tones, the brightness of lights, etc. and, like psychologists, they use both *interval* and *ratio scales* (chapter 3, p. 27). For example, the increase in energy needed to change a sound from 35 to 40 decibels (db, the scale used to measure tone intensity) is the same amount of energy needed to change from 80 to 85 db. But do we, as living organisms, perceive these two 5-unit differences as the same? We do not, as demonstrated in the following example.

Pretend you are in a very dimly lit room. If someone were to light one candle and ask you if the room appears brighter you would answer "Yes." In a dimly lighted room one candle does make the room look brighter. Now pretend you have come into a very brightly lit room and someone lights the same candle. Would the room appear brighter? Probably not. The room is already so bright that lighting the candle is unlikely to add noticeably to the room's already high level of brightness. The addition of many candles would be necessary to notice an increase in the illumination of an already well-lit room.

We can conclude that when a dimly lit room is used as a standard, the DL will be small, and when a bright room is used as a standard, the DL will be large. Thus the size of the DL is relative to the magnitude of the standard stimulus. The more intense the standard stimulus, the higher the DL will be, and the less intense the standard stimulus, the smaller the DL will be. If you are not convinced, have a friend lift two large paper shopping bags, one that is empty and one with a small book inside. Even though a small book is relatively light, your friend will be able to tell that the bag with the book is heavier. Next, leave the small book in its bag, add equal amounts of heavy books to each bag, and repeat the comparison. Even though the difference in the weights of the two bags is the same for both comparisons, determining which of the two bags is heavier is much more difficult when both are heavy than when both are light. Thus, equal intervals on an interval or ratio scale of physical measurement (the brightness of one candle or the weight of one book) do not translate as equal intervals on a psychological scale (the perception of brightness or weight).

Psychologists have sought to describe the precise relationship between the physicist's scale and the psychologist's scale with mathematical equations. By substituting appropriate values in the equations, the effects that manipulation of stimuli should have on sensation can be predicted. Historically, three formulas have been proposed to present the relationship between the physical and psychological scales. The first was Weber's law:

$$\Delta I/I = k \text{ (constant)}.$$

Δ (delta) is the symbol used for change, and I stands for intensity, so ΔI is equivalent to the DL or the change in intensity needed to detect a difference. The I in the denominator stands for the intensity of the standard stimulus. Another way of stating Weber's law is:

$$DL/standard = k.$$

Once we run an experiment to determine the DL for a given standard, we can calculate k, and once we have determined k, then we can calculate the DL for any standard. For example, if the DL is 5 and the standard is 100, then k is 5/100, or .05. If you then wanted to calculate the DL for a different standard of, say, 300, the formula would be DL/300 = .05. Solving for DL, we find that it equals 15.

Alternative equations include Stevens' power law, which can be written as a very simple formula:

$$Y = kX^n.$$

X is the stimulus intensity presented to the subject (stimulus intensity is measured on a physical scale), k is a constant, and Y is the subject's response (n is defined later). The accuracy of Stevens' law has been tested with alternative methodologies. For example, we could ask a subject to place one hand in a bucket of water that is either 5°, 10°, 15°, or 20° C (the X variable) and report how much pain he feels (the Y variable) on a scale from 1 to 10. The response for no pain would be 1, the response for moderate pain would be 5, and a 10 would be reserved for the experience of extreme pain. If we transform the X (physical measurements) and Y (psychological measurements) into logarithms (logX and logY) and plot the results, all the points would fall on a straight line if they fit Stevens' power law, and n would be the slope of the line. Once we determine n for each sense modality (tones, lights, touch, smell, taste), we can use the formula to predict the subject's response (Y) for every stimulus (X) we present.

Magnitude Estimation Technique: The subject assigns numbers to stimuli that are proportional to an initial standard.

Another method for the assignment of subjective ratings (the Y variable) is called the **magnitude estimation technique**. The subject is given a standard stimulus (the sensation of her hand in 15° C water) and is told to consider the stimulus value as a 10. The subject then experiences different water temperatures and is told to assign to the stimuli numbers that are proportional to the initial standard. For example, if the subject perceived the second stimulus to be half as cold as the 15° standard, she would give it a 5, and if it felt twice as cold, she would give it a 20. This sounds like a complicated task, but subjects tend to become quite good at it.

There are other scaling techniques that have been developed for different types of subject responses. You can learn more about this area in a course called Tests and Measurement, which is offered at most schools that have a psychology-major curriculum.

Summary

Psychologists have developed various techniques (method of limits, method of average error, method of constant stimuli, and signal detection) to determine how sensitive people are to stimuli. One measure of sensitivity is to determine the lowest level of stimulation a subject can detect (absolute threshold) and the smallest difference a subject can detect between two stimuli (difference threshold or JND). The topic of the first article presented was the difference threshold for caffeine and for sucrose in both young-adult and elderly subjects. The second article was concerned with differences in body-size judgments in obese and normal subjects.

Key Terms

Comparison Stimulus, p. 346

Magnitude Estimation Technique, p. 356

Method of Adjustment (Method of
   Average Error), p. 345

Method of Constant Stimuli, p. 345

Method of Limits, p. 345

Psychophysical Methods, p. 353

Signal Detection Theory (SDT), p. 354

Standard Stimulus, p. 346

Chapter Exercises

1. Gilmore and Murphy found that the Weber ratios were not different between the elderly and the young for the sweet taste, but that "the elderly generated larger Weber ratios than the young for both medium and high concentrations of caffeine" (Abstract).

    a. Why can't the authors conclude that age caused these differences?

    b. If the results of a 2 × 2 × 3 analysis of variance (Age × Taste × Intensity of taste) showed a main effect for age (lower Weber ratio for the younger subjects), a main effect for taste (lower Weber ratio for sucrose than caffeine), no main effect of intensity of taste, and no interaction effects, what conclusions would the authors have drawn?

2. Design a study to test if the absolute threshold for sweet and bitter tastes differs between elderly and young subjects.

3. Gardner et al. did not find that obese and normal-weight people made different body-size judgments. In the absence of a statistical difference between conditions, one must look very carefully at the experimental procedures. If you were to replicate the study, what would you do differently that might change the outcome of the study? (For example, do you think that the definition of obese (39% for the norm) is an adequate definition?

CHAPTER

19

Research in Transfer

Perhaps the most visible applications of the study of learning are directed toward increasing our capacity to learn and our ability to remember. But another equally valuable application of learning is the study of transfer, the effect the learning in one situation subsequently has on a subject's performance in a different situation. For example, when a pilot trains in a flight simulator, the initial goal is to learn and remember maneuvering and navigating skills in the simulator environment. But the ultimate objective is to be able to transfer the knowledge acquired during simulator experience to the operation of an aircraft under actual flight conditions. Similarly, therapists hope that the skills clients learn during therapy sessions will help their patients deal with a variety of life's problems, not just the particular personal problem(s) that prompted the client to seek therapy. Parents hope that what they teach their children in the home will help them outside the home in social situations, on the job, and in raising their own families when they become adults. As educators, the authors hope that what you learn in your study of research methods will help you to do well in other classes and to meet your responsibilities in your chosen profession and in your everyday life. To the extent that the challenge of mastering a new learning situation is made easier by learning in a different prior situation, positive transfer exists.

It is also possible for prior learning to interfere with performance in a new situation; a phenomenon called negative transfer. For example, your experience driving on the right-hand side of the road in the United States would likely lead to some confusion (negative transfer) if you rented a car while on vacation in England, where they drive on the left side of the road.

Psychologists who work in the subdiscipline of learning and memory are very much interested in researching the variables that affect the magnitude of positive and negative transfer. Specifically, studies of transfer are often directed to finding out how to decrease negative transfer and increase positive transfer. The study selected to represent the subdiscipline of transfer (Bassok, 1990) was designed to determine if learning how to solve banking problems using the geometric progression technique transfers positively to help subjects solve algebra problems that use the same geometric progression technique. (If you are now thinking "Oh no! Math! I'm terrible in math! I give up!," you are exhibiting a form of learned helplessness, a very unfortunate type of negative transfer. Learned helplessness is said to exist when a subject's previous inability to solve a problem inhibits attempts to solve similar problems, even when the solution is not difficult and is well within the reach of the subject.)

Every transfer experiment has at least two phases. In the first phase a group of subjects is required to learn how to perform a task (training phase). Then, in the second phase (transfer test), how readily these experienced subjects learn to do a second task is compared with control subjects who do not have a relevant prior learning experience in Phase 1. The Bassok study contained four rather than the minimum two phases, making it somewhat more complicated than the basic transfer design. The easiest way to understand complicated experiments is to outline them:

Phase 1 (pretest)	Phase 2 (training condition)	Phase 3 (posttest)	Phase 4 (next day) (transfer test)
Solve banking problems	→ Group 1: banking → Group 2: algebra	solve banking problems	algebra problems

Subjects were told that they would be "studying a chapter from finance dealing with banking transactions." First they took a pretest of banking problems to establish a skill baseline (Phase 1). Next, in Phase 2 (a training phase) they learned about geometric progressions either in a banking context or in an algebra-applied context after which, in the Phase 3 posttest, they were tested using another set of banking problems to see how well they learned the material during the training phase. The following day the experimenter evaluated the two groups of subjects for their knowledge of geometric progressions in the context of an algebra problem. The author tested for a transfer effect (Did prior training in a banking context enhance performance in solving algebra problems?) by comparing the performance of the group trained in geometric progressions in the abstract context of algebra (the control group) to the group trained in the applied context of banking. After reading the abstract of the Bassok article, you will realize that it is not easy to predict when positive transfer will occur ("The results suggest a complex interrelation between content and structure.").

The Bassok study is in the form of Basic Question 5 (Will introducing subjects to qualitatively different conditions cause them to exhibit systematic differences in behavior?). The two qualitative conditions were the way subjects were exposed to learning about geometric sequences and series (reading an algebra-applied chapter or a banking chapter).

Journal of Experimental Psychology:
Learning, Memory, and Cognition
1990. Vol. 16. No. 3, 522–533

Transfer of Domain-Specific Problem-Solving Procedures

Miriam Bassok

Learning Research and Development Center, University of Pittsburgh

Two experiments examined transfer of mathematical problem-solving procedures learned in content-rich quantitative domains (e.g., physics, finance) to isomorphic algebra word problems dealing with other contents. In spite of content-specific embedding, many high school and college students exhibited spontaneous transfer when the variables in the learned and in the transfer problems represented similar types of quantities (e.g., speed and typing rate). Spontaneous transfer to structurally isomorphic problems with variables representing different types of quantities (e.g., speed and salary) was blocked. Protocol analyses showed that for matching quantities, transfer solutions were straightforward applications of the learned methods, whereas transfer to problems with nonmatching quantities demanded a hint for retrieval followed by an effortful process of abstraction and analogical mapping. The results suggest a complex interrelation between content and structure: Many features of the embedding content may be "screened out" as irrelevant, but content features used for interpretation of variables (e.g., intensive vs. extensive) may affect both access and use.

Method

Subjects. Subjects were 20 undergraduate students from the University of Pittsburgh who had not taken an algebra class for at least 1 year and whose major did not include finance. There were 8 male and 12 female subjects. Subjects were paid for their participation.

Materials. Two chapters were constructed for the study. The mathematical material was based on an algebra chapter dealing with geometric progressions taken from a standard high school algebra text (Dolciani, Wooton, Beckenbach, & Sharon, 1983, pp. 217–230). The banking content was based on a chapter from finance (Brick, 1984, pp. 39–73). Both chapters (i.e., banking and algebra applied) started with an introduction which set the goal of understanding various financial options concerning investments and loans in order to make well-informed choices and decisions. It presented some of the basic concepts (e.g., interest rates, compounding periods) and mentioned several

laws passed for consumer protection (e.g,, the "Truth in Lending Act").

In the algebra-applied chapter, the introduction ended by stating that the following algebra chapter would introduce the relevant definitions and calculation procedures necessary for dealing with various banking transactions. The algebraic insert, labeled "Geometric Sequences and Series," covered all the relevant mathematical material, excluding infinite geometric series. To make the practice equivalent to that in the banking chapter, the algebraic material did not include numerical exercises. The algebraic insert was followed by a section labeled "Applications to Banking Transactions." For each of the two major equations, one for sequences ($a_n = a_1 r^{n-1}$) and one for series ($S_n = a_1 \frac{(1-r^n)}{(1-r)}$), there were two worked-out examples of word problems dealing with compound interest and with annuities. Also, for each equation there were three word problems given for students' own practice followed by correct worked-out solutions. Thus, the chapter included a total of 10 (5 sequences and 5 series) banking-application word problems.

The banking chapter covered the same mathematical material and presented the same set of examples and of practice problems. However, the definitions of the relevant terms and their interrelations were developed directly for the banking concepts. For example, rather than defining n as the count of number of terms in a sequence, the chapter presented p as denoting the compounding period; rather than dealing with the general term in a sequence (a_n), the chapter presented successive balances for consecutive compounding periods (b_p). The equations were developed in the banking-specific context, such as when discussing the "time value of money," "the compounding process," or the concept of annuities. The examples and the practice problems appeared within the above context and not as a separate set of applications.

Two sets of banking problems and one set of nonbanking problems were constructed. The two sets of banking problems served as pretest and posttest, and the nonbanking set served as transfer test. Each set included first two geometric sequences and then two geometric series problems. The banking and the nonbanking problems were matched in pairs with respect to the underlying structure of the problem. Each pair could be solved by using the same corresponding formula, was matched with respect to which variables were given and unknown, and presented similar numerical values. Examples of matched pretest banking and transfer nonbanking problems are presented in Table 1.

In addition to the geometric progression problems, the banking pretest and the nonbanking transfer test included a set of four problems of the arithmetic-progression type (two sequences and two series). These problems served as structural fillers, enabling assessment of subjects' sensitivity to the structural distinction between increase and a constant

Table 1

Examples of Matched Geometric-Progressions Problems From Banking Pretest and From Algebra Nonbanking Transfer Test in Experiment 1

Nonbanking	Banking
Sequence type (Given a_1, r, n, find a_n)	
1. Because of its increasing popularity, each successive year a certain craft show attracts 1.3 times more people than during the previous year. If 1,000 people came to this craft show during its 1st year, how many people came during its 12th year?	1. A certain manufacturing company invested \$10,000 in various government bonds. Each successive year the value of their investment increases 1.3 times its value from the previous year. How much will their investment be worth during the 12th year?
Series type (Given a_1, r, n, find S_n)	
1. A certain car has a leak in its exhaust system. Each successive time that the car's accelerator pedal is pressed, 0.6% more carbon monoxide is released into the air. If 0.2 ml of carbon monoxide were released with the 1st press of the pedal, how many ml will have been released into the air altogether during the first 10 presses of the pedal?	1. Mr. Daniel is repaying a loan he received from the bank. Each successive month he agreed to repay 6% more than during the previous month. If he paid \$20 during the 1st month, what is the total amount of money that he will have repaid on the loan when he makes his 10th payment?

amount and increase by a constant rate. For the banking pretest these problems dealt with the banking content, whereas for the transfer test these problems dealt with other non-banking contents (e.g., populations). The arithmetic-progressions banking and nonbanking problems were also matched in pairs according to their underlying structure and the given and unknown variables. Starting with an arithmetic-progression problem, the geometric and arithmetic progressions problems alternated in order.

Procedure. All subjects were recruited for a study described as concerning the development of new instructional materials for college curricula in the domains of biology, algebra, economics, finance, and psychology. Subjects expected to study materials from two out of these five topics. This broad range of domains was included to minimize prior expectations regarding a possible relation between the chapters to be learned. Subjects were randomly assigned to one of two training conditions according to the chapter they were to study (see *Materials* above). Ten subjects were assigned to the banking condition, and 10 were assigned to the algebra-applied condition.

The experiment was conducted individually in two sessions on 2 consecutive days. The first pretest–study–posttest session lasted between 2–3 hr, and the second transfer session lasted between 45–60 min. During the first session, subjects first filled out a questionnaire on which they marked courses taken in each of the five topics mentioned on the recruiting form and were informed that they would study a chapter from finance dealing with banking transactions. Students then proceeded to solve the banking pretest, after which they studied either the banking or the algebra-applied chapter, according to their training condition. Students studied the chapter at their own pace with minimal intervention from the experimenter. After solving each practice problem, they were given the correct solution and were encouraged to compare it with their own solution. Students could review the chapter until they felt ready to take the chapter test (i.e., the posttest). After completing the posttest, students received a questionnaire asking them to identify the major things learned and to state whether they thought the chapter would be useful to them.

During the second session, conducted on the following day, students were informed that they would study an algebra chapter. They were then given the algebra pretest, which actually served as the transfer test. Subjects were initially not informed about the relation between their previous training and the transfer test. Those students who did not show spontaneous transfer on their algebra pretest were then asked to solve again two of the transfer problems after being informed that the previously learned chapter could be helpful for the solution of the algebra problems. Finally, all subjects were informed that they would not be studying another chapter and were thoroughly debriefed.

For all problems solved during the pretest, posttest, and transfer sessions, students talked out loud, and their solutions were tape-recorded for later analysis.

Discussion of Techniques and Controls in the Bassok Study

Method

Subjects

Bassok tested students who had not taken an algebra course within the last year. Using such subjects allowed her to presume subjects had no (or minimal) prior knowledge of the geometric progression technique, to control how they learned the geometric progression technique, and therefore to be sure that the groups were equated prior to the critical transfer phase. But using no recent instruction in algebra as a selection criterion may have created a problem: Subjects who tend to avoid taking courses in algebra may also tend to have a relatively low aptitude for mathematics. If true, the results would not *generalize* (chapter 6, p. 91) to the entire population of students. The author avoided this problem in a second experiment by testing 9th- and 10th-grade students who had not yet studied the topics (if you are interested in the methodology of the second experiment, you should be able to obtain a copy of the article through your library).

It becomes clear in the procedure section why the subjects were paid for their participation: They devoted between 2 and 3 hours of their time on the first day and about 1 hour on the second day to this experiment. Unfortunately, the author does not report how much money she gave the subjects or when she gave them the money. In general, it is wise not to pay subjects the full amount on the first day of an experiment. Delaying payment helps minimize one of the major problems of multiday test sessions: *subject loss* and the resulting problems it creates (chapter 7, p. 124).

Materials

The type of material the subjects received was the *independent variable* (chapter 3, p. 30), so it is especially important that the author describe the materials in detail, including *operational definitions* (chapter 3, p. 31). She included examples of the geometric progression problems, which would be very useful if one wanted to replicate her study. If authors do not provide sufficient detail to replicate a study, it is possible to ask for the details by letter or telephone. (Scientific journals list the institutional affiliations of authors to make it easier to obtain reprints of the article or ask for additional information.)

It is equally important to describe completely the *dependent variable* (chapter 3, p. 30), so it was helpful that the author mentioned the use of **filler items**: test items that do not relate directly to the aims of a study. Sometimes filler items are used simply to provide a distraction for the subjects during an interval in the experiment; sometimes they are used to hide the true purpose of a study; and sometimes they allow the experimenter to monitor a specific aspect of the subjects' behavior. For example, in this study, filler items consisting of arithmetic progression problems (remember, the principal concern of the study is with geometric

Filler Items: Test items intended to distract the subjects to hide the true purpose of a study.

progressions) were used to assess "the subjects' sensitivity to the structural distinction between increase by a constant amount and increase by a constant rate."

Procedure

The subjects were told that they would study two of five topics, even though the experimenter knew that they would really be learning about only two topics: banking or algebra. This type of *deception* (chapter 16, p. 314) is necessary to conceal the exact nature of the experiment when such knowledge could conflict with the aims of the research. An *Institutional Review Board* (chapter 16, p. 317), charged with evaluating research methods for adherence to ethical guidelines, will typically permit the mild form of deception employed in the present study as long as the experimenters *debrief* (chapter 10, p. 176) the subjects.

The author measured a number of different dependent variables, including the percentage of times the geometric progression technique was applied in the transfer test and the percentage of correct answers. She also had the subjects talk out loud while they were solving the problems and tape-recorded their responses for later analysis. Studying the successful and unsuccessful steps and strategies subjects employ when attempting to solve a problem, as in the analysis of subjects' taped verbal responses in the present study, is called **protocol analysis**.

In this experiment subjects were tested individually rather than in groups. Individual testing is very time-consuming for the experimenter, but there are no shortcuts if the aims of the experiment are to be realized. The one-on-one arrangement is necessary for the experimenter to give subjects help and encouragement to use the material they previously learned and to record their verbal responses for later protocol analysis.

Protocol Analysis of Problem Solving: Analysis of the successful and unsuccessful steps and strategies subjects employ when attempting to solve a problem.

Additional Techniques and Control Issues in Transfer

Control Groups in Transfer Experiments

The following example should help you remember why it is so important to include an appropriate control group in a transfer experiment and what the control group's training should be. Pretend a friend of yours has just decided that he must learn tennis. There is one problem. He lives in the northern part of the United States and it is January. It is snowing, the tennis nets have been put away for the winter, and there are no indoor tennis courts available. He will have to wait until spring to learn to play tennis. You tell him that a similar game, badminton, can be played indoors, and that knowing how to play badminton is supposed to help learn how to play tennis. Your friend is skeptical, so he decides to run the following experiment:

Task 1	*Task 2*
Badminton	Tennis

All his subjects were given badminton lessons, and, after 8 weeks, were given a test to measure their ability to volley with the shuttlecock (bird). (Scores on the test can range from 0 to 100.) The mean test score for the badminton-trained subjects was 65. Then, with the arrival of spring, all the subjects were given 8 weeks of tennis lessons followed by a tennis version of the badminton volley test. The subjects scored a mean of 85 on the tennis test. A statistical test between these two means indicates that the subjects scored significantly higher on the tennis than on the badminton test, so your friend concluded that badminton did help learning how to play tennis.

When he asks you for your impression of his study, your first reaction should be to tell him about the absence of a necessary control group. (You might even recommend his taking a course in research methods before he attempts to do research.) You should explain that it makes no sense to compare the tennis score to the badminton score. It may just be easier to learn tennis than badminton. To evaluate the presence of a transfer effect it is necessary to compare the tennis score of the group with prior badminton experience (the experimental group) to a control group that did not receive training in badminton:

	Task 1	*Task 2*
Experimental group	Badminton	Tennis (score 85)
Control group	—	Tennis (score 50)

If the experimental group's tennis score (85) was significantly higher than the control group's tennis score (for instance, 50), it would be proper for you to conclude that there was *positive transfer* between badminton and tennis. If the experimental group's tennis score was lower than the control group's tennis score, you would conclude that there was *negative transfer.*

It is important to note that in this type of experiment there are two potential types of transfer: general transfer and specific transfer. Specific transfer is likely to exist when two different tasks have similar stimulus conditions and response requirements. There are many stimulus similarities between badminton and tennis: in each sport there is an airborne object, an opponent, a net, and court boundaries. There are also response similarities: running to get to the flying object, swinging a racquet, hitting the airborne object over a net, and so forth. Similarities of stimuli and responses between two tasks often result in positive transfer, but negative transfer is also possible. For example, the badminton bird is usually struck with a flick of the wrist and must be returned before it hits the ground. In tennis, the ball may bounce once before a return is attempted, and flicking the wrist is not a proper tennis stroke.

General transfer is an influence of first-task experience on second-task performance that is unrelated to the stimulus and response similarities of the two tasks. For example, if you play badminton for 8 weeks prior to tennis, the physical conditioning that results from playing badminton can contribute to learning tennis more quickly (general transfer) in addition to the stimulus and response similarities between the two tasks (specific transfer). Psychologists tend to focus on variables that influence specific transfer and therefore are unlikely to compare an experimental group to a control group that receives no training at all while the experimental group is learning Task 1. Instead, researchers give the control group a task to do that is expected to result in as much general transfer as the experimental group's prior training, but no specific transfer. If the subjects in the control group were required to do aerobic exercise equal to the exertion of the experimental group playing badminton, both groups would have equal physical fitness, but only the experimental group would experience specific transfer from badminton to tennis:

	Task 1	Task 2
Experimental group	Badminton	Tennis (score 85)
Control group	Aerobic exercise	Tennis (score 70)

In the latter design, the difference between the experimental group's tennis score (85) and the control group's tennis score (70) must be due to specific transfer, because physical exercise (and the resulting general transfer) has been equated.

If the researcher wished to evaluate the effects of both general and specific transfer, it would be necessary to run the study with both control groups: one given no prior training and another given aerobic training. It would, however, be wrong to include only the experimental group and the control group given no prior training, since one could not determine if the differences were due to specific or general transfer.

Thousands of transfer studies appear in the published literature, and many are concerned with a task called paired-associate verbal learning rather than the perceptual-motor skills of competitive sports. The paired-associate task requires the subject to give specific verbal responses to stimulus words, as when a student must learn to associate English words with their foreign-language equivalents. In this type of experiment the task is typically to learn a number of stimulus-response pairs, but the subjects do not see all the pairs at one time. First a stimulus word is presented. Then the display changes to show the same stimulus word paired with a response word. This stimulus, stimulus-response presentation sequence is followed for all succeeding verbal pairs, as shown below.

Stimulus	Response	
house		(typically shown for 2 seconds)
house	water	(typically shown for 2 seconds)
sky		
sky	tiger	
(etc.)		

After going through the list once (that is, after one trial), the subject's task is to give the correct response when the stimulus alone is presented. That is, when subjects see the stimulus word (house) alone on the display, they must anticipate the correct response word (water) before the whole stimulus-response pair (house–water) eventually appears. The experiment will typically continue for many trials, until the subject can anticipate all the responses correctly on one trial. Of course, if the experimenter were to present the items in the same order each time, the subject would probably not bother to learn which response went with each stimulus, but would just learn the order of the responses (water, tiger, etc.). To force the subject to learn the stimulus-response pairs, experimenters present the pairs in different orders from trial to trial.

Some experimenters use **nonsense syllables**, which are nonwords frequently made up of three letters (DAX, LIQ, CHJ). They are called CVC (consonent-vowel-consonant) items if they have a vowel in the center, and CCC items if they are all consonants. Nonsense syllables are used in preference to real words when the experimenter either wants to vary the similarity between the stimulus and response items by changing one, two, or all three letters or eliminate prior familiarity with vocabulary as an extraneous variable.

In some verbal learning transfer experiments subjects have to learn different responses to the same stimuli, as when a student must learn to respond with the Russian equivalent to an English vocabulary word after first learning the English-Spanish equivalent. At other times the responses may be the same for both learning tasks but the stimuli may differ, as when a student learns to give the English equivalent of a Russian word, after learning to give the same English word to its Spanish equivalent.

When diagraming a study of verbal learning transfer experiments, each list is designated with a letter. The first letter stands for the stimulus list, the second for the response list. For example, a study that followed the sequence A-D: A-B indicates that the subjects had to learn two sets of responses (B and D) to the same stimulus words, A. (Note: When you read the literature in this area, some researchers prefer the designation A-C: A-B instead of A-D: A-B.) The sequence C-B: A-B indicates that the task was to learn the same responses to different stimuli. The A-Br: A-B sequence indicates that the same stimuli and same responses are on both lists, but the stimuli are paired with different responses (re-paired). For example, here are two stimuli with different responses in List 1 versus List 2:

List 1   *List 2*
house–water   house–tiger
sky–tiger   sky–water

This would be a simple task if the lists contained only two pairs, but there are typically eight pairs of randomly re-paired stimulus-response pairs. The different types of experimental conditions are summarized in Table 19–1.

Since transfer is defined as the difference between the performance of experimental and control groups on List 2, we need appropriate control groups for every transfer experiment. To measure specific transfer, we must include a group that can experience general transfer without specific transfer. One type of general transfer is

Nonsense Syllables: Nonwords frequently made up of three letters (such as DAX, LIQ, CHJ).

	Task 1 (List 1)	**Task 2 (List 2)**
Experimental groups	A – D	A – B
	C – B	A – B
	A – Br	A – B
Control group	C – D	A – B

Table 19–1. Possible list configurations for investigating transfer phenomena using paired-associate verbal learning.

the warm-up effect: a positive influence on performance from nonspecific elements of prior experience. For example, there is no specific reason why learning an earlier pair on the list (house–water) would transfer to learning a later pair (sky–tiger) except for the subject's familiarity with the general nature of the task, which builds as the task progresses. One type of warm-up effect is called learning to learn or a learning set: an improved ability to solve problems because of prior experience with similar problems. Thus, even when separate lists contain different stimuli and responses, a general problem-solving strategy acquired from prior list-learning experience can result in a positive transfer effect.

Since general transfer from warm-up effects can occur in any type of learning experiment, a critical control group is one that has practiced learning a List 1 with items that are totally unrelated to the A-B list (List 2) that both the experimental and control subjects must learn. List 1 for the control group is called a C-D list because, compared to the List 1 options for the experimental group listed in Table 19–1, the stimuli (A versus C) and responses (B versus D) are totally different. *Positive transfer* is evident if the experimental subjects learn their A-B List 2 more quickly than the control subjects learn theirs. *Negative transfer* is evident if the experimental subjects learn their A-B List 2 more slowly than the control subjects learn theirs. *Zero transfer* is evident if there is no difference between the performance of the control and experimental groups on learning the A-B list.

Recall of List 1 versus List 2

There is another class of experiments that calls for subjects to learn the material presented in Phase 1 (List 1), learn some related material in Phase 2 (List 2), and then recall the first list. Such an experiment is diagramed in Table 19–2 (we present the design in the context of learning lists of words, but it is equally applicable to memory for any body of information). It is called the **retroactive design**:

Retroactive Design: Subjects learn the material presented in Phase 1, then learn some related material in Phase 2, and subsequently are required to recall the material presented in the first phase (diagramed in Table 19.2).

	Original Task	Intervening Task	Recall Task
	List 1	List 2	List 1
Experimental group	A — B	A — D	A — B
Control group	A — B	C — D	A — B

Table 19–2. An experimental design for detecting retroactive facilitation and inhibition.

The first task for the experimental group is to learn a list of word pairs. Then they must learn another list that has the same stimulus words but different response words. Finally, they must relearn the original list of word pairs. The control group is given the same List 1 word pairs to learn as the experimental group, but, for the second list, they must learn a totally different list of word pairs. Thus the control group performance will be affected only by *general transfer* (learning-to-learn) and not by *specific transfer*.

When, on the recall task, the experimental group recalls more A-B pairs from List 1 than the control group, the phenomenon is called retroactive facilitation: An intermediate learning experience (List 2) facilitates the recall of originally learned material (List 1). When the performance of the experimental group on the recall task is poorer than that of the control group, the phenomenon is called retroactive interference (RI, also called retroactive inhibition): Intermediately learned material (List 2) inhibits the recall of originally learned material (List 1). (Retroactive interference is a likely result with a List 2 in the form of A-D.) One can, of course, study the transfer phenomena associated with other List 2 experiences, such as a C-B or an A-Br list, to determine which type of intervening material may result in facilitation and which may result in retroactive interference.

Since experiences that intervene between original learning and relearning frequently interfere with recall, psychologists have concluded that at least some memory loss is due to interference phenomena. For example, if college students sleep after studying material, which minimizes interference from intervening experiences between original learning and a recall task, the students will remember the material better than if they stay awake after studying the material (see Grosvenor & Lack, 1984).

Can an original learning experience (List 1) interfere with or facilitate the recall of subsequently learned material (List 2)? Table 19–3 shows the type of design used to answer this question. It is called the **proactive design**:

	Original Task	Intervening Task	Recall Task
	List 1	List 2	List 2
Experimental group	A – D	A – B	A – B
Control group	C – D	A – B	A – B

Table 19–3. An experimental design for studying proactive facilitation and inhibition.

Proactive Design: Subjects learn the material presented in Phase 1, then learn some related material in Phase 2, and subsequently are required to recall the second set of material (diagramed in Table 19–3).

The experimental and control groups have different List 1 learning tasks and identical List 2 learning tasks. On the recall task, which can be a few minutes, hours, or even days after the learning of List 2, both groups must recall (or relearn) List 2. When the experimental group recalls more pairs from List 2 than the control group, the phenomenon is called proactive facilitation: Original learning facilitates the recall of intermediately learned material. When the experimental group recalls fewer pairs than the control group, the phenomenon is called proactive interference (PI, also called proactive inhibition): Original learning inhibits the recall of intermediately learned material.

The retroactive and proactive memory designs just reviewed are often used to study long-term memory (LTM): memory tested a long time (minutes, hours, days, even years) after learning has taken place. In contrast to LTM, short-term memory (STM) is tested a short time (seconds) after a single brief exposure to a stimulus (as when you look up and remember a telephone number just long enough to dial it). A common STM research design that has been used for many years is the Brown–

Peterson design (Peterson & Peterson, 1959). Subjects are presented with one nonsense syllable like CHJ, or one word like *apple*. They are then given a number and told to count backward from the number by threes or fours to prevent rehearsal: repeating of the nonsense syllable or word during the retention interval. The subjects must count backward aloud and are timed with a metronome with instructions to say one number per second. When a light comes on, the subjects must stop counting and try to recall the material previously presented. In one of the first experiments to use this design (Peterson & Peterson, 1959), the subjects were tested at six different retention intervals: 3, 6, 9, 12, 15, and 18 seconds. The authors used the *block-randomization technique for within-subject designs* (chapter 13, p. 246) was used, with eight tests at each of the six retention intervals. The results were quite surprising. Subjects were very good at recalling after 3 seconds, but memory became worse the longer the retention interval was, and only 8% of the items were recalled at the longest retention interval. These results were taken as evidence that if rehearsal is prevented there is a rapid decay of short-term memory.

Some researchers were very skeptical about this result. Their argument was that because a *within-subject design* (chapter 11) was used, the results represent the influence of proactive inhibition with longer retention intervals (Keppel & Under-wood, 1962). Since each subject was given 48 items to remember after two practice items, all items could have had interference from previous items. They also argued that at 3 seconds there was no time for the previous items to interfere with the memory of the new item, and therefore subjects could recall the nonsense syllable. With longer retention intervals the previous items would have time to interfere with the new item.

To test this hypothesis, they ran a *between-subject design* (chapter 12). All subjects were given only one item, but half the subjects had a 3-second retention interval, the other half an 18-second retention interval. If short-term memory decays in 18 seconds, then the second group should have had trouble remembering the item. If there is no decay of memory, then both groups should be able to remember the item equally well. The latter prediction was correct. Both groups were then given additional items, and only when the retention interval was 18 seconds did retention decline with repeated number of items given. Presumably, because of proactive inhibition, a memory deficit occurred only at the longer retention interval and only after a number of items had been given.

One reason we have chosen to review the classic Keppel and Underwood experiment is to highlight again the importance of deciding whether to use a *between-subject* or *within-subject design*. The results using the within-subject design could have supported both the decay and the interference theory of memory. A second experiment had to be done to determine which theory was correct. In this case it was a matter of using a between-subject design to solve the conflict between the two theories. The second reason we reviewed this experiment is because it is an example of a **crucial experiment**. Experiments are called crucial experiments if they are designed to test which of two theories is correct when they make different predictions (crucial experiments have been done in every subdiscipline of psychology, not just in the area of memory). To be a crucial experiment, one theory has to predict one outcome and the other has to predict a different outcome. Since an experiment can only have one outcome, it will support one theory and not the other one.

Crucial Experiment: An experiment to test which of two competing theories is correct.

Although the use of the word *crucial* suggests that one experiment can discredit a given theoretical viewpoint or allow us to determine which of two competing theories is correct, experiments with such influence are the exception. Instead, when a given experiment does not support a theory, the theory is far more likely to be refined and modified rather than discarded as totally without merit. Nevertheless, although controversial, the concept of a crucial experiment is useful. When you read published papers, try to determine if they report results of experiments designed to test predictions of two theories that conflict. If you learn about two opposing theories, see if you can design an experiment to test which theory is correct.

There are many other interesting research designs used to study both long-term and short-term memory, as well as other types of transfer, but they are beyond the scope of this chapter. They are, however, likely to be covered in a course specifically devoted to the topic of memory.

Summary

Transfer occurs when learning in one situation influences performance in another situation. Transfer can be positive or negative, and is measured by comparing the performance of a control group that receives training on an unrelated task that can provide only general transfer (transfer unrelated to specific stimulus and response similarities). If subjects are asked to recall the first task (retroactive design) or asked to recall the second task (proactive design), the other task can either hurt recall (interference or inhibition) or help (facilitation). The article we included tested transfer between solving algebra problems or banking problems on subsequent ability to solve banking problems.

Key Terms

Crucial Experiment, p. 370   Proactive Design, p. 369
Filler Items, p. 363   Protocol Analysis, p. 364
Nonsense Syllables, p. 367   Retroactive Design, p. 368

Chapter Exercises

1. Why would Bassok have been unable to conclude anything about transfer if she had included only the group given banking problems in Phase 2?

2. What additional control groups do you think would be interesting to include in future studies like the one done by Bassok?

3. Bassok mentioned in the Abstract that protocol analyses showed that subjects were helped when told that what they had previously learned could be helpful. What is protocol analysis?

C H A P T E R

20

Research in Neuropsychology

The brain processes the stimuli that our senses detect, stores what we have learned, and controls our behavior. Researchers in the subdiscipline of neuropsychology (also called biopsychology and neuroscience) seek to discover how the brain accomplishes such tasks. The article chosen to serve as a model for neuropsychological research (Lobaugh, Greene, Grant, Nick, & Amsel, 1989), concerns the role that two areas of the brain, the hippocampus and amygdala, play in learning when to expect reward or no reward in a runway task (running down a long narrow box). The experiments incorporate many of the controls that are indispensable to research in neuropsychology. The basic strategy, articulated in Basic Question 4, is to introduce a change into an otherwise normal context (a normally functioning brain). The "change" is to remove components that are normally functional units of the brain, and thereby disrupt the hypothetical role these structures have in mediating the learning of reward expectation.

Since purposely inflicting selective brain damage in human subjects is unethical, the researchers chose to use laboratory rats. Specifically, the researchers wanted to know if rats with damage to the hippocampus and amygdala could retain the memory of what happened on a previous learning trial and use that information to predict what would happen on the next trial. The researchers removed these two structures from the brains of baby rats (rat pups), and they measured the ability of the surgically altered pups to learn by measuring their running speed in the runway task. They rewarded the pups on every other trial and measured how many experiences (trials) with reward followed by a trial with no reward it took for the animals to learn to predict the reward outcome on the next trial—that is, to run slowly after rewarded trials and fast after nonrewarded trials (a patterning effect).

In addition to determining if removal of the hippocampus and amygdala would influence learning (Basic Question 4), the authors also manipulated a second independent variable: the time between trials. Therefore, the experiment was executed as a factorial design (chapter 14; Basic Question 7).

Please pause at this point to read the article on pages 376–79, then return to the following discussion.

Discussion of Techniques and Controls in the Lobaugh et al. Study

The description of the experimental procedures in the Method section may have seemed unusually detailed, but research reports are supposed to provide enough information to permit readers to replicate the original experiment exactly, should they so desire. An exact replication is possible only if the authors include every detail of the experimental method.

General Method

Subjects

Rat strain

Strain refers to the bloodlines or pedigrees within a species, and there are different genetic strains of rats, just as there are different strains (breeds) of dogs. Like dogs, different rat strains are noted for specific behavioral characteristics. For example, some strains (Long-Evans) tend to be more emotional and aggressive than others (Sprague-Dawley).

Psychologists do research with many strains of rats, and different strains are available through suppliers. For example, the rats used in this experiment were from Holtzman, a supplier in Madison, Wisconsin. Many laboratories obtain breeding stock from suppliers to establish their own colony so they can control all aspects of the animals' life cycle. Such control is especially necessary when doing research with rat pups, because it is neither practical nor desirable to ship newborn rat pups from a supplier to a research site.

Litters

Rats usually give birth to between 4 and 12 pups, but sometimes they give birth to more pups than they can properly nourish (in rare instances, as many as 20). They have 12 teats with which to nurse their young, but not all teats are necessarily functional. To reduce the risk of malnourishment, it is common procedure for researchers to reduce the size of ("cull") inordinately large litters to 8 or fewer pups.

It is generally undesirable to assign all the pups from one litter to one treatment condition and those from another to another treatment condition, because there are likely to be systematic genetic differences among litters as well as differences in the pups' rearing environment. If the data revealed behavioral differences between treatment conditions, it would be impossible to determine if they originated from pre-existing systematic differences between litters or if they were a result of the treatment. The between-treatment differences that are evident in the data of such an experiment would be *confounded* (chapter 1, p. 7) with any systematic differences that may exist between litters.

Many researchers randomly assign one rat from each litter to each group in the study (a **split-litter design**). This controls for variability between litters by balancing the contribution of each litter evenly across all groups. The design of Experiment I includes six groups, so, to use the split-litter design, six rats would have to be selected from each litter. Although the authors could have used this design, they instead used only three rat pups from each litter and randomly assigned the pups to three of the six groups. The net effect of the latter assignment procedure is to randomize the litter effect and thereby balance its contribution evenly among the treatment conditions.

Split-litter Design: An equal number of rats from a litter are randomly assigned to each group in the study.

Day-night cycle

Animal colonies are usually placed on an artificial day-night cycle (Lobaugh et al. used 14 hours with lights on and 10 with lights off, controlled by automatic timers). Without a controlled day-night cycle the animals, which are housed in climate-controlled windowless laboratories, would not have the normal behavioral and physiological circadian rhythms.

Surgery

Anesthesia

Animal subjects, like humans, are always anesthetized during surgery so that they will not feel any pain (chapter 16). Using information from published sources, the researcher must adjust the anesthesia dose to the weight of the animal to avoid administering too light (insufficient pain relief) or too heavy (potentially lethal) a dose.

Lesions

There are a number of ways to interfere with the normal functioning of a part of the brain. One method is lesioning, which involves damaging the tissue. Lobaugh et al. used electrolytic lesioning. The first step in the lesioning procedure is to anesthetize the rat and place it in a special head restrainer called a stereotaxic instrument. In addition to being able to hold the head firmly in place, the instrument holds an electrode — a thin piece of wire that is insulated along its entire length

Behavioral Neuroscience
1989, Vol. 103, No. 6, 1159–1167

Patterned (Single) Alternation in Infant Rats After Combined or Separate Lesions of Hippocampus and Amygdala

Nancy J. Lobaugh, Paul L. Greene, Mitzie Grant, Teresa Nick, and Abram Amsel
University of Texas at Austin

The role of the developing hippocampus and the amygdala on patterned (single) alterna-tion (PA) in the infant rat was investigated in 4 experiments. In Experiments 1 and 2, pups were given 2 bilateral electrolytic hippocampal lesions or sham surgeries at 10 or 11 days of age and were trained 6 days later in a straight runway. In Experiment 1, there were 120 trials in 1 day, with an 8-, and 15-, or a 30-s intertrial interval (ITI). PA learning occurred in lesion and sham pups at the 8- and 15-s ITIs, but it was reduced in both groups at the 30-s ITI. In Experiment 2, training was extended to 240 trials over 2 days, with a 30- or 60-s ITI. Sham and lesion pups showed PA at the 30-s ITI, but the emergence of PA was delayed in the lesion pups at the 60-s ITI. In Experiment 3, amygdaloid lesions had no effect on PA learning at the 8-s ITI. However, when pups with hippocampal and amygdaloid lesions were trained at the 8-s ITI, the emergence of PA was delayed, and its size was reduced (Experiment 4). The results of these experiments argue for a role of the hippocampus in PA learning at long ITIs and suggest that, even in 16-day-old pups exposed to an 8-s ITI, the combined hippocampal and amygdaloid lesion produces a deficit greater than either the hippocampal or the amygdaloid lesion. The results are discussed in relation to current theories that distinguish between 2 levels of memory function.

General Method

Subjects

The subjects were Holtzman Sprague-Dawley rat pups bred in our laboratory. Behavioral testing occurred during the lights-on portion of a 14:10-hr light–dark cycle (on at 8:00 a.m.). The day of birth was designated Day 0, and the litters were culled to 8 pups (4 males and 4 females) on Day 3. No more than 3 animals from a litter were used, and subjects were assigned to one of two experimental condi-tions: sham and lesion.

Surgery

All pups chosen for lesion surgery were either 10 or 11 days old and weighed between 25 and 35 g. They were anesthetized with intraperiton-eal injections of Equithesin (0.0025 ml/g body weight). Bilateral electrolytic lesions were made in hippocampus or amygdala or both, with bregma as the reference point. Two placements were used for the hippocampal lesion, and the coordinates (in millimeters) were $P = -2.3$, $L = \pm 2.4$, and $V = -2.7$ for the first, and $P = -3.6$, $L = \pm 3.9$, and $V = -3.4$ for the second. Amygdaloid lesions were made with the following coordinates: $P = -0.8$, $L = \pm 4.3$, and $V = -6.5$. The current was 1.8 mA for 14 s. The surgical treatment in the sham-operated and lesion animals was identical except that the electrode was not lowered in the shams. After surgery, pups were allowed to recover in a plastic holding box kept at nest temperature (31–33°C) with a heating pad. Collodion was applied to the sutures of the pups to minimize cannibalization by the dams. Pups were returned to their litters when they responded to a tail pinch (approximately 5 hr after surgery).

Histology

Perfusion was performed at 21 days of age with phosphate-buffered formalin. All brains were transferred to a 30% sucrose–formalin solution 3 days before sectioning. Frozen coronal sections, 20–40 μm thick, were taken through the extent of the lesion. Every 10th section was mounted and stained with cresyl violet for subsequent analysis. The size and location of the damage was examined in five matched sections through the lesion, with the atlas of Sherwood and Timiras (1970) for reference.

Hippocampus. The percentage of undamaged hippocampus was calculated for lesion brains, relative to shams, by tracing the area of intact hippocampus in each of five sections for each subject with a bit pad (Summagraphics Model MM1201) connected to an IBM-AT. The sections chosen corresponded to A3.5, A2.6, A1.6, A1.2, and A0.8 in the atlas of Sherwood and Timiras (1970). Areas of undamaged hippocampus, damaged hippocampus, and damaged cortex were traced separately. An estimate of the total area for each tissue type in the hippocampus was made by summing the areas of the five sections. The mean area of the hippocampus for the sham pups was designated as 100%, and a proportion of undamaged hippocampus from lesion pups relative to that from shams was calculated.

Overall, approximately 59.3% of the hippocampus remained on the hippocampal lesion groups in Experiments 1 and 2 for each of the five sections analyzed (Table 1). The greatest damage was to the anterodorsal areas (A3.5 and A2.6; 33.65% and 51.85% remaining, respectively), whereas the posteroventral areas A1.2 and A0.8 were least damaged (72.25% and 80.15% remaining, respectively). Animals were excluded from behavioral analysis only if there was significant extrahippocampal damage or infection. The hippocampal damage in the pups from Experiment 4, which received combined lesions of hippocampus and amygdala, is represented in Figure 1.

Table 1
Mean Percentage of Remaining Hippocampus

Section	M	Range[a]
A3.5	33.65	7.6–66.3
A2.6	51.85	3.5–92.1
A1.6	61.95	41.4–86.5
A1.2	72.25	36.0–98.6
A0.8	80.15	40.5–116.2
Total[b]	59.3	34.8–86.1

Note. The section identifications are from Sherwood and Timiras (1970).
[a]Range of the percentage of tissue remaining for each section in Experiments 1 and 2.
[b]Mean percentage of hippocampal tissue remaining across the five sections.

Amygdala. Sections chosen for analysis corresponded to the following plates for 21-day-old rats: A5.3, A4.7, A4.1, A3.5, and A2.9 (Sherwood & Timiras, 1970). Areas of damage were superimposed upon a representative sham brain to determine which amygdala nuclei were most consistently damaged by the lesion, which is often of greater relevance to behavioral findings than the actual size of the lesion (Sarter & Markowitsch, 1985).

The extent of damage in pups with amygdaloid lesions (Experiments 3 and 4) is shown in Figure 2. The damage was largest in the anterior regions of the amygdala (A5.3–A4.1). In these sections, there was consistent damage to the central, lateral, basolateral, and basomedial nuclei, with no damage to the medial nucleus. In the more posterior sections (A3.5 and A2.9), damage was restricted to portions of the basal nuclei and lateral nucleus. In Experiment 3, 5 lesion pups were found to have unilateral amygdaloid damage in the anterior sections; in all cases, the opposite placement was in the cortex. In Experiment 4, 4 pups had damage anterior to the amygdala proper in the area amygdaloidea anterior (A5.9; Sherwood & Timiras, 1970), with slight unilateral damage to the lateral portion of the medial forebrain bundle in 1 animal. Infection was found only in 1 lesion pup, which was not run because it did not gain weight. The

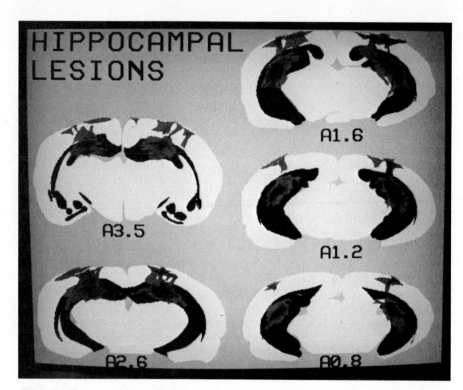

Figure 1. Computer-generated reconstruction of hippocampal damage. (Dark gray to black areas indicate regions of greatest overlap across subjects, light gray areas are regions of little or no overlap. See Plate A.)

sham and lesion pups that did not attach or acquire the approach response did not differ in terms of lesion size or placement from the other animals in their treatment group.

Apparatus

A Plexiglas runway consisted of a start box (13 × 7.5 × 12 cm), alley (60 × 7.5 × 12 cm), and goal box, covered with black cardboard on the outside and enclosed with hinged, clear Plexiglas lids. The goal box was bisected into front (8 × 27 × 12 cm) and rear (15 × 27 × 12 cm) chambers by a metal gate. The alley segment of the runway was divided into three 20-cm sections by photocell circuitry to provide three measures of the approach response, start,

run, and goal times, measured to the nearest 0.01 s. Odors were expelled from the runway by a 10-cm exhaust fan mounted on the rear wall of the goal box. During the ITI, the pup was placed in a Plexiglas box (12 × 12 × 18 cm), with sides covered with cardboard, which was located next to the runway.

General Procedure

Deprivation. All pups were tested 6 days after surgery. Twenty-four hours before the start of training, pups were removed from their litters and deprived of food and water. Each pup was weighed, then placed in a 14 × 10 × 14.5 cm compartment of a clear Plexiglas holding box that was heated to nest temperature (31–33 °C).

Each pup was fitted with an oral cannula 18–24 hr before the first session according to the procedure of Hall and Rosenblatt (1977). After cannulation, the pups were returned to the holding box for the remainder of the deprivation period.

Goal-box training. To familiarize the pups with the training situation, they received goal-box training 12–14 hr before the beginning of runway training. All pups to be run were placed in the empty runway for ten min with all doors open, allowing access to the runway and goal box. The pups were then moved to the empty goal box for an additional 10 min. After this period, each pup was placed into the goal box with an anesthetized dam and was given three 0.03-ml infusions of infant diet (Messer, Thoman, Terrasa, & Dallman, 1969) via a Harvard Apparatus infusion pump (Model 906) while suckling a nipple. The pup was first placed directly on the dam's ventrum and, after attaching to a nipple, was given the first milk infusion. For the next two infusions, it was placed in the front section of the goal box and had to crawl toward and attach to the dam. This eliminated the need to give "priming" trials before the start of the first session of runway training (see Experiment 3, Method).

Runway training. Immediately before each session, the pups were weighed after their bladders were voided. A lactating dam was anesthetized with pentobarbital sodium (Nembutal: 32.5 mg/kg body weight) and returned to her litter until the start of the session so that her nipples would be well suckled. Training consisted of 120 trials per day. There were 40 trials in each of three sessions, spaced 4 hr apart. All trials began by placing the pup in the start box facing the door. When the pup passed through the third photobeam (60 cm from the start-box door), a 30-s goal-box period commenced. If a pup remained in any of the three alley segments for more than 60 s, it was gently pushed into the goal box, and a time of 60 s was recorded for that segment and all subsequent segments. On reward trials, the gate bisecting the goal box

rose automatically, permitting access to the anesthetized dam. When the pup attached to a nipple, 0.03 ml of infant diet was infused over a 9-s period. On nonreward trials, the pup was prevented from reaching the dam and was confined to the outer portion of the goal box. At the end of each trial, the pup was placed in the ITI box for its assigned ITI.

Data analysis. Start, run, goal, and total times were converted to speeds (centimeters per second) for data analysis, and repeated-measures analyses of variance (ANOVAS) were performed on each of the four speed measures. Newman-Keuls post hoc tests were performed as appropriate.

Experiment 1

In Experiment 1, 16- to 17-day-old pups were trained to pattern their responses to a single-alternating schedule of reward and nonreward at an 8-, a 15-, or a 30-s ITI. At each ITI, the subjects either had hippocampal lesions or were sham-operated controls.

Method

Subjects. There were 38 lesion and 31 sham pups in this experiment. Seventeen animals, 8 shams and 9 lesions, with acceptable histological results, would not run or attach to the lactating dam for reward, and they were dropped from the study. Data from 4 additional lesion animals were not used, 2 because of incorrect lesion placements and 2 because of postoperative subdural infections. This left 25 lesion and 23 sham pups.

Procedure. Runway training consisted of 120 trials, and ITI was 8, 15, or 30 s.

Data analysis. For this experiment, there were two between-groups variables: group (sham and lesion) and ITI length (8, 15, and 30 s). The 120 acquisition trials were analyzed in 12 blocks of five trials of each trial type (reward and nonreward).

except for the tip. Using the stereotaxic instrument and guided by a published anatomical map of the brain (a brain atlas), the researcher can insert the electrode with great precision into the part of the brain to be lesioned.

The brain atlas for the laboratory rat indicates how many millimeters one must move the electrode to the right (lateral, L), back (posterior, P), and down (vertical, V) from a zero reference point to place the tip in the part of the brain one intends to lesion. One such zero point is an easily noticed anatomical highlight on the top of the skull. Two suture lines (where the bones of the skull join) cross on the top of the skull. One suture line goes from ear to ear and the other runs from front to back. Where the lines cross, a crude +, called the bregma, is formed. Using the coordinates from the atlas, the surgeon drills a small hole in the skull the correct distance from the zero point. The electrode is then placed on the surface of the brain and lowered just enough to place its tip in the targeted brain structure. A small amount of electrical current is then put through the electrode to destroy the cells at its tip. The amount and duration of current necessary to obtain lesions of various dimensions have been worked out in prior research and are available from published sources.

The brain is bilaterally symmetrical, so the brain has two hippocampi. Thus, the authors had to make bilateral lesions to destroy the hippocampus in both the left and right brain hemispheres. After making each lesion, the researcher removed the electrode and closed the incision. When the procedure was complete, the rat was removed from the stereotaxic instrument and placed on a heating pad to maintain body temperature. (Some anesthetics disrupt body-temperature regulation and can lead to hypothermia.) Once normal reflexes return (a response to a tail pinch, for example) the rat is sufficiently recovered from the anesthesia to be returned to its mother.

Sham controls

The procedure for lesioning an animal introduces a complex set of experiences that have the potential to alter behavior for reasons unrelated to the lesion itself. The only way to ensure that apparent experimental effects are truly due to a lesion and not some other aspect of the treatment administration (stress from the surgery, anesthesia, postoperational discomfort, or maternal reaction to the surgically modified pup) is to include a **sham-operated control group** in the experiment against which to compare the lesioned subjects. The sham control group receives the same treatment as the lesioned group, except that no electrical current is passed through the electrode, and the brain remains fully functional. For their sham-operated control group, these authors did not lower the electrode, although some researchers do.

Sham-operated Control Group: The group in brain-lesion experiments that receives the same treatment as the lesioned group, except that no lesion is made and the brain remains fully functional.

Histology

After behavioral testing of the rats has been completed, the next step is to determine if the correct part of the brain was lesioned. That is, the anatomical location of the lesion must be verified through histological analysis. The lesioned animals are anesthetized and their brains are saturated (perfused) with a tissue preservative (usually formalin). The brain is then carefully removed from the skull and made firm by freezing it or embedding it in paraffin. It is then cut into very thin slices at the presumed location of the lesion. A microtome, a knife that advances in small steps much like a meat slicer at the grocery store, takes slices of tissue so thin that light can easily pass through them. These slices are then mounted on microscope slides and are stained to highlight the structures in the tissue. The last step is to verify the site of the lesion by reading the slides under a microscope. The article describes how damaged and undamaged portions of the brain were traced, and subjects who had lesions in inappropriate anatomical locations were eliminated from the study. Authors frequently present pictures of the lesions taken from microscope slides and report a calculation of the percentage of the targeted area remaining (see Figure 1 in the reprinted article).

Apparatus

A runway is a long narrow box. A start box is at one end and a goal box is at the other end. The rat's task is to run to the goal box upon being released from the start box. These authors built their own runway and, as they should, report the exact dimensions and features of the apparatus so that other interested researchers can build one just like theirs. To measure the speed of running down the runway, photocells are wall-mounted in the beginning, middle, and end of the runway. Across from the photocell is a light. When the rat crosses through the light beam it blocks the light from reaching the photocell. This triggers a relay, which starts a clock. When the rat crosses the next photobeam, the clock stops, and the time taken to cross that section of the runway is recorded. The authors reported that the clock was accurate to the nearest 0.01 second.

To make sure that rats do not use odors in the goal box as a stimulus for drawing them to it, a fan draws the air out of the goal box and away from the runway chamber. A separate box, called the intertrial interval (ITI) box, was used to house the rats in between runway trials.

General Procedure

Deprivation

If a food reward is used, researchers usually make the subjects hungry prior to testing. In this experiment the pups were not allowed to nurse for 24 hours prior to testing in the runway.

Reward

Experimenters usually use small, uniform, commercially available food pellets to reward adult rats. Rat pups, however, drink milk. In earlier work in this research area the pup's reward was suckling on a nipple of a mother rat who was placed at the end of the runway. She was anesthetized so that she would remain still and was treated with a drug to promote the release of milk from the nipple. This method could not be relied upon to produce a constant amount of milk reward from trial to trial. To gain precise control over the amount of milk delivered as a reward, researchers began using a new technique. A small tube (oral cannula) is placed in the pup's mouth. This tube is then attached to a pump, which infuses a predetermined amount of milk formula into the mouth of the pup. As the pup attaches to the nipple of the adult female, 0.03 ml of an infant diet is delivered through the cannula. The researchers assume that the mother rats, who were well suckled by other rat pups prior to placement in the runway, do not supplement the controlled volume of infant diet with their natural milk. The authors provide a reference that describes the infant formula.

Goal-box and runway training

Rats frequently react to a novel environment by not eating, drinking, or moving around. Therefore some preliminary training is necessary to acclimate the subjects to the runway prior to actual testing to minimize the novelty of the apparatus. To make their Method section complete, the researchers described in detail the procedures for runway training, including how many trials they administered per session, how long they left the rat in the goal box, the size of the reward, and the ITI length.

Data analysis

Before analyzing experimental data, a square root, logarithm, arcsine, or reciprocal transformation is sometimes done so the data will conform to certain assumptions (such as a normal distribution of data values) of the intended statistical analysis. The distribution of time scores is typically not normal, so time is converted to speed by dividing the distance by the number of seconds needed to travel the distance (centimeters/second). To determine if the groups differed either early or late in training, the experimenters evaluated the Groups X Trials interaction with an analysis of variance (ANOVA) of the speed scores. The ANOVA was a repeated measures analysis because the same subjects were tested on each trial (chapter 14).

Experiment 1

Method

In this study the experimenters had to eliminate a large number of subjects because they did not run or drink in the runway apparatus. Experimenters must report how many subjects they eliminate from an experiment and why they were eliminated in order to convince the reader that the subjects who were retained do not constitute a *biased sample* (chapter 7, p. 114). For example, if most of the eliminated subjects had been in the lesioned group, it would be natural to suspect that their failure to run was a consequence of their being lesioned. The numbers of animals who had to be discarded in the lesioned and sham-operated control groups were almost equal (9 versus 8), so the treatment apparently did not, by itself, eliminate running behavior.

Additional Techniques and Control Issues in Neuropsychology

In discussing features of the Lobaugh et al. article, we described many of the control issues that must be addressed in experiments that use electrolytic lesioning to treat subjects. These included establishing a group of sham-operated controls, the administration and monitoring of anesthesia, and the use (in general terms) of the stereotaxic instrument, a brain atlas, and histological verification of lesion sites. There are, however, many other methods neuropsychologists use to study how the brain controls behavior: ablations (lesions), electrical stimulation, electrical recording, chemical stimulation, and chemical recording. Each of these methods has limitations, so researchers apply the principle of **converging operations**. That is, they attempt to show that many different research methods yield data that are consistent with the same conclusion. When several different methodologies yield data that are consistent in their support of a single hypothesis, we can be optimistic that we have discovered a way in which the brain controls behavior. We will now briefly review some of these other techniques and control issues.

Converging Operations: Establishing that different research methods yield data consistent with the same conclusion.

Ablation

In addition to using the electrolytic technique described earlier, an experimenter can lesion brain tissue by cutting, sucking out (aspiration), heating, freezing, or applying certain chemicals to brain tissue.

Ablation controls

Regardless of the lesioning technique used, all lesion experiments must incorporate the use of anesthesia to eliminate pain, sham-operated controls to provide an appropriate reference group against which to compare the lesioned group, and histology to verify the site of the lesion. Because the relatively recent development of the electron microscope permits viewing much smaller anatomical features than does the light microscope, researchers can now study the effects of very tiny brain lesions.

Lesions in humans

Because of ethical restrictions, we cannot evaluate the behavioral consequences of lesioning the brains of humans using the experimental method. We cannot randomly assign humans to be lesioned, or even sham-lesioned, but we can collect data from opportunistic sources and use ex post facto data to demonstrate an *association* between specific types of brain damage and behavioral consequences. For example, some humans suffer brain lesions from being victims of accidents or violence, or during surgery to remove a tumor, blood clot, aneurysm, epileptic focus, or similar circumstance. With the relatively recent invention of CAT scans (computerized axial tomography), PET scans (positron emission tomography), and MRI (magnetic resonance imaging) techniques, it is possible to determine what parts of the brain are missing or nonfunctional while the subject is still alive. Prior to using these techniques, researchers could study the behavioral deficits in head-injured human subjects, but they had to wait for the death of the subject and a postmortem examination to verify the locus and extent of the brain damage.

Testing humans with lesions is very popular with researchers interested in finding out what parts of the brain are important for short-term memory, long-term memory, and cognitive functions (thinking and reasoning processes). Researchers compare the behavior of people with brain lesions either to *norms* from the population (chapter 10, p. 169), to control subjects randomly selected from the population, or, if behavioral data happened to have been recorded for lesioned subjects prior to their misfortune, to changes in the behavior of individual subjects (*pretest-posttest design without a control group*, chapter 12, p. 206). As pointed out above, such data reveal association only. The absence of random assignment of humans to lesioned and nonlesioned groups precludes a causal interpretation of the connection between a given degree and type of brain damage and changes in behavior. Nevertheless, when experimental results from animal research correspond with the ex post facto data from research with humans, researchers are confident that they can infer a causal connection between behavioral changes in humans and the specific form and degree of brain damage they suffer.

Electrical Stimulation

When we remove a part of the brain, we expect to disrupt a certain behavior. When we electrically stimulate that part of the brain instead of removing it, we expect the electrical stimulation to initiate a behavior. To prepare an animal for electrical stimulation of its brain, we go through the same procedure described earlier for lowering an electrode into the brain. After insertion into the targeted brain locus, the electrode is attached to an electrical plug that is secured to the top of the skull with screws and a special type of glue. The skin is then sewed securely around the plug. A few days after the animal recovers from the anesthesia, the plug is attached to an electrical stimulator and a very small amount of current is applied. It is important that the current be weak, so that instead of damaging the cells at the tip of the electrode, the current stimulates them to fire (do you remember from your biology classes what a nerve cell does when it fires?).

In vitro (as opposed to **in vivo**): Literally, in the test tube. Studying live tissue outside the body.

It is also possible to use **in vitro** (as opposed to **in vivo**) techniques to study brain function. An example of an in vitro preparation would be to stimulate fresh brain tissue and record its response while it is being kept alive in a special solution. Researchers use the in vitro technique to study synaptic transmission (how brain cells communicate with each other), how memories are stored, and the influence of chemicals on these brain functions. One consequence of learning how cells communicate with each other could be a better understanding of diseases that involve memory loss (e.g., Altzheimer's disease).

Electrical stimulation controls

By measuring the behavior of a subject before, during, and after electrical brain stimulation, the researcher can use the subject as its own control. At the end of the experiment a larger amount of electricity is delivered through the electrode to destroy the cells at its tip, and histology is used to verify the electrode's location.

Electrical stimulation in humans

Sometimes, for legitimate medical reasons, even humans have electrodes implanted in their brains. For example, people who suffer from narcolepsy (inability to stay awake) can provide themselves electrical stimulation to the "wake" center by means of an electrode, which enables them to function well enough to carry on a near-normal life. Electrical stimulation of certain areas of the brain can also be used to reduce or eliminate intractable pain (see Kumar, Wyant, & Nath, 1990).

Electrical Recording

The firing of a brain cell is an electrochemical phenomenon, and the rate, duration, and intensity of firing varies as a function of the subject's behavior. The same electrode a researcher implants to stimulate a portion of the brain can also be used to record electrical activity in surrounding brain tissue.

It is possible to measure the electrical activity of a single cell (single-unit recording), or from a group of cells, by implanting an electrode so small that its uninsulated tip is confined to a very small area, such as inside a single cell (intracellular recording) or next to it (extracellular recording). It is also possible to record from a large area of the brain without doing any surgery. The technician places macroelectrodes (small circular disks) on various parts of the scalp using electrode paste to insure a firm contact between the electrode and the skull. The written record of the electrical activity of the brain is called an electroencephalogram (EEG).

Many subdisciplines in psychology use the EEG for research purposes. For example, researchers have shown that different EEG wave patterns are present during different levels of sleep and when a person is dreaming. Also, abnormal EEG patterns can be used by clinical psychologists to diagnose brain dysfunctions. Evoked potentials are similar to EEGs, except the recorded brain-wave patterns are in response to a given external stimulus such as a light or sound. Evoked potentials are also used for clinical diagnosis, and have been used to test the neurological effects of toxic chemicals in both animals and humans.

Electrical recording controls

When electrical recording is used for experimental research, subjects are tested under different treatments and changes in electrical brain activity are recorded. Either between-subject or within-subject designs are appropriate. Electrical recording is also used in ex post facto research. For example, recent research indicates that sons of alcoholic fathers and sons of nonalcoholic fathers have different brain waves (see Ehlers & Schuckit, 1990).

Chemical Stimulation

Studying the effects of drugs on human and animal behavior is a very active research area, especially since drug abuse has become a serious social problem. Drugs are frequently administered by injection, and researchers use various routes of administration, depending on how rapidly they wish the drug to be absorbed. Intraperitoneal (i.p.) means the subject is injected in the peritoneum (abdominal cavity), intramuscular (i.m.) into muscle (the thigh), intravenous (i.v.) into a vein, and subcutaneous (s.c.) under the skin. An i.v. injection results in the most rapid drug response, whereas an i.m. injection results in substantially slower absorption of the drug into the bloodstream.

Some injected substances are effective only if they are administered using the proper route. Some can even be lethal if injected incorrectly. If you observe doctors or nurses giving i.m. injections to a patient, notice that they withdraw the plunger slightly before pushing it. This is a check to make sure the tip of the needle is not in a blood vessel.

It is also possible to place an experimental drug directly in an animal's food or water supply. Sometimes drugs have an undesirable taste, which is inferred when subjects eat or drink less. Adding sugar frequently eliminates this problem but introduces the problem of evaluating the possible effects of the sugar alone (the experiment must include control subjects that are given the sugar without the chemical). Drugs can also be administered through a gastric tube (see chapter 10, p. 173). Humans frequently take medication in pill form, and control subjects are given a *placebo* pill (chapter 4, p. 53).

The injection, feeding/drinking, and pill procedures have limitations. They can only be used to test drugs that cross the blood-brain barrier, a concept that refers to the inability of certain chemicals (especially toxins) circulating in the blood to access brain tissue. In addition, the chemicals that do cross the blood-brain barrier typically affect many parts of the brain. This makes it impossible to determine the part(s) of the brain being influenced by the drug and to link the drug effects on specific nerve cells to changes in behavior.

Fortunately, it is possible to place drugs directly into the brain and thus bypass the blood-brain barrier. A cannula (thin tube) is implanted into the brain using procedures similar to those used to implant an electrode. After the animal recovers from anesthesia, the researcher passes precisely measured amounts of a chemical through the cannula directly into brain tissue. When the chemical has been totally depleted, a different chemical can be injected.

Chemical stimulation controls

Since injections can cause a small amount of discomfort and bloating, experimental designs must include control subjects who are injected with a placebo. The placebo is the drug vehicle — the fluid in which the drug is dissolved or suspended. The experimental subjects are injected with the drug suspended or dissolved in its vehicle. Saline solution, a vehicle for water-soluble drugs, is slightly salted water that matches the salinity of the water in live tissues. The amount of the drug injected is determined by the weight of the subject, and the researcher reports the amount given in mg/kg (milligrams of the drug per kilogram of body weight).

Both between-subject and within-subject designs are used in drug-behavior research. If the design of the experiment requires that subjects be injected a number of times (if the behavioral test requires multiple trials, or a within-subject design is used), it is important to be sure that the effects of the earlier injections have totally worn off before reinjecting the subject.

Chemical Recording

The brain has a large number of naturally occurring chemicals (neurotransmitters) that control behavior. It is possible to use an implanted cannula to extract these chemicals from the brain following different behavioral tests. A double-barreled micropipette is a special cannula that allows the experimenter to stimulate an area electrically and, at the same time, test which neurotransmitters are released (the method is called microiontophoresis).

Researchers also know that the amounts of different chemicals in the brain are influenced by conditions in the environment. For example, in a classic study done years ago (Krech, Rosenzweig, & Bennett, 1966), rat pups were raised in an enriched or in an impoverished environment. The animals were then sacrificed and the levels of a number of chemicals in different areas of the brain were measured. The brain chemistry of the rats raised in an impoverished environment differed from the brain chemistry of the animals raised in the enriched environment.

Summary

Psychologists use a large number of converging operations to determine how the brain controls behavior: lesions, electrical stimulation, electrical recording, chemical stimulation, and chemical recording. Histology must be done to determine which area of the brain has been influenced, but recently developed techniques (CAT and PET scans, and MRI), can test for changes in the brain in live subjects, including humans.

Key Terms

Converging Operations, p. 383   Sham-operated Control, p. 380
In Vitro, In Vivo, p. 384   Split-litter Design, p. 375

Chapter Exercises

1. It is reported in the abstract that removal of the hippocampus retarded learning how to pattern (run slow after a rewarded trial only), but only if subjects had to remember the outcome of the previous trial for a long time (60 seconds).

    a. Would you predict that electrical stimulation of the hippocampus would make subjects learn to pattern more quickly?

    b. What control group would you use if you tested the effects of electrical stimulation of the hippocampus?

    c. What basic question would you be asking if you did the electrical stimulation experiment?

    d. If we could determine what neurotransmitter was involved in this behavior, would you predict that introducing this chemical into the hippocampus would make the subjects learn to pattern more quickly? If we introduced a chemical that blocked the effects of this neurotransmitter, what results would you predict?

2. Explain the role of histological analysis in neuropsychological research.

3. How could one determine if the hippocampus is involved in patterning behavior in humans without violating ethical guidelines?

CHAPTER

21

Research in Behavioral Toxicology

Exposure to toxic chemicals has been, and for the foreseeable future will continue to be, a threat to the physical and psychological health of all living organisms. Toxic chemicals are everywhere: at home, in the workplace, and in natural surroundings. They are in the air we breathe, the water we drink, the food we eat, and the materials we touch. Man has introduced many poisons into the environment, such as the radioactive waste we put in landfills, the heavy metals we dump in our waterways, the dioxin we release into the air when burning plastic in garbage-burning steam plants, and the radioactivity released into the air by the

Chernobyl nuclear power plant accident. There are also many naturally occurring poisons (toxins) such as the poisons in some species of mushrooms and the venom from creatures that bite and sting.

Usually when we think of the harm that follows exposure to certain chemicals we think of the increased risk of diseases such as cancer and birth defects. Psychologists, however, are discovering that many chemicals, including substances once thought to be harmless, cause changes in the behavior of subjects without any corresponding symptoms of physical illness. The subdiscipline of psychology that is concerned with the behavioral consequences of exposure to toxic chemicals is called behavioral toxicology.

As important as it is to learn about the toxic potential of various chemicals and understand the mechanisms through which they produce their effects, *experimental* behavioral toxicology with human subjects is virtually nonexistent. To do an experiment one would have to manipulate which subjects would and would not be exposed to a potentially harmful chemical. This would, of course, be a violation of *research ethics* (chapter 16), which have been articulated to protect subjects' basic human rights. Thus, human research in the area of behavioral toxicology must, of necessity, be restricted to correlational studies, as when we collect data from subjects who, through unfortunate life experiences, have come in contact with actual or suspected toxins. Such exposures are the *natural treatments* and *selected variables* of correlational research discussed in chapters 3 and 9 as ex post facto variables.

Unlike experimental data, which support a causal interpretation, the results of correlational studies are limited to interpretations of association and risk. Yet, because of the important public health issues involved, many scientists have not been content to hold their interest in behavioral toxicology within the limits of correlational research. They do use the experimental approach, and they do manipulate the subjects' exposure to toxic substances, but with animal subjects rather than humans.

Of course, it is never clear how precisely experimental results from animals generalize to humans. How can we know for sure if human reaction to a toxic chemical is the same as an animal's reaction without also exposing the human to the same poison? Short of doing the ethically forbidden experiment with humans, the best solution to this problem is to show that the cause–effect relationships that emerge from experiments with subhuman species are consistent with the correlational data collected from human subjects.

The first article we have chosen is a report of a correlational study. The findings of the Needleman, Schell, Bellinger, Leviton, and Allred (1990) study reveal that a correlation exists between the amount of lead found in the teeth of six- to seven-year-old children and a number of behaviors at age 18, such as dropping out of high school and impaired eye-hand coordination. The research is in the form of Basic Question 3: Does an association exist between two (or more) variables? Lead level in the teeth is the nonmanipulated independent variable of the study, and scores on a large number of behavioral tests are the dependent variables.

Article 21-2 is a report of an animal experiment designed to test for the behavioral effects of consuming contaminated food (Daly, 1991). The data support the hypothesis that consuming Lake Ontario salmon fillets, which contain a large number of toxic chemicals, affects the behavioral response of laboratory rats to a reduction in the size of an expected food reward. This experimental research is in the form of Basic Question 4: Will introducing subjects to a specific change in an otherwise standard context cause their behavior to change? The inclusion of the word *cause* in the statement of Basic Question 4 affirms its experimental character.

Please pause at this point to read the article on pages 392–95, then return to the following discussion.

Discussion of Techniques and Controls in the Needleman et al. Study

Sample

The children in the original sample were from two school systems located in the greater Boston area in Massachusetts. The subjects were not randomly selected. Instead, their group assignment was determined by a natural treatment: the very high or very low levels of prior lead exposure, as measured in subjects' first (baby) teeth. The high and low lead groups were selected from a larger group of children whose parents were willing to give the researchers at least one of their child's naturally shed first teeth for analysis. The children with high lead levels presumably obtained the lead from the dirt they played in (deposited from the lead in gasoline) and from eating the paint chips peeling from the walls in their older homes. (Household paint is no longer formulated with lead.)

Eleven years after the original test, when the children had grown to young adulthood, the researchers were able to locate 177 of the original 270 subjects in the study. Of these, 132 were willing to resume their participation. Since not all of the 270 original subjects were retested, it is possible that the retested subjects were not representative of the original high and low lead groups. Fortunately, by comparing the smaller sample to the larger original sample on measures taken at six years of age, it is possible to evaluate the representativeness of the retested sample. Indeed, in the section called Results, Selection Bias, the authors point out that the high-lead subjects they retested were not representative: They had lower lead levels than the original group. The direction of the bias that is introduced by the reduction in the original high–low lead difference (the independent variable) is to make it more difficult to show a behavioral difference between the two groups (the dependent variable) associated with the differences in lead level.

At the end of the section called Sample, the authors state that the research design was approved by the review boards at the children's hospitals in Pittsburgh and Boston, which are the hospitals with which the researchers are affiliated, and that the subjects or their parents consented to testing. It is unusual to state in an article that permission was obtained, since *all research must be approved* by the Institutional Review Board (chapter 16).

Classification of Lead Exposure

Calculating a correlation coefficient (r value) reveals the degree of association between the lead-level scores and the corresponding behavioral measures. Since the lead levels were measured for each subject in parts per million (ppm), which is a

Vol. 322   No. 2   THE NEW ENGLAND JOURNAL OF MEDICINE   Jan. 11, 1990

THE LONG-TERM EFFECTS OF EXPOSURE TO LOW DOSES OF LEAD IN CHILDHOOD
An 11-Year Follow-up Report

Herbert L. Needleman, M.D., Alan Schell, M.A., David Bellinger, Ph.D., Alan Leviton, M.D.,
and Elizabeth N. Allred, M.S.

Abstract To determine whether the effects of low-level lead exposure persist, we re-examined 132 of 270 young adults who had initially been studied as primary schoolchildren in 1975 through 1978. In the earlier study, neurobehavioral functioning was found to be inversely related to dentin lead levels. As compared with those we restudied, the other 138 subjects had had somewhat higher lead levels on earlier analysis, as well as significantly lower IQ scores and poorer teachers' ratings of classroom behavior.

When the 132 subjects were re-examined in 1988, impairment in neurobehavioral function was still found to be related to the lead content of teeth shed at the ages of six and seven. The young people with dentin lead levels > 20 ppm had a markedly higher risk of dropping out of high school (adjusted odds ratio, 7.4; 95 percent confidence inter-val, 1.4 to 40.7) and of having a reading disability (odds ratio, 5.8; 95 percent confidence interval, 1.7 to 19.7) as compared with those with dentin lead levels < 10 ppm. Higher lead levels in childhood were also significantly associated with lower class standing in high school, increased absentee-ism, lower vocabulary and grammatical-reasoning scores, poorer hand–eye coordination, longer reaction times, and slower finger tapping. No significant associations were found with the results of 10 other tests of neurobehavioral functioning. Lead levels were inversely related to self-reports of minor delinquent activity.

We conclude that exposure to lead in childhood is associated with deficits in central nervous system functioning that persist into young adulthood. (N Engl J Med 1990; 322:83-8.)

Methods

Sample

The initial sample was chosen from the population of 3329 children enrolled in the first and second grades in the Chelsea and Somer-ville, Massachusetts, school systems between 1975 and 1978. Of this population, 70 percent provided at least one of their shed primary teeth for lead analysis. From this sample of 2335 children, 97 percent of whom were white, we identified 270 from English-speaking homes whose initial dentin lead levels were either > 24 ppm or < 6 ppm. These children (mean age, 7.3 years) underwent an extensive neu-robehavioral examination. More teeth were sub-sequently collected and analyzed, and the subjects whose teeth were discordant with re-spect to lead level according to a priori criteria were excluded from the data analysis. Also excluded from the analysis were children who had not been discharged from the hospital after birth at the same time as their mothers, who had a noteworthy head injury, or who were reported to have had plumbism.[3]

In a later reanalysis, conducted in re-sponse to suggestions from the Environmental Protection Agency,[12] the tooth lead level was treated as a continuous variable. A mean dentin lead level was computed for each subject from all the teeth collected. The exclusionary factors previously used were found not to be related to outcome scores. The subjects initially excluded were therefore not excluded from this follow-up sample.

The 270 subjects tested from 1975 to 1978 constitute the base population for this report. From old research records, telephone directories, town records, and driver's-license rolls, we located 177 subjects. Of these, 132 agreed to participate, and the remaining 45 declined. The subjects were paid $35 each and received travel expenses. Ten subjects tested in 1988 had been excluded from the analysis reported in 1979 because their parents stated at the time of testing that the children had elevated blood lead levels or had undergone chelation for lead poisoning. This group is discussed separately in this report. The mean age of the 132 subjects at the 1988 reexamination was 18.4 years; the mean length of time between the two examinations was 11.1 years. All but four subjects in the current follow-up study were white. No clinical manifestations of lead exposure were recorded in the earlier interviews for the 122 subjects who were not treated with chelating agents.

The research protocol and informed-consent procedures were approved by the institutional review boards of the Children's Hospital of Pittsburgh and the Children's Hospital, Boston. Informed consent was given by all the subjects or their parents.

Classification of Lead Exposure

All the dentin lead levels measured from 1975 through 1977 were used to compute an arithmetic mean lead concentration for each subject. The lead burden was treated in two ways: as an interval variable in linear regressions and as a categorical variable—i.e., high (> 20 ppm), medium (10 to 19.9 ppm), and low (< 10 ppm)—in the logistic regressions described below. Lead levels in venous blood were measured at the time of the reexamination to estimate current exposure. This practice was discontinued after the first 48 subjects were tested, because none had a lead level exceeding 0.34 μmol per liter (7μg per deciliter), well below the Centers for Disease Control's definition of undue lead exposure of 1.25 μmol per liter (25 μg per deciliter).

Behavioral Evaluation

The subjects were evaluated individually by a single examiner, who remained blinded to their lead-exposure status until all the data had been coded and entered into a computer data base. All assessments were carried out in a fixed order; the duration of the testing was about two hours.

Neurobehavioral Evaluation System

The subjects completed an automated assessment battery in which they used a personal computer, joystick, and response key.[13] We selected the following items from the battery for evaluation.

Continuous-performance test.[14]

Symbol–digit substitution, an adaptation of the Wechsler item for computer administration.

Hand–eye coordination. Using a joystick to move the cursor, the subject traced over a large sine wave generated on the monitor screen; deviations from the line (root mean square error) were recorded.

Simple visual-reaction time. Subjects pressed the response key when an O appeared on the screen; the interval before the stimulus was varied randomly.

Finger tapping. The subject pressed a response button as many times as possible during a 10-second period: both hands were tested.

Pattern memory. The subject was presented with a computer-generated pattern formed by a 10-by-10 array of dark and bright elements. After a brief exposure, the subject was presented with three patterns, only one of which was identical to the original pattern. The number of correct responses and the length of time to the pattern choice were recorded.

Pattern comparison. The subject was presented with three computer-generated patterns on the 10-by-10 array. Two were identical, and one differed slightly from the other two. The subject was required to select the non-matching pattern.

Serial-digit learning. The subject was presented with a string of 10 digits, then asked to enter the string into the computer. After an error, the same stimulus was presented, and the second trial began.

Vocabulary. For each of 25 words, the subject chose the word most nearly synonymous from a list of four choices.

Grammatical reasoning. The subject was presented with a pair of letters, A and B, whose relative position varied. Then the screen cleared, and the letters were replaced by a sentence that described the order of the letters. The sentence might be active or passive, affirmative or negative, true or false (examples are "A follows B" and "B is not followed by A"). The subject had to choose the correct sentences, and the number of errors was recorded.

Switching attention. The subject was required to choose which key to press in response to three different instructions. In the "side" trials, the subject had to press the key on the same side as the stimulus. In the "direction" trials, the correct choice was the direction in which an arrow pointed. Before each trial in the third set, the subject was told whether to choose the side the arrow was on or the direction in which it pointed.

Mood scales. This test was derived from the Profile of Mood States.[15] Five scores were computed for tension, anger, depression, fatigue, and confusion.

The following tests were also used to evaluate neurobehavioral functioning:

California Verbal Learning Test

The California Verbal Learning Test[16] was used to assess multiple strategies and processes involved in verbal learning and memory. Scores for immediate and delayed recall were also obtained.

Boston Naming Test

In the Boston Naming Test,[17] the subject was presented with 60 pictures in order of increasing difficulty and asked to name the objects shown.

Rey–Osterreith Complex Figure Test

The Rey–Osterreith Complex Figure Test[18] was used to evaluate visual–motor and visual–spatial skills. The subject was asked to copy an abstract geometric figure and then to draw it from memory both immediately and after 30 minutes. Accuracy and organization scores were calculated.

Word-Identification Test

Form B from the Woodcock Reading Mastery Test was used to evaluate reading skill. Grade-equivalency scores were calculated from raw scores. Reading disability was defined as indicated by scores two grade levels below the score expected on the basis of the highest grade completed.

Self-Reports of Delinquency

The subjects completed a structured questionnaire from the National Youth Survey[19] that included scales for minor antisocial behavior and for violent crimes.

Review of School Records

High-school records were obtained for all but two of the subjects tested. Class size and rank, the highest grade completed, and the number of days absent and tardy in the last full semester were recorded. Students who were still in the 11th grade at the time of testing were not included in analyses of the highest grade completed. Class rank was computed as $1 - $ (class rank/class size).

Statistical Analysis

To evaluate whether the participants in this follow-up evaluation were representative of the original cohort, subjects who were tested and not tested in 1988 were compared in terms of variables reported in 1979, including dentin lead levels, covariates not related to lead exposure, teachers' ratings of classroom behavior, and IQ scores. In addition, we carried out separate regressions of dentin lead level against IQ score as measured between 1976 and 1978 for subjects tested and not tested in 1988. We then performed a regression on both groups taken together, entering both a dummy term for participation in the current follow-up (yes or no) and a lead-level-by-participation status term.

To evaluate the relation between early exposure to lead and each of the continuously distributed outcome variables, subjects were classified according to dentin lead-level quartiles, and mean scores, adjusted for covariates, were computed. Ordinary least-squares linear regression, with the mean or log-mean dentin lead level as the main effect, was used to estimate the significance of the relation. Outcomes that were significantly associated with lead exposure in these bivariate analyses were further evaluated by multiple regression analysis. Ten covariates were included in the model. They were the mother's age at the time of the subject's birth, the mother's educational level, the mother's IQ, family size, socioeconomic status (a two-factor Hollingshead index), sex, age at the time of testing, birth order, alcohol use, and whether the subject and the mother left the hospital together after the subject's birth. The lead measure (the mean or the log of the mean) that produced the best-fitted model (highest R^2) is reported. Five of these covariates were employed in the first study of these subjects and shown to be influential. Five others (sex, age at testing, prolonged hospitalization as a neonate,

birth order, and current alcohol use) were added to the model on the basis of prior knowledge of their effects on psychometric function. Logistic-regression analysis was used to model the association of lead level and two outcomes treated categorically (failure to graduate from high school and reading disability). In this analysis, we controlled for the covariates listed above. Two indicator variables were used to represent the three exposure groups. Odds ratios and 95 percent confidence intervals, adjusted for covariates, were computed for the high-lead-level group, with the low-lead-level group used as the reference group.

Results

Selection Bias

The 132 subjects who were retested in 1988 (Table 1) were not representative of the group of 270 subjects tested in 1979. The subjects we retested tended to have slightly lower dentin lead levels, more highly educated families of higher socioeconomic status, and mothers with higher IQs and better obstetrical histories; a higher proportion of the retested subjects were girls. In addition, they had had fewer head injuries and had significantly higher IQ scores and better teachers' ratings as reported in 1979. The slope of the regression of childhood IQ on dentin lead level was steeper in the group not tested in the follow-up study, although the difference from the slope in the group we retested was not statistically significant (F = 1.82, 1,196 df; P = 0.18).

ratio-scaled variable, the Pearson *r* is the appropriate statistic to measure the strength of association. It is also possible to break the lead scores into a number of discrete categories, such as high (> 20 ppm), medium (10 to 19.9 ppm), and low (< 10 ppm). The behavioral data from the three treatment groups may be analyzed with the same ANOVA test we use to analyze the data of experiments (chapter 13), but, because lead level is an ex post facto variable instead of a manipulated variable, we must be careful to limit our interpretation of between-treatment differences to association rather than causality.

Behavioral Evaluation

Blind testing

The method of "blind" testing assures the neutrality of the data collection process by preventing the introduction of any bias that could influence the researcher's perceptions of the subject's behavior (experimenter bias was discussed in chapter 10). Therefore, the researchers who collected behavioral data took steps to ensure that they remained unaware of subjects' lead levels.

Summarizing data before all subjects are tested

Another check against bias requires that researchers not preview incomplete experimental results. Peeking at the results before all the data have been collected can affect the conduct of the study. For example, if, after half the subjects had been tested, it appeared that those with high lead levels were not behaving differently from those with low lead levels, the researcher might lose interest in the study and not test the remaining subjects with equal precision. Similarly, if the researcher became aware of a strong trend in the early data that tended to confirm the researcher's hypothesis, this too could affect the way in which the remaining testing was conducted.

Neurobehavioral Evaluation System (NES)

The authors selected a standard set of behavioral tests rather than making up their own tests. The NES is a series of tests that measure a large number of different behaviors, such as hand-eye coordination and vocabulary, and is administered by a computer. *Computers* are frequently used to present the stimuli to the subject and/ or to record and score the subject's responses, because of its many advantages. The computer presents the stimuli precisely the same way to every subject. It is perfect in timing the stimulus presentations and in recording the responses. There is also no *experimenter bias*, since the computer cannot express expectations to the subject, and no researcher is present during data collection. The disadvantage is that some subjects may not be familiar with computers and may be somewhat apprehensive.

Other behavioral measures

The subjects were asked to fill out a *questionnaire* (chapter 7) on antisocial behavior. Questionnaires are self-reports and are, by definition, subjective rather than objective measures of behavior. Nevertheless, they provide a measure of behavior that is easy to obtain. Checking all school, teacher, and police records for antisocial behavior would be very time-consuming.

Usually, questionnaire data are kept confidential to protect the privacy of subjects. It is impossible, however, in the type of correlational research presented by the present study, to maintain the anonymity of questionnaire responses. The reason is simple. If the researcher did not know the identity of each questionnaire respondent, it would be impossible to pair each subject's lead score with his or her questionnaire data, a step necessary in order to compute a correlation statistic.

One strategy that provides some degree of privacy is to assign each subject a code number. Under the coding system, the researchers who score the responses and do the analyses remain unaware of the subjects' identities. Only one person (not the experimenter) has the name and number codes hidden away. Subjects are probably less honest in their answers when the questionnaire is not anonymous, but there is no way to solve this problem.

The lead study also made use of *archival* data (chapter 6). From an examination of the subjects' high school records, various facts, such as the highest grade completed and absenteeism, were recorded.

Statistical Analysis

Reading this section of the article should convince you that, to be a researcher in the behavioral sciences, it is very important to be well versed in the methods of statistical analysis. If you go to graduate school in psychology to obtain an M.A. or Ph.D. degree, you will probably be required to take between one and three statistics courses as well as to learn how to use one or more of the large computer statistical packages (like SPSS, SAS, BMDP, or MINITAB). The more statistics you remember from your undergraduate courses, the easier graduate school will be, and the easier it will be for you to understand the research articles you read.

For the researchers to achieve their goal, which was to determine the degree of association between lead level in the baby teeth and several measures of adult behavior, it was necessary to consider other influences on adult behavior that have nothing to do with exposure to lead in early life. That is, the researchers had to be careful to avoid the pitfall of judging adult behaviors to be associated with early lead consumption when other independent variables (covariates) might really have been the factors responsible. For example, poor people (low socioeconomic status) are more likely than upper-income people to live in old houses in which leaded paint is both present and peeling. Let us assume that the children who live in substandard housing tend to eat the flakes of leaded paint. At the same time, for a variety of reasons (say, working two jobs to meet expenses) poor people may not be able to help their children with their homework. If one result of the lack of mentoring is that children from poor families are more likely to drop out of school, there would appear to be a correlation between lead level in childhood and dropping out of school in adulthood, when in fact there may really be no relationship between the two. In this example, both high lead levels and a high risk for becoming a high school dropout may both be problems that stem from a third variable (a covariate): the life-style of the socioeconomically disadvantaged.

Fortunately, there is a statistical method, called multiple regression, for measuring the strength of association between the nonmanipulated independent variable (here, lead level measured in childhood) of a correlational study and dependent behavioral measures with the influence of possible covariates removed. (*Multiple regression* was discussed conceptually in chapter 9.) Some of the covariates the authors used included mother's educational level, mother's IQ, family size, socio-economic status, and use of alcohol. These variables were identified as possible covariates because, in the judgment of the study's authors, they could be correlated with both lead level and the highest grade achieved in high school. As such, the covariates could make the correlation between lead level and, say, highest grade achieved in school look high when, in reality, those two variables may be unrelated.

In the present discussion we are centering on the utility of various research methods. But, in case you are curious, with 10 covariates used, the r value Needleman et al. found between lead and highest grade achieved in high school was .56, and the r^2 value was .319. This means that 31.9% of the highest grade achieved (the criterion available) is predictable from the knowledge of lead level in the baby teeth (the predictor variable), and 68.1 percent is not predictable from known lead levels ($1 - .319 = .681$). (See chapter 9, p. 155.)

Please pause at this point to read the article on pages 400–01, then return to the following discussion.

Discussion of Techniques and Control Issues in the Daly Study

The subjects, apparatus, and testing procedures described in the Daly article are very similar to those described in detail in chapter 20.

Method

Fish preparation

Since the type of fish diet is the independent variable of the experiment, the experimenter explained how she obtained the fish, what she did to the fish before feeding them to the laboratory rats, and how much fish she fed to the rats. Only the fillets were used. The skin and fatty body tissues, in which the fish store a large portion of the toxic chemicals they take in, were not used. Presumably, the behavioral changes would have been larger if the whole fish had been fed to the experimental animals.

The same procedure was used to prepare the experimental group's diet of Lake Ontario salmon, and the control group's diet of Pacific Ocean salmon, which contain far lower levels of toxic chemicals.

Subjects and procedure

The laboratory rats that served as subjects were 85 days old, which is young adulthood for the species. They were weighed both before and after feeding them the salmon to provide a general indication of their health. If the toxic chemicals had caused physical illness, the rats fed Lake Ontario salmon presumably would have gained less weight. Since there was no difference in weight gain (reported in the

Results section), there appeared to be no obvious negative impact on physical health from eating Lake Ontario salmon.

The food deprivation schedule was designed to reduce the weight to 80% of the rat's original weight (called ad libitum weight). This results in a hungry rat, but probably one that is no more hungry than a wild rat that must spend large parts of each day foraging for food. A 37-mg pellet is a small reward, but 15 of these pellets is a large reward, and rats run quickly to obtain it. The experimenter assumed that shifting from the 15-pellet reward to the 1-pellet reward is like having a candy machine give you one little Lifesaver when you pushed the lever for a large chocolate candy bar. Psychologists usually think of this as a negative or frustrating event. The magnitude of frustration is reflected in how slowly we approach the candy machine the next time we decide to use it. Similarly, the more frustrated the rats are, the more slowly they approach the goal with the 1-pellet reward when they were previously given a 15-pellet reward.

The experimenter tested the rats for only six trials per day so they would still be very hungry on the last testing trial of each day. Fifteen to 20 minutes after training, the rats were allowed to eat additional food in order to maintain them at 80% of ad libitum weight. The experimenter was "blind" concerning the diet condition of the animals she tested to eliminate any possibility of *experimenter bias*, (chapter 10, p. 177).

Additional Techniques and Control Issues in Behavioral Neurotoxicology

Controlled and Uncontrolled Exposures

In experimental research a precise amount of a toxic chemical is given to each subject. The chemical can be administered using any of the ways drugs can be given (chapter 20, p. 385), such as by injection, in the food or water, or in pill form. In addition, subjects can be placed in an inhalation chamber filled with chemical fumes. For all techniques, control groups that receive only the vehicle holding the chemical must be included in the experiment. For example, when experimental subjects receive a chemical dissolved or suspended in a saline solution, control subjects should be injected with saline alone.

One advantage of the controlled exposure technique is that the researcher can easily vary the amount of the chemical given and determine a **dose-response curve**. That is, by administering a large number of different levels of the chemical (*multiple-treatment design*; chapter 13) the researcher can determine the relationship between the amount of the chemical given (the dose) and the amount of change in the behavior (the response). Frequently, the higher the dose, the larger the behavioral change. Small doses of toxic chemicals usually do not result in behavior different from the behavior of an appropriate control group and are sometimes referred to as "safe." It is, however, controversial to conclude that any dose of a potentially toxic substance can be assumed to be safe. The lack of a difference in behavior between the experimental and control groups may be because the behavioral test was not sensitive enough, or two few subjects were used, resulting in inadequate statistical power (chapter 4, p. 60).

Dose-response Curve: Figure showing the relationship between the amount of the chemical given (the dose) and the amount of change in a behavior (the response).

Neurotoxicology and Teratology, Vol. 13, pp. 449–453.© Pergamon Press plc, 1991. Printed in the U.S.A.   0892-0362/91 $3.00 + .00

Reward Reductions Found More Aversive by Rats Fed Environmentally Contaminated Salmon

HELEN B. DALY

Department of Psychology, State University of New York College at Oswego, Oswego, NY 13126

Received 6 August 1990

DALY, H. B. *Reward reductions found more aversive by rats fed environmentally contaminated salmon.* NEUROTOXICOL TERATOL **13**(4) 449–453, 1991.—Pacific salmon stocked in Lake Ontario concentrate persistent toxic chemicals such as PCBs, DDT, DDE, mercury and dioxin. The present experiments support earlier findings that consumption of these salmon by laboratory rats increases their behavioral reactions to negative events. For 20 days rats were fed a diet consisting of 30% Lake Ontario salmon or a control diet of Pacific Ocean salmon or no salmon. They were then trained to run down an alley to receive a large 15-pellet or small 1-pellet food reward (6 trials/day). Following 72 trials the 15-pellet groups were shifted to 1 pellet for 90 trials, and showed a *contrast* (depression) effect: they ran more slowly than the groups always given 1 pellet. Rats previously fed Lake Ontario salmon showed a much larger contrast effect than the two control groups. These results were replicated in a second experiment, and a group fed a 10% diet of Lake Ontario salmon for 60 days showed the same size contrast effect as the group fed a 30% diet for 20 days.

Experiment 1

Method

Fish preparation. Pacific salmon, which had been stocked as fingerlings in Lake Ontario, were obtained in the fall of 1986 and 1987 from the Salmon River near Altmar, NY, a river on the eastern end of Lake Ontario which is heavily fished by sports fishermen. The salmon had swum upstream from Lake Ontario to spawn. Additional salmon, taken directly from Lake Ontario, were obtained from sports fishermen bringing their catch to a weigh station during a fishing derby in May, 1987, in Fair Haven, NY (southeastern shore). The salmon were 10–20 lb, and were filleted according to the guidelines of the Department of Environmental Conservation, which are designed to minimize ingestion of contaminants. The fillets obtained in a given season were ground together (skin excluded) and frozen in 100–400 g packages. Control Pacific Ocean salmon fillets or steaks, packaged for human consumption, were obtained from a local fish market. They were also ground and frozen.

The ground salmon was defrosted when needed, and a 30% fish and 70% ground Purina Laboratory Rat Chow mixture was combined with tap water (75 g fish-chow mixture with 75 cc of water) to form a mash. Purina Chow pellets (75 g) were combined with 85 cc of tap water overnight to form the no-salmon mash (more water was added to equate the water content of the salmon).

Apparatus. The alley was 11.4 cm wide and 14 cm high, painted white, and covered with opaque Plexiglas. The startbox was 30.5 cm, the runway 140 cm, and the goalbox 28 cm long. A timer (Hunter Klockounter, 0.01 second accuracy) was started when the start-door was opened. Interruption of photobeams

15.2, 137.2, and 157.5 cm from the door connected to Hunter Photorelays and Klockounters measured start, run, and goal times, respectively.

Subjects and procedure. Forty-five male Sprague-Dawley rats from the Oswego colony (derived from stock obtained from the Holtzman Co., Madison, WI), 75 to 93 days old (mean of 85 for each group), were weighed, placed in individual cages (41 × 24 × 18 cm high), and for 20 days fed either the 30% mixture of Lake Ontario salmon (Lake), Pacific Ocean salmon (Ocean), or the chow mash (Mash). A fresh mixture (75 g dry weight) was provided each day. The rats were then reweighed and placed on regular Purina Laboratory Rat Chow pellets. After one day on a regular diet, the rats were weighed again, moved to smaller cages (18 × 24 × 18 cm high), and placed on a food deprivation schedule. They were weighed daily, handled and petted (gentled) for 10 seconds, and fed the appropriate amount of Purina chow to reduce them to 80% of their body weight on the first day of deprivation. Following 7 days on food deprivation rats were taken to the experimental room, placed in individual cages and given the same number of pellets they would receive during alley training, to experience eating the reward pellets (37 mg each, manufactured by P. J. Noyes Co., Formula A). Alley training began the following day. The rat was placed in the startbox of the alley, and the door was opened. The rat was allowed to run to the goalbox where food rewards were given (pellets were not visible until the subject had reached the goal), and was removed when finished eating. Subjects were given either 15 or 1 pellet. These rewards were given for 12 days of acquisition training (6 trials per day). On the thirteenth day of training the subjects given 15 pellets in acquisition were shifted down to 1 pellet beginning with the second trial, for the next 15 shift days (6 trials per day) of training. Subjects were maintained at 80% of their ad lib weight by feeding them the appropriate amount of Purina Rat Chow 15–30 minutes after testing.

Subjects were run in five replications of nine rats each, three per diet. Replications 1 and 2 were fed Fall 1986 salmon, and were run in the early spring of 1987. Replications 3 and 4 were fed Spring 1987 salmon, and were run in the late summer of 1987, and replication 5 was fed Fall 1987 salmon, and run in the fall of 1987. Data were not analyzed until all replications were completed. Of the nine rats in each replication, two in each diet condition were given a 15-pellet reward, and one was given a 1-pellet reward, which resulted in 10 subjects per diet given the large reward and 5 subjects per diet given the small reward. The nine rats were run in rotation, with an intertrial interval of 5–8 minutes. The *experimenter was unaware* of which fish condition each rat was in until the end of the experiment.

In *correlational* research, which involves uncontrolled exposure to chemicals, subjects are exposed to the toxic chemicals by: (a) ingesting them through their food and drink (or in paint chips, see Needleman et al. article); (b) inhaling them if they have become airborne; or (c) absorbing them through their skin. These exposures occur because toxic chemicals are: (a) used in the production and processing of food (pesticides), and it is difficult to prevent the food from absorbing the chemicals; (b) used in the manufacture of a large number of products (e.g., mercury thermometers), and it is frequently difficult to prevent exposure of the workers; (c) released during fires (PCB releases when old electrical transformers explode and burn), (d) released from a toxic landfill into the air or water; or (e) released purposely or through accidental spills into rivers and lakes. When persistent (long-lasting) chemicals are released into the environment they can be concentrated in the food chain through bioaccumulation, a process whereby small amounts of a chemical can accumulate in significant concentrations. For example, chemicals in the water are picked up by algae, small fish eat the algae, larger fish eat many smaller fish, and concentrate the chemicals in larger and larger amounts. The largest fish have the greatest amount of chemicals, and consumption of these fish by mammals can cause behavioral changes (see Daly article).

Researchers interested in studying the consequences of exposure to toxic chemicals sometimes travel to distant locations on learning of a chemical contamination of the environment. The same opportunistic strategy is used to study behavioral changes in subhuman species. For example, researchers study wildlife living in polluted areas of the world, and they have documented many changes in their natural behaviors. Kubiak et al. (1989), for instance, have shown that the reproductive impairment of Forster's tern living on Green Bay, Lake Michigan, a highly polluted section of the Great Lakes, was due in part to lack of parental attentiveness.

You should be aware of one more method of uncontrolled exposure. The unborn baby of a female who has suffered exposure to toxic chemicals could be exposed to any toxic chemicals that happen to be present in her blood. Also, after her baby is born, toxins could be present in her breast milk. The behavioral as well as the physical development of babies appears to be highly sensitive to many chemicals. Among them are alcohol (fetal alcohol syndrome), cocaine (crack babies), and toxic chemicals found in Great Lakes fish (among them PCBs). For example, there is a correlation between mother's consumption of Lake Michigan fish, which is contaminated with a large number of toxic chemicals, and the score on the Fagen Infant Test of Intelligence of the baby tested at seven months of age. Specifically, the more fish consumed by the mother, the lower the baby's score on the Fagen test (Jacobson, Fein, Jacobson, Schwartz, & Dowler, 1985).

Measurement of Chemicals Present

To realize the goal of a correlational study in behavioral toxicology, which is to assess the association between an uncontrolled level of exposure to toxic chemicals and behavioral phenomena, it is essential that researchers determine the level of toxic exposure after the fact (ex post facto) with as much precision as possible. There are two ways to obtain the required measurements: noninvasive techniques and invasive techniques. A **noninvasive technique** is one that permits data

Noninvasive Technique: A research procedure that does not create discomfort for the subject.

collection without creating discomfort for the subject. Examples include testing of: (a) baby teeth obtained when they fall out naturally (the technique used by Needleman et al.); (b) hair; (c) urine; and (d) breath. An **invasive technique** is more likely to create some discomfort—ranging from mild, as in the case of drawing a blood sample for analysis, to significant, as when various tissues (skin, fatty deposits, and internal organs) are harvested surgically. Of course, tissues from internal organs, such as the brain and liver, are harvested for research purposes only from subhuman species or, in humans, after death (with consent).

Invasive Technique: A research procedure that is likely to create some discomfort.

Even when the controlled exposure technique is used, chemical analyses are frequently done to identify the specific tissues that store the toxic substances. For example, researchers may want to determine how much of a particular toxic substance has reached the brain, and if some parts of the brain have higher concentrations than others.

Tests of Individual versus Multiple Chemicals

Humans and subhumans are often exposed, either in a controlled or uncontrolled manner, to several toxic chemicals at the same time rather than just one. It is therefore important that researchers in behavioral toxicology be able to assess the impact of several chemicals acting in concert. Using the controlled exposure technique it is possible to assess *interaction effects* (chapter 14) between toxic chemicals. An interaction is present if the combination of two or more chemicals cause changes in behavior that are different from, or substantially larger than, the behaviors caused by each one individually (also called a synergistic reaction). In experimental research the *factorial design* (chapter 14) is used to test individual chemicals and all possible combinations. For example, consider the 2 × 2 factorial design in Table 21–1.

Using the uncontrolled exposure technique, researchers test a large number of subjects for the presence of many different chemical contaminants and use statistical analyses to determine which combination of chemicals has the greatest association with specific behavioral changes.

Selection of Behavioral Tests

Except for an accidental discovery (serendipity) that points the behavioral toxicology researcher in the right direction, it is very difficult to know the specific behaviors that different chemicals are likely to influence. In other words, selection

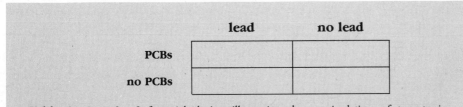

	lead	no lead
PCBs		
no PCBs		

Table 21–1. A 2 × 2 factorial design illustrating the manipulation of two toxic substances within one behavioral toxicology experiment.

of an appropriate and sensitive dependent measure for behavioral toxicological research is, to some extent, a matter of intuition and luck. For example, we know that lead is a lethal poison, but, from a behavioral standpoint, is nonlethal lead exposure likely to influence learning, or would the research prove more fruitful if the researcher studied measures of motivation, perception, or memory? Does the toxic chemical influence just one behavior, or are several behaviors affected (see Figure III–1 on page 330 to review the types of behaviors psychologists study)? It is also possible that an apparent influence of a toxic substance on one behavior is really the result of its influence on another behavior. For example, the real reason for a poor performance on a learning task may be a deficit in motivation rather than a deficit in memory capacity. Generally, to classify the effects of toxic exposure as completely as possible, researchers tend to evaluate changes in a large number of diverse behaviors.

Research Designs and "Control" Groups: Correlational Research

In correlational studies there are no "control" groups, but since the level of the chemical can vary all the way from zero to a very high level, the zero level can, in a loose sense, be considered a control condition. Also, covariates function as a type of control because they permit statistically removing the influence of confounding variables when we assess the meaning of data. Some researchers argue that if all the covariates that correlate with a dependent variable are accounted for, correlation alone is sufficient documentation of a causal relationship. For example, if a behavioral effect is noted in subjects who have been exposed to toxins and the influence of all possible confounding variables is removed, what else is there besides the toxic exposure itself to explain the behavioral effect? Other researchers are reluctant to take this position because one can never know with absolute certainty that all existing covariates have been identified and accounted for. Their position, which is the one that the authors embrace, is that the experimental method is the only one that can provide evidence for a cause-and-effect relationship (see Games [1990] for a review of the arguments).

Retrospective Study: Both the independent variable (such as chemical exposure) and the behaviors under study are in the past (*see also* Prospective study).

Prospective Study: The researcher identifies subjects who have experienced a condition (suffered exposure to toxic substances), then measures behavioral changes (*see also* Retrospective study).

Researchers use two correlational research designs to study behavioral toxicological phenomena: the retrospective design and the prospective design. A **retrospective study** is one in which both the chemical exposure and the behaviors under study are in the past. For example, if we asked a mother how many cigarettes she smoked while she was pregnant and also determined from hospital records the weight of her child at birth, the study would be retrospective. In a **prospective study**, as in a retrospective study, the researcher must identify subjects who have suffered exposure to toxic substances and then measure their level of exposure. But, unlike the retrospective study, the behavioral data are collected in the present. The Needleman et al. article is an example of a prospective study, since the children were first identified and measured for exposure to lead, and then their behaviors were measured. These researchers will probably test the same people in middle age and perhaps also in old age, to see if the effects of the lead exposure at a very young age lasts through life. Looking at the effects throughout the life of individuals is called a *lifespan* approach (chapter 17).

Research Designs and Control Groups: Experimental Research

The general principle of control, as applied to experimental research in the area of behavioral toxicology, requires the researcher to include in the experiment a group that is treated the same as the experimental group without exposing it to the toxic chemical. But the specific kinds of control measures that are appropriate depend on which type of experimental design (between-subject or within-subject) is used. Experiments designed to evaluate the effects of persistent (long-lasting) toxic chemicals are almost exclusively between-subject designs, because persistent chemicals, by definition, stay in the body. To attempt to test the effects of a second chemical while the first chemical is still present in body tissues would yield uninterpretable results. It would be uncertain which chemical is responsible for the behavioral effect. On the other hand, if it is known that a chemical is purged from the body in a relatively short period of time, then a within-subject design can be used as long as one of the *counterbalancing techniques* is employed (chapter 12, p. 210).

Summary

People are exposed to toxic chemicals, many of which cause changes in behavior. Research with humans is restricted to the correlational method because it is unethical to purposely expose people to potentially toxic chemicals. The experimental method is, however, used with subhuman animals. Article 21–1 measured the correlation between lead level in the teeth of children and behavior later in life. The experimental group of rats in the Daly study was given a diet of environmentally contaminated Lake Ontario salmon, and the control group was fed relatively uncontaminated salmon from the Pacific Ocean.

Key Terms

Dose-response Curve, p. 399

Invasive Techniques, p. 403

Noninvasive Techniques, p. 402

Prospective Designs, p. 404

Retrospective Designs, p. 404

Chapter Exercises

1. The Daly experiment showed that rats fed salmon from Lake Ontario were more frustrated when shifted from a large to a small reward. Explain why it would be impossible to use the experimental method to determine if consumption of environmentally contaminated fish caused changes in behavior using humans.

2. Explain why it is important to measure as many potentially confounding variables as possible in correlational research.

22

Research in Industrial/Organizational Psychology and Program Evaluation

Businesses, industries, and organizations must do more than manufacture a quality product or provide a useful service to maximize success. They suffer in both human and financial terms when their practices are wasteful, inefficient, and ineffective. Some psychologists are specially trained to assess the strengths and weaknesses of organizational policies and practices and make recommendations for improvements. Their findings could cause a company to: (1) adopt a good managerial style that promotes high performance and job satisfaction among the workers (organizational psychology); (2) provide an environment in which workers can be productive and safe (human engineering or human factors psychology); (3) select qualified employees, train them properly, evaluate their performance, and keep them motivated (personnel psychology); and (4) design, advertise, and market products so they can compete effectively with similar products (consumer psychology). To help industries and organizations solve problems in these four areas, psychologists in the field of industrial/organizational psychology (also called I/O psychology) are actively involved in both *basic* and *applied research* (chapter 1).

We selected an I/O article by Dalton and Mesch (1990). They tested the effects of a flexible time-scheduling program on absenteeism and turnover rate at a utility company. The flexible-scheduling program (*independent variable*) was *operationally defined* (chapter 3) by the authors in the Introduction of the paper rather than in the Method section, so we reproduce it here:

> (1) Employees must accumulate the necessary hours during the accounting period—8 hours per day/40 hours per week; and, (2) All employees must be present during "core" time . . . 9:30 A.M. to 11:00 A.M. and 2:00 P.M. to 3:30 P.M. . . . The balance of the eight-hour day could be selected anytime from 7:00 A.M. to 6:00 P.M. The choice of hours need not be contiguous [p. 371].

The flexible-scheduling program was official policy at one subunit of the utility, and employees at that subunit made up the experimental group. At the other subunit the flexible-scheduling program was never implemented, so employees at that subunit made up the *untreated control group* (chapter 11, p. 190). The research is in the form of Basic Question 4: Will introducing subjects to a specific change (here, flexible scheduling) cause their behavior to change?

It is important to notice that the assignment of workers to one or the other of the subunits was not random. Therefore, the control group was a *nonequivalent control group* (chapter 15, p. 290), making the study a *quasi-experiment* (chapter 15) as opposed to a true experiment. In addition, because the study was designed to evaluate the effectiveness of a program not previously used by the utility (flexible time-scheduling), it is also an example of program evaluation, a type of research we describe later in this chapter.

Please pause at this point to read the article on pages 410–12, then return to the following discussion.

Discussion of Techniques and Controls in the Dalton and Mesch Study

Method

The Method section begins with a long description of the research design: the *quasi-experimental time-series design with a non equivalent control group* (chapter 15, p. 295). There tend to be many potential threats to *internal validity* (chapter 10) in quasi-experimental designs, but the authors were aware of the threats and tried to show how many of them may have been neutralized in their study. For example, the authors were able to control for historical and maturation effects by measuring absenteeism and voluntary turnover of personnel (the *dependent variables*) 36 times before the intervention (once per month for three years), 12 times while the flexible-scheduling program was in effect (once per month for one year), and 24 times after the program was stopped (once per month for two years). The researchers argued that the control group was equivalent to the experimental group despite its technical nonequivalent designation: Subjects were employed by the same utility company, in subunits only 40 miles apart, in the same state, and each work site had almost the same number of employees (136 and 135).

Selection of Intervention Site, Subjects, Variables, and Analyses

Employing workers under a flexible-scheduling versus no flexible scheduling condition was not under the control of the researchers. Instead, the company and organized labor decided to try a new program for one year, and this event created a fortuitous research opportunity. The authors also point out that the two dependent variables were not specially selected by either the company or labor to evaluate the program, but were selected a posteriori by the experimenters. This should have eliminated any possible self-serving bias created by *demand characteristics* (chapter 10, p. 179) on the participants in the study. Moreover, the possibility that either labor or management would resist evaluation and incorrectly report absenteeism and personnel turnover statistics to bias the evaluation was presumably eliminated by using existing payroll records (*archival data*, chapter 6) that were not maintained at the work site.

Analyses

Specialized statistical tests have been developed to deal with time-series designs that are beyond the scope of our discussion. But we should point out that the main goal of these tests is to remove random fluctuations and those that can be attributed to other factors (such as seasonal fluctuations) in order to determine with greater precision if the major change in behavior is linked to the independent variable of the study (here, flexible scheduling versus no flexible scheduling).

Additional Techniques and Control Issues in Industrial/Organizational Psychology

Most *basic research* in I/O psychology is experimental rather than correlational or quasi-experimental. Typically subjects are randomly assigned to perform tasks under various manipulated conditions (the nature of the stimulus display, the nature of the responses subjects must give when performing, conditions that affect work stress, training strategies, and the ways in which worker performance is monitored), and the conditions that result in the highest and most reliable and sustained performance are determined. When basic research in this subdiscipline moves from the controlled environment of the research laboratory to an *applied* context in the field (say, at a factory), the approach is more likely to be *quasi-experimental.* The reason is that, in the field, it is often impossible to assign subjects randomly to the different conditions of a study and/or to manipulate variables.

If you are interested in learning more about research in this subdiscipline, we recommend a course in the area. Here we review only two points.

Administrative Science Quarterly, 35 (1990): 370–387

The Impact of Flexible Scheduling on Employee Attendance and Turnover

Dan R. Dalton
Indiana University

Debra J. Mesch
Northeastern University

The implementation of an experimental flexible-scheduling program was the basis for a naturally occurring field experiment. A six-year assessment tests the effects of a flexible-scheduling program on absenteeism and turnover for the division implementing the program as well as a comparable control group. Results indicate gross reductions in employee absenteeism after the flexible-scheduling intervention for the experimental group, while no such changes were evident in the control group. The two-year period after the program ended indicates that absenteeism immediately returned to base-rate levels. The rate of employee turnover, however, was unaffected by the intervention. The concluding section discusses the problems encountered in trying to apply flexible scheduling to a large-scale organization.

Method

The field experiment is an interrupted time series with multiple time-interval pretest measures, intervention removal, and a no-intervention, quasi-control group design (Cook and Campbell, 1979). The time-series design was proposed initially by Campbell (1963) as a means of assessing the impact of a discrete intervention on a social process. In this case, there are measures taken monthly for the three years prior to the intervention, the intervention year, and two postintervention years. The nonequivalent group received no intervention. This quasi-experimental design, particularly with a nonequivalent control group, is considered to be a very strong design with high internal validity (e.g., Hoole, 1978; Judd and Kenny, 1981). Even so, the design is not ideal, as it does not randomly assign subjects to the experimental and comparison groups. Although this study is naturally occurring and the employees of the experimental and control groups were ob-

viously not randomly assigned by the utility company to their respective locations for purposes of this "experiment," the design can still be quite powerful if the experimental and control groups are comparable and as similar as possible (Huck, Cormier, and Bounds, 1974; Cook and Campbell, 1979). These conditions were reasonably met in this case. The experimental group—the group involved in the flextime experiment—was the total employee population of that subunit. The control group selected for comparison was the total employee population of a matched subunit. The control group worked for the same organization, in the same region, some forty miles to the south, in the same state. The charter of the groups was identical; the technology employed was identical. Over a six-year period, even the mean number of employees in the experimental ($N = 136$) and the intact control group ($N = 135$) was remarkably similar. This control group was the closest division geographically, with an identical charter, and with a nearly matched number of employees. The control group was not matched with the experimental group on the basis of the levels of absenteeism and turnover. The similarity of the control group to the experimental group of these dimensions was welcomed, but serendipitous.

Selection of the Intervention Site

The intervention was done in one subunit of a large Western public utility. The "Memorandum of Agreement" between the parties concerning the implementation of this flexible-scheduling program noted, in part, that the site chosen should have several attributes. Specifically, a strong test of flexible scheduling must include its effects on the interactions between the subunit and the company's facilities as well as on those with the customer. The test unit was adopted because it was the only division within the company that met all the criteria. Its charter included direct interaction with the customer, with the outside facilities (e.g., maintenance and repair functions), as well as the inside facilities (operations) of the company. The billing function was housed there as well. The final choice of location was made by a committee composed of hourly and management personnel, a union representative, a personnel analyst from the company, and an outside consultant.

Subjects

All subjects (experimental and intact control group) were hourly employees in an essentially nontechnical, white-collar, service-oriented classification. These employees handled the assignment of facilities for new installations. In addition, they were responsible for the routing of service personnel when subscribers made complaints about their service and for matters related to customer billing.

At the beginning of the period, there were 137 employees in the test subunit; at the end of the trial period, there were 134 employees. The control group population was 135 at the onset and 140 at the conclusion. The comparability of sample size over the period, however, does not necessarily suggest employee stability in the groups. Given turnover over the six-year period,

a large number of the employees who were employed at time 1 were not employed at time 6. Such attrition would be expected and was not of great concern, because both the experimental and the control groups experienced similar rates of employee turnover over the period.

Variables

Two dependent variables are relevant to this study: the rate of unexcused employee absenteeism and voluntary turnover. Excused absence, military leave, vacation time, jury duty, and so forth were not included in the analysis. This absence variable was derived by dividing the total number of days absent by the total number of employees by month. We then focused on the total absence rate for the two groups (experimental and control) for the three years prior to the intervention, the year of the intervention, and the two years after it was discontinued. These data were derived from archival sources.

Employee turnover was the second dependent variable. By turnover, we refer only to voluntary turnover. Employees who were terminated by the organization, retired, or passed away over the period were not included in the analysis. These data were also derived from archival records. We relied on monthly absence and turnover rates. We had no access to individual-level absence or turnover data or any information on individual differences.

It should be noted that the dependent variables of this research—employee absenteeism and voluntary turnover—were not identified by management and labor as evaluative criteria for the success or failure of the cooperative flexible-scheduling program. Rather, we selected these indices a posteriori. We would argue that this provides a methodological advantage. Campbell (1969: 428), for example, argued that individuals can become so committed in advance to the efficacy of a reform that they cannot afford honest evaluation and "for them favorably biased analyses are recommended." We are reminded of Kaplan's (1964: 128) classic admonition that "wishful thinking . . . has its counterpart in wishful seeing." While we have no reason to believe that management or organized labor were under any undue pressure for the program to succeed, it seems reasonable, given that both parties agreed to the trial, that each had certain expectations for its implementation. If a prejudicial assessment could be expected, it seems that the parties would be more likely to misrepresent changes in the stated evaluative criteria. Since the parties to the intervention had no apparent interest in absenteeism or turnover, however, there would be no impetus whatever to color conclusions in these areas. Beyond that, even given such an inclination, it would have been most difficult to affect the archival data from payroll records, on which we relied. These records were not maintained locally but were monitored by organizational departments that were independent of the "experimental" intervention. Also, such records would not seem to be subject to selective deposit and survival, the two principal sources of bias in archival data (Webb et al., 1966).

The independent variable of note is the intervention itself—flexible scheduling. Strictly speaking, there are two independent variables, as there are actually two interventions: the introduction of the flexible-scheduling program and, one year later, the discontinuation of this program.

Analyses

We relied on a general class of techniques designed to assess the impact of discrete events on a time series, known as Autoregressive Integrated Moving Average (ARIMA) intervention analysis (Box and Jenkins, 1976). Such a procedure may be used to iteratively remove systematic error such as trend, aberrant oscillation, autocorrelation, and seasonality from a time series. Having done so, it is then possible to determine the impact of an intervention; in this case, the flexible scheduling program.

All ARIMA analyses are reported on the basis of 72 data points (monthly data over a six-year period). This uncommonly large number of observations provides an opportunity to estimate ARIMA models of unusual robustness. The availability of a large number of preintervention observations, for example, allows us to establish a stable base-line period. The two-year postintervention period provides similar advantages.

The Hawthorne Effect

The Hawthorne effect was documented in the late 1920s by Elton Mayo and other researchers. The studies were designed to explore the effects of changing the working conditions in an industrial setting (the amount of light in the room in one study, different supervision practices in a second set of studies) on employee performance. Surprisingly, change itself rather than the direction of the changes had the strongest positive influence on worker productivity. That is, much to the surprise of the investigators, productivity tended to increase (or remain at a satisfactory level) following any change in working conditions, whether illumination was increased or decreased. Apparently, the workers were responding to the special attention they were getting from their supervisors during the studies rather than to the advantages or disadvantages posed by working under the various manipulated conditions (called the **Hawthorne effect**). Even when the lighting was reduced to the equivalent of a moonlit night, productivity did not suffer! The Hawthorne effect is similar to the phenomena of *reactivity* (chapter 3, p. 29) and *demand characteristics* (chapter 10, p. 179), since all are examples of subject reactions to other than a manipulated variable and all can confuse the interpretation of experimental data. When evaluating any research report, the careful reader will always consider the possible contributions of reactivity and/or demand characteristics to the data. It should be pointed out, however, that criticisms of the study have been raised. According to Bramel and Friend (1981), when output fell the workers were reprimanded and two of the five workers were dismissed for low output. These factors could have confounded the experiment.

Hawthorne Effect: Workers respond to the special attention they get from their supervisors during their participation in a study rather than the manipulated conditions.

The Individual Differences Approach: Personnel Psychology

The evaluation of differences between individuals (*idiographic approach*, chapter 6, p. 95) is sometimes more relevant to the I/O psychologist than the evaluation of differences between groups. For example, in personnel selection (an important concern of I/O psychologists) the focus is on finding the most qualified person to fill a position of employment. The assessment of individual traits, such as prior experience, physical and intellectual aptitudes, stress tolerance, and assertiveness, is the primary objective—not, as is so often the case in experimental research, the comparisons among differently treated groups. By applying appropriate tests and measures, personnel psychologists seek to answer such questions as: Does the applicant have the necessary communication skills to excel in the job? Will the applicant be likely to function well as a cooperative team player? Does the applicant have the emotional stability to withstand the stresses of the work environment? Notice that all the I/O research questions listed focus on individuals and differences between individuals, not on groups. Analyses and assessments of behavior that focus on the individual are collectively referred to as the individual differences approach.

Research Issues in Program Evaluation

Industries, schools, government programs such as the criminal justice system, and human service organizations such as mental health centers can be very costly in terms of human resources, time, and money. Therefore such institutions must be carefully monitored to determine if they are functioning properly and, if modifications are introduced, if they were effective in producing the intended improvements. The need for evaluation is especially keen if there is controversy over the effectiveness with which an organization or program is fulfilling its stated purpose. It is at this point that psychologists who have received training in program evaluation are brought in to address these issues. In the following section we review some of the important research issues in program evaluation.

Formative versus Summative Evaluation

There are two major forms of evaluation, summative and formative, and each is identified with the objectives of the evaluation. The goal of summative evaluation is to determine if a given individual or program is performing adequately. The outcome of the summative evaluation is used to determine, for example, whether a program should be cut back, discontinued, maintained, or expanded with additional funding, or whether a person should be promoted with a raise, transferred, or fired, and so forth. As you may already have surmised, to the people under scrutiny a summative evaluation is likely to be threatening. The psychologist must do everything possible to minimize the perceived threat and enlist the cooperation of the people involved. Otherwise, the evaluation effort can fail.

Formative evaluation has several separate but related objectives. It begins with a formal performance evaluation of an individual or program. Then the focus shifts toward recommending changes that will improve individual or program performance. Next, the task is to evaluate the effectiveness of the newly implemented changes and provide feedback to the individual or organization. If the target of a formative evaluation is an individual, the individual is frequently the only person to see the results of the evaluation. Similarly, if the target is a particular program of an organization, the organizational members who are responsible for monitoring the program may be the only ones to see the results of the evaluation. The limited distribution of evaluation results is maintained because the objective of a formative evaluation is to improve the performance of the individual or program, not to decide on its ultimate fate. The removal of any threat of program elimination, reduction of funding, loss of personnel, or the like will promote cooperation between the evaluator and the organizational members rather than lead to an adversarial relationship.

Types of Evaluation

Within both summative and formative evaluations, there are certain subcategories: needs assessment, implementation or process evaluation, outcome evaluation, and cost-benefit (efficiency) analyses. We will review each of these within two sample contexts: the Dalton and Mesch study and the success of convict-release programs.

Needs assessment

In doing a needs assessment evaluation the aim is to describe what presently exists (the "before" or "pretest" condition), the gap between what presently exists and what ought to exist, and then prepare a plan to reduce the gap. In the context of the Dalton and Mesch study, needs assessment would have involved determining if absenteeism and turnover are creating problems in the proper functioning of the industry. In the context of a convict release program, we would measure how many convicts return to a life of crime and wind up back in prison (recidivism) after their release. If recidivism is high, this is not the result that ought to occur if a penal system is working in an ideal fashion.

After identifying a problem, the next logical step is to propose a plan to alleviate it. Trying a flexible-scheduling program is one possible solution to absenteeism and turnover. In the example of a deficient penal system, plans could include alternative sentencing (such as community service and/or weekends in jail), job-training programs, work-release programs, in-house high school certification programs, and so forth.

Implementation evaluation

The purpose of an implementation or process evaluation is to assess the degree to which the planned changes are in place and operating as intended. The reason behind an implementation evaluation is straightforward: It would be unfair and misleading to assess the effectiveness of a program before it is in place and operating as intended. For example, we would need to determine that employees were taking advantage of the flexible-scheduling opportunity before it would be appropriate to begin a formal evaluation of its impact on employee absenteeism. Similarly, we would not begin to evaluate the effect of alternative sentencing on the rate of recidivism until we had: (a) a commitment from judges to actually use alternative sentencing; (b) written guidelines to determine the eligibility of convicts for alternative sentencing; (c) firm options for placing convicts in community service environments; and (d) determined that these alternative options were being used.

During implementation evaluation it is common to become aware of unanticipated problems that are interfering or have the potential to interfere with the original program plan. For example, some community members may be against any program that would place convicts in a work environment in which they would freely mingle with other workers. To the extent that the protesters are successful in mobilizing political opposition to the program, full program implementation could be hampered. In response to the reality of partial implementation, the program evaluator usually adjusts the original evaluation plan.

Outcome evaluation

The goal of an outcome evaluation is to assess the degree to which the planned impact of a program has been realized. The most pressing problem is to determine how to measure the success of a program. The posttest condition of a *within-subject pretest-posttest quasi-experiment* (chapters 12 and 15) is really an outcome evaluation against which to compare the data from a needs assessment. An outcome evaluation would provide answers to questions such as: Were absenteeism and turnover rates lower after flexible scheduling was introduced? and Did recidivism rates decrease? An alternative strategy for an outcome evaluation is to use a *between-subject design* (chapter 11) and compare the absenteeism and turnover rates of an experimental group with a control group (or nonequivalent control group).

Cost-benefit (efficiency) analysis

The objective of a cost-benefit or efficiency analysis in program evaluation is to weigh the investment that was necessary to implement a program against the success the program enjoys in meeting its stated goals. To justify the effort and expense of a program, we must not only be prepared to demonstrate its practical benefits with hard data, we must also be prepared to argue that the degree of benefit derived from the program was worth the cost. Thus, even if the flexible-scheduling program decreased the absenteeism and turnover rates, if the program resulted in a net cost to the industry by decreasing productivity, it would probably be abandoned. Even if alternative sentencing should lead to an overall significant reduction in recidivism, a few unfortunate incidents involving further criminal behavior by program participants that involved, say, the death of innocent people could cause the program to be dropped. Following such a tragic turn of events, the risk of exposing the public to repeat offenders, who would be in prison if they were not in the alternative sentencing program, would probably be judged unacceptable.

Special Concerns in Program Evaluation

On a general level there is very little difference between the research activity of a program evaluator and that of researchers in other subdisciplines of psychology. There are, however, some concerns that are unique to program evaluation research because of the impact a program evaluation can have on the welfare of the people or organizations being evaluated. Because sloppy program evaluation research can condemn programs and people that are really effective in what they do and waste valuable resources, it is necessary to take certain steps to minimize such a possibility. We review some of these steps.

It is very important for all involved in the evaluation process to formulate carefully the goals and objectives of the program and the expectations of the evaluation. Otherwise, the evaluators can be misdirected and may evaluate an inappropriate, unintended, and/or irrelevant aspect of the program. Even if the evaluator succeeds in targeting the most important program aspects for study, it is possible for the scope of the evaluation to be too narrow or the amount of information collected too skimpy for the evaluation to be useful. Evaluators frequently face resistance to evaluation: attempts by those who will be directly affected by the evaluation findings to sabotage the evaluation process by, say, refusing to comply with the requests of the evaluator. One way to minimize resistance is for the evaluator(s) to establish a rapport with the stakeholders: the people who stand to gain or lose from the information that is revealed in the evaluation report. When the evaluator meets with the stakeholders to share information about the evaluation project, discussions should include an explanation of why the evaluation is being done and how the results will be used (that is, formative versus summative evaluation goals). As a courtesy, the stakeholders also should be informed as to whether the evaluation will be in-house (an evaluation conducted by people who work for the organization) or done by outside consultants (professional program evaluators who are not part of the organization). There is, of course, usually more resistance to evaluation when outside consultants are used. They are strangers and, therefore, potentially more threatening. To defuse stakeholder resistance to evaluation by outside consultants, it is helpful to point out that the results of the evaluation are confidential, they are not the property of the evaluator, and that outside consultants are likely to be more neutral and even-handed than in-house evaluators.

As pointed out earlier in this chapter, a summative evaluation is likely to meet with more resistance than a formative evaluation for a very obvious reason: One goal of summative evaluation is to offer a recommendation regarding the continuation, expansion, contraction, or elimination of a program or job. One tactic to minimize the perceived threat of a summative evaluation and maximize participant cooperation is to point out that a positive summative evaluation can be used by the targeted individuals to request promotions or increases in salary, or by the project directors to save their program from budget cuts. In this light the program evaluation can be seen as potentially very beneficial to the individual or program. By comparison, formative evaluation typically meets with less participant resistance because the goals are usually to improve the performance of an individual or program without the threat of program elimination or other disturbing disruptions. Also, if program evaluation is seen as a continuing process (as when evaluation leads to program adjustments followed by further evaluation, more program adjustments, and so forth) the perceived threat posed by evaluation is likely to be minimal.

Summary

It is sometimes impossible to randomly assign subjects to experimental and control conditions when doing applied research, so applied researchers tend to rely on quasi-experimental designs. The Dalton and Mesch study is an example of applied research in an industrial setting using a quasi-experimental time-series design with a non-equivalent control group. The authors selected one industry site to try a flexible-scheduling program for workers, but the workers had not been randomly assigned to the two work sites. The study was also an example of program evaluation, a type of research that measures the impact of a new program or change on an existing program.

Key Term

Hawthorne Effect, p. 413

Chapter Exercises

1. The results of the Dalton and Mesch study showed that absenteeism declined when flexible scheduling was introduced. Did you discover anything in the description of the nonequivalent control group that would make you suspect the validity of the study?

2. Why does the fact that absenteeism increased after flexible scheduling was stopped increase the likelihood that flexible scheduling caused the decrease in absenteeism?

3. Could demand characteristics have possibly influenced the results of the Dalton and Mesch study? If so, what changes would you make in the study to determine if the results were due to demand characteristics?

4. If the results were due to a Hawthorne-type effect, would the absenteeism rate have increased or decreased when the workers were taken off the flexible-scheduling program? Explain your answer.

C H A P T E R

23

Research in Social Psychology

To illustrate how behavioral diversity in the form of a personality variable affects behavior in various social contexts, we include a study by Schlenker, Weigold, and Hallam (1990) that has five independent variables in a $2 \times 2 \times 2 \times 2 \times 2$ *factorial design* (chapter 14). You may be concerned about your ability to understand the results of a study that contains five separate independent variables, especially if you had difficulty with the material covered in chapter 14. We are confident, however, that with some guidance and a refusal to be intimidated, you will have no trouble understanding the experiment.

The Examination of Complex Experiments

The simplest way to understand the design of a complicated experiment is to break down the task into steps. We will go through these steps for you before you read the Schlenker et al. article. We have numbered the steps, although researchers do not necessarily do them in any particular order.

Step 1

The first step is to identify the independent variables and write them down. The five independent variables are:

$$
\begin{array}{ccccccccc}
2 & \times & 2 & \times & 2 & \times & 2 & \times & 2 \\
\end{array}
$$

2	×	2	×	2	×	2	×	2
high or low self-esteem		high or low motivation to make positive impression		critical or supportive audience		success or failure on previous task		public or private testing

We can then calculate the number of different treatment combinations in the experimental design by multiplying the levels of each factor. Each of the five independent variables in the design has been restricted to only two levels, so the computation is $2 \times 2 \times 2 \times 2 \times 2$. The answer, 32, reveals that the design requires 32 separate treatment combinations. The chore we would have to interpret the results would be far more complicated if the authors had chosen to manipulate some of the independent variables using three or more levels. For example, running the study as a $3 \times 2 \times 4 \times 3 \times 2$ factorial design would require 144 treatment combinations.

Step 2

The second step is to determine which independent variables are manipulated variables, which are nonmanipulated variables, and how they were *operationally defined* (chapter 3, p. 31). The first independent variable was measured and not manipulated: Subjects were regarded as having high or low self-esteem on the basis of their responses on the Rosenberg Self-Esteem Scale. If the authors had decided to manipulate the self-esteem variable, they would have had to find a way to convince a random half of the subjects that they are truly wonderful people (high self-esteem) and convince the other half that they are profoundly inadequate (low self-esteem). One possible way to raise self-esteem is to tell subjects how nice they look, what a good impression they make, that they should feel good about themselves, and the like. To lower self-esteem we would give the opposite message.

The second independent variable, motivation to make a positive impression, was manipulated by telling the subjects that this "was not a test of you in any way" (low motivation) or that they should "try to make a positive impression" (high motivation). (See the procedure section for a complete set of the instructions to subjects.) To manipulate the third independent variable, type of audience, half the subjects were told that a person who was going to form an opinion about them was "very perceptive in making interpersonal judgments and skeptical about what people say" (critical audience). The other half were told that the person was "very unperceptive and very trusting" (supportive audience).

Whereas the second (motivation) and third (audience) independent variables were both manipulated by means of instructions to the subjects, the fourth variable (success or failure on a previous task) was manipulated by giving false feedback on the subject. Subjects took a test of social decision-making prior to the experiment and, regardless of how they actually scored, they were told that they scored in either the 93rd (success) or 27th (failure) percentile.

Like the second and third variables, the fifth variable was also manipulated by means of the instructions. All subjects completed a questionnaire to assess their perceptions of the social decision-making test. But the experimenter explained to half the subjects that their responses would be anonymous and confidential (private), whereas the other half had to sign the questionnaire and were informed that their responses would be viewed by others (public).

A thorough specification of the operational definition of each independent variable is essential not only for replication of one or more of the conditions reported in the study, but for interpreting the results. The interpretation of a difference between levels of a nonmanipulated variable is limited to *description*. If, on the other hand, the levels of a variable are manipulated, we can attribute results to a *causal* action of the variable.

The study clearly addressed a number of the seven basic questions. The first independent variable was not manipulted, and therefore addressed a Basic Question 4 corollary: Are there systematic differences in behavior among subjects who are identified as having experienced different conditions (level of self-esteem)? The remaining four independent variables addressed Basic Question 5: Will introducing subjects to qualitatively different conditions cause them to exhibit systematic differences in behavior? In addition, since the authors were interested in whether there were interaction effects, they also addressed Basic Question 7: Will introducing subjects to two or more systematically different conditions cause an additive and/or interactive effect on behavior?

Step 3

The third step is to determine if the design is a *between-subject design* (chapter 11), a *within-subject design* (chapter 12), or a *mixed design* (chapter 14). If a design is identified as between-subject, we must determine if subjects were randomly assigned to the different levels of the independent variable (a true experiment) or if a nonequivalent control group was used (a *quasi-experimental design*, chapter 15). In the case of a within-subject design, we must consider the possibility of *carryover effects* (chapter 11) and the adequacy of the counterbalancing procedure used to neutralize the influence of carryover effects. The present study was a between-subject design, and subjects were randomly assigned to those conditions that were manipulated. The authors also included an **offset control condition**, an extra control group that is not one of the treatment combinations defined by the core experimental design. Here, the offset control is not part of the $2 \times 2 \times 2 \times 2 \times 2$ factorial design. Subjects assigned to the offset control condition were tested with no feedback and no motivational instructions, and the type of audience was not mentioned. In the absence of any information in the article to the contrary, it is reasonable to assume that the subjects in the offset control group constituted a separate group that was not tested under any of the other conditions.

Offset Control Condition: An extra control group that is not one of the treatment combinations defined by the core experimental design.

Step 4

The fourth step is to identify the dependent variables. The ideal description of the dependent variables should, like the descriptions of the independent variables, permit the interested reader to duplicate the experiment. Schlenker et al. had a complicated set of dependent measures, which we will review later in the chapter.

Step 5

The fifth and final step is to evaluate the methodological approach. Is the design appropriate? Are rival hypotheses possible, and if so, should additional control conditions have been included to rule them out? Evaluation of the methodological approach requires complete understanding of the purpose and methods of the study. Even seasoned researchers find it necessary to read the method section of a complicated experiment a number of times before they fully understand what the experimenters did. We read the Schlenker et al. article one time to determine what the independent variables were and how they were manipulated, a second time to determine what the task was, and a third time to see if we could find any methodological flaws that would make us less interested in the results and conclusions.

If you read the entire article (look in the periodical section of your college library), you will find that in the introduction the authors predicted what effect each of the five independent variables would have and how the variables would *interact* (chapter 14). In the discussion section the authors presented their interpretations of the numerous experimental results. Do not become discouraged if you do not understand a journal article immediately. Full understanding often requires considerable time and effort. In fact, you have probably discovered that reading and developing a thorough understanding of a 10-page journal article can be more time-consuming than reading a novel.

Please pause at this point to read the article on pages 424–27, then return to the following discussion.

Discussion of Techniques and Controls in the Schlenker et al. Study

Method

Subjects

With 32 different conditions plus an offset control group, it is not surprising that the authors tested a relatively large number of subjects (272). How many subjects were assigned to each of the 33 differently treated groups? Dividing 272 subjects by 33 equals 8.24 subjects per group. This impossible result is a clear indication that all 33 treatment conditions did not contain the same number of subjects, or that some subjects dropped out of the experiment. Since it is not unusual to have to eliminate some subjects because they fail to comply with the instructions (as when a subject fails to fill in all the items on the questionnaire), the results are probably based on fewer subjects than the authors originally intended to include. If *subject attrition* (chapter 7, p. 124) was high, however, it is important to determine whether or not the remaining sample was biased.

It is not difficult to obtain 272 subjects from a typical subject pool, the population of individuals willing to serve as subjects. Since most instructors encourage their students to learn about psychological research by volunteering to serve as subjects, and since colleges and universities can have, depending on their size, up to several thousand students enrolled in introductory psychology classes, academicians who do psychological research seldom have a problem recruiting subjects.

The authors tested both males and females. Therefore, they can *generalize* (chapter 10, p. 000) their interpretations of the data to both genders. It would have been possible to include gender as another independent variable in the study, but to do so would have required adding a sixth factor (gender) to the design. This step would have further complicated the data analysis and interpretation. Because subjects were tested only in same-gender groups, we do not know if similar results would be obtained with mixed-gender groups.

Procedure

The authors present the procedure in a very clear fashion, and there is no need to review it further. You may, however, find it helpful to write down the tasks the subjects had to complete, the order in which they were performed, and at what points the subjects were given additional instructions. We review the scoring of the data in the next section, but note that the dependent variables were the "subject's perceptions of the test, responsibility of performance, and self-ratings on relevant and irrelevant dimensions." The irrelevant dimensions addressed by some questions were used as *filler items* (chapter 19) to make the purpose of asking the relevant questions less obvious to the subject.

Additional Techniques and Control Issues in Social Psychology

In the remainder of this chapter we shall stress research issues of importance to social psychology. We do not wish to imply, however, that the research issues we have selected are only of interest to this subdiscipline. Many have relevance to other subdisciplines of psychology.

Instructions

Verbal instructions are obviously not useful in experiments with subhuman subjects. Training begins immediately, and the subjects must "figure out" what is required of them. Although a noninstructional procedure can also be used with humans, it typically is not. To manipulate the levels of independent variables, as was done in the study you just read, or to inform subjects what to do, experimenters give verbal **instructions**. Instructions often end with "Do you have any questions?" If subjects do have questions, the experimenter repeats the relevant part(s) of the instructions but does not provide any additional information.

Instructions should always be written, because keeping to a set script of written instructions ensures that all subjects within the same treatment condition will receive the same instructions. Sometimes the procedure is to have subjects read their instructions, and it is routine to allow them ample time to reread any portions that may be confusing. In other studies the experimenter reads the instructions aloud to the subjects. There are two disadvantages to the latter approach. First, the

Instructions: Information for guiding subjects what to do in the study or for manipulating the levels of an independent variable.

Journal of Personally and Social Psychology
1990, Vol. 58. No. 5, 855–863

Self-Serving Attributions in Social Context: Effects of Self-Esteem and Social Pressure

Barry R. Schlenker, Michael F. Weigold, and John R. Hallam
University of Florida

This study examined the attributions of Ss high (HSEs) and low (LSEs) in self-esteem in contexts where (a) they were low or high in the motivation to make a positive impression on an audience, (b) the audience was perceived as supportive or critical, (c) Ss' accounts were public or private, and (d) Ss had succeeded or failed on a previous task. Overall, Ss displayed pronounced and pervasive egotistical biases, but the social context influenced the magnitude of the bias. HSEs were most egotistical when evaluative pressures were greatest (i.e., they were motivated to make a good impression and had the opportunity to account publicly), whereas LSEs were least egotistical under these conditions. HSEs tended to internalize success by raising their self-ratings, whereas LSEs tended to internalize failure by lowering their self-ratings. In general, a critical audience seemed to activate concerns about the defensibility of attributions, producing more caution and less explicit boastfulness. Factor analysis of subjects' responses suggested that they conceptualized the situation in terms of its implications for evaluating identity.

Method

Subjects

Two hundred seventy-two introductory psychology students (136 men and 136 women) participated in partial fulfillment of a course requirement.

Procedure

Sessions were run with 4 to 6 same-sex subjects, who worked in individual cubicles. Written instructions minimized experimenter–subject interaction and permitted each subject to be assigned to a different treatment condition. Subjects were led to believe that another person, who had not worked on the same tasks they completed, would be forming an impression of them later in the session. Specifically, half of those present supposedly would participate in a study of decision-making ability and half would participate in a study of impression-formation ability. Those in the latter study would take a test of impression-formation ability and then form an impression of a randomly selected participant from the decision-making study. The instructions noted that the two studies would normally be run separately because they addressed different issues, but running them in a single session maximized efficiency by obviating the need to recruit a separate group of subjects merely to be "stimulus persons."

In actuality, all subjects read that they would participate primarily in the social decision-making study but would later serve as a "stimulus person" in the other study. Subjects first completed a background questionnaire that included Rosenberg's (1965) Self-Esteem Scale and the (fictitious) "Lawley-Yates Decision Assessment Test." The latter was described as a frequently used and reasonably valid measure of factors underlying a person's ability to make certain types of social decisions. Scores on the test were supposedly related to such important attributes as logical thinking in social situations, mature reasoning, moral consistency, leadership, and social competence. The bogus but face-valid test consisted of descriptions of problematic social situations (e.g., how to deal with an employee who is a long-time friend and a new father but who consistently makes mistakes and costs the company money), each followed by questions in multiple-choice format asking how the subject would handle the situation.

After completing the test, subjects read that they had been randomly paired with one of the participants in the impression-formation study who, as a part of that study, would be asked to form an impression of them based on (a) their answers on a to-be-completed questionnaire about their interests, hobbies, attitudes, and so forth and (b) their responses on the social decision-making test. It was explained that although the other person would see the subject's test responses, he or she would not be given the subject's score. Thus, the other person might form an opinion about how well the subject did, but he or she could not be certain. This procedure permitted social decision-making ability to be relevant to the impression formed without exerting undue constraint on the subjects' accounts of their performance by revealing a precise score to the other (Schlenker, 1975b).

Motivation to impress the other person was manipulated by differentially emphasizing whether the focus was on the content or process of impression formation and whether subjects should be themselves or try to create a positive impression. Subjects in the low motivation condition read that the research was primarily

> interested in how people form impressions, not in the particular types of impressions they form or even whether they are remotely accurate. Hence, this is not a test of you in any way. Your responses are merely being used as a stimulus with which we can examine the process the other person uses to form impressions and to see how his or her personality, attitudes, and score on the Harkov Impression Formation Test relate to the process he or she uses. The specific content of the impression is irrelevant to our work. Thus, please act naturally, be honest, and be yourself.

In contrast, subjects in the high motivation condition read that the researchers

> are interested in the factors people take into account when they form a positive or negative evaluation of someone else. We are particularly interested in the factors that underlie positive evaluations, and hence would like you to try to make a positive impression so that the other person will see you as competent, likeable, and so forth.

The instructions went on to explain that, because the other person would receive personal information about them, it would be appropriate for subjects to know something about the other person. Consequently, subjects received a summary evaluation of the other person, ostensibly based on the other's answers to a background questionnaire completed earlier. The evaluation form contained numerical ratings of the other of five dimensions (10-point scales) indicating that he or she was about average on measures of self-esteem, esteem for others, and optimism–pessimism. In addition, the form indicated that the other was either (a) very perceptive in making interpersonal judgments and skeptical about what people say (critical audience condition) or (b) very unperceptive and very trusting about what others say, taking words at face value (supporting audience condition).

Next, subjects were given their scores from the test of social decision making, which the experimenter had purportedly graded while they were reading the instructions for their role as a "stimulus person." Subjects were again reminded that the other person would not see their scores and that the reason they were receiving them was because most prior participants had expressed an interest in learning how well they had performed. The feedback sheets provided percentile scores indicating the subject had scored either in the 93rd percentile of college students (success condition) or in the 27th percentile (failure condition).

Subjects were next asked to complete a questionnaire assessing perceptions of the test, responsibility for performance, and self-ratings on relevant and irrelevant dimensions. The written instructions explained that subjects' perceptions of the test would be useful in the continuing process of refining the instrument. Subjects in the anonymous account condition read that their responses on the questionnaire would be completely anonymous and confidential. They were told not to place their name on the form and, when finished, to seal it in an accompanying envelope; their responses would be recorded anonymously by a research assistant and would not be viewed by either the experimenter or the other subject. In contrast, subjects in the public account condition read that, because the other subject would see their responses on the decision making test, he or she would also be allowed to view the subject's perceptions of the test. Subjects were told to sign the questionnaire and were told it would be given to the other person along with the other relevant material. Thus, the manipulation of a public versus private account pertained to whether subjects' attributions about their performance would be communicated to the other *along with* their responses on the test and the information about their hobbies, interests, and attitudes. After completing the questionnaire,

subjects filled out a short manipulation check form and were fully debriefed.

In an offset control condition, subjects took the test but did not receive performance feedback, completed the questionnaire anonymously, and, although they anticipated playing the role of a stimulus person, did not receive specific motivational instructions or a description of the other's characteristics.

Results

Scores on the self-esteem scale were split at the median and entered into a 2 × 2 × 2 × 2 (Self-Esteem: high vs. low × Feedback: success vs. failure × Motivation to Impress: high vs. low × Audience: critical vs. supportive × Account: public vs. anonymous) factorial design. Self-esteem scores ranged from 17 to 50, with a mean score of 40.5 (the lowest possible score was 10 and the highest was 50). The high self-esteem group had a mean score of 44.4 (range, 41 to 50), whereas the low self-esteem group had a mean score of 36.4 (range, 17 to 40).

Table 1

Means for the Feedback × Self-Esteem × Account × Motivation to Impress Interaction Effect on Ascriptions of Task Validity

| | Performance feedback | | | |
| | Failure | | Success | |
Condition	Low motivation	High motivation	Low motivation	High motivation
Public account				
Low self-esteem	-1.05_{ab} ‡	$-.45_a$ ‡	.47	.55
High self-esteem	$-.29_{bc}$	$-.83_c$ ‡	$.41_d$	$.88_d$ ‡
Private account				
Low self-esteem	$-.69$‡	$-.89$‡	.76	.54
High self-esteem	$-.82$‡	$-.46$	$.69$‡	.52

Note. All comparisons between corresponding success versus failure conditions are significant by simple effects tests, $p < .05$. Means with common subscripts differ ($p < .05$) in tests of simple-simple-simple main effects, under conditions in which the appropriate higher order interaction was significant.
‡ Mean differs significantly ($p < .05$) from mean control condition (.75 for low self-esteem subjects; .03 for high self-esteem subjects).

Manipulation Checks

The manipulations created the desired impressions. Subjects believed they performed better on the decision task in the success condition than in the failure condition, $F(1,224) = 555.99$, $p < .001$ ($Ms = 12.4$ and 5.2; 15-point scale); control subjects differed from both groups ($M = 10.4$, $ps < .05$). Subjects in the high motivation condition tried harder than subjects in the low motivation condition to create a positive impression, $F(1, 224) = 83.28$, $p < .001$, and expressed a greater desire to make a positive impression, $F(1, 224) = 8.06$, $p < .01$ (control subjects were intermediate).

Questionnaire Factors

The questionnaire contained a range of items that provided a portrait of how subjects evaluated themselves, the test, and the situation. The 23 items tapped (a) general measures of personal and nonpersonal responsibility ("How responsible do you feel you personally are, that is, your social decision-making ability and effort, for the score you received on the test?" and "How responsible do you feel factors beyond your personal ability and effort are for the score you received on the test, e.g., your mood, distractions in the situation, luck?"); (b) the four quadrants formed by the combination of Weiner's (Weiner et al., 1971) taxonomy of locus and stability (i.e., separate ratings of how much their performance was influenced by ability, effort, luck, and task difficulty); (c) the validity of the test; (d) score reliability ("If you were to take a different version or form of the test again, do you think you would do better, worse, or about the same?"); (e) characteristics of the test, including how interesting and enjoyable it was; (f) self-ratings on five attributes previously described as closely related to social decision-making ability (e.g., social competence, mature reasoning, ability to think logically in social situations); and (g) five attributes designated as unrelated to social decision-making ability (e.g., friendliness, wittiness), which allowed for the possibility that subjects could compensate for poor test scores with inflated self-ratings on important but unrelated dimensions (Baumeister & Jones, 1978).

A factor analysis was performed to reduce the items to a smaller number of meaningful dimensions. The analysis used a principal-axis solution and orthogonal varimax rotation and yielded six factors with eigenvalues greater than 1, accounting for 66% of the variance.

experimenter may find it difficult to use the exact same intonation for each subject, and if a number of different experimenters are running the same experiment, the variability in reading style is even more likely to create a problem. Second, unintentional behavior by the experimenter while reading the instructions (facial expression, body language) can contribute to *demand* characteristics (chapter 10, p. 179), and can cause subjects to draw conclusions about specific aspects of the experiment and try to behave in a manner that they believe is expected of them. ("The experimenter smiled. I'll bet I scored a lot better than the 27th percentile, but I'll act as if I'm really concerned.") To eliminate these effects, the instructions can be recorded on tape and played to each subject.

Writing a clear and useful set of instructions can be quite difficult. No matter how simple and direct the instructions may appear to the writer, they are unlikely to be clear to everybody. To avoid misinterpretations and confusion, it is important to use very simple language, simple sentence structure, and to repeat the critical information in the instructions at least twice. Repetition is important because subjects tend to be somewhat anxious in a research setting and can have trouble attending to all the details set forth in the instructions. To make sure you have written a good set of instructions for your experiment, it is wise both to seek the advice of colleagues and *pilot test* (chapter 10, p. 182) the instructions. The ideal subjects to use for pilot work are those who belong to the same *subject pool* to be used in the actual experiment. Pretesting the instructions should reveal any parts that are in need of clarification. Important details of the instructions must be included in articles to enable others to replicate the study, but instructions are usually not presented verbatim unless used as an independent variable.

Deception

In the subdiscipline of social psychology, *deception* (chapter 16, p. 314) is a relatively common research tactic. Did you notice the use of deception in the Schlenker et al. experiment? One deception was to give the subjects a "bogus but face-valid test." To describe the test as having *face validity* (chapter 6, p. 99) means that, judging from superficial characteristics alone, the test appears to be able to measure what it pretends to measure. Administering a bogus test is a fairly mild form of deception, but telling subjects that they scored in the 93rd or 27th percentile regardless of their true performance is not as innocuous.

Experimenters are ethically bound to *debrief* (chapter 10, p. 176) deceived subjects at the end of the experiment. In fact, experimenters should provide an explanation of the entire experiment and invite subjects to request a copy of the results of the study. Of course, such openness can contaminate the subject pool if informed subjects reveal details of the experiment to as yet untested subjects. In some cases it is defensible to defer subject debriefing until all testing has been completed.

Social psychologists have tried alternatives to deception. One technique is **role playing**, also called the **as-if experiment**. Subjects are asked to pretend that certain conditions exist. For example, an alternative to the deception procedure in the Schlenker et al. study would be to ask subjects to pretend that they had failed or succeeded on the previous task, or to pretend that their responses would be made

Role Playing (also called the **as-if experiment**): Subjects are asked to pretend that certain conditions exist.

public. Would the alternative procedure modify subjects' perceptions as effectively as deception? Without doing the experiment we cannot say for sure but, in general, role-playing is unlikely to match the effectiveness of deception as a modifier of behavior.

Manipulation Checks

At the end of the next-to-last paragraph in the procedure section, the authors mentioned that the subjects filled out a "short manipulation check form." A **manipulation check** is not another dependent variable of the experiment. It is an assessment to determine if an intended manipulation actually occurred. For example, regardless of their actual scores on the social decision-making task, the subjects who were randomly assigned to the success group were told that they scored in the 93rd percentile, whereas the subjects assigned to the failure condition were told that they scored only in the 27th percentile. Did the subjects really believe the false information? Was the deception successful in creating the perception of prior failure or prior success as intended? One way to find out is to ask the subjects. If the subjects in one group react to their set of instructions or manipulation in a different way than another group, the manipulation check (usually a short set of questions) will reveal that fact.

The authors stated in the results section that they used a 15-point scale to measure the subjects' belief about their performance on the social decision task. Results indicated that the manipulation was successful: The subjects who were told they were on the 93rd percentile did indeed believe that they had performed better on the social decision task than those who were told they had scored on the 27th percentile (mean score of 12.4 versus 5.2 on the 15-point scale). If the experimenters had failed to find a significant difference between the means, it would indicate that the strategy to manipulate the experimental condition (prior success versus prior failure) had been unsuccessful. If the authors had decided to manipulate self-esteem and had used the technique we described earlier (compliments and praise to raise self-esteem and criticism to lower self-esteem), it would have been very important to give the subjects a manipulation check to determine if the giving of compliments versus criticism had the intended effects on self-esteem.

A manipulation check adds substantially to our ability to interpret data in an unambiguous fashion. When experimental data fail to show any behavioral differences between groups of subjects who experienced different levels of an independent variable, two explanations are possible. One explanation is that, contrary to the experimental hypothesis, a successfully manipulated independent variable (here, the perception of prior success or failure) did not lead to any systematic behavioral differences on the dependent variable (questionnaire responses). Another explanation is that the manipulation itself failed, which would be the case if the false feedback failed to affect subjects' perceptions of success or failure. A manipulation check allows us to determine which of the latter two explanations of negative experimental results is correct. If there is no experimental effect evident in the data (as when both the success and failure groups respond to the questionnaire items in the same way), and the manipulation check confirms that different levels of an independent variable truly did exist (say, if giving false feedback to subjects did indeed affect the subjects' perception of prior success versus prior failure), the

Manipulation Check: An assessment to determine if an intended manipulation of an independent variable actually occurred.

unambiguous conclusion would have to be that the data fail to support the experimental hypothesis.

If, on the other hand, the evidence reveals that the manipulation did not produce different levels of an independent variable (say, if false feedback failed to make the subjects think they had failed or succeeded in the test of social decision-making), we could not draw any conclusion about the accuracy of the experimental hypothesis. In other words, if the manipulation check shows that no manipulation actually existed, the attempt to do an experiment has failed. To pursue a test of the experimental hypothesis we would first have to devise a manipulation that would successfully produce different levels of the particular independent variable (the perception of prior success or prior failure), and then repeat the experiment.

An interesting issue is raised when a manipulation check is used. The manipulation check may show that the mean score of one group is significantly different from the mean score of the other group, but that does not mean that every subject in the group had a score similar to the mean. Some researchers argue that the subjects that do not have a score similar to their group should be moved to the other group. Others feel that those subjects should be dropped from the study. Most researchers, however, leave all subjects in their original group. (It is beyond the scope of this text to discuss the pros and cons of each approach, but we advise you to determine what was done in every article you read that used a manipulation check.)

Use of Standardized Tests

The authors were probably very happy to have found a *standardized test* (chapter 6) to measure self-esteem. If they had found it necessary to develop their own test instrument, they would have had to make up the test items and establish the *validity* (chapter 3, p. 29) and the *reliability* (chapter 3, p. 28) of the test. Researchers are usually more than happy to avoid the work of test development and use a published standardized test of proven quality.

There are, however, many other concerns in addition to test development that must be weighed by researchers who intend to use standardized tests.

1. Is it difficult to administer the test? Is special training and/or formal certification required to administer the test? Is special equipment, such as a computer, required to present test items and/or record responses?

2. Is it difficult to score the test? If so, how much of a problem will it be to train personnel to score the test? Will scoring be very time-consuming? Can it be done using a computer?

3. How valid and reliable is the test? Has it been used with your subject population? Is the test appropriate for the age group you want to test? Is the test current? Was it recently revised? (If the test was developed many years ago, it may be dated and its previously established reliability and validity may have eroded.)

4. How long does it take subjects to complete the test?

5. How widely used is the test? If it has been used extensively, a large data base will exist to facilitate comparisons of your results with other research.

Researchers in social psychology, personality, and abnormal psychology use many standardized tests, and you have probably heard of a number of them: the

Minnesota Multiphasic Personality Inventory (MMPI-2), the Rorschach inkblot test, and Thematic Apperception Test (TAT); the Stanford-Binet, WAIS, and WISC intelligence tests; the Taylor Manifest Anxiety Scale (TMAS); and the Beck Depression Inventory. There are thousands of tests available, and as you become more familiar with the psychological literature you will learn what various tests measure, which ones are considered the most valid and reliable, and which ones are used frequently.

Standardized tests are used both for *basic research* and in *applied* areas of psychology (chapter 1, p. 8). Clinical and counseling psychologists are trained to give a large number of tests to diagnose the problems of their patients. School psychologists test students to determine their academic strengths and weaknesses. Vocational psychologists can assess aptitudes and recommend career choices based on standardized test performance. Industrial psychologists test the suitability of job applicants for specific job placements. If you are interested in learning more about how tests are constructed, you should take a class in Tests and Measurement. Most psychology departments offer such a course.

Group Formation from Pretest Scores

Schlenker et al. used one nonmanipulated independent variable: self-esteem. They pretested all subjects on a standardized self-esteem test and found that the scores ranged from 17 to 50. There are two ways the experimenters could have used the test results to split the subjects into high and low self-esteem groups. If the validity of a test has been established, specific score values can be defended as representing high versus low levels of the variable the test measures, and subjects are placed into the high and low group based on their scores. This procedure carries a risk, however, of ending up with very few subjects in one or both of the groups. The advantage is the confidence we have that the two groups that emerge from the assignment procedure are truly high and low with respect to the measured variable.

The second method for splitting a group into high versus low scorers is called a **median split**. The procedure is to order the test scores numerically from lowest to highest and split the group of subjects in half (at the median, chapter 4). Unlike the previous method, the median split guarantees an equal number of subjects in the high and low groups. To enlarge the differences between the high and low scorers, it is permissible to divide the scores into three parts, the top, middle, and bottom thirds, and test only the top and bottom extremes.

Median Split: A method for splitting a group into high versus low scorers. The test scores are ordered numerically from lowest to highest and the group of subjects is split at the median.

Although both splitting methods are routinely used, there are disadvantages to both approaches. The subjects within each group may not be very homogeneous. In fact, subjects placed in one group may be more similar to subjects in the other group than to subjects in the same group. For example, pretend we had the self-esteem test scores for 12 subjects and used the median-split technique to form two groups:

Low group: 17, 21, 24, 25, 26, 30   High group: 31, 35, 36, 41, 49, 50.

If we lump all subjects who scored from 17 to 30 into one group, we lose important information about each individual subject: the subject who scored 30 has a higher self-esteem than the subject who scored 17, yet both are classified as having low self-esteem. In addition, the low-group subject who scored 30 is more similar to the high-group subject who scored 31 than to the rest of the subjects in his/her group. In order to avoid these two problems, we can leave the self-esteem scores as a continuous variable (*interval scale*, chapter 3), and use the *correlation statistic* (chapter 9) to analyze the data. The original self-esteem score of the subject is put into the analysis rather than an artificial low versus high designation. The statistical test and analysis of the interaction effects is more complicated when self-esteem is treated as a continuous variable rather than dichotomized into low and high groups, and is therefore not used often.

Analysis of Questionnaire Responses: Factor Analysis

In most of the experiments we have reviewed, only one score was obtained from each subject. Sometimes, however, experimenters measure the same behavior a number of times, and the scores are combined into one number. For example, in the block randomization technique for the within subject design (chapter 13, p. 246), subjects are tested under all the different levels of the independent variable in each block, and then the scores obtained under the same treatment condition in the different blocks are combined into one number by calculating the mean or median.

In the present experiment each subject provided a response to 23 separate questionnaire items. Since these items related to many different topics, it would not have made sense to combine all the responses into one score. One approach to the analysis of such data is to analyze the responses to each question separately. A second approach is to do a **multivariate analysis of variance (MANOVA)**, an advanced statistical method that permits several independent and several dependent variables to be evaluated in the same analysis. A third approach is to separate the test items into different clusters based on the common content of the questions. Sometimes, however, it is not clear which questions belong in the same cluster. One solution to the latter dilemma is the application of a technique called **factor analysis**, a statistical method for determining which questions from a test instrument tend to measure the same dimension of behavior. Patterns of correlation between responses (the extent to which subjects who score highly on some questions also score highly on others, and the extent to which subjects who score low on some questions also score low on others) are the bases for identifying the dimensions of behavior (factors) that the test instrument measures. If we assume that a cluster of test questions that correlate highly with each other are measuring the same factor, we can give it a meaningful name. In the present instance, five factors emerged from the authors' factor analysis of the answers to the 23 questions. They called them Validity, Reliability, Ability, Trying, and Unrelated Traits. The authors then did a separate $2 \times 2 \times 2 \times 2 \times 2$ factorial analysis of variance for each of the identified factors, in effect treating each one of the five as a separate dependent variable.

Factor analysis is a popular approach to data analysis in the areas of social psychology and personality research. It allows the researcher to administer a lengthy questionnaire of items that are presumed to measure several different

---

Multivariate Analysis of Variance (MANOVA): An advanced statistical method that permits several independent and several dependent variables to be evaluated in the same analysis.

Factor Analysis: A statistical method for determining which questions from a test instrument tend to measure the same dimension of behavior.

personality characteristics and determine which questions tend to measure the same personality variable.

Presentation of Results with Three-way and Four-way Interaction Effects

We have included the table of the results from the Schlenker et al. article because it summarizes the effects that four of the independent variables had on one dependent variable (the Validity Factor) and is a popular way to report the results of experiments with a large number of independent variables (see Appendix A). Notice that subscripts (a, b, c) are attached to some of the means presented in the table. This is a common way of summarizing the pattern of differences. Means with common subscripts (two means that both have an *a* subscript) are significantly different from each other. Determining which means were significantly different from each other was determined by *tests of simple main effects* (chapter 14, p. 263) following the significant four-way interaction effect in the analysis of variance test.

It is rare to see experimental results presented in the form of a figure when there are four or more independent variables. With only three independent variables, however, figures can still be used to present results without undue visual complexity and are an excellent way of highlighting the existence of an interaction effect (*nonparallel lines*, chapter 14). If the self-esteem of the subjects had not been measured and the three independent variables were restricted to prior failure versus prior success, public versus private testing, and low versus high motivation, two simple figures, each representing a two-way interaction, could have been used to represent the results. We have plotted the means for these groups in Figure 23–1. We viewed the results as 2 × 2 factorial studies, with the failure condition plotted on the left and the success condition plotted on the right. Looking at two-way interactions within specific levels of a third variable makes the higher-order interactions much easier to understand. It is clear from the figures that only small

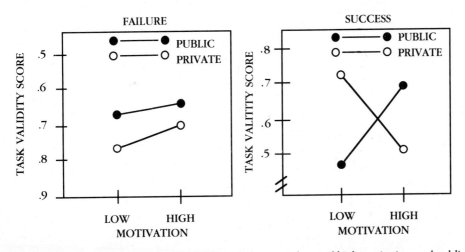

Figure 23–1. Task validity scores for the failure and success, low and high motivation, and public and private testing conditions.

differences exist among the groups in the failure condition, but there is an interesting two-way interaction under the success condition (a pattern of results reviewed in chapter 14). Task-validity scores were higher under the high motivation condition than under the low motivation condition when subjects were told their answers were public, but the opposite result occurred when they were told their answers were private.

Summary

The experiment selected to represent the subdiscipline of social psychology was relatively complex. Each of the five independent variables in the between-subject design had two levels, forming a $2 \times 2 \times 2 \times 2 \times 2$ factorial. Some of the independent variables were manipulated and some were not, so the experiment was also a mixed correlational/experimental design. We discussed several interesting methodological features of the Schlenker et al. study that have relevance to social psychology as well as other subdisciplines of psychology. These included: (a) an examination of the role of instructions in human research and the need to write them carefully so that all subjects will understand what to do; (b) the use of deception and the requirement to debrief subjects at the end of an experiment in which deception is used; (c) the use of manipulation checks to verify that the intended settings of an independent variable were achieved; and (d) the role of factor analysis in extracting important information from research data. We also presented a stepwise approach to reading and understanding a complex research report that can be applied to research in any of the numerous subdisciplines of psychology.

Key Terms

Factor Analysis, p. 432
Instructions, p. 423
Manipulation Check, p. 429
Median Split, p. 431

Multivariate Analysis of Variance
  (MANOVA), p. 432
Offset Control Condition, p. 421
Role Playing, p. 428

Chapter Exercises

1. Interpreting the results of a study with many independent variables and many dependent variables can be very difficult. The authors attempted to integrate the results using a concept of egotistical biases, also called self-serving attributions (see Abstract). It appears that subjects with high self-esteem were most egotistical when motivated to make a good impression and when in the public condition.

    a. If you had a friend with low self-esteem, how would you expect him to behave in a failure condition under low motivation with a public account on the Task Validity score? (Hint: Look at Table 1 in the Schlenker et al. article.)

    b. Would his score be significantly different if he were in the high motivation condition?

    c. What statistical tests must be done after a significant interaction effect is found in an analysis of variance test? (Hint: See footnote in Table 1.)

Communication of Scientific Research Findings

The Scientific Literature
　Finding the Pertinent Literature
Reporting Research Results
　Convention Presentations
　Written Reports

The Scientific Literature

In chapter 1 we reviewed the basic steps of research but omitted the last one: communication of the findings to others. Producing a written record of a study's purpose, methods, and results is extremely important because new research builds on the findings and methods of previously published research. Only by becoming aware of the methods and findings of all related studies can a researcher design a study that builds on the earlier efforts of others.

The practical implications of reporting results are especially obvious in the case of applied research. For example, the Dalton and Mesch (1990) finding (reviewed in chapter 22) that flexible time-scheduling decreased absenteeism could benefit a company combating absenteeism only if the results of the study were published. In chapter 21 it was reported that exposure to lead in childhood is correlated with a number of undesirable behaviors, such as decreased probability of graduating from high school. If such results were not reported to the public, then government agencies would be less pressured to decrease exposure to this persistent toxic chemical, and schools would not be aware of the need for special programs to provide assistance to lead-exposed children.

Finding the Pertinent Literature

At present, the easiest way to gain access to the literature of any subdiscipline of psychology is to use PsycLIT, a computer-based (CD-ROM) system for searching the literature published since 1973. Many college and university libraries subscribe to PsycLIT, and it is very easy to use. There are three simple commands to learn. To prepare to search for articles, press the key labeled F2. Next, type in key words that relate to your project (use the APA Thesaurus to determine appropriate key words for your topic). For example, if you are interested in the effects of transformed letters on reading speed, type in the words *transformed letters* and *reading speed*. The computer will then display how many articles have been published that contain the words *transformed letters*, how many articles have been published that contain the words *reading speed*, and how many articles contain both *transformed letters* and *reading speed*. A search can also be conducted using the name of a researcher instead of a key word. The display will show all the articles published by the researcher and, if more than one name is put in, the display will show all articles co-authored by the researchers. If you then press the F4 key, the complete reference and abstract of each of the articles that appeared during the key-word or name search will appear on the screen. If you press F6, a copy of the reference and abstract will be printed. If you have trouble using PsycLIT, read the instructions or consult with someone (such as the reference librarian) who is familiar with PsycLIT. You will find that PsycLIT will save you many hours trying to locate references that relate to your research interests.

Reporting Research Results

The obligation a researcher has to produce a formal record of a project can be satisfied in two principal ways: an oral presentation at a convention (a meeting of people with similar interests) and a published presentation in a journal (a magazine for publishing the research results of a specific subdiscipline). In Part III you read articles from a number of journals, including *Journal of Social and Personality Psychology*, *Behavioral Neuroscience*, *Perception and Psychophysics*, and *Psychology and Aging*.

The remainder of this appendix reviews guidelines for the effective oral and written communication of research findings. The need to learn these communication skills is obvious if you plan to be a research psychologist, or a professor engaging in both teaching and research. But being able to communicate in a clear and convincing manner will serve you well even if you have other career plans. You will undoubtedly have some occasion to speak before a group, to make a presentation to your boss, or to advocate your position in front of local government officials or a Parent-Teacher Association. No matter what career you choose, you will likely have to write a formal report at some point.

Convention Presentations

Conventions of professional societies differ in size and scope. At the larger conventions presentations encompass a wide range of subdisciplines. Also, large conventions usually last three or more days, are attended by a few thousand people, and are held in big cities (Boston, San Francisco, Chicago, New Orleans). At smaller conventions papers are often limited to one subdiscipline. Also, the smaller conventions are more likely to be held at universities, be limited to a few hundred attendees, and last less than three days.

The primary purpose of a convention presentation is to convey the most current research findings to fellow researchers. The presenters:

1. Review background research.
2. Introduce the problem and hypothesis.
3. Give a detailed account of the methodology.
4. Provide an overview of the results.
5. Discuss the results and their implications.
6. Answer questions (a few minutes at the end of each presentation are reserved for a question-and-answer period).

Most presentations range between 10 to 30 minutes. At some conventions, however, famous researchers are asked to give lengthier presentations (up to an hour) that review all the research they have done in a given area or provide an overview and integration of a large amount of research done both by themselves and others.

Many conventions also include poster sessions. A poster is an abbreviated paper displayed on a bulletin board. The researcher is expected to stand by the poster for about two hours and answer questions about the paper, but does not make a formal oral presentation.

Although undergraduate students seldom have an opportunity to attend national or international conventions, attendance at regional conventions (Eastern Psychological Association, Southwestern Psychological Association and others) is common. Faculty at most colleges and universities support student efforts to attend regional conventions. There are even reduced room rates and reduced registration fees for students, which helps make attendance at the convention more affordable.

Before you go to a convention, plan which presentations you want to attend. The schedule is printed in the convention program, which is distributed to registrants prior to the convention. Each paper is listed by author, title, and time of presentation, along with a short abstract. The abstracts will help you identify the papers in your area of interest. It is possible that you may want to attend two presentations that are scheduled for the same time. If this happens, try to find someone to attend one of the presentations so they can share their notes and get copies of handouts for you.

Although some undergraduate students present papers at regional conventions, it is more common for students to make conventionlike presentations at department- or school-sponsored events. At the authors' college we have Quest Day, a day devoted entirely to the scholarly presentation of faculty and student research. Typically between six and nine undergraduate psychology majors make presentations. If you should be fortunate enough to complete an interesting project and get on a convention program, remember to:

1. Outline the talk, being sure to cover the points previously mentioned (background research, etc.).

2. Prepare visual aids such as slides or overhead transparencies of the results (be sure that not too much information is presented in any one slide).

3. Prepare notecards and use them to guide your talk rather than reading directly from the paper. (Of course, if you think you may be so nervous that you cannot present using only notecards, it is acceptable to read from a prepared paper.)

4. Present your main points clearly and slowly.

5. Present major points of information using visual aids.

6. Keep your presentation as short as possible, and stay within the allotted time.

7. Practice your talk both alone and in front of other people.

8. Try to anticipate what questions you may be asked, and prepare your responses.

Written Reports

Researchers use a number of publication formats to communicate their findings. A journal is appropriate for reporting the results of only a few studies (between one and four, typically). To summarize and integrate a larger amount of related research, many researchers choose to write a chapter in a book. Researchers who are highly respected are often invited to write chapters for the annual reviews of their discipline or subdiscipline (example: *Annual Review of Psychology*). Some researchers are so productive that a book devoted entirely to their research is the logical choice.

Since most research is reported in journal articles, and because you will be asked to read many research articles as an undergraduate student in psychology, we will review the most widely adopted format for organizing and communicating information in psychology and other fields: The American Psychological Association (APA) style. The third (1983) edition of the Publication Manual of the APA reviews all the rules on general format and specific style. APA is one of the most widely used styles, with about 100,000 copies of the manual sold each year.

Your first paper using APA style will be the hardest to write. Once you learn what information belongs in which section, how much detail is needed in each section, and each picky rule (such as the rules for presenting references), it should become much easier for you to write the report.

The APA-style report typically includes seven main sections that appear in the following order: Title page, Abstract, Introduction, Method, Results, Discussion, and References. To help you learn what material should be presented in each section we have included a sample manuscript. At appropriate places in the sample manuscript, we review (using marginal notes) the rules for manuscript preparation that tend to be the most troublesome to students.

The first page of every manuscript is the title page
(see pp. 22–23 of the APA Publication Manual).

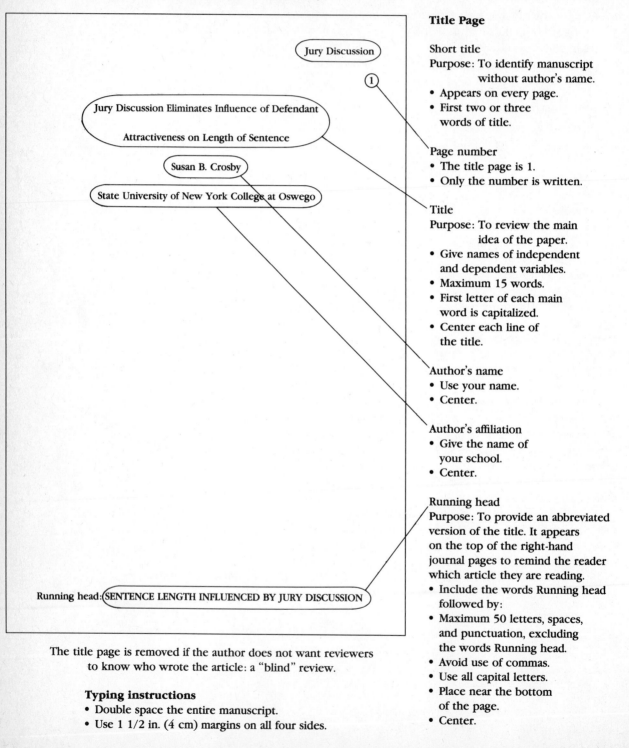

Title Page

Short title
Purpose: To identify manuscript
without author's name.
• Appears on every page.
• First two or three
words of title.

Page number
• The title page is 1.
• Only the number is written.

Title
Purpose: To review the main
idea of the paper.
• Give names of independent
and dependent variables.
• Maximum 15 words.
• First letter of each main
word is capitalized.
• Center each line of
the title.

Author's name
• Use your name.
• Center.

Author's affiliation
• Give the name of
your school.
• Center.

Running head
Purpose: To provide an abbreviated
version of the title. It appears
on the top of the right-hand
journal pages to remind the reader
which article they are reading.
• Include the words Running head
followed by:
• Maximum 50 letters, spaces,
and punctuation, excluding
the words Running head.
• Avoid use of commas.
• Use all capital letters.
• Place near the bottom
of the page.
• Center.

The title page is removed if the author does not want reviewers
to know who wrote the article: a "blind" review.

Typing instructions
• Double space the entire manuscript.
• Use 1 1/2 in. (4 cm) margins on all four sides.

NEW PAGE—The second page of every manuscript contains the abstract (see pp. 23–24 of the APA Publication Manual).

Jury Discussion

②

(Abstract)

Ten groups of six subject-jurors each were shown a videotape of a trial in which either an attractive or unattractive female defendant was convicted of vehicular manslaughter. Before any group discussion about the case, each subject-juror had to recommend a sentence for the defendant (from 1 to 25 years). After group discussion about the case, each subject-juror again recommended a sentence. Prior to group discussion the unattractive defendant received a longer sentence than the attractive defendant, but after group discussion subject-jurors no longer sentenced the unattractive defendant more harshly. These results supported a hypothesis derived from the problem-solving literature but ran counter to predictions based on information-integration theory.

Abstract

- The abstract is always the second page.

- Center the word Abstract.
- Only the first letter is capitalized.
- Do NOT underline the word Abstract.

- Do NOT indent first word of the abstract.
- Use one paragraph only.

Purpose:
1. Review problem under investigation with a single sentence (may be omitted if abstract is long).
2. Review methodology (subjects, apparatus/materials, procedures).
3. Review results, conclusions, and implications.

- Make sure the reader knows "WHAT YOU DID" and "WHAT YOU GOT."

- The length allowed was recently reduced from 100–150 words to 20 lines so that the title and abstract would fit on a computer screen and facilitate reading citations on computer-based literature reviews.

NEW PAGE—The introduction is begun on the third page of every manuscript (see pp. 24–25 of the APA Publication Manual).

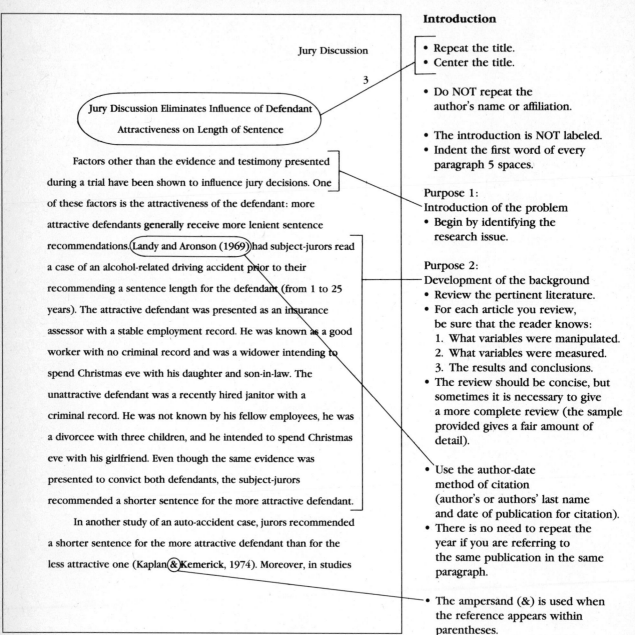

Jury Discussion

3

Jury Discussion Eliminates Influence of Defendant Attractiveness on Length of Sentence

Factors other than the evidence and testimony presented during a trial have been shown to influence jury decisions. One of these factors is the attractiveness of the defendant: more attractive defendants generally receive more lenient sentence recommendations. Landy and Aronson (1969) had subject-jurors read a case of an alcohol-related driving accident prior to their recommending a sentence length for the defendant (from 1 to 25 years). The attractive defendant was presented as an insurance assessor with a stable employment record. He was known as a good worker with no criminal record and was a widower intending to spend Christmas eve with his daughter and son-in-law. The unattractive defendant was a recently hired janitor with a criminal record. He was not known by his fellow employees, he was a divorcee with three children, and he intended to spend Christmas eve with his girlfriend. Even though the same evidence was presented to convict both defendants, the subject-jurors recommended a shorter sentence for the more attractive defendant.

In another study of an auto-accident case, jurors recommended a shorter sentence for the more attractive defendant than for the less attractive one (Kaplan & Kemerick, 1974). Moreover, in studies

Introduction

- Repeat the title.
- Center the title.

- Do NOT repeat the author's name or affiliation.

- The introduction is NOT labeled.
- Indent the first word of every paragraph 5 spaces.

Purpose 1:
Introduction of the problem
- Begin by identifying the research issue.

Purpose 2:
Development of the background
- Review the pertinent literature.
- For each article you review, be sure that the reader knows:
  1. What variables were manipulated.
  2. What variables were measured.
  3. The results and conclusions.
- The review should be concise, but sometimes it is necessary to give a more complete review (the sample provided gives a fair amount of detail).

- Use the author-date method of citation (author's or authors' last name and date of publication for citation).
- There is no need to repeat the year if you are referring to the same publication in the same paragraph.

- The ampersand (&) is used when the reference appears within parentheses.

Jury Discussion

4

in which attractiveness is defined in terms of physical

characteristics alone, results have been similar. For example,

Efran (1974) attached a photograph of a physically attractive or

unattractive male or female college student to a booklet

describing a case of student cheating. Subject-juror ratings of

the defendant on a 6-point scale indicated a desire to punish

the unattractive defendant more severely than the attractive

defendant.

Gerbasi, Zuckerman, and Hess (1977) pointed out that these as

well as other subject-juror studies (e.g., Nemeth & Sosis, 1973;

Sigall & Ostrove, 1975) are lacking in one critical respect:

subject-jurors were presented with a case and were asked to render

sentence without discussing the case with fellow jurors, which is

always the case following a real trial. The purpose of the present

experiment was to determine if attractiveness of the defendant

influences the length of sentence recommendations when group

discussion precedes a sentencing decision. It was hypothesized that

before group discussion subject-jurors would recommend a more

lenient sentence for an attractive defendant than for an

unattractive defendant, but that after group discussion the

attractive and unattractive defendants would receive equally harsh

sentence recommendations. This prediction was based on research

that has shown that group discussion leads to problem solutions

- If there are three or more authors, mention all authors the first time. After that use the "first author" and et al., as in Gerbasi et al. (1977) pointed . . .

Purpose 3:
Statement of purpose and rationale.
- Be very explicit:
  The purpose . . .
  It was hypothesized . . .
- The literature reviewed is the basis for the predictions.
- Researchers frequently base their predictions on theories.

- Limit the use of "I" or "we" in all sections of the manuscript (APA style rules just recently began to allow the use of the first person).

Jury Discussion

5

that are superior to the solutions of individual subject's (e.g.,

Shaw, 1932). So, if the extralegal variable of defendant

attractiveness does indeed result in jurors' making inappropriate

sentence recommendations when they act as individuals, group

discussion should result in rejection of attractiveness (a

superior solution) as a sentencing criterion. In other words,

attractiveness of the defendant should be less likely to influence

the length of a juror's sentence recommendation if the

recommendation follows group discussion.

Method

Subjects

Thirty male and 30 female students who were enrolled in an

introductory psychology course at the State University of New York

at Oswego volunteered to participate. They were white, primarily

middle class, freshmen or sophomores who ranged in age from 18 to

24 years ($M = 19.7$).

Materials

The questionnaire, a two-page typed booklet, contained a

cover page with the title of the case, and a second page labeled

"Years of Sentence" on which were listed numbers 1 to 25.

- There is no formal limit to the length of the introduction, but the typical range is between one and four typewritten double-spaced pages.

Method
- The method section follows the introduction—on the same page if space permits.

Heading levels: the rules for headings change when the article reports more than one experiment (see APA Publication Manual, pp. 66–67, 155–156).

- The word Method is centered and is NOT underlined.

- The Subjects, Materials, and Procedure headings are NOT centered or indented, but are underlined. The text begins on the next line and is indented five spaces.

Subjects
- Who participated.
- How many participated.
- How they were selected.

Materials
- Provide a complete description of the materials you used.

Purpose (Method Section):
To provide in great detail the characteristics of the subjects, the apparatus and/or materials used, and the procedure (what experiences the subjects had from the beginning to the end of the study). There should be enough detail in the method section to permit someone else to replicate the study. (See pp. 25–26 of the APA Publication Manual.)

Jury Discussion

6

A rectangular table with six chairs and a large screen (1 × 1 m) were set up in the experimental room for viewing the videotape of the trial. The two videotaped versions of the trial (each 12-min long) were identical except for the high versus low attractiveness of the defendant. The attractive and unattractive defendants were both acted by the same 25-year old professional actress and model. In the highly attractive condition she was physically appealing, well-groomed, and neatly dressed. In the unattractive condition she was unkempt and sloppily attired, and, through the assistance of the theatrical make-up staff, was made to look physically unappealing (stained teeth, poor complexion, etc.). The defendant was charged with vehicular manslaughter because, while intoxicated, she ran a red light and killed man who was crossing the street. For a complete description of the case, see Landy and Aronson (1969).

Procedure

Six subjects were randomly assigned to each jury group, with the restriction that there were three males and three females in each. Of the 10 jury groups included in the experiment, five were randomly assigned to see the videotape depicting the high attractive defendent (Group HI-A), and five were randomly assigned to see the low attractive defendant (Group LO-A). The groups were run on 10 consecutive days at 9:00 a.m.

Upon entering the experimental room the female experimenter asked the six subjects to seat themselves at a table. She informed them that after watching a videotape of a trial they

- Psychologists use the metric system. Therefore, all measurements are given in m, mm, or cm, NOT in inches or feet. Abbreviations for metric units are given in the APA Publication Manual (pp. 75–76).

Apparatus
Either the apparatus OR materials heading is used. The apparatus heading is used if you are primarily describing equipment. The materials heading is used if you are describing word lists, reading material, etc.
- Manufacturer's name and the model number of any apparatus commercially available must be reported.
- Report all physical characteristics (e.g., measurements, color, intensity of lights or tones) of self-made apparatus. The details provided must permit the reader to duplicate the apparatus.

Procedure
- Review what was done to the subjects from the beginning to the end of the study.
- Instructions are included verbatim only if they are an experimental manipulation. Otherwise, they are paraphrased.
- The design of the experiment and how subjects were assigned to each group are mentioned in this section.

Group abbreviations: It is easier for readers if meaningful initials or numerals are used for group names rather than meaningless letters or numbers.

- Avoid sexist language: use "they" rather than "he" or "she," except when a male or female is explicitly referred to.

Jury Discussion

7

would be asked to recommend a sentence for the defendant. The
experimenter then played the appropriate videotape. One-half of
the subjects were shown the tape with the attractive defendant,
whereas the other half were shown the tape with the unattractive
defendant. Immediately after the presentation, the questionnaire
booklet was given to each subject. The experimenter instructed
them to circle a number (from 1 to 25) on the second page of the
booklet to indicate the sentence length they thought was
appropriate for the defendant. Subjects were given as much time
as they needed, but were instructed not to say anything to the
other subjects. The booklets were then collected, and the
experimenter asked the six subjects to discuss the case freely as
if they were a real jury. They were told to notify the
experimenter (who was waiting in the next room) when, as a group,
they felt they had fully discussed the case. Once the
experimenter was notified and re-entered the room, she handed all
subject-jurors another copy of the questionnaire. She again asked
them to fill it out individually, after considering all
aspects of the case brought out in the group discussion. The
experimenter specifically told subjects not to feel bound by the
response they gave to the questionnaire prior to the opportunity
for group discussion.

Rules for Using Numbers

(See APA Publication Manual,
pp. 71–75)
• General Rule: Numbers 10 or above
are expressed as numerals. Nine or
below are written as words.

• The rules for when to write a
number as a word or as a numeral
are probably the hardest to
learn because there are many
exceptions to this rule. It
is wise to frequently refer
to the APA Publication Manual.

• Some exceptions to the general rule:
1. Measurements are always
numerals.
2. Statistical functions
are always numerals.
3. Groups of numbers with
one value above 10 are
always numerals.
4. Numbers that indicate a
specific place in a series:
Figure 1, Group 4, Trial 6 are
numerals.
5. If a sentence begins with a
number, it is always a word.

Jury Discussion

8

At the end of the experiment subjects were thanked for their participation and were instructed not to discuss the case with anyone else. They were also informed that within two weeks they could contact the experimenter to receive a detailed explanation of the research project. An additional group of six subjects was excused partway through the experiment due to a malfunction of the videotape monitor.

Results

An analysis of the sentence lengths that subject-jurors recommended for the defendants revealed that although the low-attractive defendent received a longer sentence than the high-attractive defendant prior to group discussion, attractiveness of the defendant had no effect on the sentence recommendations that followed group discussion. These results can be seen in Figure 1, which shows the mean sentence in years for Group HI-A

—————————

Insert Figure 1 about here

—————————

and Group LO-A prior to and after group discussion. This figure

Document any variations in procedures.

Results
• Center heading.

Purpose:
To summarize the results and the statistical analyses (see APA Manual, p. 27).

• Results can be summarized through figures, tables, or in the text, but can only be presented once.

• Refer to specific tables and figures in the text (e.g., Figure 1, which shows...), so the reader will know when to refer to them.

• The figures are placed at the end of the manuscript, but will be inserted in the text when printed. To let the typesetter know where to place each figure, type the instruction

—————————

Insert Figure 1 about here

—————————

on the center of the page, set off by lines above and below, shortly after the words Figure 1 appear in the text.

• The line before the instruction Insert Figure 1 about here should be a complete line.

• When a specific figure and its number are referred to, Figure is capitalized, and a numeral is used.

• If the results are summarized in a table, the words, Table 1, must be mentioned in the text, so the reader will know to look for the table.
• The typesetter must be told where to insert Table 1, by typing

—————————

Insert Table 1 about here

—————————

Jury Discussion

9

indicates that defendant attractiveness influenced the sentence lengths that subjects recorded prior to group discussion but not those they recorded after group discussion.

A preliminary analysis comparing sentences given by male ($M = 7.4$) versus female ($M = 7.0$) subject-jurors indicated no significant difference attributable to the gender of the subject-juror, $\underline{t}(58) = 1.73, \underline{p} > .20$. Therefore, the gender variable was not included in the main analysis. Results of a 2 × 2 repeated measures analysis of variance (High versus Low Attractive Defendant × No Discussion versus Discussion) showed a significant main effect for attractiveness, $\underline{F}(1, 58) = 10.88, \underline{p} < .01$, a main effect for group discussion versus no group discussion, $\underline{F}(1, 58) = 12.22, \underline{p} < .001$, and a significant interaction effect, $\underline{F}(1, 58) = 7.46, \underline{p} < .01$. Because the analysis revealed a signficant interaction effect, tests of simple main effects were done. The analysis revealed the source of the interaction effect: sentence recommendations for the low-attractive defendant were longer than for the high-attractive defendant only when they were made prior to group discussion, $\underline{F}(1, 58) = 17.54, \underline{p} < .001$, but after group discussion defendant attractiveness had no effect on sentence-length recommendations, $\underline{F}(1, 58) = 2.75, \underline{p} > .10$. The low attractive defendant received a longer sentence prior to group discussion than after group discussion, $\underline{F}(1, 58) = 19.39, \underline{p} < .001$,

- Provide a brief description of the results seen on the figure.

Statistical Results
Purpose:
  To present all results—
  even non-significant ones.

- Give a verbal description of the results, end the statement with a comma, and follow the statement with the statistical evidence. (The phase before the comma is a complete sentence.)

- The letter that represents the type of test used is underlined only if it is not a Greek letter. Note, the symbol for chi square, χ^2, is NOT underlined.

- The number in the parentheses represents the degrees of freedom (df value). Do NOT type the letters df.

- When reporting the results of an analysis of variance there are two df values.

- The p is always underlined.

- Do not confuse the $<$ and $>$ sign.

- Do NOT interpret the results in the Results section.

Jury Discussion

10

but the high attractive defendant's sentence was not significantly different before versus after discussion, $F < 1$.

Discussion

The finding that, before group discussion, subject-jurors sentenced the unattractive defendant more harshly than the attractive defendant replicates the findings of earlier research (e.g., Efran, 1974; Kaplan & Kemerick, 1974; Landy & Aronson, 1969; Sigall & Ostrove, 1975). After group discussion, however, high versus low defendant attractiveness no longer influenced the length of the subject-jurors' sentence decisions. These results support the experimental hypothesis that group discussion of the case would tend to eliminate the influence of defendant attractiveness on individual sentence decisions. Since no data were collected that reflect the content of the group discussions, future research should either monitor group discussion to determine if attractiveness was discussed, or should assess the impact of directing delibertions toward or away from a discussion of defendant attractiveness.

One prediction was not completely verified: that after group discussion the attractive defendant would receive a sentence as harsh as that received by the unattractive defendant. The results show that sentence values assigned to the attractive and unattractive defendant were equally lenient after group discussion. Apparently, the unattractive defendant had

- If the F value is less than 1, simply report $F < 1$ and omit the df and p values.

Discussion
- Purpose: To review whether the results supported or did not support your hypotheses, whether they are consistent with the published literature, and the conclusions and implications of the results. (See APA Publication Manual, pp. 27–28.)

- Center heading.

- Tie in the results of the present experiment with those reported in the literature.

- Discussion sections frequently begin with a review of the major results.

- The results are tied in with the hypotheses stated in the introduction.

Jury Discussion

11

received unduly harsh sentence recommendations when there was no

group discussion.

The effect group discussion had on the sentencing of

attractive and unattractive defendants may not generalize to other

types of defendant characterizations. For example, Myers and

Kaplan (1976) found that for defendants involved in a high- versus

low-guilt case, group discussion increased rather than decreased

the length of the sentence decisions. Perhaps group discussion

influences the effect the high- versus low-guilt variable had on

sentencing differently from the way it influences the effects of

the high- versus low-attraction variable. Alternatively,

procedural differences may have caused the difference in results.

Myers and Kaplan had subjects read booklets containing the summary

of the case, whereas in the present experiment subjects saw a

videotape of the trial. Research reported by Williams, Farmer,

Lee, Cundick, Howel, and Rookeer (1975), however, indicates that

mode of trial presentation may not be an important variable.

Williams et al. found no difference in punishment (dollar amounts

assigned in a land condemnation case) among groups seeing the

trial live versus in color video, black and white video, audio only,

or transcript only. Another procedural difference was that

subject-jurors in the Myers and Kaplan study read both high- and

low-guilt cases (a within-subject design), whereas in the present

experiment subject-jurors saw either the high- or low-attractive

• Authors frequently indicate if they believe the results can be generalized.

Reminder: Use et al. if the citation has been previously given and there are three or more authors.

Jury Discussion

12

defendant tape (a between-subject design). Additional research must be conducted to determine if the type of design used can account for the opposite effects group discussion had in the two sentencing experiments.

The opposite effects of group discussion obtained in the present study and Myers and Kaplan's (1976) study also raised an interesting theoretical question. Myers and Kaplan explained their results in terms of Anderson's (1974) information-integration theory, which predicts that group discussion should increase the difference in the length of the sentence between high- and low-guilt cases as compared with the sentence length prior to group discussion. Perhaps information-integration theory makes predictions opposite to the results obtained in the present experiment because it does not isolate the contributions of the guilt and attractiveness variables. This theory may need to be modified.

The practical implication of the results of the present experiment is that those who were concerned that attraction of the defendant may influence jury decisions should question the conclusions of earlier research. Apparently, defendant attractiveness only has an effect on juror sentence recommendations in the absence of jury discussions of the case. Because real juries always discuss cases presented to them, the extralegal attractiveness variable should not influence jury decisions about a defendant. Future investigations of the effects of attractiveness on jury decisions should allow for case discussions. Otherwise the research setting will not be representative of the real legal environment.

- Discuss problems you encountered when carrying out the research and suggestions for improving the research effort.

- Elaborate on contradictory results.

- Discussion sections frequently end with a review of the implications of the results.

NEW PAGE—The reference section always begins on a new page.

The exact format used varies among periodicals, books, chapters in books, etc., and you should look up the style in the APA Publication Manual (pp. 119–133). There are many picky rules for citing references.

Jury Discussion

13

References

Anderson, N. J. (1974). Cognitive algebra: Integration theory applied to social attribution. In L. Berkowitz (Ed.), Advances in experimental social psychology (pp. 1–101). New York: Academic Press.

Efran, M. G. (1974). The effect of physical appearance on the judgment of guilt, interpersonal attraction, and severity of recommended punishment in a simulated jury task. Journal of Research in Personality, 8, 45–54.

Gerbasi, K. C., Zuckerman, M., & Reis, H. T (1977). Justice needs a new blind-fold: A review of mock jury research. Psychological Bulletin, 84, 323–345.

Izzett, R. R., & Leginski, W. (1974). Group discussion and the influence of defendant characteristics in a simulated-jury setting. The Journal of Social Psychology, 93, 271–279.

Kaplan, M. G., & Kemerick, G. D. (1974). Juror judgment as informational integration: Combining evidential and nonevidential information. Journal of Personality and Social Psychology, 30, 493–499.

Landy, D., & Aronson, E. (1969). The influence of the character of the criminal and his victim on the decisions of simulated jurors. Journal of Experimental Social Psychology, 5, 141–152.

References
Purpose:
To provide the complete reference for every citation mentioned in the manuscript.

- Center heading.

- References are NOT numbered.

- All references are in alphabetical order.

Rules for journal articles:
- The last name appears first, followed by the initials.
- The first line of each reference is NOT indented, but subsequent lines are indented three spaces.
- The ampersand (&) is used if there is more than one author.
- There is a comma before the &.
- The year appears in parentheses and is followed by a period.
- The first letter of the first word is the only one capitalized in the title, and the title is followed by a period.
- The name of the journal article is NOT abbreviated.
- The first letter of each main words is capitalized.
- The journal title is underlined.
- The volume number and pages follow the journal title.
- All numbers are separated by commas.
- Do NOT use the words "volume" or "pages."
- Only the volume number is underlined.
- End with a period.

Myers, D. G., & Kaplan, M. F. (1976). Group-induced polarization
in simulated juries. Personality and Social Psychology
Bulletin, 2, 63–66.

Nemeth, C., & Sosis, R. H. (1973). A simulated jury study:
Characteristics of the defendant and the jurors. Journal of
Social Psychology, 90, 221–229.

Shaw, J. I. (1972). Reactions to victims and defendants in
varying degrees of attractiveness. Psychonomic Science, 27,
329–330.

Sigall, H., & Ostrove, N. (1975). Beautiful but dangerous:
Effects of offender attractiveness and the nature of the crime
on juridic judgement. Journal of Personality and Social
Psychology, 31, 410–414.

Williams, G. R., Farmer, L. C., Lee, R. E., Cundick, B. P.,
Howell, R. J., & Rooker, K. (1975). Juror perceptions of
trial testimony as a function of the method of presentation:
A comparison of live, color video, black-and-white video,
audio, and transcript presentations. Brigham Young University
Law Review, 2, 375–421.

Jury Discussion

15

Author Notes

This sample manuscript reported data published by Izzett
and Leginski (1974).

Jury Discussion

16

Table 1

Mean Sentence in Years for Low and High-attractive Defendant

With and Without Discussion

	Attractiveness	
	Low	High
No discussion	11.5	5.3
Discussion	7.2	4.8

Tables
(see APA Publication Manual, pp. 83–94).
- Each table is placed on a separate page.
- Place the code word and page number on the top of each table.

- Table number and title are placed on the top of the table.
- Table 1 is NOT underlined.
- Table 1 is NOT indented or centered.

- The first letter of each main word in the table title is capitalized.
- The table title is underlined.

This table is not part of the sample manuscript. It is provided only to show how tables are presented. Remember, results can be summarized through figures, tables, or in the text, but may only be presented once.

All figure captions are placed on the same page, with figures clearly numbered.

Jury Discussion

17

Figure Caption

Figure 1. Mean sentence in years for low- and high-attractive

defendant with and without discussion (LO-A = low attraction,

HI-A = high attractive, ND = no discussion, D = discussion).

Figure Captions
- The page is titled Figure Caption and is the title centered.

- <u>Figure 1</u> is underlined.
- Nothing is indented on the figure caption page.

REMINDERS:
1. Write clearly and concisely.
2. All pages of a manuscript are double spaced. NEVER SINGLE SPACE.
3. Check the APA Publication Manual for additional rules.
4. Plan on writing many drafts before the final one.
5. Proofread your final version and correct spelling, typing, and grammatical errors (this is very simple if you have typed the paper on a word processor).
6. Make sure you have not missed a section.
7. Be sure that the sections are in the correct order.

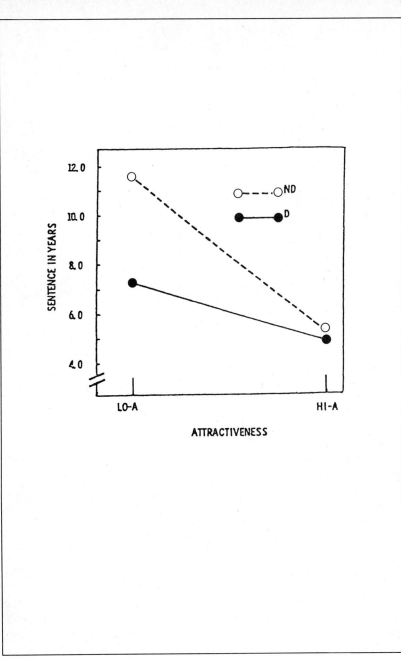

(See APA Publication Manual, pp. 96–98.)

Figures
- Each figure is drawn on a separate page and is placed after the Figure Caption page.
- Page is not titled or numbered.

- The vertical axis should be about two-thirds the length of the horizontal axis.
- If either axis does not begin at zero, a double slash mark must be made to indicate the discontinuity.
- All axes must be labeled.
- The legend that identifies the group names appears within the axes on the figure.
- Do NOT put the figure caption (same as figure title) on the figure. It is placed on a separate page at the end of the report.
  - Figures are drawn in black (NO colors are allowed).

APPENDIX

B

Statistical Analyses
of Selected Examples

Parts I and II include fictional examples of studies and experiments as well as data and the results of statistical tests. With the exception of Box 12–1, however, we reported only the computed values of statistics and whether or not results were significant. This appendix contains additional details of the statistical analyses in earlier chapters and can serve as a brief review for students who have already studied statistics and wish to reacquaint themselves with the principal features of some of the more commonly applied statistical analyses.

Since relatively simple statistical analysis is often done on a hand calculator, the necessary details for hand calculation of chi-square, Pearson *r*, and Spearman rho statistics are furnished here. For the ANOVA examples, however, we have omitted hand calculation methods because students are unlikely to forsake the speed, convenience, and accuracy of a computer-based analysis.

In most cases the data used for illustrations of data analysis are taken from tables in chapters 4, 9, and 14. For some of the experimental designs discussed in chapter

14 (single-factor experimental designs with more than two treatments, within-subject factorial design, and mixed between-subject within-subject factorial design), examples with data appear here for the first time.

Chi-Square Analysis (Table 4–1)

The 2×2 contingency table originally shown as Table 4–1 appears here as Table B–1 with the obtained frequencies (f_o) and computed expected frequencies (f_e) in parentheses. (The chi-square analysis of these data does not employ the Yates correction for discontinuity, even though some researchers prefer to include it when, as here, there is only one degree of freedom.) The expected frequencies represent the pattern of independence between the row and column variables, as stated in the null hypothesis. To compute the expected frequency for a cell, multiply the row total of the row the cell is in by the column total of the column the cell is in and then divide by the overall total. For example, the obtained frequency in the Male/Atmosphere cell, which is in the first row and the first column, is 13. The expected frequency for that cell is 37 (the column total for the first column) times 40 (the row total of the first row) divided by 80 (the overall total of all the cell frequencies). The answer is 18.5. The degrees of freedom (df) of a contingency table equal $(r - 1)(c - 1)$: the number of rows minus 1 times the number of columns minus 1. Here, $df = 1$, the critical value for χ^2 will be found in the χ^2 table in the row labeled $df = 1$ and in the column for the .05 (or .01) level of significance.

The critical value of the χ^2 statistic with $df = 1$ and the .05 level of significance equals 3.84. The result of 6.10 exceeds 3.84, so we reject the null hypothesis that the

Which is more important?

	Atmosphere	Portions	Total
Male	13 (18.5)	27 (21.5)	40
Female	24 (18.5)	16 (21.5)	40
Total	37	43	80

$$\chi^2 = \Sigma \frac{(f_o - f_e)^2}{f_e}$$

$$\chi^2 = \frac{(13 - 18.5)^2}{18.5} + \frac{(27 - 21.5)^2}{21.5} + \frac{(24 - 18.5)^2}{18.5)} + \frac{(16 - 21.5)^2}{21.5}$$

$$\chi^2 = 1.64 + 1.41 + 1.64 + 1.41$$

$$\chi^2 = 6.10$$

Table B–1. The data from Table 4–1, with expected cell frequencies and χ^2 calculations.

row and column variables are independent and recognize the significant contingency between the row and column variables. In the context of the present example, the analysis shows that the relative importance consumers place on atmosphere versus portion size when rating a restaurant depends on the gender of the consumer.

Chi-Square Analysis (Table 4–2)

In contrast to the data in Table 4–1, in Table 4–2 the row and column variables are independent (the χ^2 statistic is not significant). As in Table B–1, in Table B–2 the expected frequencies are shown in parentheses along with the obtained frequencies. Notice how close in value the expected frequencies are to the obtained frequencies when, as in the present case, contingency is absent.

The critical value of the χ^2 statistic equals 3.84 at the .05 level of significance. The result of 0.49 does not exceed 3.84, so the row and column variables are independent (that is, not contingent). The chi-square analysis of the data from Table 4–2 indicates that the relative importance consumers place on restaurant atmosphere versus portion size does not depend on the gender of the consumer.

Which is more important?

	Atmosphere	Portions	Total
Male	27 (25.5)	13 (14.5)	40
Female	24 (25.5)	16 (14.5)	40
Total	51	29	80

$$\chi^2 = \Sigma \frac{(f_o - f_e)^2}{f_e}$$

$$\chi^2 = \frac{(27 - 25.5)^2}{25.5} + \frac{(13 - 14.5)^2}{14.5} + \frac{(24 - 25.5)^2}{25.5} + \frac{(16 - 14.5)^2}{14.5}$$

$$\chi^2 = 0.088 + 0.155 + 0.088 + 0.155$$

$$\chi^2 = 0.49$$

Table B–2. The data from Table 4–2, with expected frequencies and χ^2 calculations.

The Pearson *r* Correlation Analysis (Table 9.1)

Here is the computational formula for the Pearson *r* statistic:

$$r = \frac{\Sigma XY - \dfrac{(\Sigma X)(\Sigma Y)}{n}}{\sqrt{\left[\Sigma X^2 - \dfrac{(\Sigma X)^2}{n}\right]\left[\Sigma Y^2 - \dfrac{(\Sigma Y)^2}{n}\right]}}$$

In Table B–3 the data from Table 9–1 are reproduced, as are the computations necessary to fill in the values in the formula.

$\Sigma X^2 = 2^2 + 4^2 + 5^2 + \ldots + 14^2 = 905$
$\Sigma Y^2 = 0^2 + 2^2 + 2^2 + \ldots + 12^2 = 504$
$\Sigma XY = (2)(0) + (4)(2) + (5)(2) + (11)(7) + \ldots + (14)(12) = 654$
The value of *n* equals the number of subjects, so here $n = 10$.

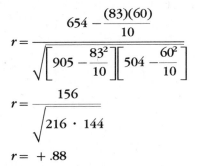

$$r = \frac{654 - \dfrac{(83)(60)}{10}}{\sqrt{\left[905 - \dfrac{83^2}{10}\right]\left[504 - \dfrac{60^2}{10}\right]}}$$

$$r = \frac{156}{\sqrt{216 \cdot 144}}$$

$$r = +.88$$

Type of Controller

Subject	(X) Keyboard	(Y) Joystick	XY
1	2	0	0
2	4	2	8
3	5	2	10
4	11	7	77
5	15	10	150
6	7	9	63
7	3	4	12
8	14	9	126
9	8	5	40
10	14	12	168
	$\Sigma X = 83$	$\Sigma Y = 60$	$\Sigma XY = 654$

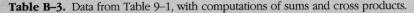

Table B–3. Data from Table 9–1, with computations of sums and cross products.

The critical value of the Pearson *r* is found in the Pearson *r* table (found in any statistics text) in the row for 8 degrees of freedom

$$df = n - 2 = 10 - 2 = 8$$

in the column for the .05 level of significance. The critical value equals .6319, so *r* = .88 represents a significant positive association between keyboard and joystick performance.

The Spearman rho Analysis (Table 9.2)

The X and Y columns of Table B–4 are the data from Table 9–2. Variable X is a rating of a patient's resistance to treatment, variable Y a rating of the pain he or she experiences.

The first step is to convert the X and Y scores to ranks. Then, for each row in the table we then subtract the Y rank from X rank and put the result in the D (difference) column. Each D score is squared and the result is entered into the D^2 column, which is then added to get ΣD^2. The *n* value is the number of subjects. For the data above, $\Sigma D^2 = 70.5$ and *n* = 12.

$$rho = 1 - \frac{6\Sigma D^2}{n^3 - n}$$

$$rho = 1 - \frac{6 \cdot 70.5}{12^3 - 12}$$

$$rho = 1 - 0.25$$

$$rho = .75$$

Subject	X	Rank X	Y	Rank Y	D	D^2
1	2	2.5	1	1	1.5	2.25
2	4	6	2	2	4	16
3	4	6	5	7.5	−1.5	2.25
4	9	12	7	10	2	4
5	5	8	3	4	4	16
6	7	9.5	9	12	−2.5	6.25
7	3	4	4	6	−2	4
8	8	11	6	9	2	4
9	2	2.5	3	4	−1.5	2.25
10	4	6	5	7.5	−1.5	2.25
11	7	9.5	8	11	−1.5	2.25
12	1	1	3	4	−3	9
						$\Sigma D^2 = 70.5$

Table B–4. Data from Table 9–2, with computations for the Spearman rho.

The critical value of the Spearman rho when $n = 12$ and the level of significance set at .05 equals .591, so a rho value of .75 represents a significant positive association between resistance-to-treatment ratings and pain ratings.

Single-Factor Between-Subject and Within-Subject Designs

Just as for the two-treatment design (see Box 12–1 for the t test formulas and sample analyses), the independent and correlated observations of single-factor between-subject and within-subject designs with more than two treatments (the topic of chapter 13) require different analyses. Here are data and ANOVA summary tables for each type of design.

A Sample Analysis of a Single-Factor Between-Subject Experiment

Responses were recorded for 20 subjects (shown in Table B–5 as S_1 to S_{20}) who were randomly divided and assigned to four different incentive conditions: no incentive, praise, food, and money. The analysis partitions the total variation among the data values to identify the respective contributions of the experimental factor (type of incentive) and chance (error) to the values.

Different computer programs require different procedures for entering data, and it is very important to follow all rules carefully. For example, one program could specify that the data be entered column by column (Group 1, then Group 2, and so on), another that data be entered row by row, and still another could accommodate either row or column input as long as the program is properly configured to match the sequence of data input. When the data above are properly entered, the computer will produce output that contains the information in Table B–6, the ANOVA summary table. The critical F values (from the F table) with 3 and 16 degrees of freedom are 3.24 ($\alpha = .05$) and 5.29 ($\alpha = .01$). Since the computed F value (6.71) exceeds 5.29, F is significant at the .01 level. (Many computer programs provide the exact probability value for the computed F statistic, which makes it unnecessary to consult an F table in a statistics text.)

	No Incentive		Praise		Food		Money
S_1	12	S_6	17	S_{11}	20	S_{16}	28
S_2	11	S_7	13	S_{12}	23	S_{17}	19
S_3	8	S_8	9	S_{13}	17	S_{18}	16
S_4	9	S_9	16	S_{14}	22	S_{19}	21
S_5	6	S_{10}	7	S_{15}	15	S_{20}	11
Means:	9.2		12.4		19.4		19

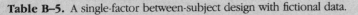

Table B–5. A single-factor between-subject design with fictional data.

ANOVA Summary Table

Source	df	SS	MS	F	p
Between Treatment	3	378.8	126.26	6.71	< .01
Within Treatment (error)	16	301.2	18.82		
Total	19	680			

Table B–6. ANOVA summary of the data from Table A–5.

Inspection of the treatment means reveals the principal source of the significant between-treatment differences: the food and money conditions (19.4 and 19) are basically equal, but they differ substantially from the no-incentive (9.2) and praise (12.4) conditions. To verify this impression formally we must do a post-ANOVA comparison, such as the Tukey HSD test discussed briefly in chapter 13. The first step is to set up a table with the ordered means as row and column labels and enter the differences between pairs of means within the table, as shown in Table B–7.

The next step is to compute the Q statistic for each difference score in the table using the following formula:

$$Q = \frac{\bar{X}_1 - \bar{X}_2}{\sqrt{\dfrac{MS_{error}}{n}}}$$

For example, starting with the cell in the upper right corner, $\bar{X}_1 - \bar{X}_2 = 10.2$. The denominator of Q is the square root of the MS_{error} from the ANOVA table divided by n, the sample size for a treatment condition:

$$\sqrt{\frac{MS_{error}}{n}} = \sqrt{\frac{18.82}{5}} = 1.94.$$

	Trt. 1	Trt. 2	Trt. 4	Trt.3
Ordered Means:	**9.2**	**12.4**	**19.0**	**19.4**
Treatment 1 (9.2)	—	3.2	9.8	10.2
Treatment 2 (12.4)		—	6.6	7.0
Treatment 4 (19.0)			—	.4
Treatment 3 (19.4)				—

Table B–7. The table of differences between all pairs of treatment means from Table B–5.

So, for the Treatment 1 versus Treatment 3 comparison,

$$Q = \frac{10.2}{1.94} = 5.26.$$

Similarly, the Q value for the Treatment 1 versus Treatment 4 comparison is:

$$Q = \frac{9.8}{1.94} = 5.05.$$

With the number of treatments (k) equal to 4 and degrees of freedom for the MS_{error} equal to 16 (see ANOVA table), the critical value of Q as published in the Q table (the studentized range statistic) is 4.05 for the .05 level of significance and 5.19 for the .01 level of significance. Thus, the two Q values above are significant because they exceed the critical values. Specifically, the Treatment 1 versus Treatment 3 comparison is significant at the .01 level (5.26 > 5.19), and the Treatment 1 versus Treatment 4 comparison is significant at the .05 level (5.05 > 4.05). None of the Q values for the other pairs of treatments (1.65, 3.61, and 3.40) exceed the critical values, so no other treatments are significantly different from each other besides Treatments 1 and 3 and Treatments 1 and 4.

Sample Analysis of a Single-Factor Within-Subject Experiment

Table B–8 represents a within-subject experiment in which target misses were recorded for seven subjects during four consecutive performances of an aiming task. The design is an extension of the test-retest design (as diagramed in Table 13–4), so each row of the table contains the data of a single subject.

Notice in Table B–9 that in processing the data of the within-subject single-factor design the two primary identifiable sources of the variation among the data values are between-subjects (individual differences) and within-subjects. Then the within-subject variation is partitioned into the contribution of the experimental

Test Sessions

Subjects	I	II	III	IV
1	11	13	8	8
2	18	12	11	12
3	14	18	5	6
4	22	24	18	13
5	9	9	8	11
6	17	14	11	4
7	21	18	15	7
Means:	16	15.43	10.86	8.71

Table B–8. A single-factor within-subject design with fictional data.
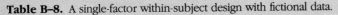

ANOVA Summary Table

Source	df	SS	MS	F	p
Between Subjects	6	296.50			
Within Subjects	21	444.75			
Between Treatment	3	263.25	87.75	8.75	< .01
Residual (error)	18	181.5	10.08		
Total	27	741.25			

Table B–9. ANOVA summary of the data from Table B–8.

factor, and the remainder (residual) is considered to be chance variability from undetermined sources. Of course, for the program to output the correct ANOVA summary, the computer user must: (1) load a program suitable for analyzing the results of a within-subject design; and (2) input the data in proper sequence so the ANOVA computations will be applied to the correct data.

The computer F value (8.75) is significant at the .01 level (the critical value for F when $\alpha = .01$ is 5.09), which indicates that there are significant differences among the four treatment means. Inspection of the means suggests that Treatments 1 and 2 both differ from Treatments 3 and 4. As with the between-subject design, such impressions can be verified statistically using a post-ANOVA test such as the Tukey HSD test.

Analysis of the Between-Subject 2 × 2 Factorial Experiment

The data in Table 14–8 illustrate an outcome of a between-subject 2×2 factorial experiment in which the Factor A and B main effects are significant, but there is no A × B interaction. The row, column, and cell means from Table 14–8 are summarized in Table B–10.

As noted in chapter 14, the ANOVA results (Table B–11) show that a $1 payment ($\bar{A}_1 = 27$) had a different effect on Task Y performance than a $20 payment ($\bar{A}_2 = 37$). Similarly, 1 point of extra credit ($\bar{B}_1 = 28$) had a different effect on Task Y performance than 20 points ($\bar{B}_2 = 36$).

Analysis of Table 14–9

In contrast to Table 14–8, the data in Table 14–9 illustrate an outcome of a between-subject 2×2 factorial experiment in which almost all the between-cell variation is due to the A × B interaction. The significant A × B interaction revealed by the ANOVA (Table B–12) indicates that the effect the two levels of cash payment had on Task Y performance depended on the operative extra-credit condition (see Figure 14–4).

Extra Credit

(Factor B)

		1 Point	20 Points	
Cash Payment	$1	23	31	$\bar{A}_1 = 27$
(Factor A)	$20	33	41	$\bar{A}_2 = 37$
		$\bar{B}_1 = 28$	$\bar{B}_2 = 36$	

Table B–10. The cell, row (Factor A), and column (Factor B) means from Table 14–8.

ANOVA Summary Table

Source	df	SS	MS	F	p
Between Cell	3	1640.0			
Cash Payment (A)	1	1000.0	1000.0	9.00	< .01
Extra Credit (B)	1	640.0	640.0	5.76	< .05
A × B	1	0.0	0.0	0.0	
Within Cell (error)	36	4000.0	111.1		
Total	39	5640.0			

Table B–11. The ANOVA summary of the data from Table 14–8.

ANOVA Summary Table

Source	df	SS	MS	F	p
Between Cell	3	1310.0			
Cash Payment (A)	1	10.0	10.0	0.09	
Extra Credit (B)	1	90.0	90.0	0.81	
A × B	1	1210.0	1210.0	10.89	< .01
Within Cell (error)	36	4000.0	111.1		
Total	39	5310.0			

Table B–12. ANOVA summary of the data from Table 14–9.

███████████████

In order to gain a clear picture of the experimental results when a significant interaction is present, it is necessary to follow the overall ANOVA with an analysis of simple effects.

Analysis of Simple Effects (Table 14–9)

A test of simple effects follows the discovery of an interaction effect, and an analysis of the data in Table 14–9 reveals a significant interaction between the two incentive conditions: cash payment (Factor A) and extra credit (Factor B). Methods for computing simple effects seldom appear in introductory statistics texts and are not covered here. Nevertheless, analyses of simple effects are routinely reported in the psychological literature, and it is important to understand the important information an analysis of simple effects can provide following the discovery of an interaction. We therefore include here the results of a simple effects analysis of the Table 14–9 data, summarizing the cell, row, and column means from Table 14–9 in Table B–13.

The analysis of simple effects shows that within Level 1 of Factor B (23 versus 33) the $20 group performed better on Task Y than the $1 group, $F(1, 36) = 4.50$, $p < .05$. Within Level 2 of Factor B (31 versus 19), the pattern was reversed: the $1 group performed better than the $20 group, $F(1, 36) = 6.48$, $p < .05$. If, instead, the analysis of simple effects focused on comparing the two levels of Factor B within individual levels of Factor A, we would find no difference between the levels of Factor B at Level 1 of Factor A (23 versus 31), $F(1, 36) = 2.88$, $p > .05$, and a significant difference at Level 2 of Factor A (33 versus 19), $F(1, 36) = 8.82$, $p < .01$. Thus, Factors A and B did exert significant effects, *but only within isolated levels of one or the other factor.*

Analysis of Table 14–11 Data

The data in Table 14–11 illustrate an outcome of a between-subject 2×2 factorial experiment in which all sources of between-cell variation are significant:

		Extra Credit		
		Factor (B)		
		1 Point	20 Points	
Cash Payment	$1	23	31	$\bar{A}_1 = 27$
Factor (A)	$20	33	19	$\bar{A}_2 = 26$
		$\bar{B}_1 = 28$	$\bar{B}_2 = 25$	

Table B–13. Cell, row (Factor A), and column (Factor B) means from Table 14–9.

ANOVA Summary Table

Source	df	SS	MS	F	*p*
Between Cell	3	9230			
Cash Payment (A)	1	4410	4410	36.69	< .01
Extra Credit (B)	1	3610	3610	32.49	< .01
A × B	1	1210	1210	10.89	< .01
Within Cell (error)	36	4000	111.1		
Total	39	13,230			

Table B–14. ANOVA summary of the data from Table 14–11.

the Factor A main effect, the Factor B main effect, and the A × B interaction. The fact that the ANOVA (Table B–14) shows both main effects and the interaction effect to be significant indicates that, overall, both Factor A and Factor B affected performance, but the influence of Factor A was different within one level of Factor B than within the other, and the influence of Factor B was different within one level of Factor A than within the other. (See chapter 14 for details.)

Sample Analysis of a 2 × 2 Within-Subject Design

The data in Table B–15 represent the result of a 2 × 2 within-subject experiment. No example of a 2 × 2 within-subject design was provided in chapter 14; one is provided here to (1) stress that every subject is tested under all treatment combinations and (2) demonstrate the special ANOVA that is necessary for a within-subject factorial design. Specifically, notice that in the ANOVA summary for the within-subject design (Table B–16), the A, B, and A × B effects require separate error terms.

Each of the six subjects experienced both levels of Factor A and both levels of Factor B, so each subject contributed four data values to the results. The ANOVA summary in Table B–16 shows the significant contributions of Factor A, Factor B, and the A × B interaction to the results. The effect of Factor A is represented by the comparison between the two Factor A means (74.5 versus 83). The effect of Factor B is represented by the comparison between the Factor B means (82 versus 75.5), and the interaction is evident from the uniformity of the cell means within Level 1 of Factor A (cell means of 74 and 75) together with the relatively large difference within Level 2 of Factor A (cell means of 90 and 76).

Factor B

Factor	Subjects	B_1	B_2	
A_1	1	66	64	
	2	73	74	
	3	70	77	
	4	73	87	
	5	80	69	
	6	82	79	
	Means:	74	75	$\bar{A}_1 = 74.5$
A_2	1	82	69	
	2	88	80	
	3	85	64	
	4	97	78	
	5	89	76	
	6	99	89	
	Means:	90	76	$\bar{A}_2 = 83$
		$\bar{B}_1 = 82$	$\bar{B}_2 = 75.5$	

Table B–15. A 2 × 2 within-subject design with fictional data. Six subjects were tested under all four treatment combinations.

ANOVA Summary Table

Source	df	SS	MS	F	p
Between Subjects	5	768.5			
Within Subjects	18	1366.0			
Factor A	1	433.5	433.5	23.95	< .01
Error (A)	5	90.5	18.1		
Factor B	1	253.5	253.5	22.43	< .01
Error (B)	5	56.5	11.3		
A × B	1	337.5	337.5	8.68	< .05
Error (A × B)	5	194.5	38.9		
Total	23	2134.5			

Table B–16 ANOVA summary of the data from Table B–14, a within-subject design.

Sample Analysis of a Mixed Between-Subject/Within-Subject Design

This example uses the same data as the within-subject design shown above. Notice, however, that in the mixed 2 × 2 design shown in Table B–17 different groups were assigned to the two levels of Factor A, and the same subjects were tested under both levels of Factor B. Under this arrangement the factorial experiment is a combination of a between-subject design (Factor A) and within-subject design (Factor B and the A × B interaction). As you inspect the results of the ANOVA in Table B–18, note that the total SS (2134.5), the SS for the A main effect (433.5), the SS for the B main effect (253.5), and the SS for the A × B interaction (337.5) are the same for both the within-subject and the mixed between-subject/within-subject examples, but the error terms are not the same. Thus, the results of statistical analyses can differ markedly when the same data are analyzed using different design assumptions, underlining the importance of selecting a computer program appropriate for analyzing the results of your research.

		Factor B		
Factor A	**Subjects**	**B_1**	**B_2**	
	1	66	64	
	2	73	74	
A_1	3	70	77	
	4	73	87	
(Group 1)	5	80	69	
	6	82	79	
	Means:	74	75	$\bar{A}_1 = 74.5$
	7	82	69	
	8	88	80	
A_1	9	85	64	
	10	97	78	
(Group 2)	11	89	76	
	12	99	89	
	Means:	90	76	$\bar{A}_1 = 83$
	$\bar{B}_1 = 82$	$\bar{B}_2 = 75.5$		

Table B–17. A 2 × 2 mixed between-subject/within subject experimental design with fictional data.

ANOVA Summary Table

Source	df	SS	MS	F	p
Between Subjects	11	1292.5			
Factor A	1	433.5	433.5	5.05	< .05
Error (between)	10	859.0	85.9		
Within Subjects	12	842.0			
Factor B	1	253.5	253.5	10.10	< .05
A × B	1	337.5	337.5	13.45	< .01
Error (within)	10	251.5	25.1		
Total	23	2134.5			

Table B–18. ANOVA summary of the data from Table B–16, a mixed between-subject/ within-subject experimental design.

G L O S S A R Y

ABBA Counterbalancing: All subjects experience both orders of both treatments in ABBA sequence.

AB/BA Counterbalancing: The treatments are administered to half the subjects in an A-B sequence, with a B-A sequence for the other half.

A Posteriori Test: A technique for executing a comparison between treatment conditions that was not planned prior to running an experiment.

A Priori Test: A technique for executing a comparison between treatment conditions that was planned prior to running an experiment.

A-B-A Design: Tracking a reversible behavior first without (A), then with (B), and again without (A) the experimental condition present.

Accidental Sample: A sample that includes subjects simply because they are available at a particular time and/or location.

Additive Result: A result of two or more variables acting in concert that equals the sum of their respective influences.

Analysis of Variance (ANOVA): A statistical procedure for comparing multiple treatments or treatment combinations.

Animal Model: A nonhuman biological preparation used as a substitute to study a phenomenon that is fundamentally human.

Anonymous Testing: Testing subjects without knowing their identities.

ANOVA: *see* Analysis of Variance.

Antagonistic Effect: A combined action of two or more variables that is less than the potential of their individual contributions.

Anthropomorphizing: Imparting human motives, emotions, and intellectual abilities to animals in the absence of carefully controlled scientific observations.

Applied Research: Research to solve practical problems and improve the quality of life.

Archival Research: Retrieval of selected information from existing data bases.

Assignment Error: A possible but statistically improbable failure of random assignment to achieve initial equivalence.

Association: The systematic and orderly paralleling of the values of different variables.

Assumptions of the Scientific Method: Premises that scientists must accept on faith.

Authority: Knowledge based on faith and trust in an individual or institution.

Baseline: The subject's level of performance prior to introducing an experimental condition or prior to making a change in an existing experimental condition.

Basic Research: Acquiring information for its own sake rather than for practical application.

Best-Fit Linear Function: *see* Line of Best Fit

Between-Subject Design: Experimental design in which each treatment condition is administered to a separate group of subjects.

Biased Sample: A subset of a population with characteristics that are systematically different from the population as a whole.

Bimodal: A distribution in which the two most frequent values occur equally often.

Block: A subgroup containing one subject per treatment condition.

Block Randomization: The random assignment of subjects to treatment conditions in blocks.

Carryover Effects: Residual effects on a subject's behavior from having experienced one or more prior treatment conditions.

Case Study: A very detailed and comprehensive study of the behavior of a single individual together with descriptions of past and present life events relevant to the behavioral record.

Cell: A row/column combination in a table.

Central Tendency: The "average" or typical value of a distribution as reflected in the mean, median, and mode.

Chi-Square Goodness of Fit Test: A statistical test to evaluate whether the deviation of obtained frequencies from expected frequencies is significant or due to chance.

Closed Questions: Survey questions that require the respondent to select a category that is most representative of his or her attitude.

Cluster Sampling: Sampling groups as opposed to sampling individuals.

Coefficient of Determination: r^2, the proportion of variability in the criterion variable that is predictable.

Coefficient of Nondetermination: $1 - r^2$, the proportion of variability in the criterion variable that is *not* predictable.

Coercion: Inducing subjects to participate or to continue to participate in an experiment against their own best interests.

Cohorts: Subjects born at the same time and therefore exposed to the same unique environmental circumstances present at that time.

Comparison Stimulus: The stimulus against which the standard stimulus is contrasted.

Confidentiality: The names of subjects are known, but in order to maintain secrecy they are assigned secret code numbers when their data are analyzed.

Confounding Variable: A factor that can influence experimental results apart from the influence of the actual experimental variable.

Construct Validity: The usefulness of a psychological concept as a measure of behavior.

Contamination (of the subject pool): The spreading of information about an experiment by former participants to future participants.

Content Analysis: The plan for evaluating an answer to an open-ended question with respect to objectively defined features of its content.

Contingency: Association between categorical (nominal) variables.

Contingency Table: A two-dimensional (rows and columns) tabular display of nominal data as cell frequencies (tally totals).

Control Groups: Standards against which we can compare the performance of experimental groups.

Converging Operations: Establishing that different research methods yield data consistent with the same conclusion.

Correlated Observations: The data of within-subject experiments, in which repeated measures are taken of the same subjects.

Correlation Analysis: A statistical technique for quantifying the strength of association between variables.

Correlational Research: Study of the relationships between nonmanipulated variables (selected variables and natural treatments) and behavior.

Counterbalancing: A method to neutralize the impact of carryover effects.

Covert Behavior: A psychological reaction or mental process that cannot be physically described or directly observed.

Criterion: A level of performance used to designate successful achievement of a task.

Criterion-related Validity: The extent of association between a set of test scores and one or more relevant performance measures.

Criterion Variable: A variable that is associated with and can be estimated from the value of a predictor variable.

Cross-lagged Panel Design: A research approach that points to the direction of a possible cause-and-effect relationship in correlational data.

Cross-sectional Design: The behavior of different-aged subjects is measured at the same point in time.

Cross-sectional Study: A study conducted within a single time frame.

Cross-sectional–Sequential Design: The cross-sectional study is repeated some time later (say, in five years) with a new set of subjects.

Crucial Experiment: An experiment to test which of two competing theories is correct.

Cultural Bias: A threat to the accurate measurement of a behavioral capacity arising from the subject's limited access to the personal and educational experiences on which the test items are based.

Data: The information research produces.

Datum: A single piece of data.

Debriefing: Explaining an experiment to a subject upon its completion, including the nature and purpose of any deception that may have been used.

Deception: The practice of describing a study to a subject with incomplete and/or false information in order to avoid contaminating the results.

Deduction: A statement of the facts a researcher should find if a theory is correct.

Demand Characteristics: Cues that lead subjects to have an impression of what an experimenter expects or wants to happen in a study.

Dependent Variable: A measurement that changes in response to different values of an independent variable.

Descriptive Corollaries: Questions that, although similar to Basic Questions 4, 5, 6, and 7, represent types of correlational rather than experimental research.

Descriptive Research: Investigations limited to describing behavior.

Descriptive Statistics: Computed values that reflect specific characteristics of data, such as central tendency and dispersion.

Designs: The various methodological approaches we use to answer formally stated research questions.

Dispersion: The extent to which the scores in a distribution deviate from the central value as reflected by the range and standard deviation.

Dose-response Curve: Figure showing the relationship between the amount of the chemical given (the dose) and the amount of change in a behavior (the response).

Double-barreled Question: A survey item that contains two queries, which makes it impossible to tell which one the respondent is answering. *See also* Loaded Question.

Double-blind Methodology: Neither the subjects nor the experimenter know any details of the experiment that could bias their behavior.

Double Negatives: A potential source of confusion from using two negatives to convey a positive thought in a survey item.

Embarrassing Questions: Survey items that request information of a personal or intimate nature.

Envelope: Sketch around the periphery of a scatterplot that indicates its general shape and trend.

Expectancy Effect: A bias in subjects that arises from some degree of knowledge about the methods and/or purpose of an experiment, or assumptions (correct or incorrect) about the experiment.

Experiment: The implementation of a formal strategy to reveal cause–effect relationships between variables.

Experimental Hypothesis: Formal statement of the effect an experimental manipulation should produce.

Experimental Research: A method for documenting cause–effect relationships between variables.

Experimentally Naive: Description of subjects who have never before participated in an experiment.

Experimenter Bias: The influence of an experimenter's fears, hopes, expectations, and/or prejudices on the conduct of the research.

External Validity: The extent to which researchers can generalize the results of carefully controlled laboratory studies to understand behavior in real-life situations.

Extraneous Variable: A variable that introduces confounding and, thereby, rival explanations of an experimental result. Another name for confounding variable.

Face Validity: Assumption that a measure is a valid predictor of behavior owing to the obvious association between the measure and the behavior.

Factor: Independent variable.

Factor Analysis: A statistical method for determining which questions from a test instrument tend to measure the same dimension of behavior.

Factorial Design: A method for exploring how two or more independent variables act in concert.

Filler Items: Test items intended to distract the subjects or to hide the true purpose of a study.

Frequency Data: Tallies in discrete categories; nominal data.

Functionally Dependent: Referring to the existence of an association between variables.

Functionally Independent: Referring to the absence of an association between variables.

Group-administered Tests: Tests that can be administered to many subjects at once.

Haphazard Sample: *see* Accidental Sample

Hawthorne Effect: Workers respond to the special attention they get from their supervisors during their participation in a study rather than the manipulated conditions.

Higher Order Designs: Experimental designs that include the manipulation of more than two factors.

History as a threat to internal validity: The attribution of pretest-posttest differences to a behavior-altering experience that occurs between pretest and posttest in addition to the significant event.

Hypothesis: A speculation about the truth.

In vitro (as opposed to **in vivo**): Literally, in the test tube. Studying live tissue outside the body.

Independent Observations: The data of between-subject experiments, in which subjects experience only one treatment condition.

Independent Variable: A manipulated variable that defines the treatment conditions of an experiment.

Idiographic Research: Research with a primary objective to describe, analyze, compare, and contrast the behavior of individual subjects.

Individual Differences: The natural physical and behavioral diversity among people.

Individually Administered Tests: Tests that must be administered one-on-one.

Induction: Integrating information from facts in order to explain why the facts are as they are.

Inferential Statistics: Procedures that permit making generalizations about population characteristics from the analysis of sample data.

Informed Consent: A subject's declaration of willingness to participate in a study with full knowledge of the potential for objectionable, inconvenient, or unpleasant consequences.

Initial Equivalence: An even distribution across treatment conditions of any pre-existing behavioral differences among subjects.

Insignificant: Description of an experimental result attributable to chance alone.

Institutional Review Board (IRB): A broad-based group of citizens entrusted with screening research proposals to make sure they comply with regulations governing the ethical treatment of human subjects.

Instructions: Information for guiding subjects what to do in the study or for manipulating the levels of an independent variable.

Instrumentation as a threat to internal validity: The attribution of pretest-posttest differences to inconsistent experimental execution rather than to the significant event.

Interaction: A result of two or more independent variables acting in concert that cannot be explained as the sum of their individual contributions.

Internal Consistency Reliability: The mean reliability measure one would obtain from all possible split-half analyses.

Internal Validity: The determination that an obtained pattern of experimental results is a direct and unambiguous consequence of the experimental manipulation.

Interobserver Reliability: The extent of agreement among observers about what did or did not occur.

Inter-rater Reliability: The degree of consistency among multiple evaluators.

Interrupted Time-Series Design: A pretest-posttest design with several pretests and several posttests before and after the significant event.

Interval Scale: Different variable values reflect different magnitudes and equal intervals between magnitudes reflect equal quantity.

Interviewer Bias: A systematic effect on the respondent's behavior that stems from the behavior of the interviewer toward the respondent.

Intuition: Knowledge based on a personal hunch.

Invasive Technique: A research procedure that is likely to create some discomfort.

Kruskal–Wallis H Test: A test used to compare differences among three or more sets of ranked data for statistical significance.

Latin Square: A square matrix (k rows and colums) that contains a subset of all the possible treatment orders in a multiple-treatment experiment.

Leading Question: A question that tends to channel a response in a certain direction.

Levels of a Factor: The specific values of an independent variable that comprise the treatment conditions of an experiment.

Likert-type Scaling: A closed-question format that expands the two-choice format to include less extreme and neutral response choices.

Line of Best Fit: The straight line that best represents the trend in a scatterplot.

Linear: Pertaining to a straight line.

Linear Progressive Error: The assumption relevant to ABBA counterbalancing that the carryover effect grows progressively and in equal amounts with each repeated testing.

Linear Regression Analysis: A statistical procedure for determining the regression constants.

Loaded Question: A question that contains emotionally charged language. *See also* Double-barreled question.

Longitudinal Design: The same people are repeatedly tested as they grow older.

Longitudinal Study: *See* Panel Study.

Longitudinal-Sequential Design: Subjects born in two different years are tested in the same year and then repeatedly tested.

Magnitude Estimation Technique: The subject assigns numbers to stimuli that are proportional to an initial standard.

Main Effects: Differences among the treatment conditions of a factorial design that are attributable to a single factor.

Manipulated Variable: An independent variable; a condition under the direct control of the experimenter.

Manipulation Check: An assessment to determine if an intended manipulation of an independent variable actually occurred.

Matched-Groups Design: Subjects are paired on the basis of some attribute or behavioral measure, then assigned to different treatment conditions.

Maturation as a threat to internal validity: The attribution of pretest-posttest differences to normal age-related developmental phenomena rather than to the significant event.

Measurement Equivalence: The application of behavioral testing procedures that are appropriate for a broad spectrum of age groups.

Measurement Scales: The four levels of information data can convey (nominal, ordinal, interval, or ratio).

Median Split: A method for splitting a group into high versus low scorers. The test scores are ordered numerically from lowest to highest and the group of subjects is split at the median.

Method of Adjustment (also called **Method of Average Error**): To determine a threshold the subject adjusts a stimulus until it can no longer be detected, then increases the intensity until it can once again be detected.

Method of Constant Stimuli: A fixed number of constant stimuli (typically between 5 and 11) that vary in a dimension (such as loudness or frequency of tones) are presented in random order to determine a threshold.

Method of Limits: To determine a threshold, stimuli, such as tones, are presented in a fixed order many times, progressing from soft to loud and from loud to soft.

Minimal Risk: Risk is minimal if a subject's participation does not increase the likelihood of a negative event occurring or the magnitude of a negative event, should one occur unexpectedly.

Mixed Design: A hybrid design with between-subject and within-subject elements.

Mixed Experimental/Correlational Design: A research design that includes both manipulated and nonmanipulated factors.

Mixed-Stimulus Counterbalancing: Neutralizing carryover effects from Type A and Type B trials by arranging the trials in random sequence.

Morgan's Canon: "In no case is an animal activity to be interpreted in terms of higher psychological processes if it can be fairly interpreted in terms of processes which stand lower in the scale of psychological evolution and development."

Multiple Baseline Designs: Small-n designs that require tracking a behavior across the introduction and withdrawal of an experimental condition that, unlike the single-subject design, do not require that the behavior be reversible.

Multiple Regression: A statistical procedure that uses several predictor variables to predict a criterion variable.

Multiple Time-Series Design: A pretest-posttest design with a nonequivalent control group that has been expanded into a time-series design.

Multiple-Treatment Single-Factor Designs: Single-factor designs in which the factor has more than two levels.

Multivariate Analysis of Variance (MANOVA): An advanced statistical method that permits several independent and several dependent variables to be evaluated in the same analysis.

Mutually Exclusive Response Categories: Nonoverlapping response categories.

Natural Setting: An environment characterized by the absence of any purposeful or controlled modification of an organism's living conditions.

Natural Treatment: Exposure to or isolation from an unplanned event.

Naturalistic Observation: The unobtrusive recording and description of animal or human behavior in an unaltered natural setting.

Negative Relationship: The direction of association between variables when pairs of measurements on the same subjects tend to be of opposite magnitudes (high, low; low, high).

Nomethetic Research: Research that has the behavior of groups as its primary focus.

Nominal Scale: Numerals name, categorize, or label.

Nonadditive Result: An interaction.

Noncomparable Successive Samples: A source of bias in the successive samples design that arises when the successive samples have different characteristics.

Nonequivalent Control Group: A group that resembles the experimental group but, because of the absence of random assignment, cannot be assumed to be initially equivalent to the experimental group.

Noninvasive Technique: A research procedure that does not create discomfort for the subject.

Nonmanipulated (Subject) Variable: A subject characteristic or experience over which the researcher has no control.

Nonsense Syllables: Nonwords frequently made up of three letters (such as, DAX, LIQ, CHJ).

Norm: The central (mean, median, or mode) or average form of a behavior derived from prior study of a relatively large group.

Null Hypothesis: A tentative assumption that exposing subjects to different treatment conditions will fail to produce systematic behavioral differences attributable to those treatment conditions.

Occam's Razor: We should avoid framing explanations based on numerous assumptions. *See also* Parsimony.

Offset Control Condition: An extra control group that is not one of the treatment combinations defined by the core experimental design.

Open-ended Questions: Survey questions that do not place limits on the content of the response.

Operational Definition: An objective definition of a variable stated in terms of the specific methods used to manipulate (independent) or measure (dependent) the variable.

Ordinal Scale: Numerals of different magnitude convey only "more" or "less."

Overt Behavior: A directly observable behavior.

Panel Study: A study that uses the same sample on successive occasions.

Parsimony: Principle that the simplest of two or more equally well-reasoned explanations is the preferred explanation.

Partial Out: Statistically remove the effects of a confounding variable in a correlational design through the use of the partial correlational technique.

Partially Treated Control Groups: Subjects who have some or all of the experiences of the experimentally treated subjects except for the treatment itself.

Pearson r: A measure of the strength and direction of association between interval- or ratio-scaled variables.

Performance Criteria: Behavioral measures against which to compare the predictions of a test.

Pilot Work: The preliminry work done before full-scale execution of the experiment.

Placebo: A bogus treatment condition in which subjects experience the elements of the treatment administration without receiving the treatment itself.

Planned Comparison: *See* A priori test.

Planned Pretest-Posttest Study: The significant event that occurs between the pretest and the posttest is planned.

Positive Relationship: The direction of association between variables when pairs of measurements on the same subjects both tend to be of the same relative magnitude (high, high; low, low).

Post-ANOVA Test: An analysis to follow the overall ANOVA that can reveal additional details about the specific pattern of differences among the treatment conditions.

Post Hoc Test: *See* A posteriori.

Potentially Testable Hypotheses: Hypotheses that are not currently testable but may one day be testable as technology advances.

Power: The capacity to detect an effect of the independent variable on the dependent variable when one truly exists.

Prediction: Estimation of one variable value from knowledge of another.

Predictive Validity: The degree to which a test can predict the type of performance it is supposed to predict.

Predictor Variable: A variable that is associated with and can be used to estimate the value of a criterion variable.

Prestige Bias: An influence on a survey response arising from references to popular people or institutions in the body of the question.

Pretest-Posttest Design: An initial evaluation occurs before a significant event and is followed by another evaluation after the significant event.

Pretest-Posttest Design with a Nonequivalent Control Group: A two-group pretest-posttest study that lacks the random assignment of subjects to the control and experimental conditions.

Pretest-Posttest Design with an Equivalent Control Group: Two groups of randomly assigned subjects receive the pretest and the posttest but only one experiences the significant event.

Proactive Design: Subjects learn the material presented in Phase 1, then learn some related material in Phase 2, and subsequently are required to recall the second set of material.

Prospective Study: The research identifies subjects who have experienced a condition (for example, suffered exposure to toxic substances), then measures behavioral changes. *See also* Retrospective Study.

Protocol Analysis of Problem Solving: Analysis of the successful and unsuccessful steps and strategies subjects employ when attempting to solve a problem.

Psychophysical Methods: Methods for determining the sensitivity of organisms to stimuli and calculating the absolute (AL) and difference (DL) thresholds (method of constant stimuli, method of limits, and method of adjustment).

Purposive Sampling: Accidental sampling combined with some selectivity to ensure that a certain type of subject is included in the sample.

Qualitative: Representing different values of a variable without reference to a quantifiable characteristic (e.g., ethnic group, job title, and brand name.)

Quantitative: Representing different values of a variable as numerically coded expressions of magnitude (e.g., intelligence, drug dosage, and time).

Quasi-experimental Designs: Research strategies that tend to minimize one or more of the threats to internal validity that arise when we are unable to apply all the controls required of a true experiment.

Quota Sampling: Sampling that fills strata quotas using an accidental sampling method.

Random: A determination based on chance alone, as in the random assignment of subjects to different groups.

Ratio Scale: Equal intervals reflect equal quantity and the variable has a true zero point.

Rationalism: Knowledge based on logical deductions from true premises.

Raw Data: Research results that have not yet been statistically described or analyzed.

Reactivity: An extraneous influence on measurement that occurs when the act of measurement produces a reaction in the subject.

Regression Analysis: A statistical procedure that uses a predictor variable to predict the value of a criterion variable. The stronger the association between the variables, the more accurate the predictions are likely to be.

Regression Constants: The slope and Y-intercept of the best-fit linear function.

Regression Line: *See* Line of Best Fit.

Regression to the Mean as a threat to internal validity: Attributing a shift from an atypical level of performance on a pretest to a more normal level on a posttest to the statistical improbability of consecutive atypical performances rather than to the significant event.

Reliability: Consistency of a measurement taken at different times.

Repeated Measures Design: Within-subject design.

Representative Sample: A subset of a population that matches the characteristics of the population.

Respondent Mortality: *See* Subject Loss.

Response Bias: A distorting influence on the representativeness of a sample caused by the failure of some sampled people to respond to the survey.

Retroactive Design: Subjects learn the material presented in Phase 1, then learn some related material in Phase 2, and subsequently are required to recall the material presented in the first phase (diagrammed in Table 19–2).

Retrospective Study: Both the independent variable and the behaviors under study are in the past. *See also* Prospective Study.

Risk: An association between variables that carries an element of danger.

Risk Factor: A variable that is predictive of an undesirable consequence.

Role Playing (also **As-if Experiment**): Subjects are asked to pretend that certain conditions exist.

Sample Size: The number of subjects in an experiment assigned to the different treatment conditions.

Sampling Frame: A relatively large, clearly defined group assumed to be an accurate microcosm of the even larger target population.

Science: The systematic collection of information according to rules and procedures that preserve objectivity and accuracy.

Selected Variable: A personal subject characteristic, such as age, years of formal education, or gender.

Selection Bias: A flaw in the sampling process that results in an over- or under-representation of some segments of the population in a sample.

Sequence and Order Effects: *see* Carryover Effects

Sham Procedure: A treatment condition that contains all the invasive elements of the experimental treatment short of the treatment itself.

Sham-operated Control Group: The group that in brain-lesion experiments receives the same treatment as the lesioned group, except that no lesion is made and the brain remains fully functional.

Signal Detection Theory (SDT): An approach to threshold measurement that accounts for both the physical characteristics of the stimulus and the characteristics of the background (noise) against which the stimulus is presented.

Significant: Conclusion that a research result is attributable to other than chance factors.

Simple Effects: A comparison of the levels of one factor within one level of another factor.

Simple Main Effects: *See* Simple Effects.

Single-Blind Methodology: Withholding methodological details of an experiment from subjects to avoid biasing their behavior.

Single-Factor Design: A research plan in which only one independent variable is manipulated.

Single-Sample Study: The behavior of a single treatment condition is compared to norms of behavior from some data base.

Single-Subject Design: Studying the effects of the introduction and withdrawal of an experimental condition on a reversible behavior using only one subject.

Small-n Experiment: An experiment that requires only a few subjects, such as a multiple-baseline design or replications of a single-subject design.

Spearman rho: A measure of the strength and direction of association that is appropriate when one or both variables have at least ordinal scaling.

Split-half Reliability: The association between responses to two equivalent halves of a test.

Split-litter Design: An equal number of subjects from a litter are randomly assigned to each group in the study.

Standard Stimulus: A reference against which the subject must contrast the comparison stimulus to determine the difference threshold.

Standardization Sample: The sample studied to determine the normative level of a behavioral capacity.

Standardized: Denotes adherence to uniform test administration and scoring procedures and the comparison of test results to norms.

Standardized Psychological Tests: Instruments that assess the behavioral characteristics, abilities, and aptitudes of individuals with reference to group norms.

Statistical Analysis: A tool for extracting, highlighting, and organizing the information in data.

Stratified Random Sampling: Random sampling conducted within defined subgroups of a population.

Subject Attrition: *See* Subject Loss.

Subject Loss: The failure of sampled subjects to participate fully in a study.

Subjective Rating: Assignment of a value to an observation based on the subject's personal perception.

Successive Independent Sample Design: A series of cross-sectional studies with different samples.

Survey Design: A strategy that guides the administration of the survey instrument.

Survey Research: A technique for exploring the nature of personal characteristics and perceptions by analyzing the answers to a set of carefully developed questions.

Symmetrical Transfer: The assumption that any carryover effect from Treatment A to Treatment B can be offset by the carryover effect from B to A.

Synergistic Effect: A combined action of two or more variables that is greater than the sum of their individual contributions.

Systematic Sampling: Inclusion of every k^{th} member of a list in the sample.

***t* test:** A statistical test for evaluating the difference between two treatment means for significance.

Testable Hypotheses: Hypotheses that are verifiable by gathering and analyzing objective data.

Testing as a threat to internal validity: The attribution of pretest-posttest differences to the subjects' growing familiarity with experimental apparatus and procedures rather than to the intervening significant event.

Test-Retest Design: Subjects are evaluated twice under the exact same set of experimental conditions and data-gathering procedures.

Test-Retest Reliability: The strength of association between original test results and a set of retest results.

Theory: A proposition or set of propositions that serve to explain and integrate a set of facts.

Time-lag Design: Subjects of the same age are tested in different years.

Treatment Effect: An influence on behavior that is attributable to the manipulation of the independent variable.

Treatments (Treatment Conditions): Conditions manipulated by and under the direct control of the experimenter.

Trial: A single unit of test experience.

Two-Sample Experiment: An experiment for comparing the effects of two different experimental conditions or comparing an experimental treatment condition to a control condition.

Two-Treatment Experiment: *See* Two-sample Experiment.

Type I Error: Rejection of the null hypothesis when it should have been retained.

Type II Error: Retention of the null hypothesis when it should have been rejected.

Unplanned Pretest-Posttest Study: The significant event that occurs between the pretest and the posttest is unplanned.

Untestable Hypotheses: Hypotheses that cannot be supported or rejected on the basis of objective data.

Validity: The capacity of a measurement to reflect accurately the variable under study.

Variable: That which is subject to change, such as an experimental condition (independent variable) or a behavioral measure (dependent variable).

Within-Subject Design: Experimental design in which two or more treatment conditions are administered to the same group of subjects.

Yoked Control: A subject whose treatment is linked to a voluntary behavior of an experimental subject.

Abel, E. (1980). Fetal alcohol syndrome: behavioral teratology. *Psychological Bulletin,* **87,** 29–50.

American Psychological Association (1990). Ethical principles of psychologists. *American Psychologist,* **45,** 390–395.

Anderson, J. R. (1974). Retrieval of propositional information from long-term memory. *Cognitive Psychology,* **5,** 451–474.

Babbie, E. R. (1973). *Survey research methods.* Belmont, CA: Wadsworth.

Babbie, E. R. (1986). *The practice of social research* (4th ed.). Belmont, CA: Wadsworth.

Bailey, K. D. (1987). *Methods of social research* (3rd ed.). New York: Free Press.

Bassok, M. (1990). Transfer of domain specific problem solving procedures. *Journal of Experimental Psychology: Learning, Memory, and Cognition,* **16,** 522–533.

Bramel, D., & Friend, R. (1981). Hawthorne, the myth of the docile worker, and class bias in psychology. *American Psychologist,* **36,** 867–878.

Campbell, D. T., & Stanley, J. C. (1963). *Experimental and quasi-experimental designs for research.* Chicago: Rand McNally.

Cook, T. D., & Campbell, D. T. (1979). *Quasi-experimentation: Design and analysis issues for field settings.* Chicago: Rand McNally.

Dalton, D. R., & Mesch, D. J. (1990). The impact of flexible scheduling on employee attendance and turnover. *Administrative Science Quarterly,* **35,** 370–387.

Daly, H. B. (1991). Reward reductions found more aversive by rats fed environmentally contaminated salmon. *Neurotoxicology and Teratology,* **13,** 449–453.

Dorfman, D. D. (1978). The Cyril Burt question: New findings. *Science,* **201,** 1177–1186.

Ehlers, C. L., & Schuckit, M. A. (1990). EEG fast frequency activity in the sons of alcoholics. *Biological Psychiatry,* **27,** 631–641.

Fink, A., & Kosekoff, J. (1985). *How to conduct surveys.* Newbury Park, CA: Sage.

Fisher, R. A. (1953). *The design of experiments* (6th ed.). New York: Hafner Press.

Fowler, F. J. (1988). *Survey research methods.* Newbury Park, CA: Sage.

Games, P. A. (1990). Correlation and causation: A logical snafu. *Journal of Experimental Education,* **58,** 239–246.

Gardner, R.M., Morrell, J. A., Watson, D. N., & Sandoval, S. L. (1989). Subjective equality and just noticeable differences in body-size judgments by obese people. *Perceptual and Motor Skills,* **69,** 595–604.

Gilmore, M. M., & Murphy, C. (1989). Aging is associated with increased Weber ratios for caffeine, but not for sucrose. *Perception and Psychophysics,* **46,** 555–559.

Grosvenor, A., & Lack, L. C. (1984). The effect of sleep before and after learning and memory. *Sleep,* **7,** 155–167.

Grundner, T. M. (1986). *Informed consent.* Owings Mills, MD: National Health Publishing.

Health and Human Services, Department of (1981). Final regulations amending basic HHS policy for the protection of human subjects. *Federal Register,* **46**(16), 8366–8392.

Jacobson, J. L., Fein, G. G., Jacobson, S. W., Schwartz, P. S., & Dowler, J. K. (1985). The effect of intrauterine PCB exposure on visual recognition memory. *Child Development, 56*, 853–860.

Joffe, J. M., Rawson, R. A., & Mulick, J. A. (1973). Control of their environment reduces emotionality in rats. *Science, 180*, 1383–1384.

Kamin, L. M. (1974). *The science and politics of I.Q.* New York: Wiley.

Keith-Spiegel, P., & Koocher, G. P. (1985). *Ethics in psychology.* New York: Random House.

Keppel, G., & Underwood, B. J. (1962). Proactive inhibition in short-term retention of single items. *Journal of Verbal Learning and Verbal Behavior, 1*, 53–161.

Kretch, D., Rosenzweig, M. R., & Bennett, E. L. (1966). Environmental impoverishment, social isolation, and changes in brain chemistry and anatomy. *Physiology and Behavior, 1*, 99–104.

Kubiak, T. J., Harris, H. J., Smith, L. M., Schwartz, T. R., Stalling, D. L., Trick, J. A., Sileo, L., Docherty, D. E., & Erdman, T. C. (1989). Microcontaminants and reproductive impairment of the Forster's Tern on Green Bay, Lake Michigan. *Archives of Environmental Contamination and Toxicology, 18*, 706–727.

Kumar, K., Wyant, G. M., & Nath, R. (1990). Deep brain stimulation for control of intractable pain in humans, present and future: A ten-year follow-up. *Neurosurgery, 26*, 774.

Likert, R. (1932). A technique for the measurement of attitudes. *Archives of Psychology, 21*, 140.

Lobaugh, N. J., Greene, P. L., Grant, M., Nick, T., & Amsel, A. (1989). Patterned alternation in infant rats after combined or separate lesions of hippocampus and amygdala. *Behavioral Neuroscience, 103*, 1159–1167.

Marsh, C. (1982). *The survey method.* London: Allen & Unwin.

Mendenhall, W., Ott, L., & Scheaffer, R. L. (1971). *Elementary survey sampling.* Belmont, CA: Wadsworth.

Michael, R. P. (1980). Hormones and sexual behavior in the female. In Krieger, D. T., & Hughes, J. C. (Eds.), *Neuroendocrinology.* Sunderland, MA: Sinauer.

Morgan, C. L. (1906). *An introduction to comparative psychology* (2nd ed.), London: Walter Scott.

Murphy, K. R., & Davidshofer, C. O. (1991). *Psychological testing* (2nd ed.). Englewood Cliffs, NJ: Prentice-Hall.

Needleman, H. L., Schell, A., Bellinger, D., Leviton, A., & Allred, E. N. (1990). The long-term effects of exposure to low doses of lead in childhood. *New England Journal of Medicine, 322*, 83–88.

NOVA (1988). *Why scientists cheat.* Public Broadcasting System, Boston: WGBH-TV.

Oppenheim, A. N. (1966). *Questionnaire design and attitude measurement.* New York: Basic Books.

Peterson, L. R., & Peterson, M. J. (1959). Short-term retention of individual verbal items. *Journal of Experimental Psychology, 58*, 193–198.

Reder, L. M., & Wible, C. (1984). Strategy use in question-answering: memory strength and task constraints on fan effects. *Memory and Cognition, 12*, 411–419.

Schaie, K. W. (1989). Perceptual speed in adulthood: Cross-sectional and longitudinal studies. *Psychology and Aging, 4*, 443–453.

Schlenker, B. R., Weigold, M. E., & Hallam, J. R. (1990). Self-serving attributions in social context: Effects of self esteem and social pressure. *Journal of Personality and Social Psychology, 58*, 855–863.

Skinner, B. F. (1953). Some contributions of an experimental analysis of behavior to psychology as a whole. *American Psychologist, 8,* 69–78.

Skinner, B. F. (1963). The flight from the laboratory. In M. Marx (Ed.), *Theories in contemporary psychology.* New York: Macmillan.

Smith, E. G., Adams, N., & Schorr, D. (1978). Fact retrieval and the paradox of interference. *Cognitive Psychology, 10,* 438–464.

Steininger, M., Newell, D. J., & Garcia, L. T. (1984). *Ethical issues in psychology.* Homewood, IL: Dorsey.

Streissguth, A. P. (1976). Psychological handicaps in children with the fetal alcohol syndrome. *Annals of the New York Academy of Sciences, 273,* 140–145.

INDEX

Page numbers in **bold** type indicate the page where the indexed term is defined.

ACKNOWLEDGMENTS

Chapter 16

Excerpts from APA Guidelines quoted throughout Chapter 16. American Psychological Association (1990). Ethical principles of psychologists (amended June 2, 1989). *American Psychologist, 45,* 390–395. Copyright 1990 by the American Psychological Association. Reprinted by permission.

Chapter 17

Method and Table pages 334–35 from Schaie, K. W. (1989). Perceptual speed in adulthood: Cross-sectional and longitudinal studies. *Psychology and Aging, 4,* 443–453. Copyright 1989 by the American Psychological Association. Reprinted by permission of the publisher and the author.

Chapter 18

Method pages 348–49 from Gilmore, M. M. & Murphy, C. (1989). Aging is associated with increased Weber ratio for caffeine, but not for sucrose. *Perception and Psychophysics, 46,* 555–559. Reprinted by permission of the Psychonomic Society and the authors.

Method and Figure pages 350–51 from Gardner, R. M., Morrell, J. A., Watson, D. N., & Sandoval, S. L. (1989). Subjective equality and just noticeable differences in body-size judgments by obese persons. *Perceptual and Motor Skills, 69,* 595–604. Reproduced with permission of the authors and the publisher.

Chapter 19

Method and Table pages 360–62 from Bassok, M. (1990). Transfer of domain-specific problem-solving procedures. *Journal of Experimental Psychology: Learning Memory and Cognition, 16,* 522–533. Copyright 1990 by the American Psychological Association.

Chapter 20

Method, Figure, and Table pages 367–79 from Lobaugh, N. J., Greene, P. L., Grant, M., Nick, T., & Amsel, A. (1989). Patterned (single) alternation in infant rats after combined or separate lesions of hippocampus and amygdala. *Behavioral Neuroscience, 103,* 1159–1167. Copyright 1989 by the American Psychological Association. Reprinted by permission of the publisher and the authors.

Chapter 21

Method pages 392–95 from Needleman, H. L., Schell, A., Bellinger, D., Leviton, A. & Allred, E. (1990). The long-term effects of exposure to low doses of lead in childhood: An 11-year follow-up report. *The New England Journal of Medicine, 322,* 83–88. Copyright 1990 by the Massachusetts Medical Society. Reprinted by permission of the publisher.

Method pages 400–01 from Daly, H. B. (1991). Reward reductions found more aversive by rats fed environmentally contaminated salmon. *Neurotoxicology and Teratology, 13,* 449–453. Reprinted by permission of the publisher.

Chapter 22

Method pages 410–12 from Dalton, D. R. & Mesch, D. J. (1990). The impact of flexible scheduling on employee attendance and turnover. *Administrative Science Quarterly, 35,* (2), 370–387. Copyright 1990 by the Administrative Science Quarterly, Inc. Reprinted by permission of the publisher.

Chapter 23

Method and Table pages 424–27 from Schlenker, B. R., Weigold, M. F. & Hallam, J. R. (1990). Self-serving attributions in social context: Effects of self-esteem and social pressure. *Journal of Personality and Social Psychology, 58,* 855–863. Copyright 1990 by the American Psychological Association. Reprinted by permission of the publisher and the authors.